PAGE 34

ON THE ROAD

YOUR COMPLETE DESTINATION GUIDE
In-depth reviews, detailed listings and insider tips

PAGE 435

SURVIVAL GUIDE

VITAL PRACTICAL INFORMATION TO HELP YOU HAVE A SMOOTH TRIP

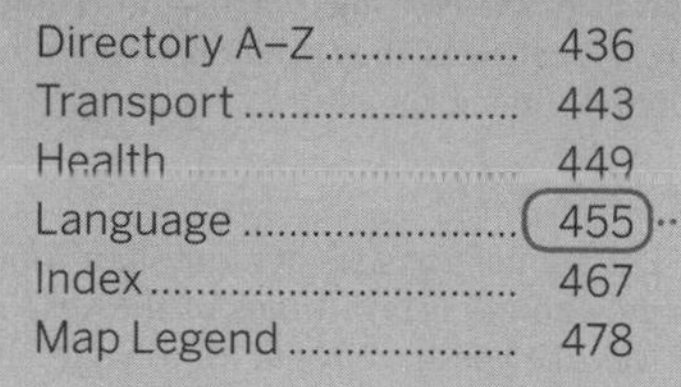

THIS EDITION WRITTEN AND RESEARCHED BY

Greg Bloom,
Michael Grosberg, Trent Holden, Adam Karlin, Kate Morgan

welcome to the Philippines

Cultural Quirks

The Philippines is a land apart from mainland Southeast Asia – not only geographically but also spiritually and culturally. The country's overwhelming Catholicism, the result of 350 years of Spanish rule, is its most obvious enigma. Vestiges of the Spanish era include exuberant town fiestas (festivals) like Kalibo's Ati-Atihan, unique Spanish-Filipino colonial architecture, and exquisite, centuries-old stone churches lording over bustling town plazas. Malls, fast-food chains and widespread spoken English betray the influence of Spain's colonial successor, the Americans. Yet despite these outside influences, the country remains very much its own unique entity. The people are, simply, Filipinos – and proud of it. Welcoming, warm and relentlessly upbeat, it is they who captivate and ultimately ensnare visitors.

Island Life

The Philippines consists of more than 7000 islands, and at certain times of the year it will feel like you have them all to yourself. The typical island boasts a jungle-clad, mountainous interior and a sandy coastline flanked by aquamarine waters and the requisite coral reef. But you'll find plenty of variations on this theme, from marooned slicks of sand in the middle of the ocean to sprawling, overpopulated mega-islands like Luzon and Mindanao. Beach bums

The Philippines is defined by its emerald rice fields, teeming megacities, graffiti-splashed jeepneys, smouldering volcanoes, bug-eyed tarsiers, fuzzy water buffalo and smiling, happy-go-lucky people.

(left) Hundred Islands National Park, North Luzon
(below) Fiesta time, Negros Occidental

and divers should head straight to the Visayas, where island-hopping opportunities abound and the perfect beach takes many forms. More adventurous travellers can pitch a tent on a deserted stretch of coastline and play solo *Survivor* for a few days.

Accessible Adventures

The Philippines isn't just about finding an isolated beach and getting catatonic. From trekking in the mountains of North Luzon, to getting airborne on a kite board in Boracay, to spelunking in the cave systems of Samar, the Philippines can capably raise any adrenaline junkie's pulse. Much of the action in the Philippines naturally takes place in and around the water. Kitesurfing and windsurfing are big in Boracay and in Daet, Bicol. While surfers are just catching on to the tasty waves that form on both coasts at certain times of the year, divers have long been enamoured of the country's underwater charms. You need only know how to snorkel to go fin deep with the gentle *butanding* (whale sharks) in Southeast Luzon. Freshwater pursuits include rafting, kayaking and wakeboarding. On terra firma, the rice terraces around Banaue are most popular for trekking, but there are peaks – including many volcanoes – to be bagged across Luzon, the Visayas, Mindoro and Mindanao.

The Philippines

Top Experiences

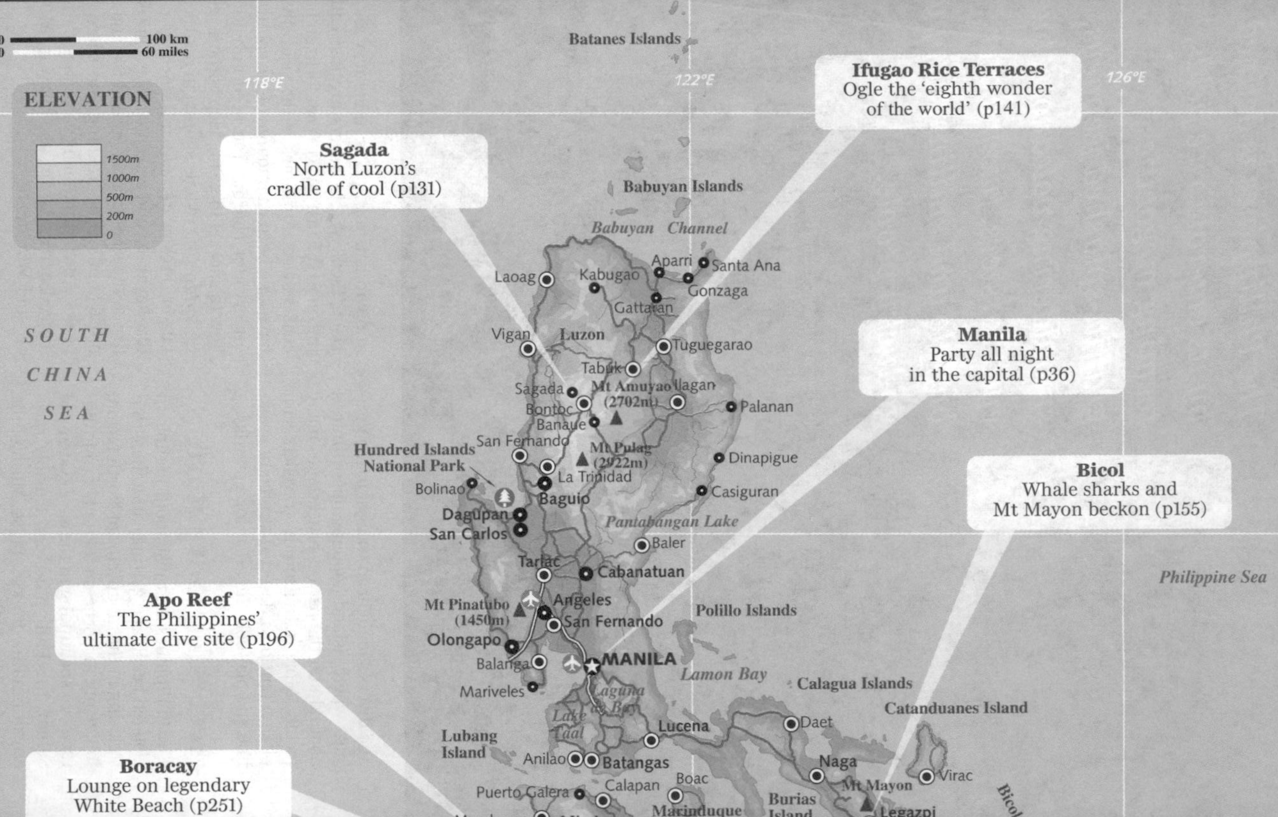

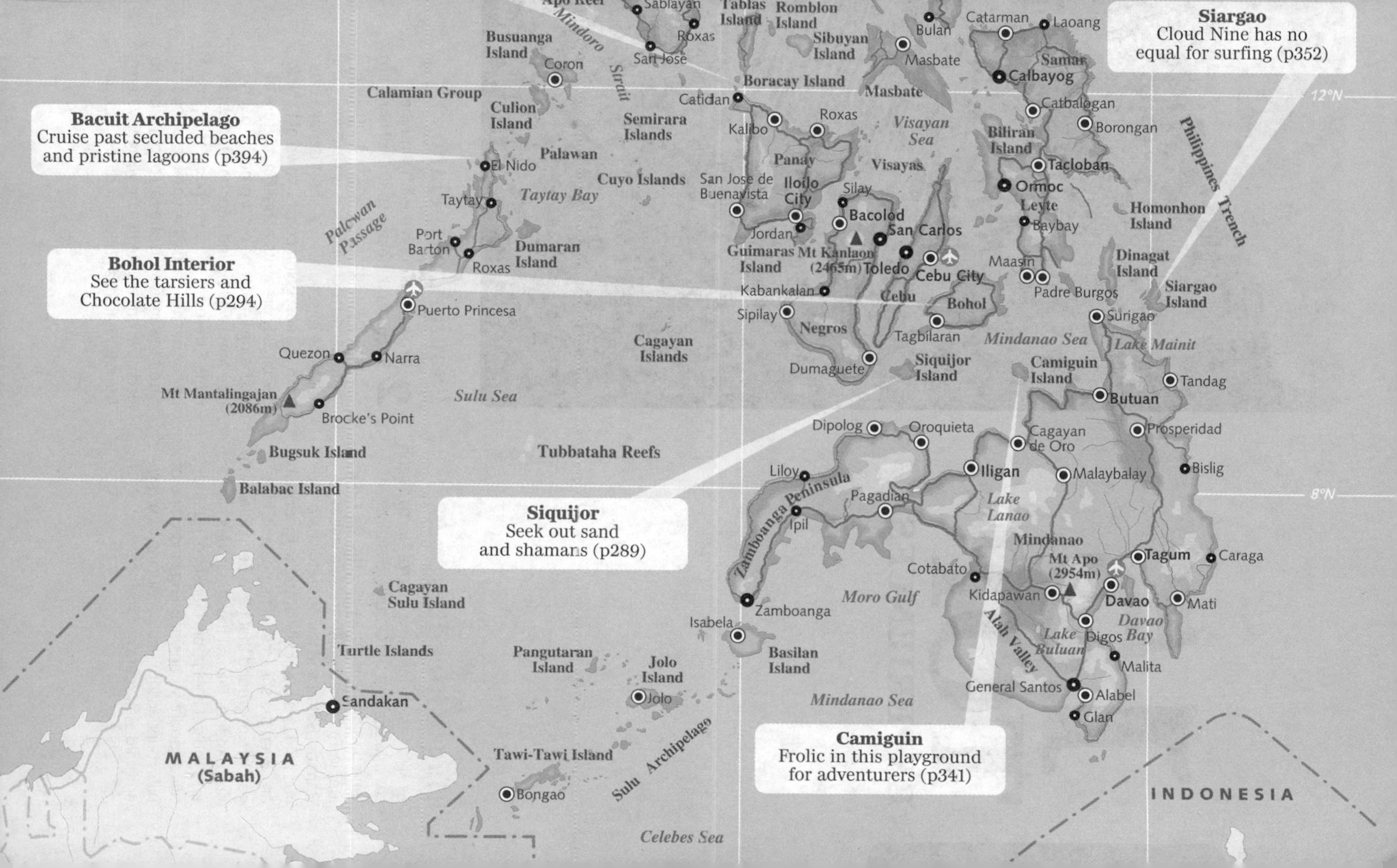
Siargao
Cloud Nine has no equal for surfing (p352)
Bacuit Archipelago
Cruise past secluded beaches and pristine lagoons (p394)
Bohol Interior
See the tarsiers and Chocolate Hills (p294)
Siquijor
Seek out sand and shamans (p289)
Camiguin
Frolic in this playground for adventurers (p341)
Apo Reef
Mindoro
Strait
Sablayan
Roxas
San Jose
Tablas Island
Romblon Island
Sibuyan Island
Bulan
Masbate
Catarman
Laoang
Samar
Calbayog
Busuanga Island
Coron
Calamian Group
Boracay Island
Catidan
Masbate
Culion Island
Semirara Islands
Kalibo
Roxas
Visayan Sea
Catbalogan
Borongan
Philippines Trench
Biliran Island
Tacloban
Palawan
El Nido
Cuyo Islands
San Jose de Buenavista
Panay
Iloilo City
Silay
Visayas
Ormoc
Leyte
Baybay
Homonhon Island
Taytay
Taytay Bay
Bacolod
San Carlos
Palawan Passage
Port Barton
Roxas
Dumaran Island
Jordan
Guimaras Island
Mt Kanlaon (2465m)
Toledo
Cebu City
Maasin
Dinagat Island
Padre Burgos
Siargao Island
Kabankalan
Cebu
Bohol
Puerto Princesa
Sipilay
Negros
Tagbilaran
Mindanao Sea
Surigao
Lake Mainit
Cagayan Islands
Quezon
Narra
Dumaguete
Siquijor Island
Camiguin Island
Tandag
Butuan
Mt Mantalingajan (2086m)
Sulu Sea
Brocke's Point
Dipolog
Oroquieta
Cagayan de Oro
Prosperidad
Bugsuk Island
Tubbataha Reefs
Iligan
Malaybalay
Bislig
Liloy
Balabac Island
Zamboanga Peninsula
Pagadian
Lake Lanao
8°N
12°N
Ipil
Mindanao
Mt Apo (2954m)
Tagum
Caraga
Cotabato
Cagayan Sulu Island
Moro Gulf
Kidapawan
Davao
Mati
Zamboanga
Isabela
Davao Bay
Alah Valley
Lake Buluan
Digos
Turtle Islands
Pangutaran Island
Basilan Island
Malita
Jolo Island
Jolo
General Santos
Alabel
Sandakan
Mindanao Sea
Glan
MALAYSIA (Sabah)
Tawi-Tawi Island
Sulu Archipelago
INDONESIA
Bongao
Celebes Sea

15 TOP EXPERIENCES

Ifugao Rice Terraces

1 It's easy to look at a map of North Luzon and assume the Cordillera is all untamed wilderness. And yes – there's rugged jungle. But what really strikes a visitor to Banaue, Batad and the other towns of Ifugao (p142) is how cultivated the mountains are. Even the sheerest cliffs possess little patches of ground that have been tilled into rice paddies. Take all those patches together and you get a veritable blanket of upland-tilled goodness, an unending landscape of hills rounded into rice-producing lumps of emerald. Batad, Ifugao Province

Bacuit Archipelago

2 Cruising through the labyrinthine Bacuit Archipelago (p394) of northern Palawan, past secluded beaches, pristine lagoons and rocky islets, is an experience not to be missed. Only a short bangka ride from the easygoing coastal town of El Nido, Bacuit Bay presents a thrilling mixture of imposing limestone escarpments, palm-tree-lined white-sand beaches and coral reefs. Overnight island-hopping trips in the bay or further north through the Linapacan Strait toward Coron offer an opportunity to bed down in remote fishing villages where the daily catch is grilled for dinner. Bacuit Bay, Palawan

1

KIMBERLEY COOLE/LONELY PLANET IMAGES ©

2

TOM COCKREM/LONELY PLANET IMAGES ©

Fiesta Time

3 The Philippines just isn't the Philippines without the colourful festivals, or fiestas, that rage across the country throughout the year. Even the tiniest little barangay (village) holds at least one annually. The granddaddy of them all is the Ati-Atihan Festival (p18) in Kalibo. At Bacolod's MassKara Festival (p20) and Marinduque's Moriones Festival (p179), mischievous masked men stir the masses into a dancing frenzy. The Easter crucifixion ceremony (p18) in San Fernando, north of Manila, produces a more macabre tableau, with Catholic devotees being physically nailed to crosses. Costumed dancers, Ati-Atihan Festival

Beaches

4 Nothing defines the Philippines more than a remote strip of pearly white sand – there's at least one made-to-order beach on each of the country's 7000+ islands. Want to be far away from everybody? It's almost too easy – most of Luzon is ringed by deserted beaches, while your own private island awaits in Palawan's Calamian Group (p395) around Coron. Seeking a good dive spot with plenty of additional diversions and a great beach? Dial up Malapascua (p221) or Sipalay (p280). Want action with your beach experience? Take kitesurfing lessons on Boracay (p251) or surf lessons in San Juan, La Union (p108). Coron Island, Palawan

Boracay

5 It wasn't that long ago that Boracay (p251) was a sleepy, almost unknown backwater. Oh, how times have changed. The world has discovered Boracay, elevating the diminutive island into a serious player in the pantheon of Southeast Asian party beaches. Yet for all that's changed, Boracay remains generally mellower than the likes of Kuta Beach or Ko Samui. And solace can still be found, in particular at the southern end of Boracay's signature White Beach, where the spirit of the old Boracay lives on. White Beach, Boracay

Bicol Adventures

6 Southeast Luzon, geographically defined by the Bicol peninsula (p155), is becoming adventure-travel central for the Philippines. Besides boasting some of the best regional cuisine in the islands, Bicol is a top draw for water and adrenaline junkies via the Camsur Watersports Complex, where wakeboarding and its derivative sports rule the roost. Daet, Camarines Norte, is a burgeoning surf and kitesurfing destination. To experience a more laid-back connection to the water, head to the edge of Luzon and snorkel alongside the gentle whale sharks of Donsol – an unforgettable highlight. Whale sharks

Sagada

7 The tribes of the Cordillera of North Luzon all seem to have impressive burial practices. In Sagada (p131), the way folks deal with bodies is both relatively simple and fascinatingly unique: hang them. Not in the gallows sense; the hanging coffins of Sagada are stacked into niches cut into rocky cliffs, shelved like old books sitting in silent elevation over the jungle valleys. Sagada itself is one of the few traditionally 'backpacker' towns in North Luzon, with a gentle, friendly budget-traveller vibe that's hard not to love. Lumiang Burial Cave, Sagada

6

MICHAEL AW/LONELY PLANET IMAGES ©

7

NOBORU KOMINE/LONELY PLANET IMAGES ©

8

9

Bohol Interior

8 It may all seem a bit touristy, but no visit to Bohol (p302) is complete without an inland detour to visit the iconic Chocolate Hills and cute bug-eyed tarsiers. Renting a car or motorbike is the way to go; get there at dusk for the memorable sight of the grassy hillocks spanning out to the misty horizon. Meanwhile, you can search for tarsiers in the wild on night safaris, but your chances are slim, so head to the tarsier sanctuary where you are guaranteed to see these extraordinarily freaky and lovable primates. Chocolate Hills, Bohol

Surfing Siargao

9 A chill-out vibe and friendly breaks for both experts and novices make this island an important player in the Philippine surfing scene. The picturesque pavilion at Cloud Nine (p352) is the community and tourism hub, but waves abound elsewhere; head to the tranquil village of Burgos (p353) in the north for an undeveloped experience or charter a bangka to seldom-visited spots. At the end of the day, regardless of your skills, nothing beats exchanging exaggerated tales of your exploits, a beachfront sundowner in your hand while you stare out at the waves rolling in.

CARLOTTA/ALAMY ©

TOM COCKREM/LONELY PLANET IMAGES ©

Climbing Camiguin

10 From the northern coastline of mainland Mindanao, the rough-hewn landscape of volcanic Camiguin (p341) is camouflaged by its lush silhouette. To truly grasp this island's inspiring topography, veer into the interior on roadways that carve through dense forests and culminate in rocky pathways that trail further up into the highlands. Made for do-it-yourself adventurers, Camiguin's peaks and valleys offer streams for scrambling, mountains for scaling, canyons for rappelling and pools at the base of thundering waterfalls in which to wash off the day's exertions.

Day Tripping in Siquijor

11 The best way to take in Siquijor's (p289) mellow vibe is to circumnavigate the nearly traffic-free island by motorbike on a day trip. Start with a morning dip at Paliton Beach, before proceeding to JJ's for awesome fruit shakes and breakfast. Arrange a visit with a folk healer, involving unique traditional herbal remedies; head to Lazi for its magnificent coral-and-wood church; then cool off in the falls or at Kagasua Beach. Check out some modern art at Olang Art Park, and finish north of Larena for a cold beer and stellar sunset. Lazi Convent, Siquijor

DENNIS M. SABANGAN/EPA/CORBIS ©

Apo Reef

12 It takes a special spot to stand out amid the Philippines' myriad dive sites. Apo Reef (p197) is such a spot. A protected, mostly sunken atoll off the west coast of Mindoro, Apo supplies divers – and snorkellers – with a smorgasbord of underwater splendour. On some dives you might lose track of how many sharks, rays and sea turtles you spot. Rogue tuna, wrasses and huge schools of jacks patrol deeper waters, while in the shallows eels, turtles and an array of macro (small marine) life patrol the dazzling reefs.

Manila's Seething Nightlife

13 You name it, it's there. That about sums up Manila nightlife. From the bongo-infused hipster hang-outs of Quezon City, to Malate's live-music bars, to the chichi nightclubs of Makati and the new Resorts World, action beckons at all hours. On any given night, open-air 'restobars' are packed with beer-swilling punters until well past midnight. On weekends, stir-crazy expats and cadres of cashed-up Makati kids keep the clubs thumping until well past dawn. Looking for something different? The drag show at Club Mwah! (p61) is classic.

Colonial Architecture

14 The Philippines isn't just about beaches and adventure; the Spanish left some wonderful architecture that combines native and European elements. The historical centres of cobblestoned Vigan (p111) in North Luzon and Silay (p276) on Negros have many well-preserved ancestral houses; many mansions in these towns have been turned into lovely hotels and restaurants. Centuries-old stone churches, such as the Unesco-recognised specimens in Paoay (p118), Santa Maria (p116) and Miagao (p246), are another Spanish legacy. Paoay Church, Ilocos

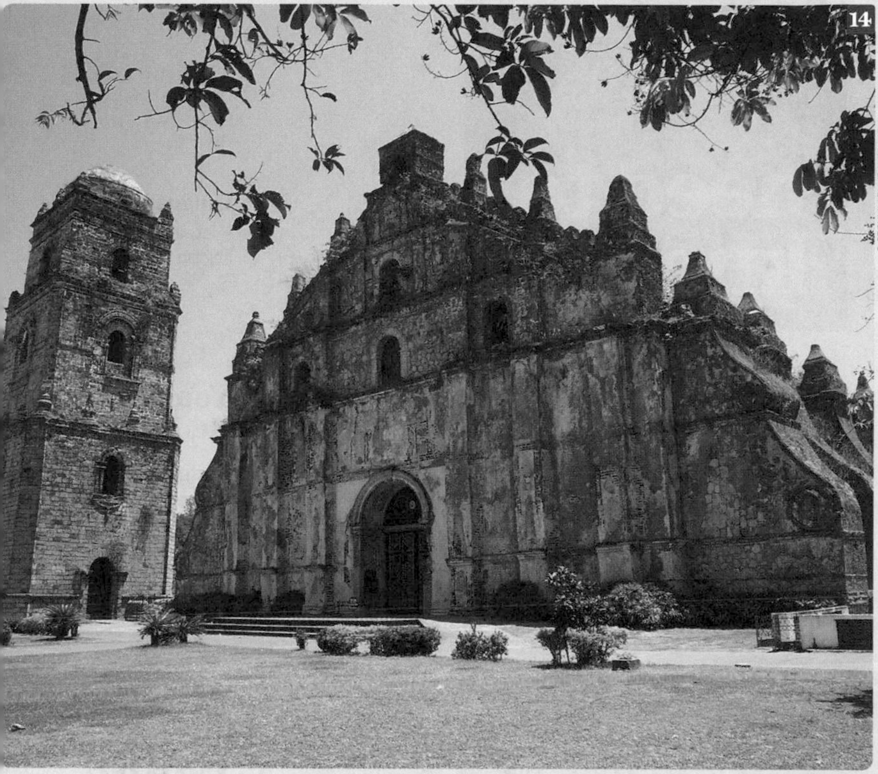

14

Volcanoes

15 Located along the Pacific 'Ring of Fire', the Philippines is a land of volcanoes. The 1991 eruption of Mt Pinatubo (p98) sent ash clouds around the globe and altered the earth's climate for a spell. Today you can venture through Pinatubo's moonscape and swim in its bright blue crater lake. Serious climbers should target Mt Kanlaon (p275) on Negros, Romblon's Mt Guiting-Guiting (p238) or, the most challenging of all, Mindoro's Mt Halcon (p191). The easiest climb is up Mt Taal (p85), while perpetually smoking Mt Mayon (p167) is postcard perfect. Mt Mayon, Bicol

need to know

Currency

» Philippine Peso (P)

Languages

» Tagalog (Filipino) and English

When to Go

Tropical climate, rain all year round
Tropical climate, wet and dry season
Shorter dry season, cooler temperatures all year round

High Season (Dec–Apr)

» High season is dry season for most of the country; December to February are the coolest, most pleasant months.

» Many resorts triple rates around New Year and before Easter.

Shoulder Season (May & Nov)

» Rising May temperatures herald the onset of the rainy season around Manila and elsewhere.

» November sees high-season rates kick in.

Low Season (Jun–Sep)

» Accommodation prices drop 30% in resort areas.

» Passing typhoons can cause days of torrential rain.

» Eastern seaboard is usually dry, if susceptible to typhoons.

Your Daily Budget

Budget less than

P2200

(US$50)

» Dorm bed or single room P250-500

» Local food and beer P500

» Hail roving tricycles P8

Midrange

P2200-6000

(US$50-138)

» Air-con room P1200-3000

» Decent meal with drinks P1200-2000

» Motorbike rental and massage P1000

Top end over

P6000

(US$138)

» Boutique resort P4000-12,000

» Champagne brunch buffet P3000

» Van rental per day with driver P4000

Money

» ATMs widely available and credit cards accepted at hotels, restaurants and some shops in all but the most remote areas.

Visas

» 21-day visas available on arrival for most nationalities. Visas are easily extended for a fee in major provincial centres.

Mobile Phones

» Local SIM cards can be used in all but American phones. Americans can roam or buy a basic phone on arrival for US$15 and up.

Transport

» Mostly boats or budget flights between islands, buses or self-driving on the main island of Luzon (drive on the right).

Websites

» **Philippine Newslink** (www.philnews.com) Thorough pile of news, views, links.

» **ClickTheCity.com** (www.clickthecity.com) A great listings site for happenings in Manila and around the country.

» **Tanikalang Ginto** (www.filipinolinks.com) Every topic under the Philippine sun.

» **Lonely Planet** (www.lonelyplanet.com/philippines) Destination information, hotel bookings, traveller forum and more.

» **MindaNews** (www.mindanews.com) Hard-hitting online news site for Mindanao.

Exchange Rates

Australia	A$1	P44
Canada	C$1	P42
Euro zone	€1	P58
Japan	¥100	P56
New Zealand	NZ$1	P34
Thailand	10B	P14
UK	£1	P68
USA	US$1	P43

For current exchange rates see www.xe.com

Important Numbers

Dial 0 before area codes when calling from a cellphone or a landline outside that region.

Country code	☎63
Emergency	☎117
International dialling code	☎00
International operator	☎108
PLDT directory assistance	☎187

Arriving

Ninoy Aquino International Airport (NAIA)

» Check which of NAIA's four terminals you are arriving in (and, especially, departing from).

» Public transport into town is complicated and involves transfers, but taxis are cheap (P225 average to most hotels) and plentiful at airport ranks.

» The four terminals are not particularly close to each other but are linked by shuttle vans (P20).

» See p80 for more detailed info.

Travelling Responsibly

Explosive population growth is exacting a huge toll on the Philippines' environment and indigenous communities. A few tips to avoid making the situation worse:

» Choose local tour companies (preferably grassroots ecotourism operators) over big firms.

» Tread softly in indigenous areas: avoid obvious displays of wealth, ask permission before taking photos and spend some time engaging with villagers.

» Fill your water bottle up at the ubiquitous water refilling stations.

» Avoid plastic bags when you can.

Lastly, we still love Boracay, but let's face it, unchecked development and explosive tourism growth aren't doing its environment any favours. Consider adding a few more remote, less touristy areas to your itinerary. They'll be grateful for your dollars.

if you like...

Island Hopping

The world's second-largest archipelago is, naturally, an island-hopper's dream. Little clusters of islets abound off all of the main islands, and in any coastal community you'll find a boatman with a bangka, just waiting to take you exploring.

Northern Palawan The labyrinthine Bacuit and Calamian Archipelagos should be top of the list for any island nut (p394 and p395)

Romblon Bouncing around by bangka is the only way to roll in this diverse province in the Sibuyan Sea, north of Boracay (p230)

Caramoan Peninsula The karsts around this wedge of land in eastern Bicol rival those of the Bacuit Archipelago (p161)

Siargao The Philippines' surf capital has a dizzying array of idyllic islets to explore when the waves aren't happening (p350)

Zambales Coast Uninhabited islands abound off this lonely stretch of coastline that's within easy driving distance of Manila (p101)

Trekking

The major islands boast mountainous interiors carpeted by forests and pock-marked by some of the largest caves in Asia. The rice terraces of North Luzon are justifiably most popular, but there are peaks to be bagged across South Luzon, Mindoro, the Visayas and Mindanao.

The Cordillera Besides rice terraces, Luzon's signature range offers multiday treks that traverse remote tribal villages and several 2500m+ peaks (p119)

Bicol 'Perfect' Mt Mayon is the region's prettiest but by no means its only volcano. Nearby Mt Isarog and Mt Bulusan make better climbs (p155)

Davao The Philippines' highest peak, Mt Apo, dominates the horizon in Southern Mindanao, tempting climbers to set out from nearby Davao (p354)

Sibuyan Island The Philippines' answer to the Galapagos, Sibuyan is a wonderland of biodiversity that also boasts a fine climb up 2058m Mt Guiting-Guiting (p237)

Mindoro Oriental The three-day grunt up Mt Halcon (2505m) is the ultimate challenge; you can trek to remote Mangyan tribal villages here, too (p191)

Water Sports

Much of the action in the Philippines naturally takes place in and around the water. Scuba diving is the big one (see p25), but the country is becoming equally renowned for surfing and kitesurfing, with sailing, windsurfing, deep-sea fishing, rafting, kayaking and wakeboarding also on the menu.

Swimming with whale sharks Snorkelling with the gentle *butanding* (whale sharks) of Donsol is the quintessential Philippine adventure (p169)

Rafting The white water around Cagayan de Oro is surprisingly brisk and can be paddled year-round (p334)

Sea kayaking Sea kayakers have miles of pristine coastline to explore in places like Northern Palawan and Hundred Islands National Park (p107)

Surfing Baler's point break, made famous in *Apocalypse Now*, is still fickle, but when it's on, it's surfing bliss (p144)

Kitesurfing and windsurfing The *amihan* (northeast monsoon) kicks up stiff breezes on Boracay from December to March, delighting sailors and turning this resort island into a kitesurfing and windsurfing paradise (p251)

JOHN BORTHWICK/LONELY PLANET IMAGES ©

» Surfing Sabang Beach (p145) in Baler, North Luzon

Ecofriendly Experiences

Twenty years of the country's natural resources being plundered under Marcos, followed by 20 years of environmental indifference, did the Philippine ecology no favours. Today the country is finally waking up to the benefits of conservation and ecotourism.

Tubbataha Hop on a live-aboard for a dive safari to this protected sunken atoll in the middle of the Sulu Sea (p379)

Puerto Princesa Pasyar Developmental Tourism organises ecofriendly dolphin-spotting tours and homestays in small rural communities in southern Palawan (p373)

WWOOF Away Go 'WWOOFing' as a willing worker on an organic farm in the Cordillera mountain villages of Acop (p127) and Pula (p144)

Pamilacan Island Spot dolphins near Pamilican Island, from boats once used by manta ray and whale fishermen (p305)

Primates and eagles For responsible bird and primate viewing, drop into the Philippine Eagle Research & Nature Center near Davao (p361), or Bohol's Tarsier Sanctuary (p302)

WWII History

Few countries endured more pain, suffering and damage than the Philippines in WWII. Although there are fewer military sights than you'd expect, somber memorials across the archipelago commemorate key battles, historic landings and gruesome death marches.

Manila The capital has several poignant WWII memorials, none more peaceful and moving than the American Memorial Cemetery in Fort Bonifacio (p61)

Bataan Peninsula Kilometre markers trace the route of the Bataan Death March, while the museum and shrine atop Mt Samat is a must for military-history buffs (p96)

Red Beach A quirky statue re-enacts General MacArthur's famous return to the Philippines (p315)

Corregidor Island Only Bataan is more synonomous with WWII in the Philippines; visit on a fascinating day or overnight tour from Manila (p84)

Lingayen Gulf Make like MacArthur's men and waltz ashore on the broad beaches around Lingayen, the site of several key American amphibious landings (p108)

Beach Resorts

Boracay is resort central, but those looking for something more subdued have plenty to choose from. Lose yourself on your own private island or pursue underwater pleasures at a low-key dive resort. With over 7000 islands, there's a patch of sand for everyone.

El Nido The mix of exquisite luxury resorts on private islands and down-to-earth backpacker beach bungalows is unprecedented (p388)

Dumaguete It's not a resort per se, but it's in range of several of the best: Siquijor, Sipalay, Dauin and idyllic Apo Island (p281)

Mactan Island A host of exclusive self-contained resorts with plenty of activities on offer make Mactan a family favourite (p216)

Malapascua Island A laid-back diving resort on the verge of big things in northern Cebu (p221)

Port Barton Ultramellow beach town on Palawan's lonely west coast has affordable resorts both on and offshore (p385)

month by month

Top Events

1 **Ati-Atihan Festival**, January

2 **Moriones Festival**, Holy Week

3 **Crucifixion Ceremonies**, Good Friday

4 **MassKara**, October

5 **Rodeo Masbateño**, May

January

New Year is a 'superpeak' period, and hotel rates can quadruple in resort areas. Away from the eastern seaboard, the weather is usually pretty good – relatively cool and dry, although rain can certainly linger into January.

Ati-Atihan

The Philippines' most famous and riotous festival is this weeklong mardi gras in Kalibo on Panay, which peaks in the third week of January. Other towns in the region, such as Cadiz on Negros and Iloilo, hold similar festivals on the weekend nearest 26 January (p265).

Sinulog Fiesta

The grandaddy of Cebu's fiestas sees celebrants engaged in a unique *sinulog* dance, a unique two-steps-forward, one-step-back shuffle meant to imitate the rhythm of the river (p207).

February

It's peak season for foreign travellers, so book ahead. The Christmas winds continue to howl, thrilling kitesurfers, while surf season continues in San Fernando (La Union) and butanding (whale shark) activity picks up in Donsol.

Chinese New Year

The lunar new year in late January or early February is popular even among non-Chinese Filipinos. Dragon dances, street parties and huge fireworks displays take place in Manila.

Panagbenga Flower Festival

During the last week in February, the streets in the northern mountain city of Baguio come alive with song, dance and a grand floral parade with spectacular floats.

April

Everything shuts down during Holy Week,which leads up to Easter, when senakulo (passion plays) and pasyon (a recitation of the Passion of Christ) are staged throughout the country. Resort prices again hit 'superpeak' levels.

Moriones Madness

Marinduque's colourful Moriones Festival is a week-long *senakulo* in which the streets are overrun by masked locals engaging in mock sword fights and playing pranks on bystanders.

Crucifixion Ceremonies

The Easter crucifixion ceremony in San Fernando (Pampanga), north of Manila, presents a more macabre tableau, with devotees literally being nailed to wooden crosses. Similar re-enactments of Christ's suffering occur in several towns (p96).

Lenten Festival of Herbal Preparation

On the 'spooky' island of Siquijor, faith healers and witch doctors gather around a big pot on Black Saturday, chanting and preparing a medicinal concoction some say cures all that ails you.

May

Scorching heat, beaches packed with vacationing locals and light winds can make this an uncomfortable time to

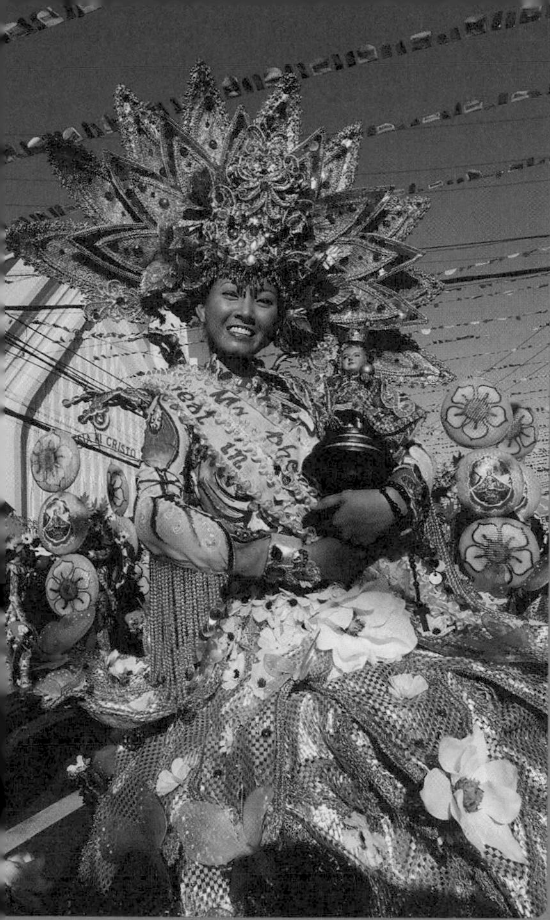

(above) Elaborate outfits are worn at the Sinulog Fiesta in Cebu
(below) Costumed participants at the Pahiyas sa Lucban fiesta in Luzon

travel. Consider highland destinations such as Batad, where the rice terraces are at their greenest. May is the last chance for whale sharks in Donsol.

Rodeo Masbateño

Cowboy up for Masbate's electric weeklong rodeo in early May or late April, with bull-riding, lasso contests and other events that will have you clicking your spurs (p173).

Flores de Mayo

Throughout the country, May sees girls in white dresses strewing flowers around an image of the Virgin Mary in a centuries-old custom known as Flores de Mayo. Makati's red-light district hosts a somewhat infamous Flores de Mayo.

Pahiyas sa Lucban

This famous fiesta takes place around 15 May in the town of Lucban south of Manila, where houses are decked out with colourful *kiping* (leaf-shaped rice wafers) decorations, which are later eaten (p92).

June

The onset of the rainy season (and low season) brings welcome respite from the heat. June also marks the onset of typhoon season, so check the radar and re-route if there's a big red blob heading your way.

Pintados-Kasadyaan

This 'painted festival' in Tacloban on 29 June

celebrates pre-Spanish traditional tattooing practices, albeit using water-based paints for the festival's body decorations.

Baragatan Festival

In the third week of June, residents of Puerto Princesa, Palawan, flood the grounds of the provincial capitol building in a massive display of merrymaking (p375).

August

It's the rainiest month (except for on the eastern seaboard, where it's the driest), so you'll get fabulous discounts on accommodation. The end of the month sees durian season begin in Mindanao and surf season launch in Siargao.

Kadayawan sa Dabaw Festival

Davao's big festival showcases its Muslim, Chinese and tribal influences with parades, performances, and fruit and flower displays. It's held in the third week of August.

October

Things start to dry out after the heavy rains of August and September, but typhoons are still common. High-season prices kick in towards the end of the month. Christmas music is already ubiquitous in the malls.

MassKara Festival

Mischievous masked men stir the masses into a dancing frenzy on the streets of Bacolod, capital of Negros Occidental, during the weekend closest to 19 October.

Todos los Santos

Families laden with food gather at the local cemetery to spend the night remembering their departed loved ones on All Saints' Day (actually commemorated on 1 November). It's a surprisingly festive occasion – check out the Chinese Cemetery in Manila (p46).

December

The Christmas music reaches a crescendo, and the northeast Christmas winds ramp up, launching kitesurfing season in Boracay and surf season in northwest Luzon.

Shariff Kabungsuan Festival

This festival in Cotabato on Mindanao from 15 to 19 December celebrates the arrival of Islam in the region and includes river parades of decorated boats.

itineraries

Whether you've got six days or 60, these itineraries provide a starting point for the trip of a lifetime. Want more inspiration? Head online to lonelyplanet.com/thorntree to chat with other travellers.

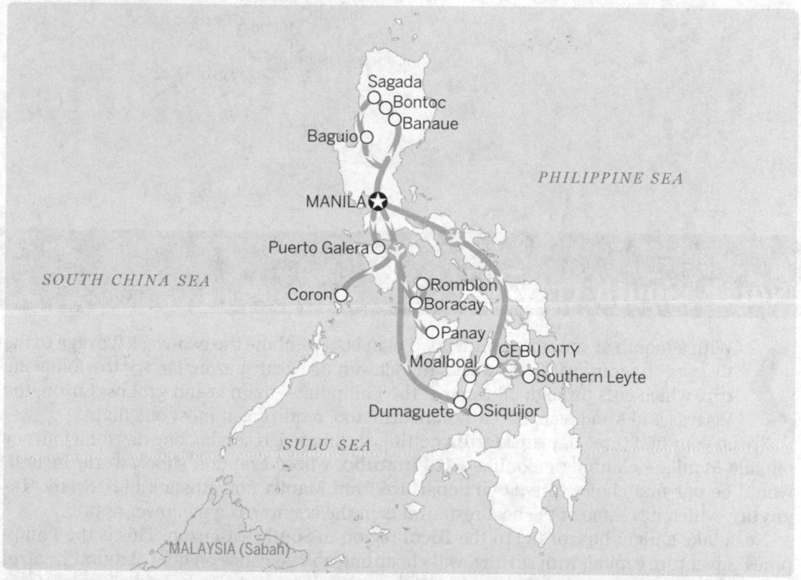

10 Days

Manila Plus One

Start off with two days in **Manila** doing a one-day tour of historic sights, such as **Intramuros**, and another day for modern Manila as embodied by **Makati City** and other centres of contemporary urban development.

Having experienced a little of Philippine life in the big city, you'll be ready to hit the countryside. Beach lovers should fly straight to **Boracay** for its unmatched White Beach and plenty of activities and nightlife. Round off your trip with a few days island-hopping around idyllic **Romblon** or circumnavigating rugged **Panay**. For a more mellow beach experience, fly to **Dumaguete** and find a secluded spot in **southern Negros** or **Siquijor**.

Divers can replace the above with a week of submersion at **Puerto Galera**, **Moalboal**, **Coron** or **Southern Leyte**, where you'll find plenty of dive buddies and fish. Prefer mountains? Go north to 'the eighth wonder of the world': the ancient Ifugao rice terraces around **Banaue** and **Batad**. Tack on a trip to nearby **Sagada** or explore more rice terraces around **Bontoc** before heading back via the Philippines' 'summer capital', **Baguio**.

One Month
North–South Traverse

With a month at your disposal, a good plan is to combine the two-week 'Voyage to the Visayas' itinerary with two weeks in Palawan or North Luzon. Or, try the following trip, which cuts through all three of the Philippines' main island groups: Luzon, the Visayas and Mindanao. It's carbon neutral too, requiring at most one flight.

Spend your first three days in **Manila** getting acclimated, reserving one day for a journey outside Manila – climbing moonlike **Mt Pinatubo**, whose eruption shook world in 1991, would be our first choice (pre-dawn departure from Manila notwithstanding). Scenic **Tagaytay**, which has some of the best restaurants in the country, is a mellower option.

Next, take a night bus (or fly) to the **Bicol** region in Southeast Luzon. This is the Philippines' adventure capital, with surfing, wakeboarding and volcanos on offer. Around Legazpi you can snorkel with the whale sharks off **Donsol** or climb the symmetrical cone of **Mt Mayon**.

Proceeding south, cross the San Bernadino Strait to the rugged islands of **Samar** and **Leyte** in the Eastern Visayas. Along the way, have the spelunking adventure of a lifetime in **Catbalogan**. Stop off in Imelda Marcos' hometown, **Tacloban**, for decent food and a dose of WWII history at nearby **Red Beach**. Then take a ferry to the Visayas' gritty capital, **Cebu City**, for some modern comforts and nightlife.

You'll be approaching week three of your trip by now, and possibly ready for some serious beach time. Take the route less travelled into Bohol, boarding a slow ferry to Talibon, then meander down the east coast to **Anda** for some serious chill time on the sand. Once you're sufficiently unwound, move south and catch another classic back-door ferry: 3½ hours from Jagna, Bohol, to **Camiguin Island**.

Camiguin can keep both adventurous travellers and beach bums satisfied for days. Spend several here, then make the short hop over to mainland Mindanao by ferry. Parts of Mindanao are no-go zones but this northern stretch is perfectly safe – and lovely. For your last few days, choose between **Cagayan de Oro**, a buzzy university town with white-water rafting, and **Siargao**, an idyllic island that also happens to be the Philippines' top surf spot.

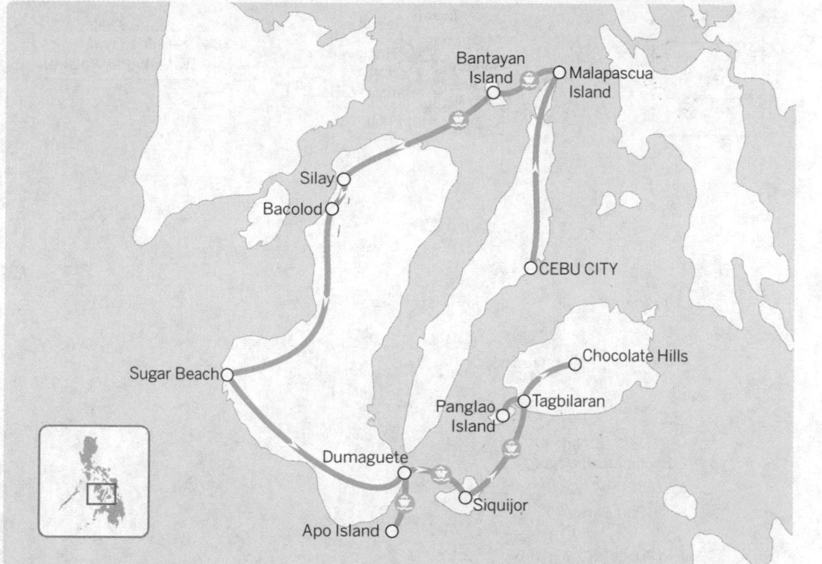

Two Weeks

Voyage to the Visayas

Kick things off in **Cebu City**, soaking up some history during the day before partying it up at its buzzing nightlife. Then it's time to hit the islands: divers will want to head straight to **Malapascua**, where you've a good chance of encountering thresher sharks; while beach bums can catch some rays on laid-back **Bantayan Island**. A day or three should do you fine, before it's time to skip across to neighbouring island Negros by ferry.

Bus it to **Silay** for a fascinating journey through haciendas and sugar-cane plantations. Spend a night in one of its ancestry homes and dine on Spanish food in the ruins of a grand 1930s mansion. An hour's journey south takes you to **Bacolod**, where you can revel in urban joys of great food and bar-hopping, and it is also the base for volcano-trekking **Mt Kanalon**. Then leg it down the coast for more beach action at the delightfully laid-back **Sugar Beach** – a divine sweep of fine white sand, perfect for lazy days in a hammock. Continue along the coast to the southeast for the university town **Dumaguete**, which is all about promenading on its scenic boulevard, great seafood and rowdy nightlife. Then it's time for more underwater delights, taking a bangka to tiny **Apo Island**, renowned for some of the finest diving in the Philippines.

Say goodbye to Negros, catching the ferry to mystical island of **Siquijor**. A day or two here is perfect, allowing you to take in a visit to one of its famed folk healers, laze on some stunning beaches, maybe try a dive or some caving, and take in its mellow island vibe.

Bohol is next on the list, a favourite of many a traveller, arriving in its lively capital of **Tagbilaran**. Spend a night here to take a memorable evening kayak trip to see fireflies, before joining the crowds at **Panglao Island** for fantastic diving and boozy nights on Alona Beach. Drag yourself away for a change of scenery and take a trip into its jungle interior. Get an early to start to catch the **Chocolate Hills** at dawn for majestic views minus the crowds. Then of course there's the tarsiers. One of the world's smallest primates, these freaky, adorable critters are best seen at the **Tarsier Research & Development Center**.

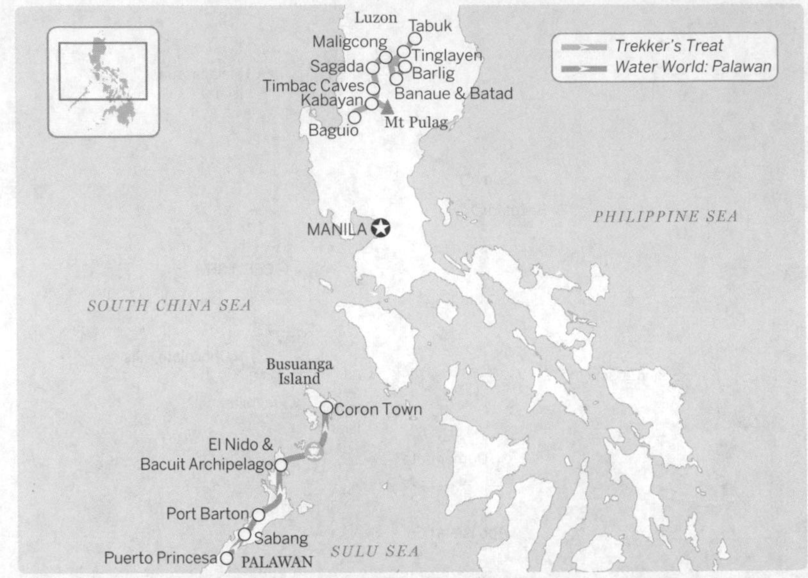

Three Weeks
Water World: Palawan

Puerto Princesa, the capital and transport hub of this long slender island, is the most convenient place to begin. Spend a few days checking out the city's culinary scene, exploring the surrounding countryside on a motorcycle and island-hopping in Honday Bay. From Puerto, organise a ride to **Sabang**, a laid-back beachfront village and the base for trips through a darkened riverine cave.

From Sabang, head to **Port Barton**, another low-key town spread out along a beach with good snorkelling and isolated coves offshore. Continue north to **El Nido**, a town sandwiched between limestone cliffs and the fantastically picturesque **Bacuit Archipelago** filled with secret lagoons, beaches and rocky landscapes. From El Nido, take a boat that winds its way through a maze of islands up to **Coron Town** on Busuanga Island. From this base you can venture out to the striking lakes of **Coron Island** and some of the best wreck diving in the world. From Busuanga, flights and ferries are available to usher you back to reality and Manila.

Three Weeks
Trekker's Treat

From Baguio, take a bus to **Kabayan** and the Akiki Trail, which leads up to the grassy summit of **Mt Pulag**. Hike from Kabayan to the Halsema Hwy, stopping to view the mummies at the **Timbac Caves**, and catch a northbound bus to **Sagada**, where there are excellent day hikes and caving. The amphitheatre-like rice terraces of **Maligcong** are your next destination. Either take a jeepney to Bontoc and explore on a day trip, or walk via Mainit from the town of Aguid near Sagada.

From Bontoc you have two choices. To really get off the beaten track, head to **Tinglayen** and trek to villages around there. From Tinglayen, travel by jeepney or white-water raft down the Chico River to **Tabuk**. Alternatively, from Bontoc head to **Banaue** and **Batad**, site of Luzon's most famous **rice terraces**. Hard-core trekkers should not miss the outstanding two-day trek to Batad from **Barlig**, outside of Bontoc, via Mt Amuyao. Stunning hikes around Batad and Banaue will keep you occupied for days.

Diving in the Philippines

Best Dive Regions

Mindoro Two hours off Mindoro's west coast lies Apo Reef (p197), arguably the Philippines' best dive site, while under the emerald-green waters of Puerto Galera (p183) are coral-rich reefs full of marine life of all shapes and sizes.

Bohol The most popular dive destination in the Visayas is Bohol's Panglao Island (p298), where the action is concentrated around Alona Beach. The entire area is festooned with wonderful dive sites, but the highlight is undoubtedly Balicasag Island (p301)

Southern Negros The city of Dumaguete (p281) is in range of several top dive sites, including the underwater paradise of Apo Island (p288), Siquijor (p289) Dauin (p287) and Sumilon Island, Cebu (p228).

Cebu In the island province of Cebu you'll find Moalboal, (p224) one of the oldest centres of diving in the country; Mactan Island (p216); an upscale resort area with good diving near Cebu City; and Malapascua Island (p221), where you can spot rare thresher sharks

Planning Your Dive

When to Go

Many parts of the country boast year-round diving, but the Philippines is affected by the annual cycles of the northeast *(amihan)* and southwest *(habagat)* monsoon winds that create a dry season (November to May, with some regional variations), and a wet season (June to October), as well as by typhoons that visit the country periodically from June to December.

Dry Season

The *amihan* winds that affect the country from November until April dispel much of the remaining rain. The sea can be quite choppy and turbid during the height of the *amihan* (late December to early March) – many dive centres have alternative sites to visit if weather disturbances are affecting specific areas. Mid-November is generally regarded as the start of the 'tourist season' by dive operators throughout the country. Christmas and New Year see most dive centres and resorts overflowing with divers, so reservations are recommended. The *amihan* dies down in late March and the sea becomes flat, calm and a brilliant azure, with incredible visibility that peaks during April and May in many areas.

RESPONSIBLE DIVING

Before embarking on a scuba-diving, skin-diving or snorkelling trip, carefully following the points below will help ensure a safe and enjoyable experience.

» Be sure you are healthy and feel comfortable diving.

» Be aware of local laws, regulations and etiquette about marine life and the environment.

» Avoid touching or standing on living marine organisms or dragging equipment across the reef. Polyps can be damaged by even the gentlest contact.

» Be conscious of your fins. Even without contact, the surge from fin strokes near the reef can damage delicate organisms.

» Practise and maintain proper buoyancy control. Major damage can be done by divers descending too fast and colliding with reefs.

» Resist the temptation to collect or buy corals or shells or to loot marine archaeological sites (mainly shipwrecks).

» Ensure that you take your rubbish and any other litter you may find away from dive sites. Plastics in particular are a serious threat to marine life.

» Do not feed fish.

» Minimise your disturbance of marine animals. Never ride on the backs of turtles.

Wet Season

The height of the rainy season for most of the country (July to September) corresponds with the height of the typhoon season, a double whammy that often results in major tropical downpours that can last for a few days. While heavy rain can cause lowered visibility, the nature of many of the diving areas is such that there are usually sheltered spots in the lee of the prevailing winds that afford reasonable diving and adequate visibility. Still, remote live-aboard and safari diving are rarely offered from July through to November, and in some areas many dive operators close down for a few months during this period.

What You'll See

The Philippines' amazing diversity of marine life is mostly of the small- to medium-sized variety. Divers who have travelled the world recognise the Philippines as one of the world's best macro (small marine life) diving locations. However, outside of Tubbataha, Apo Reef and a handful of other locations you rarely get the big pelagic (open-sea marine life) action that characterise neighbours such as Palau in the south Pacific. Still, the sheer range of marine life and the diversity of coral is among the world's best.

Sadly, that coral remains under constant threat, as destructive fishing methods such as cyanide and dynamite fishing are widely practised (see p432). The best Philippines dive sites have been given marine-protected status and have thus been spared the ravages of destructive fishing practices.

What to Bring

Dive centres are typically well stocked with a wide variety of well-maintained and reasonably new rental equipment. Technical divers will find what they need at dive centres offering technical diving, including reels and accessories, mixed gas and, in many cases, rebreathers. Many operators also sell equipment, and most internationally recognised brands can be bought and serviced throughout the islands.

Choosing a Dive Operator

The diving environment can often be deceptive in the Philippines. Clear water and great visibility can lead to disorientation and going below the planned depth easily. Currents can be a major factor on many dives, and the sea conditions and weather can change in a matter of minutes at certain times of the year, from flat, calm and sunny to big waves, wind and rain.

For those reasons, it is strongly advised that you dive with a local dive operator that displays a high degree of professionalism. A PADI affiliation can be a good indication of

» (above) Wreck diving at Monkey Beach, Mindoro Occidental
» (left) A delicate nudibranch (sea slug) in the waters off Negros island

COSTS

Dive prices vary significantly from region to region, and depend on how many people are in your group. Provided you have a few people along with you, you can expect to pay about US$23 to US$30 per dive with a divemaster, including all equipment and a relatively short boat trip. Prices go down a bit if you have your own equipment, and two- or three-tank dives usually cost less than single-tank dives. Prices go up if you're heading to dive sites located further offshore. PADI open-water certification courses vary widely from resort to resort and can cost anywhere from US$350 to US$450.

Of the major dive destinations in the Philippines, Moalboal and Dumaguete (not really a dive destination per se but within range of a lot of good diving) are generally known to have the cheapest rates. Padre Burgos in Leyte is just slightly more expensive.

Anilao, Alona Beach (Panglao Island), Mactan Island and Dauin (the jump-off point for Apo Island in Negros) are at the pricier end of the spectrum, with individual dives often costing as much as US$40 including equipment, and PADI open-water courses costing upwards of US$450.

The other popular dive centres – Malapascua, Camiguin Island, Coron, Puerto Galera and Siquijor – are in the midrange. These areas tend to have a mix of affordable dive centres and higher-end resorts that charge a premium for diving.

In Boracay, which is not known as a great dive destination but is a popular place to get certified, prices are fixed for all resorts by the Boracay Association of Scuba-diving Schools at about US$35 for a dive including full gear, and US$450 for an open-water certification course.

Of course, safety is more important than price when choosing a dive operator. Often (but certainly not always) more expensive dive outfits have better equipment and service and/or more experienced guides.

a dive operation's commitment to safety and customer service. In addition, check out an operator's safety procedures and emergency plans. Ask if the operator has oxygen, if it is brought along on dive boats, and if there are personnel that are trained to administer it on board too. Take a look at the rental equipment: is it relatively new and well maintained? Are the classrooms equipped with audiovisual aids? And finally, as there are hundreds of international dive professionals working throughout the country, find one that speaks a language you are comfortable with.

Certification

All dive centres in the Philippines require that a diver be certified by a recognised international training agency and should ask to see your card (many of them take your word for it if you forget your card). Operators rarely ask to see a log book to assess a diver's experience. Most live-aboard trips require at least an advanced certification, but the good news is that training is both widely available and great value throughout the country.

Courses

Whether you're an entry-level scuba diver looking to learn with a professional dive centre or an experienced technical diver seeking to become an instructor trainer, the Philippines is an excellent place to learn to dive and for ongoing training. The industry leader, the Professional Association of Diving Instructors (PADI), accounts for the majority of dive certifications issued here, and there are many PADI-accredited dive centres and dive resorts covering the full range of affiliate statuses, usually a good indication that a centre follows high safety, ethical and professional standards. Other training agencies represented throughout the country include the National Association of Underwater Instructors (NAUI), Scuba Schools International (SSI), Confédération Mondiale Des Activités Subaquatiques (CMAS), Scuba Diving International (SDI) and all the main international technical diving associations.

Technical Diving

Technical diving is big throughout the Philippines, and there is no shortage of deeper sites for technical training. The wrecks at

Diving in the Philippines

LIVE-ABOARDS

Live-aboards (boats that divers sleep on during dive trips) are a popular way to visit some of the Philippines' more remote dive sites, or to visit several sites in a week. They range from custom dive boats and yachts to converted fishing vessels and modified bangka boats.

Live-aboard dive safaris depart from and/or are organised by dive operators in Puerto Galera, Boracay and throughout the Visayas. In general, choosing a live-aboard boat should be as much or more a function of assessing the safety, seaworthiness and professionalism of an operation rather than the price.

Live-aboards operating out of Puerto Princesa, in Palawan, are the only way to visit the Philippines' marquee dive site, the Tubbataha Reefs in the Sulu Sea.

the bottom of Coron Bay and Subic Bay make for outstanding technical diving.

Qualified technical dive training outfits include Tech Asia (www.asiadivers.com), the technical diving arm of Asia Divers in Puerto Galera (see p185); Vasco's (p94) in the Subic Bay Freeport Zone; and PhilTech (www.philtech.net), based in Makati.

Some live-aboards also offer technical diving, mixed gas and rebreather equipment and training on request to qualified divers.

Dive Sites

Divers of all levels will find challenge and adventure aplenty in the Philippines. Whether you're more comfortable diving on a shallow coral garden or are looking for deep technical dives, the Philippines is one of the world's best diving destinations. It has a profusion of wrecks, walls and reefs, many teeming with marine life ranging from tiny, unique nudibranchs (sea slugs) to giant whale sharks.

The following dive-site descriptions represent just a few of the hundreds of sites that are visited regularly by divers throughout the Philippines.

Luzon

Not only is Luzon home to the capital, Manila, it's also home to the nation's unofficial scuba-diving capital, Anilao (p89), in Batangas province, where many Manila-based divers make their first training dives. Anilao is busy most weekends with city-dwelling enthusiasts, as it is a convenient two-hour drive from Manila. The most famous dive site in Anilao, and arguably in the country, is Cathedral Rock, a marine sanctuary just offshore. Nearby Sombrero Island presents a cavalcade of crevices and coral- and gorgonian-covered boulders which attract pelagic such as rainbow runners and yellowtails. Maximum depth here is 27m. The former US Naval Base of Subic Bay (p93) has several wrecks to dive including the impressive USS *New York* (p94). Rounding out Luzon, we must mention Donsol (p169), in southeast Luzon, where whale sharks can be found in the silty waters of Donsol Bay. The season for snorkelling with the sharks usually lasts from early December to late May or early June.

Mindoro

The Spanish named Mindoro after a gold mine, but for divers, the most exciting treasure is under the water. Puerto Galera (p183) is a major training centre, and there are over 20 professional dive operations along the two main beaches of Sabang and Small La Laguna. The isthmus that contains these beaches juts out into the Verde Island Passage, and consequently some of the sites, especially those off Escarceo (or Lighthouse) Point, can experience unpredictable sea conditions and strong currents, so diving with an experienced local guide is an absolute necessity. But there are also plenty of less challenging sites, perfect for intermediate divers and the many divers who take their basic certification course here. Two hours off Mindoro's west coast lies Apo Reef, one of the Philippines' very best dive sites, where you'll likely spot more sharks than other divers.

The Visayas

The Visayas is comprised of numerous islands, large and small, encompassing some of the country's most exciting diving. This list of dive sites in the Visayas is practically infinite. Located on the island of Cebu, Moalboal (p224) has a spectacular wall that starts just offshore. Other popular dive destinations on Cebu include Lilo-an (p228), on the island's southern tip, and Mactan Island (p216) near Cebu City. Both cater to package tourists. Just off Cebu's north coast lies Malapascua Island (p221), where a resident shoal of rare thresher sharks patrols the adjacent Monad Shoal. Over on Bohol, the waters around Cabilao Island (p302) and Panglao Island (p298) are rich with marine life, and many diving veterans consider Balicasag Island the best commercial dive site in the country outside the remote reefs systems of Apo Reef National Park and Tubbataha National Park.

Southern Negros, around Apo Island, and nearby Siquijor are two more hugely popular dive areas, although the sites are more spread out in these parts than at Alona Beach or Moalboal. Boracay (p251) is a popular training spot with a few good dives of its own. And Padre Burgos (p316), on Sogod Bay in Southern Leyte, offers reef diving on par with anything else in the Visayas, and the possibility of spotting whale sharks from February to June.

Mindanao & Sulu

Mindanao is the second-largest island in the Philippines, and, despite being known for its religious and political unrest, is also home to some excellent diving. On the south side, the area around Davao (p354), particularly Samal Island (p360) and its smaller neighbour Talikud Island (p361), has been a popular dive destination for several decades. Ligid Caves is the most famous site around Samal Island. General Santos (or 'Gen San'; p185) is home to a couple of dive centres and an extremely impressive drop-off that stretches for over 10km along the coastline. Off the central north coast of Mindanao, Camiguin Island (p341) bears reminders of its volcanic origins and more recent tectonic events at dive sites such as Jigdup Reef, a sea mount that rises from the deep sea floor to the surface.

Palawan

The long finger of Palawan points to some great diving whichever way you look at it. Coron Bay in the north, with its sunken Japanese WWII fleet (p396), is a must-see for wreck-diving enthusiasts. Aside from wreck diving, Coron has some outstanding coral reefs that often get overlooked in all the excitement, as well as a unique trek up a cliff face to dive in an inland lake. The Bacuit Archipelago (p394) is known more for what's above water than what's below, although there are a smattering of sites around El Nido. Puerto Princesa (p373) has a few dive sites in Honda Bay (p378), but is chiefly known as the jumping-off point for live-aboards visiting the remote Tubbataha Reefs (p379).

Other Resources

» *Diving & Snorkelling Philippines*, published by Lonely Planet, is a great, detailed guide to the dive sites of the Philippines. It neatly supplements the information in this book and can be purchased at shop.lonelyplanet.com.

» *Coral Reef Fishes: Indo-Pacific and Caribbean* by Ewald Lieske and Robert Myers is a useful guide to reef fish found in Philippine waters.

» The website www.divephil.com is a comprehensive source for all things dive-related in the Philippines.

» Tanikalang Ginto has a fantastic selection of Philippine dive websites at www.filipinolinks.com/Sports/Diving.

» Dive Right Coron's website at www.coronwrecks.com has detailed information about the wrecks of Coron.

regions at a glance

The Philippines consists of three main island groups: Luzon, the Visayas and Mindanao. Between them they offer something for everyone: megacity madness in Manila, hill tribes in North Luzon and Mindanao, surfing along the eastern seaboard of the entire country, and good snorkelling practically everywhere. The Visayas most embody the defining image of the Philippines: a dreamy desert island festooned with palm trees and ringed by white sand. Palawan is an island apart, a fantastic otherworld of unspoiled rainforest and surreal seascapes.

Manila

History ✓✓
Nightlife ✓✓
Food ✓✓

The steamy, seamy capital is a little in-your-face for many first-time visitors, but it can quickly grow on you with its mix of fascinating museums, raucous nightlife, varied cuisine and undeniable energy.

p36

Around Manila

Diving ✓
History ✓✓✓
Trekking ✓✓

Names like Corregidor and Bataan evoke WWII like nowhere else. For climbers there's a bevy of accessible peaks to choose from, while the south coast of Luzon has some of the country's best diving.

p82

North Luzon

History ✓✓
Outdoors ✓✓✓
Culture ✓✓✓

This region is intimidating in its diversity, with secluded bays where the surf's almost always up, romantic Spanish colonial enclaves and mountains sliced by rice terraces, inhabited by a staggeringly diverse range of indigenous tribes.

p100

Southeast Luzon

Food ✓✓✓
Outdoors ✓✓
Festivals ✓✓

After searing your tongue on the spicy cuisine of Bicol, cool down by taking advantage of numerous water sports, or heat things up more with a volcano trek. Nearby small islands are perfect for short-hop exploration.

p154

Mindoro

Diving ✓✓✓
Cultural Minorities ✓✓
Remote Places ✓✓

Diving or snorkelling at Apo Reef can't be beat, while Puerto Galera adds a party element to your diving experience. Elsewhere you can visit lost islands offshore and lost tribes in the impenetrable hinterlands.

p181

The Visayas

Diving ✓✓✓
Beaches ✓✓✓
History ✓✓

Diving and beaches are what bring the majority of visitors to the Visayas, but the region is steeped in history too – you'll encounter grisly reminders of WWII through underwater wrecks, museums or monuments.

p200

Palawan

Underwater Views ✓✓✓
Resorts ✓✓✓
Village Life ✓✓✓

From chic and exclusive private island retreats to simple beachfront bungalows, Palawan has it all. Leave your resort to explore coral reefs, WWII shipwrecks and isolated settlements where new visitors are accorded celebrity status.

p370

Mindanao & Sulu

Hiking ✓✓✓
Water Sports ✓✓
Rural Landscapes ✓✓✓

Mindanao's rugged and varied topography is a blessing for thrill seekers. This huge, largely rural island has four peaks higher than 3000m, canyoning, surfing, white-water rafting and, of course, diving and snorkelling galore.

p329

Look out for these icons:

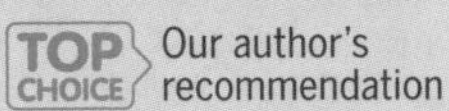

Our author's recommendation

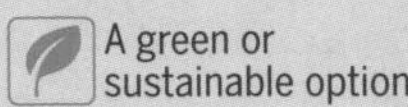
A green or sustainable option

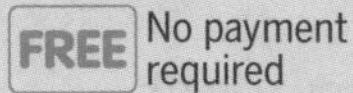

No payment required

See the Index for a full list of destinations covered in this book.

On the Road

Manila

TELEPHONE CODE 02 / POP 11.5 MILLION

Includes »

Best Places to Eat

- » Sala (p67)
- » Corner Tree Cafe (p68)
- » Seafood Market (p53)
- » Sofitel Philippine Plaza (p52)
- » Casa Armas (p53)

Best Places to Stay

- » Manila Hotel (p49)
- » Hotel Miramar (p49)
- » Makati Shangri-La (p63)
- » Casa Bocobo (p49)
- » A Venue Suites (p65)

Why Go?

Manila's moniker, the 'Pearl of the Orient', couldn't be more apt – its cantankerous shell reveals its jewel only to those resolute enough to pry. No stranger to hardship, the city has endured every disaster both human and nature could throw at it, and yet today the chaotic metropolis thrives as a true Asian megacity. Skyscrapers pierce the hazy sky, mushrooming from the grinding poverty of expansive shantytowns, while gleaming malls foreshadow Manila's brave new air-conditioned world. The congested roads snarl with traffic, but, like the overworked arteries of a sweating giant, they are what keep this modern metropolis alive.

The determined will discover Manila's tender soul, perhaps among the leafy courtyards and cobbled streets of serene Intramuros, where little has changed since the Spanish left. Or it may be in the eddy of repose arising from the generosity of one of the city's 11 million residents.

When to Go

Manila

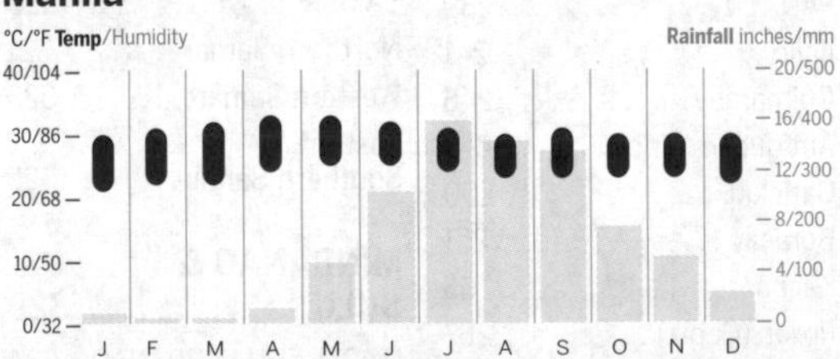

Dec–Feb The coolest, most pleasant months.

Mar–Apr Holy Week is no time to be in packed beach resorts, so spend it in sleepy Manila.

Jul–Aug Some say it rains too much; we say it's the best time to escape the searing sun.

MANILA IN...

Two Days

Wander historic **Intramuros** and **Rizal Park**. Head to **Roxas Blvd** to watch the sun set over Manila Bay, then spend some quality hours in the many bars of **Malate**. On your second morning, take the LRT up to the **Chinese Cemetery**, then backtrack to **Chinatown** for lunch. Spend the evening in upscale **Makati**, where there are oodles of restaurants, bars and nightclubs to choose from.

Four Days

Follow the two-day itinerary, then on your third day take an entertaining **walking tour** around a city neighbourhood. In the afternoon, head back to Makati for the intriguing **Ayala Museum** and some more good eatin'. On your final day, spend the morning at the **National Museum of the Filipino People**, or treat yourself to a massage at one of Manila's many spas. Explore the camp and classic **Cultural Center of the Philippines**, then take in the sunset at the **Sofitel Philippine Plaza** or at one of many bay-facing eateries at gargantuan **Mall of Asia**.

History

Early tourists, such as the 19th-century traveller Fedor Jagor, described Manila as a splendid, fortified city of wide, cobbled streets and regal town houses. Tragically, most of that splendid city was obliterated in WWII.

Manila was colonised by the Spaniard Miguel Lopez de Legazpi in 1571. Its broad sweep of fertile lands made it more attractive than Cebu, which had been the capital. King Philip II of Spain conferred on the city the illustrious title *Isigne y Siempre Leal Ciudad* (Distinguished and Ever Loyal City), but the city continued to be called by its pre-Hispanic name of Maynilad (presumed to be from *may*, meaning 'there is', and *nilad*, a mangrove plant that grew in abundance on the banks of the Pasig River), which was later corrupted to Manila.

From the late 19th century onwards, it could be argued that Manila was something approaching a Paris of Asia. It was a thriving trading centre, and its multicultural mix provided a good entry point into China and other Asian countries. In 1905 Daniel Burnham, the master planner of Chicago, was hired to produce a master plan for the city. His grand vision included Roxas Blvd, which, even today, under its somewhat shabby patina, echoes Lake Shore Dr in Chicago. The streets were lined with grand structures, many reflecting the best of Art Deco design.

WWII changed everything (see 'The Destruction of Manila' on p414). Many claim the city has never recovered. Rebuilding after the war was sporadic, and the city was never able to reclaim either its regional importance or its sense of self. Many locals complain about the scattered character of Manila; it's true that the various cities within the city feel disunified and there is no sense of a whole.

CITY OF MANILA (DOWNTOWN)

The vast urban sprawl known as Metro Manila is composed of 16 cities, but its heart and soul remains the City of Manila proper ('downtown' Manila; population 1.7 million). It was here that the city was founded on the banks of the Pasig River; it was here where the Spanish solidified their claim to the Philippines after overthrowing the Muslim rulers of Maynilad; and it was here where the city suffered its darkest hours in the dying days of WWII.

The traditional tourist belt encompasses the area immediately south of the Pasig River – specifically Intramuros, where the main tourist attractions are concentrated; and Ermita and Malate, where most tourists still stay. Immediately to the north of the Pasig are the districts of Binondo and Quiapo, gateway to Chinatown. Other districts are Paco, San Miguel, Santa Cruz, San Nicolas and slum-ridden Tondo, near the ferry docks.

Until recently most tourists had little reason to leave the downtown area, but Metro Manila's best restaurants and bars have

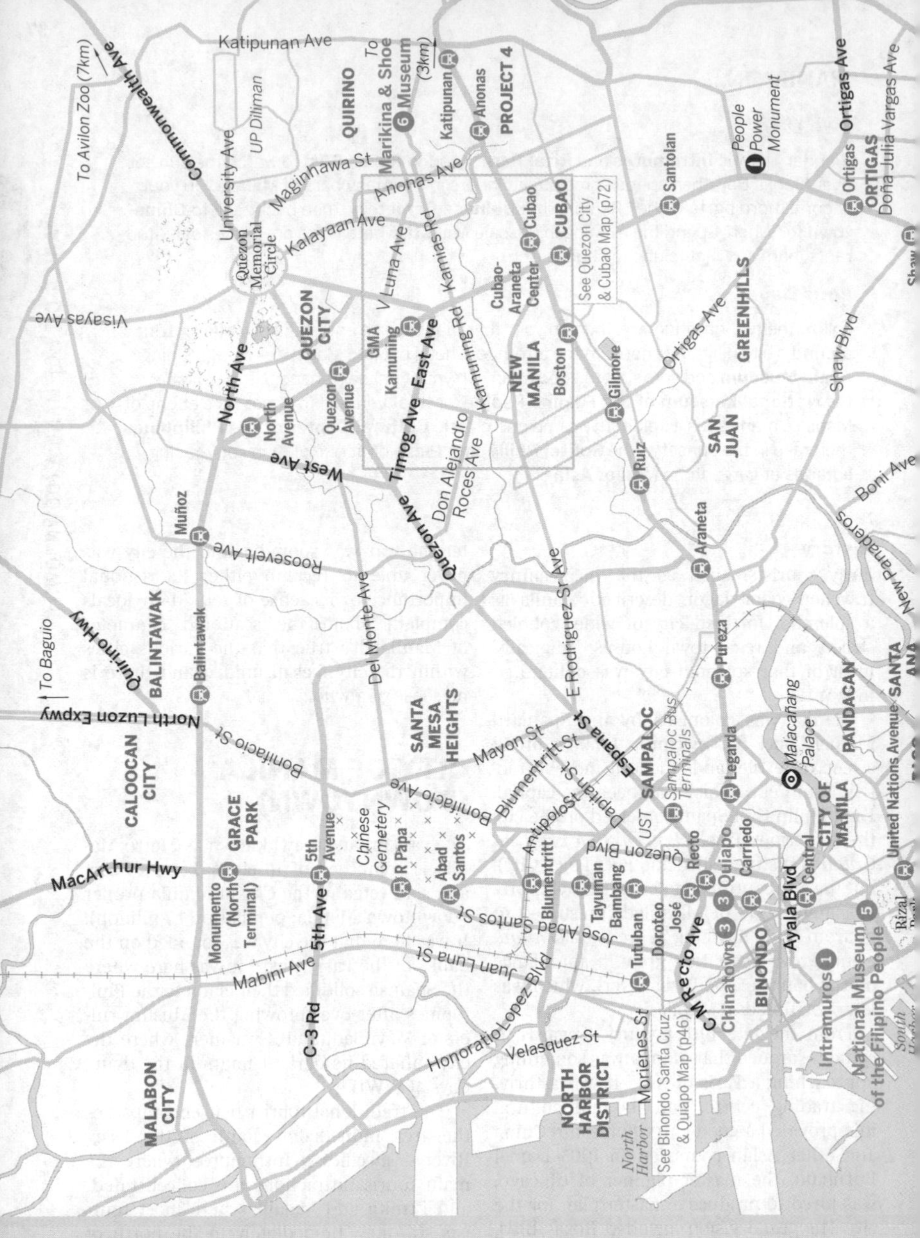

Metro Manila Highlights

1. Hear echoes of a lost past in **Intramuros** (p40)
2. Live the high life amid the upscale malls, restaurants and hotels of **Makati** (p70)
3. Prowl the markets and backstreets of **Quiapo** (p48) and **Chinatown** (p47)
4. Learn about a Manila you didn't know existed on an excellent **walking tour** (p48)
5. Take the country's cultural pulse at the wonderful **National Museum of the Filipino People** (p41)

6 Gawk at Imelda's shoes – some 800 pairs – on display at the **Marikina Shoe Museum** (p75)

7 Take in Manila Bay's famed sunset from a seaside perch along **Roxas Blvd** (p45)

8 Get lost three times while careening about the streets in a **jeepney** (p80)

gradually been migrating east to more upscale Makati over the last decade, and the visiting masses are starting to follow.

Sights

For a city that's not known as a major tourist draw, Manila sure has a lot to see. Because of its hugeness and its traffic you'll likely never see all of it – the best strategy is to go one neighbourhood at a time. Much of what's best to see isn't always at a traditional sight, but rather can be found in the life of the varied neighbourhoods.

INTRAMUROS

When Miguel Lopez de Legazpi wrested control of Manila, he chose to erect his fortress on the remnants of the Islamic settlement by the mouth of the Pasig River. The walled city of Intramuros, as it came to be called, was invaded by Chinese pirates, threatened by Dutch forces, and held by the British, Americans and Japanese at various times, yet it survived until the closing days of WWII, when it was finally destroyed during the Battle of Manila.

From its founding in 1571, Intramuros was the exclusive preserve of the Spanish ruling classes. Fortified with bastions *(baluarte),* the wall enclosed an area of some 64 hectares. Gates *(puerta)* with drawbridges provided access to and from the outside world. Within the walls were imposing government buildings, stately homes, churches, convents, monasteries, schools, hospitals and cobbled plazas. The native populace was settled in surrounding areas such as Paco and Binondo, while the Chinese were kept under permanent supervision in ghettos called *parian.*

One can still feel a strong sense of history on a visit to Intramuros. Start your walking tour at the **Intramuros Visitors Center** (☎527 2961; ⊙8am-5pm), which hands out a an excellent free guide map of the walled city. It's located on the grounds of Fort Santiago. **Anda St** is a good street for a wander; many of the buildings still have Spanish-tile street names.

Fort Santiago FORTRESS
(Map p42; Santa Clara St; adult/student P65/50; ⊙8am-6pm) Guarding the entrance to the Pasig River you'll find Manila's premier tourist attraction. Over the years it has evolved largely into a memorial to Dr José Rizal, who was imprisoned here in the final days before his execution in 1896 for inciting revolution against the Spanish colonials.

Within the fort grounds you'll find the **Rizal Shrine** (⊙8am-5pm) in the building where the Philippines' national hero was incarcerated as he awaited execution. It contains various displays of Rizal memorabilia, including a reliquary containing one of his vertebrae, the first draft of his novel *Noli Me Tangere* (Touch Me Not) and the original copy of the poem 'Mi Ultimo Adios' (My Last Farewell), which was smuggled out of his cell inside an oil lamp.

At the far end of the fort, a Spanish military barracks has been turned into a seldom-used **open-air theatre**. Rizal spent his last night in a cellblock at one end of these barracks. Brass footprints set into the pavement mark his final steps to the execution spot in Rizal Park. For more information on Rizal, see p410.

San Agustin Church CHURCH
(Map p42; General Luna St) The San Agustin Church was the only building left intact after the destruction of Intramuros in WWII. Built between 1587 and 1606, it is the oldest church in the Philippines. The present structure is actually the third to stand on the site, and has weathered seven major earthquakes, as well as the Battle of Manila. It's an active church and much in demand for weddings and other ceremonies.

The massive facade conceals an ornate interior filled with objects of great historical and cultural merit. Note the intricate trompe l'oeil frescoes on the vaulted ceiling. Be sure to check out the tropical cloisters as well as the slightly shabby gardens out the back.

To see the interior of the church for free, you must visit during a mass, or you can access it through the interesting **San Agustin Museum** (admission P100; ⊙8am-noon & 1-6pm), a treasure house of antiquities that give the visitor tantalising glimpses of the fabled riches of old Manila. Look for the vaguely Chinese-looking Immaculate Conception statue in ethereal ivory.

Casa Manila MUSEUM
(Map p42; ☎527 4084; Plaza Luis Complex, General Luna St; adult/child P70/50; ⊙9am-6pm Tue-Sun) This beautiful reproduction of a Spanish colonial house offers a window into the opulent lifestyle of the gentry in the 19th century. Imelda Marcos had it built to showcase the architecture and interior

design of the late Spanish period (the ceilings were made much higher, as Imelda is a well-above-average 178cm). The house may not be authentic but the stunning antique furniture and artwork are.

Bahay Tsinoy MUSEUM
(Map p42; cnr Anda & Cabildo Sts; adult/student P100/60; ⌚1-5pm Tue-Sun) The vast Bahay Tsinoy museum showcases the important role played by the *sangley,* as the Spanish called the Chinese, in the growth of Manila (*sangley* means 'trade' in the locally prevailing Hokkien dialect). There are three-dimensional dioramas depicting Chinese and mestizo life in the *parian,* old coins and porcelain, and an excellent collection of photos.

Ramparts RAMPARTS
Most of Intramuros' walls, gates and bulwarks are accessible, although some are weedy and a bit seedy. You can walk along the top of the ramparts for all or part of their approximately 4.5km length. There are several places inside the walls to ascend and descend.

Memorare Manila MEMORIAL
(Map p42; cnr General Luna & Anda Sts) This simple but moving memorial honours the approximately 150,000 civilian Manileños who perished in the Battle of Manila. A few faded placards nearby contain before-and-after photos of the city.

Manila Cathedral CHURCH
(Map p42; cnr Postigo & General Luna Sts) The Manila Cathedral was destroyed in WWII, but the present edifice, erected in 1951, looks suitably ancient with its weathered Romanesque facade and graceful cupola. Inside are a gilded altar, a 4500-pipe organ, and rosette windows with beautiful stained glass. The cathedral fronts **Plaza de Roma**, which was a bloody bullring until it was converted into a plaza. To one side a new Treasury Department building has been built on the ruins of the **Ayuntamiento**, once the grandest building in all of Intramuros.

Metropolitan Theater HISTORIC BUILDING
(Map p42; Quezon Blvd) Opposite the Lawton Park and Ride bus station, a few blocks south of the classic Manila Central Post Office, stands one of the few survivors of Burnham's plan. It's now in a state of disrepair but is still a stunning piece of Art Deco architecture. Nearby, beautifully illuminated at night, the clock tower of **Manila City Hall** (P Burgos St) is visible from the Intramuros golf course.

RIZAL PARK & AROUND

Rizal Park PARK
(Map p42) Still widely known as 'Luneta' (its name until it was officially changed in the 1950s), Manila's iconic park is spread out over some 60 hectares of open lawns, ornamental gardens, paved walks and wooded areas, dotted with monuments to a whole pantheon of Filipino heroes.

At dawn, various groups gather to practise t'ai chi or the local martial art of *arnis,* or *arnis de mano,* a pre-Hispanic style of stick-fighting. The long-running Concert at the Park also takes place at the **open-air auditorium**; it's free and starts at around 5.30pm on Sundays.

It was in this park that José Rizal was executed by the Spanish colonial authorities. The **Rizal Monument**, guarded by sentries in full regalia, contains the hero's mortal remains and stands as a symbol of Filipino nationhood.

To one side of the monument you will find the **Site of Rizal's Execution** (admission P10; ⌚8am-5pm Wed-Sun); at the entrance is a black granite wall inscribed with Rizal's 'Mi Ultimo Adios' (My Last Farewell). Eight tableaux of life-size bronze statues recreate the dramatic last moments of the hero's life; at night these statues become part of a light-and-sound presentation dedicated to Rizal (admission P50; ⌚7pm Wed-Sun). It's in Tagalog, but they'll do it in English if you have a big enough group (or pay them enough).

At the western end of the park is the **Quirino Grandstand**, where Philippine presidents take their oath of office and deliver their first address to the nation. At the opposite end of the park the gigantic three-dimensional **relief map of the Philippines** is worth a look – see if you can spot 'perfect' Mt Mayon.

Along the north side are several ornamental gardens and the **Chess Plaza**, a shady spot where regulars test each other and look for new blood with shouts to visitors of 'Hey Joe, do you play chess?'

National Museum of the Filipino People MUSEUM
(Map p42; www.nationalmuseum.gov.ph; T Valencia Circle; admission P100, Sun free; ⌚10am-5pm Tue-Sun) This splendid museum houses a vast collection, including the skullcap of the

Intramuros & Rizal Park

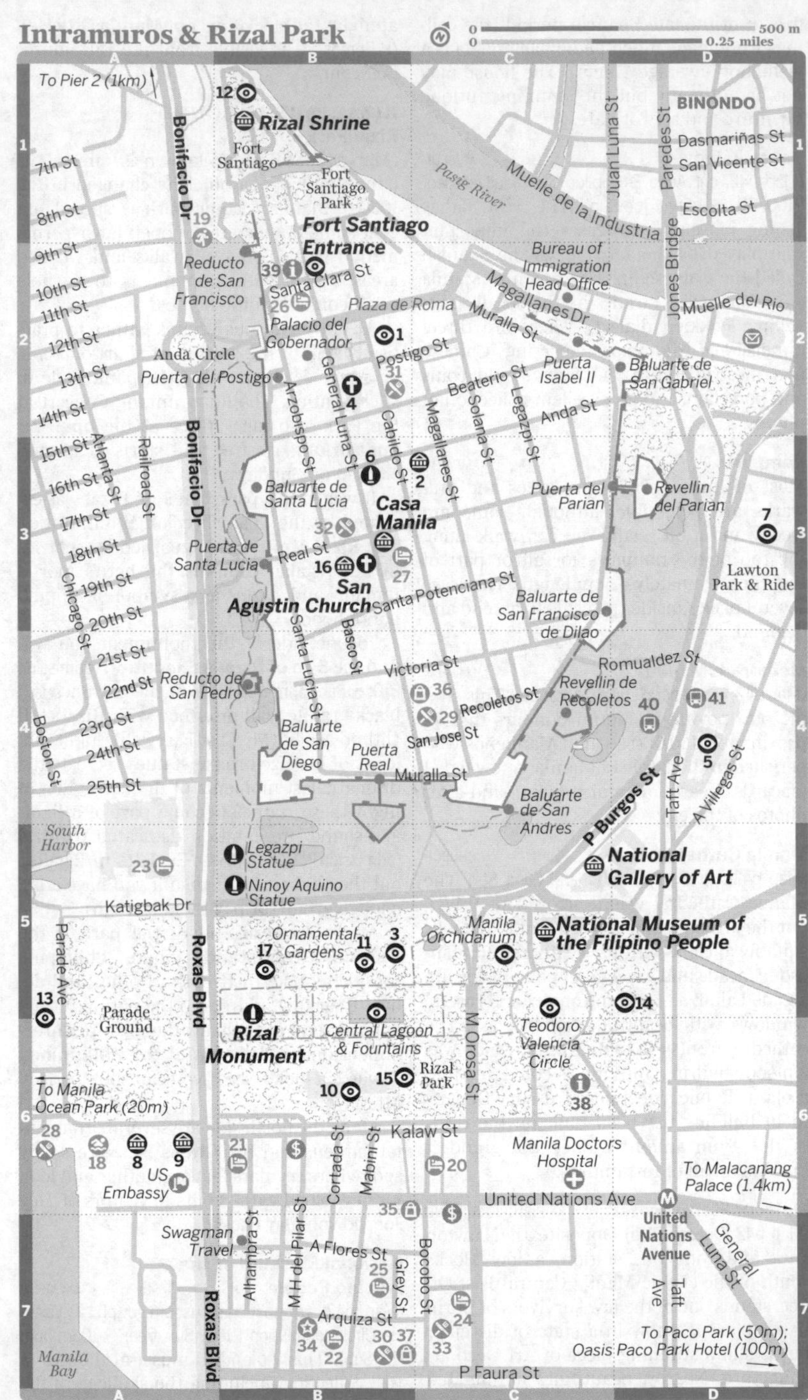

Intramuros & Rizal Park

Top Sights
- Casa Manila ... B3
- Fort Santiago Entrance ... B2
- National Gallery of Art ... C5
- National Museum of the Filipino People ... C5
- Rizal Monument ... B5
- Rizal Shrine ... B1
- San Agustin Church ... B3

Sights
- 1 Ayuntamiento ... B2
- 2 Bahay Tsinoy ... C3
- 3 Chess Plaza ... B5
- 4 Manila Cathedral ... B2
- 5 Manila City Hall ... D4
- 6 Memorare Manila ... B3
- 7 Metropolitan Theater ... D3
- 8 Museo ng Maynila ... A6
- 9 Museo Pambata ... A6
- 10 National Library ... B6
- 11 Open-Air Auditorium ... B5
- 12 Open-Air Theater ... B1
- 13 Quirino Grandstand ... A5
- 14 Relief Map of the Philippines ... D5
- 15 Rizal Park ... B6
- 16 San Agustin Museum ... B3
- 17 Site of Rizal's Execution ... B5

Activities, Courses & Tours
- 18 Army & Navy Club Pool ... A6
- 19 Club Intramuros Golf Course Entrance & Barbershop ... A1

Sleeping
- 20 Casa Bocobo ... C6
- 21 Hotel Miramar ... B6
- 22 Lotus Garden Hotel ... B7
- 23 Manila Hotel ... A5
- 24 Ralph Anthony Suites ... C7
- 25 Richmond Pension ... B7
- 26 Sailor's Inn ... B2
- 27 White Knight Hotel ... B3

Eating
- Barbara's ... (see 27)
- 28 Harbor View ... A6
- 29 Ilustrado ... C4
- 30 Kashmir ... B7
- 31 Patio de Conchita ... B2
- 32 Ristorante delle Mitre ... B3
- 33 Seafood Market ... C7

Entertainment
- 34 Hobbit House ... B7

Shopping
- 35 Hiraya Gallery ... B6
- La Monja Loca ... (see 27)
- 36 Silahis Arts & Artifacts Center ... C4
- 37 Solidaridad Bookshop ... B7
- Tradewinds Books ... (see 36)

Information
- 38 Department of Tourism Information Centre ... C6
- 39 Intramuros Visitors Center ... B2

Transport
- 40 Jeepneys to Ermita, Malate and Baclaran ... D4
- 41 Jeepneys to Quiapo, Sampaloc and Cubao ... D4

Philippines' earliest known inhabitant, Tabon Man (said by some to actually be a woman), who lived around 24,000 BC. There are extensive displays on the major Filipino indigenous groups, and a vast collection of Filipino painting and sculpture. A large section of the museum is devoted to porcelain plates, coins, jewellery etc recovered from the wreck of the *San Diego,* a Spanish galleon that sank off the coast of Luzon in 1600. Other treasures include a large collection of pre-Hispanic artefacts and musical instruments.

National Gallery of Art MUSEUM
(Map p42; P Burgos St; adult/student P100/30, Sun free; ⏲10am-5pm Tue-Sun) This proud museum contains many of the Philippines' signature works of art, including Juan Luna's seminal *Spoliarium,* which provides harsh commentary on Spanish rule. It's in the old Congress building designed by Daniel Burnham, across the street from its sister National Museum of the Filipino People (see p41; an admission ticket for both museums costs P150).

Museo ng Maynila HISTORIC BUILDING
(Map p42; South Blvd) The Museo ng Maynila is in the former Army & Navy Club, a once-posh US officers' retreat. The museum itself is closed, but it's worth strolling by to check out the building, a classic piece of

Ermita, Malate & Paco

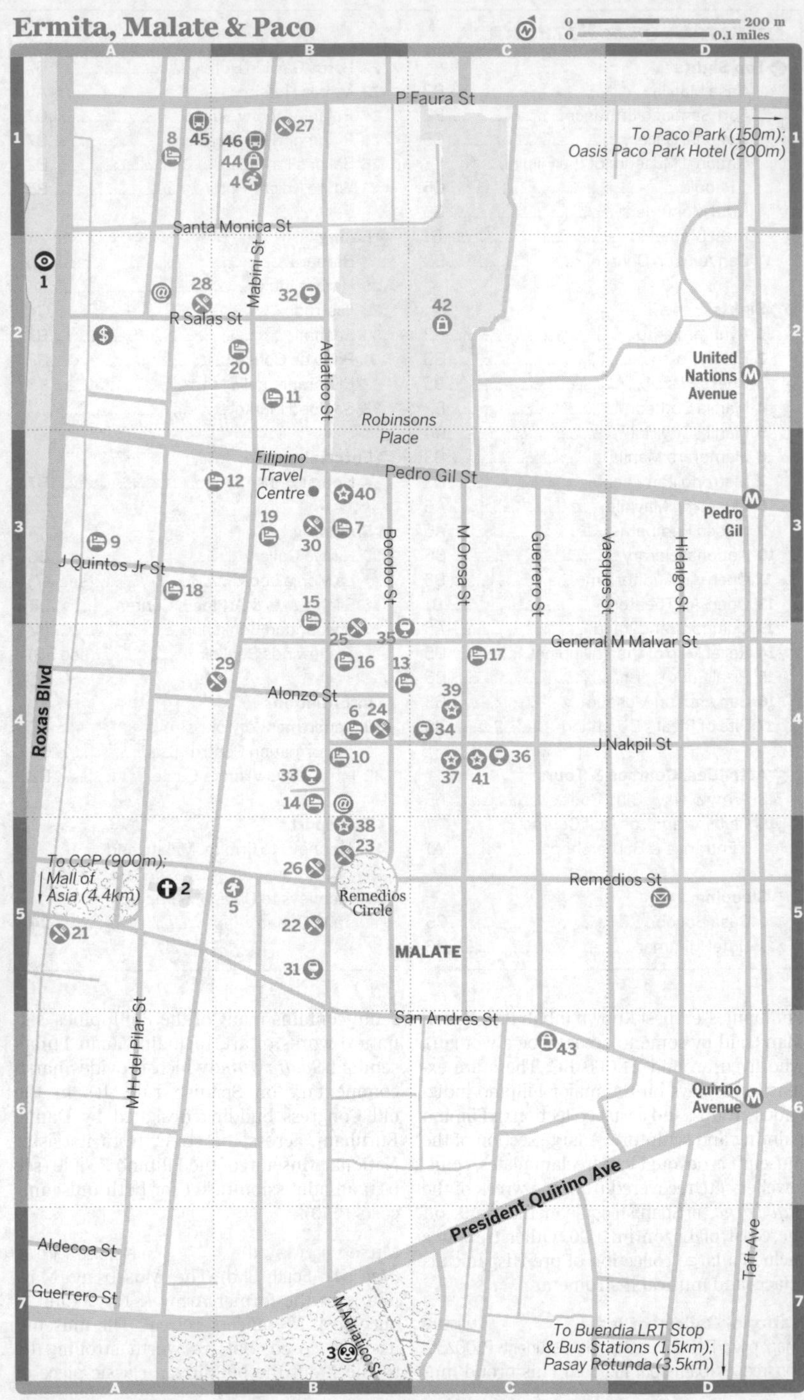

Ermita, Malate & Paco

Sights
- 1 Baywalk A2
- 2 Malate Church A5
- 3 Manila Zoo B7

Activities, Courses & Tours
- 4 Touch of Hands B1
- 5 Touch of Hands B5

Sleeping
- 6 Adriatico Arms Hotel B4
- 7 Adriatico Pensionne Inn B3
- 8 Chill-Out Guesthouse A1
- 9 Diamond Hotel A3
- 10 Friendly's Guest House B4
- 11 Hotel Vieve B2
- 12 Hyatt Hotel & Casino Manila B3
- 13 Lovely Moon Pension Inn B4
- 14 Malate Pensionne B4
- 15 Pan Pacific Hotel B3
- 16 Pearl Garden Hotel B4
- 17 Pearl Lane Hotel C4
- 18 Pension Natividad A3
- 19 Riviera Mansion Hotel B3
- 20 Stone House B2

Eating
- 21 Aristocrat A5
- 22 Bistro Remedios B5
- 23 Cafe Adriatico B5
- 24 Casa Armas B4
- 25 Hap Chang Tea House B4
- 26 Korean Palace B5
- 27 München B1
- 28 Shawarma Snack Center A2
- 29 Suzhou Dimsum B4
- 30 Zamboanga Restaurant B3

Drinking
- 31 1951 (Penguin Cafe) B5
- 32 Aqualicious B2
- 33 Erra's Place B4
- 34 Kuwagos Grill C4
- 35 Oarhouse B4
- 36 Silya C4

Entertainment
- 37 Bed C4
- 38 Bedrock B5
- 39 FAB/The Library C4
- 40 Ka Freddie's B3
- 41 O Bar C4
- Robinsons Movieworld (see 42)

Shopping
- 42 Robinsons Place Manila C2
- 43 San Andres Market C6
- 44 Tessoro's B1

Transport
- 45 Cagsawa A1
- RSL (see 45)
- 46 Si-Kat (Puerto Galera Trips) B1

American-era architecture. The tennis courts and swimming pool next door were once part of the club.

ERMITA, MALATE & PACO

Sights are not the real purpose of the adjoining areas of Ermita, Malate and Paco, south of Rizal Park. Commerce, including the bulk of Manila's tourism infrastructure, is the story here. The centre of the area's action is Remedios Circle, surrounded by numerous restaurants, bars and karaoke parlours.

Baywalk PROMENADE
(Map p44; Roxas Blvd) Splendid views of Manila Bay can be had from the pedestrian 'Baywalk' that runs along aspiring-to-be-grand Roxas Blvd. It was once a hive of activity, but the current Mayor of Manila, Alfredo Lim, cleared out the eateries, buskers, jugglers, magicians and cover bands after he assumed office in 2007, leaving the Baywalk in the category of 'peaceful place to enjoy the sunset'.

Malate Church CHURCH
(Map p44; cnr MH del Pilar & Remedios Sts, Malate) A greatly revered image of the Virgin Mary, called *Nuestra Señora de Remedios* (Our Lady of Remedies), roosts here. It was first built in 1588; this version dates from the 1860s.

Paco Park PARK
(off Map p44) For something a little leafier and historic than Remedios Circle, head over to Paco Park, where sturdy stone walls surround a pleasant circular park, popular for weddings and strolling. It was a cemetery during Spanish times; Rizal was buried here from 1898 to 1912.

BINONDO, QUIAPO & SANTA CRUZ

The teahouses of Chinatown are the big draw in this area, just over the Pasig River from Intramuros. These are some of the oldest parts of Manila, but sadly the few pieces of Spanish colonial architecture remaining are being rapidly torn down. Still, it remains the centre for trading, and there are numerous markets, especially in Quiapo. The LRT-1 Carriedo Station is in the heart of the action.

West of the old Binondo area are parts of Manila that survived the war intact. Somewhat dodgy in character, the San Nicolas neighbourhood in and around Madrid St and Lavezares St has some rundown but amazing 19th-century wooden houses with *capiz*-shell (mother-of-pearl) windows, elaborate carving and tiled street signs. Sadly, many of these buildings have been razed in recent years, and replaced with concrete structures.

Bahay Nakpil-Bautista HISTORIC BUILDING
(Map p46; http://bahaynakpil.org; 432 A Bautista St; adult/student P40/20; ⏲9am-5pm Tue-Sun) On a crowded side street just to the east, you will find Bahay Nakpil-Bautista. This is where the widow of Andres Bonifacio, the father of the Philippine Revolution, lived after his death. A historic landmark, it houses a small museum and is used for occasional cultural exhibits.

FREE **Chinese Cemetery** CEMETERY
(off Map p46; Rizal Ave Extension; ⏲7.30am-7pm) As in life, so it is in death for Manila's wealthy Chinese citizens, who are buried with every modern convenience in the huge Chinese Cemetery. There are mausoleums with crystal chandeliers, air-con, hot and cold running water, kitchens and flushing toilets (in case the interred are caught short on the way to paradise).

On 1 and 2 November (All Saints' Day and All Souls' Day), hundreds of Chinese-Filipino families gather to offer food and flowers to their ancestors, and have family reunions themselves.

Hire a bicycle (per hour P100) to get around the sprawling grounds, and consider hiring a guide (P350) for access to the best tombs. Tour guide Ivan Man Dy of Old Manila Walks (p48) does an excellent Chinese Cemetery tour. To get here take the LRT to Abad Santos then walk or take a tricycle (P25) to the south entrance.

Golden Mosque MOSQUE
(Map p46; Globo de Oro St) The Golden Mosque was constructed in 1976 as something of a welcoming gift for the late Libyan leader

Binondo, Santa Cruz & Quiapo

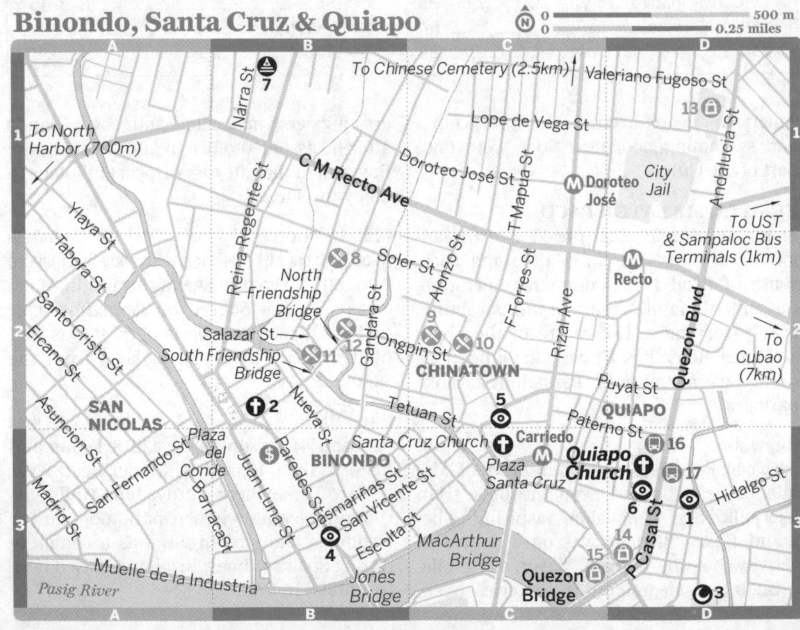

Muammar al-Gaddafi, although his scheduled visit never happened. This is still the city's largest mosque, and today it serves the growing Muslim community that has settled by the thousands in Quiapo.

Binondo Church CHURCH
(Map p46; cnr Paredes & Ongpin Sts) At the northern end of Paredes St stands the bell tower of Binondo Church, an unusual octagonal structure dating back to 1596. The rest of the church is a modern replacement for war damage. Inside there is a somewhat lurid statue of a bloody Jesus that would do Mel Gibson proud.

Seng Guan Buddhist Temple TEMPLE
(Map p46; Narra St) Further north, the Seng Guan Buddhist Temple is the centre of Manila's Buddhist community. It's not pretty but it's big.

Chinatown HISTORIC AREA
(Map p46)After centuries of suppression by the Spanish, Manila's Chinese population quickly rose on the economic and social ladder under more liberal administrations. Today the centre of the vibrant Chinese community is Chinatown, which straddles Santa Cruz and Binondo.

Chinatown is demarcated by **Goodwill Arches** (Map p46). The main street is Ongpin St; walking its length – which we recommended – will take 10 minutes, but exploring the neighbourhood can take hours. As in any other Chinese enclave around the world, you'll find dozens of goldsmiths, herbalists, teahouses and shops selling mooncakes, incense, paper money to burn for ancestors, trinkets and other curios. There are numerous places for a snack or a meal (see p54).

Activities

Golf

Club Intramuros Golf Course GOLF
(Map p42; ☎527 6613; Bonifacio Dr; nonresident green fees incl caddy day/night P1800/2750, resident P1300/1650) Just outside the walls of Intramuros in a uniquely urban venue, on what used to be the moat surrounding the city, you can golf by day or by night at the quirky 18-hole, par-66 Club Intramuros Golf Course. You can obtain the shady services of an 'umbrella girl' for P350 as well as rent clubs (P700).

Spas

It's not hard to find a massage in Manila. Use common sense to avoid getting more than you bargained for – in Malate, that usually means sticking to the nicer hotels. Five-star outfits like the Pan Pacific and Diamond hotels all have seriously swanky spas that welcome walk-in guests. Makati is more of a spa town.

Touch of Hands SPA
(www.touchofhands.com; 1hr massages P300-600) Mabini (Map p44; Casa Tesoro Bldg, 1335 Mabini St, Ermita) Remedios (Map p44; 513 Remedios St, Malate) Good-value, no hanky-panky.

Swimming

Thankfully there are many alternatives to fetid Manila Bay if you want to cool off. You can use almost any five-star hotel pool but it will cost you P600 to P1000. A thriftier

Binondo, Santa Cruz & Quiapo

Top Sights
Quiapo Church D3

Sights
1 Bahay Nakpil-Bautista D3
2 Binondo Church B2
3 Golden Mosque D3
4 Goodwill Arch B3
5 Goodwill Arch C2
6 Plaza Miranda D3
7 Seng Guan Buddhist Temple B1

Eating
8 Happy Veggie B2
9 Ling Nam Wonton Parlor & Noodle Factory C2
10 MXT Tea House C2
11 President Tea House B2
12 Salazar Bakery B2

Shopping
13 Central Market D1
14 Ilalim ng Tulay D3
15 Quinta Market C3

Transport
16 Buses to Makati D3
Jeepneys and FX to Rizal Park, Ermita, Malate and Pasay .... (see 6)
17 Jeepneys and FX to University of Santo Tomas and Quezon City D3

DON'T MISS

QUIAPO CHURCH

Lovers of markets and mayhem should cross the Quezon Bridge over the Pasig River to **Quiapo Church** (Map p46; Quezon Blvd), home of the **Black Nazarene**.

The main reason to go to Quiapo is not to see the church but to witness what's happening on and around the church square, Plaza Miranda. Here and in the surrounding markets every manner of product is sold to a throng of humanity.

Most notorious are the dubious apothecary stalls selling herbal and folk medicines, as well as amulets (carved stones and medallions believed to have magical powers). Showing admirable initiative, vendors will tell you that the 'Pampa Regla' potion is good for everything from weight loss to curing erectile dysfunction, depending on how you look. Langis Ng Ahas is snake oil – maybe.

Particularly colourful are the stalls around Carriedo St, which sell thickly padded bras, hardware, porn DVDs and just about anything else. Nearby, under **Quezon Bridge**, the area known as **Ilalim ng Tulay** (literally 'under the bridge'; Map p46), you can find really cheap junk for tourists. Across the road, at **Quinta Market** (Map p46), you'll find vendors boisterously peddling fish, meat, vegetables, fruits and other foodstuffs.

The action is particularly feverish at weekends, when the half of the population not in malls is shopping here.

Plaza Miranda has some history. This is where the common folk came to watch beauty contests, political rallies and various events and festivities, until it was destroyed by a bloody bombing in 1971 that preceded Marcos' imposition of martial law. Later it was rebuilt in the style of a Roman square with pillars, arches and decorative urns.

option is to stumble over to the Oasis Paco Park Hotel (off Map p44) and order some food, which should give you pool rights. Or you could join the masses and swim for free at the old **Army & Navy Club pool** (Map p42; South Blvd, Rizal Park; ⌚9am-3pm). It's a nice 25m pool but the attractive pricing draws crowds.

Tours

Two engaging locals offer captivating and entertaining walks around the city. These tours are the best way to see and learn a little bit about Manila, especially if you are only in town for a day or two.

Walk This Way WALKING TOURS
(☎0920 909 2021; www.carlosceldran.com; adults P1000-1100, students P500) Something of a Manila celebrity, Carlos Celdran is a hilariously eccentric one-man show of Filipino history and trivia. Highly recommended for those with a sense of humour and an open mind. His Intramuros headquarters is in his sort-of souvenir shop, La Monja Loca, opposite San Agustin Catholic Church – Carlos has been at loggerheads with the church over its opposition to the Reproductive Health Bill (see p407), even spending a night in jail for the cause in 2010 after disrupting a mass.

Old Manila Walks WALKING TOURS
(☎711 3823, 0918 962 6452; www.oldmanilawalks.com; tours P650-1100) Tour leader Ivan Man Dy has a deep knowledge of Manila and its history and culture. He's an expert at ferreting out the city's often overlooked secrets. The more expensive tours include some food. Ivan also sells walking-tour maps for those who prefer to go it alone.

Jeepney Tours CITY TOURS
(☎994 6636; www.jeepneytours.com; tours per person P2500-6000) City tours take place in a customised air-con jeepney (karaoke-enabled!), often combined with a walking tour, river-boat ride and/or sunset Manila Bay cruise.

Festivals & Events

Black Nazarene Procession RITUAL
The Black Nazarene, a life-size and highly revered black image of Christ in Quiapo Church that is believed to be miraculous, is paraded through the streets in massive processions on 9 January and again during the week before Easter (Holy Week). Thousands of frenzied devotees crowd the streets carrying the image on their shoulders.

Independence Day NATIONAL DAY
A huge parade in Rizal Park celebrates independence from Spain on 12 June.

Sleeping

Manila has accommodation to suit all price ranges, from spartan P500 boxlike rooms to luxurious US$1000 penthouse suites. The main question most people have is which district to stay in – see the boxed text, p50 for advice.

Manila's five-star hotels are truly sumptuous. There's a decent rivalry between them and you can often bag a 'promo' rate (ie discount) well below those published, especially on weekends.

INTRAMUROS

Hotels only recently started opening inside Intramuros' fabled walls. This isn't a bad choice if you want peace and quiet. Intramuros really shuts down after 10pm (or earlier).

TOP CHOICE White Knight Hotel HOTEL $$
(Map p42; ☎524 7382; www.whiteknighthotelintramuros.com; General Luna St; d P1960-2520, ste P2744;) Newly opened in a restored 19th-century building within the Casa Manila complex, the White Knight has plenty of character. Some rooms are somewhat spartan, but overall it's a good blend of history and modern amenities. Golf/stay packages make this an easy choice for early-rising duffers bound for Club Intramuros.

Sailor's Inn HOSTEL $
(Map p42; ☎527 6206; 1 Fort Santiago; dm/q/ste P350/1700/2200;) With two huge semi-compartmentalised air-con dorms (100 beds for men, 40 beds for women), this is more like a barracks. Shape up, sailor, you're in the navy now. The cold-water common bathrooms are predictably large. Both private rooms and dorms are ship-shape but basic.

RIZAL PARK

Historic hotels are the name of the game here.

TOP CHOICE Manila Hotel HOTEL $$$
(Map p42; ☎527 0011; www.manila-hotel.com.ph; 1 Rizal Park; r from P7000;) As the Mandarin Oriental is to Bangkok and Raffles is to Singapore, so is the Manila Hotel to Manila. This is one of Asia's grand and regal hotels, where everyone from General MacArthur to the Beatles to JFK has spent the night. It's more than 100 years old, yet has kept up with the times brilliantly, adding elegant Filipino touches like *capiz*-shell dividers and two-poster beds to rooms that include every modern convenience imaginable. Flat-screen panel in the bathtub? Check. Swim-up bar at the pool? Check. In a word: wow.

TOP CHOICE Hotel Miramar HISTORIC HOTEL $$$
(Map p42; ☎523 4484-86; www.miramarhotel.ph; 1034-36 Roxas Blvd; d incl breakfast P3200-4400, ste P5500-10,000;) If you're looking for a classic hotel with a little Old-Manila flavour that won't break the bank, look no further than this 1930s Art Deco masterpiece. Rooms are smartly furnished and although fully modern still have some pre-war charm. The cafe, with wall-to-wall Parisian-style murals, is excellent. Super promo rates available.

TOP CHOICE Casa Bocobo HOTEL $$
(Map p42; ☎526 3783; www.casabocobo.com.ph; 100 Bocobo St; r incl breakfast P1900-2800;) This is it: Metro Manila's best midrange hotel. Classy black-and-white photos and mounted flat-screen TVs adorn meticulously painted walls, and attractive lamps flank beds draped in soft white linens. The 'petite' standard rooms are a bit cramped, but the pricier 'superior' rooms have space galore and wonderful love seats for lounging. No lift.

MAN LOVE

For some serious and seriously affordable man grooming, it's hard to beat Club Intramuros Golf Course's **barbershop** (Map p42; ☎489 3359; Bonifacio Dr; per treatment P100-200; 8am-8pm Mon-Sat). A two-hour session in the barber's chair includes any or all of the following: haircut, shave, manicure, pedicure, ear cleansing, face treatment, foot scrub – plus a full-body massage that takes place *as* all that other stuff is going on. Total price tag? About P800. It's not uncommon for four people at once to be working on your fully reclined, utterly relaxed self.

Most barbershops offer similar services for similar prices (try any Bruno's chain), but Intramuros is more secluded than most; you won't have any voyeurs looking in and you'll often have the place all to yourself. A round of golf beforehand is decidedly optional.

WHERE TO STAY IN MANILA?

Manila's hugeness makes picking a hotel a daunting task, especially for first-time visitors. The key to accommodation enlightenment is to pick a district before settling on a hotel. A quick rundown of the major sleeping areas:

AREA	PROS	CONS
Downtown (Malate & Ermita)	Traditional tourist belt; close to main sights; 'authentic' Manila; best budget accommodation	Beggars and scam artists; street-level destitution; restaurants are average; nightlife better elsewhere
Downtown (Intramuros)	Quiet, neighbourhood feel; close to main sights	Food options limited; nightlife nonexistent
Downtown (Rizal Park)	History, charm	Expensive
Pasay & Parañaque	Close to airport and Mall of Asia; close to Pasay bus terminals	Close to Epifanio de los Santos Ave; loud, blighted; restaurants lacking
Makati	Great restaurants; great nightlife; clean streets	Expensive; too 'sanitized'; less backpacker camaraderie
Quezon City	Less touristy, more local; good restaurants and bars; close to Cubao bus terminals	Far from everything except Cubao bus terminals

Lotus Garden Hotel HOTEL **$$**
(Map p42; ☎522 1515; www.lotusgardenhotelmanila.com; 1227 Mabini St; s/d incl breakfast from P2200/2500; ❄@🛜) An impressive midranger with a glamorous curved staircase and the busy (and smoky) Cilantro Restaurant Bar commanding attention in the lobby. As you rise through the price range you gain light and amenities such as a kitchen. Extras include a gym.

Ralph Anthony Suites APARTMENTS **$**
(Map p42; ☎521 1107; www.ralphanthonysuites.com; M Orosa St; d from P2000, ste from P2400; ❄@🛜) It's primarily long-term accommodation but it provides good value for short-term guests. One-bedroom suites have kitchenettes.

MALATE, ERMITA & PACO

Despite Makati's increasing popularity, the majority of travellers still find themselves in the adjoining downtown neighbourhoods of Malate, Ermita and Paco. Malate is the better choice for most people and is where backpackers flock. Ermita offers better midrange value than Malate, but it's seedier and further away from the action on Remedios Circle and J Nakpil St. Paco has more of a neighbourhood feel.

Top-end places down here are high-rises with good views of the city and Manila Bay. Dorm dwellers should be prepared to supply their own soap and towels. Apartment places usually offer big monthly and sometimes weekly discounts.

TOP CHOICE **Malate Pensionne** HOSTEL **$$**
(Map p44; ☎523 8304; www.mpensionne.com.ph; 1771 Adriatico St; fan dm P350, d without/with bathroom P750/1100, with air-con from P1400; ❄@🛜) This beautifully maintained and grandly atmospheric travellers' centre with hardwood detail throughout is justifiably popular. It has a three-bed men's dorm, a bigger women's dorm and a variety of private rooms – although some are showing their wear. It draws a mellow crowd and has a useful traveller message board. Wi-fi costs extra.

TOP CHOICE **Oasis Paco Park** HOTEL **$$**
(off Map p44; ☎521 2371-73; www.oasispark.com; 1032-34 Belen St; r std/deluxe incl breakfast from P1825/2500; ⊖❄@🛜≋) Well removed from the hustle and bustle of Malate and Ermita you'll find this friendly neighbourhood hotel. You come here mainly because it's relatively quiet and isolated, and because it's the rare Manila midranger with a pool – a good one at that, commanding a leafy central courtyard, wi-fi enabled and surrounded by patio furniture. The stylish, well-appointed rooms are just a bonus; upgrade to a deluxe if you want a window.

Friendly's Guesthouse HOSTEL $
(Map p44; ☎489 8897, 0917 333 1418; www.friendlysguesthouse.com; 1750 Adriatico St; dm without/with air-con P325/375, s/d from P500/675; ❄@📶) Captained by the suitably friendly Benjie, this is backpacker HQ, with three large dorm rooms, a great balcony/lounge area, nonstop movies, free coffee and even free wine every other Saturday. Private rooms are small but clean and some have bathrooms.

Pension Natividad HOSTEL $
(Map p44; ☎521 0524; 1690 MH del Pilar St; dm with fan P400, d without/with bathroom P1000/1100, with air-con P1500; ❄📶) Popular with Peace Corps volunteers, this is one of the nicer budget places, but consider staying elsewhere if you plan to party hard – it advertises 'clean guest rooms for individuals, married couples and families'. Backpackers congregate most evenings on the large outdoor patio.

Adriatico Arms Hotel HOTEL $$
(Map p44; ☎524 7426; 561 J Nakpil St; r standard/deluxe P1650/1850; ❄📶) Rooms in this smart boutique hotel are good value, and the ground-floor cafe, surrounded by wrought-iron detailing, gives off an especially homey vibe. Air-con rooms are a step up from nearby Malate Pensionne.

Hotel Vieve HOTEL $$
(Map p44; ☎526 4211; info@hotelfrendy.com; 1548 Mabini St; r incl breakfast P1800; ❄@📶) Newly renovated and newly named, the erstwhile Hotel Vieve is a shiny model of contemporary class on one of Ermita's dodgier blocks. Rooms offer plenty of space, flat-screen TVs and several pieces of furniture. Drawbacks are cheap towels and imperfect plumbing.

Pearl Garden Hotel HOTEL $$
(Map p44; ☎525 1000; www.pearlgardenhotel.net; 1700 Adriatico St; d incl breakfast P2600-3400, ste P3900-5900; ❄@📶) This is the most modern and stylish of Malate's midrange hotels. Unfortunately, many rooms stink of smoke. Upgrade to the 'deluxe' doubles, which feature flat-screen TVs, separate bathtubs and showers and gorgeous king-sized beds clad in white cotton covers.

Adriatico Pensionne Inn HOTEL $
(Map p44; ☎404 2300; adriaticopensionne@yahoo.com; 1612 Adriatico St; d incl breakfast P950-1500, ste from P1700; ❄📶) There are 29 dark but sparkling-clean rooms here, some with fans and shared bathrooms. Upgrade to one of the rambling, two-floor suites with flat-screen TVs, or better yet the penthouse (P3000). Ask for a 20% discount.

Diamond Hotel HOTEL $$$
(Map p44; ☎528 3000; www.diamondhotel.com; cnr Roxas Blvd & Jr Quintos St; s/d incl breakfast from P8000/8900; 🚭❄@📶🏊) There's not much to separate Manila's five-star offerings – they are all incredibly lavish. The opulent Diamond stands out by offering the best promo rates. You might get a night in this plush palace for as little as P5000 on weekends or through online booking sites specialising in Southeast Asia, such as www.agoda.com.

Pan Pacific Hotel HOTEL $$$
(Map p44; ☎318 0788; www.panpacific.com; cnr Adriatico & Gen Malvar Sts; r from P11,500; 🚭❄@🏊) This truly luxurious five-star business hotel is Malate's solitary choice for travellers requiring British-trained butler service. The particulars of each stay can be personalised online. Standard rooms include one of the following: free breakfast, free room upgrade or free airport transfer.

Hyatt Hotel and Casino Manila HOTEL $$$
(Map p44; ☎245 1234; www.manila.casino.hyatt.com; 1588 Pedro Gil St; s/d incl breakfast from US$179/200; ❄@🏊) It doesn't get much more all-inclusive than at the Hyatt, where you can get a haircut, buy a dozen muffins, play a game of roulette, enjoy a foot massage, and take a yoga class without ever leaving the building. The high-ceilinged, contemporary-styled rooms belong in a glossy magazine.

Pearl Lane Hotel HOTEL $$
(Map p44; ☎523 2000; 1700 M Orosa St; d incl breakfast P2100-3400; ❄@📶) Just a small step down from its larger sister, Pearl Garden, with the same strengths and (smoky) weaknesses.

Riviera Mansion Hotel HOTEL $$
(Map p44; ☎523 4511; www.rivieramansion.com; 1638 Mabini St; d incl breakfast P2500-4200; 🚭❄@📶) A sleek lobby and great bathrooms, but rooms don't quite follow suit – standard rooms have too much fabric and small beds. Wi-fi is P100 per hour.

Chill-Out Guesthouse HOSTEL $
(Map p44; ☎450 8023, 0939 517 7019; Lucky 888 Bldg, 1288 MH del Pilar St; dm P350, d P800-P1340; ❄@📶) Boldly challenging Friendly's turf,

this newish hostel passes the eye test, with blissfully air-conditioned dorms plus an OK hangout/kitchen area where smoking is allowed. One drawback is the location, on one of Ermita's louder and dodgier blocks.

The following are bare bones but would serve in a pinch if everything else in the budget range is booked, as it often is:

Stone House PENSION HOUSE **$**
(Map p44; ☎524 0302; stonehouse_apt@yahoo.com; 1529 Mabini St; s/d without bathroom from P300/500; ❄) While the budget singles are shoeboxes, the better doubles are OK value. Some rooms are windowless and wi-fi is extra.

Richmond Pension PENSION HOUSE **$**
(Map p44; ☎525 3864; 1165 Grey St; 3-bed dm P290, s/d without bathroom from P390/570) Rickety old family-run house with simple rooms on an isolated side-street.

Lovely Moon Pension Inn PENSION HOUSE **$**
(Map p44; ☎524 9974; 1718 Bocobo St; d P400-850; ❄) If you are looking for that sweltering old-school Southeast Asia dive that draws a full spectrum of colourful locals and diehard backpackers, look no further.

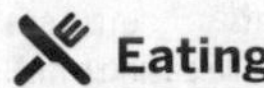

Eating

The downtown area is not the foodie haven it once was, as most of the best restaurants have moved north to Makati, where the average punter has more disposable income. A few stalwarts in Malate have resisted the move. Other than that, the best options are the unrivalled five-star hotel buffets and the teahouses of Chinatown.

Malls such as Robinson's Place in Ermita and the gargantuan Mall of Asia (in Pasay, but close to Malate) have a stupendous variety of fast-food chains, including slightly more upscale chains like Mexican food staple **Mexicali** (burritos P125), **Outback Steakhouse** (steaks P350-600) and **Kenny Rogers Roasters** (chicken with 3 sides P200).

Self-caterers will find large Western-style supermarkets in the malls, although the many outdoor markets such as Malate's San Andres Market offer more colourful grazing, especially for tropical fruits. Food stalls are conspicuously absent from the streets of Manila, but roadside *turu-turò* (basic canteens, or 'point-point' eateries) abound in Malate, Ermita and elsewhere.

Most bars listed on p54 are also good places to eat Filipino and sometimes Western cuisine. Casual wear is the order of the day everywhere.

INTRAMUROS

There are surprisingly few good choices here, and they are somewhat specialised.

Barbara's SPANISH, FILIPINO **$$$**
(Map p42; ☎527 3893; General Luna St; lunch/dinner buffet P395/425; ⏱coffee shop 9am-6pm, restaurant lunch & dinner Mon-Sat) In an elegant space within the Casa Manila complex, Barbara's does a buffet dinner that includes a cultural show (7.15pm) with traditional music and dances such as *tinikling* (see p420) on display. This is white-tablecloth fine dining for the wannabe colonialist in you.

Ilustrado SPANISH, FILIPINO **$$$**
(Map p42; ☎527 3674; 744 General Luna St; mains P450-720; ⏱lunch & dinner Mon-Sat, lunch Sun)

BEST BRUNCHES

You have not been to Manila until you've enjoyed a sumptuous five-star all-you-can-eat Sunday brunch (preferably with a Champagne component). They usually start around 11am or noon and last most of the afternoon. A few five-star hotels have daily lunch and dinner buffets that are almost as good.

Here are our top five:

» **Sofitel Philippine Plaza** (p58; lunch/Sunday brunch P2100/2700) The standard bearer; simply mind-boggling.

» **Manila Hotel** (p49; lunch/Sunday brunch P1700/1866) Shellfish bar and cuisines spanning the globe.

» **The Peninsula** (p63; lunch/Sunday brunch P1680/2087) The Escolta restaurant is the setting for the Peninsula's reliable spread, although champagne costs P700 extra.

» **Diamond Hotel** (p51; lunch/Sunday brunch P1420/1550) Just a baby step down from the Manila Hotel.

» **Oasis Paco Park Hotel** (p50; Sunday brunch P500) Not five-star, but nor is the price.

Set in a reconstructed Spanish-era house, this is fine dining of the stiff-upper-lip variety. Traditional Spanish-Filipino dishes like paella join salmon, duck and lamb chops. The adjacent Kuatro Kantos Bar is a less-formal coffee shop that stays open all day.

Ristorante delle Mitre FILIPINO $$
(Map p42; 470 General Luna St; mains P175-400; ⏲8am-8.30pm) Nuns cook up dishes named after archbishops in this unique and very attractive cafe opposite San Agustin church. The food is a mix of Filipino and Italian, and it's not a bad place for a pre-walking-tour breakfast – try the waffles.

Patio de Conchita FILIPINO $
(Map p42; cnr Cabildo & Beaterio Sts; meals P75-150; ⏲10am-10pm) For something a bit more, well, normal than the above, there's this Filipino eatery. It looks fancier than it is – it's essentially an upscale *turu-turò*, where customers can order by pointing at the pre-cooked food on display).

Harbor View SEAFOOD $$
(Map p42; South Blvd, Rizal Park; dishes from P150; ⏲lunch & dinner) This long-standing and popular fresh seafood *inahaw* (grill) restaurant juts into Manila Bay. The breezes can be delightful on sweltering days, but just check the wind direction as sometimes it sends the bay's insalubrious flotsam into malodorous piles along the piers. The fish is best enjoyed with a golden sunset and some amber refreshments.

RIZAL PARK

TOP CHOICE Seafood Market SEAFOOD $$$
(Map p42; 1190 Bocobo St; meals from P400; ⏲11am-10.30pm) The long ice counter here looks much like the seafood tank at a grocery store. Point to your preference, then watch as a team of chefs cooks your meal in a flaming wok that's clearly visible from the sidewalk outside. It's a wonderful dining experience, just ask for the price when they weigh your fish, lest you be in for an unpleasant surprise later.

Kashmir INDIAN $$$
(Map p42; ☎524 6851; P Faura St; meals P300-550; ⏲11am-11pm) Relatively small but distinctly upmarket, serving Indian specialities and a few Malaysian and Middle Eastern options. Curries are especially toothsome here.

MALATE, ERMITA & PACO

The best restaurants are in Malate around Remedios Circle and J Nakpil St, where there's plenty of neighbourhood colour to observe if you can bag a street-side perch.

TOP CHOICE Casa Armas SPANISH $$$
(Map p44; J Nakpil St; tapas P25-35, mains P300-500; ⏲11am-midnight Mon-Sat, 6pm-midnight Sun) Foodies have been enamoured with this Filipino-Spanish spot for years, where tapas, paella, seafood and even entire roast suckling pigs are on offer. There's a second branch in Makati's Greenbelt 3.

Cafe Adriatico INTERNATIONAL $$
(Map p44; 1790 Adriatico St; meals P250-500; ⏲7am-5am) This corner bistro is worth a splurge for the original Spanish fare with English, American and Italian effects, and the people-watching on Remedios Circle.

Bistro Remedios FILIPINO $$
(Map p44; Adriatico St; mains P200-400; ⏲lunch & dinner) Food from Pampanga province is the speciality here, including many exotic and unusual dishes, like fried frog legs. The nicely relaxed ambience is traditionally Filipino.

Zamboanga Restaurant FILIPINO $$
(Map p44; ☎521 7345; 1619 Adriatico St; mains P200-300; ⏲10am-11.30pm, cultural show 8.30pm) The prices here aren't bad considering many dishes feed two and that along with your dinner you get a one-hour Filipino cultural program, complete with colourful costumes and indigenous dances. Food is best described as gourmet Filipino.

Suzhou Dimsum CHINESE $
(Map p44; cnr Mabini & Alonzo Sts; dim sum P90-120, soups P120; ⏲24hr) Suzho has some of the best dim sum in Malate, plus large and wildly affordable noodle dishes and other Chinese staples. Ask for chilli sauce to liven up the soups.

Korean Palace KOREAN $$$
(Map p44; 1799 Adriatico St; mains P200-500; ⏲10am-midnight) Still the best Korean restaurant in town; try the *bibimbap* (rice with meat, vegetables, egg and chilli; P300) or Korean barbecue (P300 to P400).

Aristocrat FILIPINO $
(Map p44; cnr Roxas Blvd & San Andres St; meals P150-400; ⏲24hr) This Manila institution began life in 1936 as a mobile snack cart.

Shawarma Snack Center MIDDLE EASTERN $
(Map p44; 485 R Salas St; shawarma P55, meals P100-250; ⏲24hr) It doesn't sound like much, but this street-side eatery serves the richest

and most flavourful falafel, *muttabal* (eggplant dip), hummus, and kebabs for kilometres around. The branch across the street has more upscale dining in air-conditioned comfort.

München GERMAN $$
(Map p44; 1316 Mabini St; mains P155-500, set lunch P285) Hearty, authentic German dishes emerge from the kitchen in this cosy spot done up like a Bavarian country cottage. Think meat loaf, rump steak and red cabbage.

CHINATOWN (BINONDO)

TOP CHOICE **Happy Veggie** CHINESE $
(Map p46; 958 Masangkay St; meals P50-150; ⏲9.30am-8pm; ✎) The interior of this place is as brightly coloured as a ripe melon. Like many local places, the name leaves little doubt as to what's on offer here, and it's all scrumptious. Many items have more appealing names than the 'Fungus & Ball Soup'. It doubles as a Chinese health-food store.

Salazar Bakery BAKERY $
(Map p46; 783 Ongpin St; snacks from P30) Experience the singular joys of black mongo beans, sticky mooncakes, and all manner of odd and exotic baked goods here.

Ling Nam Wonton Parlor & Noodle Factory CHINESE $
(Map p46; 616 Alonzo St; dim sum P50-70, mains P120-150) The name alone should tell you that the noodles are fresh here. Pots steam like mad, air-conditioners roar and happy patrons lap up tasty and simple fare.

President Tea House CHINESE $$
(Map p46; 809 Salazar St; dim sum P60-100, mains P150-250) The original branch of what has become one of Manila's more popular Chinese chains; it's known for dim sum.

MXT Tea House CHINESE $$
(Map p46; 965 Ongpin St; mains P150-250; ⏲7am-midnight) More superb dim sum and noodle soups in the heart of Chinatown.

Drinking

You're rarely far from a drinking opportunity in downtown Manila. You'll find the college crowd chugging cheap suds curbside just west of Remedios Circle on Remedios St in Malate – dubbed the 'Monoblock Republic' because of the preponderance of brittle plastic furniture.

TOP CHOICE **1951 (Penguin Cafe)** CAFE
(Map p44; ☎0917 858 3009; 1951 Adriatico St; ⏲from 6pm Tue-Sat) This legendary bar-cum-gallery has reopened in Malate after a failed move to Makati. It's a magnet for bohemian types and on Fridays and Saturdays squeezes in some of the finest musical talent in the Philippines, including, on occasion, Kalayo (see p417). The official name is now 1951 but everybody still calls it Penguin Cafe.

Oarhouse BAR
(Map p44; cnr Bocobo & General Malvar Sts) Oarhouse is something of a clubhouse for Peace Corps volunteers and Filipino journalists who often linger until the sun comes up. Recently moved to a new location.

Kuwagos Grill BAR
(Map p44; 615 J Nakpil St; mains P100-200; ⏲4pm-8am) This 2nd-floor open-air restobar under a thatched roof is an ideal place to grab a drink and some Filipino bar food while watching the action on busy J Nakpil St. Buying beer in bulk nets big discounts.

Erra's Place BAR
(Map p44; Adriatico St) Cheap snacks and P29 (!!) San Miguel in a small street-side nook. If it's full the place next door has P31 San Miguel (larceny!). Both are backpacker faves.

Silya BAR
(Map p44; 642 J Nakpil St; breakfast P75, mains P110-160) This little restobar is a great place to warm up your karaoke skills before hitting the provinces.

Aqualicious WATER
(Map p44; Adriatico St; water refills per litre P5; ⏲7.30am-7pm) Water refilling station.

☆ Entertainment

The best nightlife is up in Makati or in the new Resorts World complex in Parañaque. However, Malate remains the epicentre of Manila's gay nightlife – the corner of J Nakpil and M Orosa Sts is ground zero, with the action spilling out into the streets until the wee hours on weekends and sometimes on weekdays. There are a few trendy uni clubs and lounges behind the street bars of the Monoblock Republic (aka Remedios St).

FAB/The Library CLUB
(Map p44; www.thelibrary.com.ph; 1139 M Orosa St, Malate; comedy shows P100-500, club admission varies) Two gay clubs under one roof. FAB is a club with live music on weekdays. The

LOCAL KNOWLEDGE

AIMEE MARCOS

Interview by Trent Holden

Aimee is a member of indie Pinoy band the Dorques, underground music promoter, DJ, self-confessed Star Wars nerd and youngest daughter of Ferdinand and Imelda Marcos.

You're the drummer with the Dorques, are you guys still going strong? Yeah we're still playing, but it's something we put on hold every now and again. Especially as most of us play in other bands, and it's hard to make a living out of being a musician, especially as we're all pretty weird looking – our lead singer dresses like a cow on stage, for instance. One of our songs (Le Metronome) was actually inspired by the French Lonely Planet book...

How about your band management company, Princess Batugan? We basically promote local underground bands. It's on hiatus at the moment, but we put on the occasional show for hardcore punk and metal bands. The bands are our babies.

What's your favourite place in the Philippines? My favourite place is Illoco Norte, so beautiful! One of the best kept secrets. Don't mention it, you'll spoil it! Surfing, diving and weird landscapes. We call the sand dunes here 'Tatooine', from the desert in Star Wars. I can see myself settling down somewhere in Paoay. The lake, the church, it's all so pretty.

What was it like to grow up in the Marcos household? Fun, good times. All of us were really tight. Everything I am I owe to them. My love of music, writing, art, travel. My parents always encouraged us to follow our dreams and have been really encouraging in supporting what we want to do – whether in politics or being a musician. Apart from the Marcos name, we are all pretty normal. We still joke about like we always have. We're all pretty kooky.

People are obsessed by your mum's shoe collection, have you seen them? Ha, I don't really know too much about them, other than when I was a kid I used to have a ball playing with them. Sneaking around to prance around in them, like any little girl would!

I read that your father gave you permission to be present at any meeting of his you wished? I remember hanging out, but I was only seven when we left the Philippines in 1986. Hence recollections of the discussions and things of my father would have been incomprehensible to me at the time. I just remember playing a lot around people's feet.

Would you ever consider a career in politics? I don't know, I've never really been interested in politics. I doubt I'd seriously consider it in the foreseeable future, but I will never say never. I just want to do my own thing. I don't think that we should be categorised just for one thing. I'm pretty sure we can do other stuff well too and still in one way or another help others, so I hope I get to show that in my own little humble way from behind the drums.

Library has nightly comedy shows (at 9pm) that are popular with both gay and straight audiences.

Bed CLUB

(Map p44; www.bed.com.ph; cnr J Nakpil & M Orosa Sts, Malate; ⏲9pm-6am Thu-Sat) A club with rare staying power, Bed has gone through many incarnations over the years but is still throwing its infamous gay and straight parties until the wee hours.

O Bar CLUB

(Map p44; cnr J Nakpil & M Orosa Sts, Malate; admission incl 3 beers weekday/weekend P150/250; ⏲til late) Tiny gay-friendly establishment often spills out onto the streets; drag shows happen most nights after 1am.

Bedrock LIVE MUSIC

(Map p44; 1782 Adriatico St; admission free; ⏲7pm-4am) You wouldn't want to visit the Philippines without seeing a cover band, and Bedrock is a good place for it. Any given night is lively, just stick to beer (P90) because other drinks are expensive.

Hobbit House LIVE MUSIC

(Map p42; www.hobbithousemanila.com; 1212 MH del Pilar St; admission P125-150; ⏲5pm-2am) This quality blues bar, now in a new location after 34 years on Mabini St, is staffed by little people. Some people find it a delight, others snap a lot of photos, and others find it a bit exploitative.

Ka Freddie's LIVE MUSIC

(Map p44; ☎526 7241; cnr Adriatico & Pedro Gil Sts) Filipino folk legend Freddie Aguilar owns and plays in this Ermita space every Monday, Wednesday, Friday and Saturday. Acoustic music usually kicks off at 8.30pm, followed by Freddie or another act at 10.30pm.

Cinemas

Manila's malls boast hundreds of movie houses, many of them state of the art. Hollywood blockbusters are often shown at the same time as their US release, yet it costs only P100 to P150 to watch a movie here. All of the local newspapers have extensive film listings, as does www.clickthecity.com. English-language movies are screened with their original English dialogue.

Popular choices with the latest projection gear include **Robinsons Movieworld** (Map p44; ☎632 9116; Robinsons Place, Ermita).

Shopping

Manila is a bargain-hunter's paradise. The largest variety of stores is in the shopping malls, which have the added advantages of being air-conditioned and full of other diversions like restaurants and movie theatres. Market lovers should head to the Quiapo Church area (see the boxed text, p48). In Ermita a stroll along Mabini St will often yield authentic old textiles and other antiques.

Silahis Arts & Artifacts Center SOUVENIRS

(Map p42; www.silahis.com; 744 General Luna St,; ⏲10am-7pm) This is almost more of a cultural centre than store. Intricately woven baskets, wooden Ifugao *bulol* (rice guard) statues, textiles and other crafts from around the country are sold next to beautiful antiques. A must-stop if you are in Intramuros.

Tesoro's SOUVENIRS

(Map p44; 1325 Mabini St; ⏲9am-8pm) The speciality here is woven *pinya* products, but there are also lacquered coconut-shell products, baskets, bags, coffee, dried mangoes and a few rare books on Philippine culture.

Hiraya Gallery ART

(Map p42; www.hiraya.com; 530 United Nations Ave; ⏲9am-5pm Mon-Sat) This long-established gallery has a museum-quality selection of Filipino contemporary art. Names to look out for are Leonard Aguinaldo, Norberto Carating and Eric Guazon.

SOUVENIR HUNTING

Souvenirs from all over the country are readily available in Manila. Lacquered coconut-shell products produced mainly in the Visayas – balls, bowls, placemats, vases – are the most popular souvenirs, along with baskets, and are widely available.

Other notable souvenirs include wood carvings from Ifugao province in North Luzon; betel-nut boxes from Mindanao's Lake Sebu area; and indigenous weavings from the mountain tribes of North Luzon and Mindanao. Filipino weavings are not as coveted as Indonesian weavings, but offer good value. The abaca (native hemp plant) weavings of the T'boli and other Mindanao tribes are considered world class.

One popular purchase is the *barong Tagalog*, the traditional dress-shirt (which usually includes an embroidered front) worn by Filipino men. The best *barong* are made from *pinya*, a fabric woven from pineapple fibres (see p267). *Jusi* (*hoo*-see), from ramie fibres, is more common and less expensive, while the cotton version is cheaper still. Ready-to-wear *barong* are available at most handicraft shops and department stores, and most tailors will gladly sew one to your specifications. Most shops also carry womenswear made from the finely embroidered material.

The sprawling Greenhills Shopping Center (p74) in Mandaluyong City is considered a fine place to buy pearls, both locally farmed and more expensive Tahitian and other South Pacific varieties.

For a souvenir with a difference check out the **Kilus** (www.kilus.org), available at different stores around town, which uses recycled products like juice labels to produce handbags, placemats and other knick-knacks.

Lastly, be aware that the Batangas or Laguna *balisong* (fan or butterfly knife), a popular handmade souvenir sold at numerous stalls in the Central Market in Quiapo, is banned in many countries.

THE PRESIDENT'S RESIDENCE

The official residence of the President of the Philippines, **Malacañang Palace** (Map p38; ☎784 4286; pml@malacanang.gov.ph; Kalayaan Gate, JP Laurel Sr St, San Miguel) was originally a Spanish grandee's summer house.

Tours of the palace and the **Museo ng Malacañang**, which displays memorabilia related to the Philippines' 15 presidents, along with old photos of Manila, are possible by appointment only. You'll need to write an email to Edgar Faustino at the palace email address at least seven days prior to your visit. Provide a contact number, indicate how many people are in your party, and attach copies of all passports.

Tour guide Ivan Man Dy (see p48) offers Malacañang tours.

La Monja Loca SOUVENIRS
(Map p42; General Luna St; ⏲9am-6pm Tue-Sun) Great selection of creative souvenirs at 'The Crazy Nun', run by celebrated tour guide Carlos Celdran, in the Casa Manila complex.

Robinsons Place Manila MALL
(Map p44; btwn Pedro Gil & Padre Faura Sts) Close to the tourist belt. It's a vast place and it's getting bigger.

Solidaridad Bookshop BOOKS
(Map p42; ☎254 1086; 531 P Faura St, Ermita; ⏲9am-6pm Mon-Sat) Owned by the Filipino author F Sionil Jose, this fantastic shop has a masterfully edited collection of both Western and Eastern nonfiction, international magazines such as the *New Yorker*, and hard-to-find Filipino history titles and documentaries.

Tradewinds Books BOOKS
(Map p42; 3rd fl, Silahis Arts & Artifacts Center, 744 General Luna St, Intramuros) Varied assortment of books on the Philippines and Asia, including out-of-print or hard-to-find volumes.

Markets

Go ahead and hit the malls for authentic brand-name clothing, but for a real taste of Filipino life, be sure to check out one of Manila's many excellent markets. Traditional markets are, not surprisingly, found in the oldest parts of town, such as Quiapo, where you can join the masses shopping in the vicinity of Quiapo Church (see p48).

San Andres Market MARKET
(Map p44; San Andres St; ⏲24hr) Malate's main market looks like one big cornucopia of fruits including exotic *guyabano* (soursop) and durian. It's a dark warren of treats ripe for exploration.

Central Market MARKET
(Map p46; Andalucia St) Further north of Quiapo Church, the dingy Central Market, by the Manila City Jail, sells clothes, military uniforms, knives and hardware.

PARAÑAQUE & PASAY

Lying just south of Malate, these adjoining districts straddle Manila's busy main thoroughfare, Epifanio de los Santos, universally known as EDSA. They are best know as transport hubs, as the airport and many key bus stations lie within their boundaries. The best real estate here is north of EDSA (essentially an extension of Malate) and near the waterfront. South of EDSA it gets loud and dodgy quite quickly.

Sights

Cultural Center of the Philippines (CCP) Complex HISTORIC DISTRICT
(Map p58) The main sights in Pasay are dotted around the sprawling grounds of the CCP. Conceived during the era of Imelda Marcos' grand plans for Manila, the CCP refers to both the vast collection of white elephants on reclaimed land in the bay, and the performing arts centre of the same name. The decaying excess on display here is a fascinating and fitting lasting legacy of the Marcos era.

There are numerous exhibition halls and other buildings scattered about the vast site. Some components, like the Sofitel Philippine Plaza hotel and the Philippine International Convention Center are surviving well. Others, such as the Manila Film Center (see the boxed text, p61) and the Coconut Palace (see the boxed text, p60), struggle against inglorious fates.

The CCP is a pleasant walk from Malate along the Roxas Blvd promenade, or take any Baclaran-bound jeepney on MH del Pilar St. Jeepneys ply a circular route around the complex.

FREE **Cultural Center of the Philippines** HISTORIC BUILDING

(Tanghalang Pambansa; Map p58; CCP Complex, Roxas Blvd) The centrepiece of the CCP complex is set back from Roxas Blvd and constructed in the bombastic style favoured by dictators everywhere. It never quite lived up to its promise of being a centre of culture for the masses, but the building has a grand design by noted Filipino architect Leandro Locsin. Inside is an **art gallery** (admission free; ⊙10am-6pm Tue-Sun), a **library** (⊙8am-5pm Tue-Fri) and a **museum of musical instruments** (adult/student P30/20; ⊙10am-6pm Tue-Sun). Three theatres regularly present performances by the Philippine Philharmonic Orchestra, Ballet Philippines and local and visiting artists.

Metropolitan Museum of Manila MUSEUM

(Map p58; www.metmuseum.ph; Roxas Blvd; admission P100; ⊙9am-6pm, gold exhibit to 4.30pm Mon-Sat) Manila's most underrated museum has a stunning collection of pre-colonial gold ornaments in the basement, along with ancient pottery, and occasionally superb changing exhibits of contemporary Filipino art. It's on the grounds of the Bangko Sentral ng Pilipinas (Central Bank), which bought this stuff at the height of the Marcos era in the '70s and '80s. There are some real bricks here – a few of the gold armlets and necklaces weigh upwards of 1kg.

FREE **GSIS Museo ng Sining** MUSEUM

(Museum of Art; Map p58; CCP complex, GSIS Bldg; ⊙9am-noon & 1-4pm Tue-Sat) This hard-to-find museum houses an extensive collection of contemporary Filipino art. On display are paintings, sculptures and tapestries by such famous Filipino artists as Fernando Amorsolo, Vicente Manansala and Hernando Ocampo. There's a free concert here on the last Thursday of every month that shows off *kundiman* (see p417) and other Filipino musical styles.

Sleeping

The main reason to stay in Pasay is to be closer to the airport, or to stay at the Sofitel.

TOP CHOICE **Sofitel Philippine Plaza** HOTEL $$$

(Map p58; ☎551 5555; www.sofitel.com; CCP Complex, Atang Dela Rama St; r incl breakfast from P8000;) This five-star masterpiece, with its meandering pool area right on Manila Bay, is the closest you'll get to a resort holiday in Manila. It's the same magnificent hotel that has presided over the CCP for decades now. Other highlights are the library bar and the stupendous buffet meals.

Parañaque & Pasay

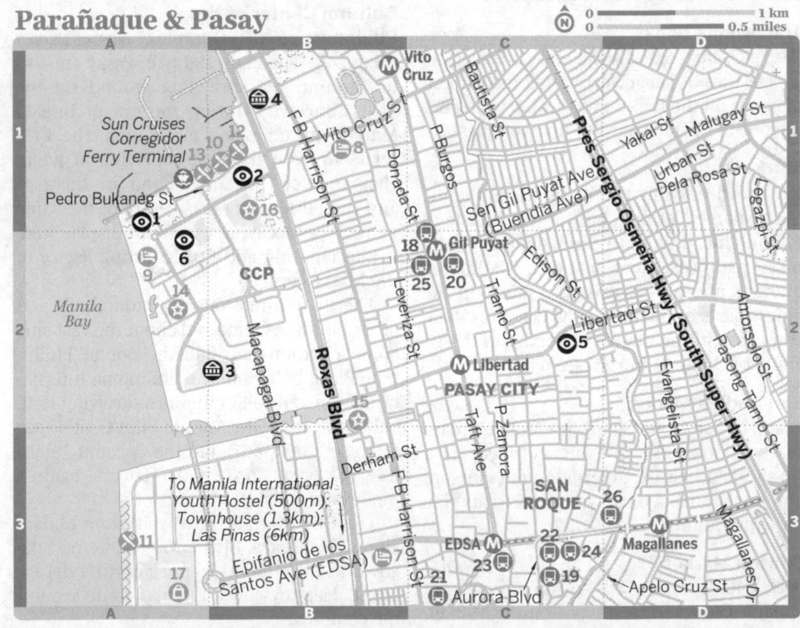

Orchid Garden Suites HOTEL $$
(Map p58; 708 9400-14; www.orchidgardenhotel.com; 620 P Ocampo Sr St; d incl breakfast from P2800;) An elegant choice that's also convenient to Malate. Guests stay in a 1980s tower block in huge rooms that have been nicely maintained. The lobby and function room are in a 1930s Art Deco mansion – one of Manila's few remaining pre-war architectural landmarks. We'd like to see more room to hang out by the pool.

Manila International Youth Hostel HOSTEL $
(off Map p58; 851 6934; 4227-9 Tomas Claudio St; dm with fan P270, d/tr with air-con P1000/1500;) This hostel near the airport has one gargantuan men's dorm (36 beds) and more manageable women's dorms (12 beds).

Copacabana Apartment-Hotel APARTMENTS $$$
(Map p58; 831 8711; www.copasuites.com; 264 EDSA Extension; studio P2700-3700, 2-room apt P4800-5300;) Convenient for the airport, the old Copacabana looks horrifying on the outside, but inside are spiffy apartments with kitchens and walls adorned with art and attractive maroon paint. Long-termers especially will be happy here if they don't mind the bleak location on EDSA. Wi-fi costs extra.

Townhouse INN $
(off Map p58; 854 3826; bill_lorna@yahoo.com; 31 Bayview Dr; dm P180, s/d from P300/400;) The only selling points of the creaky Townhouse are that it's cheap and it's close to the airport. Luckily for Townhouse, those are strong selling points.

Eating & Drinking

There's a surprising lack of restaurant options in Pasay, where hotels tend to be the best option. The best restaurants are a cab ride away from the CCP at the **Mall of Asia** (MOA; Map p58) waterfront promenade, dubbed 'San Miguel by the bay', where a long line of restobars woos customers with live music and discounted buckets of (what else) San Miguel. Closer to the CCP is **Harbour Square** (Map p58; CCP Complex, Pedro Bukaneg St), a modest food court overlooking Manila's marina. The best strategy at both of these areas is to just walk and choose.

Army Navy TEX MEX $$
(Map p58; Harbour Sq; burritos P145-170; 10am-11pm Sun-Thu, to 2am Fri & Sat) High on our list of guilty pleasures is this chain of

Parañaque & Pasay

Sights
1 Coconut Palace A1
2 Cultural Center of the Philippines B1
3 GSIS Museo ng Sining B2
4 Metropolitan Museum of Manila B1
5 Pasay City Cockpit C2
6 Philippine International Convention Center A2
Cultural Center of the Philippines .... (see 2)
15 Cuneta Astrodome B2
16 Star City B1

Sleeping
7 Copacabana Apartment-Hotel B3
8 Orchid Garden Suites B1
9 Sofitel Philippine Plaza A2

Eating
Army Navy .... (see 10)
10 Hap Chan Tea House B1
11 Harbor View Bistro A3
12 Harbour Square B1
13 Inggo's A1
Mall of Asia .... (see 17)

Entertainment
14 Amazing Show A2

Shopping
17 Mall of Asia A3

Transport
BSC/Batman .... (see 23)
18 Ceres/JAC Liner C2
DBLT .... (see 18)
19 Five Star Bus Lines Terminal C3
Genesis Pasay Terminal .... (see 23)
20 JAM Transit C2
21 Jeepneys to Airport Terminals C3
22 Partas Parsay Bus Terminal C3
23 Pasay Rotunda C3
24 Philtranco Bus Terminal C3
25 RRCG C2
Shuttle Vans to Terminal 3 .... (see 23)
26 Victory Liner Pasay Terminal D3

burrito-and-burger shacks. It's all good, but the veggie burritos bundle the best combination of value and taste.

Harbor View Bistro SEAFOOD $$
(Map p58; Mall of Asia Waterfront; mains P150-400; ⌚3pm-midnight) While it lacks the ambience, good service and dizzying seafood selection of its esteemed parent restaurant near Rizal Park, this is nonetheless one of the better choices on the MOA strip. Try the black tiger prawns cooked in crab fat.

Hap Chan Tea House CHINESE $$
(Map p58; Harbour Sq; mains P130-250; ⌚11am-midnight) Delicious, steaming platters of Macau specialities are the name of the game at the popular Hap Chan chain of teahouses. This is the only one with an outdoor patio and harbour views. There's another branch on General Malvar St in Malate.

Inggo's RESTOBAR $$
(Map p58; Harbour Sq; mains P75-300; ⌚8am-1am) We hadn't seen a beer bong for quite awhile before running into one at this harbourfront restobar. Enjoy Filipino bar faves like sizzling *sisig* and nightly live music with your funnel.

☆ Entertainment

Performing Arts

Pasay is an unlikely nexus for Manila's performing arts scene. The big draw for tourists are the transvestite revues (see the boxed text, p61), but there's also plenty of theatre, ballet and classical music, albeit rarely world class.

Cultural Center of the Philippines PERFORMING ARTS
(Map p58; ☎832 1125; www.culturalcenter.gov.ph; CCP Complex, Roxas Blvd; performance prices vary; ⌚box office 9am-6pm Tue-Sat, 1-5pm Sun performance days) Manila's major cultural guns perform here, including Ballet Philippines, the nation's premiere dance troupe; Philippine Philharmonic Orchestra, the nation's main classical orchestra; and Tanghaland Pilipino, a theatre group that performs classic and original local work, often in the original language.

Nightclubs

Manila's top nightclubs at the time of research were in the new Resorts World complex, opposite Terminal 3 at the airport.

Republiq CLUB
(Map p38; www.republiqclub.com; Resorts World, Andrews Ave, Pasay; admission varies; ⌚Wed, Fri & Sat) Metro Manila's 'it' club at the time of research, along with neighbouring **Opus Lounge** (www.opusmanila.com).

Sport

Cuneta Astrodome BASKETBALL
(Map p58; ☎831 4652; Derham St) Popular venue for professional basketball games managed by the PBA (Philippine Basketball Association), the Philippines' equivalent of America's NBA.

Shopping

Mall of Asia MALL
(MOA; Map p58; Manila Bay; ⌚10am-10pm) Metro Manila's latest and greatest mall is this monster on Manila Bay, with an Olympic-sized

THE COCONUT PALACE

Of all of Imelda's wacky schemes, the **Coconut Palace** (Map p58; CCP Complex, Pedro Bukaneg St) may be the wackiest. Hearing that Pope John Paul II was planning a visit to his flock in the Philippines, Imelda ordered that a grand palace be built. And not just any palace either, but one showcasing the nation's crafts and materials.

Huge teams of craftsmen laboured overtime to complete this edifice in time for the pontiff's arrival. As Imelda readied herself to throw open the door to welcome the pope, she got stiffed. After sternly chastising that the US$37 million cost could have gone to better uses, such as clean water for the people, the pope went elsewhere.

Left with a palace (the name derives from the extensive use of coconut materials) and no guests, Imelda eventually seized upon a couple of C-level celebrities for a gala opening: Brooke Shields and George Hamilton. As camp goes, you can't do much better. It is rumoured that Brooke got pineapple-fibre sheets for her room, while the ever-tanned George snuggled into banana-fibre sheets.

These days the palace serves as a vice presidential office and is closed to tourists, although you can still have a look from the outside.

THEY'RE HERE, THEY'RE QUEER, & THEY LOOK STUNNING!

Bangkok may have invented the concept of transsexual and transvestite variety stage shows, but Manila may do it better.

The best of the city's tranny stage shows take place at the opulent **Club Mwah!** (off Map p66; ☎535 7943; www.clubmwah.com; 3rd fl, Venue Tower, 652 Boni Ave, Mandaluyong City), an incredibly shiny, sparkly and fabulous place with obvious Las Vegas interior-design influences. Manila's gay expats give it a huge thumbs-up.

In the heart of the CCP, the Manila Film Center building stages performances of the **Amazing Show** (Map p58; ☎834 8870; www.amazing-show.com; admission P1200; ⏰8pm Tue-Sun). The one-hour revue-type shows and beauty contests star all manner of trans-people. This group caters mainly to Korean tour groups, but it's easy to piggy-back.

There are also a few low-profile transvestite shows in Malate. If you wander up and down Adriatico St and Mabini St, especially on weekend evenings, just keep your eyes open for clusters of tall 'women' wearing feather boas and slinky dresses recruiting punters outside club entrances.

ice rink and an IMAX theatre, among other diversions.

MAKATI

The business hub of Manila has also become its restaurant and nightlife centre. The towers here house the nation's major corporations and most of the major hotels. It all came about after WWII when the Ayala family seized upon the destruction of the rest of the city as a chance to start building. The heart of Makati was Manila's airport in the '30s and '40s: Ayala and Makati Aves were the runways, while the Filipinas Heritage Library was the terminal.

Today the Heritage Library sits on the perimeter of Ayala Triangle Gardens, recently converted by the Ayala family into Manila's cleanest urban park. The park forms the geographic core of Makati's central business district. Immediately south of park is the Ayala Centre, a vast, seemingly endless maze of upscale malls.

Makati seems to have boundless growth ahead of it – but just when you think you're somewhere like Singapore, a whiff of sewage will bring you down to earth! The up-and-coming Fort Bonifacio area, which lies in Taguig City but is effectively an extension of Makati, does a better Singapore impression. 'The Fort', as it is known, is included in this section.

Sights

Ayala Museum MUSEUM
(Map p62; ☎757 7117; www.ayalamuseum.org; Greenbelt 4; foreigner/resident P425/225; ⏰9am-6pm Tue-Fri, 10am-7pm Sat & Sun) This excellent modern museum has ethnographic and archaeological exhibits on Filipino culture, art and history. At the heart of the collection is a brilliant exhibit consisting of 60 dioramas that trace the nation's violent history. The museum's rotating art exhibits tend to showcase Filipino masters like Luna and Amorsolo. Guided tours (P100) of the museum are highly recommended (call ahead).

American Memorial Cemetery CEMETERY
(Map p38; Old Lawton Dr, Fort Bonifacio) This sprawling cemetery on a grassy, beautifully manicured plot is a must-see for WWII buffs. In addition to hundreds of rows of perfectly aligned white crosses, there are several excellent open-air galleries with murals and descriptions of key battles. It's a poignant and peaceful spot.

FREE **Museo Ng Makati** MUSEUM
(off Map p66; JP Rizal St; ⏰8am-5pm Mon-Fri) Down by the river, the Museo Ng Makati is a classic old Manila house from the 1800s (look for the *capiz*-shell windows), with some great photos of old Makati and murals of past mayors, among other exhibits.

Ninoy Aquino Statue MONUMENT
(Map p62; cnr Paseo de Roxas & Ayala Ave) This is a famous Ninoy Aquino statue that shows him right before he was shot. It's built on the spot where many pro-democracy rallies took place in the 1980s and 1990s.

Activities

It's not hard to find a massage in Makati, and in the central business district they are

Makati

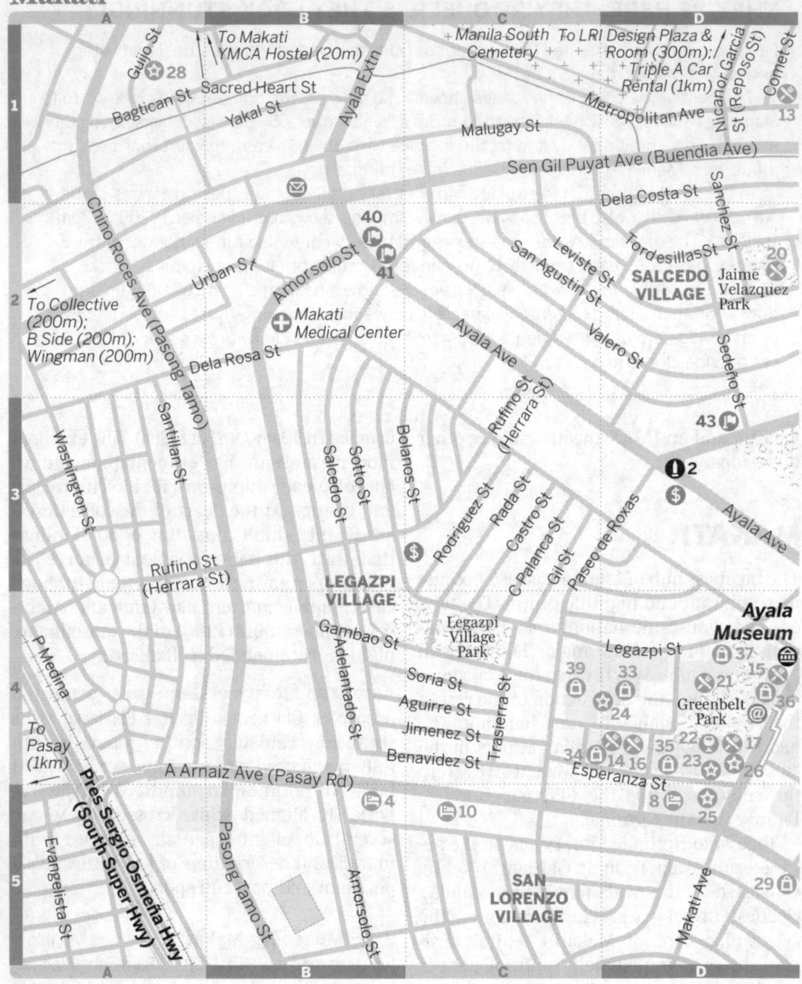

mostly on the up-and-up (the same can't be said for the P Burgos area).

Even the least metrosexual man should not leave Manila without availing himself of the full range of services on offer, for stunningly low prices, at just about any barbershop (see the boxed text, p49).

Mandarin Oriental Spa SPA

(Map p62; ☎750 8888; www.mandarinoriental.com; cnr Makati Ave & Paseo de Roxas; packages from P3200) At this five-star hotel's recently renovated spa, you'll find an array of treatments, plus regular yoga classes

The Spa MASSAGE

(www.thespa.com.ph; 1hr massage from P820) This chain has about a half-dozen locations, including Greenbelt 1 in Makati and Bonifacio High St in the Fort.

Neo Spa MASSAGE

(☎815 6948; www.neo.ph; 26th St cnr 3rd Ave, the Fort; 1hr massage P1000) A pricier option, but worth it.

Footloose FOOT MASSAGE

(various locations; www.clickthecity.com for locations; 1hr massage P350) Thorough foot scrubs. Various locations; check the website.

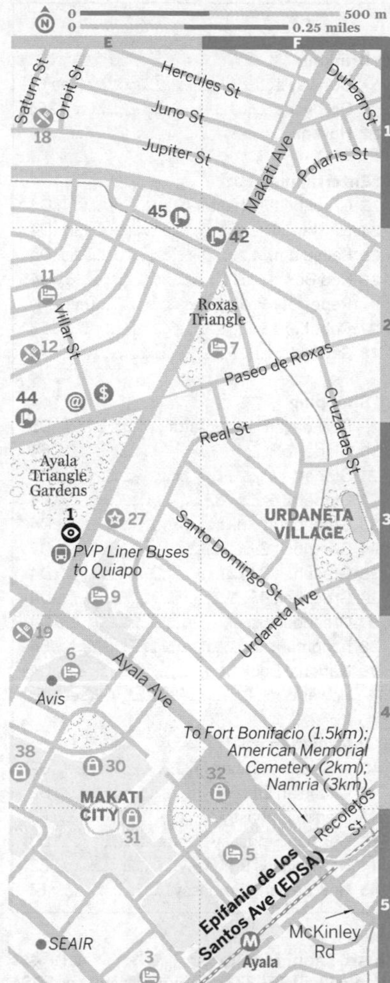

Piandré SALON

(Map p62; ☎816 3884; www.piandre.com; Greenbelt 1) The place for great, professional wax jobs (no, really).

Sleeping

Makati's five-star hotels are located in close proximity to each other near the Ayala Centre. The midrange hotels, for better or worse, are clustered around Makati's red-light area, north of the central business district. This area contains plenty of girlie bars concentrated on P Burgos St, but it is also home to a fine selection of legitimate bars and restaurants.

What little budget accommodation there is in Makati is located outside of the central business district.

AYALA CENTRE & AROUND

TOP CHOICE **Makati Shangri-La** HOTEL $$$

(Map p62; ☎813 8888; www.shangri-la.com; cnr Ayala & Makati Aves; r from P14,500;) With a jaw-dropping main entrance that faces the Glorietta mall, the beautifully done Shangri-La may very well win the award for Makati's most aesthetically stunning interior. The world-class Asian restaurants and mini-waterfalls on every floor greatly contribute to the overall Zen energy. Walk-in guests can use the pool for P600.

Peninsula Manila HOTEL $$$

(Map p62; ☎810 3456; www.peninsula.com; cnr Ayala & Makati Aves; r from P8600;) With rooms that highlight the best of Filipino design, the Peninsula is a Makati veteran that nevertheless appears brand new. The cafe in the soaring lobby has a fine Sunday brunch and is a 24-hour destination for the city's business elite. A side note: a tank drove through the front doors here in 2007 during a foiled coup attempt.

Mandarin Oriental Manila HOTEL $$$

(Map p62; ☎750 8888; www.mandarinoriental.com; cnr Makati Ave & Paseo de Roxas; r from P8000;) As with any of the world's Mandarin Orientals, the level of service here will simply astonish those who've not experienced it before. The rooms are freshly renovated and the spa is arguably Manila's finest.

El Cielito Inn HOTEL $$

(Map p62; ☎815 8951; www.elcielitohotels.com; 804 Pasay Rd; s/d incl breakfast from P2750/3150;) If you want to be near the Ayala Centre malls but don't want to pay five star rates, this is your obvious choice. A recent renovation has it looking in fine fettle, and the rooms have little things that matter like desks and ample bathroom counter space.

Pensionne Virginia GUESTHOUSE $$

(Map p62; ☎844 5228; pensionnevirginia@yahoo.com; 816 Pasay Rd; s/d P1150/1700, ste P1500-2050;) The only thing resembling a budget choice in the area is this quirky family-run guesthouse. While on the tatty and depressing side, it's nonetheless a good value for solo travellers. The suites are *huuuuge.*

Makati

Top Sights
- Ayala Museum ... D4

Sights
- 1 Filipinas Heritage Library ... E3
- Mandarin Oriental Spa ... (see 7)
- 2 Ninoy Aquino Statue ... D3
- Piandré ... (see 33)

Sleeping
- 3 Dusit Thani Manila ... E5
- 4 El Cielito Inn ... B5
- 5 Hotel InterContinental ... F5
- 6 Makati Shangri-La ... E4
- 7 Mandarin Oriental Manila ... F2
- 8 New World ... D5
- 9 Peninsula Manila ... E3
- 10 Pensionne Virginia ... C5
- 11 Picasso Makati ... E2

Eating
- 12 Army Navy ... E2
- Benjarong Royal Thai Restaurant .. (see 3)
- 13 Corner Tree Cafe ... D1
- Grappa's ... (see 17)
- 14 Masas ... D4
- 15 Museum Cafe ... D4
- 16 Nuvo ... D4
- 17 People's Palace ... D4
- 18 Queens ... E1
- 19 Sala ... E4
- 20 Salcedo Community Market ... D2
- 21 Travel Café Philippines ... D4

Drinking
- Conway's ... (see 6)
- Dillinger's ... (see 26)
- 22 Havana ... D4

Entertainment
- 23 Greenbelt 3 Theaters ... D4
- 24 OnStage Theatre ... D4
- 25 Palladium ... D5
- 26 Red Box ... D4
- Repertory Philippines ... (see 24)
- 27 Robot ... E3
- 28 SaGuijo ... A1

Shopping
- 29 Balikbayan Handicrafts ... D5
- 30 Glorietta 3 ... E4
- 31 Glorietta 4 ... E5
- 32 Glorietta 5 ... F4
- 33 Greenbelt 1 ... D4
- 34 Greenbelt 2 ... C4
- 35 Greenbelt 3 ... D4
- 36 Greenbelt 4 ... D4
- 37 Greenbelt 5 ... D4
- 38 Landmark ... E4
- 39 National Book Store ... C4
- Power Books ... (see 36)

Information
- 40 Australian Embassy ... B2
- 41 Canadian Embassy ... B2
- 42 French Embassy ... F2
- 43 German Embassy ... D3
- 44 Netherlands Embassy ... E2
- 45 New Zealand Embassy ... E1

The following are just a step below the 'Big Three' (ie the Shangri-La, Peninsula and Mandarin). They have a variety of restaurants and top-notch service, but the rooms aren't quite as modern and they lack that whiff of history.

Hotel InterContinental HOTEL **$$$**
(Map p62; ☎793 7000; www.intercontinental.com; 1 Ayala Ave; r from P8000;) The architecture here recalls a time when windows were best kept small lest political upheaval break them.

New World HOTEL **$$$**
(Map p62; ☎811 6888; www.manila.newworldhotels.com; cnr Esperanza St & Makati Ave; r from P8200;) Good promo rates are often available here.

Dusit Thani Manila HOTEL **$$$**
(Map p62; ☎867 3333; www.dusit.com; cnr EDSA & Pasay Rd; r from P8000;) Recent renovations have brought this closer to the big boys.

P BURGOS & AROUND

TOP CHOICE **Our Melting Pot** HOSTEL **$**
(Map p66; ☎659 5443, 0932 950 0255; ourmeltingpotbackpackers@gmail.com; A Venue Suites Unit 18 N-O, 7829 Makati Ave; 2-/4-/6-bed air-con dm incl breakfast P850/800/750, r incl breakfast P1000-1600;) Rarely can a humble hostel claim such a swanky address as A Venue Suites. Occupying an apartment within the revered hotel/residence, OMP delivers on minimalist style (lovely beds), yet

remains down-to-earth. It's the place to be if you want to save pesos yet be near Makati's nightlife. You get free use of A Venue's gym and swimming pool. Private rooms are in an annexe nearby on Kalayaan Ave.

TOP CHOICE A Venue Suites APARTMENTS $$$
(Map p66; ☎403 0865; www.avenuehotelsuites.com; 7829 Makati Ave; 1-/2-bedroom ste incl breakfast P6500/9000;) Here you'll find stylish, immaculate suites in a tower rising above A Venue mall. It doubles as a long-term apartment complex, so the service and amenities, while good, are not five-star. Note that with www.agoda.com you can get super deals – under US$75 – on this and sister Antel Suites.

Picasso Makati APARTMENTS $$$
(Map p62; ☎828 4774; www.picassomakati.com; 119 Leviste St, Salcedo Village; r incl breakfast from P9000;) The lofts at this suave boutique belong in the pages of *Architectural Digest*. Think mounted beds, floating staircases, space-age chairs. The standard rooms aren't far behind, and promo rates can cut the prices in half. True to its name, the entire hotel doubles as an art gallery.

Hotel Durban HOTEL $$
(Map p66; ☎897 1866; www.durbaninn.com; 4875 Durban St, Makati; r P1100-1700;) Makati's best midrange value is a tightly run ship. The immaculate rooms, with faux-wood panelling, are more than adequate for the price. It's popular so book ahead.

Makati YMCA Hostel HOSTEL $
(off Map p62; ☎899 6379; 7 Sacred Heart St; www.ymcaofmakati.com; air-con dm/r from P400/1100;) You could bounce a five-centavo coin

MANILA FOR KIDS

Heading off to Manila with a child or two in tow? Not to worry. Many jet-setting parents are surprised to learn that the city is home to a fair number of kid-friendly activities and attractions.

Cleaner, greener Makati is where most parents with kids elect to roost. Legazpi Village's central park and Jaime Velasquez Park in Salcedo Village have good playgrounds, and the malls of the Ayala Centre are full of diversions like bouncy castles and video game arcades. An even better bet is the upscale Bonifacio High Street Mall (p71) in the Fort, which has intriguing interactive sculptures for kids to play with in a pleasant outdoor walking area that's a popular hang-out zone for pets, as well.

At the respected **Repertory Philippines Children's Theatre** (Map p62; ☎571 6926; www.repertory.ph; OnStage Theatre, 2nd fl, Greenbelt 1, Makati; tickets P340-450;), productions such as *Pinocchio* and *Seussical* have been known to play.

At the charming **Museo Pambata** (Map p42; www.museopambata.org; cnr Roxas & South Blvds, Ermita; admission P100; 9am-5pm Tue-Sat, 1-5pm Sun), near Rizal Park, interactive, hands-on exhibits explore subjects as diverse as the environment, the human body and Old Manila through the eyes of kids. Efforts are made to bring everything down to size: there's even a pint-sized jeepney.

Manila Ocean Park (off Map p42; www.manilaoceanpark.com; Rizal Park; adult/child P400/350; 10am-7pm Mon & Tue, 10am-8.30pm Wed-Fri, 9am-8.30pm Sat & Sun) is Manila's latest and greatest kid-friendly attraction. It's an impressive and impressively ecoconscious aquarium, but it's a bit too popular for its own good. The place often gets mobbed, especially on weekends when there are long lines to get in. The entrance is behind the Quirino Grandstand.

The **Manila Zoo** (Map p44; www.manilazoo.org; cnr Quirino Ave & Adriatico St, Malate; admission P40; 7am-6pm) is an appealing oasis in the middle of the city with a diverse collection of animals, although the place is a bit rough around the edges these days. A better, more humane zoo, if you have wheels, is the **Avilon Zoo** (off Map p38; www.avilonzoo.ph; adult/child P300/200). It's northeast of Quezon City in the town of Rodriguez, a 40- to 60-minute drive from Makati (depending on traffic). It's damn near impossible to find so get directions on the website.

Star City (Map p58; www.starcity.com.ph; CCP Complex, Roxas Blvd; admission P60, tickets per ride from P100; 4pm-midnight Mon-Thu, 2pm-midnight Fri-Sun) is a decent amusement park right in the heart of the CCP Complex, although it also tends to get crowded. It has a good number of kiddie rides, a playground and other diversions like ice sculptures.

P Burgos Area

off the beds at the tidy Makati 'Y'. The dorm is dudes-only, but women can book the private rooms. It's in a quiet barangay, yet only a five-minute walk to Makati's central business district.

Berjaya Hotel HOTEL $$$
(Map p66; ☎750 7500; www.berjayahotel.com; 7835 Makati Ave; r incl breakfast from P4500;) This Malaysian-run place just down the street from flashy A Venue mall is very attractive and the service is excellent. It's a pretty big step down from the five-star places, but still an excellent choice for business travellers, with steep promo discounts available.

Robelle House GUESTHOUSE $$
(off Map p66; ☎899 8209; www.robellehouse.net; 4402 B Valdez St; s/d without bathroom P1000/1250, with bathroom P1495/1750;) The location in a residential neighbourhood isn't for those who are creeped out by isolated side streets. Other than that it's a brilliant choice, and entirely unlike anything else in the area. A small pool sits just off the open-air lobby, and the vibe is family friendly.

Antel Suites APARTMENTS $$$
(Map p66; ☎403 8888; www.antelsuites.com; 7829 Makati Ave; d incl breakfast P7650-8100;) Like its sister A Venue next door, this is another super-smart, half-hotel, half-residential high-rise with a gym, a spa and all the fixin's.

St Giles Hotel HOTEL $$$
(Map p66; ☎988 9888; www.stgilesmanila.com; cnr Makati & Kalayaan Aves; r from P3600;) The gym, rooftop pool and compact-but-fashionable rooms will please business travellers. Wi-fi is P300 per day.

Millennium Plaza HOTEL $$
(Map p66; ☎899 4718; www.millenniumplaza.com.ph; Eduque St; r P2800;) Smart, spacious

P Burgos Area

Sleeping

1 A Venue Suites ... A1
2 Antel Suites ... A1
3 Berjaya Hotel ... B2
4 Great Eastern Hotel ... B1
5 Hotel Durban ... A2
6 Millennium Plaza ... A2
Our Melting Pot ... (see 1)
7 St Giles Hotel ... B2
8 Sunette Tower ... A3

Eating

9 Filling Station ... B3
10 Grilla Bar & Grill ... D4
11 La Tienda ... B4
12 North Park Noodles ... A2
13 Som's Noodle House ... D4
14 Ziggurat ... A3

Drinking

15 Beers Paradise ... B4
16 Handlebar ... B4
17 Heckle & Jeckle ... A4
18 Howzat ... C3

Entertainment

19 Time ... B1

rooms with smoking balconies and kitchenettes, but few amenities. Wi-fi is extra.

Great Eastern Hotel HOTEL $$
(Map p66; ☎898 2888; www.greateasternhotelmanila.com; 7842 Makati Ave; d P1500-1900, ste P2600;) Rooms in this high-rise across from A Venue are dated and dark. Still, the price is right for functional doubles in these parts.

Sunette Tower APARTMENTS $$
(Map p66; ☎895 2726; www.sunette.com.ph; Durban St; d/ste from P2500/3000;) It's *soooo* '80s, but has a variety of plain studios and apartment suites with kitchenettes. Wi-fi costs extra.

Eating

You are only limited by your ability to choose when you eat in Makati. Unlike elsewhere in Manila, some of the best restaurants in Makati are actually in the malls, particularly in Greenbelt 2 and 3, as well as Bonifacio High St in the Fort. These all have outdoor pedestrianised areas lined with restaurants and bars. Keep walking until you see something that looks good. At most places you can choose between air-con dining rooms and large outdoor patios that are perfect for people-watching.

Outside of Makati's central business district, there's a cluster of good restaurants along Jupiter St in the P Burgos area, and more restaurants nearby along Kalayaan Ave, which terminates near the Power Plant Mall in the Rockwell Center, another upscale shopping centre with some fantastic eating options.

The big five-star hotels all have notable restaurants. The best of the lot are Red at the Makati Shangri-La, Spices at the Peninsula, and the Dusit's Benjarong Royal Thai Restaurant.

For a delightful market experience, check out the gourmet Salcedo Community Market (p69) in Makati.

AYALA CENTRE & AROUND

TOP CHOICE **Sala** FUSION $$$
(Map p62; ☎750 1555; A Locsin Bldg, cnr Makati & Ayala Aves; mains P500-1500; ⊙lunch & dinner Mon-Fri, dinner Sat & Sun) Possibly Manila's finest restaurant (with the prices to match), this refined European bistro features A-level service and an ever-changing selection of fusion dishes and creative desserts. If you can't get a reservation here try nearby Sala Bistro, next to People's Palace in Greenbelt 3.

People's Palace THAI $$$
(Map p62; ground fl, Greenbelt 3; mains from P350; ⊙11am-midnight) Nearly everything about this high-concept Thai restaurant is envelope-pushing, starting with the fact that it looks nothing like an Asian eatery. The dishes are authentic, yet so gorgeously presented you may not recognise them.

Masas FILIPINO $$
(Map p62; ground fl, Greenbelt 2; meals P300-600; ⊙lunch & dinner;) The food is a contemporary take on traditional Filipino food, specialising in cuisine from the food-rich Bicol region of Southeast Luzon.

Travel Café Philippines FILIPINO $$
(Map p62; ☎729 3366; level 2, Greenbelt 5; mains P150-450; ⊙11am-9.30pm;) Visitors to this travel-themed lifestyle cafe can enjoy an array of Filipino regional specialties before purchasing coffee from North Luzon (including *kopi luwak* – civet-shit coffee), Filipino CDs, handicrafts, guidebooks and more.

Grappa's ITALIAN $$$
(Map p62; level 2, Greenbelt 3; mains P400-1000; ⏲11.30am-11.30pm; 📶✍) Get your Italian fix at this reliable *ristorante* in a prime spot with a commanding view of Greenbelt's central park. There'a a great wine list and set lunches (P595).

P BURGOS & AROUND

TOP CHOICE **Corner Tree Cafe** VEGETARIAN $$
(Map p62; 150 Jupiter St; Fort Bonifacio; mains P200-400; ⏲11am-10pm Tue-Sun; 📶✍) The Corner Tree provides a tranquil escape from busy Jupiter St, not to mention heavenly vegetarian fare that even diehard meat-eaters will love. Dishes are designated either vegan, gluten-free or simply vegetarian. The soups, stews, spinach-feta croquettes and smoothies are our favourites, but also take a gander at the baked tofu walnut burger or the vego chilli. Delightful.

Ziggurat MIDDLE EASTERN $$
(Map p66; just off Makati Ave; mains from P200; ⏲24hr; ✍) This culinary gem is one of Makati's best-kept secrets, with an encyclopaedic menu bearing Indian, Middle Eastern and African influences. At the outside bar you can recline and enjoy a hookah in a setting that manages to slightly evoke a desert tent somewhere.

La Tienda SPANISH $$$
(Map p66; 43 Polaris St; mains P300-700; ⏲grocery 7.30am-11pm, restaurant 7.30am-3pm & 5.30-11pm) As the name implies, this smart Spanish eatery doubles as a gourmet food shop. The restaurant proper doles out fine tapas in addition to larger mains like paella and a long list of steaks. Many come just to savour a glass of red wine.

Grilla Bar & Grill FILIPINO $$
(Map p66; cnr Kalayaan Ave & Rockwell Dr; mains P150-300; ⏲11am-2.30pm & 5pm-1am, to 3am Fri & Sat) One of the better Filipino restobars, this is a fine place to sample Pinoy specialities like sizzling *gambas* (shrimp) and crispy *pata* (pork leg) and drink San Miguel by the bucketful.

Som's Noodle House THAI $$
(Map p66; ☎836 0075; 5921 A Alger St; mains P150-220; ⏲10.30am-10pm) Restaurants in the Philippines generally struggle with Thai food but not Som's, which spices staples like red curry and *tom yum* to your liking. It's a great deal, and it can deliver to your hotel.

Room FUSION $$
(off Map p62; LRI Design Plaza, 210 Nicanor Garcia St; light meals P150-300; ⏲9am-6.30pm Mon-Sat; 📶) Awash in wildly creative furniture that befits its location in the top design centre, this is a great place to settle in for the afternoon – good coffee, ambience, all-day breakfasts and light Asian fusion meals.

Queens INDIAN $$$
(Map p62; ☎895 1316; 146B Jupiter St; mains P250-450; ⏲lunch & dinner; ✍) For a city with a large Indian population, Manila is sadly lacking in world-class Indian food. Queens is probably the best of the lot, although the decor is questionable. Nonstop Bollywood flicks on the small screen rescue the atmosphere somewhat.

Filling Station DINER $$$
(Map p66; 5012 P Burgos St; burgers P410; ⏲24hr) Not even in the American heartland itself could there be a diner with as much 1950s pop-culture paraphernalia as you'll find stuffed inside this P Burgos landmark – everything from life-sized superhero statues to vintage motorcycles. Burgers and milkshakes are the specialities.

Wingman AMERICAN $$
(off Map p62; the Collective, Malugay St; 6/12 wings P180/300; ⏲noon-1am) One of the first establishments to plant its flag at the Collective, a 10-minute taxi ride east of P Burgos St, Wingman slings several varieties of buffalo wings – the best in town by far – plus burgers, beer and other things that backpackers like.

Army Navy TEX MEX $$
(Map p62; 140 Valero St; burgers P145-250; ⏲24hr Mon-Fri, 9am-11pm Sat & Sun; ✍) Convenient Makati locale of the trendy burger-and-burrito chain with call-centre-friendly opening hours.

North Park Noodles CHINESE $$
(Map p66; 1200 Makati Ave; meals P125-170; ⏲10am-4am) Tasty and affordable braised and other Chinese noodles.

FORT BONIFACIO

Pier One FILIPINO $$
(☎887 0115; www.pierone.com.ph; Fort Sq; mains P150-300; ⏲5.30pm-2am) Manila is awash in quintessentially Filipino restobars, which all serve classic Filipino food favourites and buckets of beer, but Pier One in the Fort has the best atmosphere of them all, with

A FOODIE'S WEEKEND PARADISE

During the early months of 2004, several expats living in the tight cluster of high-rise apartments in Salcedo Village, near the heart of Makati's financial district, got together to talk about food. Someone brought up the subject of Europe's quaint neighbourhood markets, and the rest of the group wondered why something similar couldn't exist in their part of the world.

Today, close to 150 separate vendors set up shop every Saturday in the **Salcedo Community Market** (Map p62; Jaime Velasquez Park, Salcedo Village; ⌚7am-2pm Sat). Here one will find a dizzying array of local specialities from food-crazy regions like Ilocos, Pampanga and Bicol, as well as French, Thai and Indonesian offerings and heaps of organic produce.

Thankfully for travellers who don't have a kitchen to cook in, pre-prepared dishes are a market staple. Visitors can sample everything from local desserts and candies to a boggling array of grilled pork, and Filipino rice-flour pancakes known as *bibingka*. The market is also a perfect place to scout for new friends and travelling companions – head towards the communal dining area, choose a chair, and dig in.

If you miss the Salcedo market there's a similar smorgasbord in Legazpi Village's central park on Sundays.

outdoor and indoor seating and plenty of camaraderie.

Aubergine FRENCH, EUROPEAN **$$$**
(☎856 9888; cnr 5th Ave & 32nd St; mains P500-1500; ⌚lunch & dinner; 🖉) This is one of Manila's top restaurants, luring a well-heeled clientele from all over the metropolis. The service is impeccable and the menu a delight – try the porcini leek fondue (P680) or the Tasmanian wild salmon (P980). Vegetarians can get out for a bit less.

Rose FUSION **$$$**
(ground fl, Grand Hamptons Tower, 31st St btwn 1st & 2nd Aves; tapas P75-200, mains P600-800; ⌚lunch & dinner Tue-Sun; 🖉) At this diminutive 'modern Japanese' food place, pieces of raw fish and other appetisers float by on little boats, set to drift along a miniature river carved into the sushi bar. The food is as creative and wonderful as the concept.

Drinking

Makati has some truly excellent bars, specifically on the streets running parallel to P Burgos St. The beer's a bit expensive in these parts (about P75 for a San Miguel) but if you get drinking early you'll be rewarded with fine happy-hour specials.

TOP CHOICE **Handlebar** BAR
(Map p66; www.handlebar.com.ph, 31 Polaris St; ⌚3pm-2am Mon-Thu, 11am-3am Fri-Sun) The motif is Harley at this expat fave, which boasts a big screen for sports viewing and a justifiably popular nightly barbecue under the big tree in front, with famous T-Bone steaks and baked potatoes. Decent cover bands, often including one or two token expats, perform on the weekends.

Museum Café LOUNGE BAR
(Map p62; Ayala Museum, Greenbelt 4; mains P400-600) Much more than a simple refuelling stop for museum patrons, 'M Café' is a magnet for Manila's chi-chi class. It's usually more of a place to warm up for the evening, either inside or outside, but on Thursday nights the beats are thrown down and M Café becomes the party. The menu is heavy on light bites and sandwiches.

Heckle & Jeckle BAR
(Map p66; cnr Jupiter & Polaris Sts; ⌚2pm-5am) For anyone needing to escape the debauchery of nearby P Burgos St, this simple and generally well-behaved pub is one of the area's best options. There's occasional stand-up comedy, and live football matches on TV.

Havana BAR
(Map p62; Greenbelt 3 Courtyard; ⌚11am-2am) The courtyard outside the Greenbelt 3 mall is a popular place for drinking and socialising, and the late-night action centres around Havana. Inside live salsa kicks off nightly at 9.30pm.

Conway's LOUNGE BAR
(Map p62; Makati Shangri-La; ⌚5pm-1am) This place gets packed with yuppies, expats and all sorts of characters out to hear top Filipino

cover bands, like the self-defined Spirit of '67. It's all-you-can-drink beer, wine and cocktails (P625) every night from 6pm to 8pm.

Nuvo LOUNGE BAR
(Map p62; ground fl, Greenbelt 2; meals P500-1000; 11am-2am) Trendy lounge draws Manila's beautiful people. Serves great, albeit pricey food too.

Howzat PUB
(Map p66; 8471 Kalayaan Ave; 10am-2am) Cross through the shaded doors and enter a world of pints and football.

Beers Paradise BAR
(Map p66; cnr Polaris & Durban Sts; 5pm-4am) Belgian beer is the speciality at this spartan drinkery. Most varieties pack quite a wallop.

Dillinger's BAR
(Map p62; level 3, Greenbelt 3; mains P200-400; 11am-4am) Serves meaty mains and classic bar appetisers to go along with an array of draft beers.

☆ Entertainment

There's plenty going on by night in Makati although finding out about it can be a challenge as there's no comprehensive listings magazine or website. Still, listings website www.clickthecity.com and free monthly pamphlets *Circuit* (www.circuitmag.net) and *24/7* (www.mag24-7.com) offer a few ideas. The Manila nightclub scene is covered at http://manilaclubbing.com.

Nightclubs

Along with Resorts World's two chi-chi clubs in nearby Parañaque, the key targets for clubbers are all up in Makati. Cover charges vary from nothing to as much as P500 or more at the prime hotspots. The scene is fickle, but these clubs were producing reliably good times at the time of research.

Time CLUB
(Map p66; http://timeinmanila.com; 7840 Makati Ave) Thumping beats inside, mellow patio overlooking Makati Ave outside.

Palladium CLUB
(Map p62; New World Hotel, Esperanza St; admission incl drink P500; Wed-Sat) A consistent choice, descending into the depths beneath the five-star New World.

Robot CLUB
(Map p62; the Peninsula, Makati Ave; 6pm-midnight, to 3am Fri & Sat) Up-and-down club was a bit down when we visited; keep an eye on it. A table charge applies on weekends.

Performing Arts

SaGuijo LIVE MUSIC
(Map p62; 897 8629; www.saguijo.com; 7612 Guijo St, Makati; admission after 10pm P150; 6pm-2am Tue-Sat) This place styles itself as an indie-rock club but it's really a cool and down-to-earth little bar where the live music is just part of the attraction. Bands are mostly of the emo and post-punk variety and kick off at 10.30pm.

B Side LIVE MUSIC
(off Map p62; the Collective, Malugay St; varies) This is the bar that makes the artsy Collective tick. It tosses a live band or two into the Collective's central courtyard on weekends and on some weeknights, and the whole complex gets jumping – especially on reggae Sundays, which kick off late afternoon.

Repertory Philippines THEATRE
(Map p62; www.repertory.ph; Greenbelt 1) Professional group performs plays at the OnStage Theatre.

Cinema

The most popular choice is **Greenbelt 3 Theaters** (Map p62; 757 3863; Greenbelt 3)

Karaoke

Belting out versions of ballads is a cultural obsession, and you won't so much need to find karaoke as eventually try to get away from it. It's in bars, cafes, buses, almost anywhere there's a person, a microphone and a dream.

Red Box KARAOKE
(Map p62; 757 6188; level 3, Greenbelt 3; per person incl 2 drinks P300-500; noon-3am) As the exclusive address implies, this is karaoke of the upper-crust variety. It may not be an authentic Pinoy karaoke experience but man is it fun, and the prices are actually reasonable. The playlists have pretty much anything you'd want to sing. Pile 15 to 20 friends into a room if need be. Reservations don't hurt.

Shopping

Central Makati can seem like one big upscale mall – you might find yourself shopping against your will. There are numerous art galleries scattered throughout Makati. See the boxed text p56 for souvenir tips.

Balikbayan Handicrafts SOUVENIRS
(Map p62; 1010 Pasay Rd; ⌚9am-8pm) The kind of place that pulls in tourists by the busload. The merchandise is of a surprisingly good quality, considering how much of it they have, and the speciality is beautiful, glazed coconut dishware, decorative balls and other products.

LRI Design Plaza ART
(off Map p62; 210 Nicanor Garcia St; ⌚9am-6.30pm Mon-Sat) A conglomeration of art galleries and contemporary furniture showrooms under one roof, showing off all that's chic in Manila's art world. Check out the **Ricco Renzo Gallery** (www.riccorenzo.com), which holds regular art workshops that are open to all.

Collective KNICK-KNACKS
(off Map p62; Malugay St) This is a collection of funky galleries and shops to go along with a few bars and restaurants. Think vintage clothing, costumes, vaguely erotic statuettes, lava lamps and tie dyes. It doesn't really awaken until early evening.

Greenbelt MALL
(Map p62; btwn Makati Ave & Paseo de Roxas, Ayala Centre) This is the high end of the Ayala Centre, with scores of delightful cafes and restaurants around a central park area. There are five sections (Greenbelt 1 to Greenbelt 5) each with its own character. A true oasis in the middle of the concrete jungle.

Landmark SOUVENIRS
(Map p62; Makati Ave, Ayala Centre) This delightfully dated department store – perfect for costume-party shopping – has an excellent selection of textiles, wood carvings and other souvenirs on the top floor.

Bonifacio High Street & Serendra SHOPPING ARCADE
(btwn 7th & 11th Aves; Fort Bonifacio) Two adjoining upscale, open-air strip malls with loads of good restaurants.

Glorietta MALL
(Map p62; Office Dr, Ayala Centre) Plenty of fast-food here along with less-ritzy boutiques than in neighbouring Greenbelt; two of its five sections (Glorietta 1 and 2) have been at least temporarily subsumed by a new '6-star' hotel going up on Pasay Rd.

Filipinas Heritage Library Bookstore BOOKS
(Map p62; Ayala Triangle Gardens, Makati Ave, Makati; ⌚9am-6pm Tue-Sat) This small bookstore is one of the best places to go for books on all aspects of the Philippines.

Fully Booked BOOKS
(off Map p66; Power Plant Mall, Rockwell, Makati) Manila's most comprehensive bookstore, with a great travel section and an outstanding selection of fiction and nonfiction. Other branches are in Bonifacio High St in the Fort and in Mall of Asia.

National Book Store BOOKS
(Map p62; ground fl, Greenbelt 1, Makati) Books, magazines and lots of stationery products. Excellent copying services. Branches all over the city.

Power Books BOOKS
(Map p62; level 2, Greenbelt 4, Makati) Another large bookstore in the mould of Fully Booked. Additional locations in most major malls.

QUEZON CITY

The country's largest municipality, with about three million people, is overlooked by most travellers because it's far from the airport and the sights in downtown Manila. If you can overlook those flaws, 'QC' has a ton to offer – stellar restaurants, a thriving music scene and cool university kids galore. Go strolling in the quiet neighbourhood west of T Morato Ave and you might feel like you're in one of Makati's exclusive gated communities – only without the gates.

QC is so different from the rest of Manila that you'd do well to look at it as a self-contained entity. If you have the time, head up here and stay for a few days.

Ortigas, a business area lying just south of QC in Mandaluyong City, is also covered in this section.

Sights

QC is more about good eating and drinking than about sights. T Morato is restaurant row, intersecting with the main commercial drag, Timog Ave, at the **Monument to Boy Scouts** (Map p72). Numerous nearby side streets were named after boy scouts after 24 of them died in a plane crash in 1963.

UP Diliman UNIVERSITY
(Map p38; www.upm.edu.ph) If you have a half-day, make the trip out to the lovely, leafy University of the Philippines Diliman campus. It has a genuine American university

feel, and the 22,000-plus students fuel QC's active nightlife. It's a great place for a walk, bike or jog, and you'll find pickup football and Ultimate Frisbee games most afternoons on the central field known as Sunken Garden.

Ninoy Aquino Parks & Wildlife Center ZOO
(Quezon Memorial Circle; adult/child P8/5; ⏲7am-5pm) This park and wildlife rescue centre runs a mini-zoo where injured wildlife are nursed back to life. A few patients who never checked out are on display, including a Burmese python and various birds, reptiles and monkeys.

Sleeping

The most attractive area by far is the T Morato area. There are a few options in the congested City Hall area south of the Quezon Memorial Circle, but we would not recommend staying there.

TOP CHOICE **Stone House** HOTEL $$
(Map p72; ☎724 7551; www.stonehouse.ph; 1315 E Rodriguez Sr Ave, Quezon City; r P1100-2500; ❄📶) Made for the discerning flashpacker, Stone House delivers on style, price and creature comforts. It's miles ahead of its sister hotel in Malate. The only flaw is that the budget rooms are windowless, but colourful tones mitigate this, and for P200 extra you get a window. Stone House is within easy walking distance to the T Morato restaurants.

TOP CHOICE **Torre Venezia Suites** APARTMENTS $$$
(Map p72; ☎332 1658; www.torrevenezziasuites.com.ph; 170 Timog Ave; r/ste from P4500/5500; ⊖❄📶🏊) The same idea as Makati's A Venue Suites here – super-sleek rooms in a towering hotel/residence. The beds, furniture and bathrooms all look mah-velous, and you'd gladly swaddle a newborn in the towels. Throw in a gym and decadent spa and you have a gem. Look for big discounts on www.agoda.com.

Edsa Shangri-La Hotel HOTEL $$$
(☎633 8888; www.shangri-la.com; 1 Garden Way, Ortigas; r from US$200; ⊖❄@📶🏊) Slightly less impressive than Shangri-La's Makati location, yet still a five-star hotel by all rights. The gardens here are truly a sight to behold, and the MRT is just steps away.

Villa Estella Hometel HOTEL $$
(Map p72; ☎371 2279; 33 Scout Santiago St; r standard/deluxe P1500/1800; ❄🏊) This is your friendly neighbourhood crash pad within the maze of silent streets west of T Morato Ave. The rooms are faded and the furniture ancient, so hang out at the poolside bar. *The* place to feel like you're not in Manila.

Quezon City & Cubao

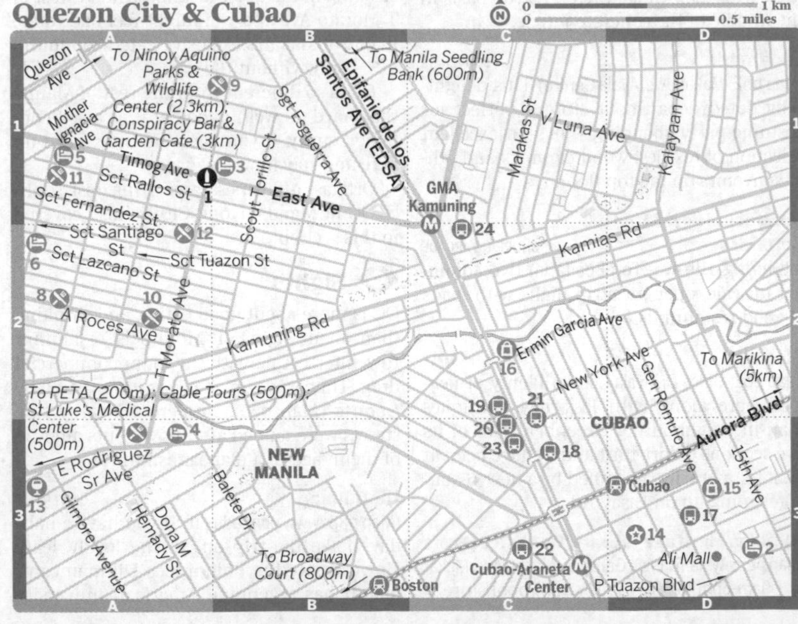

Imperial Palace Suites APARTMENTS $$
(Map p72; ☎927 8001-05; www.imperial.ph; cnr Timog & T Morato Aves; d incl breakfast P4350-4875, ste from P5915;) Well-kept if slightly dated rooms with kitchenettes and plenty of amenities, overlooking the Boy Scouts Monument. Scout the promo rates here.

Broadway Court APARTMENTS $$
(off Map p72; ☎722 7411-15; www.broadwaycourt.com; 16 Broadway Ave; d P1400-1600, ste from P5915;) These basic apartments in a quiet residential 'hood are an intriguing deal, especially for long-stayers, but location is poor. Wi-fi is paid.

Fersal Tuazon HOTEL $$
(Map p72; ☎912 2691; www.fersalhotelgroup.com; 245 P Tuazon Blvd, Cubao; r incl breakfast from P1600;) An alright midranger if you need a place in Cubao.

Eating

Quezon City is awash in restobars specialising in Filipino specialities and catering to the university crowd. They usually sell buckets of beer at a discount.

TOP CHOICE **Chocolate Kiss** EUROPEAN $$
(Map p72; 91 A Roces Ave; sandwiches P150-200, mains P200-300; 11am-10pm Mon-Sat, 9am-2pm Sun;) The continental comfort dishes fashioned by the chefs at this oddly named QC favourite might make you nostalgic for home. Chicken Kiev and Salisbury steak are among the surprises. Hit the all-you-can-eat Sunday brunch – just P350. Good sandwiches and desserts too.

Greens VEGETARIAN $
(Map p72; 92 Scout Castor St, Quezon City; 11am-10pm Mon-Sat, noon-9pm Sun;) It's almost worth the long slog up to Quezon City just to sample the wonderful vego fare here. Try the 'beef' and broccoli, and the incredible, logic-defying meatless *sisig*. Greens also does a mean chocolate cake.

Mogwai CAFE $$
(Map p72; Cubao Expo, Gen Romulo Ave, Cubao; mogwaifilm.multiply.com; mains P140-200; 6pm-2am) This painfully hip Cubao X favourite is a restaurant, bar and indie-cinema screening room rolled into one (screenings at 9pm Monday to Thursday). It has an extensive menu of Filipino food and it doubles as a bar, naturally.

Uno Restaurant FUSION $$$
(Map p72; ☎374 0774; 195C T Morato Ave; mains P300-600; 10am-9.30pm Mon-Sat;) A quaint and handsome little bistro serving complex fusion fare whipped up by the talented chef-owner Jose Mari Relucio. The menu rotates quarterly. Enter on Scout Fuentebella St.

Quezon City & Cubao

Sights
1 Monument to Boy Scouts A1

Sleeping
2 Fersal Tuazon D3
3 Imperial Palace Suites B1
4 Stone House A3
5 Torre Venezia Suites A1
6 Villa Estella Hometel A2

Eating
7 Azadi Persian Kebab A3
8 Chocolate Kiss A2
9 Gerry's Grill B1
10 Greens A2
Mogwai .... (see 15)
11 Restorante La Capre A1
12 Uno Restaurant A2

Drinking
13 Big Sky Mind A3

Entertainment
14 Araneta Coliseum D3

Shopping
15 Cubao Expo D3
16 Q Mart C2

Transport
Amihan Bus Lines .... (see 17)
17 Araneta Bus Terminal D3
18 Baliwag Transit Bus Terminal C3
Cagsawa .... (see 17)
19 Dagupan Bus Co C2
20 Dominion Bus Lines C3
21 Genesis Cubao Terminal C2
Isarog Bus Lines .... (see 17)
22 Partas Cubao Terminal C3
23 Victory Liner Cubao Terminal C3
24 Victory Liner Kamias Terminal C2

LOCAL KNOWLEDGE

CARLOS CELDRAN'S QUEZON CITY

In Quezon City you'll discover more breathing space than you would have thought possible in this chaotic city of 13 million people. First, take the MRT to Quezon Ave. At the corner, you'll find the **Manila Seedling Bank** (off Map p72; www.msbfi.com; cnr Quezon Ave & EDSA), where you can walk through rows of fruit trees, plants and flowers and check out the horticultural exhibits. It's a classroom, a salesroom and a greenhouse rolled into one. Then take a stroll or catch a jeepney down to Quezon City Hall and cross the underpass to **Quezon Memorial Circle** (Map p38), home to the dramatic Art Deco **Quezon Monument** and **Mausoleum of Former President Manuel Quezon**. If the elevator works, take in a view of the city from the top, or if the air-conditioning works, visit Quezon's grave below. Wrap up your day at leafy UP Dilliman (p71).

The best time to visit is Sunday. No traffic, no crowds, and a great time to take a side-trip to Cubao Farmer's Market (Cubao MRT station) and wander over to hipster wasteland Cubao Expo for dinner at Bellini's Italian restaurant, or have a drink at Mogwai (p73).

For more great eats, head to **Van Gogh is Bipolar** (☎394 0188; 154 Maginhawa St, Sikatuna Village). The ambience: *Alice in Wonderland* decides to move to Manila. The cuisine: apothecarically amazing. Dishes are named after famous people who the restaurant claims are 'bipolar'. The owner and chef, Jetro Rafael, will tailor a menu to your desired effect and personality. (Be sure to call ahead; it's only open when he is in the mood.) After dinner, walk around Maginhawa St. It's Manila's next up-and-coming hipster wasteland.

Big Sky Mind (cnr E Rodriguez Sr Ave & 14th St, New Manila; ⌚9pm-5am, Tue-Sun) is best known as 'the only bar I know that's open late on a Sunday night'. On the average night, you might watch a college band try out something new, see an art exhibition, or strike up a conversation with a friendly and overeducated crowd. The bartender Hank will play classic rock, British New Wave, or even Henry Rollins as you swig down cold beer, garlic peanuts and chicken lollipops (yes, it is what it sounds like).

Carlos Celdran is a renowned tour guide, best known for his tours of downtown Manila. For this interview, he went uptown to give us some insider tips on QC.

Restorante La Capre FILIPINO **$$**
(Map p72; cnr Scout Santiago & Scout Limbaga Sts; mains P150-350; ⌚10am-2am Mon-Sat) Tucked away in the quiet streets west of T Morato Ave, this little eatery has Pinoy faves and a host of exotic Pampanga specialities such sizzling crocodile and sizzling *kabayo* (horse).

Gerry's Grill RESTOBAR **$$**
(Map p72; cnr T Morato Ave & Eugenio Lopez St; meals P100-250; ⌚11am-1am;) The original location of the now-widespread Filipino restobar chain is a Quezon City institution.

Azadi Persian Kebab MIDDLE EASTERN **$**
(Map p72; 1 T Morato Ave; mains P70-160; ⌚24hr) Budget eatery near Stone House offers a quick fix for your hummus, kebab and *shisha* cravings. Popular with both students and nonstudents.

Shopping

Greenhills Shopping Center MARKET
(Ortigas Ave, Greenhills, San Juan; ⌚9am-10pm) Somewhat like an indoor/outdoor flea market, Greenhills has stall after stall selling DVDs and brand-named clothing of questionable legitimacy. But snoop around here and you'll find quality antiques and the best selection of genuine pearls in the country.

Cubao Expo ARTIST COMMUNITY
(Map p72; Gen Romulo Ave, Cubao) 'Cubao X', as it is known, is an uber-hip assortment of kitschy shops and galleries selling everything from old LPs to retro toys and housewares. There are lots of shoe vendors here too – this is a traditional selling point for shoes made in Marikina, and some still refer to it by its old moniker, the Marikina Shoe Expo.

Q Mart MARKET
(Map p72; Ermin Garcia Ave) If you want to have a truly local experience – or buy a goat – stumble over to this sprawling covered bazaar not far from the Cubao bus terminals along EDSA.

☆ Entertainment

Live music is the focus at QC's student-driven bars. For nightclubs check out what's happening on T Morato Ave north of Timog Ave, where clubs tend to come and go.

'70s Bistro LIVE MUSIC
(off Map p72; 46 Anonas St; www.70sbistro.com; admission P150, ⏲9pm-late Mon-Sat) A long-running QC bar, it's known for getting some of the best reggae acts in the country, plus classic Pinoy rock bands like the Jerks that have been around almost since the '70s. Draws a reliable crowd every night.

Conspiracy Bar & Garden Cafe LIVE MUSIC
(www.conspi.net; 59 Visayas Ave, Quezon City; admission free; ⏲5pm-2am; 🚭) Owners Cynthia Alexander and Joey Ayala and their guests play folk, jazz and various global tunes. It's more acoustic-oriented and draws an older, sit-down crowd. The inside is nonsmoking and the snacks are vegetarian, while the garden is a good place to chill with a dark San Miguel.

Philippine Educational Theater Association THEATRE
(PETA; off Map p72; ☎725 6244; www.petatheater.com; 5 Eymard Dr; ⏲shows 10am, 3pm and/or 8pm Fri-Sun) This 'open' theatre group does both comedy and tragedy, most of it original. Arguably Manila's best troupe.

Araneta Coliseum ARENA
(Map p72; www.aranetacoliseum.com; Araneta Center, cnr EDSA & Aurora Blvd) Manila is a good place to see washed-up rock acts from the '70s and '80s. Boy George, the Eagles and Duran Duran are among those to have landed in Manila in recent years. It's also popular for PBA basketball games.

ℹ Information

Dangers & Annoyances

Manila is probably no more dangerous than the next city, but it can still be dodgy. As in any big city, crime is a part of life, with foreigners sometimes targeted by petty criminals and carjackers. Be on your guard if walking around on your own at night, especially in deserted places and in rough districts like Tondo. When riding in taxis, do as your driver does and lock your doors.

Pickpocketing is rampant on the MRT/LRT, and on major bar strips where drunk tourists present easy prey.

Traffic is the big annoyance in Manila; you'll probably spend half your time either stuck in it or talking about it. Leave extra time to get to airports, bus stations and dinner dates. Noise, crowds and air pollution are the major annoyances.

Emergency

Ambulance (☎911 1121)
Fire brigade (☎522 2222)
Police (☎117)

WORTH A TRIP

MARIKINA SHOE MUSEUM

Sprawling east of Quezon City on the edge of Metro Manila, Marikina is a bit of a no-man's-land as far as most tourists are concerned, but it does have one must-see sight (at least for Imelda Marcos junkies): the **Marikina Shoe Museum** (JP Rizal St; admission P50; ⏲8am-5pm Mon-Sat).

Footwear of various Filipino luminaries is on display here, but the reason you come here is to see is Imelda's shoes – about 800 pairs of them, lined up in rows behind glass cases. That's only about 25% of the horde left behind in Malacañang Palace by the eccentric former First Lady. After spending an hour or so here it's unlikely that you'll be clamouring to see the other 75%.

Marikina is known as the shoe capital of the Philippines – some 70% of the nation's footwear was made here as recently as 1981. You can find good deals on footwear at department stores and in the **Marikina Market Mall** (Shoe Ave), about a 10-minute walk from the museum. The world's largest shoe (allegedly) is in the Riverbanks Mall on the Marikina River.

Jeepneys go right to the centre of town from Cubao – take a 'Silangan-Cubao' jeepney with a 'Marikina' placard from Aurora Blvd. Or take the LRT-2 to its last stop (Santolan) and then a 'San Mateo' jeepney to City Hall on central Shoe Ave, a short walk from the museum.

SCAM CITY

Manila is notorious for scams that target tourists. The most common scam involves confidence tricksters posing as a group of friends or a family and befriending (usually solo) travellers. They eventually invite them home or on a short excursion. The situation ends with the traveller being drugged and robbed. If you feel that a stranger is acting overly friendly to you, walk away. Beware as well of people who claim to have met you before or claim to be staying in your hotel.

Be wary of the money changers along HM del Pilar and Mabini Sts in Ermita. They've been known to use amateur-magician card tricks to cheat you.

Rigged taxi meters are becoming more common, although most taxi drivers are honest – see p81 for more taxi tips.

Internet Access

Internet cafes are ubiquitous in Malate, Ermita and the P Burgos area in Makati. All major malls have at least one such cafe. Try these if you need services beyond just browsing:

b_connected (Map p62; level 2, Greenbelt 4, Makati; per min P1; ⌚10am-10pm) Has printing, scanning, faxing, disk-burning and other computing services.

E Cafe (Map p44; MH del Pilar St; per hr P39; ⌚24hr) Big place next to notorious Manila Bay Cafe.

Station 168 (Map p44; Adriatico St; per min P1; ⌚24hr) Full computer services available.

Internet Resources

Click the City (www.clickthecity.com) Manila's online directory of businesses is getting better all the time. It contains vast listings of telephone numbers and addresses that are mostly up to date as well as web links where available. Search by name, category, location or any combination of the three.

Medical Services

Metro Manila has several large, private hospitals that are gaining traction for medical tourism. The following are both modern and conveniently located to the primary tourist zones of Malate and Makati.

Makati Medical Center (Map p62; ☎888 8999; www.makatimedcenter.com; 2 Amorsolo St, Makati)

Manila Doctors Hospital (Map p42; ☎524 3011; www.maniladoctors.com.ph; 667 United Nations Ave, Ermita)

St Luke's Medical Center (off Map p72; ☎789 7700; www.stluke.com.ph; 32nd St, Fort Bonifacio) Metro Manila's newest and most modern hospital.

Money

For general information on changing money in the Philippines, see p439. The three main Philippine banks with ATM machines that accept Western bank cards – Bank of the Philippine Islands (BPI), Metrobank and Banco de Oro (BDO) – have scores of branches strewn across the city, including in all major malls. They usually have a limit of P10,000 per withdrawal. Citibank allows P15,000 while HSBC allows up to P40,000 per withdrawal. The **Citibank main office** (Map p62; 8741 Paseo de Roxas) and **HSBC main office** (Map p62; 6766 Ayala Ave) are in Makati's central business district.

Malate and Ermita are peppered with money changers, and there are places all over the city where you can change foreign currency into Philippine pesos, but take care when using these services.

American Express (Map p62; ground fl Eurovilla 1, 142 Legazpi St, Makati; ⌚9am-5pm Mon-Fri) Exchanges US dollar Amex travellers cheques.

Post

Ermita Post Office (Map p44; Pilar Hidalgo Lim St, Malate) Most convenient to Malate's tourist belt.

Makati Central Post Office (Map p62; Sen Gil Puyat Ave, Makati; ⌚8am-5pm Mon-Fri)

Manila Central Post Office (Map p42; Magallanes Dr, Intramuros; ⌚6am-6.30pm Mon-Fri, 8am-noon Sat) A landmark; offers full services.

Tourist Information

Department of Tourism Information Centre (DOT; Map p44; ☎524 2384; www.visitmyphilippines.com; Kalaw St; ⌚7am-6pm Mon-Sat) This large, friendly office is in a beautiful pre-WWII building at the Taft Ave end of Rizal Park. Hands out maps for some interesting self-guided walking tours. There are also smaller DOT offices at the various NAIA terminals.

Travel Agencies

There are travel agencies everywhere in Ermita, Malate and Makati, but most specialise in outbound tourism. Most hotels can arrange excursions outside Manila. The following cater to foreigners and can arrange visa extensions.

Filipino Travel Center (Map p44; ☎528 4507-9; www.filipinotravel.com.ph; cnr Adriatico &

Pedro Gil Sts, Malate; ⌚8am-6pm Mon-Fri, 9am-5pm Sat) Catering to foreign tourists, this helpful and knowledgeable agency organises tours to just about anywhere in the country. Also arranges bus tickets to Banaue.

Filipino Travel Cafe (Map p62; ☎729 3366; Filipino Travel Cafe, 2nd fl, Greenbelt 5, Makati; ⌚11am-9pm Mon-Sat) A private travel agent mans a desk inside this cafe. Can arrange city tours, van rental, etc.

Swagman Travel (Map p42; ☎523 8541; www.swaggy.com; 411 A Flores St, Ermita) Helpful agency inside Swagman Hotel.

Visa Extensions

Bureau of Immigration Head Office (BOI; Map p42; ☎527 4536; Magallanes Dr, Intramuros; ⌚7.30am-5pm Mon-Fri) Offers visa extensions, although can be a painful experience here. Use a travel agent or renew in the provinces if you can.

Getting There & Away

Air

All international flights in and out of Manila use one of the three main terminals of **Ninoy Aquino International Airport** (NAIA; Map p38; ☎877 1109), while many domestic flights use a fourth, domestic, terminal. The four terminals share runways, but they are not particularly close to each other. 'Airport Loop' shuttle vans (P20, 7am to 10pm) link the four terminals.

INTERNATIONAL

For information on international arrivals and a list of international airlines flying to/from Manila and other Philippine airports, see p443 and the boxed text on p444.

A P750 departure tax is payable for international departures out of NAIA.

Several Asian discount carriers fly to Diosdado Macapagal International Airport (Clark Airport, DMIA) in the Clark Special Economic Zone near Angeles, a 1½- to two-hour drive north of Manila.

DOMESTIC

Cebu Pacific and Airphil Express use NAIA Terminal 3, Philippine Airlines (PAL) uses Terminal 2, and Zest Air, SEAIR and Sky Pasada use the antiquated NAIA Domestic Terminal (Map p58).

PAL and its budget affiliate, Airphil Express, have joint ticketing facilities at NAIA 2 and several ticket offices in town. The other domestic carriers have ticket offices at their terminal of departure and also have several ticket offices in town.

The following airlines fly domestically in and out of Manila.

Airphil Express (☎855 9000; www.airphilexpress.com) Main office at NAIA 2.

Cebu Pacific (☎702 0888; www.cebupacificair.com) Has eight offices in town, including one in Robinsons Pl mall and one at the domestic terminal.

ITI (☎851 5674; www.islandtransvoyager.com; ITI Hangar No 5-03-127, Andrews Ave, Pasay) The office is near the Domestic Terminal.

Philippine Airlines (☎855 8888; www.philippineairlines.com) Main office at NAIA 2.

SEAIR (Map p62; ☎849 0100; www.flyseair.com; 2nd fl, La'O Centre, Pasay Rd, Makati)

Sky Pasada (WCC; ☎912 3333; www.skypasada.com; Domestic Terminal)

Zest Air (☎855 3333; cnr Domestic Rd & Andrews Ave, Parañaque)

Boat

The port of Manila is divided into two sections, South Harbor and North Harbor (see Map p38). It's best to take a taxi to North Harbor, as the area isn't a place for a foreigner to be wandering around with luggage. The South Harbour is easier to get to.

There are two major shipping lines handling inter-island boat trips from Manila. Both companies have excellent websites for checking schedules and reserving tickets. For an updated list of destinations served, see their websites. You needn't go to the pier to buy tickets, tickets can be bought through virtually any travel agent and at ticketing booths in major malls.

Negros Navigation (☎554 8777; www.negrosnavigation.ph; Pier 2, North Harbor)

SuperFerry (☎528 7000; www.superferry.com.ph; Pier 15, South Harbor)

Other companies with passenger services:

Moreta Shipping Lines (☎721 4066; www.moretashipping.com; Pier 6, North Harbor) Has boats to Kalibo and Dumaguit on Panay.

WI-FI ACCESS

Wi-fi is common in chain coffee shops but there's usually a charge of P100 per hour. A notable exception is Robinsons Pl mall in Ermita. The entire building is a free wi-fi zone. Coffee shops with free wi-fi in Makati include several at Fort Bonifacio's Bonifacio High St Mall (p71), Seattle's Best in Makati's Greenbelt 3 mall, and the Starbucks opposite the main Citibank office in Salcedo Village, Makati. Most hotels in Manila offer wi-fi, usually free.

Romblon Shipping Lines (☎243 5886, www.romblonshippinglines.com; Pier 8, North Harbor) Sails weekly to Caticlan (for Boracay); to Mandaon, Masbate; and to several ports in Romblon.

Bus

Getting out of Manila by bus is harder than you might expect, as there is no central bus terminal. Instead, myriad private operators serve specific destinations from their own terminals.

The two main 'clusters' of terminals are known as Cubao, which is in Quezon City near the corner of EDSA and Aurora Blvd (see Map p72); and Pasay, which is along EDSA near the LRT/MRT interchange (Pasay Rotunda; see Map p58).

Two harder-to-reach clusters are Sampaloc, north of Quiapo near the University of Santo Tomas (UST); and Caloocan in the far north of Metro Manila.

The biggest bus company, **Victory Liner** (www.victoryliner.com), has an excellent website with route and price information for buses from all five of its Manila terminals, and you can reserve online.

If heading north, try to get buses that say 'SCTEX', as these shave up to two hours off any trip by taking the new Subic–Clark–Tarlac Expressway.

What follows is a list of some of the more important bus companies, which are organised by destination. For fares and trip durations, consult the relevant destination sections.

TO THE NORTHEAST & BANAUE

Advance reservations are highly recommended for direct night buses to Banaue. For a daytime route to Banaue involving several changes, see p140.

Baliwag Transit (Map p72; ☎912 3343; EDSA cnr New York St, Cubao) Buses to Cabanatuan (every 30 minutes); buses to Tuguegarao (four daily) via Solano.

Cable Tours (behind St Luke's Medical Center, E Rodriguez St, Quezon City) Nightly to Bontoc.

Florida Bus Lines (☎781 5894, 743 3809; cnr Extremadura & Earnshaw Sts, Sampaloc) Buses to Tuguegarao (frequent) and Santa Ana via Solano; buses to Claveria via Laoag and Pagudpud; and on-and-off buses to Banaue.

Genesis Cubao Terminal (Map p72; ☎421 1422; cnr New York Ave & EDSA, Cubao) Buses to Baler (three early morning trips, one midnight express trip).

Ohayami (☎516 0501; cnr Loyola & Cayco Sts, Sampaloc) Separate buses nightly at 10pm to Banaue and Kiangan (P450, eight hours).

Victory Liner Kamias Terminal (Map p72; ☎920 7396; cnr EDSA & East Ave, Kamias, Quezon City) Buses go to Santiago City (every 30 minutes), Tuguegarao (hourly until 11.30pm), and Tabuk (four daily). All buses go via Solano.

TO BAGUIO, ILOCOS & ZAMBALES

Several bus lines run 27-seat 'deluxe' overnight express buses to Vigan and Laoag. It's recommended to book these a day or two ahead.

Dagupan Bus Co (Map p72; ☎727 2330; cnr EDSA & New York St, Cubao) Buses to Baguio (hourly) and Bolinao (eight daily).

Dominion Bus Lines (Map p72; ☎727 2350; cnr EDSA & East Ave, Kamias) Buses to Bangued (10 daily), San Fernando (La Union) (18 daily) and Vigan (eight daily).

Fariñas Transit (☎731 4507; cnr Laong Laan & M de la Fuente Sts, Sampaloc) Buses to Laoag via Vigan (15 daily).

Five Star Bus Lines (Map p58; ☎853 4772; Aurora Blvd, Pasay) Buses to Alaminos (three daily), Bolinao (three daily) and Dagupan in Pangasinan (every 30 minutes).

Genesis Pasay Terminal (Map p58; ☎853 3115; Pasay Rotunda) Buses to Balanga and Mariveles in Bataan (every 15 minutes); San Fernando La Union (hourly).

Partas Cubao Terminal (Map p72; ☎725 7303/1740; Aurora Blvd cnr Bernadino St, Cubao) Buses to Vigan (hourly) and Laoag (every two hours) via San Fernando (La Union).

Partas Pasay Terminal (Map p58; ☎851 4025; 518 EDSA cnr Tramu St, beside Winston Hotel) Buses to Vigan and Laoag (eight daily).

Victory Liner Cubao Terminal (Map p72; ☎727 4534; cnr EDSA & New York Ave) Buses to Bolinao via Alaminos (four daily), Baguio (air-con every 30 minutes, deluxe via SCTEX five daily), Iba (three daily) and Olongapo (air-con every 30 minutes, deluxe via SCTEX seven daily).

Victory Liner Pasay Terminal (Map p58; ☎833 5020; cnr EDSA & Taft Ave) Buses to Baguio (hourly), Iba (six daily) and Olongapo (every 30 minutes).

TO ANGELES & CLARK AIRPORT

Swagman Travel (see p77) runs three daily buses to Angeles City (P600), departing at 11.30am, 3.30pm and 8.30pm. Otherwise most northbound buses (to Baguio or Ilocos) take you to

> **WHICH BUS TERMINAL?**
>
> Can't figure out which bus terminal to use? On www.clickthecity.com you can search for 'bus lines' and add in the name of your destination city. Often the correct company and terminal will come up.

Dau, which is just a short tricycle or jeepney ride from Angeles.

Philtranco (Map p58; ☎851 8078/9; cnr EDSA & Apelo Cruz St, Pasay) runs a convenient shuttle service to Clark Airport, with five daily trips originating from its Pasay station (P450, 1¾ hours) and stopping to pick up passengers at SM Megamall in Ortigas (P400, 1½ hours).

Partas runs two daily trips to Clark from its Pasay terminal and two trips from its Cubao terminal.

TO BATANGAS & PUERTO GALERA

For Puerto Galera on Mindoro, several companies run combination bus/boat services, leaving around 8am from Ermita. These take about four hours and cost roughly P350 more than going the individual route and taking a bus to Batangas pier, then a boat to Puerto Galera. Companies include the following:

Swagman Travel (see p77) Tickets P850; departure at 8am.

Si-Kat (Map p44; ☎708 9628; Citystate Tower Hotel, 1315 Mabini St, Ermita) Tickets P700. Departure at 8.30am.

Companies going to Batangas pier roughly every 20 minutes throughout the day:

JAM Transit (Map p58; cnr Taft & Sen Gil Puyat Aves, Pasay)

RRCG (Map p58; cnr Taft & Sen Gil Puyat Aves, Pasay)

DLTB (Map p58; ☎0922 817 1082; cnr Taft & Sen Gil Puyat Aves, Pasay; ☎)

Ceres/JAC Liner (Map p58; cnr Taft & Sen Gil Puyat Aves, Pasay)

TO THE SOUTH OF MANILA

BSC/Batman (Map p58; Pasay Rotunda) Buses to Nasugbu and Matabungkay via Tagaytay (every 30 minutes).

DLTB (Map p58; ☎0922 817 1082; cnr Taft & Sen Gil Puyat Aves, Pasay) Buses to Santa Cruz for Pagsanjan (every 30 minutes), Lucena via San Pablo (every 30 minutes).

Ceres/JAC Liner (Map p58; cnr Taft & Sen Gil Puyat Aves, Pasay; ☎) Buses to Lucena via San Pablo (every 30 minutes).

JAM Transit (Map p58; cnr Taft & Sen Gil Puyat Aves, Pasay; ☎) Buses to Lipa City (every 30 minutes) and Lucena via San Pablo (every 30 minutes).

TO SOUTHEAST LUZON

The hub for Bicol-bound buses is the newly relocated **Araneta Bus Terminal** (Map p72; btwn Times Sq & Gen Romulo Aves, Cubao, Quezon City). Cagsawa and RSL have coveted overnight buses departing straight from Ermita. All night buses to Bicol are not created equal. You'd be best off shooting for the pricier deluxe buses with three fully reclining seats per row. Book these in advance, if possible. To save money take one of the myriad 'ordinary' (non-air-con) buses that leave from the Araneta Bus Terminal.

Amihan Bus Lines (Map p72; ☎387 1790; Araneta Bus Terminal, Cubao) Loads of mostly night buses to Naga, Legazpi and Sorsogon.

Cagsawa Ermita (Map p44; ☎525 9756; P Faura Centre, Padre Faura St, Ermita) Cubao (Map p72; ☎913 1514; Araneta Bus Terminal, Cubao) Has two nightly deluxe buses to Tabaco via Legazpi and Naga from Ermita. More buses from Cubao.

Isarog Bus Lines (Map p72; ☎482 1600; Araneta Bus Terminal, Cubao) Runs deluxe night trips to Naga (six daily) and Legazpi (six daily). Isarog has the comfiest buses of them all.

Philtranco (Map p58; ☎851 8078/9; cnr EDSA & Apelo Cruz St) Buses to Naga and Legazpi (both daily). Philtranco also runs a masochists-only trip along the so-called 'Nautical Highway' to Davao (Mindanao) via Samar, Leyte and Surigao City (three daily, two days).

RSL (Map p44; ⊙525 7077; Padre Faura Center, Padre Faura St, Ermita) Has a nightly bus to Tabaco via Naga and Legazpi.

Car & Motorcycle

If you are driving, the North and South Luzon Expressways are the quickest ways to disentangle yourself from Manila. They are relatively expensive tollways (pricey even by Western standards) but that just serves to cut way down on traffic. See p446 for details on car rental.

Train

Philippine National Railways (PNR; ☎319 0041) runs from Tutuban Station in Tondo (Map p38) to Naga (seat/sleeper/executive P548/950/1425, 10 hours) in Southeast Luzon with five quick stopovers in Lucena, Hondagua, Tagkawayan, Cagay and Sipocot. Trains leave at 6.30pm from both stations.

ℹ Getting Around

For many the worst part of Manila will simply be getting around. Like many Asian metropolises it has enormous traffic problems. Add in rush hour, rain or both and you've got a quagmire. Fortunately there's one thing local transport isn't: expensive. Even a cab will seldom cost more than P250 for even the longest journey.

Even cheaper are the jeepneys, which go everywhere in a confusing muddle, but also find themselves stuck in the same traffic despite the best kamikaze-like efforts of the drivers.

The LRT and MRT trains are an excellent way to soar over and past traffic. The only downsides are the lack of comprehensive coverage of the city and the mobs using the trains at rush hour.

To/From the Airport & Boat Docks

As there are no direct public transport routes from either of the four terminals to Malate or Makati, bite the bullet and take a taxi, especially if you have much luggage. NAIA is quite close to the city and barring traffic you can get to Malate or Makati by taxi in 20 minutes.

Option one is the white, prepaid 'coupon' taxis that charge set rates of more than P440 to Malate and P530 to Makati. These can be found just outside the arrivals area at all four airport terminals.

Just as easy, as long as the lines aren't too long, are the special yellow airport metered taxis, which have a flagfall of P70 (regular metered taxis on the street have a P40 flagfall). There are ranks for these taxis just outside the arrivals areas of the three international terminals. Your total bill to Malate should be about P170, to Makati closer to P220.

To save a few pesos you can walk upstairs to the arrivals area of any of the terminals and angle for a regular metered taxi on a drop-off run. These will save you P70 to P100 to either Makati or Malate.

The domestic airport has an easy-to-find taxi rank with regular metered taxis outside.

Braving public transportation from the airport is tricky and involves several changes. It probably isn't worth the trouble, given how cheap taxis are, but if you insist, walk out to the main road and hail any 'Baclaran' jeepney. In Baclaran you can get on the LRT or switch to a Malate-bound jeepney.

At Terminal 3, an 'Airport Loop' shuttle bus (P20) runs every 15 minutes from 7am to 10pm straight from the terminal to the MRT/LRT exchange at **Pasay Rotunda** (cnr EDSA & Taft Ave), where public transport is readily available to take you to Malate or Makati. Walk out of the terminal and go right – don't confuse this with the other 'Airport Loop' shuttle that connects the four terminals. The van operates from Pasay Rotunda to the airport according to the same schedule.

STREET NAMES

Be aware that many streets are known by two, or even three, names. A Arnaiz Ave in Makati is universally known as Pasay Rd, its former name. P Ocampo Sr St is still called Vito Cruz St, Sen Gil Puyat Ave is Buendia, Rizal Ave is Avenida, and Chino Roces is Pasong Tamo. To make matters worse, street numbers are often unmarked. Instead, an address is usually specified as an intersection, eg 'Pedro Gil St corner A Mabini St'.

If you arrive in Manila by boat, you're also better off catching a taxi into town, as the harbour is a pretty rough area and public transport routes are complicated.

Bus

Local buses are only really useful to get to places on the main roads such as Taft Ave, España Blvd, Buendia (aka Sen Gil Puyat Ave) or EDSA, as they are prohibited from most streets in the centre of town. Depending on the journey, ordinary buses cost from P10 to P15; air-con buses cost from P10 to P25.

Like jeepneys, buses have their destinations written on signboards placed against the front windshield, for example 'Ayala' (for Ayala Centre) and 'Monumento' (for Caloocan).

Probably the most useful local bus is the air-con PVP Liner bus from Quezon Blvd by Quiapo Church to Makati Ave in the heart of Makati (P26).

Car & Motorcycle

Because of traffic and unorthodox local driving habits, renting a self-drive car or motorcycle to get around Manila is not recommended. On the other hand, a rental car is a great way to visit the attractions outside Metro Manila, many of which are hard to reach by public transport.

International car-rental companies have offices at the airport terminals and some major hotels. Rates start at about P3000 per day. Local car-rental companies tend to be cheaper. Companies include the following:

Avis (Map p62; ☎584 2463/4; www.avis.com.ph) Offices throughout the city, including at NAIA Terminals 1, 2 & 3, and the Shangri-La Hotel.

Nissan (Map p62; ☎816 3551; www.nissanrentacar.com; Peninsula Hotel, cnr Ayala & Makati Aves, Makati)

Triple A Car Rental (off Map p62; ☎895 4382, 0920 926 5750; tr-a@pldtdsl.net; 1158 Antipolo St, Makati) Hires out vehicles from P1800 per day, plus P500 for a driver (mandatory). Good, honest service.

FX

Manila has numerous air-con Toyota Tamaraw FX vans, sometimes bearing a Mega-Taxi sign, which follow similar routes to the jeepneys, picking up and setting down passengers en route. The fare is P30 for long rides and P20 for shorter hops.

Jeepney

For the uninitiated, Manila jeepneys can be a challenging experience. The long-wheel-base jeeps offer a bewildering array of destinations and, though these destinations are written on signboards stuck in the window, few people arrive exactly where they intend to on their first jeepney ride. However, if you stick to the more common routes, some of which are listed here, you shouldn't go too far astray.

Heading south from Quiapo Church, jeepneys to 'Baclaran' pass Ermita/Malate along MH del Pilar St, continue close to the CCP, cross EDSA and end up at the Baclaran LRT stop. From Quiapo Church you can also take 'Kalaw' jeepneys to Ermita.

Heading north from Baclaran, jeepneys pass along Mabini St or Taft Ave, heading off in various directions from Rizal Park:

» 'Divisoria' jeepneys take Jones Bridge, passing close to the office of the Bureau of Immigration, and end up at Divisoria Market.

» 'Monumento' jeepneys pass the Manila Central Post office and roll over the MacArthur Bridge before passing the Chinese Cemetery and the Caloocan bus terminals.

» 'Quiapo' and 'Cubao' jeepneys take Quezon Bridge, passing Quiapo Church. 'Cubao via España' jeepneys continue to the Cubao bus stations via UST and the Sampaloc bus stations.

For more on riding jeepneys in the Philippines, see p447.

Kalesa

Horse-drawn carriages known as *kalesa* are common in Binondo, Intramuros and to a lesser extent in Malate, where they are used both for tourists and as a form of public transport for locals. *Kalesa* drivers were once notorious for taking tourists for a (figurative) ride, but nowadays the Intramuros drivers have fixed rates posted on their carriages – it's P350 per 30 minutes around the walled city. In Binondo (Chinatown) locals still use *kalesa* so they are cheaper – P200 to P250 to do an hour or so of touring. Carriages usually fit two to four persons and the fee should be good for the entire carriage (not per person).

LRT & MRT

Manila's metro system is far from user friendly and huge crowds make it virtually unusable during peak periods, but it's a nonetheless a good way to avoid Manila's notorious traffic in air-conditioned comfort during off-peak hours.

The LRT (Light Rail Transit) has two elevated lines. The LRT-1 runs from Monumento in the north to Baclaran in the south, interchanging with the MRT at the corner of EDSA and Taft Ave near Pasay Rotunda. The LRT-2 runs from Recto in the west to Santolan in the east, interchanging with the MRT in Cubao.

The MRT (Metro Rail Transit) travels a south–north route along EDSA. It is handy for getting to and from the Ayala Centre in Makati and to Quezon City.

Electronic farecards are usually good for one trip only, a disingenuous system that produces huge lines at ticket booths during rush hour. Fares (P12 to P15) are dependent on distance. Some stations sell 'stored-value cards' worth up to P100, which are good for three months, but these can be hard to find.

Taxi

Taxis in Manila are cheap and plentiful. Flagfall is a mere P40 for the first kilometre, plus P3.5 for every 300m (or two minutes of waiting time) after that. A 15- to 20-minute trip rarely costs more than P150 or so.

Most taxi drivers will turn on the meter; if they don't, politely request that they do. If the meter is 'broken' or your taxi driver says the fare is 'up to you', the best strategy is to get out and find another cab (or offer a low-ball price).

Rigged taxi meters are becoming more common in Manila. If you see the meter changing within the first 500m and/or racing up suddenly, you're being had. The first five minutes in a properly metered taxi in normal Manila traffic should not bring the meter past P50 to P60.

Tricycle

Motorised tricycles are useful for short hops around town. Short journeys should cost anywhere from P30 to P50, depending on how well you bargain. Push tricycles, or pedicabs, are a cheaper alternative in a few areas, such as Malate.

Around Manila

Includes »

Best Places to Eat

- » Antonio's (p87)
- » Sonya's Garden (p88)
- » Iguana's (p97)
- » Texas Joe's (p95)
- » Vasco's (p95)

Best Places to Stay

- » Farm at San Benito (p89)
- » Kinabuhayan Cafe Bed & Breakfast (p90)
- » Discovery Country Suites (p87)
- » Arthur's Place (p90)
- » Lighthouse (p94)

Why Go?

After the urban joys of Manila have exhausted you, you'll probably be ready for some fresh air. Believe it or not, it's in ample supply in the hilly regions surrounding Manila.

The area south of Manila is home to a clutch of interesting military history sights and some of the most dramatic landscapes you'll find anywhere. Volcanoes are the speciality, with some impressive seascapes thrown in.

Head north and you'll run square into the most notorious volcano of them all, Mt Pinatubo, in the underrated Zambales Mountains. It overlooks the twin ex-military bases of Subic and Clark, now struggling to become tourism hubs.

Unfortunately, getting out of Manila can take the bulk of the morning in rush hour traffic. With the obvious exception of tailor-made day trip Corregidor, most highlights are not really day-trip material by public transport. This is one place you might consider renting a car.

When to Go

Manila

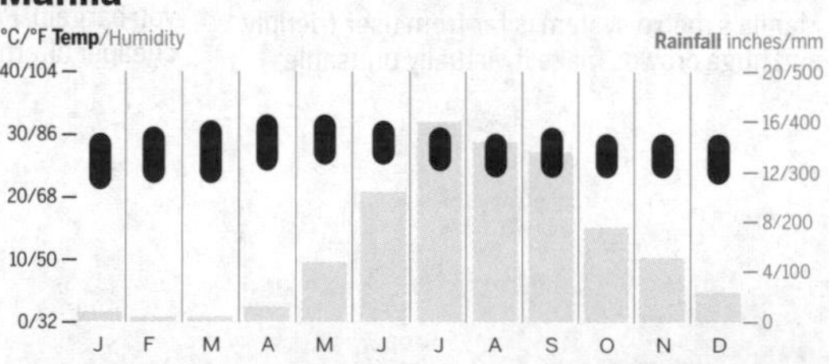

May Local peaks become places of refuge in the height of the hot season.

Dec–Feb The coolest months are particularly welcome.

Aug–Oct Some surf on the Zambales Coast within range of Subic.

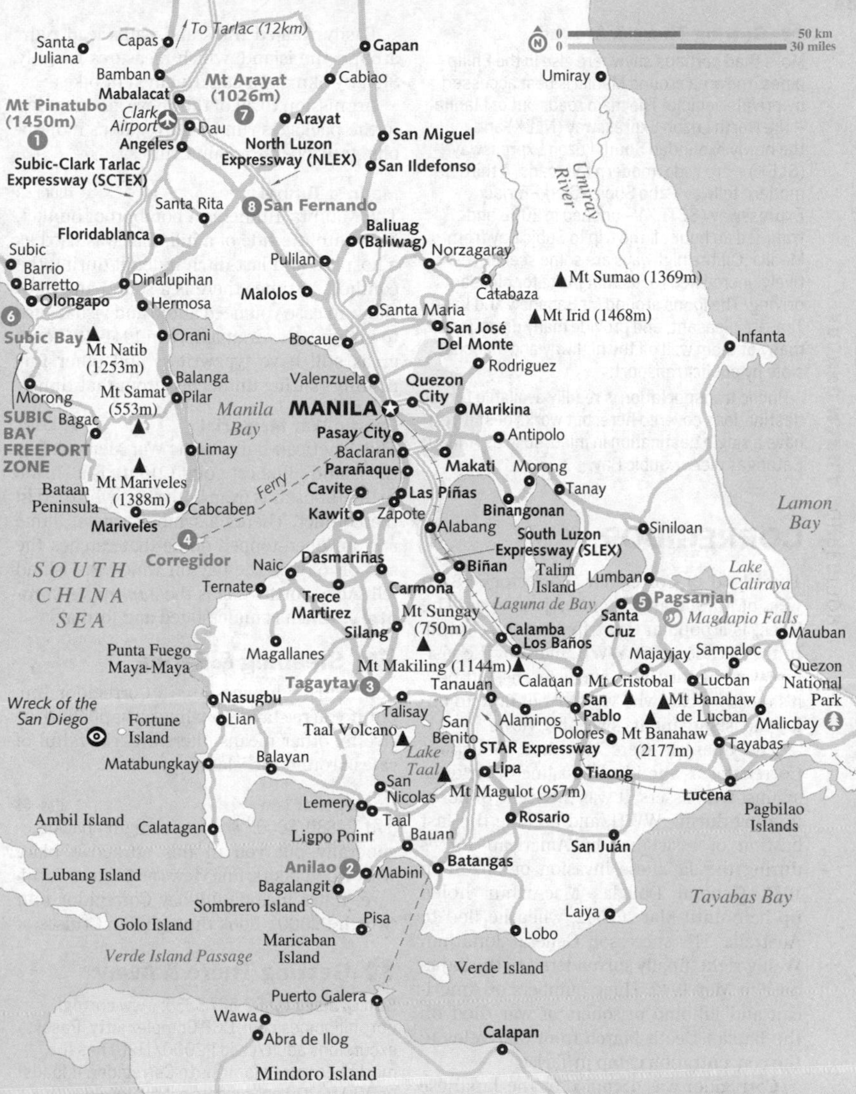

Around Manila Highlights

1. Journey to volcanic drama on **Mt Pinatubo** (p98)
2. Spend a weekend in **Anilao** (p89), the ultimate diving and snorkelling insider spot
3. Enjoy sumptuous views of Taal Volcano and sumptuous cuisine in **Tagaytay** (p85)
4. Immerse yourself in WWII history on a day trip from Manila to **Corregidor** (p84)
5. Jet through the rapids of **Pagsanjan** (p91)
6. Go to extremes amid the virgin forests and sunken wrecks in and around **Subic Bay** (p93)
7. Take a morning ultralight ride over lush **Mt Arayat** (p97), then climb the extinct volcano the same afternoon
8. Swelter through the macabre Good Friday **crucifixion ceremony** (p96) in San Fernando, Pampanga

Getting There & Around

More than perhaps anywhere else in the Philippines, the area around Manila is best accessed by private vehicle. The main roads out of Manila – the North Luzon Expressway (NLEX) and the newly expanded South Luzon Expressway (SLEX) – are wide, modern toll roads. A third modern tollway – the Subic–Clark–Tarlac Expressway (SCTEX) – opened in 2008 and trimmed an hour off the trip to Subic Bay from Manila. Off the highways are some scenic, relatively uncrowded roads that make for pleasant driving. The loops around Mt Banahaw and Lake Taal are pleasant, and provide many diversions, many of them well off the highway and inaccessible by public transport.

Public transportation is readily available for all destinations covered here, but works best if you have a single destination in mind, such as Anilao, Batangas pier or Subic Bay.

CORREGIDOR

The island of Corregidor (Corrector), 48km west of Manila and often referred to as 'The Rock,' is a popular day trip from the capital. In the decades after WWII, many of the visitors were history buffs and veterans, but now it's mostly locals who venture out here to enjoy the island and its sweeping views.

The Spanish were the first to exploit Corregidor as the ideal first line of defence against trespassers. It was the scene of fierce fighting during WWII, and became the last bastion of resistance by American forces during the Japanese invasion of Luzon in 1941. General Douglas MacArthur holed up here until March 1942, when he fled to Australia. His successor, General Jonathan Wainwright, finally surrendered to the Japanese in May 1942. Huge numbers of American and Filipino prisoners of war died on the Bataan Death March from Mariveles to the concentration camp in Tarlac.

Corregidor was occupied by the Japanese until January 1945, when MacArthur returned. The second battle for the island was no less bloody than the first, and thousands died.

Sights & Activities

There are, as you'd expect, numerous war monuments on the island. Significant sights include **General MacArthur's HQ**, the mile-long **barracks**, the **gun batteries** and the **Spanish lighthouse**, which offers good views over Manila Bay. There is also a small **museum**.

Easily walked trails and paths lead right around the island, which measures roughly 3km by 5km; you can usually rent bikes.

Admission to all of the above are included in the packages run by Corregidor's monopolist tour operator, Sun Cruises.

Malinta Tunnel BUNKER

The Malinta Tunnel is a bombproof bunker, built into the side of a hill, that was used as a hospital and last-ditch redoubt during the conflict. At times there is a sound-and-light show, in case you need audio and visual cues to imagine the drama here in 1941–42. Some areas still have typewriters and other furnishings sitting untouched from that time.

Pacific War Memorial MEMORIAL

The American-built Pacific War Memorial, at the island's highest point (210m), is a shrine to the thousands from both sides who died in the conflict. There's a symbolic metal flame and an open-topped dome that catches the sun on 6 May, the day on which the island fell. Also worthwhile is the **Japanese Cemetery**, which is understated and formal.

Sleeping & Eating

Sun Cruises' lunches are in Corregidor Inn, but if you're staying a while or happen to arrive by other means, there are a handful of cafes around the island.

Corregidor Inn INN **$$**

(s/d P2880/3000; ❄≋) Overnight packages generally put you in this attractive place with wood floors, fine views and rattan furniture. Rates include full-day Corregidor tour (worth P2000). Book through Sun Cruises.

Getting There & Away

Sun Cruises (☎02-527 5555; www.corregidorphilippines.com; CCP Complex jetty, Pasay; excursions adult/child P2000/1120) has the market cornered for trips to Corregidor. It loads up 100 to 200 passengers every morning at 7.30am; you shall return to Manila by 3.45pm, unless you stay overnight. The price includes lunch and a comprehensive tour of the island.

The only other way to get to Corregidor is to charter a bangka from Mariveles (P2500).

SOUTH OF MANILA

There is a range of day- and short-trip options south of Manila. The most popular attractions fill up with crowds from Manila on weekends, so visit on a weekday if possible.

Las Piñas

☎02

The once-tiny village of Las Piñas, 5km south of Pasay (Manila), has long been swallowed up by metro Manila, but the centre has a bit of a village atmosphere and many of its buildings have been restored using traditional methods.

The principal attraction here is the **bamboo organ** (☎825 7190; www.bambooorgan.org; Quirino Ave; admission incl tour P50; ⌚8am-noon & 2-6pm Tue-Sun, by appt Mon) in the attractive **San Joseph Parish Church** (Quirino Ave). The famous organ was built between the years of 1816 and 1821, a particularly lean period, by the Spanish priest Padre Diego Cera, who instructed bamboo to be used instead of the more expensive metal for the majority of the organ pipes. (The horizontal trumpets are made of metal.)

A short organ concert is included in the price of admission. In the second week of February, organists from around the world gather here for the **Bamboo Organ Festival**.

To get to Las Piñas, take a Baclaran–Zapote–Alabang jeepney from the Baclaran LRT stop and have the driver drop you off at the church.

Kawit

☎046 / POP 76,000

History buffs can venture another 15km south of Las Piñas to view the **Aguinaldo Mansion** (admission free; ⌚8am-4pm Tue-Sun) in the town of Kawit. Here the revolutionary army of General Emilio Aguinaldo proclaimed Philippine Independence on 12 June 1898 – a triumph soon quashed by the Americans. The alluring mahogany-and-*nara*-wood house, built in 1849, is now a shrine, and you can tour the 5ft 3in Aguinaldo's private rooms and see his much-loved bowling alley. The general died in 1964 after a very long life that included a period of chumminess with the Japanese occupiers.

Pick up buses and jeepneys to Cavite at the Baclaran LRT stop or along Roxas Blvd in Pasay.

Calamba

☎049 / POP 360,300

Calamba, southeast of Manila on the shores of the Laguna de Bay, was the birthplace of Philippine national hero José Rizal. The **Rizal Shrine** (admission free; ⌚8am-4pm Tue-Sun) is in the rebuilt (in the 1950s) Spanish colonial house where Rizal was born. On display are numerous items of Rizal memorabilia.

Tagaytay & Lake Taal

☎046 / POP 62,000

On a clear day, Lake Taal is truly a marvel to behold. From Tagaytay you can peer straight down into the simmering, multiple craters of active Taal Volcano – also known as Volcano Island – rising out of the middle of the lake 600m beneath you.

Lake Taal and Volcano Island lie within a massive prehistoric volcano crater measuring roughly 75km around. This ancient crater forms Tagaytay Ridge, upon which sits the town of Tagaytay. Like a set of Russian *matryoshka* dolls, Taal Volcano in turn encircles its own little crater lake, itself containing a small island.

Tagaytay is a relaxed town that seems to meander forever along Tagaytay Ridge. Lying just 60km south of Manila, it is everything the capital is not: cool, clean, gorgeous and oxygenated. The Tagaytay area is also known as something of a foodie haven.

The nature of the town changes dramatically on weekends, when the Manila hordes arrive and traffic jams appear.

Tagaytay Rotunda, at the intersection of the road to Silang, is a useful landmark that separates the eastern and western halves of Tagaytay Ridge. Just off the rotunda is the main commercial centre, Olivares Plaza.

Sights & Activities

The main activity in Tagaytay consists of plopping down in an establishment on the ridge and watching the mist tickle the multiple craters of Taal Volcano. Less sedentary types descend to the lake for the bangka ride out to Volcano Island and subsequent climb up the volcano. It's neither a difficult climb nor a particularly rewarding one. Notoriously dusty and hot, it's more rite-of-passage than anything else.

Taal Volcano HIKE

The bulk of Volcano Island emerged from the lake during a savage eruption in 1911, which claimed hundreds of lives. Since then frequent eruptions have sculpted and resculpted the island's appearance. With more than 47 craters and 35 volcanic cones, Taal Volcano remains one of the world's deadliest volcanos.

The main Taal crater is in the middle of the island (the obvious cone visible from the ridge is Binitiang Malaki, which last erupted in 1715). The most active crater is Mt Tabaro, on the west side, which saw dramatic lava flows in the late '60s and mid-'70s.

Several hikes are possible, but by far the most popular is the well-worn trail up to the main crater overlooking an evil-looking yellow sulfurous pool. The walk takes about 35 minutes (or you can hire a tired old horse for P500). You most definitely do *not* need a guide, even though plenty of people will try to convince you otherwise.

The launch point for bangkas out to Volcano Island is the lakeside town of Talisay, where dozens of operators vie for the attention of arriving tourists. Depending on where you hire them, bangkas to the island (20 minutes) cost P1200 to P1800 for the whole boat.

If you don't want to deal with the touts, just proceed to Taal Lake Yacht Club or to one of the many ramshackle resorts that line the lakefront west of Talisay proper and arrange your boat there. You can also arrange your excursion up in Tagaytay; it will cost more but will include transport down the hill to Talisay.

Other hiking options on Volcano Island include rigorous all-day treks up Mt Tabaro or up the south ridge of Taal's main crater, from where there's a trail leading down to the crater lake. Only a few guides make these trips; they charge around P1000, plus a bit extra for a bangka ride around to the south side of the island (P3500 for up to six people).

For all the walks bring plenty of drinking water and a hat, as there's little shelter from the relentless sun.

The **Philippine Institute of Volcanology & Seismology** (Philvolcs; ☎773 0293; Barangay Buco, Talisay; admission free; ⏰8am-5pm), on the lakeside 3km west of the junction where the road from Tagaytay terminates, can tell you if the volcano is safe to climb. It houses a monitoring station, a modest museum and seismographs of recent events. If the door is locked just knock and somebody will materialise to let you in.

Taal Lake Yacht Club SAILING
(☎773 0192; Barangay Santa Maria, Talisay) The TLYC offers parking (P100), bangka hire to Volcano Island (P1800) and a good selection of water-sport equipment, including Hobie 16 catamarans (P3200 per day), single-sail Toppers (P1600 per day) and tandem sea kayaks. They can also guide you up and down a 'secret trail' on the back side of Volcano Island (P2800 for the boat and guide). The yacht club is 1km west of the Tagaytay road junction.

People's Park in the Sky VIEWPOINT
(admission P15; ⏰8am-5.30pm) Improbably perched on a towering mound of earth at Tagaytay's eastern end, this is Ferdinand Marcos' unfinished summer home. It remains a crumbling yet appealing ruin, with a decrepit Greek-style amphitheatre and a smattering of tacky tourist attractions on the grounds. A newly constructed weather tower looms over everything. The 360-degree view of the area is indeed spectacular. Try the doughy rolled coconut snacks sold by vendors in the parking lot. It's 8.5km east of the Tagaytay Rotunda. Jeepneys go out here from Olivares Plaza.

Picnic Grove ADVENTURE PARK
(☎483 0346; Tagaytay Ridge; admission P50; ⏰7am-7pm) This is at best a moderately adventurous adventure park, with **horse-riding** (per hr P200), a **fish spa** (per 20min P200), souvenir stands, a nature walk, great views and a fairly tame 250m **zip line** (one-way/return P200/300 Mon-Fri, P320/420 Sat & Sun) over a small gorge. It's 4.7km east of the rotunda.

TOP DIY DAY TRIPS FROM MANILA

We said it was hard to do day trips from Manila without private transport. We didn't say it was impossible. The new highways certainly make it easier, so here are five doable day trips. Start early.

» **Ultralight Rides** Get yourself to Angeles by bus (easy) and they'll pick you up

» **Mt Samat Shrine** You'll need to spring for a private tricycle up to the shrine

» **Tagaytay/Mt Taal** After your climb, just pick a restaurant and don't move

» **Pagsanjan** A long way but works as an in-and-out day trip

» **Mt Arayat or Mt Makiling** Viable day climbs, although public transport tricky

Sleeping

The lakeside resorts in Talisay are by and large rundown and overpriced. You're better off staying up on the ridge in Tagaytay. Rates go down by at least 20% from Monday to Thursday – be sure to ask about promo rates.

Sonya's Garden B&B $$$
(☎0917 532 9097; www.sonyasgarden.com; cottages per person incl breakfast & dinner weekday/weekend P3000/3400;) Although Sonya's Garden is best known for its restaurant, it also runs an exquisite countryside B&B. Yoga, meditation classes and a full range of spa services are on offer. It's a ways out of town. Look for the well-marked turnoff before MC Mountain Home Apartelle, 13km west of the rotunda.

Discovery Country Suites RESORT $$$
(☎413 4567; www.discoverycountrysuites.com; 300 Calamba Rd; r incl breakfast P7400-12,300;) Tagaytay's most exclusive resort has the whole package: lake views (albeit partially obstructed), monster honeymoon-ready rooms, an outstanding continental restaurant with a fireplace, and a jacuzzi that catches cool breezes blowing off the lake. There's only seven rooms, all individually designed. Try to bag a promo rate on weekdays. It's 1.5km east of the rotunda.

Estancia RESORT $$
(☎413 1133; www.estanciatagaytay.com.ph; nipa hut/d incl breakfast from P4000/4600;) There's a huge variety of rooms at this place 1.3km east of the rotunda, including some real upscale digs in a new Mediterranean-style building. But the rooms you want are the cheaper stand-alone bamboo nipa huts in the back, which are set unobtrusively amid the jungle with balconies overlooking the lake. Wi-fi costs P90 per hour.

Taal Vista Hotel HOTEL $$$
(☎413 1000; www.taalvistahotel.com; km 60 Aguinaldo Hwy; r incl breakfast from P6500;) Faded no more, this 1970s relic has been smartly renovated and now boasts king-sized beds, downy linens and fancy bath products to complement outstanding views. Generous weekday promo rates are usually available. Wi-fi costs extra. It's 4km west of the rotunda.

Keni Po HOTEL $$
(☎483 0977; http://keniporooms.blogspot.com; 110 Calamba Rd; d P1200-1500;) This valleyside place, 3.5km east of the rotunda, is the best of the lower midrange hotels, with small, well-kept doubles that include minibars, cable TV and shared balconies. The small pool out back is a nice touch.

Java Jazz B&B HOTEL $
(☎860 2699; http://javajazzcoffee.blogspot.com; 442 Calamba Rd; r incl breakfast P980-1400;) This artistically inclined espresso shop rents out four colourful rooms at backpacker prices. Each pair of rooms shares a bathroom. It's 3.3km east of the rotunda, on the valley side of the ridge road.

Tagaytay Econo Hotel HOTEL $$
(☎483 4284; www.tagaytayeconoinn.com; Calamba Rd; r incl breakfast P1500-4000;) This well-kept place 2.7km east of the rotunda is great value, although the budget rooms are somewhat dark. It overlooks the lake but sits on a busy intersection, so noise is a potential problem. Pricier rooms are further from the road and have lake views.

San Roque Paradise Resort RESORT $$
(☎773 0271; Barangay Buco, Talisay; r P1500-2500;) Just east of Philvolcs in a well-kempt compound in Talisay, this is by far the best option down by the lake. The 11 rooms are clean and the friendly family management will happily organise both local and out-of-town excursions. There's a swimming area on the lake. Meals cost P200 to P350.

Talisay Green Lake Resort RESORT $$
(☎773 0247; Barangay Sta Maria, Talisay; d/tr/q P1500/2000/2500;) Next to the Taal Lake Yacht Club, this is an adequate second choice in Talisay, mainly because of the decent swimming pool.

Eating & Drinking

Tagaytay boasts some of the country's best restaurants. Surprisingly, many of them are located nowhere near the volcano, but rather are nestled in secluded gardens north of the ridge road

TOP CHOICE **Antonio's** CONTINENTAL $$$
(☎0917 899 2866; Barangay Neogan; set meals from P1500; ⏲lunch & dinner, closed Mon) This upscale eatery offers the chance to rub elbows with politicians and oligarchs over delicious and delightfully presented full-course meals – if you can get a reservation. Seating areas include some lovely tables overlooking lotus ponds and a sprawling garden. Book months ahead for weekends. The turn-off

is 7.6km west of the rotunda. Antonio's has two satellite restaurants along the ridge in Tagaytay proper that, while good, should not be confused with the original.

Sonya's Garden ORGANIC $$$
(☎0917 532 9097; www.sonyasgarden.com; meals P610; ⊙lunch & dinner) Tagaytay's most beloved restaurant serves up famous set-menu, several-course lunches: they feature homemade pasta and produce grown organically in a sprawling garden that practically envelops diners. Reservations are essential. Look for the well-marked turnoff before MC Mountain Home Apartelle, 13km west of the rotunda.

Josephine FILIPINO $$
(km 58 Aguinaldo Hwy; mains P175-400; ⊙7am-10.30pm) Views just don't come better than at Josephine, a long-running favourite that serves up some of the best food on the ridge. The menu is huge and has all the classics, from tangy *adobo* dishes to *sisig* (crunchy fried bits of pork), and grills up everything under the sun. It's 3km west of the rotunda.

Bag of Beans BAKERY $$
(115 Aguinaldo Hwy; mains P200-500; ⊙6am-9pm) Dine among hanging angel trumpets, begonias and other exotic flowering plants on the garden patio of this superb bakery-restaurant specialising in English meat pies and scrumptious desserts. It's 6.5km west of the rotunda.

Leslie's FILIPINO $$
(Aguinaldo Hwy; mains from P200) The central portion of Tagaytay ridge (around Starbucks) is dominated by several large Filipino *inahaw* (grill) restaurants where you can sample *tawili,* a tiny fish found exclusively in Lake Taal. Leslie's is the most famous of the lot, with some truly outstanding views of the lake. It's 1.8km west of the rotunda.

Mushroomburger VEGETARIAN $
(Aguinaldo Hwy; burgers P60-100) A Tagaytay institution known for its incredibly cheap and tasty eponymous burgers. It's 300m west of Taal Vista Hotel.

Information

There are several internet cafes around Olivarez Plaza as well as banks and ATMs.

Getting There & Away

BSC/Batman buses from Pasay Rotunda in Manila rumble through Tagaytay (P80, 1½ hours) on their way to Nasugbu or Calatagan. To return to Manila, hail a bus from the streetside shed at Olivarez Plaza or Mendez Crossing in town.

Getting Around

Frequent jeepneys traverse the ridge road from one end of town to the other.

To get to Talisay take a jeepney (P35, 25 minutes, hourly) or tricycle (P200, 30 minutes) straight downhill from the Talisay turnoff, 4km east of the rotunda.

Taal

☎043 / POP 51,500

Taal is a historic small town with a number of old Spanish colonial buildings. The truly massive **Basilica of St Martin de Tours** (built 1849–65) dominates **Taal Park** at its base. Numerous nearby shops sell the town's famous embroidery and *balisong* (butterfly knives). Some of the historic homes have irregular opening hours. The town is 3km off the main road between Batangas and Tagaytay but it is a worthy stop, especially if you have your own transport.

Batangas

☎043 / POP 295,000

The busy industrial port of Batangas holds little appeal to travellers but is the jump-off point to Puerto Galera and a few other ports on Mindoro and Romblon.

Sleeping

If you are unfortunate enough to miss the last ferry try the following.

Travellers Inn HOTEL $
(☎723 6021; Rizal Ave; s/d from P625/700; P ❄) The best of the cheap hotels, it has 25 very basic rooms and is 500m from the ferry terminal. Deluxe rooms add cable to your TV experience.

Pontefino Hotel HOTEL $$$
(☎723-3466; Pastor Village, Gulod Labac; d weekday/weekend from P3850/5200; ❄@) The best of Batangas' business hotels, it's located just outside the centre, a 10-minute walk from SM Mall.

Getting There & Away

Bus

Most Batangas-bound buses from Manila go to the pier but double check with your driver. Make sure you get on an express bus to the pier via

GET WELL SOON

The Philippines' signature wellness and detoxification centre is the **Farm at San Benito** (☎02-884 8074; www.thefarm.com.ph; r from US$190; ❄@≋), a peaceful paradise hidden in the jungle less than a two-hour drive south of Manila, near Lipa City. Besides a bevy of detox and spa treatments like therapeutic coffee scrubs and traditional Hilot massages, the resort has a mouth-watering vegan restaurant specialising in surprisingly filling five-course raw-food meals. Follow it up with a shot or two of organic wheat grass and a colon or liver cleanse. The tropical hardwood and bamboo cottages are lovely, and the grounds meticulously landscaped. The place occasionally draws A-list international celebrities.

the speedy SLEX and Star expressways (P180, 1½ hours). These are signboarded 'Batangas Pier' and/or '*derecho*' (straight). See p79 for bus companies in Manila serving Batangas. Pick up buses to Manila right at the pier.

Boat

ABRA DE ILOG & CALAPAN (MINDORO)

SuperCat (☎723 8227) has seven daily fastcraft to Calapan (P300, one hour) during daylight hours. **Montenegro Lines** (☎723 8294; www.montenegrolines.com.ph) and several other companies send car ferries to Calapan around the clock (P192, 2½ hours). Montenegro also has six daily car ferries to Abra de Ilog (P260, 2½ hours).

PANAY ISLAND & ROMBLON

Montenegro Lines has a late-afternoon boat from Batangas to Odiongan (P752, eight hours) daily except Tuesday (daily except Wednesday in the other direction). On Mondays, Thursdays, and Saturdays the same boat continues on to Romblon town (P960, 12 hours).

Super Shuttle Ferry (☎722 1655) Has Monday, Wednesday and Friday trips to Dumaguit, near Kalibo (P750, 17hrs), via Odiongan.

CSGA Ferry (☎02-742 6148) Has two weekly ferries to Romblon town that continue to San Fernando on Sibuyan Island.

PUERTO GALERA (MINDORO)

Speedy bangka ferries to Puerto Galera town (P220, one hour), Sabang (P230, one hour) and White Beach (P250, 1¼ hours) leave regularly throughout the day from Batangas pier until about 4.30pm. After 4.30pm you may have to hire a 'special trip' (ie private bangka).

The boats usually sail unless there's a tropical storm brewing, but be prepared for a rough crossing – in 2009 an overloaded bangka sank en route to White Beach from Batangas, and 12 of the 60 passengers drowned. If it looks nasty, you might consider a sturdier car ferry to Calapan.

There used to be a Montenegro car ferry (2½ hours) that sailed daily between Batangas to Balatero Pier, 2.5km west of Puerto Galera town, but it was suspended at the time of research.

Anilao

☎043 / POP 650

Anilao, 30km west of Batangas on a small peninsula, is where the Philippines' first scuba-diving operators started back in the 1960s. While it has since been overtaken by places like Puerto Galera and Alona Beach (Bohol), it remains an extremely popular weekend destination for Manila-based divers.

The area empties out during the week and many resorts close. If you're not a diver, there's not a whole lot to keep you entertained, although the fine views and midweek solitude might appeal to some. Accommodation and dive prices are high by Philippine standards, and resorts tend to work by advance booking. Most places will look at you like you're from another planet if you walk in bedraggled on a weekday with a dog-eared copy of this book in your hands.

Anilao is the generic tourist name for the 13km peninsula that extends south from Anilao village (a barangay of Mabini). The dive resorts are strung out along the rocky western edge of the peninsula, linked by a winding sealed road.

Activities

Anilao is famed for its colourful corals and rich species diversity, which yield excellent macro photography. There are good dive sites scattered around Balayan Bay and around the Sombrero and Maricaban Islands. Most resorts listed here offer diving and some form of certification program.

Sleeping & Eating

Most Anilao resorts are isolated from each other and you may face 100 or more steps getting down to the resort from the road – two reasons people tend to stay put. Rates are inclusive of all meals unless otherwise indicated.

Arthur's Place Dive Resort RESORT **$$**
(☎0919 716 7973; www.arthurs-place.com; d without meals & fan/air-con P1200/2500; ❄) This and Ligaya are really the only dive-oriented places that approaches the budget category, yet you hardly lose a thing by staying here. You still get good views from the restaurant, not to mention basic but very liveable rooms with little patios around a grassy courtyard. It's 9.5km south of the turnoff in Anilao village.

Ligaya RESORT **$**
(☎02-622 8111; www.philtech.net/VillaLigaya; dm/d per person from P1650/2100) Newly renovated Ligaya has long been among our favourites for both the quality of the dive in-

MISTY, MYSTIC MT BANAHAW

Descriptions of the vast dormant volcanic cone of Mt Banahaw (2177m), which looms over the entire southwest Luzon region, are almost always accompanied by the term 'mystic'. The mountain is said to be inhabited by a host of deities and spirits – most famously Filipino revolutionary hero and poet José Rizal, who was executed by the Spanish in 1896. A group called the 'Rizalistas' believe that Rizal was the reincarnation of Christ. No less than 75 cults have taken up residence on the mountain's lower reaches, living their lives dedicated to the spirits of Rizal and others that supposedly dwell in Banahaw's crater.

Mt Banahaw offers some of the most impressive hiking in southern Luzon. The weather is an important consideration, however, as the awe-inspiring views from the rim down into the 600m-deep crater can vanish entirely in low cloud. Even in the dry season, cloud can suddenly rise up from the crater bottom, adding to the spooky atmosphere. Some locals are convinced they've seen UFOs.

Mt Banahaw is closed from time to time to prevent environmental damage caused by unchecked trekking and mass pilgrimages up the lower slopes of the mountain. You should contact **Protected Areas and Wildlife Bureau** (PAWB; ☎02-928 1178; www.pawb.gov.ph) in Manila to see if it's open.

A trip to the Banahaw area is worth it whether you plan to climb the mountain or not. The long drive around the base of the mountain via San Pablo, Tiaong, Tayabas and Lucban is one of the prettiest in the country, with the misty mountain and its foothills – Mt Banahaw de Lucban (1875m) and Mt San Cristobol (1470m) – constantly looming.

You can also visit the religious cults on Banahaw's lower slopes. One such group, the Suprema de la Iglesia del Ciudad Mistica de Dios, maintains a rather impressive compound on Mt Banahaw. A brief word of warning: always ask for permission before photographing cult members, and never pull out your camera inside their places of worship.

The ideal base for trips to Mt Banahaw is the town of **Dolores**. From Dolores a rugged dirt road leads you through several cult villages to the village of Kinabuhayan, which is home to the obscure Tres Persona sect, which worships 'the three personalities of God'. The main trailheads for both Mt Banahaw and Mt Cristobal are near Kinabuhayan.

Dolores has a fabulous accommodation option in the form of Jay Herrera's quirky **Kinabuhayan Cafe Bed & Breakfast** (☎0916 221 5791; http://kinabuhayancafe.multiply.com; Dolores; snacks P100-200, large set meals P750, r incl 3 meals P2250). If the weather is too rainy to climb, you can while away the time here playing pool, drinking beer and eating. Herrera's cooking is world class and it's worth showing up just to gorge on his generous repasts, which span several styles. Be sure to call ahead. Accommodation is in a pair of eccentric open-air tree-house-style cottages. A short walk away are several hidden swimming holes.

Besides Mt Banahaw, Mt Cristobal and Mt Banahaw de Lucban, another good hiking option in this mountainous region of Southwest Luzon is flora- and fauna-rich **Mt Makiling** near Los Baños. Leeches are rampant on all of these peaks in the wet season.

Buses from Manila to Lucena pass through San Pablo, where you can pick up a jeepney to Dolores (35 minutes, frequent during daylight hours) at the public market. See p93 for details on buses to Lucena. From Dolores there are infrequent jeepneys to Kinabuhayan village, or you can hire a tricycle (P500 return).

struction – the owner is one of the country's top technical divers – and the backpacker-friendly dorm-style rooms. The accommodation is understated but comfortable. Late arrivals pay just P450 for a dorm bed (including breakfast only). It's 6km south of the turnoff.

Balai Resort RESORT $$
(☎02-240 2927, 0919 857 1005; www.balai-resort.com; d with fan/air-con per person P2250/2550; P❄) Simple yet attractive, Balai has 15 rooms set in its own little cove. The design is modern and there are many decorative touches, especially in the breezy common areas. The fresh and tasty dinners are recommended. Located 12.5km from the turnoff, this is one of the furthest places from town.

Dive & Trek RESORT $$
(☎0910 936 4556, 02-851 8746; www.diveandtrek.com; r incl unlimited diving per person P4000, non-diver per person P3500; ❄@≋) Accessible only by boat, this is where you come to really get away from it all. The unlimited diving and snorkelling on the house reef doesn't hurt. The simple but comfortable rooms are in a pair of hillside bamboo-and-nipa complexes. Call ahead for a free boat transfer from the Dazu by Dazl resort, 1.5km south of the Anilao turnoff.

Mayumi RESORT $$
(☎0919 420 2231, 0918 930 8922; www.mayumiresorts.com; d per person weekday/weekend from P1200/2200; ❄) Another player at the budget end of the spectrum, Mayumi shines because of discounted weekday rates and an inviting Balinese-style hangout area down by the sea. Good thing because there is nowhere to hang out in the rooms, although they have nice bathrooms and small verandas.

Dive Solana RESORT $$$
(☎0908 876 5262; www.divesolana.com; r per person from P3490; ❄@) This reliable old standby is beautifully decorated with local arts and crafts. It's such a throwback to the glory days of Filipino style that, as you sit on your porch overlooking the water, you fully expect to see a Pan American clipper boat set down in the calm waters beyond. It's 10km south of the turnoff.

Pacifico Azul RESORT $$
(www.pacificblueasia.com; r per person without meals & without bathroom P1600, with bathroom P2500-3600; ❄) The budget rooms are quirky but accommodating tree houses, or spend a little more for the well-appointed air-con rooms. The restaurant and common area, under a soaring canopy, is great; too bad there are no views. It's about 200m south of Ligaya.

Vivere Azure LUXURY RESORT $$$
(☎02-771 7777; www.vivereazure.com; r per person from P6800; ❄≋) This exclusive preserve is nice but for these prices we expect more.

ℹ Getting There & Around

To get to Anilao from Manila take a bus to Batangas pier (see p79 for details) and get off just before the bridge leading over to the pier. From here frequent jeepneys head west to Anilao proper (P30, 30 to 45 minutes).

From Anilao proper, tricycles cost P40 for short trips, or P150 to P200 to the far resorts. The little **Tourist Office** (☎410 0607) on the pier in Anilao can help you get a good price.

Pagsanjan

☎049 / POP 35,900

The town of Pagsanjan (pag-san-*han*), 100km southeast of Manila, is where the popular canoe trips up the Pagsanjan River to Magdapio Falls begin.

Sights & Activities

Magdapio Falls BOAT RIDE
Some of the final scenes of Francis Ford Coppola's epic Vietnam War movie *Apocalypse Now* were filmed along this stretch of river.

The first step is to secure a canoe from the **tourist office** (☎501 3544; ⏲8am-5pm), in the Pagsanjan municipal hall building near the bridge over the Pagsanjan River in the centre of town. Then two *bangcero* paddle you upriver for 1½ hours through a dramatic gorge hemmed by towering cliffs and vegetation. At the top, the *bangcero* will take you under the 10m-high falls on a bamboo raft for an additional P100. From here, you let the water do the work. The trip downstream is fast and exhilarating.

The height of the wet season (August to October) is the best time to ride the rapids. At any time of year it's best to avoid weekends, as half of Manila seems to descend on Pagsanjan. You should bring a plastic bag for your camera, and prepare to get very wet.

Be wary of the touts that stand along the highway offering boat trips to arriving tourists. They may try to coax you into paying more than the going rate for a boat (P1250 per person at the time of research) and pocket the difference after leading you to the official jumping-off point. Only *bangcero* licensed and employed by the town government are allowed to operate boats. The tourist office and the hotels listed here are your best bets for securing boats and *bangcero*.

The P1250 per person rate consists of P1000 for the boat trip and a P250 landing fee at the falls. You should tip your *bangcero*. Boats fit three passengers; P100 per person is the suggested tip.

Sleeping & Eating

There's not much to keep you in Pagsanjan besides the trip to the falls, but sleeping here allows you to secure a coveted early start time the next morning (boat trips start at 7am). Sleeping options are decidedly simplistic.

Willy Flores Guesthouse GUESTHOUSE **$**
(☎0948 679 3000; Garcia St; r with fan/air-con P600/800) As much a homestay as a guesthouse, it's run by an affable family with heaps of area knowledge. Breakfast is a mere P50 extra. It's 400m west of the bridge in the centre of town.

Yokohama Hotel GUESTHOUSE **$$**
(☎501 7608; Garcia St; r without bathroom P1000-1500; ❄) This unobtrusive wooden house 300m west of the bridge has a handful of homey, basic rooms set around a lovely common area with a big pool table. It's behind Kurisa Bar & Restaurant (they share the same Japanese owner).

La Vista GUESTHOUSE **$**
(☎501 1229; Garcia St; d without bathroom P350, with bathroom & air-con P1200; ❄) This place is right on the river in town, 150m west of the bridge. It has four clean if unremarkable doubles, plus six passable fan rooms in a house across the street.

Calle Arco FILIPINO **$**
(National Hwy; mains P70-150; ⏲10am-9pm) The best restaurant in town adds uniquely Pagsanjan touches to Filipino fare. Try the chicken *sisig* fajitas.

Aling Taleng's Halo Halo FILIPINO **$**
(169 General Luna St; halo-halo P65, meals for two P200-300; ⏲9am-8pm) What's better after a hot day on the river than the national icy treat? This simple place right by the bridge has been making dreams come true for decades.

Getting There & Away

There are no direct buses to Pagsanjan, but regular DLTB buses link Manila with nearby Santa Cruz (P140, 2½ hours). Santa Cruz' bus terminal is on the highway, about halfway to Pagsanjan; there are frequent jeepneys to/from Pagsanjan.

Pick up jeepneys to Lucena and Lucban heading east along the main road in Pagsanjan.

Lucban

☎042 / POP 45,500

Hidden away in the foothills of Mt Banahaw, the quiet mountain town of Lucban comes alive on 15 May for **Pahiyas**, the annual harvest festival and feast of San Isidro Labrador. Locals compete for a prize by covering their houses in fruit, vegetables and wildly elaborate decorations made from multicoloured rice-starch decorations called *kiping*. Giant papier-mâché effigies are marched through the streets to the town church. It's a great festival and, best of all, locals are delighted to have foreigners join them in the bounty (if you want a room, book a year in advance).

At other times of the year, Lucban is pleasant enough, with narrow streets lined with some old Spanish town houses, and views of Mt Banahaw to the west.

Patio Rizal Hotel (☎540 2107; 77 Quezon Ave; d P1600-2100, deluxe from P2600; ❄📶) is right in the centre of town, with an excellent cafe overlooking a small plaza. Unfortunately all rooms beneath the deluxe category are windowless, so upgrade if you can afford it.

Pick up regular jeepneys to Lucena (P30, 45 minutes) and Pagsanjan (P40, one hour) from central Rizal St.

Lucena

☎042 / POP 236,500

Lucena, the capital of Quezon province, is the departure point for passenger boats to Marinduque. Our best advice is to avoid this gritty, tricycle-mad city, but if you get stuck for a night – and many do – there are a few OK sleeping options. Stay well outside the centre if you value sleep.

Sleeping

Queen Margarette HOTEL **$$**
(☎373 4889; Diversion Rd, National Hwy; d incl breakfast P1100-3300; ❄📶🏊) With a quiet location on the outskirts of town, plenty comfortable rooms (as long as you upgrade) and

on-site Chinese restaurant, the Queen Margarette ticks off the essential boxes.

Sulu Plaza Hotel HOTEL **$$**
(☎660 5400; Diversion Rd; d incl breakfast P1500-5000; ❄@≋) Comparable to the Queen Margarette, it's a better pick if you want to be near the bus station; it's right next door.

Fresh Air Hotel & Resort HOTEL **$**
(☎710 2424; Tagarao St, Isabeng; r P320-800; ❄≋) Not even Hitchcock could dream up something this creepy, but at least it's cheap. It's out of the centre on the road to Batangas.

Getting There & Away

There are rumours that the South Luzon Expressway will be extended to Lucena, which would cut travel time from Manila to about 1½ hours.

Boat

Boats to Marinduque depart from Dalahican port, which is 5km south of the huge Shoe Mart at the east end of Lucena. Your nostrils will tell you that Dalahican port is not only a major port for travellers, but also for fishing.

For info on ferries to Marinduque, see p180.

Kalayaan Shipping has three weekly ferries to Magdiwang on Sibuyan Island in Romblon Province (P800, 17 hours) via Banton Island and Romblon town.

A tricycle to the port from Lucena costs from P50 to P75.

Bus & Jeepney

JAC Liner and DLTB run frequent buses between Manila's Buendia LRT stop and Lucena Grand Central terminal (ordinary/air-con P180/210, 3½ hours). From Grand Central, 5km north of town on Diversion Rd (National Hwy), there are also frequent buses to Bicol and jeepneys to Lucban (P30, 45 minutes).

Regular jeepneys connect Grand Central with the centre and Dalahican port.

On the road to Batangas (near the Fresh Air Hotel & Resort) you can flag down frequent ordinary Supreme Lines buses to Batangas.

NORTH OF MANILA

The Bataan Peninsula north of Manila is the destination for those wishing to recall the fateful 1942 Death March. Otherwise the big draw north is the Subic Bay area, with its nascent resort centre and many activities. Angeles remains utterly unreformed and unreconstructed, although nearby Clark Airport is now home to a growing number of bargain airlines.

Looming over it all and easier than ever to access is volcanic Mt Pinatubo in the Zambales Mountains.

Olongapo & Subic Bay

☎047 / POP 227,300

Until 1992, Subic Bay was the base for the huge 7th Fleet of the US Navy. The adjoining town of Olongapo was known for its sex industry, and not much else.

These days authorities are busy trying to remould the Subic Bay Freeport Zone (SBFZ), as the former military base is now known, into a legitimate business hub and family-friendly tourist destination.

While the tourism component of that plan hasn't been a huge hit, the potential is there. The main attractions are a gorgeous bay, renowned wreck-diving, large tracts of pristine jungle and a smattering of amusement parks for kids.

One thing that keeps mass tourism at bay is the pungent canal dividing Olongapo and the Freeport Zone, which feeds a slow-and-steady stream of raw sewage into Subic Bay. The Americans dubbed it 'Shit River' and it still goes by that moniker today.

With a hired car, Subic Bay is also a good base from which to explore Bataan, the Mt Pinatubo area and the Zambales coastline (p101).

Sights & Activities

Subic's main Waterfront Beach and most hotels are in the Central Business District (CBD). Bridges link the CBD with, respectively, the rest of the Freeport Zone, which snakes around the bay to the south; the National Hwy heading north to Zambales; and Olongapo centre via the SBFZ main gate and the Shit River.

The better beaches are north/northwest of town, in Barrio Barretto (where the remnants of Olongapo's sex industry survive) and beyond in Zambales.

Trekking

Illegal logging was nonexistent in the Freeport Zone during the American years and as a result the area has some fantastically pristine **jungle trekking**. The SBFZ Tourism Department can help steer you to walks in the large rainforest south of the SBFZ (you'll need a private vehicle to reach these). Within the zone there are some fine walks in **Subic**

Bay Nature Park, a vast tract of coastal forest south of the Cubi district. There are two main trails here – a 30-minute **nature walk** (admission P20) and the much longer **Apallin Trail**, which takes you to the coast (2½ to three hours return). Take a taxi to the well-marked trailhead, 7km south of the airport.

From the residential area of Binictican Heights, a 40-minute walk along the pretty **Pamulaklakin Forest Trail** leads to the Aeta village of Pastolen ('Aeta' is the term given to the indigenous Negrito population in the area). To get to the trailhead take a 'Binictican' Winstar from the Transportation Terminal.

At the Pamulaklakin trailhead you can pick up an Aeta guide who can lead you into the forest and teach you fire-making and a few other handy jungle survival techniques (per person P50 for 30 minutes). Ask about longer ecology tours or even overnight trips.

The Cubi district (near the Subic airport) is home to the biggest known roosting site of the world's largest **bats**: the Philippine fruit bat and the golden-crowned flying fox. Dubbed the 'Bat Kingdom', the roosting site moves around from year to year but it isn't hard to find; just follow your ears. Around dusk hundreds of bats take to the sky in this area.

Diving

Wreck diving is the other big adventure draw in Subic. Of the seven wrecks commonly visited by divers, the **USS New York** (at a depth of 28m) is probably the most impressive. The battle cruiser was built in 1891 and was scuttled by American troops in 1941 to keep it out of Japanese hands. The *New York* wreck is penetrable, but this is a huge ship and it is easy to get fatally lost in the endless corridors and passageways. Appropriate training and an experienced guide are vital.

Other wrecks in the harbour include the *El Capitan* (20m), a well-preserved site favoured by photographers for its general intactness, penetrability and prolific marine life; and the *San Quintin* (16m), home to larger fish such as wrasse, tangs, glasseyes and sweetlips. Both are suitable for beginners. Advanced divers might try the LST, an American landing craft at 37m.

The *Oryuku Maru* (20m), or 'Hell Ship', in which 1600 US prisoners of war were imprisoned and mistakenly killed during an air attack, was off limits to divers at the time of research.

Visibility in Subic is not what it is elsewhere in the country. The best time for water clarity is from February to April.

Dive prices aren't bad in Subic – P1000 to P1500 for a dive (not including equipment), and P16,000 to P18,000 for an open-water course.

Boardwalk Dive Center DIVING
(☎252 5367; www.ss719.com; Waterfront Rd) Professional outfit with a technical-diving arm.

Subic Scuba 719 DIVING
(☎252 9428; www.boardwalkdivecenter.com; 664 Waterfront Rd) Friendly and laid-back place has heaps of knowledge about the wrecks and good dive prices.

Vasco's Dive Center DIVING
(☎252 1843/5; www.vascosresort-museum.com; Lot 14, Argonaut Hwy, SBFZ) The dive shop associated with the estimable Vasco's pub. It's one of the best technical-diving facilities in the Philippines and is popular among more advanced divers.

Horse Riding

El Kabayo STABLES
(☎0915 537 1169; horse riding per hr P700) Peeps with equestrian instincts make the trip from Manila just to go here. They have plenty of horses and riding options around Subic are legion. Rates include a guided trip to a nearby waterfall. It's in Binictican Heights.

Theme Parks

Ocean Adventure AMUSEMENT PARK
(☎252 9000; www.oceanadventure.com.ph; Camayan Wharf, West Ilanin Forest Area; adult/child P500/420; ⏲9am-6pm) At this open-water marine park 20km south of the CBD you can swim with dolphins and see sea lions and other aquatic critters. It's a 20-minute taxi ride from the CBD (P500 round trip).

Zoobic Safari ZOO
(☎252 2272; www.zoobic.com.ph; adult/child P395/295; ⏲8am-4pm) Get up close and personal with dozens of tigers on a jeepney safari tour. It's a bit north of Ocean Adventure.

Sleeping

The top hotels are near Waterfront Beach in the CBD.

Lighthouse HOTEL $$$
(☎252 5000; www.lighthousesubic.com; Waterfront Rd, CBD; r incl breakfast from P6000;) Miles ahead of anything else in Subic Bay in terms of comfort, design,

service – and price. The spacious rooms are truly luxurious, with super-sized flat-screen TVs. More could be done with the verandas overlooking the bay.

Subic Park Hotel HOTEL $$
(☎252 2092; www.subicparkhotel.com; 93 Moonbay Marina, Waterfront Rd; r P2100-3500;) Next to the ritzy Lighthouse at the far end of Waterfront Beach, Subic Park has more style and panache than most and is an adequate second choice among the bayfront hotels. Upgrade to the 'Oceanfront' rooms, with sea-facing balconies and king-sized beds.

Court Meridian HOTEL $$
(☎252 2366; www.courtmeridian.com; Waterfront Rd; r incl breakfast P2600-4500;) Across the street from the waterfront, you don't lose much in location and you gain in value by staying here. Rooms are extremely well appointed and have furniture; make yourself at home. Upgrades yield rich rewards, such as flat-screen TVs and verandas with mountain views.

Sheavens Seafront Resort BEACH RESORT $$
(☎223 9430; www.sheavens.com; Barrio Barretto, Olongapo; d P990-1850, deluxe P2250 3800;) This is by far the best value in the area, sublimely placed over the rocks on the far southeast end of Barretto's signature Baloy Long Beach. There's a huge variety of rooms, including some exquisite deluxe rooms with sea views. While not a family place, it's at least somewhat removed from Barrio Barretto's sleazier side.

Kong's Hotel HOTEL $
(☎224 1516; 32 Magsaysay Dr, Olongapo; r with fan/air-con from P450/900;) For true budget accommodation, head to Olongapo. Kong's makes no pretence at lavishness but the generous use of wood and clapboard keeps untoward scents at bay.

Eating & Drinking

The restobars along Waterfront Beach are popular and often get live music.

TOP CHOICE **Vasco's** PUB
(☎252 1843/5; Lot 14, Argonaut Hwy, SBFZ; mains P200-300; 24hr;) Also known as Magellan's, this wonderfully charismatic 'pirate' bar and restaurant hangs over the bay near the port. Owner Brian Homan is an accomplished shipwreck explorer who has been diving in the Philippines forever. Some of the porcelain and other treasures salvaged by Homan are on display in a small museum. It's a wonderful place for a breezy breakfast, and there are also a few rooms for rent. From the CBD take an 'Airport-Cubi' Winstar to Vasco's (P9).

Texas Joe's RESTAURANT $$
(☎252 3189; Waterfront Rd; ribs P389) The Philippines' best ribs are right here, in good company on a menu of meaty mains from the American heartland. It's almost worth the trip from Manila just to dig into the humongous ribs. Sit outside or inside.

Rama Mahal INDIAN $$
(☎252 3663; Sampson Rd; meals P250-300; 10am-10pm) Jovial Nepalese owner Ram serves up large portions of delicious South Asian specialities and some Middle Eastern dishes. If you're not into Indian food at least stop by for Ram's legendary mango lassi. It's across from the Freeport Exchange strip mall.

Information

Internet cafes and banks are concentrated along Rizal Ave in Olongapo.

Getting There & Away

Heading to/from Manila, be sure to take express buses with 'via SCTEX' placards to shave at least an hour off the trip. **Victory Liner** (☎222 2241; cnr W 18th St & Rizal Ave) has seven such buses daily, while **Genesis** (Perimeter Rd) has a handful as well (P240, 2¼ hours). Genesis is a two-minute walk from the main gate while Victory Liner is a 10-minute tricycle ride. Both companies run local buses to Manila hourly (P210, 3½ hours).

Victory Liner also has frequent buses north to Iba (P140, two hours) and Santa Cruz (P240, four hours), plus hourly buses to Baguio.

Getting Around

'Winstar' buses are unique to the SBFZ and perform the role that jeepneys perform elsewhere. They leave from the Transportation Terminal near the SBFZ main gate and travel only within the Freeport Zone.

In Olongapo, blue jeepneys for Barrio Barretto and Subic town are sign-boarded 'Castillejos'.

Taxis are based at the Transportation Terminal and cost P50 for short trips, or P100 to P150 to Vasco's or the Bat Kingdom.

Rental-car rates average about P2500 per day without a driver. Arrange one through your hotel or try **Subic Bay Taxi** (☎0929 675 347).

WORTH A TRIP

BATAAN PENINSULA

For WWII veterans of the Pacific campaign, few places have such bitter associations as the Bataan Peninsula. Both sides saw some of their darkest moments in the jungles around Mt Mariveles.

Few are left who experienced the Bataan Death March first-hand, a grisly affair that began when 70,000 US and Filipino troops surrendered to the Japanese in April 1942. The victors marched the prisoners, many sick and diseased from months of fighting, 90km from Mariveles to San Fernando, Pampanga, where they were loaded into box cars and brought by train to the Camp O'Donnell POW camp near Tarlac. Along the way some 15,000 to 25,000 American and Filipino troops perished.

For history buffs, Bataan has a smattering of sites that make for easy day trips from Angeles or Subic Bay (or even Manila in a pinch). Poignant 'Death March' markers appear along the national highway at 1km intervals starting in Mariveles and ending 102km away at the train station in San Fernando. Annual commemoration events on or around Bataan Day (9 April) include an organised walk along part of the route, and an ultramarathon that covers the entire route.

The peninsula's most interesting site is the **Dambana ng Kagitingan** (Shrine of Valor) on Mt Samat near Balanga. Atop the mountain is a 90m-high **crucifix** with battle scenes carved around its base. You can take a **lift** (P10; ⌚8am-noon & 1-5pm) to the top of the cross, where there is a long viewing gallery with great views out over Mt Mariveles, Manila Bay and the South China Sea.

From the base of the cross steps lead 50m down the hill to the shrine proper, where the stories of the Battle of Bataan and the ensuing Death March are carved into a marble **memorial wall**. In a bunker beneath the shrine is an excellent and blissfully air-conditioned **museum** (admission free; ⌚8am-noon & 1-5pm), with an impressive range of weaponry on display, battles scenes depicted in drawings and in dioramas, and a brilliant relief map of the Bataan Peninsula.

Every 9 April, relatives of American and Japanese veterans of the battles and Death March (plus a few last remaining veterans) gather at the shrine proper and pay tribute to the thousands of their comrades who fell in the surrounding jungles.

Getting There & Away

To get to the shrine you must first travel to Balanga, linked by Genesis and Bataan Transport buses from Pasay Rotunda in Manila (P210, three hours) via Angeles' Dau bus terminal. You can also take a Victory Liner bus to/from Olongapo (P80, 1¼ hours).

From Balanga head south a few kilometres then turn right (west) off the highway toward Bagac. From the turnoff it's 4.5km to the Mt Samat turnoff, then another 7km up a steep but nicely paved road to the cross. Tricycles wait at the Mt Samat turnoff (P200 round-trip). You can reach the turnoff from Balanga on a Bagac-bound jeepney.

Hiring a van in Balanga for a half-day trip to Mt Samat costs P1000. The **Gap Plaza Hotel** (☎047-237 6757; www.gapplaza.com; cnr Capitol Dr & Sampaguita St; d incl breakfast P2300-3000; 🅿❄📶) can get you sorted and also has the best rooms in the area – the priciest include a free Mt Samat tour.

San Fernando (Pampanga)

☎045 / POP 269,400

The industrial town of San Fernando – not to be confused with San Fernando (La Union), northwest of Baguio – is the capital of Pampanga province.

About the only reason people come here is to see fanatical Christians taking part in a **crucifixion ceremony** every Easter. At noon on Good Friday, in barangay San Pedro Cutud, volunteers with a penchant for pain are nailed to wooden crosses and whipped till they bleed.

Victory Liner has buses to San Fernando from its Cubao terminal (P100, one hour, every 30 minutes). Be aware that buses from Manila to points further north take the NLEX and bypass San Fernando. Jeepneys go north to Angeles.

Angeles & Clark Airport

☎045 / POP 314,500

Angeles is a name synonymous with the sex industry in the Philippines. The strip of tacky clubs and bars is strung out along Fields Ave in barangay Balibago. The 10,000 girls and women working here now are only the vestiges of the time before the American pullout, when it was estimated that 10 times as many were employed.

Angeles remains tied to the fortunes of the US Air Force's former station, Clark Airbase (now known as the Clark Special Economic Zone). Recent success in luring budget airlines to Clark Airport and the increasing popularity of Mt Pinatubo tours have given the area new relevance for travellers who aren't seeking sex.

Activities

Believe it or not, there are a few *legitimate* activities in the Angeles area. Trekking and ultralights top the list. If you are planning to climb Mt Pinatubo, sleeping in Angeles instead of Manila allows you to get a couple more hours of shuteye in the morning before setting off.

Mt Arayat National Park TREKKING
(admission P50) Many people arriving in Angeles mistake the towering volcanic cone of Mt Arayat (1026m) for Mt Pinatubo, as it dominates the skyline. But Arayat is a great trek that's doable in a half-day even for less-serious climbers. It's not easy to get to without your own transportation, however. To go it alone, look for a jeepney at the Dau terminal heading to Arayat town, then take a tricycle to the park entrance, where you pay your fee and pick up a guide (mandatory). There are dining facilities and kiosks selling water at the park base, along with several natural swimming pools fed by a natural spring which, legend has it, produces the purest water on earth.

Angeles City Flying Club ULTRALIGHTS
(☎802 2101, 0918 920 3039; www.angelesflying.com; 10/20min flight P1650/2900) Also called microlights, ultralights are a bit like motorised hang-gliders, only with wheels and open cockpits. The flights over Pampanga may be short, but they seem longer and provide a bird's-eye view of the Philippines in microcosm: verdant rice paddies, basketball courts, bustling school courtyards, carabaos and churches. Even the shorter trips soar right over the bushy slopes of Mt Arayat. It's not actually in Angeles (it's 25 minutes away in Magalang), but it offers free morning pickups.

Sleeping & Eating

There are dozens of hotels along Fields Ave and Don Juico Ave, but most are geared to prostitution.

Clark Star Hotel HOTEL $
(☎624 5882; 1st St, cnr MacArthur Hwy; d P700-950; ❄📶) So you're stuck in Angeles and want a hotel that does not have a girlie bar in the lobby. You can pay a huge premium to stay on the base in a resort geared toward package golfers, or you can stay here. A park and boulevard form a psychological as well as a physical divide between the hotel and nearby Fields Ave. Just be aware that no place escapes the sleaze entirely in Angeles. This is also about the best value around.

Clarkton Hotel HOTEL $$
(☎322 3424; www.clarkton.com; 620 Don Juico Ave; r P1650-3900; ❄@📶🏊) The Clarkton is large and popular, with a competent travel agency and an unusual mirrored ceiling in its lobby. A modest upgrade gets you a quite-swanky room, and the pool is a very nice touch. It's on the perimeter of the Balibago 'entertainment' zone, near the best restaurants.

Angeles Beach Club HOTEL $$$
(☎892 2222; www.angelesbeachclubhotel.com; Don Juico Ave; r incl breakfast P4900-17,518; 🚭❄@📶🏊) This would basically be the opposite of the Clark Star: big, bold and in the centre of the action. The impressive wraparound pool has a swim-up sushi bar among several swim-up options. Rooms look like something out of a Russian oligarch's dream. It's spring-break-party ready.

Eating

Reservations aren't a terrible idea at the following restaurants.

Iguana's MEXICAN $$
(☎893 3654; Don Juico Ave; mains P200-350; ❄) A short walk west of the Clarkton Hotel you'll encounter some of the best Mexican food in the country – and definitely the best margaritas. The enchiladas are recommended and you won't get cheated on portions either.

Cottage Kitchen AMERICAN $$
(☎322 3366; 382 Don Juico Ave; mains P300-800; ⏲10am-11pm Tue-Sun; ❄) The Cottage Kitchen, also near the Clarkton, is a good place

MOVING ON FROM CLARK AIRPORT

Southbound

Philtranco and Partas each run four daily direct trips from Clark to Manila, usually stopping in both Cubao (P400, 1½ hours) and Pasay (P450, two hours). Philtranco buses pick up/drop off at Megamall in Ortigas as well.

If your timing is poor, head to the Dau bus terminal in Angeles and hop on any Manila-bound bus.

Northbound

If you are heading to North Luzon, first go to the Dau terminal (or to Angeles proper if you plan to hire a car).

At Dau you'll find plenty of buses going to Baguio, Vigan and elsewhere in North Luzon. The trickiest destination is Banaue because there are no direct buses. If you're comfortable with several bus/jeepney changes, the recommended route is Dau–Tarlac–San Jose (or Cabanatuan)–Solano–Lagawe–Banaue. Otherwise backtrack to Manila and take the direct night bus to Banaue from Sampaloc.

to get your steak on. St Louis style pork ribs, black bean soup and Southern fried catfish are other highlights. The mashed potatoes are a buttery delight.

 Information

There are loads of internet cafes and banks on the main drag, Fields Ave, and its extension, Don Juico Ave.

City Guide (☎892 1623; www.city-guide.ph; Stall 79, Fields Ave; ⊙8.30am-7pm) A private company that runs the prominent 'Tourist Information' booth on Fields Ave. Gives out good free advice and can handle whatever tour you want. Can also match you with a group to Mt Pinatubo to cut costs.

AAA (☎0929 782 2966; 30 Fields Ave) Has very reasonable rates on both car (P1800 per day) and motorbikes (P300 per day).

 Getting There & Away

Air

Diosdado Macapagal International Airport (Clark Airport; www.clarkairport.com) is in the Clark Special Economic Zone.

In theory air-con shuttles meet all flights and drop passengers off either at the Clark freeport zone main gate in Balibago (P30), or at the Dau Terminal (P45). If these aren't around, look for a jeepney to the main gate, or take an overpriced fixed-rate taxi (P400/500 to Angeles/Dau).

Bus

Angeles' bus terminal is in Dau, near the terminus of the NLEX, where you'll find scores of buses heading to Manila (P140, 1½ hours) and just about anywhere else in North Luzon.

Swagman Travel (☎892 6495; www.swaggy.com) and **Southern Cross Shuttle** (☎892 5475) operate shuttles directly to Subic Bay Freeport Zone (P600, one hour). There are also shuttles to Manila.

A constant stream of jeepneys connects Dau and Angeles.

Mt Pinatubo

For centuries, the residents of Angeles took the nearby volcanoes of Mt Pinatubo and Mt Arayat for granted. That changed suddenly on 15 June 1991, when Pinatubo, the larger of the two volcanoes, literally blew itself apart, sending a column of ash and rock 40km into the air. The mountain lost 300m in height, and fine dust and fist-sized fragments of rock rained down on nearby Angeles, Clark Airbase and Subic Bay. Compounding the catastrophe, a savage typhoon chose this moment to lash northern Luzon, turning the ash into lethal lahar (mobile volcanic mud), which flooded downhill from the volcano with dire consequences. In Zambales province to the west of Mt Pinatubo, lahar flows rerouted rivers and sank entire villages under newly formed Lake Mapanuepe.

The easily eroded lahar flows have created a stunning landscape around the volcano that only now is starting to recover some of its vegetation. The Abacan and Pasig-Potrero Rivers have both cut channels through the sediment, which has led to the formation of towering pinnacles of lahar, hanging valleys and canyons.

The Climb

The journey up Mt Pinatubo (1450m) is one of the country's most accessible adventures, but don't attempt it in dodgy weather: flash floods during the remnants of a typhoon in 2009 swept away a convoy of Jeeps, killing seven, including five European tourists.

After the accident, the mountain was closed for a spell, and when it opened the rules had changed so that excursions to the summit must begin by 7am or 8am (heavy rains are more frequent in the afternoon). In the height of the dry season that might be extended to 10am.

All of this means that organised excursions to Pinatubo start at a ridiculously early hour – pre-dawn in Manila and just a little after that in Angeles and Subic. If you plan to go it alone, you should also plan an early departure.

The jumping-off point for the climb is Santa Juliana, near the base of the mountain's north slope, about a 40km journey from Angeles. From there you take a 4WD most of the way up then walk the final two hours to the crater, where you can take a dip in the chilly blue waters of the crater lake.

In theory you can climb the whole way on foot, but since the accident authorities have been wary of allowing longer hikes that linger into the afternoon.

It's possible to take less-travelled paths up the south and west slopes of Mt Pinatubo from the Aeta villages around Lake Mapanuepe (see p104).

The main point of contact for the climb is Marisa at the **Sta Juliana Tourism Council** (☎0906 462 3388). Call her in advance to make sure they are allowing climbs on the day you want to go up. They can handle bookings with the two tour operators: the **Santa Juliana 4x4 Association** (☎0919 608 4313; www.mtpinatubowyne4x4.com) and **PDC** (☎045-493 0031, 0929 702 5058), which operates out of Korean day spa/restaurant Pinatubo Spa Town.

In Sta Juliana, Alvin, a member of the Santa Juilana 4x4 Association offers a **homestay** (☎0919 861 4102; bognothomestay@gmail.com) for P400 per person per night including breakfast. PDC also has rooms for a similar price.

Getting There & Away

Most people go on organised excursions. The cost of excursions with Angeles-based tour companies varies according to group size; a group of three costs P2500 to P3000 per person. From Manila you'll pay quite a bit more than that.

You can go it alone. There are sporadic jeepneys to Santa Juliana from Capas (one hour) or take a tricycle from Capas (P500). If you get there on your own, expect to pay P1500 per person for a group of one to four people (including lunch), or P1000 per person for groups of five or more.

North Luzon

Includes »

Best Places to Eat

» Log Cabin (p134)
» Uno Grille (p115)
» Bliss Cafe (p126)
» Hill Station (p126)
» Oh My Gulay (p126)

Best Places to Stay

» PNKY (p125)
» Villa Angela (p114)
» Pacita Batanes (p151)
» Casa Vallejo (p125)
» Sagada Homestay (p133)

Why Go?

North Luzon encapsulates a nation in miniature. A mountainous spine studded with machete-toting hill tribes who are quick to smile and quicker to share their rice wine. Surfers racing waves onto sunny beaches. A stormy fist of land inhabited by the Philippines' earliest inhabitants. Spanish colonial cities where sunlight breaks through seashell windows. The lonely, fortress-flecked edge of the archipelago.

For most travellers, the main event is the emerald rice terraces of the Cordillera, a mountain range that hides hanging coffins, mummified ancestors and the old ghosts of the forest. Trekking is a prime activity in this wild frontier, and outdoor activities of all stripes shape the experience of exploring North Luzon. Culturally, this is humanity at its most diverse, as the peoples of the mountains, Zambales, Ilocos and beyond are notable for a mindboggling diversity of language and ritual. Yet a similarity is shared by all these groups: an unrelenting, almost overwhelming friendliness to guests.

When to Go

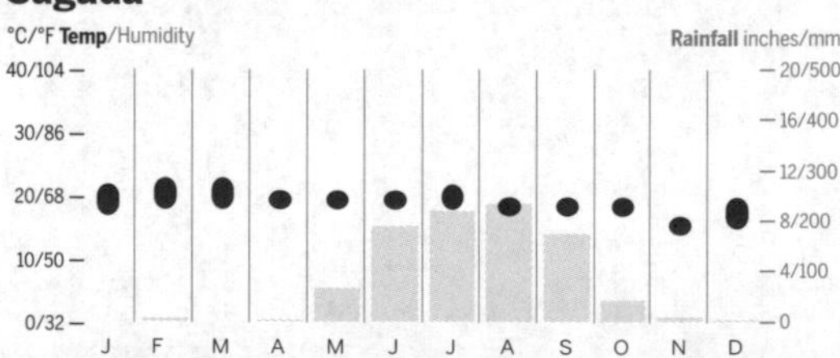

Nov–May A nice time to experience the best weather the Philippines has to offer – you won't be alone!

Apr–Jul The heat is on but the crowds are down.

Jul–Oct Rice terraces are green, but typhoons can be a problem.

Language

Myriad languages are spoken in North Luzon, including dozens of dialects in the Cordillera alone. The language jumble is most confusing in Kalinga, where just about every village has its own dialect. In the Cordillera, people are more likely to understand Ilocano or even English than the national language, Tagalog.

In the lowlands, the principal languages are Tagalog and Ilocano, which is the predominant language not only in Ilocos but also in Cagayan, Isabela and La Union. Other common dialects include Pangasinan and Sambal, the language of the Zambales people.

Dangers & Annoyances

There are sporadic shootouts between the government and the New People's Army (NPA) in mountainous areas of North Luzon. Such violence usually occurs way off the beaten track in provinces such as Aurora and Isabela, and rarely, if ever, affects tourists.

Tribal wars occasionally break out between villages in Kalinga and Mountain Province. Not even the Philippine government bothers intervening in these squabbles, some of which go back centuries. The last thing mountain tribes want to do is involve tourists in their internal quarrels; still, before heading to Kalinga, check with the police in Bontoc to see if there are any hot spots you should avoid.

Getting There & Away

Regular flights connect Manila with Baguio, Baler, Basco (Batanes), Cauayan (Isabela Province), Laoag, San Fernando (La Union) and Tuguegarao. Air-con buses link Manila with the major North Luzon cities, including comfortable deluxe buses to Laoag, Vigan and Baguio.

Driving is a great way to see Luzon's more remote regions, such as the Zambales coast and the Cordillera. Keep in mind that you'll need a pretty good 4WD for much of the latter, although most of the Halsema Hwy linking Baguio with Bontoc is now paved. You can rent cars in Manila.

ZAMBALES COAST

The lonely Zambales coast lies between a rock and a wet place. The rock? The angry massif of Mt Pinatubo. The wet? Well, the sea of course, with some fine surfing (especially around Pundaquit), and often as not the rains that unrelentingly lash this 100km of coastline every summer. Outside this season you'll find sunny days, offshore islands and beach resorts, many of them small and family run. At all times you will find small villages populated by intensely friendly locals, and you may see the area's diminutive Negrito Aeta tribespeople.

Pundaquit & Capones Island

☎047 / POP 2450

Just a three-hour drive from Manila you can sleep under the stars on hourglass-shaped Capones Island, a 20- to 30-minute bangka (outrigger canoe) ride from the small fishing village of Pundaquit. Hiring a bangka for a day of island hopping is P1200; if that doesn't appeal, see if your accommodation can arrange a discount fare. It's a short hike up to the island's scenic **lighthouse**.

Pundaquit also has a beach but it's too dirty and crammed with fishing boats to appeal.

Activities

July to October are the peak months for surfing, but decent swells linger into February. March to May is the flat season. The best spots are the south side of Capones Island, Anawangin Cove (south of Pundaquit) and San Narciso (7km north of San Antonio). Anawangin Cove is accessible only on foot or by boat. Call Crystal Beach for wave reports before you set out.

Crystal Beach Resort & Campsite SURFING
(☎913 4309; www.crystalbeachzambales.com) Part evangelical retreat, part surf camp, Crystal Beach Resort & Campsite in San Narciso gives new meaning to the word 'bizarre', but it does have Zambales' steadiest waves, boards for rent (P200 per hour) and surfing instruction (P200 per hour). From Manila, these are your closest surfing lessons. There's basic accommodation here but you're better off in nearby Pundaquit or in Subic, just 30km south.

Sleeping

'Resorts' in Zambales usually consist of low-slung apartment blocks near the sea. See the **Zambales Resort Owners Association** (www.zambalesresort.com) for a comprehensive list. During low season (June to September), many of these places go into hibernation;

North Luzon Highlights

1. Feasting your eyes on the awesome rice terraces around **Banaue** (p138), **Batad** (p141) and **Bontoc** (p135)
2. Stepping back in time in the lovely **Mestizo District** (p111) of Vigan
3. Chilling out for days – or weeks – in **Sagada** (p131), aka backpacker HQ
4. Taking in the music, fine food and cool mountain air of **Baguio** (p121)
5. Getting up close and personal with the mummies of **Kabayan** (p129)
6. Learning to surf in **San Fernando (La Union)** (p108)
7. Dangling your legs off the end of the world in **Batanes** (p149)

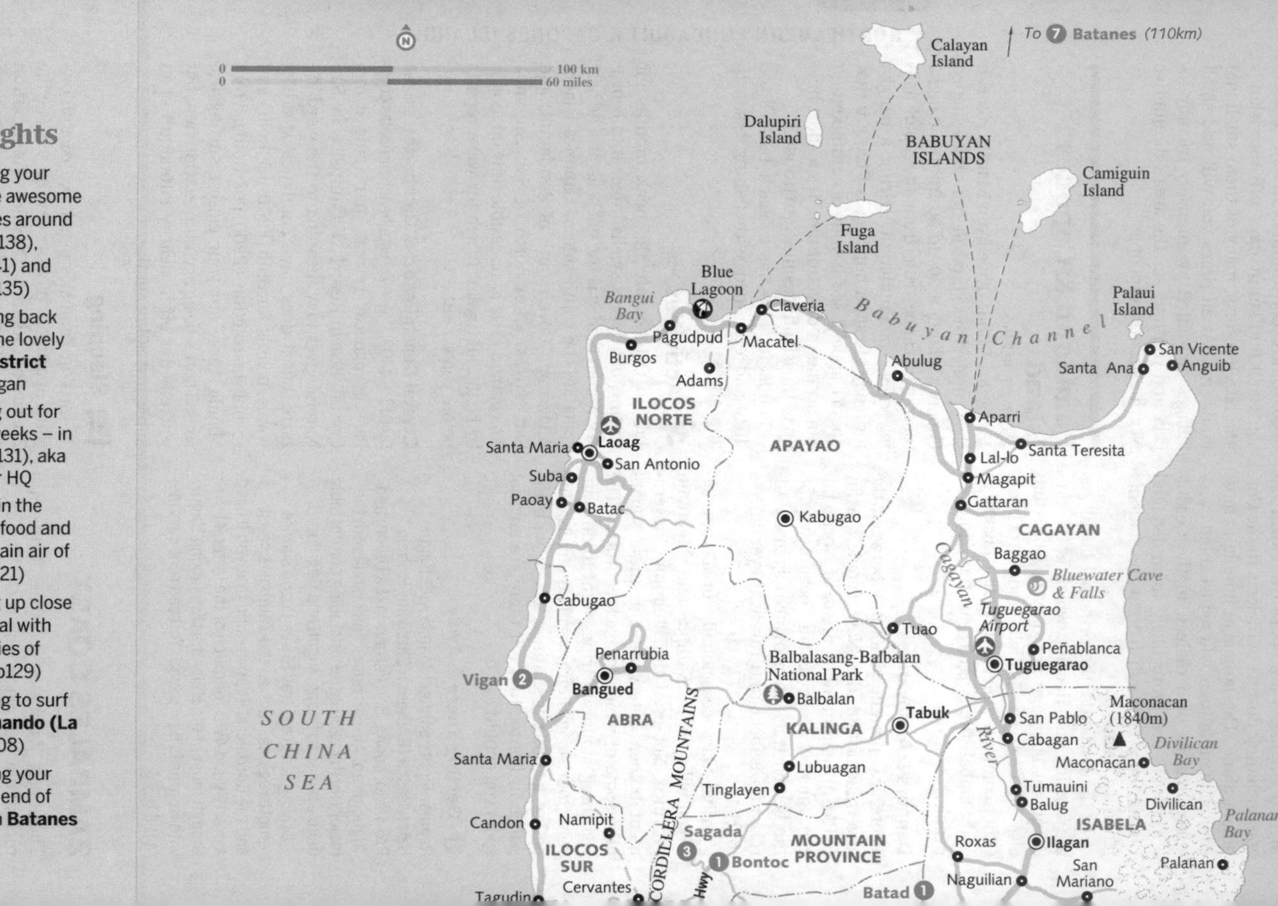

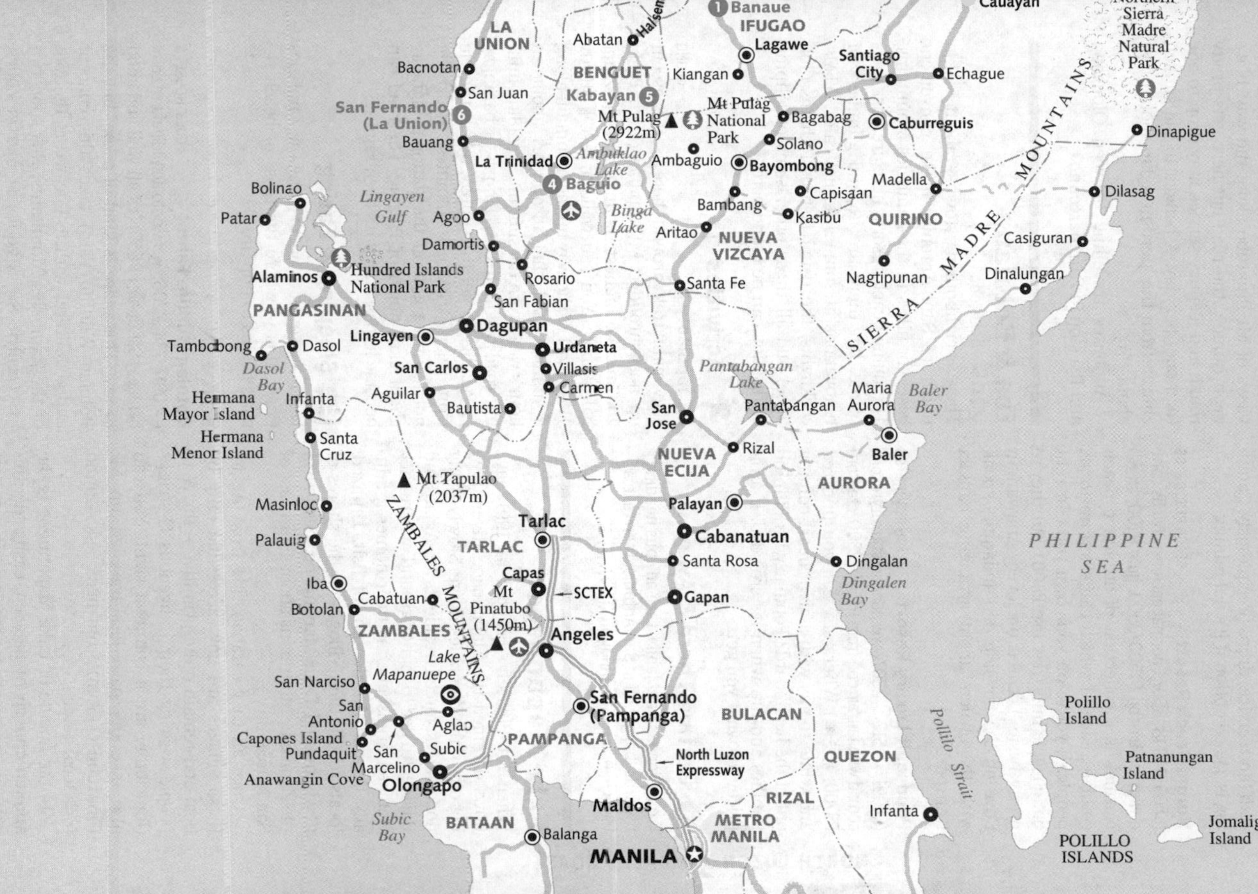

LA UNION
BENGUET
IFUGAO
Banaue
Lagawe
Cauayan
Northern Sierra Madre Natural Park
Abatan
Halsema
Bacnotan
San Juan
Kiangan
Kabayan
San Fernando (La Union)
Mt Pulag National Park
Mt Pulag (2922m)
Santiago City
Echague
Bagabag
Caburreguis
Solano
Dinapigue
Bauang
La Trinidad
Ambuklao Lake
Ambaguio
Bayombong
Baguio
Madella
Capisaan
Dilasag
Bolinao
Lingayen Gulf
Binga Lake
Bambang
Kasibu
QUIRINO
Patar
Agoo
Aritao
NUEVA VIZCAYA
Casiguran
Damortis
SIERRA MADRE MOUNTAINS
Hundred Islands National Park
Rosario
Nagtipunan
Dinalungan
Alaminos
Santa Fe
San Fabian
PANGASINAN
Dagupan
Lingayen
Urdaneta
Tambobong
Dasol
Dasol Bay
San Carlos
Villasis
Pantabangan Lake
Carmen
Aguilar
Maria Aurora
Baler Bay
Hermana Mayor Island
Infanta
Bautista
San Jose
Pantabangan
Hermana Menor Island
Santa Cruz
Rizal
Baler
NUEVA ECIJA
Mt Tapulao (2037m)
AURORA
Masinloc
Palayan
Tarlac
Cabanatuan
Palauig
TARLAC
PHILIPPINE SEA
Santa Rosa
Dingalan
Iba
Capas
Dingalen Bay
Mt Pinatubo (1450m)
SCTEX
Cabatuan
Gapan
Botolan
ZAMBALES MOUNTAINS
ZAMBALES
Angeles
Lake Mapanuepe
San Narciso
San Fernando (Pampanga)
BULACAN
Polillo Island
San Antonio
Aglao
Capones Island
PAMPANGA
Pundaquit
San Marcelino
Subic
North Luzon Expressway
QUEZON
Patnanungan Island
Anawangin Cove
Olongapo
Pollilo Strait
Maldos
RIZAL
Infanta
Jomalig Island
Subic Bay
BATAAN
METRO MANILA
POLILLO ISLANDS
Balanga
MANILA

they may still take guests, but the level of staff (and service) drops precipitously. Camping is a good option if it's not raining.

Norma Beach Resort BEACH RESORT **$$**
(0910 948 8607; normabeachresortwebs.com; d with fan/air-con P1500/3500, huts P700;) Norma's is a collection of attractive beach cottages, each of which can sleep up to six people. If you're on your own you can rent out cheapie huts (day use P500), but they're pretty basic. Located on lovely Anawangin Cove on the far side of Pundaquit; speak with the owners about arranging bangka transport.

Pundaquit Luxury Resort BEACH RESORT **$$**
(0917 512 2307www.pundaquitluxuryresort.com; d with fan/air-con from P1500/2300, ste from P3700;) Where else can you find red and white rooms with a giant heart coming out of the headboard? Popular with Filipino families and fun when it's crowded, if a bit pricey for what you get.

Getting There & Away

From Olongapo or Manila, take any bus heading towards Iba, get off in San Antonio, then take a tricycle 4.5km to Pundaquit (P75).

Lake Mapanuepe

When Mt Pinatubo erupted in 1991, lava flows dammed the Mapanuepe River flowing out of the Zambales range. Slowly rising floodwaters forced residents of Aglao and Bajaoen to flee to higher ground, where they watched in disbelief as their homes gradually became the domain of fish. Unfazed, locals rebuilt their villages on the shores of newly minted Lake Mapanuepe, nestled in the Zambales Mountains about 15km east of San Marcelino.

Once an easy carabao ride from Aglao, these villages are now accessible only by boat and remain quite primitive – the Aeta people wearing their indigenous G-strings (loincloths) are a common sight. You can also take the path less travelled up **Mt Pinatubo** (1450m) from here; ask around for a local guide.

In the middle of Lake Mapanuepe is the **sunken church** of Bajaoen, easily identifiable by its maroon cross sticking out of the water. You can try snorkelling over the church, but visibility can be extremely poor.

If the weather is dry, there are two or three daily jeepneys to Aglao from San Marcelino (45 minutes), with wonderful views of Mt Pinatubo along the way. If it's been raining, the road out here gets pretty rough and jeepney service may drop to one (or none) per day. A bangka to the sunken church from the 'port' in Aglao should cost about P700.

All buses travelling between Olongapo and Iba stop in San Marcelino.

Iba & Botolan

047 / POP 96,000

These neighbouring towns, about 45km north of San Antonio, make convenient bases for hikes in the Zambales Mountains. The many beach resorts here are past their prime, but there are hopeful glimmers of renovations at some. Internet cafes, ATMs, cockfights, the usual fast-food chains (Jollibee) and all those other signs of Filipino civilisation can be found here.

Activities

Mt Tapulao HIKING
The main trek around here is the ascent up mist-shrouded Mt Tapulao (High Peak; 2037m), the highest mountain in the Zambales range. You can walk or take a sturdy 4WD most of the way up the mountain along a mining road that terminates about an hour's walk from the summit. The 18km mining road originates in Dampay, a barangay of Palauig. To get to Dampay, take a tricycle from Palauig (P150, 40 minutes). If driving north, turn right off the national highway about 2km north of Palauig. The road can become impassable if it's been raining.

Sleeping & Eating

If driving south to north along the Zambales Coast, this is where the mass of beach resorts begins to pop up.

BOTOLAN

Botolan Wildlife Farm GUESTHOUSE **$**
(0917 734 2206; www.botolanwildlifefarm.com; barangay San Juan; r P650) It's all well and good to say, 'This place is kind of a zoo,' but the Botolan Wildlife Farm takes this concept and gets literal with it. Located at the foot of the Zambales Mountains, this spot, run by eccentric Swiss zoologist Martin Zoller, is both tourist accommodation and humane **sanctuary** (adult/child P75/65) for an array of rescued beasts, including a massive Siberian tiger. The rooms have great views of the ani-

mal pens and the mountains. To get there, take a tricycle (P75) 4km east from a well-marked turn-off on the National Hwy, just south of Botolan centre.

Zoller has also launched a community development program to revive the depressed Aeta village of Cabatuan, some 20km east of Botolan and accessible only by carabao-drawn cart. Ask about visiting the village or volunteering.

Rama Beach Resort BEACH RESORT **$$**
(☎0918 910 1280; www.ramabeach.com; d P1400, s with fan/air-con P900/1000, cottages from P1200; ❄📶🏊) If you want to sleep in Botolan sans tiger, Rama is your best bet. There's pretty accommodation and a nice restaurant with a library and pool table at this Australian-owned resort, on a quiet stretch of beach 8km south of Botolan proper. Turtles nest here from October to February.

IBA

Iba's beach resorts are clustered in barangay Bangantalinga, 3km north of Iba proper.

Sajorda River Park BEACH RESORT **$$**
(☎811 3665, 0908 881 2148; www.sajordariverpark.com; d/q/ste from P1500/1800/3500; ❄📶🏊) Around a kilometre north of Iba (look for signs pointing off the main road), Sajorda is a professional resort about 3km inland from the beach. Rooms are colourful and cheerful in an oh-so-Filipino way (lacy frills, pictures of flowers) and tours to nearby attractions are easily arranged.

Palmera Garden Beach Resort BEACH RESORT **$$**
(☎811 2109, 0917 464 1377; www.palmeragarden.com; s/d/f P1200/2500/3040; ❄📶🏊) This Swiss-owned resort is the most service-oriented in the area, with the best restaurant around and snappy staff. The rooms are mediocre, if good quality compared to the rest of Zamables.

Tolyo Pension GUESTHOUSE **$**
(☎811 1266, 0910 273 4260; www.cafetolyo.8k.com; National Hwy; s/d from P450/750; ❄📶) Avoid paying a premium to be situated on Bangantalinga's mediocre beach by staying at this simple place next to the provincial capitol building in downtown Iba.

ℹ Getting There & Away

Victory Liner (☎811 1392) has frequent buses (hourly from 5am to 6pm) from Iba to Caloocan in Manila (P342, five hours) via Olongapo (P145, two hours). Buses also run from Pasay, Manila (P357), at 5am, 10.30am, noon, 2pm and 11pm via the same route. Its buses also head north every 20 minutes to Santa Cruz (P83, 1½ hours).

North of Iba

If you're into island-hopping and beach camping, head to the border of the Zambales and Pangasinan provinces. Off Santa Cruz, **Hermana Menor Island** is fringed by a postcard-worthy white beach with some decent snorkelling just offshore. The island is privately owned, but bangka excursions there (P2500) and to neighbouring **Hermana Mayor Island** are possible through SeaSun Beach Resort (see p105).

Just south of here, **Potipot Island** (admission P50) is more accessible and more popular. It has a white beach where you can camp. SeaSun Beach Resort can arrange trips out here for P800.

Continuing north, Tambobong is the jumping-off point for the beautiful snorkelling haven of **Snake Island**, 25 minutes offshore by bangka. The difficulty involved with getting here almost ensures that you'll have the island to yourself (well, you and the snakes. Kidding! We didn't detect any more snakes here than anywhere else in the Philippines). From the market in Dasol, there are two or three daily jeepneys along the rocky coastal road to Tambobong (P35, 45 minutes), or take a tricycle (P600, one hour). Negotiate with local fishers for the bangka trip to Snake Island (about P800), and make sure to arrange a pick-up if you're staying overnight.

Danish-owned **SeaSun Beach Resort** (☎0917 409 3347; www.seasun.com.ph; barangay Sabang; d with fan/air-con P600/2000; ❄) in Santa Cruz fronts a pleasantly secluded sliver of beach in view of Hermana Menor and Hermana Mayor. Rooms run the gamut from bare-bones fan cells to fancier digs with minbars and satellite TV. The resort is 1.5km off the main road – spot the well-marked turn-off 2km south of Santa Cruz.

Victory Liner has frequent buses south to Iba and Olongapo and north to Alaminos and Lingayen. Local (non air-con) buses run up and down the same road through the day.

LINGAYEN GULF

This pretty pocket of water, a scattershot of emerald islands on azure and turquoise, dominates the coastline of Pangasinan Province.

Lingayen Gulf

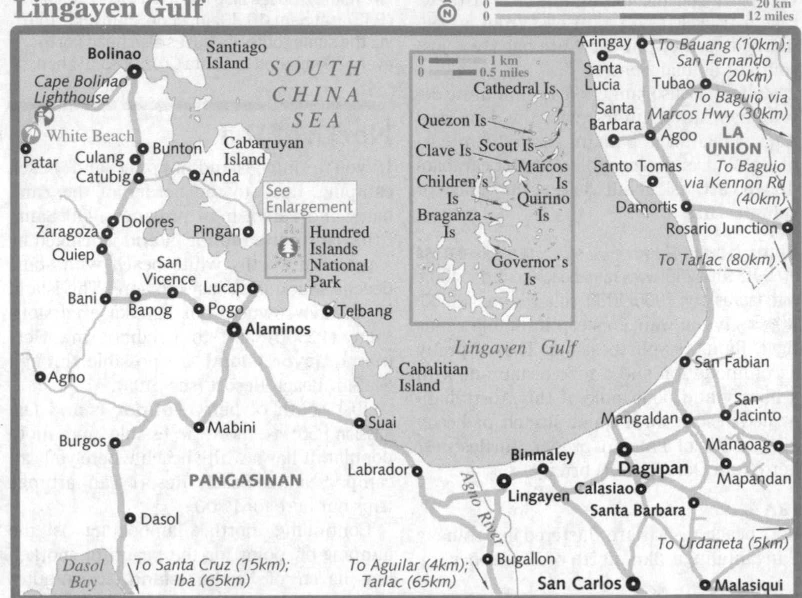

Lingayen (*leen*-gay-en) Gulf played a central role in WWII, overseeing the exit and entrance of both Axis and Allies to the Philippines. In December 1941 invading Japanese troops made their first major amphibious landing in the Philippines along the coast south of Bauang, La Union. Three years later, liberating American forces came ashore a bit further southwest, at Lingayen and San Fabian.

Sadly, the coral reefs have been all but destroyed by dynamite and cyanide fishing. Still, there is no shortage of beach resorts scattered along the coastline from Bolinao to San Fernando (La Union), which has become a popular spot to learn how to surf.

Bolinao & Patar Beach

☎075 / POP 69,500

Bolinao has a palpable end-of-the-road feel to it – unsurprising, as it is basically located at the end of everything. Depending on your point of view, local beach resorts can feel romantically isolated or a bit forlorn.

If you come out this way, your destination will likely be Patar Beach, a long stretch of narrow sand linking Bolinao with barangay Patar, situated 18km to the south. There are a few decent beaches for swimming; the best is White Beach in Patar proper, overlooked by the towering Spanish-built Cape Bolinao Lighthouse.

Internet cafes are plentiful in Bolinao, but at the time of research there were no ATMs. There are said to be various sunken Chinese junks and Mexican merchant vessels lying offshore.

Sights & Activities

TOP CHOICE **University of the Philippines Marine Science Institute** RESEARCH CENTRE

(☎554 2755; www.msi.upd.edu.ph/bml; admission P10; ⏲8am-5pm Mon-Fri) By far the best use of your time in Bolinao is coming to this research facility-cum-visitor centre. Researchers at the laboratory of the University of the Philippines Marine Science Institute cultivate coral-producing giant clams and transplant them to Hundred Islands National Park and as far away as Australia and Malaysia. The institute is about 1.5km east of Bolinao wharf; look for a marked right turn 200m before the pier.

The marine institute can arrange snorkelling trips to the gardens, as can most resorts on Patar Beach. You can check out the clams and/or local shipwrecks with **Bolinao Diving Centre** (☎0929 307 7515; lopecaacbay@yahoo.com; Celino St, Bolinao; per dive P500).

Church of St James CHURCH

Built by the Augustinians in 1609, the Church of St James in the town plaza is notable for its Mexican influences. On its antique altar are two protruding-tongue, Aztec-like statues said to have been brought to Bolinao by early traders (but they're almost certainly not from the Americas). The wooden *santos* (religious statues) on the church's facade are also rare, as many *santos* in the Philippines have been pilfered.

Sleeping & Eating

BOLINAO

Sundowners Bistro Bolinao SEAFOOD $$

(☎554 2800; d P900; ❄) In addition to being the finest restaurant in Bolinao by a considerable margin, this outdoor seafood eatery (mains P100 to P150) with views over the wharf has two rarely occupied 3rd-floor rooms.

PATAR BEACH

Treasures of Bolinao BEACH RESORT $$$

(☎696 3266, 0921 564 2408; cottage/d/ste from P4000/4800/5800; ❄≋) 'Treasures' is as opulent as Bolinao (indeed, this part of Luzon) gets. Located some 17km from Bolinao proper, the resort features posh villas, upscale coconut cottages and cavernous, exquisitely furnished suites with ocean views. The beach down here is powdered-sugar soft.

Punta Riviera BEACH RESORT $$$

(☎696 1350; www.puntarivieraresort.com; r from P3000; ❄≋) The closest thing in Bolinao to a full-service resort. Free sea kayak usage for guests.

Getting There & Around

Victory Liner and Five Star have several morning buses and a couple of afternoon buses to Cubao in Manila (P432, 6½ hours).

Frequent buses and minibuses shuttle to Alaminos (P45, one hour).

A tricycle to the resorts on Patar Beach should cost P150 to P175 one way, depending on how far you are going.

Hundred Islands National Park

☎075

This small **national park** (☎552 7777; www.hundredislands.ph; entrance fee day/overnight P20/40, boat fee P800/1400) off the coast of Alaminos, 35km southeast of Bolinao, actually consists of 123 separate islets (some are just large rocks). Over the centuries the tides have eaten away at the bases of some of these limestone islands, giving them a distinctive mushroomlike appearance.

Unfortunately, the Hundred Islands may be too popular for their own good. Visitors and fishing have taxed the local ecology. Thus it can be difficult finding the right island where the coral hasn't been damaged by dynamite fishing or typhoons. This is not a place for a casual day trip, which will likely leave you feeling disappointed; the Hundred Islands demand some patient exploring.

Environmentally, the situation has been improving since the Alaminos city government took control of the park in 2005. Speedboats patrol in search of illegal fishers, while the University of the Philippines Marine Science Institute in Bolinao has been repopulating the decimated giant clam population, which has helped coral recovery.

Sights & Activities

To enter the park, head to the Lucap wharf and pay the entrance fee at the tourism office (day trippers can stow their bags here). The three most popular islands are **Quezon Island**, **Governor's Island** and **Children's Island**. The beaches on these main islands are nothing special, although Governor's Island has a nice lookout point. On weekends you're better off finding your own island, as the main ones fill up with large families and beach vendors. Children's Island is aptly named, with calm, shallow water that attracts Filipino families.

You can snorkel at one of the giant clam sites but they are hard to find; get directions from the park office.

100 Islands Ocean Sports WATER SPORTS

(☎551 2246; Lucap waterfront) By far the best way to experience the park is in a rented tandem kayak (per day P500) from 100 Islands Ocean Sports; you can bring it with you on your bangka, or hire one on Quezon Island (P650 per hour).

The company also leads cave jumps from Imelda Cave on Marcos Island, a fun activity made infinitely better by geographic nomenclature that suggests you're about to leap into a pile of shoes.

You can also scuba dive, and even try 'snuba' diving (diving with a 40ft hose attached to a tank on the surface). Jim, the American owner, also runs parasailing and deep-sea fishing trips in his speedboat.

Sleeping & Eating

You can camp anywhere in the national park for P200. Quezon Island has six simple, two-person nipa huts (P500 to P1100) with no electricity. Governor's Island has a guest-house (P10,000) that sleeps eight to 10 and has air-con when the electricity is working (from 6pm to 6am). Bring your own food and supplies. Make reservations and pay at the Hundred Islands National Park office in Lucap.

Information

The **Hundred Islands National Park office** (☎552 7777; www.hundredislands.ph; ⊙8am-5pm) is near the pier in barangay Lucap, the jumping-off point to the national park. The office collects the park entrance and camping fees, and publishes official rates for bangka hire.

BDO (Banco de Oro), BPI (Bank of the Philippine Islands) and Metrobank have ATMs in Alaminos, and there are a couple of internet cafes.

Getting There & Around

Five Star and Victory Liner have frequent departures to Pasay, Manila (ordinary/air-con P370/450, 5½ hours), and to Santa Cruz (P180, 1½ hours), where you transfer to Olongapo. Victory Liner also has buses to Baguio (P200, 3½ hours, four daily).

It's a 10-minute tricycle ride (P60, 5km) from Alaminos centre to Lucap's resorts.

Hiring a boat from Lucap to Hundred Islands National Park costs P800 return for a five-passenger boat (day trip). Island-hopping costs a couple of hundred pesos extra.

Lingayen

☎075 / POP 95,800

The provincial capital of Pangasinan is best known as the site where US troops came ashore to liberate Luzon in January 1945, thus fulfilling General MacArthur's famous pledge, 'I shall return'. The small open-air **Lingayen Gulf War Memorial Museum**, on the beachfront behind the provincial capitol building, pays tribute to the soldiers with photos and descriptions of the US landing. An American fighter plane on display had its wing and tail blown off by Typhoon Cosme in 2008.

Lingayen's coastline comes alive every 1 May with a raucous waterborne parade in celebration of **Pista'y Dayat**, a fiesta that pays homage to local fishers. Outside of festival week you'll have little reason to stay overnight here. You're better off in Alaminos or Dagupan, a bustling provincial hub 15km east.

San Fernando (La Union) & Around

☎072 / POP 115,000

Surfers, look no further. Most travellers heading here are bound for barangay Urbiztondo in San Juan, an unassuming beach village 6km north of San Fernando that gets the country's most consistent waves from November to March. During the season a legion of bronzed instructors offer beginners some of the world's cheapest surf lessons (P400 per hour) on the perfect learners' waves that stroke the shore.

Sights

Ma-Cho Pagoda — TEMPLE

(Map p109) The Ma-Cho is one of the most striking Chinese temples in Luzon. A loud collision of Taoism and Chinese Catholicism (think bright red imperial Chinese decor mixed with the iconography of a Latin American church and you get the idea), the pagoda sits atop a hill just north of San Fernando. The original image of the Virgin of Caysasay, the patron of San Fernando's Filipino-Chinese community, is brought to the temple from Taal, Batangas, in the second week of September as part of the week-long activities in celebration of the Feast of the Virgin (a replica is on display for the rest of the year).

Freedom Park — PARK

(Map p109) Freedom Park, near the Provincial Capitol Building, has panoramic views of the city. You can access it via Zigzag Rd or walk the 153 steps up **Heroes Hill**, which is lined with statues of national heroes and presidents.

Activities

Unless you're a gambler, **surfing** is the main attraction around here. Instructors are easily found through the resorts in barangay Urbiztondo, which also rent boards (P200 per hour). The best beginners' break is usually at the 'cement factory' in Bacnotan, 6km north of San Juan proper. Urbiztondo's main beach break and neighbouring Mona Liza Point tend to get bigger waves.

If you're a beginner, it pays to shop around for an instructor who you're comfortable communicating with, as the level of English speaking varies immensely.

San Fernando (La Union)

Sleeping

SAN JUAN

If all budget accommodation in Urbiztondo is booked out, surf instructors can usually scare up a bed for as little as P500.

Sebay Resort BEACH RESORT **$$**
(Map p110; ☎888 4075, 0910 739 5698; Urbiztondo; tr/q with fan P1200/1400, d with air-con from P1600; ❄📶) Sebay's an excellent option with a great restaurant and chilled-out vibe. It's on a wide patio with front-row views of the surfing action. The rooms are basic but clean, while the newer bungalow section represents a decent deal.

Little Surfmaid BEACH RESORT **$$$**
(Map p110; ☎888 5528; www.littlesurfmaidresort.com; d from P2500, beachfront ste P3900; ❄📶) It's Danish owned, as the name implies, offering a high level of service and one of the best restaurants on the beach. The two-room beachfront suites with balconies facing Mona Liza Point are worth the extra expense. The same can't quite be said for the standard doubles.

San Juan Surf Resort BEACH RESORT **$$**
(Map p110; ☎720 0340, 0917 880 3040; www.sanjuansurfresort.com.ph; Urbiztondo; d/q with air-con from P1500/1920, fan only P890; ❄) Run by Aussie Brian Landrigan, a 25-year veteran of the area, this place has expanded from humble beginnings into a veritable surfers' village, with everything from mildewy holes-in-the-wall to semiluxury 'penthouse suites'. The latter are set back in a tall concrete edifice within sight of the main beach break.

San Fernando (La Union)

Sights
1 Heroes Hill D2
2 Ma-Cho Pagoda D1

Sleeping
3 Oasis Country Resort D3
4 Sea & Sky Hotel C1

Eating
5 Cafe Esperanza D2
6 Taipan Garden Restaurant C1

Information
7 Bureau of Immigration B3
8 DOT Region I Office D3

Transport
9 Buses to Vigan and Laoag C1
10 Jeepneys to Bauang and San Juan D1
11 Minibuses to Baguio C1

Sunset German Beach Resort BEACH RESORT **$$**
(Map p110; ☎888 4719, 0917 921 2420; www.sunsetgermanbeachresort.com; barangay Montemar; d with fan/air-con P800/1100, ste P2100; ❄) Cosy, attractive rooms with exposed brickwork, a quiet beach that gets OK surf of its own and owners who make their own German sausage at this lush little resort located 3.5km north of Urbiztondo. The turn-off to the resort is exactly 1km north of San Juan proper.

Final Option BEACH RESORT **$$**
(Map p110; ☎888 2724, 0929 448 5505; www.finaloptionbeach.com.ph; barangay Montemar; r/ste with air-con P2100/3000, fan only P1000; ❄🏊) While the name of this resort is oddly ominous, the place itself – another German-run collection of clean apartments and bungalows north of Urbitzondo – is anything but. There's a light-hearted, summery vibe here, plus an impressive swimming pool and decent German food to boot.

Lola Nanny's HOTEL **$$**
(Map p110; ☎0915 418 4934; d with fan & shared bathroom P800, s/d with air-con P1200/2500; ❄) Bare bones and clean, this is a basic option but perfectly serviceable for those here to surf.

Around San Fernando

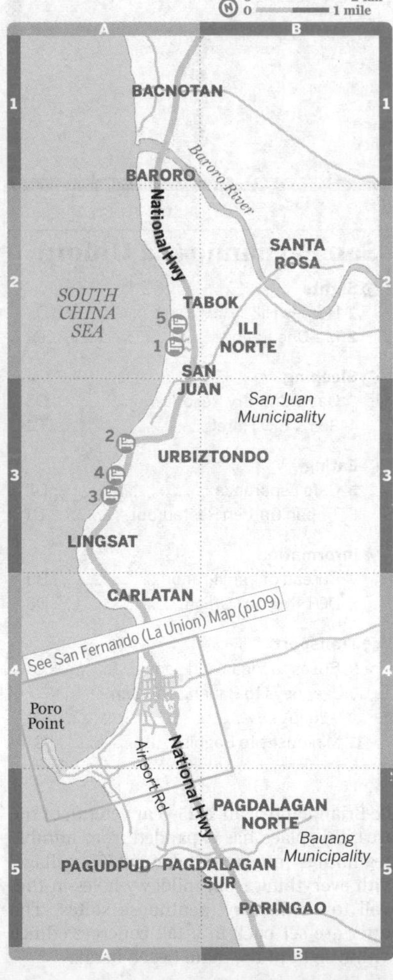

SAN FERNANDO

Oasis Country Resort HOTEL **$$$**
(Map p109; ☎242 5621; www.oasiscountryresort.com; National Hwy; s/d from P2100/3000; 🚭❄📶🏊) Don't let the name fool you – this is a business hotel, and a good one too. The doubles are sizeable if characterless, and there are a few poolside *casitas* (little houses), which make for interesting business digs. Its restaurant features sushi and themed all-you-can-eat buffet dinners.

Sea & Sky Hotel HOTEL **$$**
(Map p109; ☎242 5579; Quezon Ave; s P600, d basement/standard P1000/1300; ❄📶🏊) The doubles in this airy concrete block either overlook the sea or the National Hwy. And they cost the same. Guess which side we chose. Wi-fi in the lobby only.

Eating & Drinking

The best places to eat in San Juan and Bauang are the resorts. There are plenty of bars on Pennsylvania Ave out towards Poro Point, most less than wholesome.

Taipan Garden Restaurant CHINESE **$$**
(Map p109; Purgos St, San Fernando; mains P80-340; ⏰lunch & dinner; ❄) The best of several blissfully air-conditioned Chinese restaurants in San Fernando. The speciality is steamed *lapu-lapu* (grouper) and stinky tofu.

Around San Fernando

Sleeping

1 Final Option A2
2 Little Surfmaid A3
Lola Nanny's .... (see 4)
3 San Juan Surf Resort A3
4 Sebay Resort A3
5 Sunset German Beach Resort A2

Cafe Esperanza CAFE $
(Map p109; Gomez St, San Fernando; sandwiches under P100) Overlooking the city plaza, this mellow cafe serves coffee, desserts and a smattering of Filipino and Chinese dishes.

Information

Bureau of Immigration (BOI; Map p109; ☎888 4515; Pennsylvania Ave, Poro Point, San Fernando) Quick, efficient visa extensions.

Department of Tourism Region I Office (DOT; Map p109; ☎888 2411; National Hwy, San Fernando; ⏰8am-5.30pm) Next to Oasis Country Resort.

Getting There & Around

Partas (☎242 0465; Quezon Ave) and **Viron** (☎888 2089; Quezon Ave) are the main companies serving Manila (P500, six to seven hours, at least hourly).

Partas also serves Laoag (P380, five hours) and Vigan (P250, three hours). Cheaper, more frequent ordinary buses head to Laoag and Vigan from Quezon Ave in front of the town plaza.

Minibuses to Baguio (P70, 1½ hours) leave every 10 minutes from Gov Luna St.

Jeepneys to Bauang and San Juan (P18) can be picked up along Quezon Ave.

Both Seair and Zest used to connect San Fernando to Manila; flights may have resumed by the time you read this.

ILOCOS

Vigan

☎077 / POP 49,000

Within the consciousness of Filipino tourism, Vigan is a Spanish-colonial fairy tale of dark-wood mansions, cobblestone streets and clattering *kalesa* (horse-drawn carriages). The truth about this Unesco World Heritage site is a little more complicated. Yes: Vigan is the finest surviving example of a Spanish colonial town in Asia. But outside of well-restored Crisologo St (closed to vehicular traffic) and a few surrounding blocks, it's a noisy Filipino town like many others. We're not knocking Vigan, as it can be supremely romantic, but realise the preservation is not everywhere and you may find it easier to appreciate the places where history is alive, where you can smell the aroma of freshly baked empanadas wafting past antique shops, pottery collectives and capiz-shell windows.

History

Located near where the Govantes River meets the South China Sea, Vigan became a convenient stop on the Silk Route, which linked Asia, the Middle East and Europe, and a thriving trading post where gold, logs and beeswax were bartered for goods from around the world.

In the year 1572, Spanish conquistador Juan de Salcedo (who was the grandson of Miguel Lopez de Legazpi, one of the first conquistadors) took possession of the bustling international port. Juan de Salcedo became the lieutenant governor of the Ilocos region, and Vigan became the centre of the political, religious and commercial activities of the north. It became a hotbed of dissent against the Spanish when, in 1762, Diego Silang captured Vigan and named it the capital of Free Ilocos. He was eventually assassinated (the Spanish paid a close friend of Silang to shoot him in the back), and his wife, Gabriela Silang, took over. The first woman to lead a revolt in the Philippines, she was eventually captured and publicly hanged in the town square.

The city avoided destruction in WWII when Japanese troops fled the city just ahead of American carpet bombers, who aborted their mission at the last second.

Sights

Vigan has two main squares located near each other at the north end of town: Plaza Salcedo, dominated by St Paul Cathedral, and the livelier Plaza Burgos, where locals stroll and hang out. The historic Mestizo District is centred on nearby Crisologo St. The main commercial drag is tricycle-congested Quezon Ave, which runs south to the public market.

Mestizo District HISTORIC AREA
Vigan's old town, the Mestizo District, is where you can wander lost in a historical daze among ancestral homes and colonial-era architecture. The mansions here are simply beautiful and architecturally unique, marrying two great aesthetic senses: Chinese and Spanish. The latter were once Vigan's colonial masters; the former were merchants who settled, intermarried and, by the 19th century, became the city's elite.

In fact, Spanish and Chinese are themselves limiting terms when it comes to describing Vigan architecture. Spain itself has either influenced or been influenced by Mexico, the Caribbean and North Africa, and these regions make their presence known in the form of airy verandahs, leafy inner courtyards and wrought-iron balconies. At the same time, Asia also makes an appearance with dark wooden accents, polished floors and sliding capiz-shell windows.

In most mansions, the ground floor has stone walls and is strictly for storage and/or work, while the wooden 1st floor, with its large, airy *sala* (living room), is for living. The capiz-shell windows are as tall as doors, while the wide window sills are good spots for a siesta. The capiz is a flat bivalve found in the coastal waters of the Philippines. It came into fashion in the 19th century because it was cheaper than glass and sturdy enough to withstand typhoon winds and rain. Light shines through capiz in a particular way that is almost impossibly romantic.

While a couple of mansions have been converted into B&Bs or museums, most are private homes. You can knock on the door (note the hand-shaped brass knockers on some doors) and see if the owner will give you a tour, but there's no guarantee. Two houses to look out for are the **Quema House** and the **Syquia Mansion** on Quirino Blvd. The latter was recently turned into a **museum** (admission P20; ⏲9am-noon & 1.30-5pm) filled with old furniture and exhibits dedicated to the life of Vigan native Elpidio Quirino, the Philippines' sixth president, who was born in the nearby provincial jail. As historic homes go, this one is dusty but one of the best preserved, and a good place to get a sense of what the traditional interior of a Chinese-Spanish mansion resembled.

St Paul Cathedral CHURCH

(Burgos St) This church was built in 'earthquake baroque' style (ie thick-walled and massive) after an earlier incarnation was damaged by two quakes in 1619 and 1627. The construction of the original wooden, thatched church is believed to have been supervised by Salcedo himself in 1574. The

Vigan

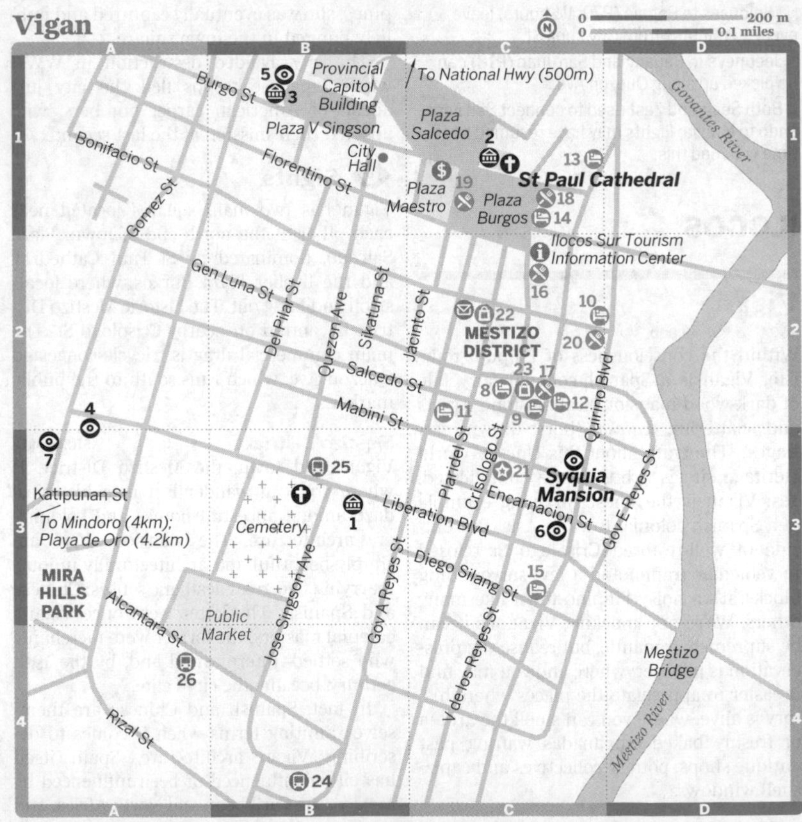

brass communion handrails were made in China, and faint Chinese characters can be seen at the points where they connect to the building. The octagonal design of the church is supposedly rooted in *feng shui* design principles (keep in mind that Vigan's wealthy Chinese merchant class were mainly Christian).

Museo San Pablo MUSEUM
(admission P10; ⏲9am-noon & 2-5pm Tue-Sun) The Museo San Pablo, in St Paul Cathedral, has a religious theme and is a good place to see old *santos* (religious statues). Make sure to have a look at the wonderfully aged photo collection of a German pharmacist who lived in Vigan for a number of years in the late 1800s.

Padre José Burgos National Museum MUSEUM
(Ayala Museum; Burgos St; admission P10; ⏲8.30-11.30am & 1.30-4.30pm Tue-Sun) Built in 1788, the Padre José Burgos National Museum is in the ancestral home of Father José Burgos, one of the three martyr priests executed by the Spanish in 1872. It houses an extensive collection of Ilocano artefacts, including a series of 14 paintings by the locally famed painter Don Esteban Villanueva depicting the 1807 Basi Revolt. Weavings, Tingguian (Itneg) jewellery, musical instruments, pottery, and farming and fishing implements are also on display.

Next door is the preserved **provincial jail**, built in 1657; if you've ever wondered what a colonial-era S&M club would look like (and really, who hasn't?), this place may match your mental image.

Pottery Factories CRAFT
Prior to the arrival of the Spanish, Chinese settlers took advantage of the abundant clay in the area and pioneered a still-active pottery industry. The *burnay* (earthen jars) are used in the fermentation of *basí* (sugar cane wine) and *bagoong* (fish paste), but you are more likely to see them scattered about in homes and gardens. You can visit a couple of pottery factories on Liberation Blvd, near the corner of Gomez St. The 50m-long kiln at **RG Jar** (Gomez St), which was made in 1823 and can hold nearly 1000 jars, is a wonder to behold. A resident carabao is employed as a mixer at RG Jar and periodically walks on the clay. Local potters are happy to take a cigarette break and watch tourists make fools of themselves as they attempt to sculpt their own earthenware. Be nice and buy a small clay souvenir if you visit.

Weavers CRAFT
Vigan weavers are known for using *abel*, a locally produced cotton fabric, to hand-weave shawls, tablecloths, napkins and

Vigan

Top Sights
- St Paul Cathedral ... C1
- Syquia Mansion ... C3

Sights
- 1 Crisologo Museum ... B3
- 2 Museo San Pablo ... C1
- 3 Padre José Burgos National Museum ... B1
- 4 Pottery Factories ... A2
- 5 Provincial Jail ... B1
- 6 Quema House ... C3
- 7 RG Jar ... A3

Sleeping
- 8 Cordillera Inn ... C2
- 9 Gordion Inn ... C2
- 10 Grandpa's Inn ... C2
- 11 Hem Apartelle ... C2
- 12 Hotel Salcedo de Vigan ... C2
- 13 Vigan Hotel ... C1
- 14 Vigan Plaza Hotel ... C1
- 15 Villa Angela ... C3

Eating
- 16 Cafe Leona ... C2
- Cafe Uno ... (see 10)
- 17 Leila's Café ... C2
- 18 Royal Bibingka ... C1
- 19 Street Stalls ... C1
- 20 Uno Grille ... C2

Entertainment
- 21 Legacy ... C3

Shopping
- 22 Mira Furniture ... C2
- 23 Rowilda's ... C2

Transport
- 24 Buses to Bangued ... B4
- 25 Dominion Bus Lines ... B3
- 26 Partas Bus Terminal ... A4

barong (traditional Filipino shirts). In barangay Camanggaan, just a 10-minute tricycle ride southeast of Vigan, you can watch *abel* handweavers in action at **Rowilda's weaving factory**, which is actually just a house.

In barangay Mindoro, near Playa de Oro beach resort, you can watch weavers on backstrap looms making *binakol* blankets that incorporate a traditional psychedelic-looking design.

Higher-quality *binakol,* including some antique blankets from nearby Abra Province, are for sale at Mira Furniture and at many shops lining Crisologo St.

FREE **Crisologo Museum** MUSEUM
(Liberation Blvd; ⌚8.30-11.30am & 1.30-4.30pm Tue-Sat) The Crisologos, Vigan's most prominent political dynasty, have converted their ancestral home into a strange but interesting family shrine, the Crisologo Museum. In addition to the usual fare of books, photos and other personal items, there is the old Chevy that Governor Carmeling Crisologo was in when she was (unsuccessfully) ambushed by gunmen in 1961.

Festivals

Viva Vigan Festival of the Arts CULTURE
A grand celebration of the town's cultural heritage takes place in the first week in May. There is street dancing, a fashion show, a *kalesa* parade and, of course, lots of food.

Vigan Town Fiesta CULTURE
Held in the third or fourth week of January, the fiesta commemorates the town's patron saint, St Paul the Apostle, with a parade and musical performances.

Sleeping

Rates decrease by about 20% from June to October.

TOP CHOICE **Villa Angela** HISTORIC HOTEL $$
(☎722 2914; www.villangela.com; 26 Quirino Blvd; dm/d/q incl breakfast from P700/1500/2800; ❄📶) This hotel is more than 130 years old and retains every morsel of its old-world charm. The massive rooms and fabulous antique furniture, which includes wooden harps and king-sized *nara*-wood canopy beds, will blow you away. This is where Tom Cruise, Willem Dafoe and other celebs spent the night while filming *Born on the Fourth of July* in the vicinity in 1989, and there is no shortage of pictures on the walls to prove it.

Hotel Salcedo de Vigan HOTEL $$$
(☎722 1200; www.hotelsalcedodevigan.com; cnr V de los Reyes & Salcedo Sts; standard/deluxe/ste incl breakfast from P2340/3510/3960; ❄📶) Filipino presidents have stayed in this new (yet historically kitted out) hotel: how about you? Rooms have high ceilings, mustard-yellow faux aged walls and fluffy beds. Service is professional and prompt.

Grandpa's Inn HISTORIC HOTEL $$
(☎722 2118, 0917 580 2118; 1 Bonifacio St; d with/without air-con incl breakfast from P1350/800; ❄📶) With an impressive array of rooms and good service, Grandpa's is solid value; the only drawback is that some of the rooms offered in that variety are pretty small, with even tinier bathrooms. All rooms have brick walls, capiz-shell windows, wooden beams, antique furnishings and rustic flavour. There are a couple of rooms where you can sleep in *kalesa*.

Hem Apartelle GUESTHOUSE $
(☎722 2173, 0917 519 1888; 32 Gov A Reyes St; r from P600; ❄) No heritage-style lodging here: the Hem is just an air-conditioned guesthouse that's the best budget deal in town. Rooms are sparse, but there are TVs, clean sheets, clean floors and clean toilets you can sit on – win!

Cordillera Inn HOTEL $$
(☎722 2727; www.cordillerainn.cjb.net; 29 Crisologo St; d with fan/air-con from P1050/1500; ❄📶) You can't beat the location, but you can probably top the decor, unless you really go in for bright pink paint (then again, towels are folded into swan shapes; nice touch). At the time of research, wi-fi was only reliable in the lobby and nearby rooms.

Gordion Inn HOTEL $$
(☎722 2526; gordionhotel@yahoo.com; cnr V de los Reyes & Salcedo Sts; d with fan P900, d with air-con incl breakfast from P1800; 🚭❄📶) This B&B is easy to spot with its bright blue-and-yellow facade. There's a new concrete building with smart, spacious rooms, and an older ancestral home with slightly worn if more character-laden rooms.

Vigan Plaza Hotel HOTEL $$$
(☎722 8552; vphotel@pldtdsl.net; Plaza Burgos; s/d/ste incl breakfast from P2300/3100/4400; ❄📶) A legitimate high-end option, the

Vigan Plaza combines mod-cons with old-world flourishes.

Vigan Hotel HOTEL $
(☎722 1906; Burgos St; fan s/d without bathroom P395/495, air-con d with bathroom incl breakfast P1395; ❄) 'The aristocrat of the north' is basic and cheap, and the owner swears he will not raise his rates.

Eating & Drinking

The Ilocos region is known for its food, and local specialities include *pinakbét* (stir-fried mixed vegetables), *bagnet* (deep-fried pork knuckle) and *puqui-puqui* (a roasted eggplant dish). For quick, cheap Ilocano fare, check out the collection of street stalls that lines Florentino St along Plaza Burgos. They specialise in empanadas, *okoy* (deep-fried shrimp omelettes) and *sinanglao* (beef soup).

Uno Grille FUSION $$
(Bonifacio St; mains P100-180; 📶) Run by neighbouring Grandpa's Inn, the food is of the same high standard as at Grandpa's fine restaurant and, unusually for a restaurant with a big menu, it does everything well. The takes on local Illocano cuisine are your best bets. Its sister restaurant is **Cafe Uno** (1 Bonifacio St; cakes P60; 📶).

Leila's Cafe CAFE $
(Gen Luna St; mains P30-80; ⏲7.30am-9.30pm; 📶) Leila's is the sort of cafe every city deserves: an airy interior, comfortable squishy chairs and couches, young people all abuzz over the issues of the day, folks reading in the corner, and fast internet. Food is a nice selection of tasty baked goods.

Cafe Leona FILIPINO $$
(Crisologo St; meals P100-300) This popular eatery that spills out onto Crisologo St is a godsend for weary travellers in search of libation and sustenance after a long hot day of sightseeing. Pluses: excellent Japanese and Ilocano specialities, and frequent all-you-can-eat pasta buffets. Fusses: plastic patio furniture and a loud adjoining open-air karaoke bar.

Royal Bibinkga BAKERY $
(8 Florentino St; bibingka P20) Vigan is famous for producing some of the best *bibingka* (rice flour cakes) in the Philippines. Royal is the spot to indulge your *bibingka* sweet tooth; its version is sweet, heavy and chewy.

Legacy CLUB
(Crisologo St) Legacy is conservative Vigan's concession to nightlife. On the inside it resembles a New York lounge misplaced in Ilocos. Thumping bass and electronic music shakes the walls; Wednesday is ladies night (one free beer, girls), and on Thursdays there's ballroom dancing.

Shopping

Antique and textile shops line the sides of Crisologo St. Bargain hard and you can score some pretty decent deals out here.

Mira Furniture FURNITURE
(cnr Plaridel & Bonifacio Sts) Has a good selection and takes orders for custom-made pieces.

Rowilda's CRAFT
(Crisologo St) Woven *abel* goods produced in barangay Camanggaan can be found in many of the souvenir and antique shops that line Crisologo St. This place has a particularly good selection.

Information

Plenty of internet cafes and banks with ATMs are clustered on Quezon Ave.

Ilocos Sur Tourism Information Centre (☎722 8771; 1 Crisologo St; ⏲8am-noon & 1-5pm) In the ancestral home of poet Leona Florentino, the highly informative staffers here give free guided tours of Vigan.

Post office (cnr Bonifacio & Gov A Reyes Sts)

Getting There & Away

Interisland Airways (☎02-852 7789; www.interislandairways.com) flies to Vigan from Manila.

Buses to Manila (P700, nine hours) are plentiful. Try **Dominion Bus Lines** (☎722 2084, 741 4146; cnr Liberation Blvd & Quezon Ave) to Cubao and Sampaloc, or **Partas** (☎722 2350; Alcantara St) to Cubao and Pasay. Partas has three nightly 29-seat deluxe express buses (P820, eight hours); the company also has frequent buses to Laoag (P180, two hours) and Baguio (P350, five hours). **Florida** (☎02-743 3809) has three nightly 29-seat deluxe/super deluxe/sleeper buses (P550/750/850) leaving every morning for Manila. Reliable and with a good service record, **Ancieto** (☎02-73 3809) is the best deal of the bunch, with regular (but comfy) buses leaving every morning for P420.

Many more buses bound for Laoag and Manila stop at the Caltex Station on the National Hwy just outside Vigan. Southbound buses go via San Fernando (P210, 3½ hours), with departures roughly every two hours.

Buses to Bangued (P100, 1½ hours, every 30 minutes until 4.30pm) depart from the main bus and jeepney terminal near the public market.

Getting Around

Vigan is one of the few remaining towns in the Philippines where *kalesa* are still in use (P150 per hour). Whole day tours will run you around P1000, but pick your driver wisely, as English is not always strong. A tricycle ride should cost P10 within town (more at night).

Around Vigan

Worth the one-hour drive south of Vigan is the **Santa Maria Church**. A massive baroque structure built in 1769, this Unesco World Heritage site is utterly unique. It has an imposing brick facade and sits alone on a hill – rather than in the town square like most Spanish churches – overlooking the town of Santa Maria, giving it an Alamo kinda vibe. It's not hard to see why it was used as a fortress during the Philippine Revolution in 1896.

Located in Magsingal, 11km north of Vigan, a branch of the **National Museum** (admission free; ⏲8am-noon & 1-5pm Mon-Fri) displays Ilocano and Cordillera relics. An ancient-looking belfry (1732), part of the remains of a ruined old church, still stands in front of the museum, which itself was once a convent for a ruined church. The church was replaced in 1827 by the nearby **Magsingal Church**, which houses two sculptures of (wait for it) pregnant-looking angel mermaids.

Laoag

☎077 / POP 102,500

Like Vigan, this is a town with some history behind it. Unlike Vigan, said history is pretty much nowhere to be seen, and Laoag comes off as a noisy step to something better. This is still loyal Marcos country, and around here the old dictator is still referred to somewhat reverently as 'President Marcos'.

Sights

St William's Cathedral CHURCH

The Italian Renaissance–style St William's Cathedral was built in the 1870s, presumably long before the McDonald's that sits right in front of it. Its weathered **bell tower** is gradually sinking into the soft riverside loam; note the low-slung entryway.

Museo Ilocos Norte MUSEUM

(☎770 4587; www.museoilocosnorte.com; Gen Antonio Luna St; admission P20; ⏲9am-noon & 1-5pm Mon-Sat, from 10am Sun) Housed in the historic Tabacalera warehouse, the snazzy Museo Ilocos Norte is one of the better ethnographic museums in the Philippines. It houses a large collection of Ilocano, Igorot and Itneg cultural artefacts and has a half-decent souvenir store to boot.

Sleeping

Isabel Suites HOTEL $

(☎770 4998; www.isabelsuites.com; Gen Segundo Ave; s/d from P850/1300; ❄📶) The doubles at the Isabel aren't exactly roomy, but they are tidy and have comfy queen-sized beds. The soundproofing is slightly better than at most places, which means you might be able to sleep until 6.30am instead of 6am.

Java Hotel HOTEL $$$

(☎770 5596; javahotel@gmail.com; Gen Segundo Ave; r/ste incl breakfast from P2180/3200; ❄📶🏊) The petrol station in the parking lot isn't exactly in keeping with the 'Balinese-Moroccan' theme (yeah, we were confused too), and the rooms aren't true to the theme either, but they are roomy and comfortable by Ilocos standards.

Texicano Hotel HOTEL $

(☎772 0606; Rizal Ave; fan s with/without bathroom P400/250, d with/without air-con from P800/4000; ❄📶) Even the ever-optimistic folks at the Laoag tourism office admit the Texicano is 'a bit...old'. Yes, it's not winning awards for, well, anything, but this is still a popular backpacker flophouse.

Eating & Drinking

Dap-ayan ti Ilocos Norte FOOD COURT $

(cnr Rizal Ave & V Llanes St; dishes from P50) An outdoor food court, this is a great place to sample local fare such as *bagnet*, empanadas and the legendary Ilocos *longganisa* (sausage).

Macy's Diner FUSION $

(Gen Segundo Ave; mains from P80; ⏲breakfast, lunch & dinner) This 1950s Americana diner (!) located below Isabel Suites may well be the only restaurant in the world where you can get a plate of dried, fermented shrimp to go along with your burger and fries.

La Preciosa FILIPINO $$

(☎773 1162; Rizal Ave; mains P150; ⏲lunch & dinner) Laoag's most elegant restaurant is high-

LEAD-ING THE WAY

Once you get up to Laoag, be sure to get in touch with the folks at the **Laoag Eco-Adventure Development Movement** (LEAD; ☎077-772 0538, 0919 873 5516; http://leadmovement.wordpress.com). The good people of LEAD are all about facilitating journeys into Ilocos Norte that are environmentally friendly and sustainable. Many of their activities focus on teambuilding and school trips, but casual tourists will want to contact LEAD to go sandboarding near Laoag. It's incredibly good fun to slice across what appears to be the Sahara. You'll want to contact the LEAD-affiliated **Wen! Travel & Tours** (☎077-770 3420, 0917 511 1050; wentravelandtours.tripod.com); rates run around P2500 for groups of up to four people. Wen! can also arrange treks, rafting and other eco-adventures across the whole of Ilocos Norte.

ly recommended for its large portions of delicious Ilocano specialities like *pinakbét* and grilled pork liver.

Information

The big banks all have branches around the intersection of Gen Segundo Ave and Rizal Ave, Laoag's main commercial thoroughfare. Gen Segundo Ave and Primo Lazaro Ave contain many internet cafes.

BOI (☎771 6855; Alejandro Bldg, AG Tupaz St) Visa extensions.

Getting There & Away

PAL and Cebu Pacific fly daily to Manila from the airport 7km west of town. Airport jeepneys (P15, 10 minutes) leave from Fariñas St; most say 'Laoag-Gabu'.

There is no shortage of buses to Manila (from P650, nine to 11 hours). Companies include **Partas** (☎772 1615; Gen Antonio Luna St), **Fariñas Trans** (☎772 0126; FR Castro Ave) and **Maria de Leon** (☎770 3532; AG Tupaz St). Most run a few deluxe overnight express buses.

Partas has frequent buses to Baguio (P500, seven hours). All buses heading south stop in Vigan (P140, two hours).

GMW/GV Florida (☎771 6466; Gen Segundo Ave) has five daily buses to Tuguegarao (around P500, seven hours) via Pagudpud (P120, 1½ hours) and Claveria (P240, three hours). Minibuses to Pagudpud (around P80) leave every 30 minutes from behind the Provincial Capitol Building.

Laoag–Batac–Paoay jeepneys leave from Hernando Ave. Laoag–Nagbacalan–Paoay jeepneys take the coastal road to Paoay (45 minutes) via the Fort Ilocandia turn-off and Malacañang of the North (30 minutes). They depart from Fariñas St.

Jeepneys bound for Fort Ilocandia (25 minutes) say 'Calayab' and depart from in front of St William's Cathedral.

Around Laoag

FORT ILOCANDIA

Located near the beach in the barangay of Calayab, 9km south of central Laoag, the sprawling **Fort Ilocandia Resort & Casino** (☎02-839 1390; www.fortilocandia.com.ph; r from P3920;) draws in hordes of baccarat-hungry tourists from Taiwan, just a one-hour flight away. The complex was originally built by the Marcos family for their daughter Irene's wedding reception. Rooms, service and restaurants are all GBG: good but gaudy.

There are some fun activities going on here that are open to both guests and non-guests. Immediately south of the resort the unique and seemingly endless **Suba Sand Dunes** sprawl south all the way to Paoay. Scenes from *Mad Max, Born on the Fourth of July* and many a Filipino movie have been filmed here. The resort rents out all-terrain vehicles (P550 per 20 minutes). Another option is to fly over the dunes in the resort's **hot-air balloon** (P1400 per person), but we prefer exploring this area with the folks from the LEAD movement.

BATAC

The embalmed body of Ferdinand Marcos (1917–89) is laid out on a mattress and lit by floodlights in an otherwise dark room at the **Marcos Museum & Mausoleum** (barangay Lacub; admission free; 9am-noon & 1-4pm). Full creepiness is achieved by eerie choral music played on a continuous loop.

It's a sign of the family's continued political influence that the body was allowed to be returned to his boyhood home. And it's testament to the ambivalence (and often outright hostility) to Marcos' legacy that prompts many Filipinos to suspect the body is simply a wax figure, one last-ditch con by the master puppet master.

The impressive **Marcos ancestral home** is next door, with some reverential displays out front.

PAOAY

From Batac it's just 4km west to Paoay (pow-*why*), where you'll find North Luzon's most famous church. **Paoay Church** was built in classic earthquake-baroque style, with massive brick reinforcements running along its sides. The walls are made of thick coral blocks and stucco-plastered bricks, sealed with a mixture of limestone mortar and sugar-cane juice. Begun in 1704 and finished 90 years later, it's architecturally unique: an incongruous, yet beautiful blend of Gothic, Chinese, Japanese and even Javanese influences (notice how the layered profile bears resemblance to the famous stepped pyramid of Borobudur). Unlike other beautiful churches of the region, Paoay Church is not encroached upon by shops, schools or food stalls. Along with its towering belfry, it stands in a wide-open square, revealed in all its splendour and glory. Unesco named it a World Heritage site in 1993.

Heading back north to Laoag via the coastal route takes you through Suba, home to scenic Paoay Lake and **Malacañang of the North** (admission P20; ⊙9-11.30am & 1-4pm Tue-Sun), the opulent former residence of the Marcos family. The impressive house, with its cavernous *sala,* capiz-shell windows and other colonial touches, provides a glimpse into the family's lavish lifestyle.

Pagudpud & Around

☎077 / POP 20,400

Straight up: Pagudpud is incredible. White-sand beach, swaying green palms, water that shimmers through every cool shade of blue. Singing frogs at night, friendly locals by day. Plus: a clutch of stylishly renovated hotels and 'next big thing on the surfing circuit' street cred are finally putting this lonely stretch of coastline on the tourist map, although it remains decidedly sleepy compared with Boracay (hooray, we say).

Sights

Pagudpud actually consists of three vast beaches, strung along Luzon's northern edge and hemmed in by headlands. Coconut-palm-backed **Saud Beach** is where most resorts are to be found. Idyllic Blue Lagoon is a few headlands east. Deserted **Pansian Beach** is still further on, near the border of Cagayan Province.

About 30km to the west of Pagudpud is the impressive **Cape Bojeador Lighthouse**; closer by are the **windmills** of beautiful Bangui Bay. **Kabigan Falls**, located in the interior jungle, is 120m of crashing white water accessible via group tours by all hotels or private tricyle hire (around P650 return).

Blue Lagoon BEACH

At Blue Lagoon, Luzon's whitest sand and bluest water conspire majestically to compete for a place on your desktop screensaver. There's terrific snorkelling here and despite the recent opening of a few resorts, the beach is rarely crowded. It's 16km from Saud to the beach turn-off, then another 4km down a sealed road.

Lovers Rocks LANDMARKS

Near Barangay Balaoi you can spot **Dos Hermanos**, a pair of inaccessible offshore islands that local legend claims are the remains of two sibling fishermen lost at sea. Past here are the most Freudian geographical formations in Pagudpud: **Bantay-abot** ('Mountain with a hole'), an offshore hole in a rocky islet, and **Timmangtang Rock**, a stubby lump of rock and jungle. Collectively, the two formations are known as the Lovers Rocks. Don't make us spell out why. You can walk to either of these islets in low tide, but *ask a local,* be it your resort or trike driver, if it's safe, lest you risk getting stranded or worse when the tides change.

Activities

Pagudpud is growing in popularity as a **surfing** spot – some real giants occasionally form at Blue Lagoon, and Saud also gets well-shaped if fickle waves. The peak surf season is August to October. Boards (P200 per hour) and lessons (P400 per hour) are available at Kapuluan Vista Resort. Be careful about swimming when conditions are rough as there's a nasty undertow.

Almost all resorts rent out **mountain bikes** (per hr P60) and Terra Rika Beach Resort has a dive centre.

The pleasant mountain town of **Adams** has good trekking and several waterfalls. A stretch of the Bulu River recently opened for inner-tubing. **Wen! Travel & Tours** (☎0917 511 1050) can help arrange tubing trips. The best rapids occur from August to October. The rough 14km road to Adams starts near

Pansian Beach. Motorcycle taxis (around P170) await passengers at the turn-off.

Sleeping & Eating

Accommodation rates drop precipitously in low season (June to December); the following reviews list high-season rates (January to April). A lot of homestays have opened in the village that abuts Saud Beach (follow the road past the big bend near Saud Beach Resort). The going rate at the time of research for fan/air-con rooms was P600/1000.

SAUD BEACH

The following resorts are clustered at the more attractive west end of Saud Beach. All accommodation bases are covered here.

Apo Idon BEACH RESORT $$$
(786 1491, 0917 510 0671; www.apoidon.com; r/ste from P4800/6000;) The fanciest resort along Saud Beach, with nicely designed rooms featuring Ifugao art, capiz-shell windows and Western-style mod-cons.

Terra Rika Beach Resort BEACH RESORT $$
(676 1599, 0918 937 1752; www.terrarika.com; r from P2500;) There's a large range of rooms on offer at Terra Rika. The somewhat disingenuously-dubbed 'deluxe' rooms are not worth the price, but more expensive cottages, with dark wood and white linen sheets, are a solid bet.

Evangeline Beach Resort BEACH RESORT $$
(655 5862, 0929 878 0335; www.evangelinebeachresort.net; d/q incl breakfast from P2600/3700;) Evangeline has upped its game, transforming previously Spartan rooms into Bali-chic style accommodation. Aim for the suites, which tend to be the best deal on the property.

Saud Beach Resort BEACH RESORT $$$
(in Manila 02-921 2856; www.saudbeachresort.com; d/tr/q incl breakfast from P3620/3950/4312;) The service here is on the ball, but the tiki-chic rooms are a bit overpriced for what you get. That said, the resort has lots of space and rooms spread out over one of the largest properties on the beach.

Villa Del Mar Beach Resort BEACH RESORT $$
(0921 295 8196; www.villadelmarpagudpud.com; tr with fan/air-con from P1590/1890, cottage from P4500;) A nice upscale option, the Villa has pretty exteriors with thatch roofs and polished timber eaves. The interiors don't quite live up to the promise – they're a bit austere, to be honest – but are clean and comfortable.

Northridge Resort BEACH RESORT $$
(0920 220 5089; http://northridgeresort.com; r without/with air-con P1200/1500;) A good backpacker option, the Northridge has clean, well-kept doubles and helpful staff who are happy to arrange bicycle rentals and transportation.

Jun & Carol Beach Cottages BEACH RESORT $$
(0920 574 0136; http://juncarolbeachresort.com; r from P2500;) Another good choice, Jun & Carol has a good spread of cosy rooms, a thatched dining arcade and an easy-breezy tropical vibe.

BLUE LAGOON

Hannah's Beach Resort BEACH RESORT $$$
(0928 520 6255; www.hannahsbeachresort.com; r/ste from P2500/6000;) Hannah's is a high-end slice of heaven, overlooking a beautiful cove, sprinkled with plush little cottages and villas. Some are admittedly a bit bare bones, but as you move up the considerably large ladder of price options, you can find some frankly luxurious lodgings, all the while served by a huge menu of activities and professional service.

Kapuluan Vista Resort BEACH RESORT $$$
(0920 952 2528; www.kapulanvista.com; dm per person without bathroom P600, d incl breakfast from P2700;) This urbane resort was conceived as a surf resort but now caters to all types. It's an excellent all-round option, with stellar food and a good variety of attractive rooms set around the well-kept grounds.

Getting There & Away

The highway around here is spectacular in spots. If you're coming from Laoag, get a seat on the left side of the bus.

Frequent buses travel the coastal road to Laoag (P80 to P100, 1½ hours) and Claveria (P70, 1¼ hours).

There are also plans for new services: by the time you read this (and if you're feeling especially fond of bus travel in the Philippines), you'll be able to take Florida buses from Pagudpud (or even Claveria) all the way back to Manila.

THE CORDILLERA

To many travellers, North Luzon is simply the Cordillera. These spiny mountains, which top out at around 2900m, are beloved, worshipped and feared in equal doses by those who witness them and those who live among them.

The Cordillera

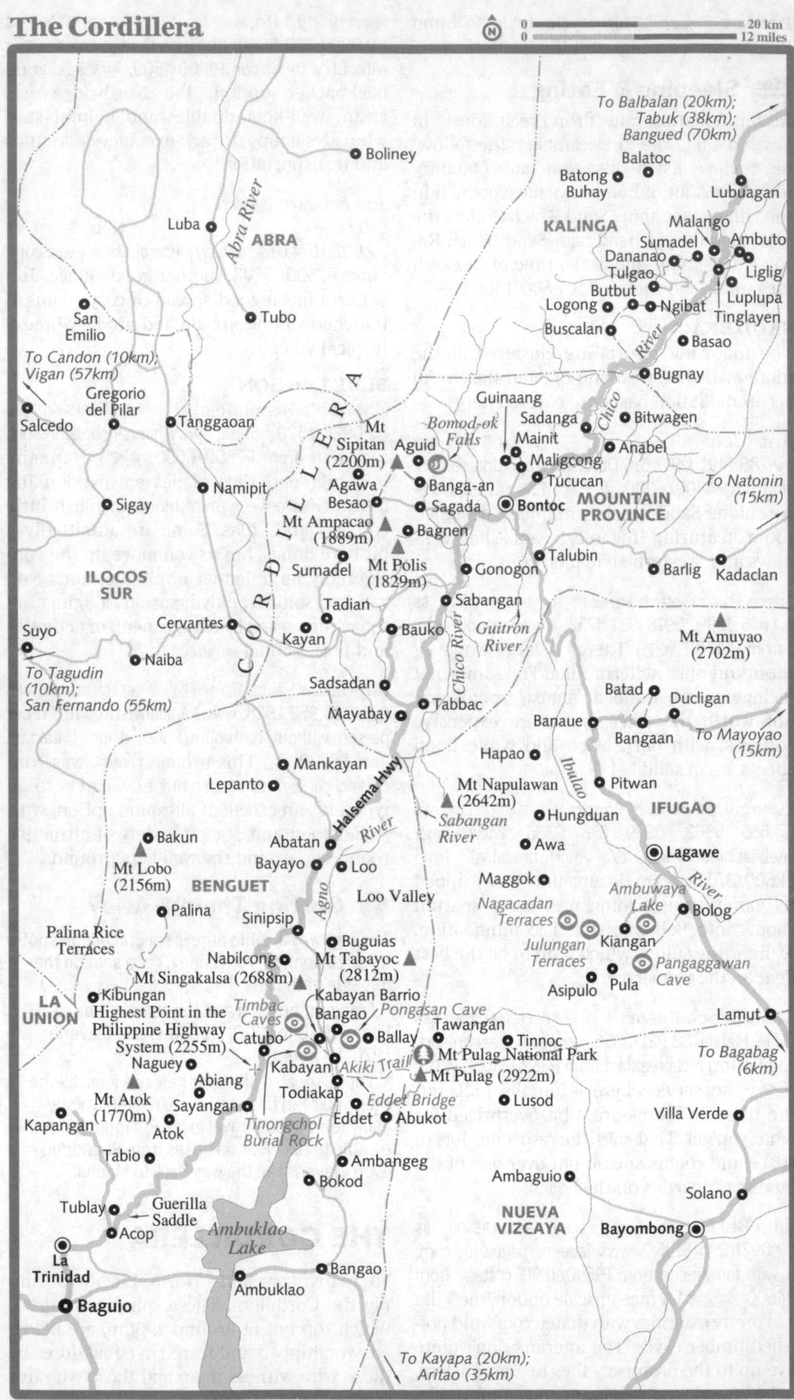

NORTH LUZON THE CORDILLERA

The people of the Cordillera, collectively known as the Igorot, own a fascinating culture that is reflected in the area's varied and multitudinous attractions. Banaue's renowned rice terraces have been dubbed 'the eighth wonder of the world', and they thoroughly deserve the label. Lesser-known but no less spectacular terraces exist throughout Ifugao, Mountain Province and Kalinga.

Baguio

☎074 / POP 305,000 / ELEV 1450M

Every country in Southeast Asia has an upland, pine-clad retreat from the heat and dust of the lowlands, and Baguio (*bah*-gee-oh) is the Philippines' exemplar of the genre. Like other hill stations, Baguio is a university town that boasts one of the Philippines' largest student populations (a quarter of a million!), and is also a crossroads between hill tribe culture and lowland settlers. For most travellers, Baguio serves as the primary gateway to backpacker bliss up north in Sagada, Banaue and Kalinga.

Sadly, thousands of jeepneys, taxis and trikes are responsible for almost unbearable levels of smog in the city centre, and long-time Baguio dwellers wax nostalgic about the days before SM Mall marred every view and traffic clogged every street. Away from the traffic-snarled city centre, Baguio is airy and pleasant. If you're returning from the mountains, the small-scale urban mayhem, nightlife and burgeoning restaurant scene are actually refreshing.

Sights & Activities

The city radiates in all directions from Burnham Park. The character of the city changes dramatically south and east of the centre as chaos gives way to green parks, towering Benguet pines, lavish summer homes and winding roads with spectacular views. The Baguio Botanic Gardens, Wright Park, Camp John Hay and Mines View Park are among the many (free) wide-open spaces in this part of town offering peace, quiet and fresh mountain air.

TOP CHOICE BenCab Museum MUSEUM

(☎442 7165; bencabmuseum.org; Km 6, Asin Rd, Tadiangan; adult/student & senior P100/80; ⏲9am-6pm Tue-Sun) The museum dedicated to the life, times and work of Benedicto Reyes Cabrera – otherwise known as BenCab – is as fascinating as the man who is its subject. Located on the outskirts of town, the BenCab gallery is a mix of high glass panes slanting light into modern art colonnades offset by walls of traditional animist wood carvings, rice Gods and jungle spirits (plus, there's a saucy erotic art section tucked away in a corner). To come here is to experience Filipino crafts and modern art displayed in tandem, in a space that evokes both ultramodernism and is partly modelled after a traditional rice terrace. To get here, either take a jeepney to Asin and ask to be let off at BenCab, or hire a cab (P150).

Tam-awan Village CULTURAL VILLAGE

(☎446 2949; www.tam-awanvillage.com; Long-Long Rd, Pinsao; admission P50) Eight traditional Ifugao homes and two rare octagonal Kalinga huts were taken apart and reassembled at this artists' village on the northwest edge of the city. On a clear day you can see the South China Sea, hence the name Tam-awan, which means 'vantage point'.

The Chanum Foundation, headed by well-known contemporary artist Ben Cabrera ('BenCab'), developed the project in line with its mission to preserve and teach the art and culture of the Cordillera people. The foundation sponsors several local artists who paint and show their works here. Chit Asignacion, the vice-president of the foundation, is a great source of historical and practical information about the area.

Guests at Tam-awan Village can participate in art workshops, learn dream-catcher making and see indigenous music and dance demonstrations. Workshops should be arranged in advance (P400 per session). You can also stay here; spending the night in one of these **huts** (single/double P500/900) is a rare treat.

To get here, take a taxi (P7) or a Quezon Hill–Tam-awan or Tam-awan–Long-Long jeepney from the corner of Shaghem and Kayang Sts. Combine your trip here with a visit to the Easter Weaving Room (p127), which is roughly on the way.

FREE St Louis University Museum MUSEUM

(☎442 3043; ⏲7.30am-noon & 1.30-5pm Mon-Sat) The St Louis University Museum, in the basement of the campus library, is run by Ike Picpican, one of the country's foremost authorities on the history and culture of the Cordillera people. There's a strong collection of weapons, basketry and other hill tribe ethnographic artefacts, and the placards are

Baguio

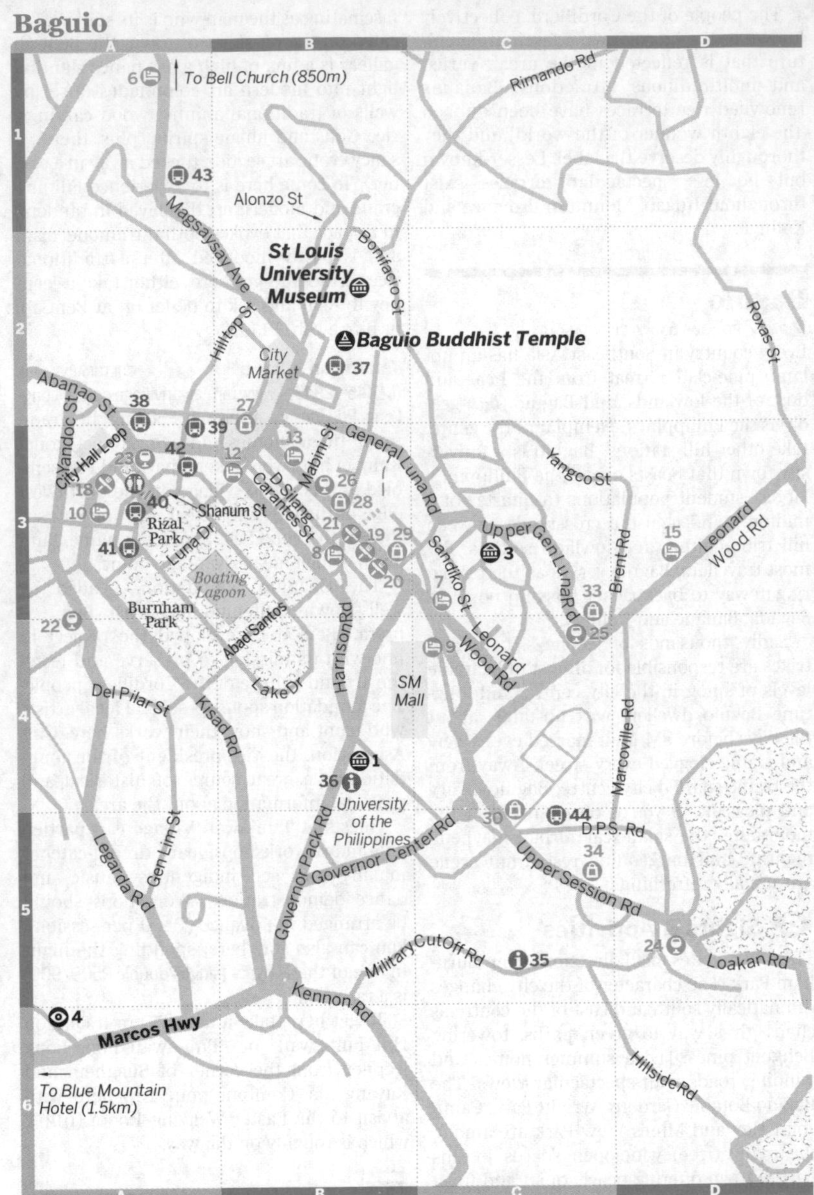

well written, but it helps if Ike is around to explain their context. Free tours end with participatory native-instrument jam sessions. To get here, you leave some form of ID with the front security folks at St Louis University.

Emilio Aguinaldo Museum MUSEUM
(Aguinaldo Park, Gen Luna Rd; admission P10; ⏲10am-noon & 1-4pm Wed-Sun) More of a 'repository of stuff' as opposed to an inquisitive museum, this is nonetheless a good spot to gain some insight into the life and times of

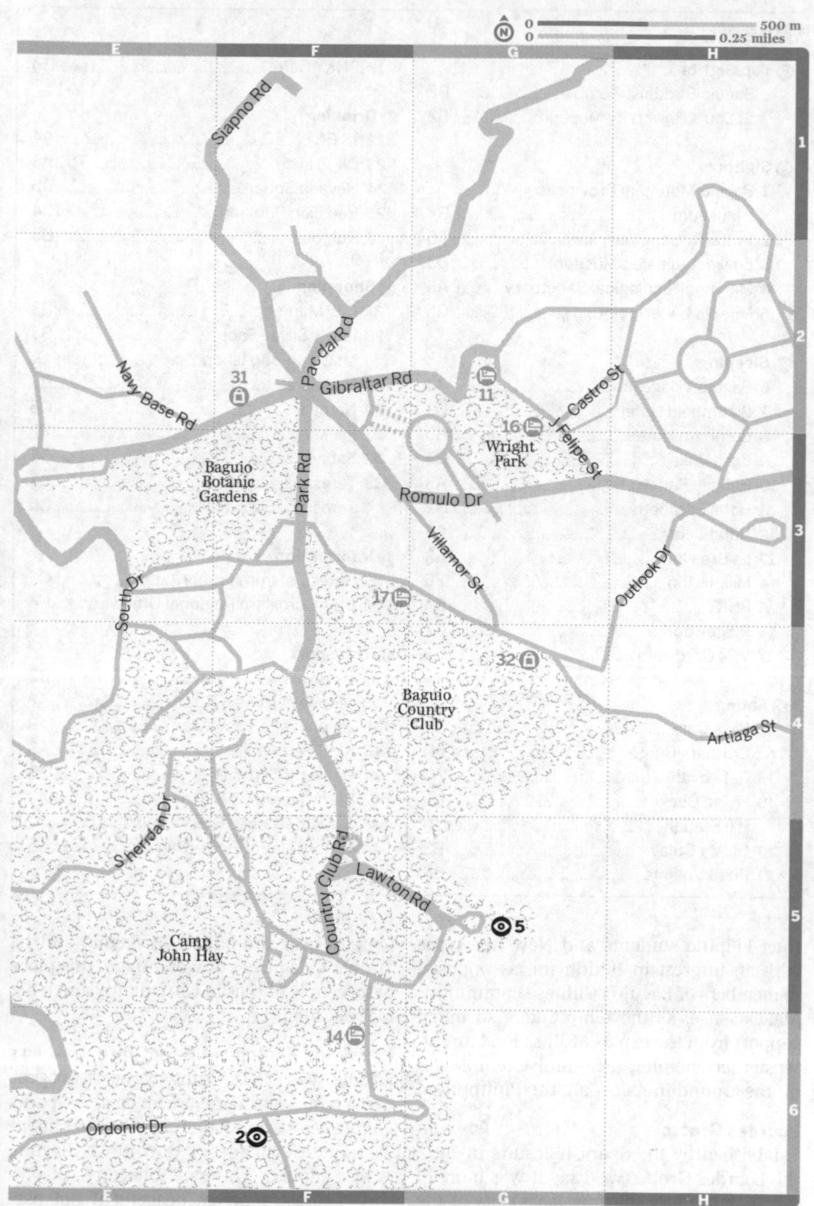

independence leader Emilio Aguinaldo. The main event is a collection of Aguinaldo's personal effects and the Philippines' first national flag. Visitors will get a better sense of the events surrounding the independence fight against the Spanish, and then Americans.

Baguio Buddhist Temple TEMPLE

This tough-to-find Buddhist temple is near the campus of St Louis University, and is located off Assumption Rd. There's a 6m sitting Buddha and interesting views of the city-market area. The temple tends to at-

Baguio

Top Sights

Baguio Buddhist Temple B2
St Louis University Museum B2

Sights

1 Baguio Mountain Provinces Museum B4
2 Butterfly Sanctuary F6
3 Emilio Aguinaldo Museum C3
4 Maryknoll Ecological Sanctuary A6
5 Mile High Viewpoint G5

Sleeping

6 Baguio Village Inn A1
7 Bloomfield Hotel C3
8 Burnham Hotel B3
9 Casa Vallejo C4
10 Holiday Park Hotel A3
11 Hotel Elizabeth G2
12 Hotel Veniz B3
13 La Brea Inn B3
14 Mile-Hi Inn F6
15 PNKY D3
16 Ridgewood G2
17 Villa Cordillera F3

Eating

Bliss Cafe ..... (see 11)
Brothers Burger ..... (see 14)
18 Cafe by the Ruins A3
19 Flying Gecko B3
Hill Station ..... (see 9)
20 Oh My Gulay B3
21 Pizza Volante B3
PNKY Cafe ..... (see 15)

Drinking

22 18 BC A4
23 City Tavern A3
24 Nevada Square D5
25 Red Lion Pub/Inn C4
26 Rumours B3

Shopping

27 City Market B3
28 Ibay's Silver Shop B3
Mt Cloud Bookshop ..... (see 9)
29 Namaste B3
30 Narda's C5
31 Pilak F2
32 Sabado's G4
33 Teresita's Main Shop C3
34 Teresita's Showroom C5

Information

35 Bureau of Immigration C5
36 DOT Cordillera Regional Office B4

Transport

37 Dangwa Bus Terminal B2
38 Jeepneys to Asin Rd A2
39 Jeepneys to Tam-awan A3
40 KMS Terminal A3
41 Ohayami Terminal A3
42 Plaza Jeepney Terminal A3
43 Slaughterhouse Bus Terminal A1
44 Victory Liner Bus Terminal C5

tract Filipino students and New Age types with an interest in Buddhism, as opposed to members of Baguio's Chinese community. Makes sense, as the temple gets so much support from the expats at Bliss Restaurant. Westerners helping a Buddhist temple get off the ground in Asia – ah, the Philippines.

Lourdes Grotto MONUMENT

Established by the Spanish Jesuits in 1907, the Lourdes Grotto (we'd say it was more of a cave, but who's splitting hairs) sits at the top of 252 steps. From the top, there's a nice view of the city's rooftops. Sometimes the approaches are enhanced with life-size statues of famous saints.

Bell Church CHURCH

(La Trinidad Rd; 6am-5pm) The Bell Church consists of several ornate, pagoda-roofed temples near the border of Baguio and La Trinidad. As places of worship go, this place has a couple of toes in Christianity and a big foot in China.

Maryknoll Ecological Sanctuary PARK

(0912 431 4622; http://maryknollecological.weebly.com; Camp Sioco; 8am-5pm) As parks go, the Maryknoll Sanctuary, located about 25 minutes outside of downtown Baguio, is nice enough. There's 2.8 hectares of preserved forest – pretty, peaceful if not particularly striking. What does wow us about Maryknoll is the 'Cosmic Journey', a pathway that threads through a series of art installations that measures the evolution of humanity in the Philippines via hill tribe artefacts, surreal sculpture and a maximum amount of New Age discourse. Appreciating this 'journey' almost inevitably involves bridging a cultural gap; most Filipinos find the journey reverential, while most foreigners tend to find it kitschy in the extreme.

Camp John Hay MOUNTAIN RESORT
(☎442 7902) Formerly a US military rest-and-recreation facility, 246-hectare Camp John Hay has been reinvented as a mountain resort with restaurants, hotels, shops and a fantastic golf course sprinkled amid rolling hills and stands of Benguet pines. The Historical Core is worth a visit, with the attractively landscaped Bell Amphitheatre and some walking trails. Nearby is the unique Choco-Laté de Batriol restaurant. There's a nice panorama from the **Mile High viewpoint**, and the **Butterfly Sanctuary** is also worth a look. It's free to enter Camp John Hay, although modest admission fees apply to some sights.

Baguio Mountain Provinces Museum MUSEUM
(☎444 7541; Governor Pack Rd; ⌚9am-5pm Mon-Sat) The collection of Cordillera artefacts at the Baguio Mountain Provinces Museum isn't quite as impressive as the showcase in St Louis, but the museum also has a compelling exhibition on the history of Baguio, with some superb old photos and placards chronicling the city's role in WWII. There's also one Kabayan mummy on display.

Mt Santo Tomas HIKING
The highest peak around Baguio, 2200m Mt Santo Tomas, just south of the city off the Marcos Hwy, affords good mountain-biking and hiking opportunities. It's a two-hour walk to the top from the trailhead up an easy-to-navigate road.

Sleeping

Consider staying out of the centre to escape Baguio's notorious noise and air pollution. Be sure to ask for the 'promo rate' (or just a discount) in the off-season.

The most unique budget choice is Tamawan Village (p121), but note that it's at least a 15-minute ride from the centre.

TOP CHOICE **PNKY** B&B $$
(☎444 5418, 0922 818 4247; pnkyhome.com; 13 Leonard Wood Rd; r summer/winter P2480/3100; wi-fi) There's so much creativity and intellectual energy in Baguio – and none of it seems to extend to the accommodation scene. The PNKY puts paid to this stereotype. This B&B has four rooms that resemble hip Soho lofts, all highly individualised (the Van Gogh room, for example, is decorated in rich oranges and painted sunflowers). Plus: there's a gorgeous common room decorated with items for sale from an art-and-handicraft store downstairs.

Casa Vallejo BOUTIQUE HOTEL $$$
(☎424 3397; www.casavallejobaguio.com; Upper Session Rd; d/ste from P2700/3600; non-smoking, air-con, internet) A beautiful beast of a boutique hotel, situated in a classic historical building that looks like the sort of spot where colonial-era gentlemen with floppy white moustaches rabbit on about having a grand spot of tiger hunting. The rooms don't quite fulfil the grand promise of the exterior, but they're attractive studies in classy understatement, with off-white floors and dark wood accents.

Burnham Hotel HOTEL $$
(☎442 2331; www.burnhamhotelbaguio.com; 21 Calderon St; d from P1000; wi-fi) This old-fashioned hotel in the city centre has a wonderful common area festooned with indigenous handicrafts, antiques and old photos. The rooms are also attractively decorated, although some are looking a little threadbare these days. Request one away from the noisy street.

Ridgewood HOTEL $$$
(☎446 6295; www.ridgewoodhotel.com; 17 J Felipe St; d/ste P2800/3900; non-smoking, air-con, wi-fi) This wood-and-brick number out by Wright Park offers top-end conveniences at midrange prices. If you don't mind being away from the city centre – and in Baguio, you shouldn't – you'll enjoy this refreshingly quiet gem, which boasts soft duvet covers, twice-per-day cleaning service and access to Baguio Country Club's golf course.

Baguio Village Inn HOTEL $
(☎442 3901; 356 Magsaysay Ave; r without bathroom per person P300, d with bathroom from P850) This warm and inviting backpacker special is reminiscent of the cosy pinewood guesthouses in Sagada and Banaue. Request a room at the back.

Blue Mountain Hotel HOTEL $
(☎0917 507 2030, 443 8411; Marcos Hwy; d from P600; wi-fi) The colour scheme of the exterior lives up to its name: powder blue and standing tall. Inside you'll find a take-and-give-no-guff owner and pretty, well-furnished rooms.

Hotel Veniz HOTEL $$
(☎0917 506 0701, 446 0700; www.hotelveniz.com; 1 Abanao St; s/d from P1200/1400; wi-fi) A bit

plain, but a solid midrange option for those who love their wi-fi, cable TV and functional if boring rooms.

La Brea Inn HOTEL **$$**
(☎446 6061, SMS 0917 508 7800; labrea.webs.com; 24 Session Rd; d from P1100; 📶) This spick-and-span, no-frills option manages to seal the noise off better than most hotels in the centre. Free wi-fi in the lobby.

Villa Cordillera HOTEL **$$**
(☎619 2062; villacordillera.com; 6 Outlook Dr; d/tr/q P1600/2400/3200; 📶) There's a cabin-in-the-woods feel to this lodge overlooking Baguio Country Club. Well removed from the centre, it's so quiet you'll hardly realise you're in Baguio. Rooms are spiffy with wood floors and tightly made single beds. Make sure to sample the scrumptious raisin bread.

Mile-Hi Inn HOTEL **$**
(☎446 6141; Mile-Hi Center; dm/d P600/1800) Its motto is 'clean, cosy, comfy', and frankly it would be hard to argue with that. Located in Camp John Hay's duty-free shopping centre, it has four four-bed dorm rooms.

Bloomfield Hotel HOTEL **$$$**
(☎446 9112; www.bloomfieldhotel.com; 3 Leonard Wood Rd; d/ste from P2140/3390; 🚭❄📶) This snazzy spot near SM Mall has tastefully austere rooms with inviting, duvet-covered beds. The suites, with king-sized beds, are worth the splurge.

Holiday Park Hotel HOTEL **$$**
(☎619 2807; 129 Abanao St Extension; r/ste P1800/3800; 🚭❄📶) One of the more modern properties in town falls just short of Bloomfield Hotel in terms of panache, but it has bigger rooms, better soundproofing and, in general, a more professional vibe.

Hotel Elizabeth HOTEL **$$$**
(☎619 0367; www.hotelelizabeth.com.ph; 1 J Felipe St; r from P3800; 🚭❄📶) This enormous hotel is Baguio's most service-oriented, and gives 20% off-season discounts. Lacking in soul but overwhelming in amenities like swimming pools, gyms etc. The mustard and purple colour scheme in the rooms works surprisingly well.

Eating

Baguio has arguably the best dining in the Philippines pound-for-pound. The Mile-Hi Center in Camp John Hay has several good eating options, including the always reliable **Brothers Burger** (☎446 5702; black Angus burgers P250), which delivers.

TOP CHOICE **Cafe by the Ruins** FUSION **$$**
(☎442 4010; 25 Chuntug St; mains P150-325; ⏰7am-9pm; 🖉) Baguio's most beloved restaurant is a relaxing refuge in the middle of the bustling city. The interior is awash in art, foliage and sculpted wood. It specialises in Cordillera-inspired Filipino dishes: try the eggplant omelette with carabao cottage cheese for breakfast, or the *suman at tsocolate* (hot chocolate and sticky-rice cake) for afternoon tea.

Hill Station FUSION **$$$**
(Casa Vallejo, Upper Session Rd; mains P250-450; ⏰lunch & dinner; 🖉) The Hill Station is certainly the most creative and ambitious restaurant in Baguio. The menu reads like a foodie's fantasy tour of the world: crispy slow-cooked duck flakes, beef stewed in cinnamon and oregano, and roasted Mediterranean vegetables. Not all dishes win, but the food is pretty wonderful overall, and custom cocktails are even better.

PNKY Cafe FUSION **$$**
(☎444 5418; 13 Leonard Wood Rd; mains P150-350; ⏰lunch & dinner) Belgian *frites* and fried tofu share the starters page, setting the East meets West tone of this hip eatery. To be fair (or is that fare?), the main courses are more European in origin, which you may find a relief after too much *sisig*. Our favourite selections on this menu come from the pasta page.

Bliss Cafe VEGETARIAN **$$**
(☎619 0367, 0917 846 4729; www.blissnbaguio.multiply.com; mains P150-250; ⏰11am-9pm; 🖉) There are Buddhas on the tables, Chinese art on the walls, modern decor in the niches and a general sense of delicious funkiness at this earthy lacto-vegetarian restaurant at Hotel Elizabeth. Owner-chef Shanti home-cooks delectable vegetarian pasta and a few Indian dishes. You may want to call ahead before arriving to make sure it's open.

Oh My Gulay VEGETARIAN **$$**
(La Azotea Bldg, Session Rd; mains P150-250; ⏰11am-8.30pm; 🖉) Baguio's most creative interior is five storeys up under a vast atrium. It's like a giant tree fort, with bridges, ladders and little nooks to hide in. The mercifully compact all-vegetarian menu is equally creative – try the tofu *lumpia* (small spring rolls) salad.

WWOOFING AWAY IN BENGUET

Vegetarian restaurants and organic produce are all the rage in Baguio, but you can do more than just eat the wonderful veggies plucked from the earth in surrounding Benguet province. Fulfil your farming fantasies as a WWOOF (World Wide Opportunities on Organic Farms) volunteer on the Cosalan family's organic **Enca Farm** (☎0919 834 4542; www.encaorganicfarm.com) in Acop, Benguet, an hour north of La Trinidad on the Halsema Hwy. You can also try to arrange your trip via Enca's USA office at ☎+1 425 698 5808.

The contact person at the farm is Marilyn Cosalan, whose family has been farming for generations using indigenous Ibaloi methods. The family lost its original *kintoman* (red) rice farm in nearby Itogon to unchecked copper mining, which destroyed hectares of farmland and killed several rivers in southern Benguet in the Marcos era. The family's new farm grows beans, lettuce, broccoli, carrots, radish and coffee. Volunteers usually do about eight hours of farm work per day. Accommodation is in rustic but cosy lodging onsite and is very cheap – P250 a night. Short-term visitors are highly encouraged to check the farm out. On off-days you can go hiking or explore the nearby Bengaongao and Paterno caves.

Marilyn can meet volunteers in Baguio or you can get there on your own – take a Baguio-Acop jeepney from the Dangwa terminal to Acop (1½ hours). From the jeepney stop in Acop it's a 3km walk or jeepney ride to the farm. Contact Marilyn or the **Benguet Provincial Tourism Office** (☎422 1116) in La Trinidad for help getting to the farm.

Pizza Volante PIZZA $$
(☎445 0777; 82 Session Rd; 6/10in pizzas P100/200; ⊙24hr) The pan pizza here is tops in town, and it's not a bad place for a beer either, especially after everything else has closed. It also has a delivery service.

Flying Gecko FILIPINO $$
(☎444 9372; 102 Session Rd; sandwiches P145-220) Tranquil oasis on Session Rd that does decent Filipino fusion fare.

Drinking & Entertainment

Red Lion Pub/Inn PUB
(☎304 3078; tonyperlas54@yahoo.com; 92 Upper Gen Luna Rd; ⊙24hr) The 24-hour bar here is filled up with beer-swilling expats and travellers just about any time of day. It serves up good steaks and bad karaoke.

City Tavern BAR
(Abanao St; ⊙8am-3am) Live music is the name of the game at this creatively designed, open-air bar, a local favourite. Catch regular act Petune and its unique brand of tribal-infused reggae sung in various Cordillera dialects.

18 BC BAR
(16 Legarda Rd; ⊙6.30pm-late) Another local favourite for live music. Friday is reggae night, Saturday alternative night. Always crowded and fun on weekends.

Rumours BAR
(☎442 8153; Session Rd) A mellow, sophisticated place that draws its fair share of tourists, expats and local students. Some of the bar's speciality drinks will, in no uncertain terms, lay you on your arse but good.

Nevada Square CLUB
(off Military Circle, Loakan Rd) This innocuous-looking collection of bars and clubs turns into one wild and crazy fraternity party on weekends, complete with shooters, bar sports and inebriated Filipina students dancing on tabletops until the wee hours. It can be pretty quiet during the week.

Shopping

Baguio is a shopping mecca known for woodcarvings, traditional weavings, baskets, silver, and temperate fruits and vegies such as strawberries and cabbages.

Various hotels and boutiques in town hawk Ifugao *bulol* (rice guard) woodcarvings and rattan-laced baskets, but you can save up to 50% by buying such items wholesale from one of the many workshops that line Asin Rd, 7km west of the city centre. You can also watch Ifugao craftspeople doing their thing at these workshops. Take the Asin Rd jeepney from Kayang St. In Baguio, **Teresita's** (Main Shop 90 Upper Gen Luna Rd) and **Sabado's** (16 Outlook Dr) sell similar carvings, as well as antique *bulol* and, in Teresita's case, Igorot textiles and beads. Teresita's also has a showroom at 221 Upper Session Rd.

For genuine Igorot weavings and garments, both **Narda's** (151 Upper Session Rd;

BAGUIO & THE 'N' WORD

Filipinos are famously friendly people, but their attitudes towards race, civility and discourse are not always, shall we say, the most enlightened. The most egregious example we can cite from our research is frequent use of the 'N' word to describe Africans and people of African descent. Although we encountered casual use of this word everywhere in Luzon, the phrase seemed particularly common in Baguio, where there are many African (especially Sudanese) students attending local universities and some African-American US Peace Corps volunteers.

We talked with some of these volunteers (of all races), and their (and our) jury remains out as to whether this language is racist, or ignorant, or both. Some people said that Filipinos were simply unaware of how offensive the word was, yet continued using it despite gentle reminders. Others said that Filipinos were fully aware and simply don't care.

We can offer no good advice here except to be aware of the problem and keep patient. If you feel you must speak up, try to do so in as civil a manner as possible – in a situation where it is difficult to determine if the source of a comment is ignorance or malice, it's likely best to err on the side of caution.

⌚8am-7pm) and **Easter Weaving Room** (2 Easter School Rd) carry a broad selection of high-quality, locally made items. Easter Weaving Room sells everything from hand-woven bookmarks to *tapis* (woven wrap-around skirts). It's well organised and prices are clearly marked. In the basement factory you can watch women hard at work on their looms.

There are several silver shops in town, the best being **Ibay's Silver Shop** (☎444 2652; cnr Session Rd & Assumption Rd) and **Pilak** (☎442 3686; 37 Leonard Wood Rd). Both also have outlets at Mines View Park. For Tibetan and Nepalese jewellery and crafts, check out **Namaste** (Porta Vaga Bldg, Session Rd; ⌚10am-7pm).

Mt Cloud Bookshop BOOKS

(Casa Vallejo, Upper Session Rd). Is this the only boutique bookstore in Luzon? We can't claim for sure, but it's by far the hippest bookstore we found on the island, with a fantastic selection of Western and Filipino titles, with a trend towards historical and ethnographic nonfiction, although there's plenty of fiction too.

City Market MARKET

(Magsaysay Ave) Baguio's city market is a 3-sq-km maze of a 'useful things' market where vendors sell everything from lettuce to live poultry to low-quality crafts and souvenirs. Be prepared to haggle. There are some good eating options – find a spot that's crowded, pull up a stool, point at something that smells good and chow down.

Information

Banks and ATMs are all over the centre. Session Rd and its arteries are flooded with internet cafes.

BOI (☎447 0805; 38 Military Cut Off Rd) Visa extensions. At the time of writing, there were no BOI signs or address numbers on the building (sigh); look for the Greenwood School/Alex and Jenny, Inc. building and the Bureau is in the lobby.

DOT Cordillera Regional Office (☎442 6708/7014; Governor Pack Rd) Has information on tours and treks throughout the Cordillera.

Getting There & Away

Sky Pasada (WCC; ☎912 3333; www.skypasada.com) operates flights to and from Manila (P3426) and Batanes (P5285); by the time you read this, routes should be open to Tuguegarao as well.

The quickest, most comfortable buses to Manila are the nonstop, 29-seaters run by **Victory Liner** (☎619 0000; Upper Session Rd) to Pasay (P715, four to five hours, five daily). Many buses take the comfortable, fast SCTEX (Subic-Clark-Tarlac Expressway), but at the time of research only Victory Liner offers nonstop service. Reserve bus tickets ahead of time. Victory also has slower buses to Manila every 20 minutes (P455, 6½ hours); it accepts credit cards. **Genesis** (☎421 1425, 709 0545) also makes frequent trips to Manila from Governor Pack Rd.

Partas (☎725 1740, 410 1307) has hourly buses to Vigan (P350, five hours) from 8am till about 6pm, and San Fernando (La Union; P100, 1½ hours). In Vigan, you can switch over to frequent buses to Laoag (P180). Minibuses to San

Fernando (P70) leave frequently from the Plaza jeepney area east of Rizal Park.

GL Lizardo (☎304 5994) has hourly trips to Sagada (P230, six to seven hours) departing 6am to 1pm from the Dangwa terminal. **D'Rising Sun**, based at the Slaughterhouse terminal on Slaughterhouse Rd, has buses to Bontoc (P220, six hours) hourly from 6am to 4pm. Both of these services head along the Halsema Hwy. Also at the Slaughterhouse terminal you will find A-Liner, which services Kabayan (P170, four to five hours); buses leave from around 7am till 10am hourly, and a last bus makes the trip at 1pm. This scenic drive takes you along a paved road to Ambuklao Dam, from where it's an intensely bumpy 30km north to Kabayan. If the rains have been intense, this road may be washed out.

Remember: it takes as much time (eight to nine hours) to bus from Manila to Banaue as from Baguio to Banuae! Ohayami and KMS each have daily trips to Banaue (P480, 8½ hours) along the paved southern route, via San José, starting at about 7am and lasting until 2pm. Their terminals are near each other on Shanum St. A faster way to Banaue is to take an air-con van from the Dangwa terminal to Bambang (P200, four hours) via Ambuklao Rd. Bambang is about 2½ hours from Banaue by three jeepneys.

Kabayan

☎074 / POP 1300 / ELEV 1200M

Nestled amid dramatic, rice-terraced slabs of mountain terrain and watched over by its world-famous mummies, Kabayan remains a virtually untouched jewel.

If mummies aren't your thing, Kabayan is a nice place to hike, stargaze, breathe in exhaust-free air and marvel at the voluntary 7pm curfew. Kabayan is also the centre of Ibaloi culture, and many Ibaloi traditions and animistic beliefs linger, especially in the surrounding hills. The area is also known for strong Arabica coffee and tasty red *kintoman* rice.

You can find guides for Mt Pulag and the mummy caves through the Coop Lodge, Rockwood Cafe or the tourism department at the Municipal Hall.

Sights & Activities

Hiring a guide (P500 to P1500 for the day, depending on your activities) through the Coop Lodge is a good idea. Local guides are professional, courteous and can clue you in on all sorts of cultural background that would otherwise go over most travellers' heads.

Kabayan National Museum MUSEUM

(admission P20; ⌚8am-noon & 1-5pm Mon-Fri) This small 'museum' is more of an annex of Ibaloi, Kankanay and Ikalahan ritual artefacts, plus one lonely-looking mummy.

Mummy Caves CAVES

Although the forests around Kabayan are said to hide dozens of mummy caves that only Ibaloi elders can locate, there are only two main sites where you can see mummies: the Timbac Caves, 1200m above Kabayan, and the more accessible caves near *sitio*

MEETING TIMBAC'S MUMMIES

The centuries-old mummification procedure used in Kabayan is different from that of the nine other cultures that have practised mummification worldwide, because here the internal organs were not touched. The corpses were dried using the heat and smoke of a small fire, then meticulously bathed in herbal preservatives. Tobacco smoke was periodically blown into the abdominal cavities to drive out worms and preserve the organs. The whole process took up to six months.

The mummies have been frequently stolen and vandalised over the years, so the main caves are now under lock and key. The best-preserved mummies are in the **Timbac Caves** (admission P100). Located about 1200m above Kabayan proper, these are Kabayan's most sacred caves, and locals customarily make offerings of gin and *pinikpikan* before entering them. *Pinikpikan* is a local chicken dish, made by beating a live chicken to coagulate its blood. If this makes you uncomfortable, ask if you can replace the offering with cigarettes or rice.

Walking up here from Kabayan with an Ibaloi guide (P1500) is one of the most rewarding and culturally sensitive ways to experience the unique folkways of the Cordillera.

Be warned, however: it's a four- to six- hour, pretty much straight-up ascent to Timbac. You need to be in shape to make this trek, especially as you'll likely be doing so with your pack on your back.

(small village) **Bangao** in the foothills of Mt Tabayoc (2812m), 7km north of Kabayan. The most interesting is the **Pongasan Cave** (admission free), a half-hour climb straight up from Bangao, where you'll find five coffins with mummies. However, the mummies here are not as well preserved as those at Timbac.

Tinongchol Burial Rock CAVES

(suggested donation P20) About 3km northwest of Kabayan, near barangay Kabayan Barrio, is the Tinongchol Burial Rock, where several coffins have been leveraged into cut holes in a boulder. Getting here takes you past some stunning mountain vistas via a one-hour walk along a footpath that starts behind the national museum; the last portion of the walk is a steep uphill ascent. Either get the gate key and pay your donation to the barangay captain in Kabayan Barrio, or come here with a guide, which is probably the best option if you don't want to ask random villagers for directions to the spot.

Opdas Mass Burial Cave CAVE

(suggested donation P20) On the southern edge of town (indeed, practically in someone's backyard) is the spooky charnel house of Opdas Mass Burial Cave, containing hundreds of skulls and bones between 500 and 1000 years old.

Sleeping & Eating

Stores along the main road serve chicken and rice with whatever vegetable is in season. At night you'll likely hear locals drinking at some unofficial bottle house at night; they'd love to have you join, but it could be uncomfortable for female travellers.

Coop Lodge GUESTHOUSE $

(d without bathroom per person P200) This quaint spot on the main road has half-a-dozen simple doubles with bunk beds and tiny toilets designed for Smurfs. When it's full, the Municipal Hall makes its dorm rooms (P200) available.

Getting There & Away

Kabayan is well linked to Baguio's Slaughterhouse terminal by bus (P170, four to five hours); buses leave from around 7am till 10am hourly, last bus departs at 1pm.

The road north to Abatan makes the Halsema Hwy look like an autobahn. It's truly breathtaking but you'll need a good 4WD with high clearance.

For a more adventurous escape, hike to Timbac Caves and walk out to the Halsema Hwy, where you can flag down a bus going south to Baguio or north to Bontoc or Sagada.

Around Kabayan

MT PULAG NATIONAL PARK

Mt Pulag (2922m), considered sacred ground to the Ibaloi and Kalanguya, is the third-highest peak in the Philippines and anchors the Cordillera's largest national park. The **Protected Areas Office** (PAO; ☎0919 631 5402; www.pawb.gov.ph/protected/mt_pulag/pulagmain.htm) in Ambangeg, 1½ hours south of Kabayan, doubles as the park's visitor centre. There's a hefty P750 entrance fee for nonresidents, or P100 for residents, payable here or at other points of entry.

From the visitor centre a rough road climbs 11km to the start of the **Grassland Trail** near the Department of Environment & Natural Resources (DENR) ranger station, where you must hire a guide (P500) to navigate the final two to three hours to the summit. About 30 minutes beneath the summit is the 'grassland' campsite (P50).

A more interesting two- to three-day hike is the **Akiki Trail** – also known as the 'killer trail' – which starts 2km south of Kabayan in Todiakap, a *sitio* of Duacan. From the trailhead it's two hours to Eddet River and another six hours to the 'cow country' camping site. You can camp there or continue on another four hours and camp at the 'saddle grassland' campsite. It's just 30 minutes from there to the summit. A guide for this route costs P1200 per day.

There are still-longer routes up Mt Pulag that take you around the back of the mountain through Tawangan or Lusod, home of the Kalanguya. Call the PAO or ask guides in Kabayan for details. Visibility is best in March and April, and the area sees regular heavy downpours from June to November.

The remarkably large and well-kept PAO has a big dorm room (P150) upstairs and a kitchen for guests to use.

To get to the visitor centre, jump off the A-Liner Baguio–Kabayan bus in Ambangeg. If coming by bus from Baguio, you'll arrive too late to launch an assault on Mt Pulag, as it's often raining by 2pm, so plan to sleep a night in the PAO or in Kabayan and start early the next morning.

Sagada & Around

☎074 / POP 1550 / ELEV 1477M

Imagine: mists shredding through dark jungle valleys, lizards carved into coffins stacked like soda cans, bodies hanging from boulders and hot rice wine washing down sweet oatmeal cookies. Got that image in your head? Cool. Very cool, actually – you're imagining Sagada, and in terms of vibe and temperature, this is as cool as the Cordillera gets.

Sagada is the closest thing the Philippines has to a Southeast Asian backpacker mecca, but it's certainly no Sapa. This tranquil mountain town may get packed with travellers at times, but there's always a sense of calm and peace (partly due to the widespread consumption of cheap local pot). There is just one time of year that's incredibly busy here: Sagada fills up during Holy Week and the week between Christmas and New Year's, so book way ahead if you insist on visiting at these times.

Try to time your visit for a *begnas* (traditional Kankanay community celebration), when women wear *tapis* and older men don G-strings and gather in the *dap-ay* (outdoor patio); chickens are sacrificed, gongs are played and general merriment ensues. Sagadans are of Applai (northern Kankanay) ancestry and their native language is Kankanay, although, as in the rest of the Cordilleras, Ilocano and English are widely spoken.

Sights

Caves CAVES

On the road to Ambasing, near the spot where the road takes a hard curve to the right (if heading downhill), you can see the **Sugong hanging coffins** suspended from the cliff face. A short distance further, the road forks at the Right Turn Cafe. Take the left fork, follow it for 200m and look for a path to your left that leads down to the **Lumiang Burial Cave**. Over 100 coffins are stacked in the entrance, the oldest believed

Sagada

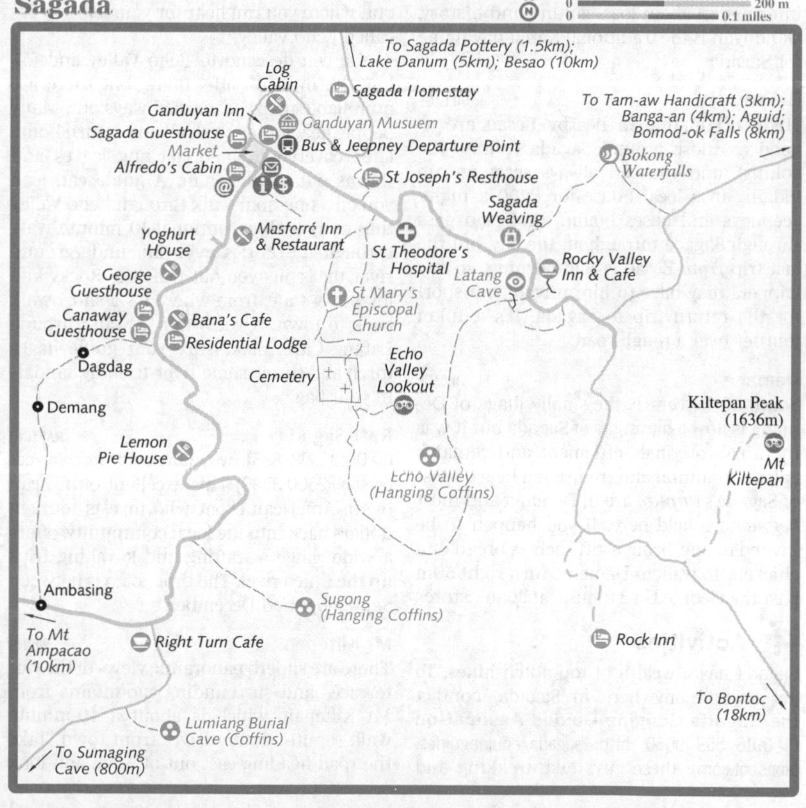

to be about 500 years old. Many are carved with images of lizards, which are symbols of long life and fertility.

Nine hundred metres further down the road, a path leads to the exhilarating **Sumaging Cave** (Big Cave). You'll need a guide to tour the cave (roughly two hours); the guide will provide a gas lantern. It's quite slippery in parts and you'll get wet; wear river sandals or other shoes with nonslip soles.

The king of Sagada's cave adventures, suitable for the reasonably fit and courageous, is the **cave connection**, an underground passage that links Sumaging and Lumiang caves. This three- to four-hour tour is definitely *not* for the claustrophobic, and there's a fair chance you'll get to swim through some underground pools.

Ganduyan Museum MUSEUM

(admission P25; ⌚8am-7pm) This small museum is nonetheless packed with an anthropologist's dream of sculptures, jewellery and other Kankanay artefacts. Be sure to chat to owner Christina Aben, who is a fount of information about local culture and history. Ganduyan is the traditional Kankanay name for Sagada.

Besao VILLAGE

Hikes originating in nearby Besao are as good as those around Sagada (minus the coffins), and you can always scrounge up lodging in a local house for P200 a night. Jeepneys and buses bound for Besao pass through Sagada throughout the day, but the last trip *from* Besao is midmorning, so day trippers may have to hire private transport for the return trip to Sagada. It's a 10km journey over a rough road.

Demang VILLAGE

South of the centre, the small village of Demang is now a barangay of Sagada but it was the area's original settlement and remains Sagada's cultural and traditional heart. Most of Sagada's *dap-ay* are in Demang and most *begnas* are held here. If you happen to be invited to one, bring a gift such as bread or a chicken. To walk to Demang, turn right 50m past the George Guesthouse, at Joan's store.

Activities

Sagada has a wealth of top-notch hikes. To get around anywhere in Sagada, contact the **Sagada Genuine Guides Assocation** (☎0916 559 9050; http://sagadagenuineguides.blogspot.com); these guys take trekking and customer service seriously. Their lives rely on tourists, and they do their best to take care of each and every one of their charges. As in most of the Cordillera, your guide will be wearing flip-flops; do *not* use him as a role model.

Echo Valley HIKING

Most of Sagada's famous hanging coffins are high on the limestone cliffs surrounding Echo Valley. Some hanging coffins are centuries old; others were put there recently. Animistic Applai elders continue to be entombed in the caves surrounding Sagada – if they can afford it. The gods demand the sacrifice of more than 20 pigs and three times as many chickens for the privilege of being buried in the caves.

To get to the Echo Valley **lookout**, walk behind St Mary's Episcopal Church and take a hard left on a dirt road that winds uphill to a cemetery. Continue uphill straight to the top of the cemetery and beyond; the path leads by a mobile telephone tower. From here it's a short stumble down to the lookout, where you can hear for yourself why it's called Echo Valley.

You can descend to Echo Valley and follow the myriad paths there, but there are no reliable maps or marked ways out. Many people head out for a stroll and return hours later covered in mud, picking leaves and thorns out of their hair. A guide can lead you on a one-hour walk through Echo Valley that ends with an optional 10-minute walk through **Latang Cave**, an underground river that spits you out near the Rocky Valley Inn & Cafe, from where it's a short walk back to town. If you want to walk through Latang Cave, make sure your guide has a torch and throw some river-friendly sandals in your bag.

Raft Sagada RAFTING

(☎0919 698 8361; www.luzonoutdoors.com; per person P2500-3500) This excellent outfit, run by an American expat who invests tourism dollars back into the local community, offers a wide range of rafting and kayaking trips up the Chico river. The time to go is between September and December.

Mt Kiltepan HIKING

There are superb panoramic views of the rice terraces and surrounding mountains from Mt Kiltepan, which is about a 40-minute walk (or 10-minute drive) from town. Take the road heading east out of town and look for a left turn about 500m past the turn-off to Rock Inn.

Bokong Waterfalls HIKING

About a half-hour walk from town are the small Bokong Waterfalls, where you can take a refreshing dip. To get here, follow the road east out of town and take the steps just after Sagada Weaving on the left. Follow the path through the rice fields down to a small river. Cross the river and continue upstream to the falls. The path continues up to the road leading to the town of Banga-an, 4km away.

Bomod-ok Falls HIKING

Banga-an is where the excellent 45-minute walk to the much larger Bomod-ok Falls (Big Waterfall) begins. You'll need a guide for this one, as the walk traverses rice terraces and access is sometimes restricted because of traditions associated with the planting and harvest seasons.

On the way back, ask your guide or villagers to point you in the direction of **Aguid**, a picturesque village located about 3km beyond Banga-an. From Aguid, walk back to Banga-an along the road. Two daily jeepneys go from Sagada to Banga-an, but they aren't much use to day trippers as they both depart midafternoon. Walk or hire a jeepney instead. Jeepneys from Banga-an to Sagada depart early in the morning.

Mt Sipitan HIKING

You can bag a few peaks around here, including Sagada's highest mountain, Mt Sipitan (2200m), although it's said to be rife with hunters' booby traps; don't try it without a guide. The majority of this rigorous, full-day hike, which starts near not-quite-idyllic Lake Danum on the way to Besao and ends in Banga-an, is through mossy forest. **Mt Ampacao** (1889m), 10km south of town beyond Ambasing, is a much easier conquest via a dirt road.

Sleeping

Accommodation in Sagada is exceptional value. Common bathrooms tend to have cold water only, but you can purchase hot water by the bucket (P50). In-room wifi is rapidly becoming the norm.

Sagada Homestay GUESTHOUSE $

(☎0919 702 8380; r without bathroom per person P250; wi-fi) Funny name considering it is not a homestay (it's a guesthouse), but it's nonetheless friendly, eminently affordable and loaded with character born of polished pinewood. It also boasts righteous views.

Residential Lodge GUESTHOUSE $

(☎0919 672 8744; www.geocities.com/residential_lodge; dm/r P200/250) 'Tita' (Aunty) Mary, a retired teacher, will treat you like the long lost child you are if you decide to stay at her lodge. The rooms are lovely, and her care and attention are wonderful, but if you don't fancy being spoiled by a doting Filipina woman, look elsewhere.

Sagada Guesthouse GUESTHOUSE $

(☎0929 680 7849, 0919 300 2763; r without bathroom per person P250, d with bathroom P600) The rustic, cheerful doubles here overlooking the central square are excellent value. As you go higher in the building, room rates increase all the way to P1200, but keep in mind these larger rooms can house three to five guests.

Canaway Resthouse GUESTHOUSE $

(☎0918 291 5063; r per person P250; wi-fi) You'll find exceptional value rooms here, with friendly service, clean sheets and reliable wi-fi.

George Guesthouse GUESTHOUSE $

(☎0918 548 0406; r per person from P250; wi-fi) The George is located in a candy-coloured building next to the Canaway and offers very much the same level of service and amenities (and even decor). A large double room with a TV costs P600 – a veritable splurge in Sagada.

Ganduyan Inn GUESTHOUSE $

(☎0921 273 8097; r without bathroom per person P250, d with bathroom P600; wi-fi) It's not quite as rustic as some guesthouses of this ilk, but it's serviceable and cheap.

Rock Inn HOTEL $

(☎0920 909 5899; www.rockfarmsagada.com; attic/dm/r/q P250/450/1500/1800; wi-fi) If you have a car, you might consider this option in a citrus grove 2km from the town centre. It has a huge, beautiful banquet hall and top-notch doubles overlooking a rock garden and *dap-ay*. There's a bit of variety to the rooms here (rare in Sagada). You can book out the dorm for groups, and up to 18 people can sleep on the floor of the attic.

Alfredo's Cabin GUESTHOUSE $

(☎0918 588 3535; s/d without bathroom P350/600) The simple doubles, better than most in town, are fine value, and the restaurant, while a bit mediocre in terms of food, has immense charm – woody and fragrant, with a big fireplace.

St Joseph's Resthouse HOTEL $
(☎0918 559 5934; d/q with cold water from P500/900, cottages with hot water P1700) This is the most versatile place in town, with a wide variety of rooms distributed among several structures overlooking a garden and the mountains beyond. Rooms vary enormously in quality.

Eating & Drinking

There's good food to be had, but Sagada's idea of service is somewhat peculiar – take the initiative and go to the counter to place your order.

TOP CHOICE **Log Cabin** FUSION $$
(☎0920 520 0463; mains P150-250; dinner) One of Sagada's many wonderful surprises is this aptly named eatery. The Western-style food is hearty and elegantly presented, and on Saturday evening there's a buffet (P250; prepaid reservations only) prepared by a French chef, who also bakes fresh bread for the restaurant. To top it all off there's good wine and a fireplace. You must drop by in the morning to place your order; sometimes closed on Tuesdays or if there are no guests around.

Yoghurt House FUSION $$
(breakfast P60-140, mains P85-160; 7am-8.30pm;) Fuel up here with mountain coffee and delicious homemade yoghurt before a long day of hiking or caving. Then return for dinner to carb-load on delicious vegetarian pasta dishes or *rösti* (shredded fried potatoes). The home-baked oatmeal cookies are to die for.

Masferré Inn & Restaurant FUSION $$
(☎0948 341 6164; sandwiches P80, mains P150-220; breakfast, lunch & dinner) The food here is among the best in town, but what really makes this place stand out are the awesome, powerful prints of the late Sagada-born photographer Eduardo Masferré.

Bana's Cafe CAFE $
(breakfast P100, mains P130-150; breakfast, lunch & dinner;) This artsy place specialises in coffee and breakfast (great omelettes). Its narrow balcony overlooks a gorge and catches the morning sun.

Lemon Pie House CAFE $
(pie from P35, mains from P50; breakfast, lunch & dinner;) There's more than lemon pie at this cute cafe – there's egg pie too! And some basic Filipino and Western fare, although we suspect they're using the same noodles for *lumpia* as they are for spaghetti...nonetheless, a tasty choice, and the pies really are great.

Shopping

Sagada Weaving CRAFT
(7am-6pm) Produces backpacks, money belts and other practical items in the traditional patterns of the region.

Tam-aw Handicraft CRAFT
(barangay Madongo) You'll find a smaller selection but better prices here, on the road to Banga-an, where the weavers are deaf and/or mute.

Sagada Pottery POTTERY
On the way to Besao you'll pass Sagada Pottery, which creates labour-intensive earthenware pottery that takes 30 hours to fire. It's 1.5km north of Sagada.

Information

The **tourist information centre** (7am-5pm) in the municipal building is the dispatch centre for all the guides in Sagada. The fixed rates for guides and private jeepney rates (Banga-an return P550) are clearly posted; you can expect to pay around P600 to P1000 for a day of caving or trekking, depending on how far you want to go.

Downstairs from the information centre are the **post office**, an **ATM** that works about half the time (with half the international cards) and **Sagada Rural Bank** (8-11.45am & 1.15-4.45pm Tue-Sat). The bank changes cash at very poor rates.

Across from the municipal building is the **Sagada Newsstand**, which sells all the big domestic newspapers and used novels.

Golinsan Internet Cafe (per hr P40; 8am-8.30pm) is below Alfredo's Cabin.

Getting There & Away

Morning jeepneys to Bontoc (P50, one hour) are frequent but peter out at noon. GL Lizardo has hourly buses to Baguio (P230, 6½ hours) until 1pm.

For Manila you can either backtrack to Baguio and transfer there, or take the Cable Tours bus from Bontoc. Both routes take a good 12 hours. Transfer in Bontoc for Banaue.

Bontoc

☎074 / POP 3500 / ELEV 900M

Bustling Bontoc is one of the most important market towns in the Cordillera, but it doesn't hold much appeal to travellers except as a transportation hub. There is an excellent museum on-site, but if it's hiking, rice paddies and mountain vistas you crave, best head on to Sagada or Banaue. Today you still may see an occasional old woman with tattooed arms or an old man in a G-string, but Bontoc is best known as the gateway to Maligcong, Mainit and Kalinga.

Sights

Bontoc Museum MUSEUM
(admission P50; 🕗8am-noon & 1-5pm) The wonderful Bontoc Museum is, quite simply, the best in North Luzon. Powerful black-and-white photos and indigenous music accompany the exhibits – one for each of the region's main tribes. Naturally, the headhunter exhibits, which display axes used to do the deed and *gansa* (gong) handles made with human jawbones, are the most fascinating. There are some grisly photos of headhunters and their booty. The Bontoc huts outside are definitely worth a look – check out the 'bedroom' in one.

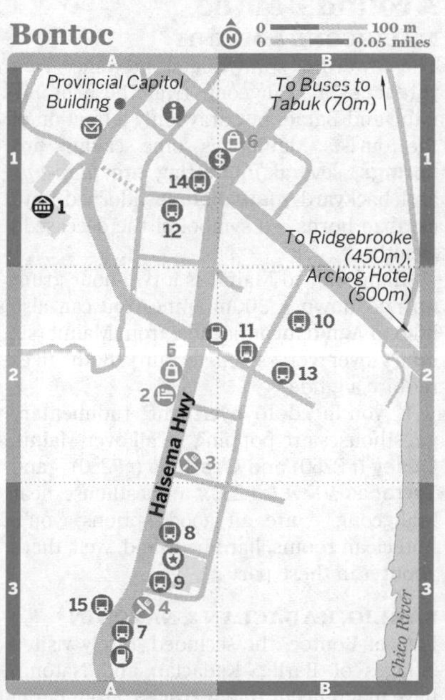

Tours

Both these guys can be hired to lead you around Sagada or just about anywhere else in the mountains.

Raynoldo 'Kinad' Waytan TOURS
(☎0929 384 1745) Kinad is an experienced guide who is also Bontoc's de facto tourist information centre (as well as a former candidate for town councillor). He tailors trips to Maligcong, Mainit and further afield for around P1000 per day for groups of one to four, excluding food. If Kinad's number isn't working, you can find him through most hotels.

Francis Pain TOURS
(☎0915 769 0843) Francis is a stand-up fellow who leads excellent tours and literally speaks over a dozen local dialects, making him the Prince of Polyglots out here in the Cordillera.

Sleeping

For a modicum of comfort you have to cross the bridge to the quiet eastern side of the Chico River.

Bontoc

Sights
1 Bontoc Museum.......A1

Sleeping
2 Churya-a Hotel & Restaurant.......A2

Eating
3 Cable Cafe.......A2
4 Tchayapan.......A3

Shopping
5 Luisa's Antique Shop.......A2
6 Mountain Province Trade Centre.......B1

Transport
Cable Tours.......(see 3)
7 Dadance Bus Terminal.......A3
8 D'Rising Sun Bus Terminal.......A3
9 Jeepneys and Buses to Banaue.......A3
10 Jeepneys to Barlig, Kadaclan and Natonin.......B2
11 Jeepneys to Mainit.......B2
12 Jeepneys to Maligcong.......A1
13 Jeepneys to Sagada.......B2
14 Jeepneys to Tinglayen.......A1
15 Von Von Terminal (Buses to Banaue).......A3

Churya-a Hotel & Restaurant HOTEL $
(☎0906 430 0853; darwin_churyas@yahoo.com; dm/d/tr P250/400/700) This is the best guesthouse in town, though that's not saying much. It scores points with its tastefully adorned common area and cafe, set on a balcony overlooking the main street. Front-desk staff can help arrange guides into the mountains.

Archog Hotel HOTEL $$
(☎0918 328 6908; www.archoghotel.com; d P700-1000, ste P1100-1800; ❄📶) The Archog is connected to the fading Ridgebrooke Hotel and is the closest thing Bontoc has to a business hotel. The clean doubles without bathrooms are a decent deal.

Eating & Drinking

The Churya-a and Tchayapan hotels have the best food in town. There's plenty of dog meat to be found in Bontoc. Your author couldn't bring himself to eat any, but we're sure you can find some if you bark up the right tree (sorry, had to).

Cable Cafe BAR $
(☎606 8013; meals P90; ⏲7am-3pm & 6-10pm) This place has no real competition. There's live music every night – OK, it's mostly '80s pop and Pinoy love songs, but it's something. No other place stays open past the 10pm curfew and you can snack on wings and drink beer until who knows when, maybe even 11pm.

Shopping

Luisa's Antique Shop ANTIQUES
(⏲6.30am-6.30pm) Mostly carries reproductions of Igorot artefacts, but savvy buyers will find the occasional bargain such as a genuine old woven blanket or a Samoki *tapis*.

Mountain Province Trade Centre SOUVENIRS
(⏲8.30am-6pm) Has woven materials from Sagada, Sadanga and Samoki, all with their own distinctive styles.

Information

There are several internet cafes on the main road.

Landbank (⏲9am-7pm) Near the Mountain Province Trade Centre; changes money.

Tourist Information Centre (Town Plaza; ⏲8am-5pm Mon-Fri) Has some detailed maps of the region but little else.

Getting There & Away

Cable Tours (☎0918 521 6790, 0908 207 8465) has daily 'air-con' (more like 'break-con') buses to Quezon City, Manila (P650, 12 hours), at 11am and 3pm; these buses stop in Banaue on the way (P120). Bonbon bus makes the trip to Banaue every hour from 10am to noon for the same rate. The bus from Manila to Bontoc is operated by Cable and departs between 8pm and 9pm. D'Rising Sun has hourly buses to Baguio (P220, six hours) until 4pm.

There is a jeepney to Banaue that leaves when full, usually around noon (P150).

Jeepneys depart every hour to Sagada (P50, one hour) from 7am to 5pm (that last '5pm' trip may or may not go, so we suggest getting here a little earlier). There's at least one bus and one jeepney every day to Tinglayen (P100, 2½ hours); the best option is usually to catch the 8.30am bus, which continues to Tabuk (P210, six hours). Maligcong is served by two morning and two afternoon jeepneys (last trip back to Bontoc at 4pm).

Jeepneys tackle the rough roads to Mainit (P40, one hour, 2.30 and 4.30pm), Barlig (P90, 1½ hours, 1.30pm) and Kadaclan (P130, four hours, 4pm to 5pm). Jeepneys head to Natonin (P170, six hours) when full. Dadance has one early-morning bus to Paracelis that goes through all three villages.

Around Bontoc

MALIGCONG & MAINIT

The towering, sprawling stone-walled **rice terraces** of Maligcong rival those of Banaue and Batad, but draw only a fraction of the tourists. Mainit has some scalding **hot springs**, several interesting **ato** *(dap-ay)*, and backyard **mausoleums** adorned with carabao horns – a symbol of the deceased's wealth.

Maligcong to Mainit is a two-hour grunt up and down a 300m spine. You can also hike to Aguid, near Sagada, from Mainit (six hours over very steep terrain). Both hikes require a guide.

If you need to overnight, rudimentary guesthouses are popping up all over Mainit. **Odsey** (r P250) and **Geston's** (r P250) – and **Terraces View** (r P250), a guesthouse near Maligcong – are all good options; you'll find clean rooms, hard beds and, well, that's about it in these parts.

BARLIG, KADACLAN & NATONIN

East of Bontoc, the secluded, rarely visited villages of Barlig, Kadaclan and Natonin have magnificent **rice terraces**. From Barlig it takes only about four hours to summit this region's highest peak, **Mt Amuyao** (2702m). The walk from Barlig to Batad, over Mt Amuyao, is one of the best two-day hikes in the Cordillera. Natonin to Mayoyao is a two- or three-day trek. Guides around here typically charge P800 per day and can be found in Barlig's Municipal Hall or in Bontoc.

There are a few *extremely* basic guesthouses and homestays in the villages; our favourite is the curiously named **Sea World** (r P250) in landlocked Barlig.

Kalinga Province

It's a bit disingenuous of Filipino tourism companies to advertise the Cordillera with pictures of half-naked, tattooed tribespeople, but if you are going to see that cliché in person, likely it will be in Kalinga.

Kalinga is a place where weekends aren't even a concept, let alone a reality; where animals are frequently sacrificed in *cañao* (ritual feasts), and where traditional law still trumps the contemporary world. You might meet a headhunter or tattooed tribeswomen with snake bones in their hair. You'll dwell amid free-ranging livestock and hike along ancient mountain trails to villages enveloped in rice terraces as spectacular as those in Bontoc and Ifugao.

Travel here has risks. If you get hurt you're a long way away from modern medical care (tribal remedies should be easier to come by). Plumbing is rudimentary if it exists at all. Landslides can foul up any trip, especially in the wet season.

The practice of headhunting ceased decades ago but tribal wars do break out occasionally. While warring tribes rarely bother foreigners, it helps to be cautious.

Gifts go a long way in Kalinga, so stock up on matches, gin and, if you really want to be popular, live chickens.

TINGLAYEN

074 / POP 865 / ELEV 900M

The best starting point for treks in Kalinga is Tinglayen, 2½ hours north of Bontoc on the Chico River. Victor Baculi, the barangay captain of Luplupa (just across the hanging bridge from Tinglayen), can set you up with guides; look for him at the Luplupa Riverside Inn, which he owns. You should also enquire at the **Churya-a Hotel** (0906 430 0853; darwin_churyas@yahoo.com) in Bontoc and with any guide organisations in Banaue or Sagada. Guide rates average P800 per day.

Activities

There's little point in coming here if you're not willing to go **trekking**. There are several exceptional routes – some are half-day forays into nearby villages, others are several-day grinds terminating as far away as Tabuk or Abra province. For the following treks, your guides will arrange accommodation and transport to the trailhead where necessary.

Headhunting has died out; you hear rumours of the practice continuing every now and then, but none of these can be confirmed. Every now and then you'll see staunch traditionalists, distinguishable by elaborate chest tattoos, but by and large the people of the hills are forgoing the old ways for the modern world. Among villages where you can meet them are **Sumadel**, a three-hour hike from Tinglayen, and **Dananao**, which is best combined with the three-hour trek to **Tulgao**, near where you'll find hot springs and a 30m waterfall. One early-afternoon jeepney goes most of the way to Tulgao (40 minutes).

Another excellent one-day hike southwest of Tinglayen is Ngibat–Butbut–Buscalan–Bugnay. You have to be in reasonably good shape and prepared to negotiate a few precarious sections with steep drop-offs on one side. **Buscalan** is a beautiful village with pretty stone-walled rice terraces and many traditional houses.

East of the Chico River, **Tanudan** municipality sees fewer visitors than the villages west of Tinglayen. This is extremely isolated and rugged terrain.

For a shorter walk, try the Tinglayen–Ambuto–Liglig–Tinglayen loop, which takes you through some small **rice terraces**, as well as villages where a few indigenous houses remain.

Sleeping & Eating

The **Sleeping Beauty Resthouse** (r per person P250) in Tinglayen and the **Luplupa Riverside Inn & Restaurant** (r per person P250) serve food and have a few basic rooms. Sleeping Beauty also has a store where you can stock up on water and snacks for the trail.

Most of the villages around Tinglayen have a multipurpose cooperative or modest homestay.

Getting There & Around

The daily Tabuk–Bontoc bus passes through at around 11am heading north (to Tabuk) and around 10.30am heading south (to Bontoc).

There is also at least one daily jeepney heading to both Bontoc and Tabuk. For the best views, sit on the roof.

TABUK

☎074 / POP 88,000 / ELEV 200M

The capital of Kalinga Province is a flat, dusty, sweltering university town on the banks of the Chico River. There's not much happening here, but **Chico River Quest** (☎0920 205 2680; www.chicoriverquest.com; lower/upper Chico River trips incl transport & accommodation P4000/7000) runs rafting trips on the Chico River from June to December. The more thrilling up-river run includes a night at the Sleeping Beauty Resthouse in Tinglayen, where the rafting trip starts.

The best hotel in Tabuk is the altogether lovely **Davidson Hotel** (☎0918 930 0830; http://davidsonhotel.com.ph; Provincial Hwy; r from P1500; ❄📶), with immaculate doubles and a sense of colonial hill station chic. A plain budget option is the **Kalinga Youth Hostel** (dm P250), near Chico River Quest.

Autobus and Victory Liner have a few daily buses to Manila (around P700, 11 hours), and there are frequent vans to Tuguegarao (P80 to P100, 1½ hours).

Morning buses and jeepneys to interior Kalinga villages and Bontoc originate in barangay Dagupan, 7km north of town.

THE KALINGA–ABRA ROAD

On the way from Tinglayen to Tabuk, about 7km north of Lubuagan, a fork off the main road takes you through hidden **Balbalasang-Balbalan National Park** and on into Abra Province. It's about four hours' drive from the turn-off to Abra's capital, **Bangued**. Public transport along this road is limited to one Saturday- or Sunday-morning jeepney to/from Tabuk, and another to/from Bangued; otherwise you'll need a private 4WD or mountain bike.

The two-hour drive from Balbalan to Balbalasang is one of the most scenic in the country, dipping into yawning gorges and cutting across jagged peaks, each hairpin seeming to bring into view a new waterfall, rice terrace or river. Just try to keep your eyes on the road, because there are lots of twists and turns, and chances to plunge to oblivion.

Balbalasang-Balbalan National Park was established to commemorate Kalinga opposition to government-backed logging operations in the area in the 1970s. There are a couple of good camping spots – one of the best is along the river in Balbalasang.

Banaue

☎074 / POP 2594 / ELEV 1200M

If you say 'rice terraces' to a Filipino, they're likely going to think of Banaue. Lipped in on all sides by fuzzy green steps, Banaue is directly accessible from Manila, and as such it is no idyllic getaway like Sagada. But don't give Banaue grief. The local mud-walled rice terraces have a pleasing, organic quality that differentiates them from the stone-walled terraces in most of the Cordillera. World Heritage listed, they are impressive not only for their chiselled beauty but because they were created around 2000 years ago.

The Ifugao, once headhunters, built the terraces and were as skilled at carving wood as they were at carving terraces. Their carved *bulol* statues are a Philippine icon, albeit a misunderstood one: *bulol* are rice guards, not rice gods, as many would have you believe.

While Banaue remains the centre of the rich Ifugao culture, tourism now shapes the town. Fortunately, it's easy to leave the tourists behind by escaping to villages like Batad, which have their own incredible rice terraces.

Sights & Activities

Viewpoint LANDMARK

It's a 10-minute tricycle ride up to the viewpoint (return P200), which is the best place to observe Banaue's terraces. The 'viewpoint' actually consists of four viewpoints lining the road to Bontoc at 200m intervals. The higher you go, the (duh) better the view. There are souvenir shops at most of these points, and at one you can get your photo taken with old Ifugao women decked out in full tribal regalia for around P20.

Museum of Cordillera Sculpture MUSEUM

(admission P100; ⏲8am-5pm) Located next to Spring Village Inn, this museum has a fabulous collection of *bulol* and other Ifugao woodcarvings, including some rare originals. There are also some fascinating old books that you can read here, including a 1912 *National Geographic* on Ifugao headhunters.

Banaue Museum MUSEUM

(admission P30; ⏲by request) The Banaue View Inn runs the Banaue Museum, which contains books written decades ago by anthropologist Otley Beyer and Igorot artefacts collected by his son William. Beyer's massive ethnography of the Igorot is a must-peruse for anyone with even a passing interest in the social sciences in general, and anthropology in particular.

Tam-an, Poitan, Matanglag & Bocos HIKING
The hikes between these villages traverse rice fields in the immediate vicinity of Banaue. You'll see traditional Ifugao houses in all of these villages.

The 45-minute hike from Tam-an to Poitan starts near Banaue Hotel's swimming pool and follows a century-old irrigation canal. Once you reach Poitan, ascend to the road, go left towards Banaue, then hang a right at a staircase a few minutes later and start climbing. In 30 minutes you'll reach Matanglag, where a few bronzesmiths work. From here it's another half-hour to Bocos, known for its woodcarving. Along the way you'll pass the waterfall visible from Banaue. From Bocos you can descend to Banaue or head north across yet more rice terraces and end up at the viewpoint. Ask for directions frequently or bring a guide if you don't want to get lost.

Sleeping

TOWN CENTRE

Uyami's Greenview Lodge HOTEL $
(☎386 4021/2, 0920 540 4225; www.ugreenview.wordpress.com; d without bathroom per person P250, d without/with view P800/1500; wi-fi) The Greenview is the most popular place in town, which is unsurprising since it covers all the usual backpacker bases: clean, comfy, equipped with a decent restaurant, good views of the terraces and wi-fi. There's nothing exceptional about this place, but it's a good spot to meet other travellers.

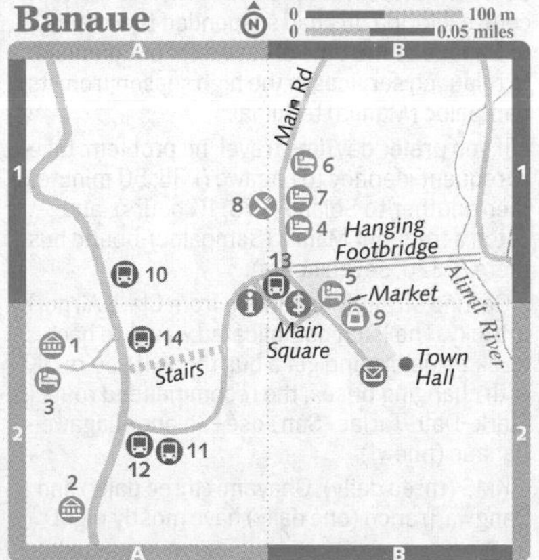

People's Lodge & Restaurant HOTEL $
(☎386 4014; d without bathroom per person from P250, d with bathroom from P600; wi-fi) The second-most popular place in town after Greenview has exceedingly friendly staff to offset its exceedingly ugly restaurant. The views from the restaurant balcony also don't hurt, nor do the reasonably priced rooms. Again, a good spot to meet fellow travellers.

Sanafe Lodge & Restaurant GUESTHOUSE $
(☎386 4085, 0920 950 4644; sanafelodge.com; s/d/ste P400/700/1200) An enigma if ever there was one, the Sanafe Lodge has the best-looking restaurant in the centre, extremely cosy rooms, a splendid leafy patio and bar stools that stare straight at the terraces (a happy-hour must). But outside of peak season, it's dead. You decide if that's good or bad. The 'deluxe' suites are pretty posh (for Banaue), if a bit overpriced.

Stairway Lodge & Restaurant GUESTHOUSE $
(d without bathroom per person P250, d with bathroom P500) A little north of Greenview, Stairway Lodge has acceptable rooms for the price.

RIDGE ROAD & ELSEWHERE

Native Village Inn HUTS $$
(☎0916 405 6743; www.nativevillage-inn.com; 2-person huts from P1250) These lovely huts,

Banaue

Sights
1 Banaue Museum ... A2
2 Museum of Cordillera Sculpture ... A2

Sleeping
3 Banaue View Inn ... A2
4 People's Lodge & Restaurant ... B1
5 Sanafe Lodge & Restaurant ... B1
6 Stairway Lodge & Restaurant ... B1
7 Uyami's Greenview Lodge ... B1

Eating
8 Las Vegas ... A1

Shopping
9 Montana & Tex ... B2

Transport
10 Buses to Bontoc ... A1
11 Dangwa Tranco Bus Terminal ... A2
12 KMS Bus Terminal ... A2
13 Main Jeepney Departure Point ... B1
14 Ohayami Bus Station ... A2

situated 9km out of town, offer stunning views onto the rice terraces and are ensconced in an atmosphere of splendid isolation. Unfortunately, the spot really is on an unpaved road and is pretty isolated; make sure you arrange pick-up logistics with the owners before you arrive.

Banaue View Inn GUESTHOUSE **$**
(☎386 4078, 0916 405 6743; banaue _view_inn@yaho.com.ph; dm without bathroom P200, d/tr/f with bathroom P800/900/1500) This inn sits at the top of Magubon hill, overlooking town and the rice terraces. Rooms are pleasant and clean, and service is friendly. You might ask the owner, Lily, to regale you with stories about her grandfather, renowned Yale anthropologist Otley Beyer, who wrote extensively about Ifugao culture, or her father, William, a swashbuckling antiques dealer who sired 16 children.

Banaue Hotel HOTEL **$$**
(☎386 4087; standard/deluxe r from P2800/3500; 🏊) This concrete hulk looks better inside than out. The capacious lobby features lots of wood and a humongous fireplace. Rooms are large, and the wood-panelled deluxe quarters even have some character, along with stunning views. The restaurant serves decent wine, steaks and other continental cuisine. It's a tour-group favourite, with services to match.

Eating & Drinking

The best guesthouses double as the best restaurants; we prefer the Sanafe. In general, mains range from around P60 to P150; the more expensive meals are Western fare pushed through a Filipino mould press. Along the ridge road north of Banaue Hotel are several low-key cafes with great views. Most kitchens close by 9pm.

Las Vegas FILIPINO **$**
(mains P60-90) One of the few restaurants that tends to stay open later than 9pm. The owners are friendly and dish up so-so Filipino food. The Las Vegas kitsch decor is awe inspiring.

Shopping

Ifugao woodcarvings and crafts are everywhere, but **Montana & Tex**, near the plaza, has the best selection. There are a couple of workshops on the main road towards Bocos where you might find better deals.

Information

Stock up on pesos as there are no international ATMs in Banaue. Convenience store RSR, Greenview Lodge and People's Lodge change dollars at poor rates. There are several **internet points** in town, including People's Lodge.

The main **post office** is near the entrance to Banaue Hotel.

Visitors to Banaue are supposed to pay a P20 environmental fee, payable at most lodges or the Banaue Tourist Information Centre. We were not asked to foot this fee during our visit, but hoteliers assure us it is usually collected. Batad has its own network of guides.

Banaue Tourist Information Centre (☎386 401; ⏲6am-7pm) Manages a network of accredited guides, sells a map (P15) and maintains the definitive list of guide and private transport prices to selected locations. Guides average P1200 for full-day hikes.

Marcial Cuision (☎0918 522 5049) Marcial is a friendly local guide who can get you around via his van or his feet.

Tam-an Guides Organisation (☎0919 500 1028; ⏲6am-7pm) Next to the post office, this guides' association was launched by a group of freelance guides. Elvis, one of the founders, can whisk you to Sagada and just about anywhere else in the Cordillera on his off-road motorcycle (P1500 per day plus petrol), and has a spare motorbike if you prefer to drive yourself.

Getting There & Away

Ohayami run one night bus per evening between Banaue and Sampaloc, Manila (P450, nine hours); the bus also stops at Cubao. In the peak season buy your tickets well ahead of time. It's a P20 trike ride from the bus station to the town centre. Florida bus had suspended their route to Banaue at the time of research, but planned to relaunch services in the high season from its Sampaloc (Manila) terminal.

If you prefer daytime travel, no problem: take a frequent jeepney to Lagawe (P35, 50 minutes), then another to Solano (P75, 1¼ hours), and catch a frequent Manila (Sampaloc)-bound bus there (P320, seven hours).

Getting straight to Banaue from Clark Airport is tricky. The least complicated way is to backtrack to Manila and get a bus there. If you're OK with changing buses, the recommended route is Clark–Dau–Tarlac–San José–Solano–Lagawe–Banaue (phew!).

KMS (three daily), Ohayami (three daily) and Dangwa Tranco (one daily) have mostly night buses to Baguio (P465, 8½ hours) via Solano and San José. The least complicated way to Vigan (at least 12 hours) is to take one of those buses, get off in Rosario, La Union, and transfer to a northbound bus. You could also go north to Tuguegarao, then loop around the north coast of Luzon to Laoag, then on to Vigan. That's about a 15-hour trip with three to four bus changes, but it's scenic as hell.

Buses to Bontoc (P150, 2½ hours) every morning and three additional buses pass through. A jeepney to Bontoc (P70) departs at 8.30am. Connect to Sagada in Bontoc.

Most jeepneys leave from the main square.

Around Banaue

Five Ifugao rice terraces are included on the Unesco Word Heritage list: Batad, Bangaan, Mayoyao, Hungduan and the Nagacadan terraces near Kiangan.

Of those, Batad's are the most famous, but Mayoyao gives Batad a run for its money. Mayoyao's not covered here but is accessible from Banaue (three hours) or Santiago (five hours) in Isabela Province.

BATAD & AROUND

074 / POP 1100

OK. You've been through Baguio. Wandered past the hanging coffins of Sagada. Hiked to Banaue viewpoint and even peeped at a few mummies in Kabayan. You've *done* the Cordillera. Well, think again, because there's rice terraces and then there's Batad and its amphitheatre of rice terraces. Seriously: this place looks like a mega-concert stadium venue where the bleachers are row after row of perfectly sculpted green terraces. Batad is only accessible by your feet and some sweat, and remains a quintessential backpacker mecca, although some say the expansion of guesthouses and the arrival of electricity have 'spoiled' it (funnily enough, most locals find the increased income and access to power a boon). There are several nearby villages, such as Cambulo, which beckon travellers who wish to escape other tourists altogether.

Activities

What follows are just a few of the many hikes in the area; the Banaue Tourist Information Centre or any guide can recommend longer treks. Batad has a network of guides called the Batad Environmental Tour Guides Association. Twenty per cent of all fees these guides collect goes towards restoring the rice terraces. Not all hikes around Batad require guides, but most do, and besides you'll find their local knowledge a huge asset, especially for locating local craftspeople.

At Ramon Homestay, the owner maintains a traditional hut built by his grandfather and adorned with the skulls of deer, monkeys and pigs. Inside you'll find an anthropologist's dream: a mini museum of spears, rice wine barrels and traditional carvings; the place looks like a set piece from an *Indiana Jones* movie. If you visit, it'd be nice to make a donation (say, P20 to P40).

Tappia Waterfall HIKING

It's a 40-minute hike across the terraces to the 30m-high Tappia Waterfall, where you can sunbathe on the rocks or swim in the chilly water. To get here from the main guesthouse area, walk down to the village and then up to the promontory, just to the left of the Waterfall Side Lodge.

Around Banaue

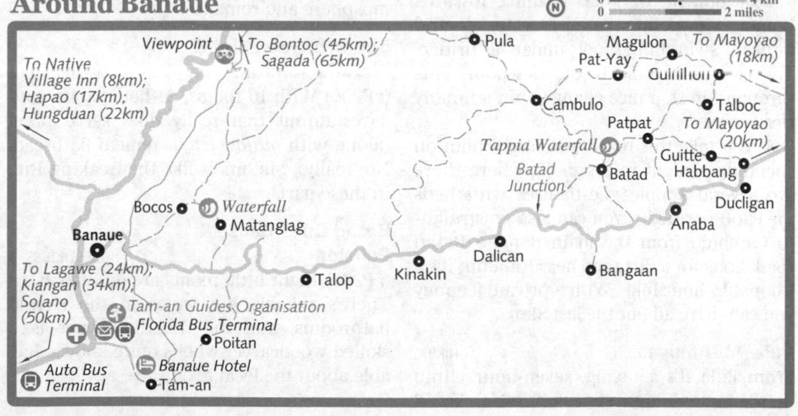

IFUGAO'S TERRACES

The Ifugao rice terraces are incredible any time of the year, but they are at their best one to two months before harvest, when they become bright green before gradually turning gold. Around planting time, the terraces take on a barren, naked look that is also appealing. In Banaue, the best viewing period is from June to July (before harvest) and February to March (cleaning and planting time). In Batad, which has two plantings a year, the fields are at their greenest from April to May and October to November. If you're interested in efforts to preserve the terraces or just want to learn more about them, check out Save the Ifugao Terraces Movement (sitmo.org).

Batad–Bangaan HIKING

This 2½-hour hike is a recommended route out of Batad or, if you prefer, in. From Batad, take the path behind Rita's guesthouse down to the small river. Cross to the other side, then head across the small bridge to the left and pick up the path. When it forks after 10 minutes go right. From there it's smooth sailing, so you can relax and enjoy the stunning panoramas of the mountains and rice terraces, bisected by a river hundreds of metres below. Eventually you'll walk through a rice terrace and hit the main road, from where it's 2km to Family Inn overlooking Bangaan, and another 1.5km from there to Batad junction.

Batad–Cambulo–Pula–Banaue Viewpoint HIKING

You'll need a guide for this one. From Batad to Cambulo is around 1½ hours, from Cambulo to Pula is about three hours, and from Pula to the viewpoint it's an easy four-hour walk.

Much of this hike is through rice terraces. The section from Cambulo to Pula follows a winding river, with terraces carved high into the mountains. Pula is a tiny collection of Ifugao houses on a hilly outcrop.

Just outside of Pula, heading towards Banaue viewpoint, there's a waterfall and a deep swimming pool under a bridge. The path from Pula to the viewpoint cuts through forest, a nice change after so many rice terraces.

If you take this route, you might plan on spending a night in Cambulo, where there are several simple guesthouses with beds for P200 per night. You can also go straight to Cambulo from the main Banaue–Batad road. Look for a dirt road near Kinakin; it's a 13km, 3½-hour hike. With a private jeepney you can drive all but the last 3km.

Pula–Mt Amuyao HIKING

From Pula it's a taxing, seven-hour climb up the region's highest peak (2702m). You'll need a guide (P800 per day) and a healthy amount of courage. Be prepared to sleep at the radar station on the top. Amuyao is much easier to scale from Barlig, near Bontoc.

Sleeping & Eating

Mobile phone reception barely reaches Batad, and the 11 guesthouses usually cannot be contacted by phone. This normally isn't a problem, but from March to May, many Filipinos arrive on tour groups, and accommodation can fill up. If you visit during this period, you may want to arrive in Batad early to find a place to stay.

All lodging is very similar: basic rooms, (usually) shared bathrooms and an on-site restaurant serving basic Filipino and Western fare for around P40 to P80 per main. Don't expect a full menu.

Hillside Inn GUESTHOUSE $

(☎0917 757 4411; r P150) Yes, the Hillside has a phone! It also has clean rooms and a lovely verandah.

Batad Kandagyan Lodges HUTS $

(r P200) These are genuine native huts, so while there's no electricity, there's lots of atmosphere and romance.

Simon's View Point & Pizza Restaurant GUESTHOUSE $

(r P200) With 16 rooms, 24-hour power and a restaurant that really does serve pizza (along with *malawach,* a Yemeni flatbread. No, really), Simon's is like the freaking Ritz in these parts.

Batad Guesthouse & Pension GUESTHOUSE $

(r P200) Eight little rooms are on offer here. There's reliable hot water in the shared bathrooms, and the friendly owner is a skilled woodcarver who is quite knowledgeable about the local region.

Ramon Homestay GUESTHOUSE $

(r P150) Besides basic rooms with 24-hour electricity that are otherwise like every other accommodation in Batad, Ramon offers a native hut for P200. Another on-site hut is a sort of mini museum of Batad culture.

Waterfallside Lodge GUESTHOUSE $

(r P150) The most isolated lodge in Batad is also one of the most beautiful, situated just by Tappia Waterfall. There are two rooms and fantastic views wherever you turn.

Cristina's Main Village GUESTHOUSE $

(r P150) We're not sure where Cristina's secondary village is (ha ha), but she's so friendly, and runs such a spick-and-span place we don't care.

Getting There & Away

From Banaue, it's 12km over a very rocky road to Batad junction, where a 4WD track leads 3km up to the 'saddle' high above Batad. No vehicles were capable of making the ascent all the way to the saddle at the time of research; trikes dropped folks off a steep 1.5-hour hike from the saddle, and from there it's a 40-minute hike downhill to Batad.

From Banaue, three or four jeepneys per day pass by Batad junction (P50, one hour). From there you'll have to walk to the saddle. Alternatively, you can team up with other travellers and hire a private jeepney to Batad junction (return P2000). Tricycles also make the trip to the junction (return P700).

To return to Banaue, either arrange transport in advance, walk (taking one of the hikes outlined earlier), or catch a passing jeepney anywhere along the main road to Banaue (traffic heading back is 'heaviest' early in the morning).

HAPAO & HUNGDUAN

Spread out over the valley floor, the rice terraces in Hapao and Hungduan are dazzling.

To walk to a small **pool** beside a river in Hapao (population 2200), a barangay of Hungduan 17km northwest of Banaue, take the concrete steps behind the viewpoint and turn left at the bottom. Follow the paved irrigation canal for about 10 minutes until you reach a small group of houses. It's another 15 minutes to the river, where you can cool off in the refreshing water.

Five kilometres beyond Hapao is Hungduan *poblasyon* (town centre; population 1500), the site of the spectacular **Bacung spider web terraces** and the jumping-off point for the six-hour climb up **Mt Napulawan** (2642m), the final hiding place of General Yamashita at the end of WWII.

You can inquire about more hikes at the Hungduan tourism information centre, a few kilometres from Hapao. You can secure guides at the Hungduan Municipal Hall, where there's also a guesthouse. Guide rates start at P800 per day.

Jeepneys to Banaue leave Hungduan (P70, 22km, two hours) and Hapao (P65, 17km, 1½ hours) around 8am and return between 2pm and 3pm. There is at least one jeepney per day to/from each town. Hapao is within tricycle range of Banaue (return P700, 1½ hours).

Kiangan

074 / POP 1600 / ELEV 1200M

Kiangan is where Ifugao and American troops helped force General Yamashita, the 'Tiger of Malaya', to make his informal surrender in WWII.

Sights & Activities

A pyramid-shaped **War Memorial Shrine** marks the spot where Yamashita surrendered in 1945.

Across the lawn from the shrine is the **Ifugao Museum** (8am-noon & 1-5pm Mon-Fri), which houses a small collection of Ifugao artefacts. **Ambuwaya Lake**, 3km east of town, is a good spot for a swim. The World Heritage–listed **Nagacadan terraces** and **Julungan terraces** are about 10km west of town, accessible by tricycle. You can hike up into the Nagacadan terraces and then descend to Maggok village (three hours). If you arrive here around the last weekend of August, you may be able to participate in the **Bakle'd Kiangan**, a local festival that celebrates a bountiful rice harvest; during this time, locals doff modern clothes in favour of traditional dress and the entire area resembles (well, more so than usual) a *National Geographic* photo spread.

Pangaggawan Cave is a three-hour hike from Kiangan; there are other caves in the vicinity. From town, a classic (ie steep) Igorot trail leads 1½ hours straight up **Mt Kapugan**, from where there are exceptional views of the surrounding terraces.

To secure guides or discuss more ambitious hikes in the area, talk to tourism council head Ani Dumangeng at the Kiangan Municipal Hall. Another great source of information is Ibulao, Ibulao Bed & Breakfast, which recently started sporadic rafting trips on the Ibulao River and guides overnight treks to caves in the area. However, as of this writing, rafting trips were only available for large groups.

The **Save the Ifugao Terraces Movement** (SITMO; http://sitmo.org) is based in Kiangan. It runs occasional ecotours on which you actually work in the rice fields of Kiangan, Hungduan and elsewhere.

Sleeping

Ibulao, Ibulao Bed & Breakfast B&B **$$**
(☎0919 694 5964; totokalug@yahoo.com.ph;) Roberto Kalungan, a practising doctor, has built a house fit for the pages of *Architectural Digest* overlooking the Ibulao River at the junction of the Lagawe–Kiangan road. There's a wonderfully unique family room built right into the rock foundation downstairs in the main house. Massive windows provide amazing views and blur the lines between interior and exterior. Note that the good doctor does not accept walk-in guests; you must book ahead.

Kiangan Youth Hostel HOSTEL **$**
(☎0910 324 3296; dm/d P250/400) Has passable rooms.

Getting There & Away

Kiangan is an easy jeepney ride from Lagawe (P25, 25 minutes, every 20 minutes until dark). Ohayami has a night bus from Kiangan to Manila and KMS has one to Baguio.

Around Kiangan

In barangay Pula in the town of Asipulo, a 48-hectare organic coffee forest has been turned into the **Julia Campbell Agroforest Memorial Park** (http://juliacampbellpark.wordpress.com). Julia Campbell was a US Peace Corps volunteer whose murder at the hands of a local man on the main trail to Batad in April 2007 shocked the country.

The park is the site of a working organic coffee farm, **Bantai Civet Coffee** (☎in the US 210-859 4342; www.bantaicivetcoffee.com), that produces common Robusta, as well as a rare and expensive type of coffee derived from the excrement of the coffee bean-eating civet. Whereas most commercial coffee plantations are on clear-cut plots, here trees have been planted amid natural forest. It is precisely this natural environment that draws shade-loving civets, which means the farm has an economic, as well as ecological motive for preserving native forest.

The park is the Philippines' second World Wide Opportunities on Organic Farms project (the first one is in Acop, near Baguio). It accepts both volunteers and regular tourists to experience electricity-free life in a small Ifugao village surrounded by natural forest. Accommodation here is in basic Ifugao huts that lack plumbing and running water. You can bathe in one of the area's many natural (cold) springs. The cost is P250 per night, or it's free if you're volunteering. You can also buy a limited amount of roasted, civet-excreted coffee on the farm for a cut rate.

Jeepneys to barangay Pula (P70, two hours) originate in Lagawe, pass through Kiangan, and continue another hour to Pula. There are usually three afternoon jeepneys. Additional jeepneys from Lagawe and Kiangan terminate in Asipulo proper, from where you can take a motorcycle taxi to Pula. From Pula it's a steep 20-minute walk up to the park. Gerald can meet you in Lagawe and guide you to the park with a little advance warning.

THE NORTHEAST

Get yourself to northeast Luzon and you're deep in the Filipino frontier. Hill tribes, huge swathes of forest, small towns connected by smaller lumber tracks – you won't find many Filipinos, let alone foreigners, out this way. The Cagayan River, the country's longest inland waterway, cuts a swathe through this famously fertile region. East of the river are the Sierra Madre, among the country's most impenetrable mountains and home to wild and woolly Northern Sierra Madre Natural Park. To the west the mighty Cordillera looms.

Baler & Around

☎042 / POP 36,000

Baler (bah-*lehr*) has never needed city walls for protection; the Sierra Madre and the Philippine Sea cut the capital of Aurora Province off from the outside world effectively enough. Today Baler is best known as the location of the surfing scene in *Apocalypse Now;* the minuscule waves on display in that scene are a testament to the area's fickleness. The government has been touting local adventure credentials, but travellers have yet to catch on.

Sights & Activities

Museo de Baler MUSEUM
(Quezon Park; admission P20; ⏲8am-noon & 1-5pm) Has some interesting photos and exhibits on the history and culture of the area.

Cemento Beach SURFING
Offshore typhoons kick up big swells for surfing between July and October. From November to March, onshore breezes make conditions challenging. The biggest waves are over a reef at Cemento Beach, 6km east of town off Cemento wharf.

Sabang Beach SURFING
The town hosts the Aurora Surfing Cup every February on Sabang Beach, an endless strip of fine dark sand extending north from Baler proper to Charlie's Point, the river-mouth break that spawned the famous 'Charlie don't surf' line in *Apocalypse Now*.

Aliya Surfshop SURFING
(☎0920 253 4814; board rental/lessons per hr P200/400) Near the central lifeguard stand dubbed Baywatch, Aliya offers boards and instruction, and also has a dive shop.

Dicasalarin Cove HIKING
If you continue 4.5km past Cemento wharf, you will come to Digisit, where a hiking trail through the jungle leads south to an isolated white-sand beach at Dicasalarin Cove. It is a two- to three-hour hike (take a guide), or you can hire a bangka (P1000 return) from the fishers near the San Luis River mouth at Sabang Beach. A nonmotorised bangka (P3) takes passengers across the river to barangay Castillo, from where you can walk to Cemento wharf. Otherwise take a tricycle from Sabang or Baler centre (P120 one way).

Ditumabo Falls HIKING
An easier hike is to Ditumabo Falls (Mother Falls), which drop 15m into a small reservoir above an unfinished hydroelectric dam. The turn-off to the trail is in Ditumabo, 5.7km west of San Luis. From there, walk or take a tricycle 2km along a 4WD track to the trailhead, from where it's a somewhat technical 45-minute hike to the falls up a creek bed next to a water pipeline.

Sleeping & Eating

Most of Baler's accommodation is along the beach in Sabang.

Aliya Surfshop HOTEL $$
(☎0920 253 4814; aliyasurfcamp.multiply.com; r P1200-2000; ❄📶) Aliya offers some of the finest surfer accommodation in Baler...which admittedly isn't saying much, the competition considered. That said, the rooms here are bright, lit by stained-glass windows, with

Baler

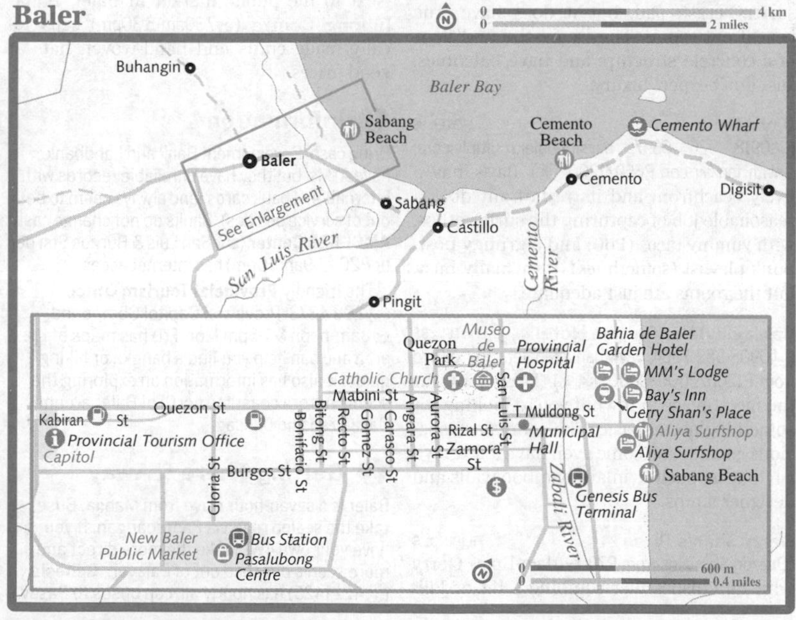

LOS ULTIMOS DE FILIPINAS

Baler's **Catholic Church** is Aurora Province's attempt at wowing history and film buffs in one shot. Built in 1611, the church facade itself is pretty enough, if nothing new to anyone who has seen other colonial churches in the Philippines. But more has gone down here than four centuries of confession and confirmations.

In June of 1898, during the Spanish-American war, 50 Spanish soldiers led by Captain Enrique de las Morenas y Fossí garrisoned themselves in the church. The Spaniards were soon besieged by hundreds of Filipino freedom fighters. In the hot, cramped church compound, disease took a toll, killing Fossi and his underlings until command passed to Lt Saturnino Martin Cerezo. The siege carried on into 1899; the Spanish themselves surrendered the Philippines to the USA in December of 1898.

Despite entreaties by Filipinos, Spanish civilians and even soldiers, Cerezo refused to surrender. He was only brought to heel when he was shown a newspaper from Madrid that contained news of the surrender and the marriage of an officer he knew; the latter detail allowed him to accept Spain's loss. Oh, and did we mention US marines tried to rescue the Spanish after the surrender, but were stopped and imprisoned themselves for eight months by Filipino nationalists? When Cerezo decided to surrender, local crowds called his men 'amigo' and president Emilio Aguinaldo sent his congratulations. The garrison members were known as Los Ultimos de Filipinos – roughly translated, 'The Last of the Philippines'.

The entire event was the subject of *Baler*, a Filipino movie released in 2008. *Baler* was incredibly popular in the Philippines and features the usual melodramatic, overacted love stories of Filipino cinema; that said, there are some pretty kick-butt explosions...

modern clean beds, hot water and working internet. Ah, luxury.

MM's Lodge GUESTHOUSE **$**
(☎0919 537 9405; d with/without bathroom & air-con from P800/350; ❄) Basically a budget surfers' crash pad, but it does have true beachfront rooms. They're on the 2nd floor of a concrete structure and have balconies. Just don't expect luxury.

Bay's Inn HOTEL **$**
(☎0918 926 6697; baysinnbaler.multiply.com; d with fan/air-con P650/1200; ❄) Bay's has a lively beachfront and its restaurant does a reasonable job of capturing the surfer ethos, with yummy tacos (P60) and a grungy post-punk playlist (sometimes). It's usually busy, but the rooms are just adequate.

Bahia de Baler Garden Hotel HOTEL **$$**
(☎0908 982 7064; www.bahiadebaler.com; d/tr/q from P1200/2000/3000; ❄📶) This is by far the nicest place in town if you're looking for something above basic. The rooms are spacious enough and some even have a few stylish touches such as inlaid-bamboo walls and designer lamps.

Gerry Shan's Place FILIPINO **$**
(Quezon St; mains from P70; ⏲11am-11pm) Gerry whips up dishes that combine a bit of Filipino love, Chinese edge and even Western richness. Fantastic Chinese seafood is the norm.

Shopping

Next to the public market in Baler, **Pasalubong Centre** (⏲7.30am-5.30pm) sells locally made crafts and hand-woven hats at good prices.

Information

Bring cash. Development Bank and Landbank have ATMs, but they have unreliable records with international bank cards (and always seem to be out of service besides). Banks do not change cash.
AMCI-B2B Center (cnr San Luis & Burgos Sts; per hr P20; ⏲9am-10pm) has internet access.

The friendly **Provincial Tourism Office** (☎209 4373; Provincial Capitol Compound; ⏲8am-noon & 1-5pm Mon-Fri) has maps of the area and can help you find a bangka or hiking guide. It also has information on exploring the scenic Aurora coastline north of Baler around Casiguran and Dilasag.

Getting There & Away

Baler is a seven-hour drive from Manila. Buses take the sealed road via Pantabangan. If you have your own 4WD, take the more direct and more scenic dirt road out of Palayan. **Genesis** (☎421 1425) has hourly air-con buses to Pasay,

Manila, until 3pm (P500, six to eight hours). Buses leave Cubao, Manila, for Baler every hour from 4.30am till 7.30am. Genesis also runs a nonstop, deluxe night bus from Manila (P650).

From other points in Luzon, you must travel first to Cabanatuan. Air-con vans link Cabanatuan and Baler (P241, four hours) every hour or so during daylight hours. Vans depart from the main bus station near the new public market. Also at the bus station, D'Liner has four morning buses that tackle the rough road to Dilasag (P420, six hours), the jumping-off point for boats to Palanan.

SEAIR used to fly here from Manila, but as of this research that service was no longer offered.

Santiago City

078 / POP 128,000

This typical, tricycle-blighted provincial city in Isabela Province is a key transport hub and jumping-off point for two exceptional off-the-beaten-track journeys: the bus-and-boat journey to Palanan in Northern Sierra Madre Natural Park, and the back-door route into Mayoyao in Ifugao Province. There are a few hotels in town if you get stuck here, all of which charge around P500/800 for singles/doubles; they're of a pretty uniform(ly bad) quality.

The **Santiago City Terminal** (Pantranco-Sagana Rd) is the hub for most public transportation, including at least two morning buses to Mayoyao (P150, six hours). To get to Palanan, board one of the three early-morning Dinapigue-bound buses and get off in Dilasag (P340, 10 hours) in Aurora Province. One boat in Dilasag waits for buses to arrive from Santiago City before departing to Palanan.

Victory Liner has hourly buses to Manila (P391, 8½ hours).

Northern Sierra Madre Natural Park

OK. You wanted to prove that you get off the beaten track. Congratulations – because out here, in the vast expanse of mountainous, critter-infested rainforest that dominates North Luzon's east coast, there's hardly a track to beat.

The Northern Sierra Madre is big. It's Switzerland-sized big. Longest mountain chain in the Philippines big. More than 60% of the country's plant species are found here, and 29 threatened species of animal, including the critically endangered Philippine eagle, the country's national bird; the largely harmless Philippine crocodile, a freshwater reptile that is the world's most endangered crocodile; and the Northern Sierra Madre Forest Monitor Lizard, a rather beautiful lizard that can grow 2.2 metres long and dines exclusively on fruit.

What won't you find out here? That many people. Not that the area is uninhabited. The park's unspoiled coastline is home to the Dumagats, a seminomadic Negrito group whose lifestyle has been relatively unchanged for millennia. This region was also a refuge for the last remaining rebels during the Philippine Revolution – American-led forces captured General Emilio Aguinaldo in the coastal town of Palanan on 23 March 1901.

With a capable guide you can trek through the heart of the park to **Palanan**. The starting point for this three-day walk is **San Mariano**, about 30km east of Naguilian. Arrange a guide (expect to pay at least P800 per day, and more if vehicle hire is required) through San Mariano's mayor's office. Before entering the park you'll need to get a permit from the DENR protected areas superintendent offices in Balug (5km south of Tumauini) or Palanan.

Endangered Philippine crocodiles tend to hang out near San José, two hours east of San Mariano by logging truck (one per day... hopefully). If you want to see the crocodiles, the **Cagayan Valley Program for Environment & Development** (CVPED; 0916 553 2998; www.cvped.org/croc.php), at Isabela State University in Cabagan, has a crocodile conservation project and arranges guided observation treks for visitors.

There's a DENR guesthouse (P200) and a few restaurants in Palanan, which is otherwise a sleepy town with a very end-of-the-world feeling to it; Dumagat men set up thatch lean-tos on the beach, Aeta tribespeople sell monitor lizards for lunch and, in general, there's a sense you're far removed from civilisation. There are beaches in **Dicotcotan** and **Didadungan** that are isolated and pristine, but getting to them will require some legwork and asking around on your part.

Getting There & Around

To enter the park you can fly, take a boat or walk in from San Mariano. To get to San Mariano, catch a jeepney or bus in Ilagan, Cauayan or Naguilian.

Cyclone Airways (☎in Cauayan 078-652 0913; www.cycloneairways.com) flies six-seaters to Palanan and Maconacan from Cauayan, and to Maconacan from Tuguegarao. **Chemtrad Airlines** (☎in Tuguegarao 078-844 3113) also has flights to Maconacan from Tuguegarao. All flights leave when full, usually daily. They cost P4000 and take 20 to 30 minutes.

To get a boat to Palanan you should first make your way to Dilasag; there are regular buses to Dilasag from Baler and Santiago City. From Dilasag there are one or two daily boats to Palanan (P300, six to seven hours). One departs in the evening, a few hours after the buses from Santiago City arrive. The other departs around 4am. There are a few simple guesthouses in Dilasag if you need to spend the night.

Tuguegarao

☎078 / POP 132,000

The political and commercial capital of Cagayan Province, Tuguegarao (too-geg-uh-row; the last syllable rhymes with 'wow') boasts a bucolic setting that's in the process of being overwhelmed with cars, trikes and jeepneys. The city serves as a convenient base for forays into the country's largest cave system, located 25km to the east, and into Kalinga Province to the west.

Sights & Activities

More than 300 caves have been discovered in the municipality of Peñablanca, about 40 minutes northeast of town.

Callao & Sierra Caves CAVES

The seven-chambered Callao Cave and the more challenging Sierra Cave nearby are both accessible by car. Callao Cave is reached by walking up 184 steps. Several sinkholes illuminate the cavernous chambers, one of which houses a little chapel with pews and an altar. To get here, catch a jeepney from Don Domingo Market, just north of the city.

A must-do excursion if you're in the area is to hire a bangka (P500) near Callao Cave and head 15 minutes upriver to watch tens of thousands of bats pour out of the caves for a flight over the **Pinacanauan River** at dusk. There is a pebble beach with a picnic table near here. You can rent kayaks (P200 per hour) from Callao Caves Resort, across the Pinacanauan River from Callao Cave.

Odessa Cave CAVE

Further afield, Odessa Cave, estimated to be at least the second-longest cave system in the country at 12.5km (it still hasn't been explored to its terminus), is for advanced cavers only. Access requires a 7km hike from Callao, followed by a 30m rappel into a sinkhole.

Tours

Kalesa KALESA

Horse-drawn *kalesa* still ply their way around Tuguegarao's commercial centre; you can flag one down and take a tour around the city for a half-day/full day (P1200/1800). Local *kalesa* are colourful and distinctly fashioned compared to carriages in other parts of the country; they're made of rubber and wood, and are a bit bigger than their counterparts The city of Tuguegarao tries to give *kalesa* drivers good English training, with mixed if admirable results. Tours can accommodate up to eight people, so costs can be shared.

Adventures & Expeditions NATURE

(☎844 1298, 0917 532 7480) Run by veteran area guide Anton Carag, the company offers kayaking trips on the Pinacanauan, where clean green waters cut through the limestone cliffs. This involves taking a bangka 5km upstream, then navigating the return trip via no-flip kayaks over light rapids. Adventures & Expeditions also organises multiday trips that include caving, kayaking and rafting on the Chico River in nearby Kalinga Province.

Sleeping & Eating

All of the following hotels are attached to good restaurants. For something more downscale just roam along Bonifacio St, loaded with fast-food and street food.

Hotel Lorita HOTEL **$**

(☎844 1390; www.ivoryhotelandsuites.com/lorita.html; 67 Rizal St; s/d P700/1000, matrimonial deluxe P1400; ❄📶) Tuguegarao's best deal, especially if you bump up to the huge, rear-facing 'matrimonial deluxe' rooms. Rooms are surprisingly modern and well kitted out, and quiet to boot.

Las Palmas de San José HOTEL **$$**

(☎844 1661; www.lasplamas.com.ph; Bagay Rd; r from P1850; ❄🏊) If you fancy some posh digs out here, head to Las Palmas. There are pruned palms, Mediterranean-style pathways and uniformed staff, and while the digs are so modern they're sometimes a little sterile, the whole package could be considered romantic after a few whiskies in the excellent hotel bar.

Hotel Delfino HOTEL $
(☎844 1314; Gonzaga St; s/d from P500/700; ❄) It is a bit old and vulnerable to street noise, but the rooms here are big, clean and cheap. Its Chinese restaurant has some of the best eats in town.

Information

Tuguegarao's main thoroughfare is Bonifacio St. It has plenty of ATMs and internet cafes.

The well-staffed **DOT Region II Office** (☎844 1621; Rizal St; ⏰9am-6pm) is an excellent source of information not only for Tuguegarao and Cagayan, but also for the Batanes and Babuyan island chains, Nueva Vizcaya and Northern Sierra Madre Natural Park.

Getting There & Away

PAL Express, Cebu Pacific and Air Philippines have daily flights to/from Manila (one hour). There are also flights to Batanes and Maconacan in Northern Sierra Madre Natural Park.

Victory Liner (☎844 0777), **Baliwag** (☎844 4325) and **Florida Liner** (☎846 2265; Diversion Rd) are the most comfortable options to Manila (P650, 12 hours). **GMW/Florida** (Diversion Rd) has buses to Laoag (P500, seven hours) via Claveria and Pagudpud. Florida also runs deluxe 10-hour night buses (P900).

Babuyan Islands

If you want to be way ahead of the pack, brave a wild bangka ride out to this quintet of islands in the fish-rich waters just off Luzon's northern tip. Humpback whale sightings are frequent in the Babuyan waters during the February-to-May breeding season. Due to typhoons and general awful weather conditions, we were not able to visit the Babuyans on this trip. **Manang Awit** (☎0910 789 4120) organises small-scale whale-watching trips on the easternmost island, **Camiguin**, and offers a homestay to visitors. Volcanic Camiguin is also known for its hot springs.

Jotay Resort (☎096 478 1270, 078 372 0560; www.jotayresort.com; r from P700, ste P2000), in the town of Santa Ana, has spare, comfortable rooms and spotty service. The resort can organise boat trips out to the Babuyans; the base trip lasts two days, involves snorkeling and camping on the islands and costs P12,000. which can be split between six guests.

Uncharted Philippines (☎02-621 5399; www.unchartedphilippines.com; 8-day tours US$700) runs tours out this way from Manila that include whale watching, trekking over the islands and skin diving; they're pricey but come well recommended. You can also contact **Balyena** (☎03-531 8604; www.balyena.org), a local educational and conservation organisation in Bohol that studies cetaceans (marine mammals), and see if you can accompany one of their survey trips. You can also pay local fisherfolk to take you out from Aparri or Santa Ana. Even if you don't see any whales, you'll almost certainly spot dolphins. Head out before sunrise and expect to pay at least P2000.

The undeveloped islands of **Fuga** and **Dalupiri** have beautiful white-sand beaches but no electricity or accommodation. Ask around for a homestay or just camp. Homestays are readily available on the most developed Babuyan island, **Calayan**, which boasts an incredible natural cover.

April to June is the best time to visit. The Babuyan Channel is generally too rough for crossings from December to March and during peak typhoon season (August to October).

Weather permitting, there are a few bangka per week from Aparri to Calayan (P600, six hours) and Camiguin (P500, four hours).

Irregular bangkas link Calayan with the other inhabited Babuyans or you can hire bangkas to jump between the islands.

BATANES

Well, this is it. You can't get further away from the Philippines without leaving the Philippines than Batanes: a group of 10 islands floating off in the 'Here be Dragons' corner of the map. To be honest, in a lot of relevant ways, once you get to Batanes you *have* left the Philippines. Only three of these specks are inhabited. With its verdant, rolling fields divided by hedgerows, the main island, Batan, looks more like the Scottish Highlands than the Philippines. Sabtang Island, with quaint villages of traditional stone houses, looks like it fell out of a fantasy novel. Itbayat, the northernmost inhabited island, is essentially a huge rock in the middle of the ocean.

Batanes experiences a lot more rain than most of the country and occasionally gets battered by typhoons. The locals, most of whom are of indigenous Ivatan stock and converse in their native Ivatan tongue, build their traditional houses typhoon tough, positioned slightly underground with metre-thick limestone walls and bushy roofs made of *cogon* grass.

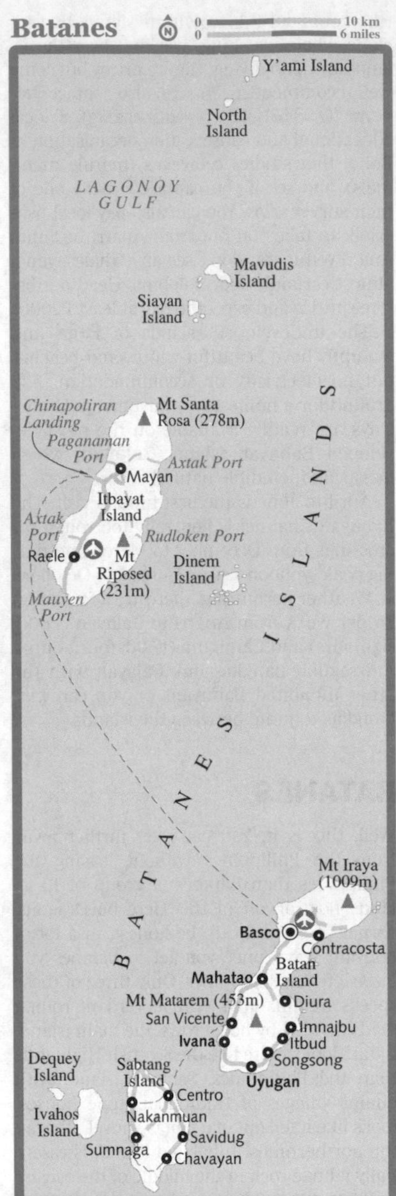

That quirky, bushy headpiece that some Ivatan women wear is called a *vakul*. It is made from the fibre of the *voyavoy* palm, found only in Batanes. Each item takes three weeks to make but lasts a lifetime, protecting the wearer from the sun and rain.

The best time to visit is between March and May, when the weather is relatively dry and typhoons are unlikely.

Getting There & Away

The only way to get to Batanes is by air. **SEAIR** (flyseair.com) has daily flights (7.50am) to Batan Island from Manila (1¾ hours).

Chemtrad Airlines (in Basco 0920 514 5274, in Tuguegarao 078-844 3113) and **Batanes Air** (in Basco 0905 927 8326, in Tuguegarao 0929 963 9162; www.cycloneairways.com) fly eight-seat planes to Basco on Batan Island (P5600, 1¼ hours) from Tuguegarao. Chemtrad flights are Monday, Wednesday and Friday. The Monday and Friday flights continue to Itbayat (P1800, 12 minutes). Batanes Air planes depart when full, usually daily.

Batan Island

078 / POP 12,000

Virtually all visitors to Batanes enter through Batan, the commercial centre and site of the provincial government. You'll want to spend at least a day circumnavigating the island, taking in the fabulous scenery and greenery, and visiting its villages. Batan is blessed with ample natural beauty, but for raw Ivatan culture, Sabtang Island is a better bet.

BASCO

With a wealth of accommodation options and a few decent restaurants, Batanes' capital makes an excellent base for exploring the rest of Batan Island. Abad St is the main drag, with several canteens and a couple of hardware stores renting motorbikes and mountain bikes.

Sights & Activities

Radar Tukon LANDMARK

From Basco it's a 1½-hour walk or a tough 30-minute bike ride up to Radar Tukon, an abandoned US weather station on a hilltop with great 360-degree views.

Pacita Abad Foundation RUINS

(www.fundacianpacita.ph) About 500m downhill beyond Radar Tukon is the Pacita Abad Foundation, in a magnificent stone house perched on a bluff overlooking Marlboro Country. The artist Pacita Abad lived and painted here until she died in 2004. Today the house serves as a lodge as well as a destination in its own right. The turn-off to Radar Tukon is on the National Hwy opposite Batanes Seaside Lodge.

Mt Iraya HIKING

North of Basco, Mt Iraya (1009m), a dormant volcano that last erupted in AD 505, can be climbed in about five hours and descended in three, though the summit is usually obscured by clouds. Your hotel can help you find a guide (P1000).

Sleeping

Batan Island's few hotels are all located in Basco. Air-con rooms tend to have hot water and fan rooms have cold water.

TOP CHOICE **Pacita Batanes** HOTEL $$$

(☎0927 290 2404; www.fundacionpacita.ph; r from P6300; ❄) You pay the price of luxury at Pacita Batanes, but you're rewarded with staying in a quirky, bohemian arts mansion perched on the edge of the earth. Fair trade, in our book. Other benefits include a lovely, grassy hilltop setting with sweet views to a stormy ocean, simple but beautiful rooms done in dark and light monochromes, and excellent on-site dining.

ShaneDel's Inn HOTEL $$

(☎0920 447 0737; shanedels@yahoo.com; cnr National Hwy & Abad St; r with fan & shared bathroom per person P500, s/d/tr with air-con P900/1500/1800; ❄) This family-run hotel, led by amiable and informative matriarch Del, is the cosiest, cleanest place in town and by far the best value. It offers game-fishing excursions (P3500) and staff can capably cook your fresh-caught fish. Locally done artwork speckles the walls.

Ivatan Lodge HOTEL $

(☎0930 851 1884; cnr National Hwy & Castillejos St; s/d/tr with fan P300/400/600, d with air-con P1000; ❄) The drab rooms here practically define 'basic', but it's cheap and 'popular' with other travellers, or those few who make it out here. It's near ShaneDel's, looking over the pier.

Eating

An abundance of fresh seafood and vegetables makes for good eating in the Batanes. *Tatus* (coconut crabs), the islands' tastiest delicacy, are becoming increasingly rare, but large ones can still be caught and eaten legally. Lobster is also popular.

Doque Grill Xaus FILIPINO $$

(National Hwy; meals P150; ⏲lunch & dinner) With some advance warning, chef-owner Salvatore can whip up exotic local concoctions such as *vunung* (a yellow rice dish), *vunes* (dried *gabi* stalks) and heavenly *uved* (banana root balls with bits of garlic and fish).

Pension Ivatan FILIPINO $$

(National Hwy; meals P150-200; ⏲lunch & dinner) Another good place to try Ivatan food.

Information

There are a few banks along the National Hwy that change dollars, but no functional ATMs as of this writing. Hotels can also arrange all-day guided tours around the island (around P4000).

Amboy Store (cnr Nunez & Abad Sts; mountain bikes/motorbikes per hr P30/150; ⏲7am-7pm)

Click (cnr Castillejos & Santana Sts; per hr P25; ⏲9am-9pm) The best of several internet cafes. It's Skype-ready.

Philippine Information Agency (☎0929 466 5794; Town Plaza; ⏲9am-6pm Mon-Fri) Manager Necitas Alconis is a receptacle of knowledge about Ivatan culture and can help arrange guides, transport and homestays (particularly in her native Itbayat). It's opposite Santo Domingo Church.

AROUND THE ISLAND

The island's main road, called National Hwy, follows the coastline anticlockwise from Basco to Imnajbu. From near Imnajbu, a steep dirt road ascends to Marlboro Country, eventually bringing you back to Mahatao.

Just south of Mahatao you'll find **White Beach**, one of the few beaches on Batan that's generally considered safe for swimming. Continuing south, you'll come to barangay **San Vicente**, the jumping-off point for Sabtang Island, before entering the town of **Ivana**, where a few traditional houses still stand (although most are in ruins). The road flattens out on the way to **Uyugan**, where there are a few more traditional houses.

On the left about halfway between Itbud and Imnajbu (barangays of Uyugan), an unmarked dirt road brings you up to a green, rolling pastureland populated by undomesticated carabao and cattle. This is Racuh Apayaman, better known as **Marlboro Country**. From here there are fantastic views of Batan's eastern coastline, Mt Iraya and a **lighthouse** near the dorado fishing village of Diura.

Continuing along the dirt road you'll pass through two gates, then hit a fork. Go right and descend to the intersection of the Mahatao–Diura road. Turn left to return to Mahatao (3km) or right to descend to **Diura** (1.5km). In Diura, have locals point you in the direction of the dark narrow **Crystal**

Cave (a 30-minute walk) and the ancient settlement of Diura (15 minutes).

There's a homestay (P100) available in Diura – set it up through the **tourism information office** (National Hwy; ⏲8am-5pm Mon-Fri) in Mahatao, which shares space with the Treasurers' Office.

Around the island there are various small canteens that serve premade dishes and may be able to whip up something fresher if you ask.

Getting There & Around

There are several ways to negotiate this loop. You can walk it, picking up jeepneys as you like. The walk from Imnajbu to Mahatao via Marlboro Country should take about three hours (there are no jeepneys along this stretch). If you're in good shape, renting a mountain bike is a fine option. Riding the entire loop takes four to six hours, not including stops. This is a difficult, undulating ride punctuated by a steep, 45-minute ascent to Marlboro Country. For a less strenuous tour, hire a motorbike, jeepney or van in Basco.

Jeepneys regularly ply the road between Basco and Itbud from around 4.30am to 8.30pm. In Basco, wait for jeepneys in front of ShaneDel's.

Sabtang Island

☎078 / POP 1500

Travelling to Sabtang from Basco increases the feeling that you've left the Philippines even further. Ivatan culture survives virtually intact here. Old ladies still walk around in their *vakul* and, unlike on Batan, the traditional limestone houses and their bushy roofs have been well preserved. Dramatic headlands, white beaches and a striking mountainous interior round out the feast for the eyes that is Sabtang.

The hike around the island is amazing. From **Centro**, where the ferry docks, hike south on the road to **Savidug** for about an hour (6km). Just south of Savidug look for a grassy *idjang* (fortress), which dates to pre-Hispanic times.

It's another 4km from Savidug to picturesque **Chavayan**, which the local authorities have nominated to be a World Heritage site because of its exceptionally well-preserved traditional Ivatan architecture. Handwoven *vakul* can be bought at the **Sabtang Weavers Association**, along the main road.

The road ends in Chavayan, but a two-hour walk through the interior brings you to **Sumnaga**, where there are more stone houses crammed up to the shoreline. From Sumnaga a paved road leads north to **Nakanmuan**, around the northern tip of the island, and back to Centro via pretty **Nakagbuan Beach**. An interior walking trail also connects Nakanmuan and Centro (45 minutes).

You can hire a motorbike (P800 to 1000), private jeep (P1500 to P2000) or bicycle (P200) to explore the island, minus the Chavayan to Sumnaga leg. Ask the helpful mayor or the tourism information centre in Centro for assistance.

There are two sleeping options in Centro. The **tourism information centre** (d with bathroom per person P300) runs a guesthouse. Next door, the School of Fisheries has a well-kept **dormitory** (dm P150).

A few *sari-sari* (neighbourhoods) in Centro have canteens and will cook up whatever is available. Nights are quiet on Sabtang, as the electricity is shut off around 8pm.

Weather permitting, round-bottomed boats *(falowa)* make several daily trips between San Vicente on Batan and Centro (P60, 35 minutes in good weather). There are usually three morning trips, the first departing from Centro around 5am. Sometimes an afternoon trip is added. If you get stuck on Sabtang you can stay the night or hire a *falowa* to make a special trip (at least P3000). Be warned: this crossing can be rough.

Itbayat Island

☎078 / POP 3100

It's a thrilling 12-minute plane ride from Basco to Itbayat, a rocky platform of an island that is the Philippines' final inhabited frontier.

Trails criss-cross the centre of the island, making for good trekking. There are nice views from **Mt Riposed** (231m), east of Raele. It's a beautiful half-hour walk from the main town, **Mayan** (Centro), to Paganaman Port, where at dusk you'll see farmers returning from the fields, and fishers with their day's catch. If you arrive at low tide, you can soak in a little natural swimming pool in the rocks next to the port.

The mayor, who can be found at the municipal building, will let you stay in Mayan's **Municipal Hall Guesthouse** (dm P150), with access to a kitchen, or ask around for Faustina Cano, who runs a homestay.

Like Sabtang, Itbayat only gets about 12 hours of electricity per day. If the weather acts up you could get stranded on Itbayat for a few days, so build some flexibility into your schedule.

Chemtrad Airlines has Monday and Friday flights between Basco and Itbayat (P1670, 12 minutes), and occasionally adds extra flights. The landing strip is near Raele, 10km south of Mayan. From there you will be transported to Mayan in a dump truck.

One or two *falowa* ferries depart Basco for Itbayat between 6am and 7am, and then turn around and leave Itbayat around noon. This is a rough crossing at the best of times and may be cancelled altogether when seas are particularly perilous.

Southeast Luzon

Includes »

Best Places to Sleep

- Sirangan Beach Resort (p168)
- La Playa Camp (p163)
- Ticao Island Resort (p174)
- Giddy's Place (p170)
- Avenue Plaza Hotel (p159)

Best Places to Eat

- Geewan (p161)
- Small Talk Cafe (p166)
- WayWay Restaurant (p165)
- Bistro Roberto (p160)
- Casa de Don Emilio (p179)

Why Go?

It's de rigueur in travel writing to describe a place as shaped like something – Vietnam is an oxbow, Thailand a kite. The crazy coastline of southeast Luzon is shaped like nothing, except maybe a mess. But what a beautiful mess. Between the dagger heights of volcanic Mt Mayon and the leviathan-studded sea depths near Donsol, there's a lot of variety here.

Plus: islands like Masbate and Catanduanes, where the pace of life is so slow as to be (cheerfully) comatose; the university-driven youth of Naga and the medieval Catholicism of Marinduque; surfing in Daet and limestone cliffs on the Caramoan Peninsula. And the food. Bicol brings the spice, and a welcome dash of taste, to the oft-bland Filipino table. Best of all, southeast Luzon is close enough to Manila to benefit from good infrastructure, but far enough away to feel removed from the capital region's grind.

When to Go

Naga City

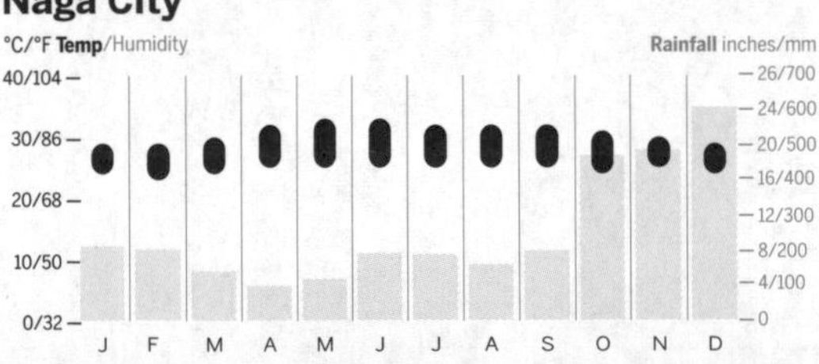

Feb–Apr Good weather and festivals.

May–Jul This is generally a sunny (and hot!) time of year.

Nov–Jan Severe rains hit the Pacific Coast; Bicol has better weather and few tourists.

Climate

Southeast Luzon's wet season begins and ends a little later than in Manila and the rest of Luzon. It kicks in around late August and lasts until February, but rain is likely at any time of the year, especially on the eastern (Pacific) side. Typhoon season is July to November. Most typhoons pass by a couple of hundred kilometres offshore, but they occasionally make landfall on the eastern shore and regularly affect Catanduanes.

Getting There & Away

If you're coming from Manila, the best way to get to southeast Luzon is to take a comfortable 29-seat deluxe bus. These travel at night and cost only about P200 more than regular air-con buses. You can also fly to Naga, Legazpi, Catanduanes and Marinduque. See those sections for specifics.

The islands of Marinduque and Catanduanes are served by frequent ferries. You can also take ferries from Matnog, at the southern tip of Bicol, to Samar, and from Pilar, near Donsol, to Masbate. See those sections for details.

BICOL

Bicol technically includes Luzon's south eastern peninsula and the islands of Catanduanes and Masbate, but this section of the chapter covers peninsular Bicol only. Catanduanes (p175) and Masbate (p171) are covered in separate sections later in this chapter.

Daet & Bagasbas

☎054 / POP 94,180

There's little to hold travellers in Daet (it kinda sounds like what to do when you want to lose weight) once the banking/internet chores are done (head for Vinzons Ave), but it's the access point for Bagasbas Beach, a laid-back surfie, barfly and karaoke-crooner hang-out 4km north of town.

Activities

Gorgeous **Bagasbas Beach** stretches for a couple of white sandy kilometres. The **surfing** is best when typhoons churn up the Pacific's waters between August and October, but fickle is a good word to describe the waves.

This is a good spot for newbie surfers, as waves are pretty small for much of the year. Instruction is available from any of the local surfing whiz kids (P400 per hour). Fair warning: while these kids can surf, their English skills aren't always great, so you may want to shop around until you find an instructor you're comfortable communicating with. That said, the locals here are beyond friendly; this is one of those places where we've seen them happily inviting international travellers over for lunch, drinks, etc.

There are equipment rental shacks all along the beach; the going rate for a surfboard is P200/hr. It can be rippy here – take care when swimming. If you're interested in kiteboarding (think wakeboarding, except you use a kite instead of a boat to propel you forward), head to **Mike's Kites** (☎0921 457 2299, 0919 209 9191; www.mikes-kites.com; 2hr intro US$60; 1-day kiteboard rental US$20) run by American Mike Gambrill, alongside a restaurant/bar of the same name.

Speaking of nightlife, Bagasbas is known as one of the videoke capitals of the country, which is pretty full-on considering that the bar strip is just 500m long. The beach is dead as a dodo until about 4pm weekdays, then crazy busy until about 4am; weekends are lively 24/7.

Sleeping & Eating

On Bagasbas Beach, **Kusina ni Angel** is still going strong. Run by the charming Angel de la Cruz, it has a creative menu specialising in seafood with a decent veg selection – the okra and eggplant is good. **Catherine's** restaurant is a buzzing spot overlooking the beach, but we think it's a bit overpriced.

Zenaida's Palace HOTEL $$
(☎0921 224 0461, 441 6286; james_auro@yahoo.com; s/d P600/1200; ❄) The friendly owner of the 'palace' has turned her yellow-and-white house with tiled floors and clean rooms into a good value midrange surfer spot.

Mike's Kites FILIPINO $$
(☎0919 209 9191; www.mikes-kites.com; Bagasbas Rd; air-con/fan bungalow P1200/800, s/d hut P300/500; ❄📶) The bar/restaurant is a good spot for Western and Filipino food, beer and the chance to meet travellers, expats and the Filipinos who love them. The on-site bungalows and native huts are good value.

Bagasbas Surfer's Diner HOMESTAY $
(☎0916 475 9053; r with fan/air-con P500/1000; ❄) In Bagasbas a few houses offer homestays – ask around or look for signs – or stay in the clean and simple rooms behind the

Southeast Luzon Highlights

1. Snorkel alongside Bicol's gentle giants, the **whale sharks** (p169) of Donsol
2. Watch the cattle hustlers round up some doggies at the **Rodeo Masbateño** (p173) in Masbate
3. Wait for Catanduanes' legendary **Majestics surf break** (p177) to kick
4. Boat the limestone cliffs and beaches of the beautiful **Caramoan Peninsula** (p161)
5. Dive the rays' cleaning station in the **Manta Bowl** (p170) at Ticao Pass
6. Sample the best of **Bicol's fiery cuisine** (p162) and hot nightlife in Naga
7. Mask up at Marinduque's wild **Moriones Festival** (p179)

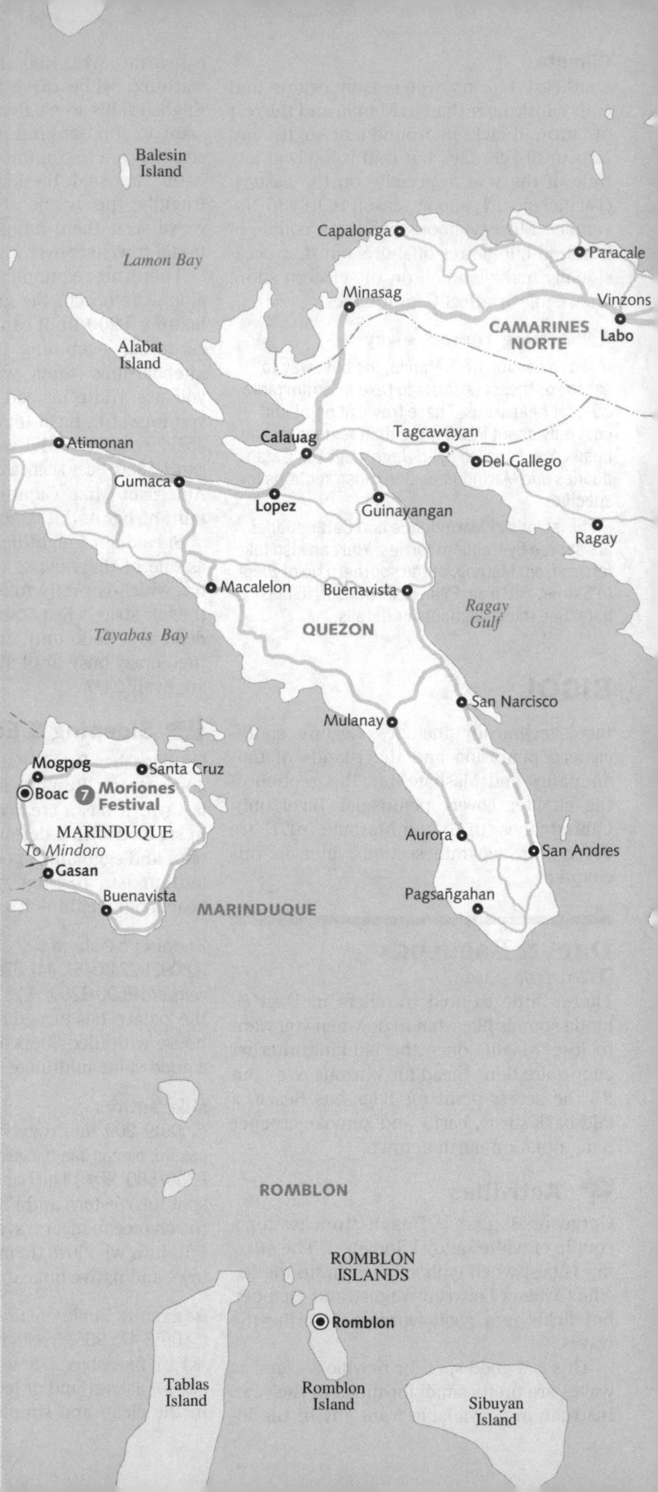

0
50 km
0
30 miles
PHILIPPINE SEA
Calagua Islands
San José
Bagasbas
Apuao Grande Island
Mercedes
Daet
Basud
Siruma
Barana
Caramoan Peninsula
4
Lahuy Island
CATANDUANES
Garchitorena
Caramoan Peninsula
San Miguel Bay
Paniman
Caramoan National Park
Caramoan
CATANDUANES
Guijalo
Presentacion
Sipocot
Bagacay
Mt Isarog National Park
Sabang
Majestics Surf Break
3
Tigaon
San Andres
Virac
Mt Isarog (1966m)
Naga
6
Sagnay
Pili
Lagonoy Gulf
Mt Iriga (1470m)
CAMARINES SUR
Pasacao
Lake Baao
Iriga
Lake Buhi
Tiwi
San Miguel Island
Cagraray Island
Bato
Tabaco
Batan Island
Rapu Rapu Island
Lake Bato
Libon
Ligao
Mt Mayon (2462m)
Rapu Rapu
Santo Domingo
Guinobatan
Camalig
Daraga
Legazpi
Manito
ALBAY
Bacon
Jovellar
Burias Island
Pio Duran
Putiao
Sorsogon
Dumadlangan
Abuyog
Gubat
Castilla
Pilar
Donsol
1
SORSOGON
Luban
Mt Bulusan (1560m)
Magallanes
Mt Juban (730m)
Bulusan
MASBATE
BICOL
Monbon
San Roque
Irosin
Bulan
Santa Magdalena
Monreal
San Jacinto
Ticao Pass
Matnog
5
Ticao Pass
Ticao Island
MASBATE
2
Masbate
NORTHERN SAMAR
To Samar

pleasant Bagasbas Surfer's Diner. Take your earplugs.

Getting There & Away

Air-con buses (P750) run by Philtranco leave Pasay, Manila at 8am, 8pm and 9pm for Daet (eight hours). Air-con buses leave for Pasay at 8:30pm. Ordinary buses to Manila are easier to come by, but are obviously not nearly as comfortable.

There are frequent minivan services to Naga (P150, two hours) from the Central Terminal northeast of town. Transfer in Naga for Legazpi and points south.

Naga

☎054 / POP 165,500

As midsized Filipino cities go, friendly Naga, in Camarines Sur, is an exemplar of the genre. Students are ubiquitous in this university town, as are the services that follow students: coffee shops with wi-fi, cheap, good restaurants and good nightlife. Then there's Camsur Watersports Complex, which draws local and international visitors, plus nearby mountain biking and hiking and, further out, the jungly, beautiful appendage of the Caramoan Peninsula. Downtown Naga is built around **Plaza Rizal**, a popular hang-out spot for students and idlers.

In September, thousands of devotees come to Naga for the **Peñafrancia Festival** in celebration of the Virgin of Peñafrancia, Bicol's patron saint. The town's population swells at this time; you need to book accommodation at least two months in advance.

Sights

FREE Naga City Museum MUSEUM

(Room 309, Dean Antonio N. Sison Hall; ⏰8am-noon & 2-5pm Mon-Fri, 8am-noon Sat) This small museum, located on the campus of the University of Nueva Caceras, is the one of the oldest museums in the country. It's ethnographic in focus, filled with crafts, tools and other artefacts of pre-colonial Bicol.

FREE Peñafrancia Museum MUSEUM

(Balatas Rd; ⏰9am-noon & 2-5pm Mon-Fri, 8am-noon Sat) If you can't make the Peñafranica festival, this little museum may be the next best thing. Located in the Peñafranica Basilica, the central point of the festival, the exhibits here consist of pictures and glass displays of religious pageantry and some entertaining dioramas of the main procession – it's a nice window into the devotion to Mary that is central to many Filipino Catholics. The actual image of Our Lady of Peñafranica is inaccessible; the 30cm-tall statue

Naga

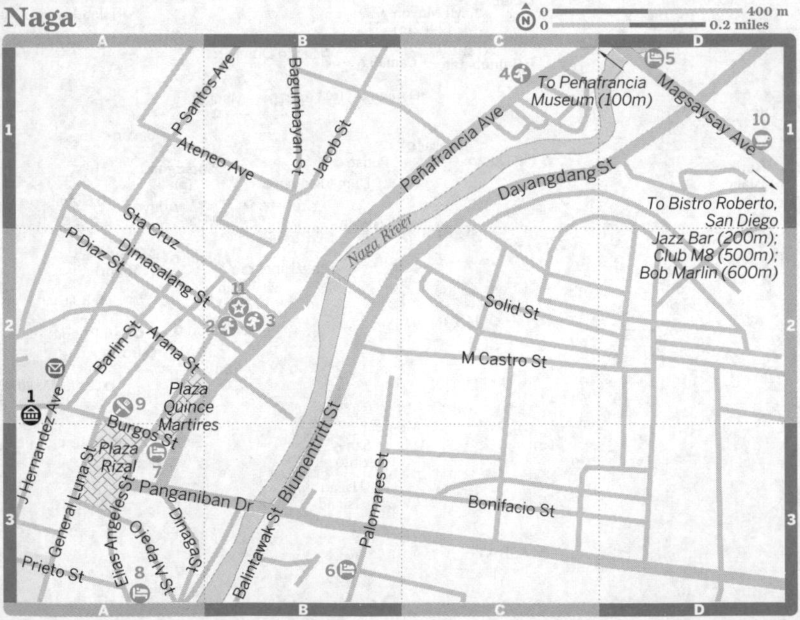

0 400 m
0 0.2 miles

P Santos Ave
Bagumbayan St
Jacob St
Ateneo Ave
To Peñafrancia Museum (100m)
Magsaysay Ave
Peñafrancia Ave
Dayangdang St
To Bistro Roberto, San Diego Jazz Bar (200m); Club M8 (500m); Bob Marlin (600m)
Naga River
Sta Cruz
P Diaz St
Dimasalang St
Solid St
Barlin St
Arana St
M Castro St
Plaza Quince Martires
J Hernandez Ave
Burgos St
Plaza Rizal
General Luna St
Panganiban Dr
Blumentritt St
Palomares St
Bonifacio St
Elias Angeles St
Ojeda St
Dinaga St
Balintawak St
Prieto St

was stolen in 1981, only to be returned a year later by an antiques dealer.

Activities

The outdoor pursuits available around Naga are one of Luzon's best-kept secrets, and centre mainly on Mt Isarog and the Caramoan Peninsula. There's also good diving in the Ragay Gulf to the west.

Kadlagan Outdoor Shop & Climbing Wall OUTDOORS
(☎0919 800 6299, 472 3305; http://kadlagan.i.ph; 16 Dimasalang St; ⊙store 9am-7pm, climbing wall 3-7pm) For gear rental, guides and tips on hiking and climbing, this is the place to go. Shop owner Jojo Villareal is a wealth of information, knows all the local rocks and routes (and won't recommend those he thinks are overused) and is usually here in the evenings. He can organise guides for hikes up Mt Isarog and takes groups to the Caramoan Peninsula – we'd recommend touring with these guys if you don't feel like dealing with low levels of tourism infrastructure out that way. Also has a location selling hiking gear in the SM City Mall.

Steady Eddie DIVING
(☎472 7333; www.steadyeddiedivecenter.com; 2nd fl, Edventure Bldg, Peñafrancia Ave; ⊙8am-7pm) This is where divers should head. You can call a few days ahead and try to join one of the weekend dive expeditions to sites such as Pasacao, on the Ragay Gulf, and Catanduanes. Costs run from US$130 for three dives. Provides open water and advanced levels of diving instruction.

Naga

Sights
1 Naga City Museum A2

Activities, Courses & Tours
2 Kadlagan Climbing Wall B2
3 Kadlagan Outdoor Shop B2
4 Steady Eddie C1

Sleeping
5 Avenue Plaza Hotel D1
6 CBD Plaza Hotel B3
7 Crown Hotel A3
8 Naga Regent Hotel 1 .... A3

Eating
Crown Hotel .... (see 7)
9 Geewan A2

Drinking
10 Beanbag Coffee D1

Entertainment
Lolo's Music Bar .... (see 5)
Westpark .... (see 5)
11 Wharf Galley B2

Sleeping

Naga has some excellent midrange accommodation if you need a base for exploring southeast Luzon.

Avenue Plaza Hotel HOTEL $$$
(☎473 9999; www.theavenueplazahotel.com; Magsaysay Ave; r from P4400; ❄@📶🏊) Over by the bar and restaurant cluster is the best hotel in town – although you pay for the privilege. Rooms are spacious, easily the match of a Western business-class hotel, with fluffy beds, flat-screen TVs, a downstairs coffee shop, gym and big pool with sundeck and loungers.

CBD Plaza Hotel HOTEL $$
(☎472 0318; www.cbdplazahotel.com; Ninoy & Cory Ave; s/d from P600/1000; ❄@📶) A good midrange selection, the CBD is painted in bright colours and is about the closest thing Naga has to a boutique hotel. Rooms are plain, bordering on sterile, but very clean and comfortable. The cheapest economy rooms are pretty cramped. Six-bed family 'suites' go for P3600. The hotel is located off Palomares St, just south of SM City Mall.

Crown Hotel HOTEL $$
(☎473 1845; www.crownhotelnaga.com; Burgos St; d from P1200; ❄@📶) This old standby hotel still gives you bang for your buck in Naga, with extremely friendly staff, solid rooms, attractive common areas and free breakfast in the comfortable restaurant overlooking the plaza. Request a room off the busy street, and note that the wi-fi service can be iffy.

Naga Regent Hotel HOTEL $$
(☎472 2626; http://nagaregenthotel.com; Elias Angeles St; dm P400, s/d P1100/2000; ❄@📶) This business-class hotel has the goods, but cheaper rooms are small and the 3rd floor vibrates thanks to an attached bowling alley. Across the street is an annexe with tatty but good-value rooms and dorm beds. By the time you read this, the properties may be joined into a single hotel. Breakfast is included at both.

WAKING UP TO WAKEBOARDING

You can't leave Naga without checking out the **Camsur Watersports Complex** (CWC; ☎477 3172; www.cwcwake.com; ⏰8:30am-7pm Tue-Thu, 8:30am-9pm Fri-Sun, 8am-7pm Mon), 'the best cable park in the world', according to *Wake* magazine.

No idea what we're talking about? Welcome to the niche – but growing – world of wakeboarding. Think snowboarding on water. Your feet are strapped to a board and you're pulled around a watercourse on a cable. Sound easy? Wait till you see the pros on the six-corner course, where the tight cable allows for big tricks over a series of obstacles and an artificial beach allows for a water surface smooth as glass. Beginners are welcome here, and a big swimming pool, restaurant and coffee shop, gear shops and lots of cheery young staff complete the very cool and hip atmosphere. Prices are complicated and depend on what you want to do and what gear you need to do it. An hour/half-day on the water, including helmet, vest and board, will cost around P250/750; if you just want to hang out, watch the action and use the pool the fee is P165.

Enthusiasts chill here for weeks or months. There's a range of accommodation on site, from very comfortable private **villas** (P5000), a short walk from the water, to cosy **cabañas** (from P1250) and **family trailers** (from P2850) right on top of it. 'The Ecovillage', also in the Capitol complex, offers more budget options, including tiny **cabins** (with/without air-con P500/350).

To get here, take a jeepney from Naga 10km or so to the CWC turn-off at Pili, then hop in a pedicab (P10) for the ride into the complex. A special-ride tricycle from Naga costs P300 one way. A free shuttle service into town operates for overnight guests.

Eating & Drinking

MAGSAYSAY AVENUE

There's a couple of clusters of trendy bars, clubs, restaurants and coffee shops centred on the Dayangdang St end of Magsaysay Ave, and at Avenue Sq, which shares the same space as the Avenue Plaza Hotel. Bars generally open around 4pm and stay open til 1am (sometimes later on weekends).

During our visit, a new food-shopping-bar-videoke-club complex called the **Westpark** (www.thewestpark.net) had opened on Magsaysay Ave; it seems packed with young Filipinos seeking good grub and good times. The top-floor **Penthouse** is a chic nightclub attracting Naga's glitterati.

Bistro Roberto FILIPINO $
(Magsaysay Ave; meals from P70) Live jam bands, Bicol cuisine, lots of booze, drunk Filipino students and (of course) videoke equals fun times all around.

Lolo's Music Bar BAR
(⏰4pm-1am) On the 2nd floor of Avenue Sq; a cool bar with plenty of room to breathe, and live music from 9pm. It caters to a more mature crowd than Club M8, but, like its rival, frowns on shorts and sandals.

San Diego Jazz Bar BAR
(Magsaysay Ave) If you're not into the rowdy, get-blasted drinking scene popular with so many young Naga residents, consider kicking back here and listening to lounge singing and smooth jazz.

Beanbag Coffee CAFE
(Magsaysay Ave; ⏰9am-midnight; 📶) Does a great imitation of Seattle's best, only much cheaper and quite artsy. The cakes are delicious. Late at night, students gather here to smoke cigarettes and discuss the vagaries of life; religion, politics and the NBA.

Bob Marlin BAR
(Magsaysay Ave) Another good spot for live music, dancing, cold brew and greasy finger food – the crispy fried pork is a delicious means of soaking up the booze.

Club M8 DISCO
(Magsaysay Ave; ⏰7pm-4am) This disco sees dance-happy revellers carousing till the wee hours, especially on weekends. Caters to a younger crowd; dress to impress.

CENTRE

Come evening you'll find a good crop of food stalls popping up around the squares that dot downtown. When we visited there seemed to be an overwhelming profligation of fishball vendors, but locals assure us you can find good Bicol cuisine here most nights.

Geewan FILIPINO $
(Burgos St; dishes from P70; ⊙lunch & dinner) Although it was under renovation at the time of writing, locals say this spot does the best Bicol cuisine in town. Try the Bicol *exprés* (see the boxed text, p162).

Crown Hotel FILIPINO $
(Burgos St; dishes from P100; ⊙lunch & dinner) They do some very fine Bicol cuisine here, although you may have to ask for specific regional specialties from off the menu (see p162). Also does good Chinese food.

Wharf Galley BAR
(Elias Angeles St; www.wharfgalleyrockcafe.com) Bills itself as a 'rock cafe' with live music every night, an acoustic night on Wednesday, and – unusually – mostly original music rather than covers from the performers. Check website for the weekly lineup.

 Information

All the major banks are well represented.

Downtown Post Office (University of Nueva Caceres)

Main Post Office (City Hall Complex, btwn J Miranda Ave and Maria Cristina St)

Naga City Visitors Center (☎473 4432; www.naga.gov.ph/tourism; City Hall Complex, btwn J Miranda Ave and Maria Cristina St; ⊙8am-noon & 1-5pm Mon-Fri)

 Getting There & Away

Air

The airport is in Pili, 14km south of Naga. Cebu Pacific and Airphil Express fly daily between Manila and Naga.

Bus & Jeepney

All bus services use Naga's central bus terminal, located near SM City, just south of Panganiban Dr. Cagsawa and **RSL** (☎472 6885) bus lines have air-con night buses that go directly to Ermita in Manila, while several others go to Cubao; most comfortable are **Isarog** (☎478 8804) and Amihan. Philtranco goes to Pasay. Most air-con and deluxe services are at night (air-con/recliner P600/700).

Jeepneys and air-con minivans leave about 100m from the central terminal. There are frequent air-con bus/minivan services to Daet (P75/150, 2½/2 hours) and Legazpi (P100/150, 2½/two hours). Avoid the 'ordinary' bus to Legazpi, which can take up to six hours. Transfer in Legazpi for Sorsogon and Donsol. Air-con minivans also serve Tabaco (P145) and Sabang (P90). Jeepneys head to Panicuason (P20, 30 minutes) and Pili (P10).

Mt Isarog National Park

Dominating Camarines Sur's landscape is Mt Isarog (1966m), Bicol's (dormant) second-highest volcano. From Panicuason (pan-ee-*kwa*-sone), a steep, half-hour walk along a rough road (passable if it's dry, but a regular car will struggle) leads to the entrance of **Mt Isarog National Park** (⊙8am-5pm). There is an admission fee (P100) at the base of the mountain. To the right, a short walk leads down some very steep stone steps to **Malabsay Falls**, where you can swim with a view of Mt Isarog – the experience is amazing. At Panicuason, **Mt Isarog Hot Springs** (admission P100; ⊙7am-6pm) has five natural hot-to-tepid pools – a nice way to relax after a trek in the park. The springs are a 1.3km walk off the main road, just before the road to the national park.

Climbing Mt Isarog

We highly recommend hiring a guide for the two-day return trek up Mt Isarog. The six- to eight-hour hike up takes you through the last virgin tropical forest in Luzon. As you get higher, the vegetation turns to mossy forest, which sheds into sparse grassland and stony alpine shelves closer to the summit.

Traditionally, late February to early June has been the best time, weather-wise, to climb. Two trails make their way up the mountain: the (often overused) trail from Panicuason, and a less used and more environmentally friendly trail starting at Consocep. Talk to Jojo at Kadlagan Outdoor Shop (p159) in Naga; hiking packages (P5000 for one person, P7000 for two) include both an experienced English-speaking and local guide, camping gear and food, and all transport and permits. Keen climbers should also ask about routes on **Mt Lobo**, in Camarines Norte (Cam Nor), and **Mt Asog**, near Iriga.

To travel to Mt Isarog from Naga, take a jeepney to Panicuason. Note that the last jeepney back to Naga leaves Panicuason around 5pm; you can always try hitching, but if traffic is light (a possibility after dark) you might get stuck.

Caramoan Peninsula

About 50km from Naga, a lonely appendage of land rubs the teal underbelly of the ocean with a sugar-sand coast, limestone cliffs and dark tufts of jungle. This is stunningly beautiful scenery that reminds one of

The Beach, *Dr No* or anywhere in Northern Palawan. And soon, we reckon Caramoan will be shouted across travel circles, rather than whispered about – the French, Israeli and Bulgarian versions of *Survivor* have all already been filmed here.

With that said, it still remains quite possible to spend quiet time close to nature here. Island-hopping is the big drawcard; highlights include the pretty islands of **Matukad** and **Lahus**, offshore from Gota, plus postcard perfect **Aguirangan**. The V-shaped **Sabitan Laya** offers long stretches of white sand and a limestone outcrop at the base of the V – there's good **snorkelling** here. The largest of the dozen or so islands is **Lahuy**, with beaches, local gold panners and a fruit bat colony; it's best accessible from barangay Bikal. So is **Tabgon**, set among onshore mangroves, and with a 500-step climb up to an enormous **statue of Mary of Peace**; it's a popular place of pilgrimage for Filipinos. White-sand **Gota Beach** lies just 4km from Caramoan town, and east of this lies **Pitogo Bay** with its unusual lagoon surrounded by nipa palms (another rumoured site of Japanese treasure). Inland from Gota, **rock climbing** and **caving** beckon, as does the nearby swimming hole at **Bolang-Bogang Spring**. Clear and refreshing in the dry season, it's murky after rain.

Caramoan Kayaks (☎0921 987 3157; www.cki-inn.com; 1hr/day P150/1900), based out of the CK Inn rents out sea kayaks and can help guide paddlers around the islands.

You may be able to rent a *sibid-sibid* (small fishing boat) and paddle yourself around, but bangka are more readily available. A full day of island-hopping in a seven-person bangka will cost you at least P2000.

Sleeping & Eating

If you're not looking for resort life, base yourself on the eastern edge of the peninsula, around Caramoan town or in the coastal barangay of Paniman.

Consider camping at Paniman if you can live with a lack of creature comforts. There's a quiet stretch of beach about 400m from the village (be prepared to haul water), where river meets sea under a limestone overhang; ask permission from the barangay captain. You can rent tents from Kadlagan Outdoor Shop (p159). Homestays are possible – ask for the school teacher Mr Boyet, or tricycle-driver Islaw can help.

There are a few hotels in relaxed and rural one-street Caramoan town (away from the beach). New homestays seem to pop up on a monthly basis. The going rate at the time of research was P500 per person per night.

THE FIRE DOWN BELOW

There may be no more roundly vilified cuisine in all of Asia than Filipino food. Bicol, with its smorgasbord of fiery fish, pork and vegetable concoctions, is the country's answer to that criticism.

Bicolanos hardly have the Philippines' monopoly on coconuts, but for some reason they are the only ones who cook predominantly with coconut milk. Wise choice. Anything cooked in coconut milk is known as *ginataán*. Squid *(pusít)* cooked in coconut milk is thus *ginataán pusít* (and it's highly recommended). *Ginataán santol* (a pulpy fruit) and *ginataán* jackfruit are also tasty. The other key ingredient in Bicol cuisine is *sili* (hot chilli pepper). There are many varieties of *sili*, among them the tiny but potent *labuyo*, which you can order in bars mixed with tender, almond-shaped *pili* nuts.

Two dishes you'll definitely notice are Bicol *exprés* and *pinangat*. The former is a fiery mishmash of ground pork, *sili*, baby shrimps, onion, garlic and other spices cooked in coconut milk. *Pinangat* is green *gabi* (taro) leaves wrapped around small pieces of fish, shrimp and/or pork, and a chopped, leafy green vegetable known as *natong (laing)*, which is also commonly served on its own as a side dish. Lastly, there's the surprisingly palatable *candingga* – diced pork liver and carrots sweetened and cooked in vinegar.

The odd thing about Bicol food is that you have to work a bit to find it. Most hotels and restaurants stick to all-too-familiar Filipino staples. Street-stall buffets in Naga are good places to find local food, though you may have trouble getting instruction on what is what. In Legazpi try Small Talk Cafe (p166) for great Bicol-Italian fusion dishes and Way-Way Restaurant (p165) for an authentic Bicol buffet.

Residencia de Salvacion B&B $
(☎0939 310 1135; http://residenciasalvacion.multiply.com; r from P800; ❄📶) The Residencia is a wonderful B&B with clean rooms, flat-screen TVs and, most importantly, great staff who go out of their way to make your stay as comfortable as possible.

La Playa Camp CAMPGROUND $
(☎0919 813 6766; www.eyeoncaramoan.com; cabanas from P800, camp sites P300) A pretty collection of beach huts with shared bathrooms and lovely views out onto the islands, La Playa is good choice for those who don't mind foregoing creature comforts for a bit of rustic tropical beauty. The same people also run **Vista Del Mar** guesthouse, with similar rates, for those who prefer sleeping in a house.

Villa Juliana GUESTHOUSE $
(☎0917 763 3167; http://villajuliana.multiply.com; r from P750; ❄📶) This bright pink guest house (with lemon yellow extension) is popular with domestic tourists. Rooms are clean, comfy, come with TVs and are as colourful as the exterior (which you may find off-putting unless you bring sunglasses) but this is a friendly place that takes care of its guests.

CK Inn B&B $
(☎0921 987 3157; www.ck-inn.com; ❄📶) An airy home that's been converted into a pretty guesthouse, the CK is a tad bit overpriced, but with its helpful staff, spick-and-span rooms, free breakfast and leafy location, it's still a lovely option. There's an eight-bed family room that goes for P2500 if you're in a big group. Run by the folks at Caramoan Kayaks.

La Casa Roa GUESTHOUSE $
(☎811 5789, 0917 580 1850; lacasaroa@yahoo.com, momieperez@gmail.com; s/d P950/1550; ❄) This 1950s house is a decent option if you don't mind staying in town. There's polished floorboards, a garden to chill in and clean rooms.

Rex Tourist Inn GUESTHOUSE $
(☎0919 882 1879; s/d P700/1400; ❄) Long-standing and showing its age, but has retained helpful and cheery staff.

Gota Village Resort RESORT $$$
(☎02 817 0831, 0928 308 3969; http://caramoanislands.com; cabanas from P3500; ❄) Gota Village is the big resort in Caramoan, located about 20 minutes from Caramoan town. We're not huge fans of the clusters of cabanas and beach huts. The same owners manage **Hunongan Cove**, a more isolated and generally beautiful cluster of cabanas/villas that run for the same price; we'd opt for this latter option.

ℹ Getting There & Away

Getting to Caramoan town is half the adventure, and the fun. There are great views of Mt Isarog on the overland leg of the journey, and of the seductive coastline – including, on a clear day, perfect Mt Mayon across the Lagonoy Gulf – on the ocean leg. The best time to visit is late May to early September, when sea conditions are generally good.

From Naga, take an air-con minivan to Sabang (P90, 1½ hours). From Sabang, boats leave when full to Guijalo pier (P120-150, two hours), the last leaving around 1pm. Go for the bigger 'Harry' boats (when the shade tarpaulins are drawn down on the small boats it's a bit like travelling blind in a hot and steamy plastic bag).

Gota Beach Resort runs a fast catamaran service from Sabang to Guijalo (P350, 45 minutes) that departs at 10am and 1:30pm. You could also hire your own boat for between P1500 and P2000 if you negotiate well.

From Guijalo, it's a 10-minute jeepney or tricycle ride to Caramoan town.

A very poor road from Sabang to Guijalo (35km, currently four hours) has been under construction for years now; when finished it will reduce road travel to Naga to about two hours. Don't hold your breath. You can drive to Sabang and leave your car there by the jetties for P100 a day.

If you're travelling from Legazpi or Tabaco, an alternative jeepney route runs along the coast road via Tiwi to Tigaon, where you can pick up a jeepney for Sabang.

Legazpi

☎052 / POP 180,000

This gritty provincial capital is situated right at the foot of Mt Mayon (2462m), justifiably dubbed the world's most perfect volcano. It's a friendly enough place, clogged with traffic and Jollibee fast-food restaurants, but oddly charming nonetheless.

Legazpi is divided into Albay District and Legazpi City. Most government offices, the airport, and the fancier restaurants and hotels are situated in Albay District. Legazpi City is a noisy, convoluted maze of street stalls, markets, bars and exhaust-stained buildings. The bus terminal and cheaper accommodation are located here. Hundreds of jeepneys per day connect the two districts, which are 3.5km apart along the National Hwy.

City officials are transforming a chunk of the waterfront into the ritzy **Embarcadero**, a shopping-dining-nightlife complex/mall serviced by a small fleet of electric jeepneys.

Sights

The **Legazpi City Museum** (City Hall Annex; ⌚8am-5pm Mon-Fri) houses a nice collection of archaeological treasures and cultural bric-a-brac donated by locals throughout the years. There are cool photographs of occupied Legazpi during the WWII plus the destruction wrought by Mt Mayon through the years.

Mt Mayon unexpectedly pops out behind every corner, and the views are lovely. To get a really good glimpse of the volcano (and the city), haul your butt up **Lignon Hill** (or drive, or take a trike; expect to pay around P300 for a roundtrip). It's a steep, but paved, 20-minute walk up the hill; we'd recommend going in the morning before it gets too hot. At the top you'll find a small **nature park**, an observation post run by the Philippine Institute of Volcanology and be treated to a superlative view of both Legazpi and Mt Mayon. The way up is by the tennis courts near **Albay Wildlife Park**, more of a municipal park than anything else (there's a playground with dinosaurs!).

Activities

Legazpi is a good base for exploring the nearby adventureland of Bicol. Climbing Mt Mayon (p167), snorkelling with whale sharks in Donsol (p169) and diving Manta Bowl (p170) top the list.

Most hotels can set you up with vans and drivers, some of whom are also tour guides. The going rate for day tours within Albay province is around P3000.

Bicol Adventure & Tours TOURS
(☎480 2266; www.freewebs.com/bicoladventures; V&O Bldg, Quezon Ave, Legazpi City; ⌚8am-5pm Mon-Fri, to noon Sat) A professional operation

Legazpi

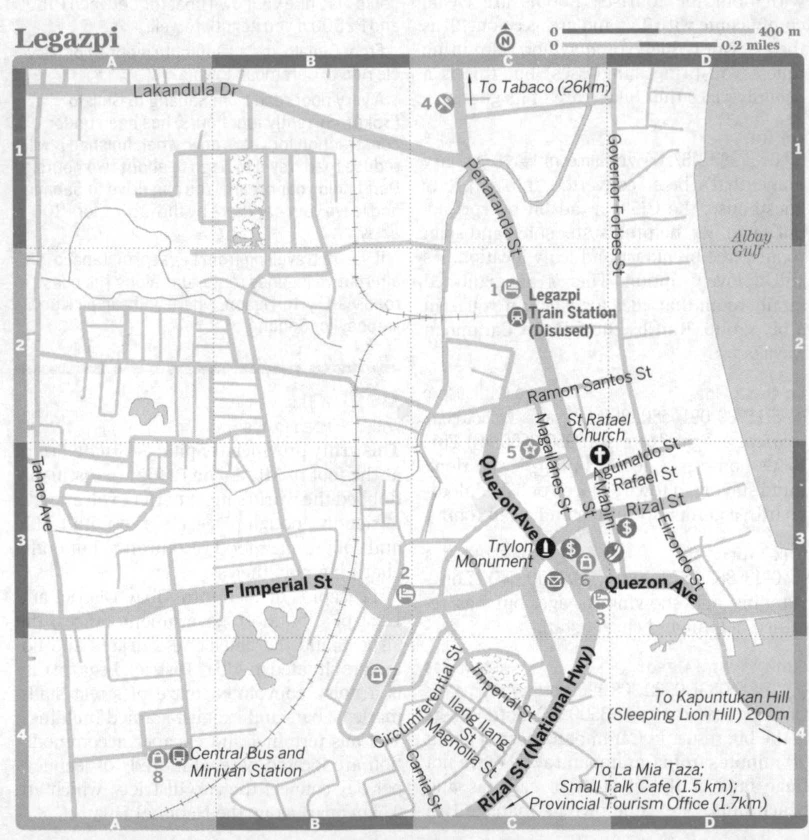

that can tailor a range of tours, from diving to climbing, and has been leading hikers up Mt Mayon for several years.

Mayon Outdoor Guides Association GUIDES (☎0915 422 4508; pinangat2001@yahoo.com) Consists of a group of highly experienced outdoor enthusiasts and guides, with an Everest climber among their number. They run tours throughout the Bicol region, including to Mt Mayon. Talk to George Cordovilla.

Sleeping & Eating

The accommodation scene in Legazpi City is a pretty dire collection of budget hotels. You can find rooms for around P300, and sometimes cheaper, but they're often filthy.

LEGAZPI CITY

Hotel Villa Angelina HOTEL $$ (☎480 6345; www.villaangelinahotel.com; Diego Silang St; r from P1800; ❄📶) This is your best bet if you want to stay in Legazpi City. The rooms are a bit dainty (OK, some look like doilies) but they're well kept and come with a free breakfast. Deluxe rooms have step-in baths that looks straight out of a hip-hop video. The downstairs restaurant serves very good Filipino and Western food.

Legazpi Tourist Inn HOTEL $ (☎820 4880; V&O Bldg, Quezon Ave; s/d with fan P550/600, with air-con P800/900; ❄📶) The Tourist Inn represents decent budget accommodation. It boasts modern, well-kept rooms with private bathrooms, TVs and lots of mirrors, but the staff were laughably incompetent when we visited. Located in the heart of the city.

Legazpi

Activities, Courses & Tours

Bicol Adventure & Tours.............(see 3)

Sleeping

1 Casablanca Hotel.......................C2
2 Dreams Inn & Café.......................B3
3 Legazpi Tourist Inn.......................C3

Eating

4 WayWay Restaurant.......................C1

Entertainment

5 Bar 101.......................C3

Shopping

6 LCC Mall.......................C3
7 Pacific Mall.......................B4
8 Satellite Market.......................A4

Dreams Inn & Cafe HOTEL $ (☎820 0885; F Imperial St; s with fan/air-con P350/500, d with air-con P700; ❄) The clean basic rooms at this extra-value place come with optional TV, hot water, air-con, private bathroom and window. Pick what you want and adjust the price. Don't plan on throwing a party in the singles or eating at the cafe – it's closed.

WayWay Restaurant FILIPINO $ (Peñaranda St; dishes around P100; ⏰lunch & dinner, closed Sun) The city abounds in fast-food eateries and *carinderias* (local restaurants, often serving just a few dishes, sometimes an extension of a home or a grill in a backyard), but for an authentic experience of Bicol food, head here for a splendid buffet of spicy coconut-milk-cooked specialities. It's 1km north of Legazpi City.

ALBAY DISTRICT

There are several good hotels within walking distance of the airport.

Hotel Venezia HOTEL $$$ (☎481 0888, www.hotelvenezia.com.ph; Renaissance Gardens, Washington Dr; d from P5000; ❄@📶) The classiest hotel in town has ultra-modern rooms decked out in muted greys, beautiful linen and private balconies with views of Mt Mayon. Staff are professional and courteous, and the surrounds are green and pleasant.

Alicia Hotel HOTEL $$ (☎481 0801, 0918 625 3696; www.aliciahotel.com.ph; Washington Dr; d from P1950; ❄📶) This is a nice midrange option near the airport, with the definite advantage of a small pool with mountain views. There's a variety of modern, well-appointed rooms, some smaller than others, so check around.

Pepperland HOTEL $$ (☎481 8000; pepperlandhotelbikol@yahoo.com; Airport Rd; r from P2184; ❄📶) This is a buzzing and busy business class hotel, with a pleasant, cool coffee shop and outdoor courtyard. Check out the Middle Eastern–influenced decor, courtesy of the Lebanese owner. Rooms at the back can be musty and dark – go for the top floor if you can.

Casablanca Hotel HOTEL $$ (☎480 8334, 820 1428; Peñaranda St; s/d from P1600/2000; ❄@📶) A big, corporate style business hotel with clean rooms, carpeted floors and cable TV. A nice splurge if you want a fresh spot to unwind.

DON'T MISS

SLEEPING LION HILL

The view that holds everyone's attention in Legazpi is of Mt Mayon, but there's another beautiful panorama many visitors miss: the pretty port of Legazpi itself. If you're into having a very satisfying glimpse of this regional capital, hike up **Kapuntukan Hill**, located near the waterfront. Locals have nicknamed this bit of elevation Sleeping Lion hill, and the rump-ish rise does bear a vague resemblance to a snoozing cat. This is strictly a footslog and we don't recommend sandals; the 30-minute ascent goes up a rough path and culminates with a great view of the waterfront and nearby islands. Legazpi Blvd leads directly to the foot of the lion. An aside: Legazpi tourism officials like to compare Kapuntukan to Rio de Janeiro's iconic Sugarloaf Mountain, which may be the most ambitious bit of tourism promotion in the Philippines.

Around these three hotels is a range of eateries as well as in-house restaurants. Try **Cafe Cubaña** (Airport Rd) beside Pepperland for snacks, coffee and free wi-fi, or **Smoke 'n' Grill** (Airport), a local beer-and-BBQ favourite.

A tricycle ride away is the truly fantastic **Small Talk Cafe** (51 Doña Aurora St; ⏲11am-10pm), which defines the notion of Bicol-fusion cooking, with dishes such as its 'Bicol express' pasta, *pinangat*-filled ravioli, great salads and *pili* nut desserts. There's great decoration, too, with old local photos displayed on the walls. Around the corner on the National Hwy is **La Mia Taza**, a popular coffee and cake joint, with free wi-fi. Several modern restaurants cluster around the City Hall square.

Drinking & Entertainment

If it's booze you choose, head to the bar at Pepperland hotel for live music from 8pm to midnight, Wednesday to Saturday, or to **Bar 101** (Magallanes St; ⏲4pm-midnight Mon-Sat), above the Bichara Silverscreens cinema, which was the place to hang out and listen to music when we passed through.

Shopping

Satellite Market, next to the bus station, is a good place to buy abaca handicrafts and products. **Pacific Mall** and **LCC Mall** can provide most other consumer goods that your heart desires.

Information

There are plenty of internet cafes all over, and ATMs in Legazpi City, but not yet in Albay District.

Provincial Tourism Office (☎820 6314; http://tourism.albay.gov.ph; Albay Astrodome Complex, Capt F Aguende Dr) Offers an excellent free map of the city and not much else.

Wow! Legazpi (http://wowlegazpi.com) Legazpi city's tourism website is a) a good portal and b) notable for its great, nerdy name.

Musings of the Midnight Writer (http://goldimyrr.repolles.com) This website, run by a Legazpi-based author, is an excellent window unto the cultural calendar of the Bicol region.

Getting There & Away

Air

Cebu Pacific, Airphil Express and Zest Air each fly at least once daily to/from Manila.

Bus

Most air-con and deluxe services to Manila (around P800, 10½ hours) depart between 6.30-8pm, although dodgy 'ordinary' (non air-con) buses depart throughout the day. **Cagsawa** (☎480 7810) and RSL bus lines run comfortable night buses to Ermita in Manila. **Isarog** (☎481 4744) and **Penafrancia** (☎820 0518) head to Cubao, while **Philtranco** (☎820 2794) serves Pasay.

There are frequent minivans during daylight hours to and from Naga (P150, two hours), Sorsogon (P70, 1½ hours), Tabaco (P30, 30 minutes) and Donsol (P80, one hour, 5pm). Buses take 30% longer (no buses serve Donsol).

Around Legazpi

Daraga Church CHURCH

Set on a hill splendidly overlooking Mt Mayon is the baroque-style Daraga Church, constructed completely from volcanic rock in 1773 and with detailed sculpted reliefs on the columns. Beside the church, stop for a cold drink or lunch at the very stylish **7 Degrees Grill & Restaurant** (dishes from P100; ⏲lunch-late), where several indoor-outdoor terraces offer fantastic views. From Legazpi take any Daraga-bound jeepney from the National Hwy.

Cagsawa Ruins RUINS

About 8km northwest of Legazpi, the remains (basically the belfry and tops of walls) of the sunken **Cagsawa Church** (admission P10) look out over a wiry plain of dusty grass at the sleek curves of Mt Mayon. Twelve hundred people who took refuge here during Mayon's violent eruption of 1814 were buried alive; this tragic loss is tackily commemorated with ice-cream stands, souvenir stalls and restaurants. With that said, if you can get a moment away from the hawkers and experience some silence, Cagsawa takes on a lonely, sad sort of beauty. Next door, a couple of big clean **swimming pools** (admission P50) are refreshing before the return jeepney trip.

To get from Legazpi to Cagsawa, take any jeepney headed to Camalig, Guinobatan or Ligao. Ask the driver to drop you off at the ruins, and walk in about 500m from the road.

Hoyop-Hoyopan Cave CAVE

Pottery dating from 200 BC to AD 900 (some is on display in nearby Camalig church) has been found in this easily accessible limestone cave, set on a quiet hillside above a pretty rural valley. The name means 'blow-blow', a reference to the cool and somewhat eerie wind that blows through the cave. Guides are available at the entrance (admission P150 including lantern; add another P150 if you want the electric light turned on). Not much of the admission fee goes to the guide, so tips are appreciated.

A tour will take around 30 minutes; look for **Maripe** (☎0915 286 7221), who is following in her father's footsteps as a local guide. There are many rock formations inside the cave, and this being the Philippines, locals believe many resemble either the Virgin Mary or the Devil. Hoyop-Hoyopan is privately owned, which is one of the reasons why a dance floor has been placed inside one chamber; guides tell us functions are sometimes held here. If the weather's kind (ie not prone to flash flooding) and you're up for adventure, you can also visit the more challenging **Calabidongan Cave** (literally, Cave of the Bats), about a 2.5km walk away.

Hoyop-Hoyopan is about 25km from Legazpi. To get here, take any jeepney heading towards Camalig, Polangui, Guinobatan or Ligao and get off in Camalig, 14km northwest of Legazpi. From Camalig, things get harder. Jeepneys towards Cotmon are few and far between, but you might be able to hitch a ride on a motorbike (P250 one way). It's much easier to hire a car and include these caves as part of a day tour.

Mt Mayon VOLCANO

One of the Philippines' most photographed sights, Mt Mayon (2462m) rises dramatically from the flat Albay terrain, and can be seen from as far away as Naga and Catanduanes. The volcano's name derives from the Bicol word *magayon,* meaning 'beauty', and it wholeheartedly deserves the moniker.

This is no sleeping beauty, however. One of the world's most dangerous volcanoes, it has erupted about 15 times since 1900. The last fatalities directly related to an eruption were in 1993, when eruptions continued for two months and a team of American vulcanologists doing research on its slopes was among the 77 people killed. Shortly after lava flows subsided in 2006, a biblical typhoon triggered mudslides on Mt Mayon that killed more than 1000 people.

Mayon emits a constant plume of smoke and is carefully monitored by **Philvolcs** (☎824 8166, 02 426 1468; www.phivolcs.dost.gov.ph), located near Lignon Hill in Legazpi, where there's a small and interesting exhibition about volcanoes. Long-time staff member Alex (alexbaloloy2002@yahoo.com) will genially answer your questions if he's not in the field.

The institute closes an area of between 6km and 10km around the volcano when there is a danger of eruption. In quieter times, you can climb part of the way up. Philvolcs strongly recommends you don't climb beyond 1800m, although some guides will take you to 2000m. Go much higher than that and you'll be overwhelmed by the sulphurous gases.

Climbing Mt Mayon

The southeastern route starts from near barangay Buyoan, 15km north of Legazpi City. From there it's a two-hour climb to 'camp one' and another 2½ hours to 'camp two', at 1800m, beyond which is the 'knife edge'. You can start early and do the climb in one day or make it a two-day climb with an overnight stay at either camp.

Traditionally the best time to climb has been from February to April. From May to August it's unbearably hot, and from September to January it's very wet – though climate change is shifting these parameters. A guide for a Mayon hiking package costs around P7000 for a two-day climb, P4500 for a one-day climb. This fee covers all food, transportation, gear and porters. If you want to climb Mt Mayon, there's plenty of guides hanging out in Legazpi; a good one is **Eugene Bañares** (☎0921 651 8851; eugene_banares@yahoo.com).

Another popular excursion is to drive to (the never-opened and now derelict) **Mayon Skyline Hotel** (810m), also known as the Mayon Rest House on the northwestern side of Mt Mayon. Renovation is talked about, but don't hold your breath. The view over the Pacific is spectacular on a clear day, and there are picnic tables, a smart cafe (due to open shortly after we visited) and the **Mayon Planetarium & Space Park** (admission free), which houses an eclectic array of NASA photos and volcano information.

The road up to the Skyline from Legazpi is in shoddy condition; at the time of research, vehicles were using the longer but better road via Tabaco. There is no public transport, so you'll have to hire a van in Legazpi (around P2500 round-trip, allow four hours). See p164 for details of tours to Mt Mayon.

Tabaco

☎052 / POP 123,500

Tabaco, in the shadow of Mt Mayon, is the departure point for boats to Catanduanes. The lovely 19th-century facade of the **Church of San Juan Batista** is a must for colonial architecture buffs; some of the bricks bear individual masons' marks, which is a rarity in this country. Otherwise, an early boat departure is the only reason to stay here.

Near the market you'll find a cluster of hotels offering rooms for P400 or sometimes less; they're all pretty tatty, but if you're on a budget, they'll serve. Across the road, **Tabaco Gardenia Hotel** (☎487 8019; Riosa St; r from P1000; ❄) has friendly service and 30 solid, clean doubles. Choose between a quiet, windowless room and a noisy street-side room. You can also opt for the **Casa Eugenia Hotel & Restaurant** (☎481 8334; Tagas St; r from P1100; ❄), which is similarly clean and comfortable. The pier is a short pedicab ride (P10) from all of the above.

Cagsawa, Amihan and Raymond Tours run buses to and from Cubao, Manila (air-con/deluxe from P850/1100, 11 hours). Frequent buses, jeepneys and minivans go to and from Legazpi (from P25, 30 minutes), and minivans go to Naga. For information on ferries to Catanduanes, see p175.

Sorsogon

☎056 / POP 151,450

The eponymous capital of Bicol's southernmost province lies in a beautiful area of endless beaches, natural springs and rice fields that sprawl beneath jungle-clad volcanoes like vast, bright-green runways. There's good **trekking** to be had nearby on the province's highest volcano, Mt Bulusan.

Sleeping & Eating

Sirangan Beach Resort RESORT $$$

(☎0919 582 2732; www.sirangan.com; r from P4000; ❄📶🏊) Ten kilometres out of town at the wonderfully named Bacon Beach, you'll find this decidedly elegant and upmarket accommodation option. The eight rooms' private balconies, stylishly crafted local wood furnishings, classic white linen and astonishing bathrooms are popular with local and international visitors; additional rooms are underway.

Villa Kasanggayahan GUESTHOUSE $

(☎211 1275; Rizal St; r P700-950; ❄) The lovely garden, green walls, breezy balconies and outdoor sitting areas make this quiet place a treat to stay in. Rooms are big if somewhat tatty, and occasional barking frenzies from neighbourhood dogs disturb the peace.

Fernandos Hotel HOTEL $$

(☎211 1357; www.fernandoshotel.com; cnr N Pareja & Rizal Sts; d/tr P1600/1800; ❄📶) A bit overpriced, the Fernandos is still a good option. The top-end rooms are spacious and have walls tastefully decorated with abaca and other indigenous fibres; cheaper rooms are functional if small (and are above the music bar). The indoor/outdoor lobby garden and breakfast area is a pretty spot to lodge in.

Fritz Homestay HOTEL $$

(☎0921 396 0852; http://fritzhomestay.multiply.com; Block 21, Executive Village; r from P1300; ❄📶🏊) Not really a homestay at all, Fritz is more of a standard Filipino midrange hotel with clean rooms, friendly owners and reliable air-con and wi-fi, which is more than most spots can boast. The little swimming pools in the garden are a supremely relaxing touch.

Villa Kasanggayahan and Fernandos are both walking distance from eating places in town (try **Jane's Fast Foods** for good cooked-to-order Filipino dishes).

Information

Several banks in town – PNB, BPI and BDO among them – have ATMs, and there are several internet cafes on Rizal St, the main road through town.

The energetic Cecilia Duran and daughter Angie at Fernandos Hotel provide all the information you need on hiking, mountain biking and diving. They can arrange rental of camping gear, mountain bikes, mopeds or cars, and provide guides for climbing Mt Bulusan or snorkelling with the whale sharks at Donsol.

Getting There & Away

Philtranco runs night buses (4am!) to Manila (ordinary/air-con/deluxe P430/750/1300, 14 hours). There are regular buses/minivans to Legazpi (P50/70, 1½ hours).

For Donsol, you have to take a jeepney to Putiao (P35, 45 minutes) and get on another jeepney to Donsol (P30, 45 minutes).

Bulusan Volcano National Park & Around

South of Sorsogon is **Bulusan Volcano National Park** (admission P10; ⏲7am-5.30pm). Just inside the park, **Bulusan Lake** is a popular picnic spot, and there's a 1.8km **walking trail** around the crater lake. When the mist is lying low over the surrounding forest and the birds are singing, it's a lovely, peaceful spot and the clear, still water makes for an inviting swim or a relaxed hour's fishing for tilapia. Climbers must get a permit and go with a guide; get organised through Fernandos Hotel (p168), or ask the barangay captain in San Roque for assistance with finding a local guide. Be prepared for leeches here.

A successful conquest of Mt Bulusan deserves a soak in the **Palogtoc Falls** (admission P10). This grotto is accessible by a 500m walk from a trailhead off the main road between the park entrance and San Roque (it's also on the Bulusan–Irosin jeepney route). It features a gorgeous cold-water pool fed by falls beside a shady river, with mercifully no visible concrete, just a few low-key bamboo and nipa huts. It's a lovely spot, especially if you luck out and are there alone. Nearby **Masacrot Springs** (admission P20) offer the same sort of pool, but with concrete huts and videoke.

Mateo Hot & Cold Springs Resort (admission P20), outside Irosin at the foot of Mt Bulusan, has – as you'd expect from the name – hot and cold pools. It often gets crowded and noisy (and, on weekends, a bit grubby).

Villa Luisa Celeste (☎0920 906 0969; r from P850; ❄📺) is a decent hotel north of the town of Bulusan, but it was up for sale at the time of research, so your best accommodation options may be in Gubat or Sorsogon.

Getting There & Away

The entrance to the park is near San Roque, about 10km west of Bulusan town. A day trip to the lake is feasible if you don't want to take an organised tour; take a jeepney from Sorsogon to Gubat (about 45 minutes), then from Gubat to Bulusan town (about 45 minutes). In Bulusan town, look for the Bulusan-Irosin jeepney; this will drop you at the park entrance track 6km from town, and you can walk the 2km in from there. Alternatively, hire a tricycle from Bulusan directly to the lake (about P200, including waiting time). It's 6km from Bulusan or 8km from Irosin to the park entrance; you can also make this trip from Sorsogon via Irosin.

Donsol

☎056 / POP 44,000

Until the 'discovery' of whale sharks off the coast here in 1998, Donsol, about 45km southwest of Legazpi, was an obscure, sleepy fishing village in one of Sorsogon's more remote areas. In 1998 a local diver shot a video of the whale sharks and a newspaper carried a story about Donsol's gentle *butanding*. Since then Donsol has become one of the Philippines' most popular tourist locations.

Only one resort accepts credit cards and there are no international ATMs here. Come prepared with plenty of cash. There are a couple of internet cafes in town.

Activities

Whale Shark Spotting

Swimming with these huge, blue-grey, silver-spotted creatures is a truly exhilarating experience – but you do need to be a decent snorkeller and in relatively good shape to keep up with them! Whale sharks are relatively slow swimmers, but still pretty fast compared to you, so unless you're quite lucky, you likely won't experience a slow ballet with these leviathans (especially if you're on a crowded boat).

AMAZING MANTAS

March to May are the peak months to dive the **Manta Bowl**, a 17m to 22m dive where you hook at the bottom to take a rest from the strong currents. It provides the perfect conditions for a manta ray cleaning station, where mantas positively queue up for cleaner wrasse to remove parasites from their skin. Whale sharks may be seen here too, and thresher sharks, among others. This is an advanced dive, though operators will take less-experienced divers as long as they pay for a dive master (P600) to go one-to-one with them. Geographically part of Masbate, it's logistically easier to dive from Donsol on mainland southeast Luzon (see p170). To get with good Manta Bowl dive operators, contact Bicol Dive Center (p170). At the time of writing, the cost per person for a two-person, three-dive trip at Manta Bowl (all gear included) was P6,500.

During the peak months of March and April, the question isn't whether you will see a shark, but how many you will see. Occasionally the sharks migrate here as early as November and stay until around late June, but you shouldn't bank on it. Like everything else in the Philippines, whale shark spotting is also subject to the vagaries of weather – if the sea is rough or a typhoon is on the way, the boats will not go out. Be sure to check the weather conditions to avoid disappointment.

When you get to Donsol, head to the **Donsol Visitors Center** (nenitapedragosa@yahoo.com; ⏲7.30am-5pm) situated 1.5km north of the river bridge (P30 by tricycle from town).

This is how the process went when we visited. You pay your registration fee and arrange a boat (good for seven people) for your three-hour tour. The Visitors Center does its best to ensure each boat is full, at a cost of roughly P1500 per person. Then off you go! The centre may close earlier (in the day or the season) if weather is bad or otherwise if there are no visitors.

Only snorkelling equipment is allowed; scuba diving is prohibited. Snorkelling equipment is available for rent (P300 per session), though it may be limited in peak season. Each boat has a spotter and a *Butanding* Interaction Officer on board – tip them a couple of hundred pesos, especially if you've had a good day.

The experience is quite regimented – it has to be, given the well-being of the animals, the number of visitors and the need to rotate boat crews fairly – and access to the whale sharks is limited to a maximum of 25 boats per day. During the busy Holy Week, you will be lucky to get a look in.

Diving

Divers come in droves to explore the Manta Bowl (see p170) and other macro dive sites closer to shore. Each resort has a dive centre with a floating population of experienced freelance dive masters; the longest-standing of these is **Bicol Dive Center** (☎0921 929 3811; www.bicoldivecenter.webs.com), located just across from the Donsol Tourism Office. A day package of two dives in the Donsol area will cost one person P6500, and there are discounts for larger groups.

Snorkelling & Island-Hopping

Boats can be hired for day trips to the exquisite San Miguel Island off Ticao, and there's good snorkelling a short boat ride north of the resorts.

Firefly Watching

An unexpected but increasingly popular evening experience is to spend a couple of hours on the river after dusk, as masses of fireflies emerge. Boat trips cost P1250 for a maximum of six, and leave from the river bridge at 6pm.

Sleeping & Eating

Many places shut up shop during the off season, from about June to about December.

Other seaside eating options in tourist season include La Meza Taza, a restaurant readers recommend, just behind the visitors centre. Popular Baracuda, between Vitton and Woodland Farm, does cocktails and dinner on the water's edge.

Budget travellers can stay in town, 10 minutes by tricycle from the visitors centre.

Giddy's Place HOTEL **$$**
(☎0917 848 8881; www.giddysplace.com; d with fan/air-con P600/2500, q P4500; ❄📶🏊) Giddy's has significantly upped the game in Donsol lodging. With a good bar and restaurant, wi-fi, cable TV, modern, clean rooms, on-site spa, professional service and a pool, this is, by Donsol standards, pretty plush. And it's

open year-round. Giddy's takes credit cards, but bring cash just in case. Unfortunately the cheap backpacker rooms are do not have air-con and have shared bathrooms.

Amor Farm Beach Resort HOTEL $
(☎0921 245 4028, 411-3180; rasyl_r_amor@yahoo.com, amorfarmbeachresort@gmail.com; r with fan/air-con from P800/2200; ❄) The Amor is a bucolic resort with cottages scattered around a garden. The fan rooms are the best value in the visitors centre area. Open year-round. The onsite bar and restaurant are nice places to chill and meet other travellers, Filipino and international.

Casa Bianca Beach Resort HOTEL $
(☎0906 309 9372; http://casabiancadonsol.multiply.com; d with fan/air-con from P800/1500, tr/q from P1800/2000; ❄📶) A 10-minute walk from the visitors centre, the resort's rooms are looking just a bit tired and the canteen is strangely situated away from the water. It's a lovely location though, with a big garden.

Woodland & Vitton Resort HOTEL $$
(☎0927 912 6313, 0915 420 3285; http://whalesharksphilippines.com; q from P2000; ❄🏊) These two resorts are managed by the same family: each has a lovely garden, clean accomodation and friendly service. Of the two resorts, we definitely prefer the newer Vitton, which has a bar and a pool, whereas the older Woodland's rooms are showing their age.

Aguluz Homestay HOMESTAY $$
(☎0918 942 0897, 0917 209 4757; razormarilyn@yahoo.com; r with fan/air-con P700/1600; ❄📶) Aguluz is the fancy homestay option in Donsol and quite a lovely sleep besides. Marilyn is your loving if sometimes intimidating host, a little tornado of energy, and she'll do what she can to arrange all your tours and onward transportation.

Santiago Lodging House HOMESTAY $
(r P700) Basically a homestay with three good, clean rooms in a beaten-up wooden house. Right across the street is **Hernandez Guesthouse** (☎0906 431 4173; r P700-1200; ❄), which has a few simple fan rooms. Other homestays of similar pricing and quality are scattered around town, usually open only during the main tourism season.

Elysia Beach Resort RESORT $$$
(☎0917 547 4466; http://elysia-donsol.com; d from P3150; ❄🏊) Elysia is the only dedicated top-end resort in Donsol. There's attractively manicured cabanas with thatched roofs and air-con arranged around a chlorine pool, but frankly, we think this place is a little overpriced, especially compared to what you get at other resorts.

ℹ Getting There & Away

There are direct air-con minivans to and from Legazpi (P80, one hour) every hour until about 4pm. Jeepneys go via Pilar and take at least twice as long. If you are stranded past 4pm, make your way to Pilar via jeepney, and connect with more frequent minivans and buses there. Buses leave Cubao, Manila for Donsol/Pilar (12 hours) at 3:30pm on Philtranco (P800), and head back to Manila at noon. It may be easier to bus to Donsol from Manila via Legazpi.

There are four fast craft boats per day between Masbate and Pilar (see p172), and connections between Pilar and Ticao Island (p174).

Matnog

Matnog is a one-road town where you catch the ferry bound for Samar, although there are some nice offshore islands. You probably won't want to spend the night here. If you get in late, it's better to get the ferry across to Allen (p322) on Samar and stay there. Another option is to head 9km north of Matnog to the pretty white beach outside Santa Magdalena (P120 by tricycle), where New Port Beach Resort and Villa Veronica advertise rooms.

Frequent ferries ply the route 24/7 between Matnog and Allen on Samar, with fares as low as P120.

Jeepneys make the run to and from Sorsogon (P60, 1½ hours). A number of jeepneys and buses run from Matnog to Bulan, 60km away, where there's a boat connection to Masbate.

MASBATE

☎056 / POP 771,000

Masbate possesses a gentle kind of beauty. An Irish or a Welsh traveller might feel at home here, at least as long as they could suspend disbelief and convert the climate of their green and hilly homelands into the tropics. There's a laidback vibe in the air, especially evident in the locals, but there's a sense of change about as well. Partly that's to do with an enthusiastic local government supported by Manila, especially in terms of Masbate's continued development as a shipping hub of the National Nautical Hwy. It's

Masbate

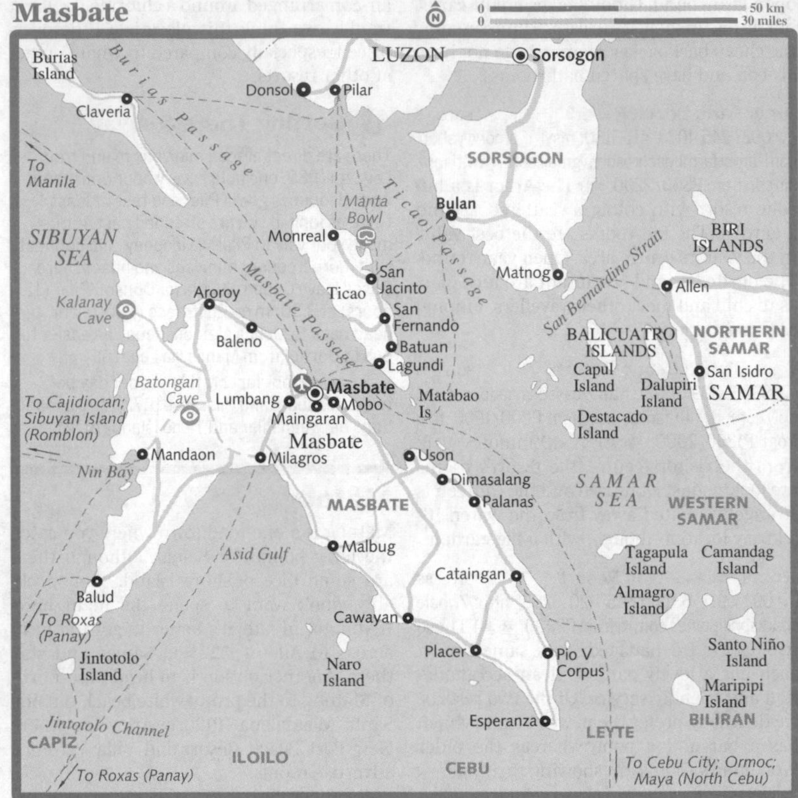

also partly to do with the growing popularity of the Manta Bowl – off Ticao Island's east coast – as a diving destination.

Getting There & Away

Air

Zest Air and Airphil Express flies to and from Manila daily.

Boat

Roll-on-roll-off (RORO) ports are under way in Esperanza and Mandaon, and by the time you read this there may be more options. Check out the shipping movements board in the Port Authority office at Masbate pier for up-to-date weekly schedules.

Pumpboats also go several times a day between Pilar and Monreal or San Jacinto on Ticao Island (P110, two hours), between Bulan and San Jacinto, and – we hear – between Donsol and Claveria on Burias Island.

CEBU **Trans Asia** (☎032 254 6491; www.transasiashipping.com; 2nd/1st/cabin class P575/850/1465) leaves Cebu for Masbate on Monday and Wednesday, leaving at 6pm and arriving at 7:30am. Return service is at the same time Tuesday and Thursday.

Asia Marine (☎02-888 6550; 2nd/1st/cabin class P600/800/1000) leaves Bogo for Cayawan at 10pm daily, and leaves in the opposite direction at noon daily.

LEYTE Ormoc and Calubian are served once a week by **Sulpico** (☎056 333 2205; P290).

MANILA Sulpico ferries comes from Manila (19 hours) on Mon and Wed (5pm). Expect fares for fan/air-con/sleeper class to run P905/1155/1280.

ROMBLON At the time of research, boats were scheduled between Mandaon and Cajidiocan on Sibuyan Island every Wednesday and Sunday morning. Ferries from Cajidiocan to Mandaon left on Tuesday and Friday mornings. Note that this timetable changes often.

SOUTHERN LUZON The quickest and most comfortable option is the Montenegro fast craft between Pilar and Masbate (P360, two hours).

Daily ferries (P288) leave on **Montenegro Lines** (☎043 723 6980; www.montenegrolines.com.ph) at 5am, 8am, noon and 4pm. Pumpboats also go from Bulan and Masbate. **Philharbor** (☎775 0480; 3rd/2nd/1st P220/264/308) also departs from Pilar at 7am and 7pm.

From Bulan, **Santa Clara** (☎0918 900 5450; P250) leaves for Masbate at 8am daily.

VISAYAS Montenegro operates boats (3rd/2nd/1st class P350/420/525) from Naval, on Biliran, to Cataingan, Masbate; boats depart Naval at 6am and Cataingan at 9am.

Masbate Town

Like a ramshackle finger clawing at the ocean, Masbate Town beckons you to the island it governs. Arrival at the pier involves the usual sense of chaos and busyness common to most Filipino towns, and there's nothing much to recommend the crowded area immediately around the port. But just a few minutes' tricycle ride away the chaos lessens, and you'll find a wide sweep of mangrove bay filling the skyline, and a few welcoming and quiet hotels and restaurants.

Sights & Activities

Close to town, check out **Buntod sand bar**, which is located in the **Bugsayon marine sanctuary**; Jaja at the interpretation centre will point you in the right direction. The sandbar is about a 20- to 30-minute bangka ride (around P250) out into the water. Once you get out here, you can pick around the sandbar island before it gets swallowed by high tide.

Pawa Mangrove Nature Park consists of some 300 hectares of mangroves threaded through with a 1.3-kilometre boardwalk. It's a lovely, quiet place for a stroll, and there's a good chance you'll spot flocks of wading birds. To get here, take a jeepney to Maingaran and follow the track past the Santos Elementary School. Low tide's a good time to come here, when life on the mudflats is active and wading birdlife is at its most dense concentration.

Festivals

Rodeo Masbateño CULTURAL

Whoop, yip, rant and roar with all the local cowpokes during the second week of April. Events include bull riding, barrel racing (a kind of slalom for horse and rider) and tie-down roping. The town gets packed – book accommodation well in advance. If you've got animal ethics issues with rodeos, obviously you may want to avoid this event.

Sleeping & Eating

MG Hotel & Restaurant HOTEL $$

(☎333 5614; Punta Nursery; r P1050-1800; ❄≋) We don't want to traffic in stereotypes, but this German-run place is the most efficiently operated hotel in Masbate. The 3rd (top) floor rooms here are very welcoming – big and airy, with huge beds, plenty of natural light and a balcony overlooking the water. The downstairs restaurant is where you'll find wi-fi and good food, though the extensive menu may not bear any resemblance to what's actually available. The nearby **Sea Blick Hotel** (☎333 6911) is run by the same folks and offers similar rooms and rates, minus the MG's excellent views.

Balay Valencia HOTEL $

(☎333 6530; Ibañez St; r from P400/650; ❄) Oozes character, from its polished floorboards to its simple furniture. Rooms are in an old, beautifully maintained house (despite the unlikely exterior), with lattice breezeways just below the ceilings. Noise may be an issue from the night food stalls below on Ibanez St, but they make for an easy dinner. Everything else is charmingly old-fashioned.

Bituon Beach Resort RESORT $$

(☎333 2242, 0918 346 4987; bituonbeach.com; r P1000-1800; ❄≋) Out of town some 14km, near Mobo, the island's only beach resort remains popular and has a range of accommodation. Day use huts and cottages are also available, and day visitors are welcome (entrance fee is P50). A tricycle ride to the resort will cost around P200.

Minlan Restaurant FILIPINO $

(Osmeña St) In town, this place will cheer a vego's heart with its offerings, including crispy tofu (P60) and grilled eggplant (P90).

Information

Tara St – parallel to the pier – and Quezon St above it are the main thoroughfares. Quezon St is where you'll find several banks – including the PNB and Metrobank with ATMs – and internet cafes.

The excellent **Coastal Resource Management Interpretation Center** (☎0906 212 5684; esperanza danao@yahoo.com) is in the City Hall compound. There's lots of good info, as well as hands-on displays aimed mostly at local school kids, and the centre's interpretation officer, Jaja, is helpful about all things marine.

DON'T MISS

TIKLING ISLAND

Matnog is not the kind of town that strikes you as a hidden, underrated gem of Filipino tourism. **Tikling Island**, on the other hand, could potentially claim that crown. Sitting 4km offshore from Matnog, Tikling is a green clump of loveliness wreathed in rare, rose-hued pink sand, with shady groves of palm trees, good snorkelling and not a tourist to be seen. You can come here and camp (you'll be expected to pay around P100 to the local village headman) and basically bliss out with nothing to do. To get here look for bangkas at the Matnog waterfront or call Eddie (☎0926 140 4577); the going rate is P1500 for a return trip to Tikling.

Across the park opposite City Hall is the Capitol Building, where the province's enthusiastic tourism officer will fill you in on the rest.

Around Masbate Island

Going anticlockwise from Masbate town, the island's points of interest include the oldest **lighthouse** in the province in the gold-mining town of Aroroy; **Kalanay** and **Batongan caves** near Mandaon, and visits to **working ranches** nearby; a vegie and dairy farm, **Facenda da Esperanza**, run as a rehab centre at Milagros; the 30-year work-in-progress **stone house** at Esperanza; **waterfalls** at Palanas; and **old Spanish houses** at Uson. A caveat, though: the island's tourism development and infrastructure is in its infancy. Finding these spots requires a bit of DIY spirit or a call to the Masbate tourism office, which can also help you arrange accommodation (where it exists).

Ticao Island

Ticao feels on the edge between laissez-faire island time and rapid tourism development. For now: the sweet, rotting scent of copra weaves through the trees and – except in the few small townships – concrete barely interrupts the bamboo and thatch structures. The island's one road bumps and winds and slopes its way through villages such as Batuan, where you can stop and check out the **mangrove boardwalk**, and **San Fernando**, where a visit to the extraordinary Dr Roger Lim is full of unexpected delights (see p177).

In **Monreal**, hire a pumpboat for the day (P3500 to P5000) and head along the coast to waterfalls and to island-hop. A couple of **old Spanish houses** and a **cannon** remain in San Jacinto.

Sleeping & Eating

Ticao Island Resort RESORT $$
(☎893 8173, 0917 506 3554; www.ticao-island-resort.com; s/d/tr per person with full board US$60/65/94, budget s/d US$65/40; ❄) In Tacdogan, about 8km north of San Jacinto, nine plush cabanas front a perfect and secluded cove, while four fan-only budget rooms huddle off the beach. Divers will enjoy the island's proximity to the famed Manta Bowl dive site. Out of season it's a bit like coming across the *Mary Celeste*: silent, becalmed and deserted. Road access is bone shattering.

Altamar Ticao Island Beach Resort RESORT $$
(☎817 7463, 0917 812 8618; www.ticaoaltamar.com; cottages per person with full board P2000-2700; ❄) The Altamar consists of a series of tastefully decorated beachfront cottages; some are built for couples while other can sleep up to eight people (a three-storey lemon-hued villa can sleep up to 15 people for P20,000 a day). Staff are attentive and dish up some seriously delicious grub, and the friendly owners can arrange diving trips, massages and other fun activities.

Getting There & Away

Three or four big pumpboats a day go between Lagundi and Masbate town (P70, one hour), between San Jacinto and Bulan or Pilar on southeast Luzon, and between Monreal and Pilar (P120, two hours). The last trip is usually around 1pm.

Burias Island

Even less developed than Ticao – and with even more body-jarring roads – Burias has Bicol's oldest church, dating from 1560, in San Pascual. It looks like a set piece from an old Western film surreptitiously dropped into the tropics. **Caves** can be found at Claveria and San Pascual, along with an ancient burial site where Ming dynasty porcelain shards have been found. Offshore, Sombero Island is a **turtle reserve**. There's absolutely no tourist infrastructure.

Pumpboats go to Claveria (P150, three hours) from Masbate town in the mornings.

CATANDUANES

☎052 / POP 234,000

Ireland and England are green because they are lashed by rains. Catanduanes is whipped by typhoons, and while her infrastructure suffers as a result, she is also that much more green, shaggy and wildly beautiful thanks to the *bagyo* (typhoons). Those storms roll in from the months of July to November, when heavy rains are eagerly absorbed by lush rainforests that have been mercifully preserved due to both Catanduanes' isolation and sparse population.

Most foreign visitors to Catanduanes are surfers looking to ride the world-famous-if-fickle Majestics surf break. The best waves are during the typhoon season, especially between August and October – but prepare to be patient.

Getting There & Away

Air

PAL Express flies daily from Manila to Virac (1¼ hours) and Zest Air also flies this route. The airport is 3.5km from town; the tricycle trip there will cost about P35.

Boat

Regina Shipping Lines (☎811 1707) has three ferries a day between Tabaco and San Andres, 17km west of Virac (ordinary/air-con P185/240, three hours). The boats leave Tabaco at 5.30am, 8am and 1.30pm, then make the return journey at 9.30 and noon. Jeepneys meet the ferry in San Andres and go to Virac (P20, 30 minutes).

The other option is to take the MV *Eugenia*, a slower ferry from Tabaco to Virac (ordinary/air-con

Catanduanes

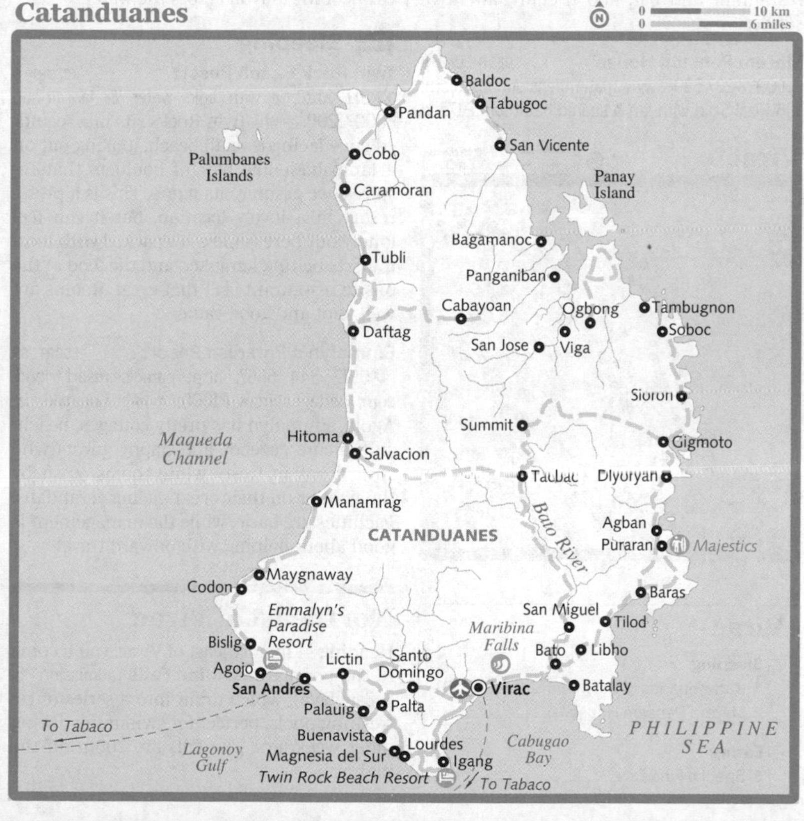

P196/252, four hours), leaving at 6.30am and returning at 1pm. All are car ferries.

Virac

The capital of Catanduanes does not offer much for travellers, but it has some creature comforts and is a convenient base for day trips to nearby beaches.

There are a few internet cafes in town, and the PNB and BDO on either side of the town plaza have ATMs.

Sleeping & Eating

Virac is not a culinary hot spot. You can eat at **Special Finds** across the road from the Midtown Inn, or at your hotel.

Monte Karlo Waterfront Inn HOTEL **$**
(0928 698 9559; San Vicente St; r from P800;) OK: there's no gambling, no racing, no Princess Grace. On the other hand, there's a shocking pink exterior, cosy rooms with porches that catch the sea breeze, a nice restaurant and bar, and friendly, attentive service.

Marem Pension House GUESTHOUSE **$**
(0928 237 5398; www.marempensionhouse.com; 136 Rizal St; d with fan & shared bathroom P175, d with air-con & private bathroom P775;) This mazelike building, home to many an aquarium, has an informal atmosphere and a labyrinth of natty rooms. It's very laid-back – a nice thing when it comes to the friendliness of staff, although service can be inconsistent.

Catanduanes Midtown Inn HOTEL **$$**
(811 0527; http://catmidinn.tripod.com; San José St; s/d from P900/1200;) This is a popular place in the middle of town, as you'd guess. Its large doubles have classic touches and parquet floors; some have balconies, but the upmarket 'deluxe' rooms aren't worth it. Beware the neighbouring videoke and disco – go for an inner room.

Virac

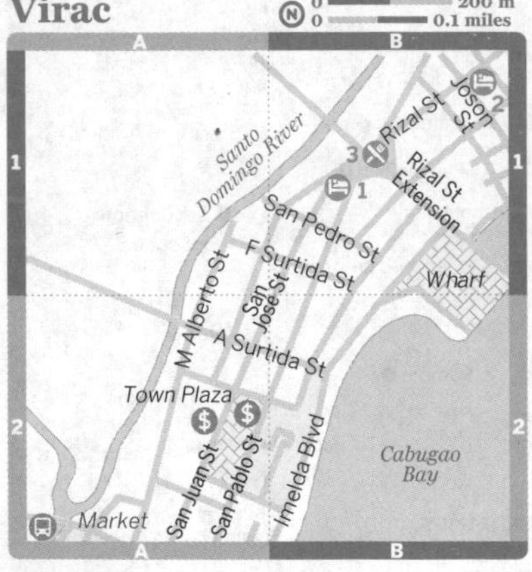

Virac

Sleeping
1 Catanduanes Midtown Inn B1
2 Marem Pension House B1

Eating
3 Special Finds B1

Southwest of Virac

The area southwest of Virac is dotted with bushy, humplike karst formations, similar to Bohol's Chocolate Hills. The landscape offers up white-sand coves making punch holes along the coast and, on a clear day, great views of Mt Mayon across the water.

Sleeping

Twin Rock Beach Resort RESORT **$**
(811 3122; r with cold water & fan/air-con P800/1200;) Twin Rocks sits in a secluded cove facing a small beach, looking out on a lampshade-like pair of boulders that inspires (we assume) its name. This is a pretty resort in a lovely location, but it can feel lonely out here (unless it's packed with local tourists belting karaoke), and the food at the onsite restaurant isn't that great. Rooms are well kept and good value.

Emmalyn's Paradise Resort RESORT **$$**
(0917 344 6667; http://paradise.resort.tripod.com; cottages from P1000;) Located in Agojo, Emmalyn has pretty cottages, beachside picnic gazebos and happy guests who sprawl out in frosty white rooms or sit by the pool or on their ocean-facing verandahs. Facilities are basic, while the management is good about helping with onward travel.

Northeast of Virac

Heading 4km northeast of Virac, you'll come to the popular **Maribina Falls** (admission P5; 8am-5pm), which drain into a series of refreshing pools, perfect for swimming during quiet weekdays. The falls are 200m off the highway.

DOCTOR DO MUCH

He carves and paints and writes and directs plays. His murals and artwork creep across the walls of his surgery. In the house behind, display cabinets showcase religious icons and coins, and eclectic found-and-restored Spanish and earlier shipwreck items that include celadon pots, Ming porcelain, ivory baby bangles and glass beads. Dr Roger Lim, San Fernando's devoted local doctor and aesthete, is erudite, charming and welcoming.

He's around most afternoons after 3pm and will show his collection in return for genuine interest and conversation (though a donation to the local church restoration fund won't go amiss). Everyone knows where to find him.

PURARAN

Northeast of Bato the paved road turns to a road from hell (the road may or may not be sealed by the time you read this) and, 20km on, leads to the stunning wide bay of Puraran, home to **Majestics surf break**.

It's an idyllic spot, with coconut trees swaying in the breeze, white sand and a coral reef for **snorkelling** just offshore. There are two excellent cheap resorts, where surfers and nonsurfers alike often stay for weeks, basking in the casual ambience of the place.

A reef break 200m offshore, Majestics is no beginner's wave. When it's working, it's perfect. But like most breaks on the country's Pacific coast, Majestics usually only works when there's a typhoon lurking offshore during the *habagat* (southwest monsoon). This is most likely to occur between August and October. The *amihan* (northeast monsoon) kicks up powerful onshore breezes from October to March, making conditions too choppy for all but the most die-hard surfers. In the calmer March to May period, local surfers run cheap one-to-one surf training sessions (P100 per hour).

Sleeping & Eating

It's advisable to book ahead from July to October. Both resorts serve set-menu meals for around P100.

Majestic Puraran RESORT $
(☎0918 497 9188; http://majesticpuraran.com; cottages P500) This friendly, family-run place is mellow in the extreme. It has simple, comfortable bamboo cottages with private porches, hammocks and great ocean views. There are board games and books for rainy days, one cable TV in the bar area and a surpassingly family friendly vibe. Snorkelling equipment costs P50 per day.

Puting Baybay Beach Resort RESORT $
(☎0919 512 9938; http://puraran-surf-putingbaybay.webnode.com; r P400) It's hard to get more idyllic, laid-back and better value than this. Puting Baybay offers cute, basic cottages, plus a couple of new rooms with shared bathroom in the (less comfortable and less private) main concrete building.

Getting There & Away

The easiest way to get here is to hire a van; it costs P1000 for a one-way trip from Virac to Puraran and takes an hour or so, depending on the road conditions.

There is one daily jeepney from Virac to Gigmoto via Puraran (P60, two hours, 32km). It leaves around 10.30am. The trip in the other direction passes through Puraran at around 7am.

You can also take a regular bus or jeepney from Virac to Baras (P40, one hour) and hire a tricycle (P170) to Puraran.

West Coast

The road leading from Virac to **Pandan** is a bumpy, beautiful and at times hair-raising race along a stretch of dagger-jawed coastline. You'll pass farms, fishing villages, great views across the Maqueda Channel and the rhythms of rural Filipino life. There is no commercial lodging in Pandan, so you'll have to ask around for a homestay (around P300).

There are three daily buses to and from Pandan (P120, five hours). The last bus from Virac leaves at noon; the last bus from Pandan leaves at 9am.

MARINDUQUE

☎042 / POP 231,600

You may think you've experienced the Philippines at its sleepiest and most rural, but if you haven't been to Marinduque yet, take heed: this place makes Palawan and Leyte look like Manhattan during rush hour. The 'Duque is a heart-shaped island bound by a

Marinduque

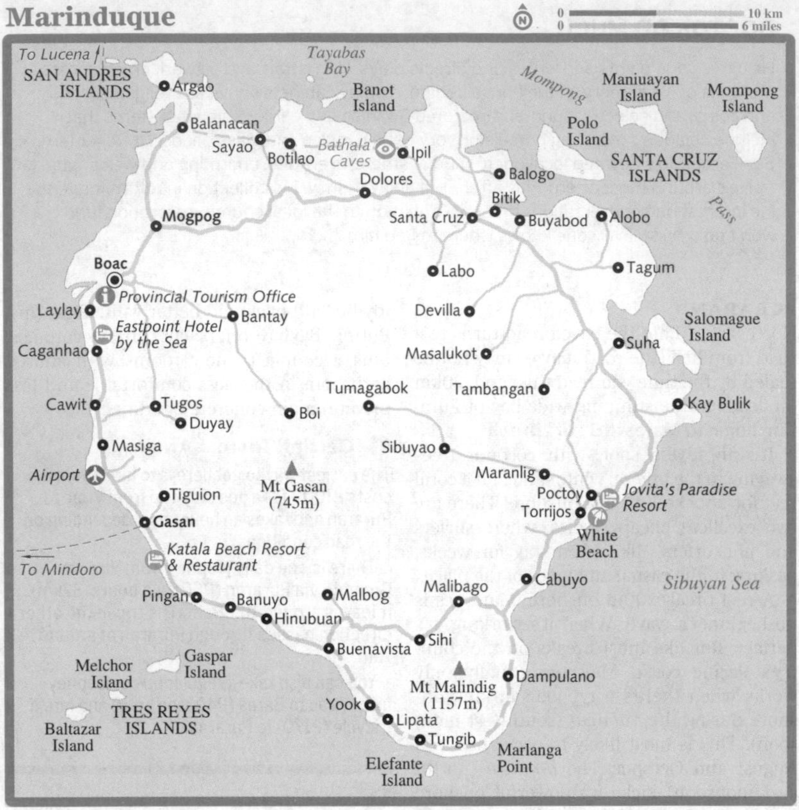

scenic 120km paved ring road, and it seems the only time this island is alive is at Easter during the quirky Moriones Festival (p179). The rest of the year visitors must content themselves with bumpy roads and beautiful scenery, dormant Mt Malindig volcano, a handful of beach resorts, hot springs in the interior and wildlife-filled caves. Perhaps Marinduque is busy after all!

Getting There & Away

Air

Zest Air (www.zestair.com.ph) flies daily from Manila to Masbate.

Boat

Montenegro Shipping Lines (☎723 6980; www.montenegrolines.com.ph) operates boat services from Lucena to Balanacan (3rd/2nd/1st class P208/250/270, 2½ hours), 30 minutes north of Boac. Boats leave at midnight, 2am, 10am, noon & 4pm.

Boac

☎042 / POP 51,300

A dusty crossroads framed by palm trees, pot plants and some dilapidated Spanish-era wooden houses, Marinduque's capital has a whiff of character. The beautiful cathedral, built in 1792 on a rise in the centre of town, and its attached convent, are the focal points.

Sights & Activities

The **museum** (Mercador St; ⏲8am-5pm) and **cathedral** in Boac showcase some Moriones memorabilia.

A hired jeepney or van with driver for trips around the (very bumpy) scenic southern end of the island costs around P3500 per day. You could also rent a 4WD from the **Eastpoint Hotel** (☎332 2229) for P350 per hour.

Sleeping & Eating

Boac Hotel HOTEL $$
(☎332 1121; Nepomuceno St; d with fan/air-con/ste P1000/1200/1800; ❄📶) Next to the cathedral, this hotel has an excellent, funky interior, decked out with vintage records, photos and handbags, plus reliable wi-fi and hot water. Best of all are the boutique suites, decorated with flowing curtains, dark colours, sensual lighting and funky pictures; they look like surreal love nests, and we kinda love them.

Tahanan Sa Isok HOTEL $
(☎332 1231; 5 Canovas St; r P800-1500; ❄📶) Located on a quiet side street just off Magsaysay St, this remains easily the best-value place in town, with clean, simple rooms, a pretty garden restaurant and very helpful front desk. There's a small book exchange, and original artworks are on display.

Happy Bunny GUESTHOUSE $
(☎332 2040, Mercado St; r with fan/air-con P300/650; ❄) This is a very basic guesthouse where the rooms are, well, pink and decorated with cartoon characters. Including the eponymous happy bunnies. Funnily enough, given all the cartoon animals around, the owner cooks up some mean roast chicken and pork.

Across from the museum you'll find **Casa de Don Emilio**, which also whips up Pinoy and Western meals for around P150 per main. The setting, a dark wooden dining room sandwiched into an old Spanish residence overlooking Boac square, is wonderful.

There's not much nightlife in Boac, but if you need a drink, just wander around until your hear the sound of karaoke, then follow the crooning to the San Miguel.

Information

The **PNB** (Gov D Reyes St) has an ATM. A few internet cafes are scattered along the side streets.

The **Provincial Tourism Office** (www.marinduque.gov.ph; ⏲8am-5pm Mon-Fri) is located in the Capitol Compound, 2km out of town on the main road south.

Getting Around

There are jeepneys to Boac from the ferry dock in Balanacan (P40, 25 minutes).

From Boac, jeepneys go south to Gasan (P20, 30 minutes) and Buenavista (P40, one hour) via the Capitol Compound. Frequent jeepneys also head northeast to Mogpog (10 minutes), Balanacan (45 minutes), Santa Cruz (P35, one hour) and Torrijos (P70, two hours).

All transport leaves from around the central terminal area near the intersection of Nepomuceno and Magsaysay Sts.

Gasan & West Coast

☎042 / POP 34,500

A few stretches of pebbly, debris-strewn beach and a motley selection of beach resorts spans 17km from Boac to south of Gasan's town proper. The further south you travel, the better the scenery and the beaches become.

MORIONES MANIA

You know something strange goes on in Marinduque when your first sight is a display of larger-than-life and very colourful plaster statues of Roman centurions – moriones – on the roundabout at Balanacan pier. And then there's the island's ring road, fringed with posts on which are mounted moriones' heads fashioned into flowerpots – some with wildly overgrown grass hair, some crumbling and sadly neglected.

Marinduque's **Moriones Festival** began in 1807 when Padre Dionsio Santiago, a Mogpog parish priest, organised a play based on the story of Longinus, one of the Roman centurions assigned to execute Christ. A drop of Christ's blood miraculously restored sight in Longinus' blind right eye during the crucifixion. Longinus instantly proclaimed his faith, whereupon he was chased around town, captured and summarily beheaded.

These days, a fabulous Easter festival combining folk mysticism with Catholic pageantry turns Marinduque's streets into a colourful re-enactment of those events, drawn out over the seven days of Holy Week. Each municipality in Marinduque holds its own festival, in which hundreds of moriones don centurion masks and costumes and arm themselves with wooden swords, spears and shields. The masks take months to prepare and are kept secret from even close friends and family so that the moriones' true identity is never known.

Throughout the week moriones take to the streets and run amok, engaging in sword fights, dances and sneaky pranks on bystanders. You have been warned!

In Gasan you can hire a boat to visit the **Tres Reyes Islands** (named Melchor, Gaspar and Baltazar after the biblical three kings); expect to pay around P2000 for a few hours of island-hopping. Gaspar Island is a marine reserve and you can **snorkel** off the northern beach, but you'll need to bring your own equipment.

Sleeping & Eating

Eastpoint Hotel by the Sea HOTEL $$
(☎332 2229; www.eastpointhotel.com; s/d/q from P850/1000/1800; ❄📶) Eastpoint offers the best waterfront facilities close to Boac. Rooms are well furnished, well maintained and very good value, there's a wellness centre with minigym and massage, thatched outdoor seating cottages dot the landscaped grounds, and the restaurant overlooks the ocean.

Katala Beach Resort & Restaurant RESORT $$
(☎0915 512 4784; www.members.tripod.com/katala.beach.resort; r with fan/air-con P1000/1500; ❄) This German-run establishment, 3km south of Gasan proper, is perched on a wall overlooking a private pier, with a floating pontoon and the Tres Reyes Islands beyond. The rooms are in good shape and you can enjoy the sound of waves lapping against the shore as you watch the sunset from your private balcony or in the pretty restaurant – which serves German sausages.

Getting There & Away

Two morning boats go from Marinduque to Pinamalayan (P200, 2½ hours) on Mindoro. Both leave from Gasan pier around 8am; be there early. Both return from Mindoro late morning.

Buenavista & Around

Buenavista is where the beautiful **coastal drive** around Mt Malindig begins. You'll need to hire a car or tricycle for the trip.

A couple of kilometres inland from the town are the **Malbog Hot Springs** (admission P70), where a series of bathing pools have been constructed to tap the water; development here is ongoing.

Elefante Island, offshore from Lipata and once a simple fishing spot, is undergoing a lengthy transformation (10 years so far, and counting) into a humongous resort with a golf course.

The five-hour hike up and down **Mt Malindig** follows a usually clearly marked trail from Sihi, a barangay of Buenavista. Take a tricycle to Sihi from Buenavista (P400 return), or any jeepney towards Torrijos.

A morning jeepney occasionally makes the pleasant (and slow) drive over the mountains to Poctoy (P48, one hour). A more sensible plan to get to and from Poctoy is to hire a tricycle (P800, one hour). There are regular jeepneys from Buenavista to Boac via Gasan.

Poctoy & East Coast

The whitest and longest beach in Marinduque is well-named **White Beach** (which happens to have a teal oceanfront) in Poctoy, where there are also views of Mt Malindig's conical snout. You'll find some day-use cottages here, and it gets pretty busy on weekends. **Jovita's Paradise Resort** (☎0918 773 8154; r with fan/air-con P800/1500; ❄), a few kilometres north of White Beach at Cagpo, is a peaceful spot with overgrown gardens and dilapidated rooms that are just out of earshot of the music from the restaurant. It's right on the beach.

Mindoro

Includes »

Best Places to Stay

» Pandan Island Resort (p197)

» Coco Beach Island Resort (p187)

» Apo Reef Club (p196)

» El Galleon Beach Resort (p186)

» Tambaron Green Beach Resort (p194)

Best Places to Eat

» Luca's Cucina Italiana (p189)

» Hemingway's (p188)

» Casa Italia (p188)

» Full Moon (p188)

» Puerto Galera Yacht Club p189

Why Go?

Bisected by a virtually impassable mountain range – aptly named the High Rolling Mountains – rugged Mindoro is part tropical paradise, part provincial backwater. Forming a dramatic backdrop almost everywhere, the mountains separate the island's two provinces: Mindoro Oriental to the east and Mindoro Occidental to the west.

Most tourists head to the dive resorts around Puerto Galera on the north coast, but there is much more to Mindoro. If you prefer remote to resort, venture into Mindoro Occidental where Sablayan, jumping-off point for the pristine dive mecca Apo Reef, awaits its destiny as the next big thing in Philippine tourism. Better roads are making this once hard-to-reach province more accessible than ever.

Mindoro's south coast has unforgettable island-hopping, while in the mountainous interior you can hike to remote villages populated by one of one of Asia's most primitive tribes, the Mangyan.

When to Go

San José

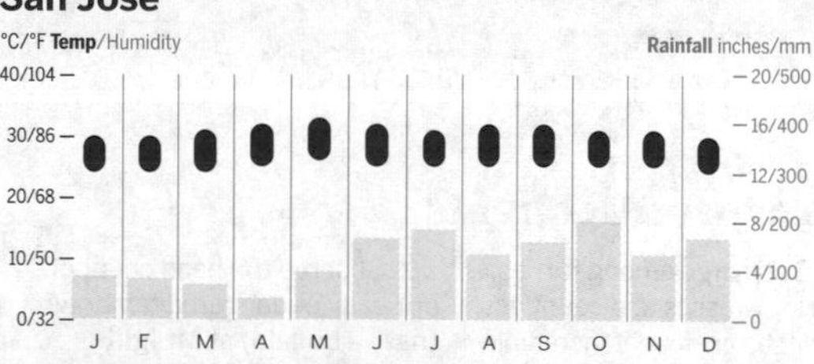

Apr-May The rainy season has yet to begin and the winds are at their calmest.

Feb-Apr The driest months and the best season for climbing Mt Halcon.

Oct-Nov Another transitional period, wind-wise, meaning more flat seas for divers.

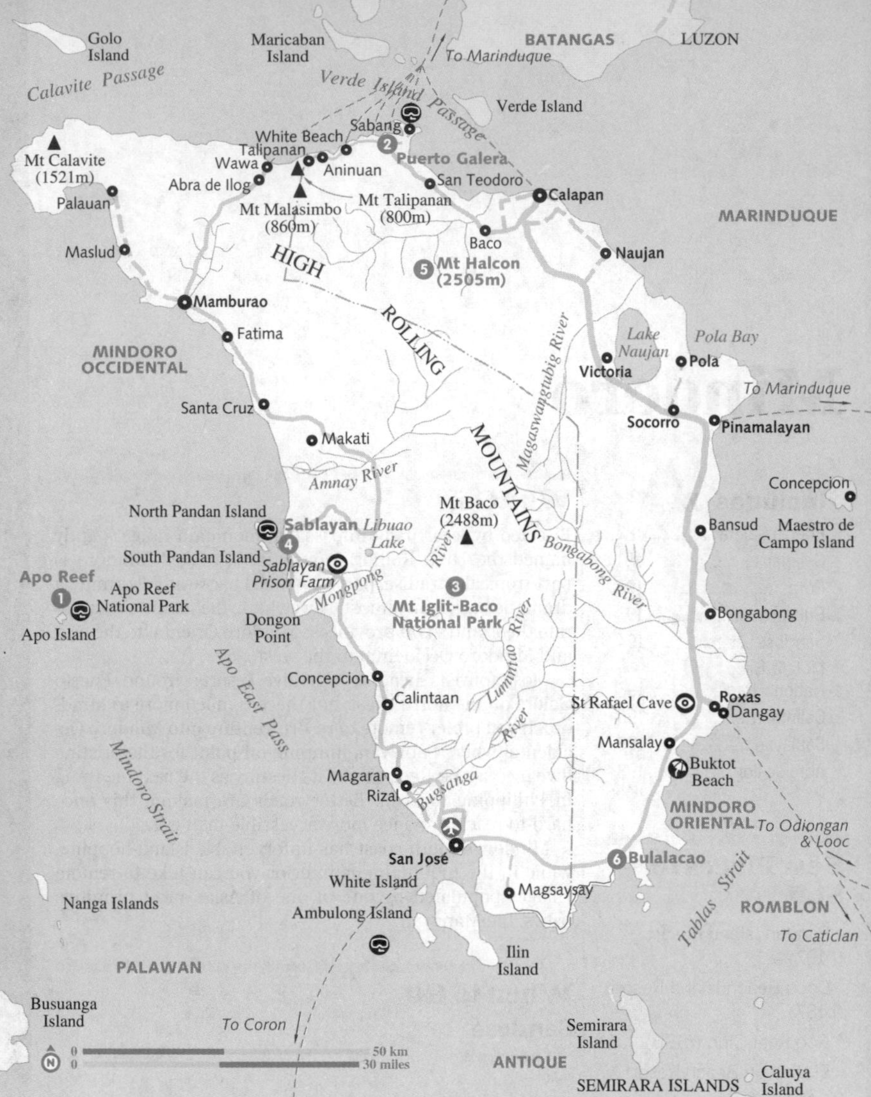

Mindoro Highlights

1. Submerge among turtles, sharks, wrasses and countless other sea critters at incredible **Apo Reef** (p197)
2. Explore the coves and beaches of **Puerto Galera** (p183) and dive its underwater wonders
3. Observe the head count of critically endangered *tamaraw* (native buffalo) at **Mt Iglit-Baco National Park** (p195)
4. Discover the unexpected attractions around **Sablayan Prison Farm** (p198)
5. Launch an assault on **Mt Halcon**, the Philippines' ultimate climb (p191)
6. Be the first person you know to island-hop reef-fringed **Bulalacao** (p193)

Getting There & Away

You can fly into San José but most people arrive by boat.

BOAT

LUZON The usual tourist route to Mindoro is by fast bangka from Batangas to Puerto Galera, but there's also a fleet of fast- and slow-craft connecting Batangas with Calapan in Mindoro Oriental. Car ferries link Batangas with Abra de Ilog, the gateway to Sablayan in Mindoro Occidental.

MARINDUQUE One or two daily bangkas leave around 11am from Pinamalayan (P200, 2½ hours) on Mindoro's southeast coast to Gasan.

PANAY & ROMBLON Roxas in southern Mindoro Oriental is linked by frequent car ferries to Caticlan (for Boracay) and less frequent boats to Odiongon, Romblon.

PALAWAN At the time of research, the only boats to Palawan were sporadic bangkas from San José to Coron and the Cuyo Islands.

BUS

If travelling from Manila, it's common to travel by bus straight through to Calapan or Abra de Ilog and points south, with your bus rolling onto a car ferry for the Batangas–Mindoro leg.

Getting Around

The road around Mindoro is mostly paved and traversed by a sizeable fleet of buses and jeepneys. However, there is still no road link between Puerto Galera and Abra de Ilog in the north of the island; travel between the two is by boat. A new road here has long been in the works, but had not been started at research time.

MINDORO ORIENTAL

Of the two provinces on the island, Mindoro Oriental is by far the wealthier and more populous. Calapan is its administrative capital, but of most interest to visitors is the northern group of resort towns collectively known as Puerto Galera ('PG', or 'Puerto'). On the southern tip of the island, Bulalacao may just have the makings of a beach-and-diving resort, especially if direct boat trips to/from Palawan materialise from its new ferry pier.

Puerto Galera

043 / POP 28,035

Just a few hours' travel time from Manila, this gorgeous collection of bays and islands is one of the country's top dive destinations. Puerto Galera is Spanish for 'port of the galleons'. Its deep natural harbour, sheltered on all sides, was a favoured anchorage well before the Spanish arrived in 1572, and today it remains a favoured anchorage for long-term yachties and short-term vacationers.

Puerto Galera typically refers to the town of Puerto Galera and the resort areas surrounding it – namely Sabang, 7km to the east, and White Beach, 7km to the west. Each has its own distinct character, spanning the range from sleaze to sophistication; you'd be well advised to choose carefully.

Sights

Tamaraw Falls WATERFALL

(admission P10; 7am-4pm) This waterfall drops from a forested ravine into pools off the main Puerto Galera–Calapan road, about 14km out of town. It gets busy at weekends, but otherwise you'll be just about the only person here – take a picnic and chill out. Jeepneys headed for Calapan will drop you here (P25, 30 minutes).

Talipanan Falls WATERFALL

(Map p184) From Talipanan beach you can hike to Talipanan Falls. Walk out on the beach access road and across the tiny bridge; just opposite the Sari-Sari store is a small concrete road heading right. Walk 500m or so to the (authentic and interesting) **Iraya Mangyan village**, where a track behind the school winds for about 40 minutes uphill and through forest to the swimmable falls. Villagers don't get much chance for extra income, so hire a guide (P200) if you can.

Excavation Museum MUSEUM

(P Concepcion St, Puerto Galera town; admission by donation; 8-11.30am & 1.30-5pm) The tiny, sweltering one-room museum displays some burial jars and ancient Chinese pottery mostly recovered from shipwrecks. It's in the grounds of the church.

Activities

Around Puerto Galera, diving is king (with drinking coming a close second). Nondiving companions will find enough to do on land for a few days, and most dive operators offer a snorkel option if you prefer to stay afloat. Still, the lack of 'real' resort-style white-sand beaches around Puerto Galera town and Sabang limits the sun, sea and sand activity somewhat; head beyond White Beach to either Aninuan or Talipanan if you're a beach junkie.

Keen or even novice sailors can head over to the **Puerto Galera Yacht Club** (Map p184;

Puerto Galera Beaches

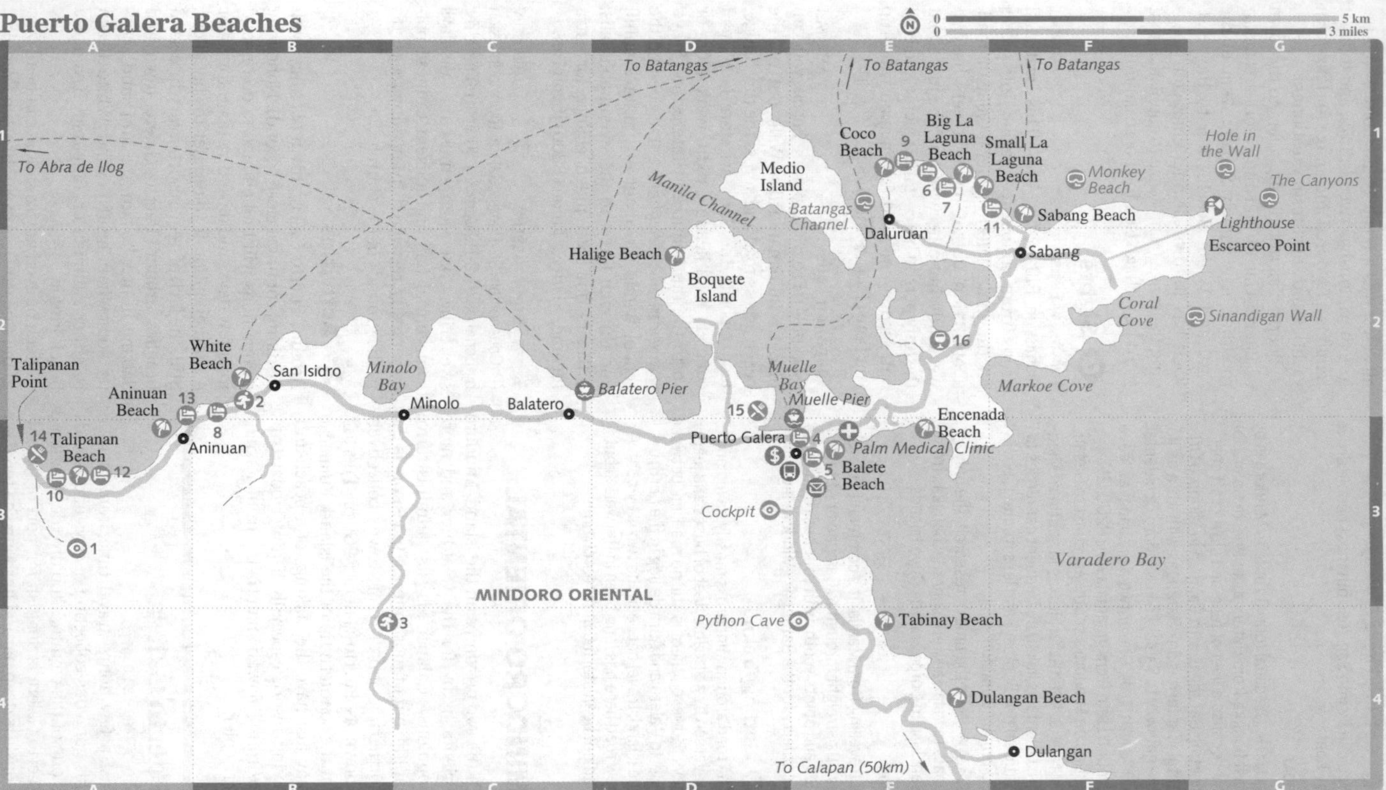

☎442 0136; www.pgyc.org; Puerto Galera town), which will team you with an experienced sailor for its 'Wet Wednesday' afternoon fun races (P450). Start time is 1pm.

Golfers can take their hacks at one of the quirkiest courses you'll find anywhere, the **Ponderosa Golf & Country Club** (Map p184; ☎0915 507 6348; 9 holes incl gear & caddy P1200). The diminutive track is cut into a steep mountain 300m above PG town, with dramatic views. Expect some odd lies.

Every Saturday at 3.30pm, the local branch of the **Hash House Harriers** meets at Capt'n Gregg's for a fun run usually followed by a drinking session.

Puerto Galera Beaches

Sights

1 Talipanan Falls A3

Activities, Courses & Tours

Asia Divers .... (see 11)
Badladz .... (see 4)
Blue Ribbon Divers .... (see 11)
2 Pacific Divers B2
3 Ponderosa Golf & Country Club B4
Puerto Galera Yacht Club .... (see 15)

Sleeping

4 Badladz E3
5 Bahay Pilipino E3
Blue Ribbon .... (see 11)
6 Campbell's E1
7 Cataqui's E1
8 Coco Aroma B2
9 Coco Beach Island Resort E1
10 El Canonero A3
11 El Galleon Beach Resort F1
Luca's .... (see 14)
12 Mountain Beach Resort A3
Sha-Che .... (see 11)
13 Tamaraw Beach Resort A2

Eating

Full Moon .... (see 11)
Hangout Bar .... (see 4)
Le Bistro .... (see 4)
14 Luca's Cucina Italiana A3
15 Puerto Galera Yacht Club D2

Drinking

16 View Point E2
Point Bar .... (see 11)

Information

Bureau of Immigration .... (see 5)
Tourist Information Center .... (see 4)

Diving & Snorkelling

The Philippines sits in a hot spot of marine diversity, and Puerto Galera offers some of the country's prime underwater real estate. Special critters that live among the coral include frogfish and mandarin fish, pygmy sea horses, ghost pipefish and nudibranches, and there's diving to suit all levels of experience. Some of the best diving is around Verde Island, a few kilometres offshore.

Dive prices vary wildly so shop around. Blue Ribbon and Dive VIP charge P1000 per dive, including equipment; others charge up to P1800. An open-water course will set you back P15,000 to P20,000, with the best rates once again at Blue Ribbon and Dive VIP.

Snorkellers shouldn't feel excluded as many of the top dive sites are well-suited for **snorkelling**. P1200 is the going rate for a three-hour snorkelling tour.

Dive operators abound, offering a range of dive and accommodation packages. The following dive operators are recommended for having a good reputation and/or being good value:

NORTHEASTERN BEACHES

Asia Divers DIVING
(Map p184; ☎287 3320; www.asiadivers.com; Small La Laguna)

Blue Ribbon Divers DIVING
(Map p184; ☎0920 823 5452; www.blueribbondivers.com; Small La Laguna)

Capt'n Gregg's Dive Shop DIVING
(Map p189; ☎287 3070; www.captngreggs.com; Sabang)

Dive VIP DIVING
(Map p189; ☎287 3140; www.divevip.com; Sabang)

PUERTO GALERA TOWN & WEST BEACHES

Badladz DIVING
(Map p184; ☎0927 268 9095; www.badladz-adventure-divers.com; Muelle Pier)

Pacific Divers DIVING
(Map p184; ☎0919 888 6763; www.philippines-diving.com; White Beach)

A few resorts and tour operators offer day tours taking in the Talipanan Falls, Tamaraw Falls, Mangyan villages and/or island-hopping. Tours are usually for a minimum of six people and cost around P1200 per head; put your name on a list and be prepared to wait a day or so if there are few takers (or pay extra for a smaller group).

Sleeping

You might try negotiating at the cheaper places. The high and low seasons aren't so defined in Puerto Galera, as divers come in droves throughout the year.

The three beaches of Sabang, Small La Laguna and Big La Laguna sweep from east to west along the north coast. Don't expect swaths of white sand lined with deck chairs and sun shades; these are slivers of sand mostly covered with bangkas pulled up on shore, and a rocky bottom where local people search for shellfish at low tide. There are many resorts up and down the hillsides, dropping (along with sometimes alarming flows of liquid detritus) almost into the ocean.

The cheapest lodging is on the eastern end of Sabang beach, where you also might be able to get a homestay in the P500–600 range.

SABANG

Sabang struts its stuff along the eastern shore. By day it's relaxed while divers dive and drinkers sleep; around sunset a metamorphosis takes place as watering holes open, barflies settle in, music cranks up, and all types – and we mean all types – of nightlife emerge.

Steps Garden Resort RESORT $$
(Map p189; (287 3046, 0915 381 3220; www.stepsgarden.com; d P1200-1900);) A delightful cluster of stand-alone cottages with private balconies in an overflowing and colourful garden, this resort sits high above the beach. It has breezes and views and is away from the noise. And yes, there are a lot of steps. The lovely pool is a pleasing new addition.

Reynaldo's Upstairs GUESTHOUSE $
(Map p189; 0917 489 5609; rey_purie@yahoo.com; r P500-1200;) Run by the nicest family you'll ever meet, Reynaldo's has a splendid mix of more-than-passable budget fan rooms and large (if tackily designed) 'view' rooms with kitchenettes and private balconies on a hillside. Only the bathrooms really disappoint.

Capt'n Gregg's Dive Resort DIVE RESORT $$
(Map p189; 287 3070, 0917 540 4570; www.captngreggs.com; r with fan/air-con from P800/1200;) This Sabang institution recently expanded after 24 years in business. The compact but cosy wood-lined 'old' rooms, right over the water, still have the most charm and are also the cheapest. Most of the new rooms are upstairs in the back.

Big Apple Dive Resort DIVE RESORT $
(Map p189; 287 3134; 0919 449 8298; www.divebigapple.com; d with fan/air-con from P500/1100;) Smack-dab in the middle of Sabang Beach, this is party central, with some noisy and tatty fan rooms to go with swankier digs around the pool in back.

Tina's Reef Divers DIVE RESORT $
(Map p189; 287 3139, 0917 532 4555; www.tinasreefdivers.com; d with fan/air-con P800/1200;) This relaxed family-run guesthouse has a few squeaky-clean teal cottages with balconies and hot water at the budget end of the beach.

Dive VIP DIVE LODGE $
(Map p189; 287 3140; www.divevip.com; r P500;) The four rooms are basic but in fine shape, with patios, hot water and TVs.

At-Can's Inn APARTMENTS $
(Map p189; 287 3659; 0920 567 9300; d with fan/air-con from P800/1200;) Flash they ain't, but for serious self-caterers these semi-apartments have some of the better kitchenettes of the many in Sabang.

SMALL LA LAGUNA

Rounding a headland, Small La Laguna is more restrained. Resorts are bigger and greener, bars and restaurants are brighter and lighter, and a quiet night's sleep is more likely; all this just five minutes walk from Sabang.

TOP CHOICE **El Galleon Beach Resort** RESORT $$
(Map p184; 0917 814 5170; www.elgalleon.com; d incl breakfast from US$51, villas US$105-300;) Elegant hut-style rooms with wicker furniture and verandahs creep up a beachfront cliff and slink around a pool. There's a fine restaurant and a top technical dive school on premises, not to mention the Point Bar, one of the country's best bars. For a modest splurge, ask about the incredible villas.

Blue Ribbon RESORT $$
(Map p184; 0920 823 5452; www.blueribbondivers.com; r P1400-2300;) This newly renovated place next to El Galleon is doing good things with prices. Not only are the rooms terrific value, but dive rates and dive/accommodation packages are as attractive

as it gets. Extras are everywhere: gym (free for guests), pool, kitchenettes (in pricier rooms) and a beachfront bar with satellite chairs plopped on the sand.

Sha-Che APARTMENTS $$
(Map p184; ☎0917 641 0112; shacheinn@yahoo.com.ph; r P1500-2500; ❄) A collection of good value, small, self-contained units with patios and kitchens, which lie in concrete rows just off the beach, next to the Full Moon restaurant.

BIG LA LAGUNA

Big La Laguna is an eclectic mix of big dive resorts and small homestay-style cottages. No wild nightlife here; it's a five-minute hike over a hilly outcrop from Small La Laguna beach – or a few minutes bangka ride from Sabang.

TOP CHOICE **Coco Beach Island Resort** BEACH RESORT $$
(Map p184; ☎0919 540 1698; www.cocobeach.com; r US$30-50; ❄@📶) From a long private beach around the point from Big La Laguna, this ideal family resort sprawls through the jungle, offering up functional bamboo- and rattan-laced standard rooms as well as more luxurious native-style hillside suites. There are two pools, a few restaurants, kiddie movie nights and activities galore. It's absurdly good value, far removed from Sabang's sleaze. It's a 10-minute jungle walk from the end of a long access road, or take a bangka from Sabang (P250, 10 minutes).

Campbell's RESORT $$
(Map p184; ☎287 3466, 0920 416 0502; www.campbellsbeachresort.com; std/deluxe incl breakfast P1280/2000; ❄📶) The westernmost place on Big La Laguna beach, right at the water's edge, is its best all-arounder. The standard rooms are nothing special, but upgrade to the deluxe and you're in business, with plump sea views from your balcony, a flat screen TV and comfy linens. You'll sleep like a rock here.

Cataqui's RESORT $$
(Map p184; ☎0920 223 8219; r with fan/air-con P1000/1200; ❄) You get no services here (the 'restaurant' is more like a *sari sari*), but the stand-alone concrete cottages, in two separate clusters near where you enter Big La Laguna Beach, will appeal to some. A couple of them are flush with the beach; the nicer ones are tucked into the trees in back.

PUERTO GALERA TOWN

Some visitors prefer the comparative calm of the waterfront around Muelle pier in Puerto Galera town to the busy resort areas of the beaches. It's where yachties tend to drop anchor and has become an enclave for older ex-pats.

Badladz DIVE RESORT $
(Map p184; ☎0927 268 9095; www.badladz-adventure-divers.com; r with P800-1200; ❄📶)
In a great location slap on the waterfront, Badladz has a well-regarded dive shop, functional if unspectacular rooms, and tasty Mexican faves like *huevos rancheros*.

Bahay Pilipino GUESTHOUSE $
(Map p184; ☎442 0266; d shared bathroom P420) Near the public market, this is the cheapest place to stay in the area. It has simple clapboard rooms, cold water only in the bathroom, and a German restaurant.

WHITE BEACH & AROUND

About 7km west of Puerto Galera are three neighbouring beaches. First up is popular **White Beach**. It does a much better impression of a beach than Sabang, but accommodation is overpriced and it fills up with mobs of Manileños on weekends and in the March–May 'summer' season. During non-summer weekdays it can be quiet and pleasant, although the monolithic resorts continue being eyesores. Try bargaining during these times.

To escape the girlie bars of Sabang, a better option is around the headland from White Beach at mellower, cleaner **Aninuan Beach**, which is almost entirely occupied by two resorts. A bit further west is **Talipanan Beach**. Flanked by Mt Talipanan to the west, and the domed peak of Mt Malasimbo to the south, this is the furthest frontier of Mindoro Oriental. Here, beach bumming, snoozing on the sand and walking the hills behind hold equal sway with diving – and nightlife means a couple of drinks and conversation over dinner.

Luca's RESORT $$
(Map p184; ☎0916 417 5125; www.lucaphilippines.com; Talipanan; r from P1500; ❄) Luca's is ideally positioned at the isolated west end of Talipanan beach. It's best known for its restaurant, but the rooms are large and functional, and the setting can't be beat – this is the nicest strip of beach in the entire area, although it occasionally gets rough.

El Canonero RESORT $$

(Map p184; ☎0915 845 4399; www.divingresortelcanonero.com; Talipanan; r incl breakfast P1300-2500; ❄@📶) Right next to Luca's, this is a newer resort, also Italian-owned, with a bigger focus on activities. It has a dive centre and a nice pool flanked by a bar. Rooms aren't spectacular, but there's a good variety, including some sea-facing rooms with verandas.

Tamaraw Beach Resort RESORT $$

(Map p184; ☎0927 597 5588; www.tamarawbeachresort.com; Aninuan; r P1000-4000; ❄📶) This ever-expanding resort sprawls along sandy Aninuan beach, with shady gardens and a relaxed vibe. A few cosy cottages front the beach, while the cheaper rooms are in a large, concrete edifice.

Coco Aroma RESORT $$

(Map p184; ☎0919 472 8882; www.cocoaromawhitebeach.com; White Beach; r without/with bathroom from P1000/1500; ❄) A rare highlight on White Beach, Coco's is rustic and relaxed at the quiet western end of the beach. The cheapest rooms are tiny – more like camping. The restaurant is vegetarian-friendly and live music happens on weekends.

Mountain Beach Resort RESORT $$

(Map p184; ☎0906 362 5406; http://mountainbeachresort.com; Talipanan; d with fan/air-con from P500/1500; ❄@📶) This is the best (and easternmost) of a cluster of small family-owned resorts on Talipanan beach. We prefer the fan rooms, in a long wooden row house with thatched walls and a long, lazy veranda.

Eating & Drinking

Almost everywhere has a happy hour, anytime between 2pm and 7pm.

SABANG & AROUND

Restaurants in Sabang are, in a word, expensive. But the quality is good compared with most Philippine resort areas. Be loose with the purse strings and you won't be disappointed. Watering holes aren't hard to find in Sabang, and some of the classics are listed here.

TOP CHOICE **Hemingway's** INTERNATIONAL $$$

(Map p189; Sabang; mains P320-1000; ⏲10.30am-10.30pm) Has some tasty Caribbean flavours in its menu to go with more traditional imported steaks and German sausages, all cooked to a T. Bonus points for mellow atmosphere and waterfront location

Full Moon INTERNATIONAL $$$

(Map p184; Small La Laguna; mains P200-500) It's worth a walk down here from Sabang just for the chili con carne – it's the real McCoy. Pastas, steaks and curries are other specialties. The uberfilling 'Full Moon breakfast' contains every breakfast ingredient you could dream of.

Casa Italia ITALIAN $$$

(off Map p189; mains P580-850; ⏲11am-11pm) Another Sabang eatery to file away in the 'damn, that was good but how did I just drop P1500?' category. A robust wine selection tempts oenophiles, while epicureans will relish the food and relaxed ambience. The bruschettas make a fine appetiser. It's on the way to the public market.

Tamarind Restaurant INTERNATIONAL $$$

(Map p189; mains P300-600) This offers a few Thai classics such as green chicken curry on its extensive menu, and it's a good sunset spot. It has a great waterfront location in the thick of – but apart from – the bustle of Sabang's walk-through lane.

Mira's Bakery BAKERY $$

(Map p189; burgers P200-250; ⏲6am-midnight) A hole-in-the-wall bakery and deli with fancy meats, cheeses and other imported picnic supplies.

Teo's Native Sizzling House FILIPINO $

(Map p189; mains P150-300; ⏲24hr) Low-key place with a comprehensive menu of sizzling dishes, Filipino classics and steaks.

Tina's FILIPINO $$

(Map p189; mains P155-400) Tina's has some of the best food on the beachfront, although it's not the bargain it once was. Do try the schnitzel.

Small Shot FILIPINO $

(Map p189; meals P120-300; P50; ⏲6am-3.30am) A *turu-turò* restaurant where you can also order a la carte.

TOP CHOICE **Point Bar** BAR

(Map p184; El Galleon Resort, Small La Laguna) Our favourite bar. The Point Bar is a mellow sunset-and-beyond meeting place with great views and eclectic music. It's relaxed, and one of the few bars in town where solo women travellers can feel comfortable.

Floating Bar BAR $$

(Map p189; ⏲9am-7pm Nov-May) Moored just offshore. Free shuttle boats leave from in

Sabang

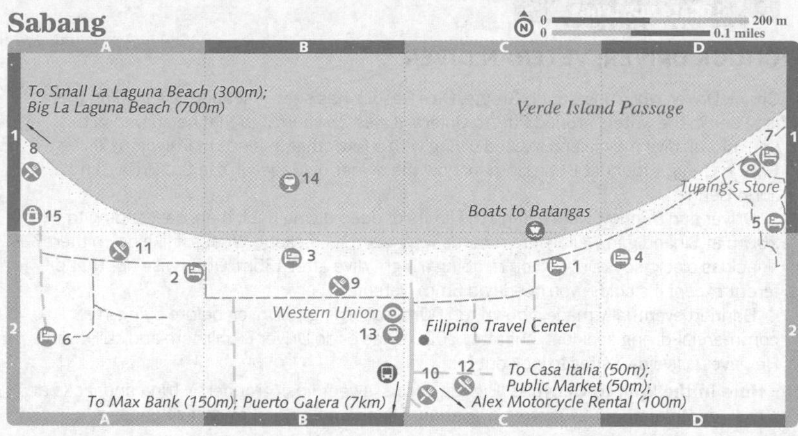

front of Capt'n Greggs for those who choose to imbibe while bobbing under a blazing sun.

Aquabest WATER STATION $
(Map p189; Sabang; ⌚7am-7pm) Water refills: P5 for a 1L bottle.

PUERTO GALERA TOWN & WESTERN BEACHES
Bars and restaurants front the gorgeous harbour west of Muelle pier, offering a range of local and western foods. Try **Hangout Bar** (Map p184) for quality pub grub and internet access (P60 per hour), or **Le Bistro** (Map p184; mains P300-500) for authentic French faves like steak tartare and bouillabaisse.

TOP CHOICE **Puerto Galera Yacht Club** INTERNATIONAL $$
(Map p184; seafood & steaks from P250-400; ⌚noon-9pm) This is a hidden gem, perched in the trees on the west edge of Muelle Bay. A free shuttle boat (three minutes) operates from the Muelle pier waterfront, from 9am to 9pm, or you can drive there easily enough. Sunset drinks and a barbecue are the traditional way to celebrate Friday.

Luca's Cucina Italiana ITALIAN $$
(Map p184; Talipanan; mains P180-280) Does great Italian food, usually cooked by the Italian owner. The pizzas (P300-400), cooked in an outdoor brick oven, are especially toothsome and feed three. The restaurant is perched over the beach, with cliffs above and mountains behind. Lovely.

View Point BAR
(Map p184; mains P175-275; ⌚9am-9pm) Atop a ridge on the winding road between PG town and Sabang, you come here for the views of PG harbour and stay for English faves like steak and 'shroom pies.

Sabang

Activities, Courses & Tours
- Capt'n Gregg's Dive Shop .... (see 3)
- Dive VIP .... (see 4)

Sleeping
- 1 At-Can's Inn C2
- 2 Big Apple Dive Resort A2
- 3 Capt'n Gregg's Dive Resort B2
- 4 Dive VIP D2
- 5 Reynaldo's Upstairs D1
- 6 Steps Garden Resort A2
- 7 Tina's Reef Divers D1

Eating
- 8 Hemingway's A1
- 9 Mira's Bakery B2
- 10 Small Shot C2
- 11 Tamarind Restaurant A2
- 12 Teo's Native Sizzling House C2
- Tina's .... (see 7)

Drinking
- 13 Aquabest B2
- 14 Floating Bar B1

Shopping
- 15 Frontier Handicrafts A1

Shopping

Frontier Handicrafts SOUVENIRS
(Map p189; ⌚6.30am-9pm) A really good souvenir store tucked in among the restaurants

LOCAL KNOWLEDGE

CHUCK DRIVER: VETERAN DIVER

Chuck Driver, who runs Capt'n Greggs Dive Resort, has seen just about everything there is to see in the waters around Puerto Galera. It was 25 years ago that he arrived in this unexplored dive mecca and started diving with a few other legends of Philippine diving – Capt'n Gregg's founder Brian Homan, now the owner of Magellan's in Subic Bay, and John Bennett.

Driver and Bennett were testing the limits of deep diving back then, descending to 200m at Sinandigan Wall before records were even being kept. What's it like down there? 'Black as black,' says Driver. 'You're doing a night dive after 135m. Otherwise not that different except it's cold – you need two 6mm wetsuits.'

Bennett eventually made it down to 300m, according to Driver, before dying in a commercial-diving accident, but after 8000 dives or so Driver is still here and still diving. He gave us five dive sites to look out for.

» **Hole in the Wall to Canyons** 'Big fan corals, sweet lips (groupers), tuna and jacks at a max depth of about 27 metres.' Location: Escarceo Point, 3km east of Sagang.

» **Sinandigan Wall** 'A good multilevel dive with lots of macro life, nudibranches and things like that. Lots of swim throughs ... the light is best in the morning, start at 42m and go multilevel all the way up.' Location: Sinandigan Point, 3km east of Sabang.

» **Monkey Beach** 'Another good multilevel. Start at 30m and gradually go up and up all the way to 4m. Great fish life and lots of different corals.' Location: off Sabang.

» **Verde Island Dropoff (aka 'Spanish Fort')** 'A big wall that goes all the way down to 70m. Lots of jacks and pelagics. Bad-ass currents though. It's a great night dive but nobody does it anymore because it's far away.' Location: Verde Island.

» **Washing Machine** 'You get a big current and man, it's fun. Go with it, then climb your way back through the canyons, pulling yourself by the rocks. I've seen people get blown away. A real adventure dive.' Location: Verde Island.

of Sabang. Lots of wooden Ifugao (North Luzon) statuettes plus local handicrafts.

Information

Internet Access

There are internet cafes along Sabang's covered lane and in PG town (including at Hangout Bar).

Money

Puerto Galera finally has ATMs – an Allied Bank in PG town, and a Max Bank in Sabang just up the hill from Tropicana Resort. Both are friendly with foreign cards. Bigger resorts take credit cards but may add a percentage fee.

Tuping's Store (Map p189; Sabang; ⏲7am-7pm) and **Western Union** (Map p189; Sabang; ⏲7.30am-11pm) change cash and give cash advances for a 7% fee.

Post

Post office (Map p184; E Brucal St, Puerto Galera town)

Tourist Information

Tourist Information Center (Map p184; ☎287 3051; Muelle pier waterfront, Puerto Galera town) Quite useful public office is up on boat schedules and hands out a good area map.

Filipino Travel Center (Map p189; ☎287 3108; ⏲9am-9pm Mon-Sat) On the main road in Sabang, it has information on transport and hotels and can recommend companies for local tours.

Visas

Bureau of Immigration (Map p184; ☎288 2245; Public Mkt, 2nd fl; ⏲9am-5pm Mon & Tue, to 12.30pm Wed) Processes visa renewals within a day.

Getting There & Away

Boat

Frequent bangka ferries connect Puerto Galera with Batangas on Luzon (see p89). Be aware that the last trip to Batangas from Sabang leaves at 1pm or 2pm (on Sundays and in peak periods there's a later boat). From White Beach the last trip is usually 3pm, and from Puerto Galera town it's 3.30pm.

A convenient way to travel between Ermita, Manila and Sabang (via Batangas) is the combined air-con bus and boat services offered by Swagman Travel and Si-Kat. Both companies have offices in Ermita (see p79) and at desks at the pier in Sabang. These cost P700 (Si-Kat) to

P850 (Swagman), compared with P430 if you go it alone. Each company has one daily departure. Both use public bangkas, then put you on private buses in Batangas.

Weather permitting, there's a 10.30am big bangka daily from the Balatero pier, 2.5km west of PG town, to Abra de Ilog (P200, one hour).

Jeepney & Van

Jeepneys (P80, 1½ hours, every 45 minutes until 4.30pm) and air-con vans (P100, 1¼ hours, hourly) service Calapan, 48km southeast of PG town, along a winding road with spectacular views across Verde Island Passage. Jeepneys depart from the Petron station in PG town. The vans aren't allowed to pick up passengers in PG proper and depart from a lot 2km southeast of the Petron station on the road to Calapan.

To reach Roxas, you must transfer in Calapan.

Getting Around

Regular jeepneys connect Sabang and PG town during daylight hours (P20, 25 minutes). A tricycle between the two costs P100 (more at night); from Sabang to Talipanan it's P300. Motorcycle taxis ('singles') are cheaper.

You can rent motorcycles in Puerto Galera at a cluster of shops around **Alex Motorcycle Rental** (off Map p189; Sinandigan Rd) east of the public market. Negotiate, but figure on P500 for a small motorbike and P700 for a trail bike.

Calapan

043 / POP 117,000

Calapan, the bustling capital of Mindoro Oriental, is a feeder port for Batangas, Luzon and – as far as most tourists are concerned – one of the stops on the bus-boat route between Manila and Boracay. It is also a good base for hiking formidable Mt Halcon and for getting to know a little about Mangyan culture.

Sights & Activities

Mangyan Heritage Center CULTURAL CENTRE

(288 5318; www.mangyan.org; Quezon Blvd; admission free; 8.30am-noon & 1.30-4.30pm Mon-Fri, weekends by appointment) Run by a small NGO, it's essentially a research centre and library, but also has a terrific small exhibition of photos with books, and a souvenir shop with greeting cards, Mangyan Jew's harps (P20), baskets, belts and necklaces – direct-traded at fair prices. It's 1km northeast of the centre on the main road to the pier, with a faded sign outside that says 'Calero Mangyan Mission'.

Mt Halcon TREKKING

Mt Halcon (2505m), which looms over Calapan to the west, is considered by many to be the most challenging big peak in the Philippines. Authorities frequently close the mountain because of environmental concerns, but it was open at the time of research. If you're keen, drop by **Apâk Outdoor Shop** (288 3391; richard.alcanices@yahoo.com; Quezon Blvd). The owner, Richard, is a member of the Mt Halcon Mountaineering Association and can tell you how to get up the mountain. You'll need to secure a guide and a permit first from the municipal office in Baco, the next town north from Calapan. Plenty of advance notice is a good idea.

The standard trip is two days up, two days down, taking in the perilous Monkey Bridge (a tangle of tree trunks spanning the Dulangan River), a breathtaking Knife Edge ridge walk and, finally, the peak itself, often jutting well above the clouds.

Local mountaineers have an arrangement with Mangyan tribespeople in the area, who are employed as porters (per day P350); on top of that expect to pay from P1800 to P2000 per day for a guide and equipment. Ask Richard about alternative outdoor activities – hikes, mountain and trail-bike rides – in and around Mindoro.

Apâk is directly opposite the Land Transportation Office (LTO), about 1.5km east of the centre on the road to the pier.

Sleeping & Eating

Calapan is no gourmand's delight. Eat at the new **Robinson's** mall near the provincial capital compound, or in the centre at chicken chain **Mang Inasal** or one of the many *carenderias* (small-scale eateries).

Filipiniana Hotel HOTEL $$

(286 2624; www.filipinianacalapan.com; M Roxas St; r with fan/air-con from P1000/1500;) Helpful staff, comfortable, well-kept rooms, a large pool in lush grounds, and a location opposite Robinson's mall make this a good choice. Be sure to ask for the 'promo rate'. Wi-fi costs P100 per hour.

Calapan Bay Hotel HOTEL $$

(288 1309; calapanbayhotel@ymail.com; Quezon Blvd; r P1100-1200;) Just a five-minute walk west of the pier, this waterfront hotel has large, cheerful rooms and a terrace

THE MANGYAN

The Mangyan were the first settlers of Mindoro, arriving around 800 years ago. They are a proto-Malay people, derived from the same ethnic stock as the majority Malay. The Mangyan comprise seven – some say eight – linguistically similar tribes spread along the length of the island's mountainous interior.

The Mangyan have preserved their culture to a much greater extent than many of the other Philippine indigenous groups. Many tribespeople still wear traditional costumes, such as the trademark loincloth *(ba-ag)*, that is worn by males. Animism – belief in the spirits that inhabit nature – remains a potent force in Mangyan cosmology, though often now with some Christian influence.

Most Mangyan are swidden farmers. During the dry season they burn scrub and forest to clear the ground and fertilise the soil; they then plant a succession of crops, including tubers, maize, pulses and 'mountain' rice (a dry rice variety). In the wet season, if there is enough game, they will hunt pigs, monkeys, birds and other small animals.

The Mangyan descend to the lowlands on market days to trade crops and handicrafts with non-Mangyans. Visitors to Puerto Galera may come across the skilfully woven, hexagonal *nito* (woody vine) baskets of the Iraya Mangyan, who live mostly in the mountains around Abra de Ilog.

The Mangyan have a long history of being persecuted by newcomers to the island or otherwise being involuntarily caught up in their wars. The Spanish punished the Mangyan for their close relations with the Moros, and the Americans put the Mangyan to work on sugar estates or forced them into reservations. In more recent times, Mangyans have been caught in the crossfire in conflicts between the Philippine Army and the New People's Army (NPA).

That they are still able to hold on to their culture despite centuries of incursions from outsiders is a testimony to their vitality and tenacity. If you are interested in finding out more, visit the Mangyan Heritage Center in Calapan (p191).

where you can dine while admiring the offshore islands. Pick a room as far from the road as possible.

Marco Vincent Hotel HOTEL $
(☎441 0239; Ivaba St; r P1000-5000; ❄) Stay in this quiet and clean lodge if you need to be near the centre. Super deal but only five rooms.

Riceland 2 Inn HOTEL $
(☎288 5590; MH del Pilar St; d with fan & shared bathroom P390, with bathroom & air-con from P700; ❄📶) Cheapie and loudie in the centre.

Information

BDO, BPI and Metrobank have functional ATMs along the main drag in the centre, JP Rizal St, and internet cafes are plentiful too.

Getting There & Away

Boat

The pier is 4km from the town centre (P20 to P30 by tricycle). The only destination from Calapan is Batangas, Luzon. All tickets are purchased at the pier. It's a swift one-hour journey to Batangas on the SuperCat fastcraft (P300, seven day trips). Slower RORO (roll-on-roll off, or car) ferries run at least every hour around the clock (P192, 2½ hours). Montenegro and Starlite are fastest and have the most trips.

Bus & Jeepney

Jeepneys to Puerto Galera (P80, 1½ hours, every 45 minutes) mainly leave from the jeepney terminal next to the Flying V petrol station on JP Rizal St, 1.5km south of central Calapan. Vans (plus a few jeepneys) to PG depart from the Calapan City Market on Juan Luna St (P100, 1¼ hours, every 45 minutes). Trips dry up after 5pm.

Also from the Calapan City Market, vans leave to Pinamalayan (P100, 1½ hours), Roxas (P200, three hours) and San José (P500, 5½ hours), departing regularly from 7am to 6pm. To Roxas or San José you could also try hopping on a southbound Dimple Star bus rolling off the ferry.

Roxas

☎043 / POP 10,000

Roxas is a dusty little spot with ferry connections to Caticlan. About the only reason to stay here would be to plot a visit to remote Mangyan villages in Mindoro's rugged interior.

Buses terminate near the lively **market** in the town centre. It's at its best on Wednesday and Sunday mornings, when Mangyan people and other villagers come to sell their wares. An even better market is barangay Bait's Friday market.

Roxas Villa Hotel & Restaurant (☎289 2026, 0921 962 0844; roxasvillahotel@yahoo.com; Administration St; s/d from P350/450; ❄@) has basic, blue rooms and a restaurant in the town centre. If he's in town, the gregarious host Bhoy Villaluna will tell you all there is to know about Roxas.

Getting There & Away

Roxas' **Dangay pier** is about 3km from the centre (P10 by public tricycle or P50 for a special trip). Vans arriving from points north do drop-offs at the pier before heading into the centre.

If you are heading to Caticlan (P400, four hours), call the **Ports Authority** (☎289 2813) at the pier, about 3km from the centre, to check the car-ferry schedule, as it changes often and departures are infrequent during the day. At the time of research **Montenegro Shipping** (☎0932 461 9096, 0909 8567 6559) had a 2pm departure, a 4pm departure and several night trips; other companies had night trips only. It's crucial to get to Caticlan before the bangkas to Boracay stop running at around 10pm.

Besides Caticlan, Roxas also has services to Odiongon, Romblon, by bangka (P300, three hours, every other day at 10am) or RORO (P300, four hours, Wednesdays at 11am).

Vans to Calapan (P180, three hours) meet the ferries at the pier. More vans depart from several points in the town centre throughout the day. Going the other way, vans leave roughly hourly from the centre to Bulalacao (P100, 1¼ hours) and San José (P350, 2½ hours) until 4pm or so.

From the highway, a few passing Dimple Star buses per day head south to San José and north to Calapan and Manila (P600, eight hours – with a little help from a ferry).

Around Roxas

Near **Mansalay**, a small coastal township 18km south of Roxas, you'll encounter a gorgeous sweep of white-sand beach and clean, calm water at **Buktot**. Behind the caretakers' house, a small green enclosure contains three pretty and basic bamboo overnight cottages (per night P350); there are beds, linen and toilets, but no screens or electricity. Take your own food, lighting and mosquito coils; haul water from the pump in the garden. We visited during the week and had the beach to ourselves, but apparently it's packed at weekends. It's 11km south of Mansalay to the turnoff, then 2km more to the beach.

Bulalacao

This unassuming coastal town is one of two places in Mindoro (the other is Sablayan) that might be on the verge of a mini (or major) tourism boom. In Bulalacao's case, this is mainly to do with location and infrastructure (see boxed text below). Its main tourist appeal is lots of lost coves and practically uninhabited islands for the plucky independent traveller to explore. Many Mangyans come to town on market days (Tuesdays and Saturdays).

BORACAY TO PALAWAN VIA BULALACAO?

The buzz in Bulalacao when we visited was all about the new RORO (car ferry) terminal. Bulalacao is hoping to compete with Roxas on the popular Mindoro–Caticlan (ie Boracay) route. Once operational, the terminal will cut the distance that car ferries have to travel on this route. An even sexier rumour was that a Bulalacao–Coron (Palawan) RORO route might open. If that happens, it would enable easy travel by sea between the country's two trendiest locales, Boracay and Palawan – a Holy Grail of sorts in Philippine tourism circles.

Bulalacao is well poised to benefit from any increased tourist traffic (although hopefully it will avoid the ills and vices that plague most port towns). Indeed all of Mindoro stands to benefit. The roads around Mindoro's south and west coasts, which were notoriously awful for decades, are now almost completely sealed. Travel to Sablayan and Apo Reef by road is no longer an intimidating proposition. Some passengers arriving from Boracay might rethink heading south to Palawan, and head west to Mindoro Occidental instead.

Sleeping & Eating

Some intriguing higher-end resorts were being built on some of the islands offshore at the time of research. The **tourist office** (☎0939 532 3761; Municipal Hall) has information on resorts old and new.

Tambaron Green Beach Resort BEACH RESORT $
(☎0929 893 7871, in Manila 02-781 2306; www.tambaron.com; r per person P200-300) This resort on nearby Tambaron Island is almost too good value to be true. The island has four private white-sand beaches that you can walk to and snorkelling at your doorstep. Rooms are simple thatched concrete affairs, and buffet meals (P150 to P175) are all-you-can-eat. Hire a bangka from Bulalacao (P600, 30 minutes) or Balatasan (P400, 15 minutes) on the Balatasan peninsula, 20 minutes southeast of Bulalacao by 'single' (motorcycle taxi).

J Felipa Lodge II LODGE $
(☎099 332 0734; r P500) This is an exceptional deal on the water 2km west of town near the new RORO terminal. Rooms can sleep four in two queen beds. Request a mosquito net.

South Drive Grill HOMESTAY $
(☎0920 436 6481; r P800-850; ❄) Not only is the sea-facing restobar by far the best place to eat in town, it also rents out two comfortable and welcoming air-con rooms.

Getting There & Away

A few vans leave to San José but you're better off flagging down a more comfortable Dimple Star bus on the main road (P250, about 1¼ hours). Vans are more frequent in the other direction to Roxas (P100, 1¼ hours), or flag down a Manila-bound Dimple Star to Roxas or beyond.

MINDORO OCCIDENTAL

The province of Mindoro Occidental is more isolated and less developed than its neighbour to the east; in most places you're as likely to be taken for a missionary as a traveller. Most tourists make a beeline for Sablayan, the entry point for the diving mecca of Apo Reef. Another attraction is ruggedly beautiful Mt Iglit-Baco National Park, a popular hiking destination and home to the endangered *tamaraw* (native buffalo).

San José

☎043 / POP 137,000

The southernmost town in Mindoro Occidental, San José has a cluster of three pretty islands – White, Ambulong and Ilin – just off-shore. It's notable for having an airport, and its position as a transport hub is what brings most travellers through. It's also the place to restock on cash from the only ATMs in Mindoro Occidental, including **Metrobank** (C Liboro St). There are several internet cafes along Rizal and C Liboro Sts, including **Geox** (per hr P20, ⏲8am-8pm).

Sleeping & Eating

The best that can be said of the accommodation in noisy, fumy San José proper is that it's better than the food. We recommend staying on Aroma Beach, just a 2km tricycle ride (P20) north of town. It's clean and good for walking, with decent swimming at high tide.

Sikatuna Beach Hotel HOTEL $
(☎491 2182; Airport Rd; d with cold/hot water from P900/1000; ❄📶) This big place on Aroma Beach is a huge step up on anything in the centre; fan rooms are clean but not flash, and the newer (check a few) air-con rooms are light and bright. The restaurant does good fresh Filipino meals.

White House Beach Resort HOTEL $$
(☎491 1656; edithpark@yahoo.com; Airport Rd; r P2500-3500; ❄) Another Aroma Beach option, this one is more like a well-to-do and classy relative's mansion than a hotel. It's the most luxurious place in town, with balconies and huge marble bathrooms (and bidets!), but is somewhat sleepy and overpriced.

Jazmine Royal Hotel HOTEL $
(☎491 4269; Sikatuna St; d P800-1800; ❄) A step up in comfort from Midtown Plaza if you need to be in the centre, with cleaner bathrooms. Close to boats to Coron and the public market.

Mindoro Plaza Hotel HOTEL $
(☎491 4661; P Zamora St; s/d with fan from P300/400, with air-con from P750/8500; ❄) The fan rooms will appeal to budget travellers; otherwise this place is unspectacular, with maintenance issues even in the pricier rooms.

Kusina Restaurant FILIPINO $
(Sikatuna St; mains P50-220) One of the few cook-to-order places in town, and maybe the only one – except for Jollibee – with air-con.

San José

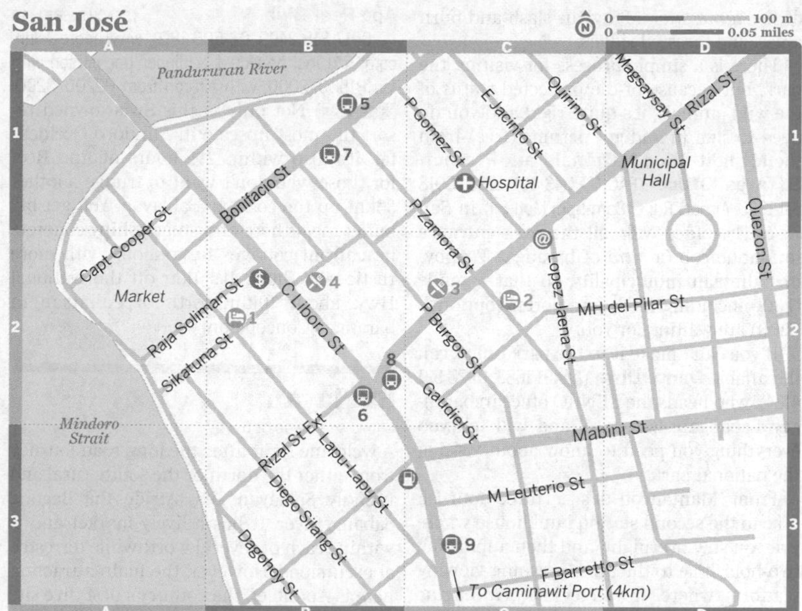

Chowder FILIPINO $
(Rizal St; mains P50-150; ⌚24hr) This restobar near Mindoro Plaza Hotel passes for trendy in San José.

ℹ Getting There & Away

Air

San José's airport, about 5km northwest of town (P50 by tricycle), is served by Cebu Pacific (two daily), Airphil Express (daily) and Zest Air (daily) flights to/from Manila.

Boat

Bangkas to Coron town in northern Palawan (P600, eight hours) leave from a wide beach in San Roque, just over the bridge heading north from the centre. Departures are Tuesday and Friday mornings.

From San José's main Caminawit Fish Port, 4km south of town, there's a twice-weekly boat to Manamok in the Cuyo Islands (P500, eight hours).

Bus & Jeepney

Air-con **Dimple Star** (Bonifacio St) buses to Manila (P950, 12 hours) go via either Abra de Ilog (eight trips daily) or Calapan (three daily). Northbound buses get you to Calintaan (P60, one hour) and Sablayan (P140, 2½ hours). Cheaper jeepneys and rickety ordinary buses are slower options to Calintaan and Sablayan.

San José

Sleeping
1 Jazmine Royal Hotel....B2
2 Mindoro Plaza Hotel....C2

Eating
3 Chowder....C2
4 Kusina Restaurant....B2

ℹ Transport
5 Dimple Star Bus Terminal....B1
6 Jeepneys and Minibuses to Sablayan....B2
7 Jeepneys to Mamburao....B1
8 Vans to Calapan....B2
9 Vans to Roxas and Calapan....C3

Eastbound Dimple Star buses transit Bulalacao (P250, 1¼ hours) and Roxas (P350, 2½ hours). Similarly priced vans, with several departure points, are another eastbound option.

Mt Iglit-Baco National Park

Travellers who trek to this remote area may be rewarded with a sighting of the elusive wild *tamaraw*, the Philippines' endangered native buffalo. The national park is made up of sweeps of grassland (the favoured habitat of the *tamaraw*), Mangyan slash-and-burn areas, and forested ridges.

There is a simple process for visiting the park, but because of the protected status of the wild animals, it's quite rigid and you do need to sign in and get permits (free) from the **Mt Iglit-Baco National Park Protected Area Office** (PAO; ☎043-491 1236, 0918 511 1323; Airport Rd; ⊙8am-5pm Mon-Fri) in San José. The office will call the park entrance in Mantancob (a *sitio* of barangay Poypoy) in Calintaan municipality, so that a guide (P300 including food) and porter (optional, P200) are waiting for you.

If you can't make it to the park office, call the affable **Dante Diwa** (☎491 1683, 0928 521 4124), who heads the CENRO office in barangay Labangan, San José, and will tell you everything you need to know about visiting the national park.

From Mantancob it's a three-hour-ish hike to the second station bunkhouse where you can stay overnight, and then a morning two-hour hike to the Mt Magawang viewing platform where, if you're lucky, *tamaraw* will be gambolling on the plains below. You will need your own gear for these hikes. December to April is good climbing time, and in April you may coincide with and observe the annual *tamaraw* count. Dante will know when it's scheduled.

The PAO office in San José shares a space with the **Tamaraw Conservation Program**, which has a small *tamaraw* information exhibition and runs a breeding station known as the Gene Pool, inside the park, that you can visit. Here captive-bred *tamaraw* are raised. It's in barangay Manoot, Rizal municipality, about 1½ hours by 'single' from San José. You can hike from the Gene Pool station in Manoot to the Mt Magawang viewing platform (about four hours).

Getting There & Away

There are a few direct jeepneys to Poypoy from San José that go straight to Mantancob, or take a bus to Calintaan (P60, one hour) and a tricycle to the park entrance in Mantancob (P75, 35 minutes).

Calintaan

About 40km north of San José, **Calintaan** is a potential launch point for both Mt Iglit-Baco National Park and Apo Reef. You could depart from Manila on an early-morning flight and be diving at Apo Reef the same morning out of Apo Reef Club.

Apo Reef Club BEACH RESORT $$
(☎0917 815 2499, 02-506 1801; www.aporeefclub.com; s/d incl breakfast & dinner per person with fan P1500/2000, with air-con from P2200/3200; ❄@≋) Not only is this Swiss-owned resort the most upscale in Mindoro Occidental, it's also within 2½ hours of Apo Reef for those who don't want to trudge another 33km up the coast to Sablayan. You get big buffet meals here and smart, shiny concrete beachfront cottages to go along with more rustic nipa huts. It's 1km off the National Hwy, about 10km north of Calintaan in barangay Concepcion.

Sablayan

☎043 / POP 90,000

A welcome sight after the long road journey from either the north or the south, rural and friendly Sablayan sits astride the Bagong Sabang River. It has a lively market and is within reach of several worthwhile terrestrial excursions. However, the main attraction here is Apo Reef, the country's best dive site not named Tubbataha, less than two hours offshore.

For years Sablayan was effectively cut off from the rest of the country by horrendous roads heading north to Abra de Ilog and south to San José. With those roads now sealed and smooth, it would seem only a matter of time before Sablayan is discovered in a big way. Try to get here before that happens.

Sights & Activities

Apo Reef Natural Park DIVING
At the time of research only three operators were doing dive and snorkelling trips to Apo Reef: North Pandan Island Resort and the Ecotourism Office in Sablayan; and Apo Reef Club in Calintaan. Small groups looking to split costs with other divers are advised to go through the ecotourism office. The costs for a day trip are P8000 per group for the boat (up to 15 people, two hours each way); an entrance fee of P350/1300 per person for snorkelers/divers; P500 for a divemaster; and P125/1600 per day for snorkel/dive equipment. Bring your own lunch, water and snacks. We hooked up with a group and paid only P4400 for a full day of diving (three dives), including transport. You'll pay more with the other two dive operators, but you'll benefit from better equipment and divemasters. All three operators can arrange

APO REEF

At 35 sq km, Apo Reef Natural Park (not to be confused with Apo Island off the south coast of Negros) is the largest atoll-type reef in the Philippines. The crystal clear waters abound with life, including 285 species of fish and 197 species of coral. It's the only readily accessible dive site in the Philippines where snorkellers and divers alike are practically guaranteed heavy pelagic (large fish) action – mostly white-tip and black-tip sharks, reef sharks, wrasses, jacks and tuna – on a day trip from Sablayan we saw so many sharks we lost count. You stand a chance of seeing trophy creatures like hammerhead sharks, whale sharks and manta rays out here, although we were not so lucky. The three islands of the reef play host to a variety of turtle and bird species, including the endangered, large-chicken-sized Nicobar pigeon.

Apo Reef is two hours sailing time from Sablayan in flat seas (a bit less from North Pandan Island, a bit more from Calintaan). Liveaboard trips from Anilao and especially Coron also make it out here.

The best time to make the trip to Apo Reef is when the seas are flattest – April–May and October–November. The journey is roughest in December–March and July–September. Just remember that there are exceptions to any rule, especially when it concerns Philippine weather patterns.

overnight trips, sleeping in hammocks or on the floor of the open-air park ranger station on Apo Island (or on boats). But be wary of sleeping on Apo Island during the *amihan* (northeast monsoon, from mid-November to mid-May), as the sandflies can be unbearable.

Tours

Ecotourism Office (☎0928 465 9585; www.sablayan.net, amazingsablayan@yahoo.com; Town Plaza, P Urieta St; ⏰8am-5pm, closed Sat & Sun Jun-Dec) This office is unique in that it actually runs tours as opposed to just dishing out pamphlets and advice. Apo Reef dive trips are the big one, but they can arrange excursions to Sablayan Prison Farm, Mt Iglit-Baco National Park and a two-day forest trek taking in several Mangyan villages.

Sleeping & Eating

A few decent lodging options have opened in Sablayan; one can only pray that decent eating options will follow.

TOP CHOICE **Pandan Island Resort** BEACH RESORT $
(☎0919 305 7821; www.pandan.com; budget r P750, bungalows P1500, q cottage from P2500) This postcard-perfect, privately owned resort island is a low-key tropical paradise. Several prime dive spots surround the island, and you'd be unlucky not see a green turtle as you snorkel. Early mornings are prime bird-watching times; listen for the Philippine pygmy woodpecker pecking away. The resort itself is on a long, curving, white-sand beach. Rooms are a combination of rudimentary budget rooms with shared bathroom, and comfortable bungalows. There's limited, solar-powered electricity, which unfortunately means no fans at night (hope for a breeze). Tasty buffet meals cost P450 and guests are required to take at least one; full board is P900. It costs P150 to visit the island for the day – a free shuttle waits on the Sabang River just southwest of the Emily Hotel, or hire a bangka (P150 to P350 per person each way, 20 minutes).

Sablayan Adventure Camp RESORT $
(☎0917 850 0410; embabia@yahoo.com; r P800) We're not sure where the 'adventure' tag comes from, but it's nonetheless a good all-around choice, with pleasantly unkempt grounds, a beach frontage of sorts, and large, stylish semi-open-air rooms with mozzie nets. It's at the mouth of the Sabang River 1km southwest of the centre.

Country Woods RESORT $
(☎0920 805 7255; r P2000; ❄🏊) On a quiet stretch of beach 3.5km south of Sablayan, Country Woods has a huge pool and the spiffiest rooms in town. The concrete cottages have hot water, big bathrooms and private balconies, but lack TVs. All rooms can sleep four in two queen-sized beds.

GVD Kubo FILIPINO $
(Town Plaza, P Urieta St; mains P50-80; ⏰6am-10pm) About the only real eatery in the centre, they offer a mix of pre-made and

LOCAL KNOWLEDGE

PETER, PRISONER

You could be forgiven for thinking that the Sablayan Prison Farm is some kind of 'Club Fed', given the engaging personalities of some of the prisoners. But it's not all fun and games. Peter (we are withholding his full name because prisoners are not authorised to do interviews) gave us the low-down on prison life.

What are you doin' time for? Falsification of public documents.

How long have you been in? Since 2001. I got 12 to 16 years but I'm being paroled in June [2011].

What are you looking forward to the most about freedom? Seeing my brother in Makati. But he is not answering my texts!

Are you going to miss prison life? Yes. In prison you bond with fellow inmates. We are like brothers who share everything. A cup of coffee is shared with 10 inmates. I've never experienced anything like that before.

But you do want to leave? Yes of course. Life is difficult here. We still can't go anywhere we want. I want to be free!

What's your least favourite thing about prison life? Guards are treated like gods here. They feel so superior. Sometimes they treat us like animals. I've heard they even joke that prisoners are their 'carabaos', doing all of their work [in the farm]. Of course that was before. Now we have tractors.

Any messages for the outside world? I want this penal farm to be changed. I wish I had evidence to show the world that this is not a really nice place. Overall it's good that you foreigners come here – it brings us outside of the prison walls in a way, and that makes us happy. But just realise that life is hard here. Can't you see how skinny we all are? We need more food. In a week they give us only 3.5 kilos of rice, plus some dried fish, four eggs, one sardine tin, some mongo beans and a small packet of macaroni. That's it!

cooked-to-order dishes. You can cobble together a takeaway lunch of cold chicken legs and other snacks for your Apo Reef trip the next day.

Other accommodation options:

Along D' Beach HOTEL $
(☎0921 404 9242; National Hwy; r with fan/air-con P350/700; ❄) On the highway just south of the centre, this place is dishevelled but has great views, and the fan rooms are good value.

Land Manz HOTEL $
(☎0928 219 7011; C Salgado St; r with fan/air-con from P400/800; ❄) Nice only by the standards of the loathsome Emily Hotel. Rooms are still pretty basic, but big enough. It's in the centre near the town plaza.

Emily Hotel HOTEL $
(☎0919 337 9492; Gozar St; r with shared/private bathroom from P200/300) Downright awful, but cheap and well located opposite the boats to North Pandan Island.

Getting There & Away

Air-con Dimple Star buses rumble through town every two hours or so on their way to Cubao in Manila (P800, nine hours, about eight daily) via Abra de Ilog (P220, 3½ hours), and in the other direction to San José (P140, 2½ hours). You can also take a more frequent but much slower ordinary bus north to Abra de Ilog or south to Calintaan and San José.

You can rent motorbikes (P400 per day) at the *habal-habal* stop next to the public market, which fronts the Sabang River near the Emily Hotel.

Around Sablayan

SABLAYAN PRISON FARM

A wonderfully quirky experience, the **Sablayan Prison Farm** (admission free) offers much more than a chance to meet-and-greet prisoners in their element. There are also a host of prisoner-guided excursions on offer in the lush forests around the farm, and you can even sleep out here within earshot of snoring prisoners in the **prison guest-**

house (Siburan subprison; r with two bunk beds P500).

You must secure a permit (P50) from the ecotourism office in Sablayan to enter the prison grounds. A half-day of activities might combine an hour or so guided hike in **Siburan rainforest** (admission P50) with a visit to **Libuao Lake** (admission P50), some time talking to prisoners at the **central subprison** and a visit to **Pasugi subprison**, where you can buy prisoner-made handicrafts. Siburan forest and Libuao Lake are prime birdwatching spots, and one of the prisoner-guides knows birds and can point out endemic black-hooded coucals, imperial pigeons, white-spotted doves and white-billed and serpent eagles if you're lucky. The lake is famed for its lotuses, and is a popular spot for fishing, boating (P150) and bird-watching. Take a picnic and relax. Secure a guide (P150) at the Siburan subprison barracks, 5km northeast of the central subprison.

Prisoners throughout the compound greet visitors cheerfully, wearing uniform T-shirts that say 'minimum' or 'medium inmate'. Maximum-security inmates are kept away from tourists, but the orange 'Maximum' shirts sold discreetly by some inmates make great souvenirs.

The prison farm makes a perfect half-day excursion from Sablayan by single (about P800) or self-drive motorbike. Turn off the National Hwy 17km south of Sablayan and proceed east 7km to the central subprison.

Abra de Ilog

☎043 / POP 25,150

The dusty town of Abra de Ilog is the northern gateway to Mindoro's west coast. If you arrive by water you'll see why there's no usable road west of Puerto Galera: a cloud-scraping wall of jagged mountains runs right to the shore.

You likely won't linger long in Abra. If you're not aboard one already, try to hop a San José-bound Dimple Star bus that's rolling off the ferry, which will take you via Sablayan (P220, 3½ hours). Otherwise, take a tricycle south 5km from the port to the town proper and jump on a southbound jeepney or ordinary local bus to Mamburao, and change there for Sablayan or San José.

Montenegro ROROs depart six times daily to Batangas (P260, 2½ hours), and there's a daily bangka to Puerto Galera's Balatero pier (P200, one hour).

The Visayas

Includes »

Best Places to Eat

» Rosita's Native Restaurant (p318)

» Angelina (p223)

» STK (p211)

» L'Elephant Bleu (p301)

» Baybay Seafood Buffets (p268)

Best Places to Stay

» Villa Marmarine (p291)

» Nami Boracay (p260)

» Takatuka Lodge & Dive Resort (p280)

» ChARTs Resort (p300)

» Harold's Mansion Tourist Inn (p284)

Why Go?

Forming the geographical heart of the Philippines, the Visayas is a star-studded collection of islands that has managed to slip under the tourist radar. While they have a common ground in offering world-class diving and fantastic beaches, each has its own unique personality. One has bug-eyed tarsiers, the next volcano trekking or killer surf, while further along there's heritage architecture or shaman folk healers. It's this diversity that makes this underrated region worth exploring in more depth.

By far the most visited part is Boracay – the Philippines' most famous beach. It's brash, crass and overdeveloped, yet remains one of the most beautiful white-sand beaches in the world and the country's biggest tourist magnet.

This suits the other less flashy islands just fine, who are more than happy to laze in its shadow. Islands like Negros, Bohol, Siquijor and Samar are far from household names, yet continue to win over visitors as their favourite spot in the Philippines.

When to Go

Cebu

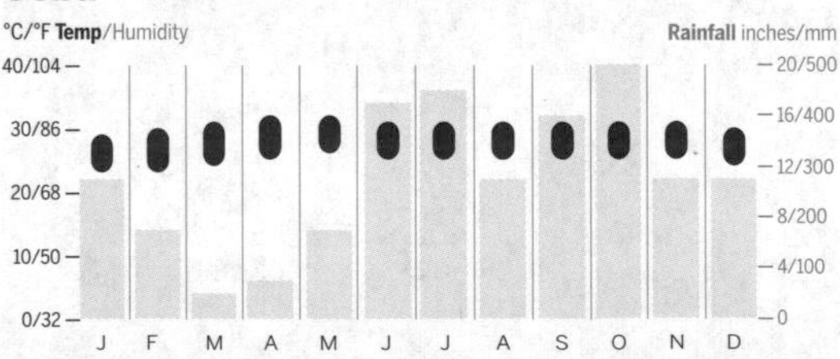

Dec–Apr Generally good weather, perfect for diving.

May–Oct It may be 'rainy season' but crowds are fewer and there's often not much rain.

Aug–Dec Best time to catch waves in Guiuan.

CEBU

POP 2.4 MILLION

Simply being from Cebu carries a certain cultural heft, and it's not hard to see why. Cebu is the hub around which the Visayas revolve. It is the most densely populated island in the Philippines and is second only to Luzon in its strategic and economic importance to the country. Cebuano, spoken on Cebu, is considered to be the standard or 'prestige' variety of Visayan, a heterogeneous language counting over 20 million speakers throughout the central Philippines.

The main attractions are its white-sand beaches and spectacular diving, namely off the northern tip of the Cebu at Bantayan and Malapascua islands, as well as on the southwest coast at Moalboal.

Getting There & Around

Cebu City is the gateway to the Visayas. It has the nation's busiest port and its second-busiest airport. If you happen to be travelling from Asia, it's an attractive alternative to entering the country at Manila, with several direct international flights to Cebu City. There also many domestic flights connecting Cebu with at least a dozen destinations in the Philippines, Manila of course included.

Cebu City is the busiest port with boats bound for almost every destination (though not always directly and often not daily). Negros is best accessed from towns on the west side of the island, with numerous places up and down the coastline with regular ferry services; via Lilo-An is the most popular route, linking it to Dumaguette. Alternatives to Cebu City for accessing neighbouring islands include Siquihor via Mainit, Bohol from Argau, Camotes via Danau and Leyte from Maya.

Air-con buses and vans provide good, reliable connection between towns.

Cebu City

032 / POP 798,809

Cebu City is like an entrée-sized Manila; it's energetic, exciting and fast-paced, or loud, dirty and ruthless, depending on your perspective. On the surface, it does its worst to attract tourists, with its honking jeepneys spluttering exhaust fumes, shopping-mall culture and lack of world-class sights. While it lacks any amazing attractions, you can have a good time here by focusing on its great clubbing, friendly Cebuanos and rich history before escaping to a more appropriate 'holiday' spot.

With its vast seaport, the city is the best-connected hub in the region and as such it is something of a vortex, sucking in travellers and spitting them out again at destinations throughout the Visayas. The average foreigner here is your long-term male visitor – a retiree with a much younger Filipina clinging to his arm.

History

When Ferdinand Magellan sailed into the Port of Cebu on 7 April 1521, an eyewitness account relates that he was already a latecomer: 'Many sailing vessels from Siam, China and Arabia were docked in the port. The people ate from porcelain wares and used a lot of gold and jewellery...'

He may not have been the first outsider to visit Cebu, but Magellan brought with him something that nobody else had: missionary zeal. Even his death at the hands of warrior chief Lapu-Lapu on Mactan Island, a few weeks later, would only afford the natives temporary respite from the incursions of the conquistadors. The arrival of avenging Spaniard Miguel López de Legazpi in 1565 delivered Cebu – and eventually the whole of the Philippines – to Spain and Catholicism. The founding in 1575 of Villa del Santisimo Nombre de Jesús (Village of the Most Holy Name of Jesus) marked Cebu City as the first Spanish settlement in the Philippines, predating Manila by seven years.

Sights

The city is divided roughly into uptown and downtown; the latter has more impoverished, vice-strewn streets and most of the 'sights' are here. A visit to the city's principal attractions – Fort San Pedro, Magellan's Cross and the Basilica Minore del Santo Niño – is an ideal way to sample the chaos and sordidness of downtown before beating a hasty retreat. As well as Museo Sugbo, there are a number of smaller museums worth checking out if you have the time – Cebu Normal University Museum, University of San Carlos Museum and Cebu City Museum all have some interesting pieces.

Basilica Minore del Santo Niño CHURCH

(Map p206; admission free; Pres Osmeña Blvd) This holiest of churches is a real survivor. Established in 1565 (the oldest church in the Philippines) and burnt down three times, it was rebuilt in its present form in 1737. Perhaps it owes its incendiary past to the perennial

The Visayas Highlights

1. Snorkel with massive turtles in the shallows of **Apo Island** (p288), before plunging into the riotously colourful reef

2. Explore nature's time capsule on biologically diverse **Sibuyan Island** (p237)

3. Dive with the swirling vortex of sardines off **Moalboal** (p224)

4. Sea-sport and sun on the stunning beaches of **Boracay** (p251)

5. Go spelunking in the extensive underground network around **Catbalogan** (p324) in western Samar

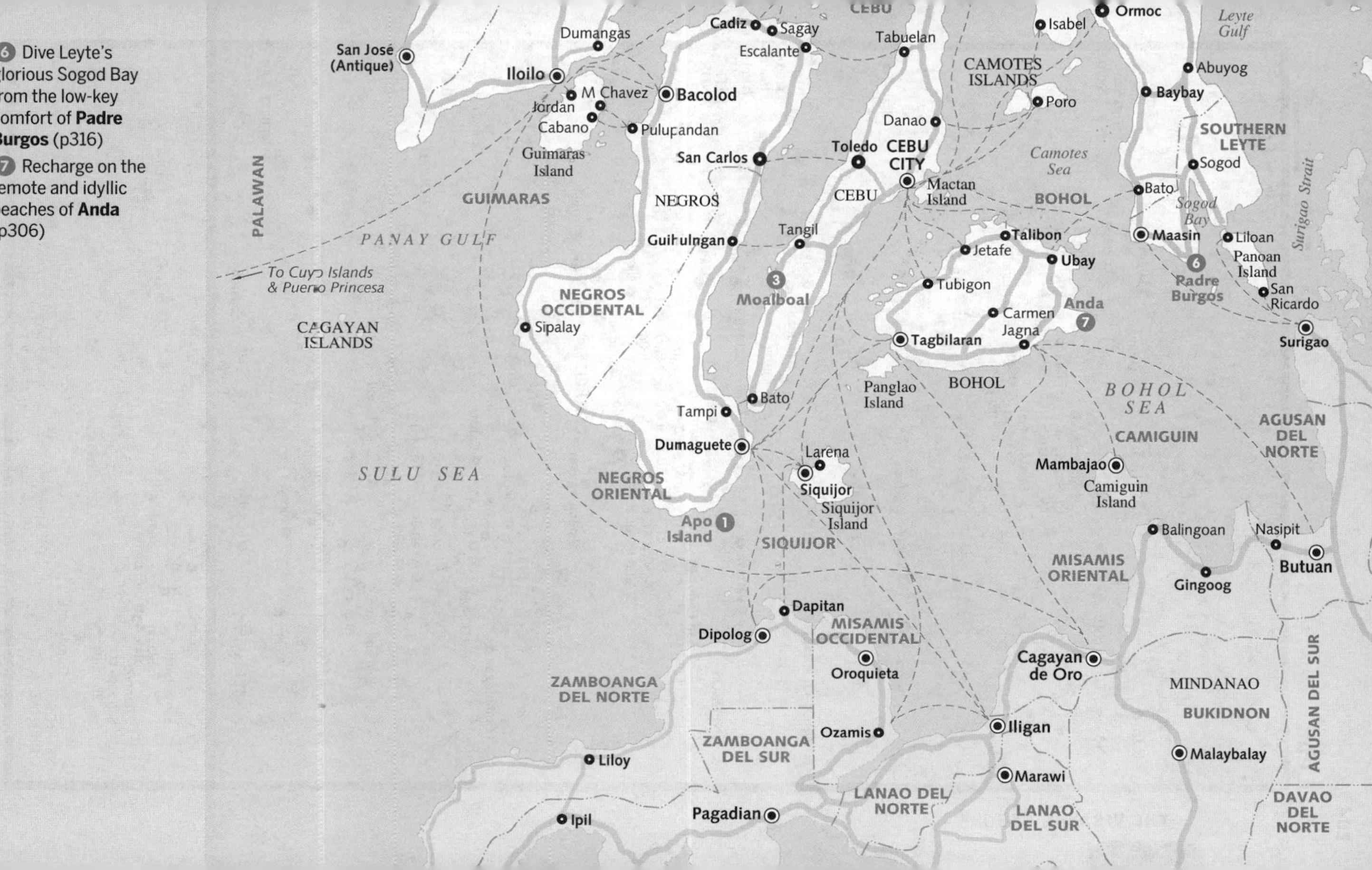

6 Dive Leyte's glorious Sogod Bay from the low-key comfort of **Padre Burgos** (p316)

7 Recharge on the remote and idyllic beaches of **Anda** (p306)

Cebu

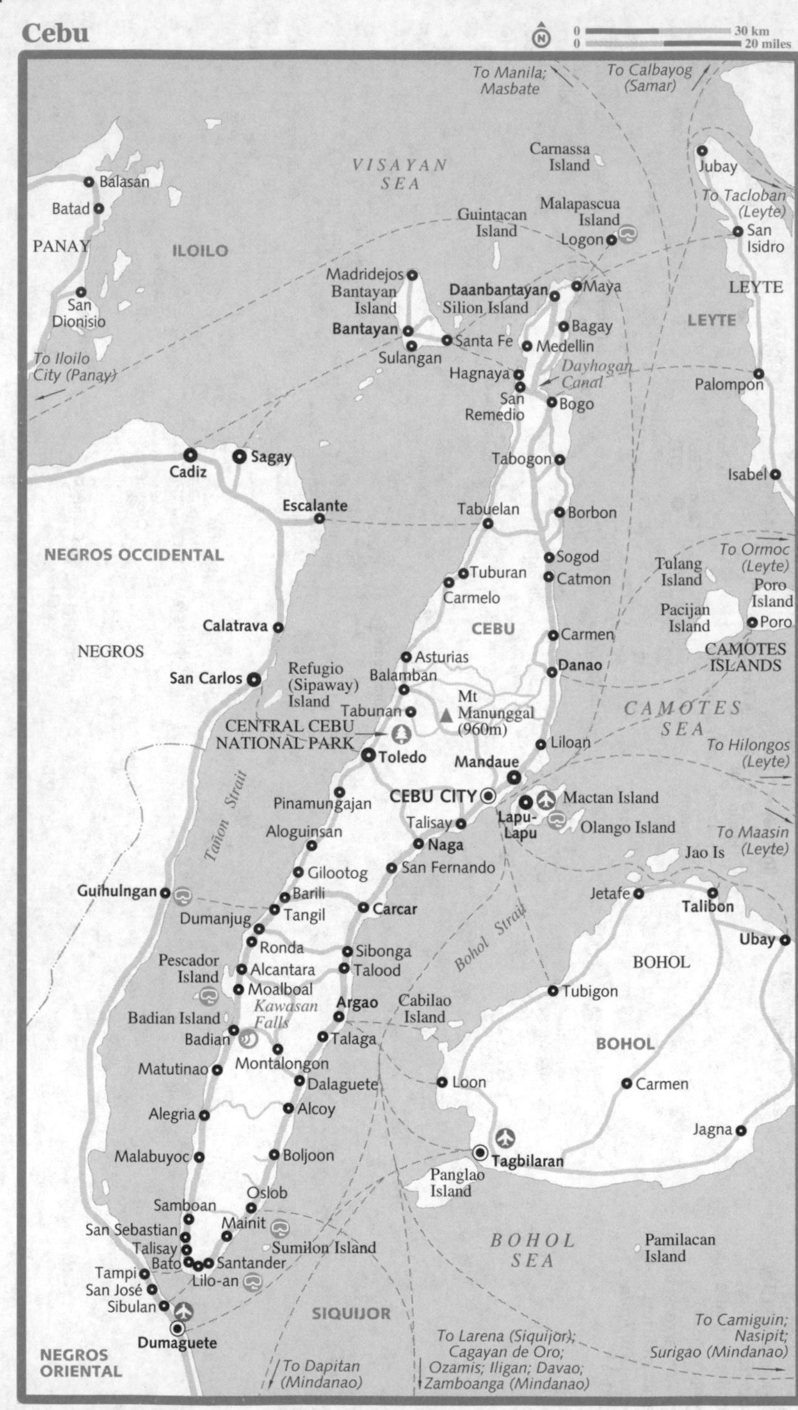

0 30 km
0 20 miles
To Manila; Masbate
To Calbayog (Samar)
VISAYAN SEA
Carnassa Island
Jubay
Balasan
Batad
PANAY
ILOILO
Guintacan Island
Malapascua Island
Logon
To Tacloban (Leyte)
San Isidro
Madridejos
Bantayan Island
Daanbantayan
Maya
Silion Island
LEYTE
LEYTE
San Dionisio
Bantayan
Santa Fe
Bagay
Medellin
Sulangan
To Iloilo City (Panay)
Hagnaya
Dayhogan Canal
San Remedio
Bogo
Palompon
Tabogon
Cadiz
Sagay
Isabel
Escalante
Tabuelan
Borbon
NEGROS OCCIDENTAL
Sogod
Tuburan
Catmon
Carmelo
Tulang Island
To Ormoc (Leyte)
Poro Island
Pacijan Island
Poro
Calatrava
CEBU
Carmen
NEGROS
Asturias
Danao
CAMOTES ISLANDS
San Carlos
Refugio (Sipaway) Island
Balamban
Tabunan
Mt Manunggal (960m)
CAMOTES SEA
CENTRAL CEBU NATIONAL PARK
Toledo
Liloan
Mandaue
To Hilongos (Leyte)
Tañon Strait
Pinamungajan
CEBU CITY
Mactan Island
Lapu-Lapu
Talisay
Olango Island
Aloguinsan
Naga
To Maasin (Leyte)
Jao Is
San Fernando
Gilootog
Guihulngan
Barili
Jetafe
Talibon
Tangil
Carcar
Dumanjug
Ubay
Ronda
Sibonga
Bohol Strait
Pescador Island
Alcantara
Talood
BOHOL
Moalboal
Kawasan Falls
Argao
Cabilao Island
Tubigon
Badian Island
Badian
Talaga
BOHOL
Montalongon
Matutinao
Dalaguete
Loon
Carmen
Alcoy
Alegria
Jagna
Malabuyoc
Boljoon
Tagbilaran
Panglao Island
Oslob
Samboan
Mainit
San Sebastian
Talisay
Sumilon Island
BOHOL SEA
Pamilacan Island
Bato
Santander
Tampi
Lilo-an
San José
Sibulan
SIQUIJOR
Dumaguete
To Camiguin; Nasipit; Surigao (Mindanao)
To Larena (Siquijor); Cagayan de Oro; Ozamis; Iligan; Davao; Zamboanga (Mindanao)
NEGROS ORIENTAL
To Dapitan (Mindanao)

bonfire of candles in its courtyard, stoked by an endless procession of pilgrims and other worshippers. The object of their veneration is a Flemish image of the infant Jesus, sequestered in a chapel to the left of the altar. It dates back to Magellan's time and is said to be miraculous (which it probably had to be to survive all those fires). Every year, the image is the centrepiece of Cebu's largest annual event, the Sinulog festival.

On Sundays the basilica turns into a spectacle of pilgrims, water sellers and replica Santo Niño salespeople.

Magellan's Cross HISTORIC SITE
(Map p206) Ferdinand's Catholic legacy, a large wooden cross, is housed in a stone rotunda (built in 1841) across from Cebu City Hall. The crucifix on show here apparently contains remnants from a cross Magellan planted on the shores of Cebu in 1521. A painting on the ceiling of the rotunda shows Magellan erecting the cross (actually, the locals are doing all the work – Magellan's just standing around with his mates). After the Santo Niño, this is the most venerated religious relic in Cebu.

Museo Sugbo-Cebu Provincial Museum MUSEUM
(Map p206; M Cuenco Ave; adult/child P75/50; ⌚9am-5.30pm Mon-Sat) Opened in 2008, Museo Sugbo sits on the site of the former provincial jail and is a complex comprising three museums. Most interesting is Museo Sugbo itself, which is made up of four galleries showcasing precolonial, Spanish colonial, American-era and WWII-era Cebu. Notable exhibits include the artificial cranial deformation displays depicting 16th-century native Cebuanos who practised skull deformation on infants as a concept of beauty. We'll let you be the judge of that. The upstairs WWII gallery highlights include an American bomb that was dropped in Cebu, a Purple Heart medallion and propaganda posters. The buildings surround a lovely courtyard area with a coffee shop and souvenir store.

Fort San Pedro FORTRESS
(Map p206; S Osmeña Blvd; adult/child P30/20; ⌚8am-7.30pm) Built in 1565 under the command of Miguel López de Legazpi, conqueror of the Philippines, Fort San Pedro has

THE GENTLE ART OF BUTTERFLIES

Julian Jumalon (1909–2000), a renowned Cebuano artist and avid butterfly collector, set up the **Jumalon Butterfly Sanctuary** (☎261 6884; admission P50; ⌚9am-5pm) at his home west of downtown, which makes for a fascinating visit. His knowledge was all acquired through his observations during expeditions into the forests to study butterflies, rather than any formal scientific training (he is credited for discovering new Philippine butterfly species and won countless awards in the field of biology). Along with these achievements, he was a widely respected artist and persistent active campaigner for the restoration and preservation of Cebu's historical landmarks.

The most interesting reason to visit the sanctuary is for the attached small art gallery displaying Jumalon's lepido-mosaic works – artworks made entirely from damaged butterfly wings that he collected from lepidopterologists around the world. Jumalon's original watercolour paintings are shown side-by-side with the lepido-mosaic versions, which are superb.

At the outbreak of WWII, Jumalon was commissioned by the Philippine government to design emergency currency notes; these notes are now considered collectors' items and can be seen on display at Museu Sugbo.

The sanctuary itself is a must for butterfly lovers. The best time of day for viewing is the morning, particularly during breeding season from August to January. The sanctuary is now run by his equally passionate son and daughter, who provide an informative tour of the garden, including the living display of the life cycle of the butterfly and Jumalon's exhaustive collection of butterflies and moths in the main room.

To get to the sanctuary, catch a jeepney (number 9 or 10) from N Bacalso Ave, which turns into Cebu South Rd, and hop off at Macopa St (after the second pedestrian overpass). Walk up Macopa St, and take the first left after Basak Elementary School. The sanctuary is on the corner at the end of this street (at the time of writing there were plans under way for this street to be renamed after Jumalon). A taxi will get you there from downtown for around P80.

served as an army garrison, a rebel stronghold, prison camp and the city zoo. These days it's retired as a peaceful, walled garden and handsomely crumbling ruin. It's a perfect retreat from the chaos and madness of downtown Cebu, especially at sunset.

Casa Gorordo Museum MUSEUM

(Map p206; 35 L Jaena St; adult/child P70/10; ⌚9am-6pm Tue-Sun) Downtown, in a quieter residential area, Casa Gorordo Museum was originally a private home built in the 1850s and purchased by the Gorordos, one of Cebu's leading families. The lower part of the house has walls of Mactan coral stone and the stunning upper-storey living quarters are pure Philippine hardwood, held together not with nails but with wooden pegs. As well as having Spanish and native influences, the house incorporates principles of feng shui, owing to the Chinese ancestry of Gorordo matriarch Donna Telerafora. Items on display include kitchen implements, antique photos and furniture. Ask to be shown the *carrozza* carriages parked outside.

Tops Lookout VIEWPOINT

(admission P100) Mt Busay makes a mighty backdrop for Cebu City, but the best view is from the mountain itself at Tops Lookout. Better known simply as 'Tops', this modernist, fortresslike viewing deck provides spectacular views, especially at sunrise or sunset. There are snack stalls and beers sell for P60. To get to Tops, jump on a jeepney from the Capitol Building (marked O4H Plaza Housing) to JY Square Mall. From here you can get a *habal-habal* (motorcycle taxi; round trip P300 to P400) up the steep winding road to the top. A round-trip taxi ride will cost around P1000 to P1500; negotiate a fixed price before you head off.

There's also a lookout at Mountain View nearby, and adrenaline junkies and brave souls might want to make a stop at the Doce Pares zipline park en route.

Cebu City – Downtown

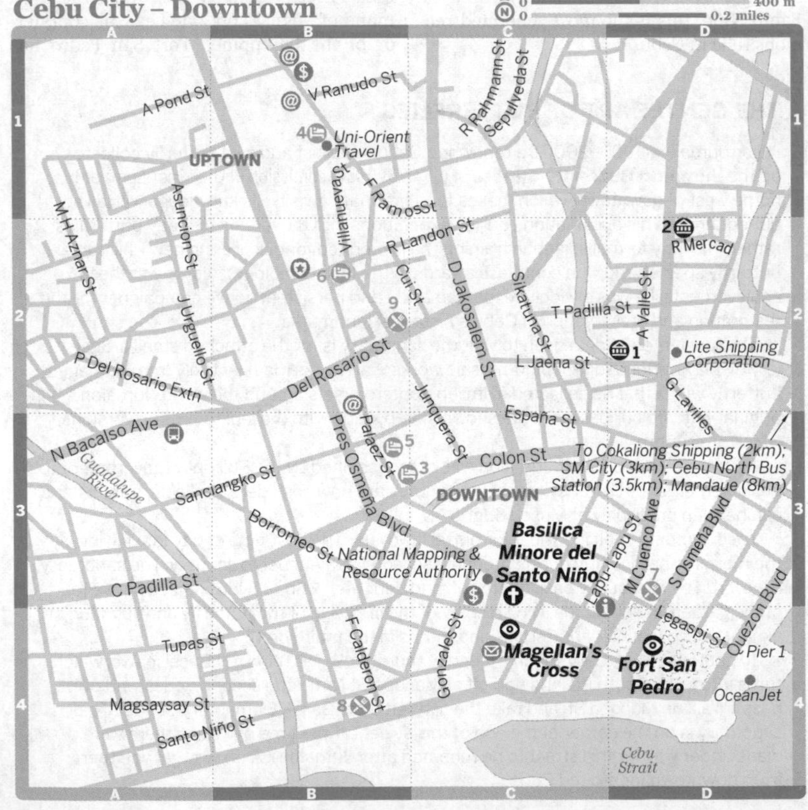

Cebu Provincial Detention and Rehabilitation Center REHABILITATION CENTRE (CPDRC) This is where you can catch the inmate dance performances that became an internet sensation on YouTube several years back with a performance to Michael Jackson's 'Thriller'. The performance was the brainchild of chief warden Byron Garcia, whose love of '80s pop inspired him to groove up the regular prison exercise drill. There are free performances on the last Saturday of each month; first register your name with the **Capitol Building** (☎254 1882) offices. Free transport is provided and runs from the Capitol Building to the CPDRC.

Festivals & Events

Cebu's epic annual **Sinulog festival** draws pilgrims from around the Philippines. Celebrated on the third Sunday of January, the Sinulog, or Fiesta Señor, is the Feast of Santo Niño (the Christ Child) and is marked by a colourful procession bearing the basilica's venerated image of Santo Niño.

The word *sinulog* is a Visayan term for a dance that imitates the rhythm of the river. It originated as an animist ritual, but after the Cebuanos' conversion to Christianity it morphed into a dance to honour the image of the Santo Niño.

Sleeping

You certainly won't suffer from a lack of accommodation choices in Cebu City. If you're planning on staying uptown, which we recommend, in most cases it's best to book ahead. Hotel choices downtown are generally just a notch up from a night in the gutter, though they provide an option for the super budget-conscious

Cebu City – Downtown

Top Sights

	Basilica Minore del Santo Niño	C3
	Fort San Pedro	D4
	Magellan's Cross	C4

Sights

1	Casa Gorordo Museum	D2
2	Museo Sugbo	D2

Sleeping

3	Century Hotel	B3
4	Diplomat Hotel	B1
5	Hotel de Mercedes	B3
6	Teo-Fel Pension House	B2

Eating

7	AA BBQ	D3
8	Carbon Market	B4
9	Elicon Cafe	B2

DOWNTOWN

Diplomat Hotel HOTEL $$
(Map p206; ☎253 0099; www.diplomathotelcebu.com; 90 F Ramos St; d P1300-2100; ❄📶) With efficient reception staff and smart leather couches, Diplomat has an air of international confidence. Rooms are a little dated but practical, with ample desk space and good lighting. Charging for wi-fi is a drawback for this otherwise business-class hotel.

Teo-Fel Pension House PENSION HOUSE $
(Map p206; ☎253 2482; 4 Junquera St; s/d from P450/650; ❄) Doubles have hot water and an extra P100 will get you a TV in the single standard rooms at this tall, slim hotel. For those who value a quiet and central location, this is good value.

Hotel de Mercedes HOTEL $
(Map p206; ☎253 1105; www.hoteldemercedes.com; 7 Pelaez St; s/d from P490/670; ❄) There's nothing flashy about this place on the dodgy side of town. The functional rooms come with air-con and cable TV as standard, and there's an attached restaurant/bar area.

Century Hotel HOTEL $
(Map p206; ☎255 1341; www.cebucenturyhotel.com; cnr Colon & Pelaez Sts; s/d/tw P550/630/740; ❄) The fluoro-illuminated corridors are a hospital blue and hot water is on a regimented schedule in the mornings and evenings. A bit on the grubby side but good value for Downtown shoestringers.

UPTOWN

TOP CHOICE **Premiere Citi Suites** HOTEL $$
(Map p208; ☎266 0442; www.premierecitisuites.webs.com; 62 M Cristina St; r P995-1895; ❄📶) Incredible value, top central location, friendly staff – no surprise this stylish, fresh new kid on the block books out in advance. Expect bright rooms with crisp white linen, flat-screen TVs and paper lampshades. There's complimentary filtered water on each floor or, for something stronger, head up to the rooftop bar and take in the mountain views. This is undoubtedly the best value in town.

Cebu R Hotel HOTEL $$
(Map p208; ☎505 7188; www.ceburhotel.com; 101 M Cui St; s/d from P1020/1360; ❄@📶) There's a distinct air of justifiable confidence at this

Cebu City – Uptown

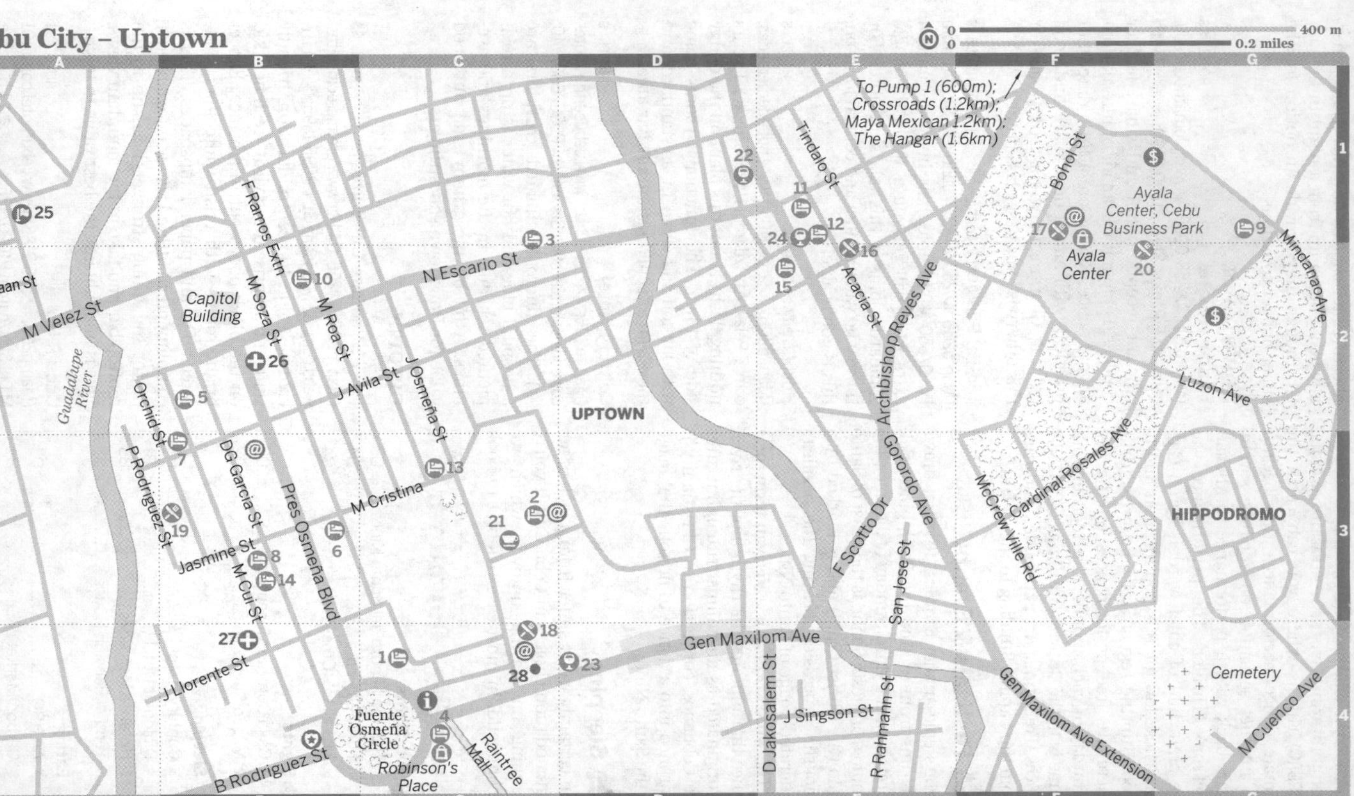

Cebu City – Uptown

Sleeping

1	Apple Tree Suites	C4
2	Casa Rosario	C3
3	Cebu Grand Hotel	C1
4	Cebu Midtown Hotel	C4
5	Cebu R Hotel	B2
6	Fuente Oro Business Suites	B3
7	Hotel Asia	B3
8	Jasmine Pension House	B3
9	Marriott Hotel	G1
10	Mayflower Inn	B2
11	Myra's Pensionne	E1
12	Pensionne La Florentina	E1
13	Premiere Citi Suites	C3
14	Travelbee Pension	B3
	Verbena Pension House	(see 8)
15	West Gorordo Hotel	E2

Eating

16	La Buona Forchetta	E2
17	Persian Palate	F1
18	Persian Palate	C4
19	STK ta Bay! Sa Paolito's Seafood House	B3
20	Terraces	F2

Drinking

21	Cofifi Café	C3
22	Kukuk's Nest	D1
23	Mango Square	D4
24	Wineshop	E1

Shopping

	Fully Booked	(see 20)

Information

25	Canadian Consulate	A1
26	Cebu Doctors' University Hospital	B2
27	Chong Hua Hospital	B4
28	National Bookstore	C4

popular newcomer close to Capitol Building. Everything is tasteful here, from the smartly uniformed staff to the lobby's lime and dark-wood colour scheme. Rooms are kitted out with desks and flat-screen TVs, and some have mountain views, while all have clean, modern tiled bathrooms. Deluxe rooms are a jump up in size.

Fuente Oro Business Suites BOUTIQUE HOTEL **$$**
(Map p208; ☎268 7912; www.fuenteoro.com; 173 M Roa St, s/d from P1200/1700; ❄@📶) This place is more cutesy boutique chic than stuffy business, with its attached Cupcake Society coffee shop. It does come with a business centre for the workaholics though. Suites are a real treat and offer comfortable large rooms, separate sitting areas and good lighting at a great price. Soft beds are perfect for lazing on after one too many sweets from downstairs.

Mayflower Inn HOTEL **$$**
(Map p208; ☎255 2800, 0919 438 7111; www.mayflowerinn.multiply.com; A Villalon Dr; s/d/tr P896/1232/1568; ❄📶) A cheerful, Mexicana-themed place near the Capitol Building, the Mayflower feels like home sweet home. Rooms are bright, clean and comfortable enough for the price. The downstairs restaurant offers native Filipino dishes in an attractive leafy courtyard.

Apple Tree Suites HOTEL **$**
(Map p208; ☎253 4236; www.appletreesuitescebu.com; 22 J Llorente St; d/tw from P998/1398; ❄📶) The shabby exterior here might have you turn on your heel but once inside you'll find simple and bright rooms – maybe too bright thanks to the Carmen Miranda–style Tropicana bedspreads. Standard rooms come windowless but the view's probably not worth the extra cash anyway. There is free wi-fi in the lobby and a bamboo-walled rooftop cafe.

Pensionne La Florentina PENSION HOUSE **$**
(Map p208; ☎231 3318; 18 Acacia St; r from P900; ❄) On a quiet street, this family-run place is a good uptown budget option and a charming alternative to a stuffy hotel. No on-site restaurant but it hardly matters when you're only a five-minute walk from the Ayala Center. Downstairs rooms are a bit on the dark side. Head up for the nicer rooms; 3A is the pick of the bunch.

Marriott Hotel LUXURY HOTEL **$$$**
(Map p208; ☎411 5800; www.marriottcebu.com; Cardinal Rosales Ave; d from P6260; ❄📶🏊) Brushing up against the Ayala Center is the ultraplush Marriott. No piped muzak or cheesy white-suited pianist will intrude on your thoughts here. The comfortable rooms are tastefully decorated with contemporary artworks and bathrooms are fitted out with rainfall showerheads. For more water action, hit the Oasis pool, which is especially ambient lit up at night.

Casa Rosario PENSION HOUSE **$$**
(Map p208; ☎253 5134; www.casarosario.multiply.com; 101 R Aboitiz St; d from P1100; ❄@📶) Don't

let the tasteless lobby put you off, as things smarten up once you get to the living quarters. This is a squeaky-clean establishment with friendly service. The brightly painted rooms vary in quality though, so ask to look at a few before settling. Try to nab one upstairs at the front of the building.

Myra's Pensionne PENSION HOUSE $
(Map p208; ☎231 5557; 12 N Escario St; d with cold/hot water from P896/1008; ❄) Blue floral wallpaper and flowers in the hall may bring back childhood memories of staying at grandma's. Not a bad option for an overnight stay despite the traffic noise, but if you're on a budget ask about the cheaper dorm rooms in the sister-owned house near JY Mall at P336 per night.

West Gorordo Hotel HOTEL $$
(Map p208; ☎231 4347; http://westgorordohotel.multiply.com; 110 Gorordo Ave; s/d/tr from P1150/1650/2150; ❄📶) A night here should lift your spirits with motivational art a standard in all rooms, along with soft comfy beds, magazines and free wi-fi going a long way too.

Cebu Grand Hotel HOTEL $$$
(Map p208; ☎254 6331; www.cebugrandhotel.com; N Escario St; d from P3300; ❄🏊) Flowers cascade from the balconies of this out-of-the-way hotel that's sensibly set a little back from the main street. Rooms are cosy with lavish bed covers and decent bathrooms. Pay a bit extra for a deluxe room to get a balcony.

Cebu Midtown Hotel HOTEL $$$
(Map p208; ☎253 9711; www.cebumidtownhotel.net; Fuente Osmeña Circle; s/d from P2700/3000; ❄📶🏊) This tightly managed place is so well insulated from the traffic noise you'll forget where you are – right in the middle of the action. The difference between standard and deluxe rooms is a matter of altitude, with better views in the latter. Cool off at the end of the day in the rooftop plunge pool. Wi-fi costs extra.

Hotel Asia HOTEL $$
(Map p208; ☎255 8534; www.hotelasiacebu.com; 11 J Avila St; s/d from P1400/1700; ❄) An elegant Japanese-owned hotel with rooftop *yakiniku* (barbecue) restaurant boasting impressive night city views. Character-filled rooms are clean and quiet; economy and standard don't offer the best value though. Pay a bit extra for deluxe and superior features – heavy wooden antique furniture, silk bed linen and deep Japanese-style stone baths.

Verbena Pension House PENSION HOUSE $
(Map p208; ☎253 3430; www.verbenapensionhouse.com; DG Garcia St; s/d/tr P750/800/1150; ❄📶) This family-owned ex-boarding house is one of the oldest pension houses in Cebu, and a reliable place to hang your hat if you're pinching pesos. All rooms are basic and a trifle poky but come with wi-fi and decent beds.

Travelbee Pension PENSION HOUSE $
(Map p208; ☎253 1005; 294 DG Garcia St; d from P400; ❄) Rooms are mostly windowless and shared bathrooms on the tiny side, but attentive staff and a bright, cheery lobby make this a solid budget choice.

Jasmine Pension House PENSION HOUSE $
(Map p208; ☎253 3757; cnr DG Garcia & Jasmine Sts; d/tw from P680/720; ❄📶) Well placed in a quiet back street north of Fuente Osmeña, the Jasmine Pension House has basic, tidy and moderately sized rooms. Great value with no unnecessary frills.

Arbel's Pension House PENSION HOUSE $
(☎253 5303; 57 Pres Osmeña Blvd; s/d from P375/500; ❄) This is about as cheap as it gets in Cebu without venturing into 'disgusting' territory. Rooms are predictably basic but at least they have windows and the location is relatively quiet.

LAHUG

Waterfront Hotel & Casino LUXURY HOTEL $$$
(☎232 6888; www.waterfronthotels.com.ph; 1 Salinas Dr; d from US$110; ❄🏊) Misleadingly named, as it is more than 2km from the water, the Waterfront is Asian high-roller city. It appeals to those taken by the thought of a 24-hour casino and countless food and beverage outlets, discos, gyms, piano bars etc. The deluxe and superior rooms boast the finest views in Cebu.

Eating

For a city its size, eating options in Cebu City are relatively disappointing. Fast-food joints line the streets and many of the city's better eateries are in the malls, where the food is generally good but the atmosphere is lacking. If the idea of eating out in a mall robs you of your appetite, don't despair as there are a few hot spots around town. For shoestringers there's a generous serving of budget food stalls set up around town and in **Carbon Market** (Map p206; MC Briones St).

DOWNTOWN

Elicon Cafe FILIPINO $
(Map p206; www.eliconcafe.multiply.com, Del Rosario St; dishes P35-120; ⏲6am-9pm Mon-Fri, to midnight Sat & Sun) This mosaic-tiled cafe is a welcome hideout when sightseeing downtown. Potted plants and board games give it a homely feel and it's part of a permaculture initiative using local food and sustainable options. Vegetarians won't want to miss the delicious *rellonong talong* (eggplant fried with egg and vegetables).

AA BBQ BARBECUE $
(Map p206; Manalili St; dishes P70-120) Vegetarians have nowhere to hide at this popular outdoor chain restaurant where diners choose their own raw meat or seafood and have it charcoal grilled on the spot. This is a top spot for a chilled beer after an evening stroll along Fort San Pedro.

UPTOWN

TOP CHOICE **STK ta Bay! Sa Paolito's Seafood House** SEAFOOD $$
(Map p208; ☎256 2700; 6 Orchid St, Capitol Site; meals P95-300; ⏲9am-2.30pm & 5-10pm) Ask a Cebuano where to dine in Cebu City and those in the know will say, 'STK'. Family heirlooms leave no space unfilled in this large ancestral home-turned-restaurant and it's hard to shake the feeling you might be dining in an antique store. Tuna belly cooked on the charcoal grill comes smoky and crisp. Jerry's crab curry is a favourite but the not-to-miss dish is hot 'n' spicy *calamares* – tender calamari fried in a spice coating and topped with green chillies.

Aranos SPANISH $$
(☎256 1937; 31 Fairlane Village, Gaudalupe; meals P100-300; ⏲11am-1.30pm & 6-10pm Mon-Sat) Direct your driver to Fairlane Village in the Guadalupe district and keep your eyes peeled for the wooden door hiding among the leaves. Upon entry at this authentic Basque/Spanish restaurant you'll be greeted by the elderly and impressively moustached Spanish owner, Senor Arano himself. The cosy front room is all gingham tablecloths and Spanish memorabilia, and leads out to an intimate fairy-lit garden dining area where you can feast on home-cooked paella and *caldereta* (beef stew).

Terraces MALL $$
(Map p208; Ayala Center, Cebu Business Park) There's a surprising array of decent food outlets at this new dining precinct attached to the Ayala Center. Standouts include **Laguna Garden Cafe** (mains P115-300) for a healthy fix of native Filipino dishes like *guso* seaweed salad washed down with freshly squeezed carrot juice; **Tsim Sha Tsui** (mains P40-200), a hot pink and lime dim sum and tea bar that's perfect for a yum cha fix; and **Red Kimono** (mains P120-500) for contemporary Japanese.

La Buona Forchetta ITALIAN $$$
(Map p208; Advent Business Center; 139 Acacia St; meals P150-500; ⏲11am-2pm & 6-11pm) Set at the back of a peaceful block, La Buona Forchetta serves up wholesome Italian food. There are no surprises on the menu, just generous servings of authentic pizza and pasta dishes. Try the ravioli funghi, bulging pouches of creamy mushroom filling topped with a cheesy tomato sauce. Perfect for a lazy lunch with a bottle of Italian wine.

Persian Palate MIDDLE EASTERN $$
(Map p208; Mango Sq Mall, General Maxilom Ave; meals P45-300; ✎) A popular franchise dishing up generous helpings of reasonably authentic Indian and Middle Eastern food. It advertises spicy food, but even the 'hot' curries are quite mild. Its menu includes a rarity in Cebu City – a large vegetarian selection. Other branches at Ayala Center and Asiatown IT Park.

LAHUG

For high-class, international-style dining, you can't go past **Crossroads** (M Cuenco Ave), a mini mall in the 'foothills' of the Waterfront Hotel. A metered taxi from Fuente Osmeña Circle will cost you P80.

Maya MEXICAN $$$
(☎238 9552; Crossroads, Banilad; mains P300; ⏲4pm-late Mon-Fri, from 11am Sat & Sun) Enter through heavy carved wooden doors to what would be a classy restaurant – candlelit with tasteful Mexican decor – but the loud music makes conversation a little difficult. The food is Tex-Mex, but a few authentic hits like lime and coriander grilled-fish soft tacos and a range of 100% agave tequila earns it kudos. Also offers tequila tasting tours.

Golden Cowrie Native Restaurant FILIPINO $$
(☎233 4243; Salinas Dr; mains P230; ⏲11am-2pm & 6-10pm) There is no better place to

challenge an ambivalence towards Filipino cuisine. Chefs conjure up exquisite regional delicacies from all over the country, with an emphasis on Cebuano specialities such as *manok halang halang* (spicy chicken soup). Long tables and colonial-era lattice windows create an informal atmosphere. There's another branch at the Terraces.

 Drinking & Entertainment

Cebu City has a deserved reputation as a party town and there's no shortage of pumping nightspots scattered about the place. The hottest places are clumped together, so pick your precinct, jump in a taxi and when you tire of one club, just roll out the door and into the next.

Wineshop WINE BAR
(Map p208; www.thewineshopcebu.com; 51 Gorordo Ave; ⌚10am-2pm) With a mixed crowd of Filipino and foreign clientele, the Wineshop is a convivial and unpretentious Spanish-owned wine bar. If you're excited by the idea of genuine tapas (P65 to P140), you'll be disappointed by the *sardinas* (straight from the tin) and bemused by the inclusion of *kinilaw* (Filipino-style ceviche). Monday to Saturday live music is on offer so grab yourself a carafe of the house red (P135) and settle in for the night.

Kukuk's Nest RESTOBAR
(Map p208; 124 Gorordo Ave) This grungy 24-hour restobar has an interesting mix of locals and expats, complete with resident armless charcoal sketcher. Plastic tables and chairs out front provide a laid-back atmosphere ideal for meeting people and a convenient place to finish up after all the other bars close. If you've had one too many, ask about the budget accommodation on offer.

Cofifi Café CAFE
(Map p208; R Aboitiz St; coffee P50-75; ⌚7.30am-midnight; 📶) Polished concrete floors, good coffee and funky furniture – there's nothin' Starbucks about this cool little hideaway. Hip young locals sit solo with Macbooks taking advantage of the free wi-fi and sipping on cookie-crumble ice blend (P85). There are standard breakfasts on offer as well as sweet treats and Italian sodas in cherry, cucumber and mint. Next door to Calda Pizza; look for the sign.

Mango Square NIGHTCLUB
(Map p208; Mango Sq Mall, Mango Ave; admission per club incl 1 drink P50-100) A clubber's heaven attracting a fun, lively crowd, though try to turn a blind eye to the occasional older male expats. It gets going around 10pm and the more popular places stay open until sunrise. The **Beat**, a two-storey club with live music and DJs, attracts mainly local students. You might catch a glimpse of them in the thick fog of the smoke machines. Head up the stairs for **Hybrid**, a popular newcomer that packs out on a Friday and Saturday night. If VIP rooms and velvet rope is more your style, you won't want to miss the hottest of them all, **Juliana's**. Expect to queue and get the once-over from the tight security here. If deemed cool enough you'll be dancin' it up to house, techno and R&B in one of the most professionally run places in town. **Numero Doce** is a gay-friendly bar.

Asiatown IT Park NIGHTCLUB
Popular with the young professional crowd who may have just knocked off from their IT jobs, the long stretch of street here is full of upmarket restaurants, bars and clubs. We're assured **Loft** (☎231 3284; Skyrise Bldg, Lahug) is a popular spot, but it was undergoing renovation at the time of research. On the 3rd level of the same building is **Penthouse** (☎231 3284), where DJs spin mainly house, techno and R&B tunes up high on their pedestal.

Pump 1 NIGHTCLUB
(off Map p208; ☎232 3637; Archibishop Reyes, Lahug) Behind the Grand Convention Centre is the original Pump, a stayer in the fickle Cebu City club scene attracting the student crowd. After a workout on the dance floor, groups spill onto the pavement to take a seat at plastic chairs under umbrellas, where the table service allows you to concentrate on people-watching while you catch your breath.

Hangar NIGHTCLUB
(Salinas Dr, Lahug) You can't miss this nightlife precinct in Lahug flagged by a giant plane suspended at the entrance. Sometimes referred to as Sunflower City (referring to the

PROSTITUTION IN THE PHILIPPINES

Prostitution, including child prostitution, is a major social issue in the Philippines. Various estimates put the number of sex workers in the Philippines at about 400,000, with up to 20% of those children. Most prostitutes come from impoverished provincial families and are easy prey for the girlie bars, which take a majority cut of their earnings in exchange for bare-essentials living arrangements.

Female Prostitution

The sex business grew up around the American military bases at Clark and Subic Bay, reaching its heyday during the late Marcos era. The Americans were booted out in 1991, but prostitution remains rampant in areas like Angeles, Subic, Cebu City and certain districts of Manila. In some European and Japanese magazines, the Philippines is actively promoted as a sex-tourism destination.

Although prostitution is officially illegal in the Philippines, you don't have to be a detective to find it being practised. The red-light districts of most big cities operate openly and freely, with karaoke bars, 'discos', go-go bars and strip clubs all acting as fronts. The call girls are euphemistically called GROs – guest relations officers. The police, many of whom are paid off by the sex industry operators, tend to turn a blind eye to the problem.

The Asia-Pacific office of the **Coalition Against Trafficking in Women** (☎02-426 9873; www.catw-ap.org) is in Quezon City, Manila. Its website has information about prostitution in the Philippines, and several useful links. In Angeles, the **Renew Foundation** (www.renew-foundation.org) works to keep former sex workers and trafficked women off the streets by teaching them alternative work skills and providing safe shelter.

Child Prostitution

A culture of silence surrounds child sex abuse in the Philippines. While *hiya* (shame) plays a big role in the silence, for the most part this silence is bought. There's big money in paedophilia, both for ringleaders who arrange meetings between paedophiles and children, and for law enforcers who get paid to ignore it.

Child-sex tourism is a criminal offence in many countries around the world. Extraterritorial laws in Australia, New Zealand, the USA and many EU countries mean that prosecution and punishment can occur in an offender's country of residence. In addition to these laws, tougher action (including imprisonment) is now being taken in countries that have been documented as centres for child sexual exploitation.

ECPAT Philippines (☎02-920 8151; ecpatphil@gmail.com) in Quezon City works to promote child-safe tourism and end the commercial sexual exploitation of children such as child prostitution, child pornography and the trafficking of children for sexual purposes. To report an incident, contact ECPAT, the **Philippine National Police Women and Children's Division** (☎0919 777 7377) or the **Human Trafficking Action Line** (☎02-1343).

average club towards the back), it's a semi-outdoor space with independently owned bars and clubs competing for the attention of the younger rowdy crowd. First in line is **Tonyo's Bar & Resto**, the kind of place you can fill up on a 3L tube of beer delivered to your table (P225) while seeing live bands thrash it out. Moving on, **Nuvo** is more your typical nightclub complete with sweaty dance floor, DJs and fluoro lights.

Shopping

Fully Booked (Map p208; www.fullybookedonline.com; the Terraces, Ayala Center) and **National Bookstore** (Map p208; www.nationalbookstore.com.ph) are good places to stock up on maps as well as local and international fiction, nonfiction and magazines. Fully Booked is at the Terraces in the Ayala Center, while National Bookstore can be found in most malls.

Information

A full list of consulates in Cebu City can be found in the brochure *Your Guide to Cebu*, available from most bookstores.

The **Bureau of Immigration Office** (BOI; ☎345 6442; www.immigration.gov.ph; cnr Burgos St & Mandaue Ave, Mandaue; ⏲8-11.30am

& 1-4.30pm Mon-Fri) is behind the Mandaue Fire Station, opposite the Mandaue Sports Complex. Mandaue is a satellite suburb of Cebu City; it lies on the other side of the bridge to Mactan Island, on the way to the airport. It's best to get here early to avoid a lengthy wait.

Decent enough tourist maps can be picked up free from the airport, the Department of Tourism office and most hotels. The more in-depth, widely sold *E-Z Map for Cebu* (P100) covers Cebu City, Mandaue, Mactan and Moalboal.

For nautical and topographical maps and charts, set a course for the **National Mapping & Resource Authority** (NAMRIA; Map p206; ☎505 9945; Room 301, 3rd fl, Osmeña Bldg, cnr Pres Osmeña Blvd & D Jakosalem St; ⏲8am-noon & 1-5pm Mon-Fri).

Emergency

Cebu City Tourist Police Station Fuente (☎253 5636); R Landon St (☎231 5802)

Report Child Sex Tourism National Hotline (☎in Manila 02-524 1660)

Task Force Turista (☎254 4023; ⏲24hr)

Internet Access

You won't have to walk far to find an internet cafe (P15 to P30 per hour), especially in the busier streets uptown and around the universities. The branches of Bo's Coffee Club on Pres Osmeña Blvd and in the Ayala Center offer free internet with coffee. Both the Ayala Center and SM City have internet cafes.

Le Internet Cafe (☎254 1181; Mango Plaza, General Maxilom Ave; ⏲8am-midnight)

Ludan's Internet Cafe (F Ramos St; ⏲8am-1am) Opposite Chinabank.

Prints & More (☎254 2467; Pelaez St; ⏲9am-6pm)

Medical Services

Cebu Doctors' University Hospital (Map p208; ☎253 7511; Pres Osmeña Blvd)

Chong Hua Hospital (Map p208; ☎255 8000; M Cui St)

Money

You'll find the major banks around Fuente Osmeña and in the Ayala Center – HSBC has the highest withdrawal limit (P40,000). Credit-card-friendly ATMs with the standard P10,000 withdrawal limit abound in the malls.

Bank of Commerce (Fuente Osmeña Circle) Between Rodriguez St and Pres Osmeña Blvd.

Citibank (Cebu Business Park, Mindanao Ave) Near Ayala Center. Changes cash and travellers cheques; P15,000 withdrawal limit at the 24-hour ATM.

HSBC (Cebu Business Park, Cardinal Rosales Ave) Near Ayala Center. Changes cash and travellers cheques, and has a 24-hour ATM.

Post

The city's **main post office** (☎253 8892) is in the downtown area, near Pier 1 and Fort San Pedro. Uptown there's a post office next door to the Capitol Building. Hole-in-the-wall sub-branches can be found at many of the universities around town. Outside the main entrance to the Ayala Center are the branch offices of international couriers.

Tourist Information

Airport Tourist Information Desk (Mactan-Cebu International Airport) At the arrivals terminal; open 24 hours and staff are eager to help.

Department of Tourism (DOT; Map p206; ☎254 2811; www.visitmyphilippines.com; ground fl, LDM Bldg, Legaspi St; ⏲7am-5pm Mon-Fri) Free maps and pamphlets, including *Where at Cebu*, transport schedules and accommodation bookings.

Travel Agencies

You'll find a few agencies in the foyer of the Diplomat Hotel, as well as in most of the shopping malls.

2GO Modern Teknika (☎254 6741; 98 F Ramos St) Other branches are in Ayala Center and Mandaue City.

Grand Hope Travel (☎254 0343; Rajah Park Hotel, Fuente Osmeña Circle)

Uni-Orient Travel (Map p206; ☎253 1866; Diplomat Hotel, 90 F Ramos St)

ℹ Getting There & Away

Air

Cebu's user-friendly **Mactan-Cebu International Airport** (MCIA; ☎340 2486; ᯤ) is on Mactan Island, 15km east of Cebu City. The airport is second only to Manila in terms of air traffic. Airport terminal fees are P200 for domestic flights and P550 for international flights, payable in cash.

Within the Philippines, the four major domestic airlines service Manila and an ever-growing list of provincial cities, including Bacolod, Cagayan de Oro, Caticlan, Davao, General Santos, Iloilo, Puerto Princesa, Ozamis, Siargao, Tacloban and Zamboanga.

A new airline, **Mid-Sea Express** (www.midseaexpress.com), does short hops a few times per week to a handful of not-so-distant destinations, including Bantayan, Siquijor, Camiguin and Tagbilaran.

The following airlines have offices at MCIA:

Airphil Express (☎341 0930; www.airphilexpress.com)

Cebu Pacific (☎230 8888; www.cebupacificair.com)

Mid-Sea Express (☎495 6976; www.midseaexpress.com)

Philippine Airlines (PAL; ☎340 0422; www.philippineairlines.com)

South East Asian Airlines (SEAIR; ☎268 5670; www.flyseair.com)

Zest Air (☎341 0226; www.zestair.com.ph)

Boat

A veritable armada of boats links Cebu's vast, multipiered port with the rest of the country. They take the form of speedy so-called 'fastcraft' passenger ferries, popular on shorter routes; slower 'roll-on, roll-off' (RORO) car ferries; and large multidecked passenger vessels.

All shipping information is vulnerable to change. The *Sun Star* and *Cebu Daily* newspapers publish a schedule that is generally reliable, but it is always good to double-check your schedules directly with the shipping companies. Also confirm the pier from which your boat is departing, or you might be in for a last-minute scramble when you arrive at the port. You can eliminate some of the uncertainty by buying your ticket from the pier itself as opposed to a travel agent. In most cases the shipping company's booking office is at the pier from which its boats depart.

You can purchase tickets for SuperFerry, SuperCat, Negros Navigation and Cebu Ferries at **2GO** (Aboitiz Express; ☎233 7000; ⏲10am-6pm), which has offices in Robinson's Plaza, Ayala Center and SM City.

Cebu City passenger-ship companies:

Cebu Ferries (☎233 7000; www.cebuferries.com; Pier 4)

Cokaliong Shipping (☎232 7211-18; www.cokaliongshipping.com; Pier 1)

George & Peter Lines (☎254 5154; Pier 2)

Golden Express (☎255 7560; Pier 1)

Island Shipping (☎416 6592; Pier 3)

Kinswell Shipping Lines (☎038-512 1195; Pier 3)

Lite Shipping Corporation (☎416 6462; www.lite-shipping.com; Pier 1)

Montenegro Shipping Lines (☎in Batangas 043-723 6980; www.montenegrolines.com.ph; Pier 5)

Negros Navigation (☎02-554 8777; www.negrosnavigation.ph; Pier 4)

Oceanjet (☎255 7560; www.oceanjet.net; Pier 1)

Palacio Shipping Lines (☎255 4538; Pier 1)

Philippine Span Asia Carrier Corp (PSACC; ☎232 5361; Sulpicio Go St, Reclamation Area)

Roble Shipping (☎232 2236; Pier 3)

SuperCat (☎233 9630; www.supercat.com.ph; Pier 4)

SuperFerry (☎233 7000; www.superferry.com.ph; Pier 4)

Super Shuttle Ferry (☎232 3150; www.supershuttleferry.com; SM City) Book through Travellers' Lounge.

Trans-Asia Shipping Lines (☎254 6491; www.transasiashipping.com; Pier 5)

VG Shipping (☎238 7635; Pier 3)

Weesam Express (☎412 9562; Pier 4)

The following destinations are serviced from Cebu City:

BILIRAN Roble Shipping has an evening boat to Naval (P450, nine hours) every Saturday and Monday, while the Super Shuttle passenger ferry (P430) departs Wednesday at 8pm.

BOHOL Tagbilaran is the main point of entry, with Oceanjet (P520, two hours), SuperCat (P520, one hour 45 minutes) and Weesam Express (P500, one hour 45 minutes) having regular fastcraft departing several times daily. There are also slow and less frequent passenger boats with Cokaliong (P210, five hours), Lite Shipping (P220, four hours) and Palacio Shipping (four hours).

Less-accessed points of entry include Tubigon, serviced by Island Shipping (P150, 1½ hours) and Kinswell Shipping (P180, one hour 15 minutes) among other companies, while Talibon is accessed by VG Shipping (P240, three hours) twice daily.

CAMOTES Golden Express has a daily 5.30pm passenger ferry to Poro (P380, two hours).

LEYTE Cokaliong has three or four passenger ferries a week to Maasin (P320, six hours), Baybay (P250, six hours) and Palompon (P320, 5½ hours). Fastcraft to Ormoc include SuperCat (P895, three hours) and Weesam (P650, two hours 15 minutes) several times a day, while Cebu Ferries (P400 four hours) and Lite Shipping (P400, five hours) have slower services. Roble Shipping has a 9pm daily service to Hilongos (P250, five hours).

LUZON SuperFerry has four boats a week to Manila (P1600, 24 hours), PSACC (P1005, 24 hours) has two boats on Sunday and Wednesday, while Negros Navigation has a weekly passenger service to Manila (P1128, 21 hours) on Wednesday at 8pm.

MASBATE Trans-Asia Shipping Lines heads to Masbate town three times a week (P575) at 6pm.

MINDANAO Cebu Ferries has two or three evening services a week to Cagayan de Oro (P935, 10 hours), Nasipit (P825, 12 hours), Surigao (P825, seven hours), Ozamis (P850, 11 hours) and Iligan (P850, 14½ hours). SuperFerry has a similar schedule to Cagayan, Nasipit and Surigao, and also has a Sunday-evening passenger boat to Camiguin. George & Peter Lines has boats to Dapitan (P600, 11 hours) and Cagayan, while Trans-Asia services Cagayan, Ozamis and Zamboanga (six hours). PSACC also heads to Cagayan and Butuan, while Cokaliong has a regular service to Surigao, Dapitan and Zamboanga.

NEGROS Cokaliong (P300, six hours) and George & Peter (P300, six hours) both have daily ferries to Dumaguete, while Ocean Jet has a fastcraft (P970, four hours) that goes via Tagbilaran.

PANAY Trans-Asia (P710, 12 hours, six weekly) and Cokaliong (P550, 12 hours, three weekly) serve Iloilo.

SAMAR Roble Shipping has a weekly boat to Catbalogan (P650, 12 hours) departing Friday at 7pm. Boats to Calbayog are with Palacio (P780, 12 hours) and Cokaliong (P690, 11 hours) at 7pm three times a week.

SIQUIJOR Cokaliong has a weekly ferry to Larena at 1pm Monday (P280, eight hours)

Bus

The main bus company servicing the Cebu area is **Ceres Bus Liner** (☎345 8650). Cebu's **South Bus Station** is a short taxi ride from downtown (around P50); otherwise take the Basak–Colon, Urgello–Colon or Labangon–Colon–Pier jeepney. From here, buses leave all day for Argao (P70, two hours); Bato via Moalboal or Oslob (P168, 3½ hours); Toledo (P68, three hours); and Moalboal (P112, three hours). Air-con vans ('V-hires') leave for Moalboal (P100, two hours) and Toledo (P100, two hours) from the Citi-link station near the terminal.

If you're after a public bus north, Cebu's **North Bus Station**, servicing several bus lines, is beyond SM City. A Mabolo–Carbon or Mandaue–Cebu City jeepney will take you there. The station is on Wireless St, in the desolate Reclamation Area.

From here, buses depart to Maya (P163, 3½ hours, every 20 minutes), the gateway town for boats to Malapascua until 7pm; and to Hagnaya (P132, around three hours), the gateway town to Bantayan Island. Hagnaya buses leave frequently from 7.30am to 5pm, but some only go as far as Bogo (P120, three hours), from where you must take a tricycle to Hagnaya pier (P50, 20 minutes). The last boat departs Hagnaya for Bantayan at 5.30pm.

If you want to do some sightseeing along the coast, you can hop off on the way and wait for another bus to come. Waving one down from the highway is usually not a problem, although they'll often be standing room only.

Getting Around

To/From the Airport

As you leave the terminal, you'll be greeted by a fleet of yellow airport taxis, with rates starting at about P450 for destinations within Cebu City (or P70 flagfall). If you pass these by, a pedestrian crossing leads to a flight of stairs that will take you to the 'white taxi' rank, with a P40 flagfall, and will generally charge you a 'fixed price' of P200 to any destination in Cebu City – very reasonable in light of the traffic and distance. Theoretically, a metered trip would cost around P175, but few drivers will agree to this.

To/From the Pier

To get uptown from the ports, catch one of the jeepneys that pass by the piers to Pres Osmeña Blvd, then transfer to a jeepney going uptown. Taxis are plentiful at all of the piers and cost about P70 to Fuente Osmeña.

Jeepney

Cebu City has no local buses, so jeepneys and taxis pretty much rule the road. As in Manila, most jeepneys have a set route, and this is displayed in the front window and along the side. You'll pay P8 to travel up to 5km within the city, and the longer journeys shouldn't cost more than P15. If in doubt, locals are always very helpful and well informed on these matters.

One important thing to remember with jeepneys – they travel a circular route, so don't expect to take the same jeepney back the way you came. Also, if a jeepney has just passed a destination written on the side, it will have to do the full circuit before returning – a long way to get to a place that may only be a 10-minute walk.

Taxi

Taxis are out-and-out the easiest way to get around the city. Drivers are mostly honest and their service is cheap and quick – streets are clogged during peak hour but rarely gridlocked. Unless a big ship has just docked, or it's serious festival time, catching a taxi in Cebu City couldn't be easier. Flagfall is P40 and then P3.50 for each additional 300m (or two minutes waiting time). Most drivers will stick to the metered price for anything other than the airport or out-of-town destinations. And before you suspect your driver of taking the long way around, remember there's a huge number of one-way streets here, especially in the downtown area.

The usual negotiated price is around P1000 for a day.

For many out-of-town destinations, taxis will fix a price that may seem way above what the meter would give. This is to cover petrol and the return drive for which the driver may not get a fare.

Mactan Island

☎032 / POP 337,596

If you're flying into Cebu City, nearby Mactan (sometimes referred to as Lapu-Lapu) is where you'll actually land. Connected to Cebu City by the Mandaue-Mactan Bridge (the 'old bridge') and Marcelo B Fernan (the 'new bridge'), this little island doesn't offer much for the independent traveller; there are no decent natural beaches as most resorts actually import their whiter-than-white sand from Boracay. Unless diving is your interest, you're more likely to come here for some resort relaxation or island hopping. It does make for a nicer place to hang out than Cebu City itself and is just a short taxi ride away. For twitchers there's birdwatching on nearby Olango Island.

Sights & Activities

Mactan Shrine HISTORIC SITE

Mactan is the improbable site of one of the defining moments in the Philippines' history. It was here, on 27 April 1521, that Ferdinand Magellan made the fatal mistake of underestimating the fighting spirit of Chief Lapu-Lapu. As the standard-bearer for Spain, Magellan had managed to curry the favour of all the most powerful chiefs of the region, with the single exception of Lapu-Lapu. So with 60 of his best soldiers, Magellan sailed to the island to teach him a lesson in gunboat diplomacy. But Lapu-Lapu and his men defended their island with unimagined ferocity, and Magellan was soon back on his boat – fatally wounded by a spear to his head and a poisoned arrow to his leg. This event is commemorated at the Mactan Shrine on a stone plinth bearing the date that Magellan was felled. Next to it is a statue of a ripped and pumped Lapu-Lapu, looking like a He-Man action figure.

Alegre Guitar Factory HANDICRAFTS

(☎340 4492; ⏲7.30am-6.30pm Mon-Sat, 8am-6pm Sun) For a peek at a guitar factory, ask a tricycle driver to take you to Alegre Guitar Factory in Abuno, where guitars are handmade on site and range from the P2500 decoration 'cheapie' to the P70,000 'export quality'. The most expensive model is made from exquisite black ebony imported from Madagascar. Beautiful native mandolins, some carved from a single piece of wood and inlaid with polished abalone shell, go from anywhere between P4000 and P14,000. Kids will love the cutesy *cocoleles* from around P1800 made from, you guessed it, coconut shells.

Diving

There's some surprisingly decent diving on the reefs off Mactan but sadly great swaths of coral have been destroyed by a lethal combination of typhoons, crown-of-thorns starfish and dynamite fishing. To protect against the latter, a couple of excellent marine reserves are maintained off Nalusuan and Hilutungan islands, with their upkeep being paid for by dive fees (Hilutungan/Nalasuan P300/200 per diver).

Diving companies include **Kontiki Divers** (☎495 2471; www.kontikidivers.com; Club Kon Tiki, Maribago Beach; US$35 per boat dive, incl equipment) and **Tropical Island Adventures** (☎492 1922; www.cebudive.com; Buyong Beach, Maribago; US$50 for 2 dives and gear).

Sleeping & Eating

NORTHWEST COAST

The northwest coast of Mactan is where you'll find Mactan-Cebu International Airport. Consider staying here if you have an early-morning flight.

Hotel Cesario HOTEL $$

(☎340 0211; ML Quezon Hwy; d from P1400) Good value, excellent service and a great perk – you get free use of the spa and pool at its sister hotel next door, the Bellavista. The viewless rooms have cable TV and hot water in big bathrooms. With breakfast for one and airport transfers included, this is one of the better deals on the island.

Waterfront Airport Hotel & Casino LUXURY HOTEL $$$

(☎340 4888; www.waterfronthotels.net; Airport Rd; d from P6590) For those who like a little splash of ritzy fun in their airport stopovers, this is the younger, less flamboyant sister of the Waterfront Hotel in Lahug, Cebu City. Prices and facilities are comparable but the airport branch is more low-key.

EAST COAST

A dozen or so beach resorts have staked out the southeastern coast of Mactan. All resorts have their own restaurants and diving facilities, and most of them provide free airport transfers.

Club Kon Tiki BEACH RESORT $$

(☎495 2434; www.kontikidivers.com; Maribago Beach; d with fan/air-con P1220/1460) This is the closest approximation of 'budget' accommodation on Mactan and the ideal place to stay for a quick diving fix before moving on to bluer waters. It's a long walk off the main road but makes for a peaceful isolated spot with coconut palms and a breezy open-air restaurant. There's no beach here but if you want luxurious views of turquoise waters then opt for a deluxe room near the rocky waterfront – 'deluxe' means you get air-con and cable TV.

Abacá Boutique Resort & Restaurant BEACH RESORT $$$
(☎495 346; www.abacaresort.com; Punta Engano Rd; ste & villas P14,500-26,500) The ultimate in boutique luxury, Abacá has it all. With its secluded oceanfront position, infinity pool and butler service, you might expect to see James Bond sipping a martini at the poolside bar (draped in a flower garland, of course). Suites and villas showcase the work of local designers in dark woods, warm tones and cooling slate and stone. This could well be *the* reason to visit Mactan Island, despite its lack of beach. It's one for the honeymooners.

Maribago Grill & Restaurant SEAFOOD $$$
(☎495 8187; Bagumbayan, Maribago; mains P200-800; ⏲10am-10pm Mon-Sat, from 2pm Sun) If you need a change of scenery from your resort restaurant, Maribago Grill is a good option. Individual nipa hut tables are set amongst lush fairy-lit gardens attracting a mix of locals and tourists to this dining oasis. Opt for the seafood and get your hands dirty ripping into meaty garlic crabs or decadent lobster (from P1095). Not far from the Maribago Bluewater Resort.

Inday Pina's Sutukil SEAFOOD $
(Manna STK; ☎495 7776; Mactan Shrine; ⏲11am-10pm) The best of the rustic seafood restaurants hidden behind the market area near the entrance to Mactan Shrine. Pick up your seafood, sniff it and hand it to the chef. Squid, grouper, lobster and crab are available daily at market price (P180 to P250 per kilo).

ℹ Information

ATMs are a little hard to find but your best bet is out the front of Gaisano Mall, Marina Mall and at the airport.

Megalink ATM (Gaisano Mall; ⏲24hr) Takes most Western cards; P200 international transaction fee and P10,000 withdrawal limit.

ℹ Getting There & Around

Jeepneys run all day to Cebu City from Lapu-Lapu (P12). The going rate by taxi from Cebu City to Lapu-Lapu or the airport is P200; to the eastern beach resorts you'll pay around P300. Be prepared for a slow crawl through heavy traffic.

If you're a foreigner on Mactan, it's assumed you're loaded so don't expect a tricycle fare anywhere for less than P100, which is usually more expensive than taxis. Bear in mind that tricycles are not allowed on the main highway.

Lapu-Lapu proper (eg ML Quezon Hwy) is serviced by jeepneys. Local taxis run the length and breadth of the island.

Olango Island & Around

☎032 / POP 6943

The story of Olango Island is a familiar one in the Philippines: a fragile and diverse ecosystem under enormous pressure from human predation. Combining salt flats, mangroves and coral reefs, it would be an ecotourism dream – except that it is facing an uphill battle for its existence.

Much of the reef on the western side of Olango was buried by a typhoon in 1993. Dynamite and cyanide fishing never gave it a chance to regenerate. The reef on the eastern side of the island is in a better state, although currents make it dangerous for inexperienced divers. Twitchers will want to head straight to **Olango Island Wildlife Sanctuary** (☎0915 386 2314; www.olangowildlifesanctuary.org; San Vicente; admission P100). Taking in 1030 hectares of sand flats and mangroves on Olango's southern shores, the sanctuary supports the largest concentration of migratory birds found in the Philippines – 48 species (including the endangered Chinese egret and Asiatic dowitcher). The birds prefer Olango to neighbouring islands because of the abundant food and ideal nesting sites, and the best time to catch them (not literally, of course) is between September and April. Viewing is better at low tide when the birds take to the mud flats. The only accommodation option for keen birders is the camping available near the sanctuary office; enquire within.

If all that twitching leaves you ravenous, there are a few eating options on the island. Ask a tricycle driver or *habal-habal* to take you to the floating restaurants near Talima. **Arnold & Candie's** (☎492 6121; ⏲8am-4pm) is one of a few. At high tide a boat will take you out to the row of rickety open-air places on stilts where you can pick the catch of the day – abalone, rock lobster, crab. At low tide you can make the sludgy walk out – be careful on the seaweed and keep your eyes out for sea urchins.

A bit further afield is the marine sanctuary off neighbouring **Hilutungan Island**.

Around the outskirts of the sanctuary, the reefs were endangered by fishing fleets and their dynamite, cyanide and – more recently – chlorine. However, the sanctuary itself is now well protected, thanks in part to money collected from a diving fee of P300 per person. Those seeking an escape from life's distractions will want to book some time out at the **Island & Sun Beach Resort** (238 1878; www.islandandsun.com; deluxe r from P8000) on Hilutungan itself. Roosters wander about this tiny island scattered with fallen coconuts from swaying palms, and there's a great island community feel. The resort features concrete bungalows perched on stilts over the glistening water and low tide brings a small stretch of sandbar. There's not too much to do here, in a good way, so just grab a drink at the thatched-roof bar and take in the spectacular ocean views.

South of Hilutungan, the private resort island of **Nalusuan** (http://nalusuan.mencaresorts.com) has arguably the best-preserved coral in the Olango Reef. Those not staying on the island's resort are charged P200 to dive Nalusuan's reef, which goes towards its ongoing conservation. Dive centres on Mactan can arrange trips.

Those after a more Robinson Crusoe experience might want to make a stop on their island-hopping trip at the lesser known, and more remote, Japanese-owned **Caohagan Island** (www.caohagan.com). Beachfront accommodation is basic and a bit overpriced.

Getting There & Away

Most resorts on Mactan will organise a day trip of island hopping, including to Olango, or you can make your own way from either Angasil Pier, just south of the Shangri-La resort, or the pier near the Hilton. Boats bound for Santa Rosa (P10, 30 minutes) depart hourly from 6am to 6pm. From Santa Rosa, a tricycle to the bird sanctuary should cost around P80 for non-residents.

It's also possible to arrange island hopping through Sunrise Watersports near Plantation Bay on the southeast of Mactan, which can hire out boats and snorkelling equipment for around P2000 for the day.

Toledo

032 / POP 152,960

The port city of Toledo, due west of Cebu City, presents a cheap and quick way to travel between Cebu and San Carlos, Negros. This nondescript little city has little to offer the traveller, though with frequent ferry services, no one should be forced to stay the night. If you do get stuck, your best bet is **Aleu's Lodge** (322 5672; Poloyapoy St; r with fan & shared bathroom from P250, with air-con P650;), located above a general store in a quiet neighbourhood. It's 1.5km from the pier (P8 by tricycle).

Getting There & Away

Regular ferries ply the Toledo–San Carlos route. **Aznar Fastcraft** (467 9447) has five daily boats (P200, 40 minutes), with the last at 3.30pm; **Montenegro Shipping Lines** (0922 774 8199) has three boats at 6am, 2pm and 4pm (P225, 45 minutes); **Lite Ferry** (467 9604) has three daily services at 7.30am, 1pm and 6pm (P190, 1½ hours).

Buses run every hour or so between Cebu South bus station and the Toledo bus terminal (P70, 2½ hours); the last bus is around 4pm. There are also quicker V-hire air-con minivans to Cebu City (P100, 1½ hours). Toledo's bus terminal is at the end of the long pier (P8 tricycle ride if you have heavy bags).

Those headed to Moalboal will need to catch a bus inland to Naga (P50, one hour) and then another bus to Moalboal.

Danao

032 / POP 109,354

With a scenic mountainous backdrop, the coastal town of Danao is known for its gracious, coral-stone **St Tomas de Villanueva Church**, built in 1755 and restored from near ruin in 1981. However, most visitors are here to catch a ferry to the Camotes Islands.

Several ferry companies run to various townships on the Camotes (P180 two hours), leaving early morning, midmorning and midafternoon from the port in front of the church.

Regular buses run between Cebu City and Danao (P30, 50 minutes).

Bantayan Island

032 / POP 71,655

Those looking for a place where there's nothing to do other than laze on a beach will love Bantayan Island. Located off the northwest tip of Cebu, here you don't need to get the guilts for not maximising your time with active pursuits: there's no diving, no canyoning or volcanoes to scale, just a blinding white-sand beach, fantastic food and lively drinking spots. The relaxed, bucolic town of Santa Fe on the island's southern coast is where you'll find the nicest stretch of beach and low-key resorts.

For 51 weeks of the year, the town is a sleepy retreat. And then there's Holy Week. During Easter, ferryloads of Filipinos are drawn to the island for an epic fiesta. The tourist influx is so great that people sleep on the beaches, locals rent out their houses, and hotel prices double, triple and even quadruple.

Activities

Although there is no decent snorkelling around Bantayan Island, it's possible to make a day trip to **Virgin Island** (admission P150) which has coral outcrops, though the snorkelling is still disappointing by Philippine standards. It's a 30-minute bangka trip (P900 to P1500, depending on how many people).

In addition to sleeping and reading, a popular activity is exploring Bantayan's quiet, shady roads. Most resorts can organise a bicycle for P200 per day, or a motorcycle from P300.

Sleeping

The resorts of Santa Fe are strung along the beach, north and south of the pier (which is a little north of the town proper).

St Bernard Beach Resort BEACH RESORT **$**
(☎0917 963 6162; www.bantayan.dk; cottages with fan/air-con P850/1300) About 1km north of Santa Fe pier, the Danish-owned St Bernard has a wonderfully relaxed island vibe with rows of thatched-roofed cottages set in a tropical garden of palm trees and aviaries of parrots. No two cottages here are exactly alike, but all feature polished wood, throw rugs and lace curtains.

Marlin Beach Resort BEACH RESORT **$$**
(☎438 9093; www.marlin-bantayan.com; r from P1750; ❄📶) One of the best midrange options, Marlin's large motel-style rooms may not inspire, but its attractive beachside location, complete with bar and restaurant, is very much its saving grace. Call to arrange free pick-up from the pier.

Bamboo Oriental Beach Villas BEACH RESORT **$$$**
(☎0910 419 0447; www.bamboo-oriental.com; ste/villa incl full board P5550/9950; ❄📶) Sophisticated polished bamboo-and-wood bungalows right on the beach are the closest you'll find to luxurious accommodation on the island. The villas are huge and well suited to families or groups.

Budyong Beach Resort BEACH RESORT **$**
(☎438 5700; www.budyong.net; cottages with fan/air-con from P500/1500; ❄📶) A great budget choice on the beach, with clean and basic nipa huts that mostly have prime ocean views through the swaying palms. The downside is its disinterested staff.

Yooneek Beach Resort BEACH RESORT **$$**
(☎438 9124; www.yooneekbeach.com; r from P1300; ❄📶) A popular and well-maintained resort that has spacious rooms close to the beach, some with balconies and ocean views. There are also newer and nicer garden rooms, just back from the resort. It boasts one of the best laid-back beach bars on the island. Has free pick-up from the pier.

White Beach Bungalows BEACH RESORT **$$**
(☎0921 362 7499; www.white-beach-bungalows.com; r from P1100; ❄📶) Set away 5km north of Santa Fe, White Beach is sought out for its exclusivity and relaxed environment. There's no restaurant here, but food can be arranged in town or there are cooking facilities if you want to visit the market. Free use of bicycles and hotel transfers means you won't be stranded here. And there's a small gym if you feel things are getting too relaxed.

Hard Kock Kafe 'n' Kottages NIPA HUTS **$**
(☎0920 668 1268; www.kiwikottages.com; huts with fan/air-con P550/750; ❄📶) One of the few budget options on the island, the large nipa huts here are incredible value if you can handle living without a beach, and with the fact it's a blokey expat hangout.

Eating & Drinking

For such a small island, Santa Fe has an impressive strip of lively restaurants just off the main road near Marlin Beach Resort.

D'Jungle INTERNATIONAL **$$**
(mains P80-300; 📶) It's hard not to be lured in by the display of salivating-inducing skewered meats and seafood that greet you at this popular outdoor eatery. Run by a charismatic German, the central barbecue kitchen overflows nightly with a cornucopia of seared fish in sweet marinade, Singapore noodles, Italian garlic potatoes, steamed shellfish and chicken done in every imaginable way. Service can be on the slow side.

Marisquera O' Portuguese RESTOBAR $$
(meals from P135; ⏰10am-late; 📶) The menu at this atmospheric restobar matches the flags on the walls and spans the globe from pricey Portuguese bacalhau cod and Basque-inspired tapas (spicy tuna) to dishes from Mozambique.

Cou Cou's INTERNATIONAL $$
(pizzas from P300; 📶) The place for thin-crust pizzas, with the Hungarian (Hungarian sausage, black olives and mushrooms) our favourite. Has a good wine list.

Le Petit Bonheir FILIPINO $$
(meals from P150; ⏰10am-late; 📶) Atmospheric cottages draped with white curtains serve up a sumptuous five-course Filipino banquet (P495) comprising shrimp and scallop curry and *ube* (purple yam) ice cream for dessert.

Floating Bar BAR
(www.thefloatingbar.com; ⏰10am-6pm) Swedish-owned bar on the water, open during the high season (December to May).

ℹ Information

About 10km west of Santa Fe is Bantayan town (P15 by jeepney), the island's beautifully preserved administrative heart. There is an Allied Bank ATM in the main plaza, but it's highly advisable to cash up before you arrive.

There are several internet cafes in Santa Fe, with **SFEC** (per hr P20; ⏰11am-10pm) the cheapest.

For regularly updated island info, have a look at www.wowbantayan.com.

ℹ Getting There & Away

It's now possible to fly to Bantayan, with Mid-Sea Express running flights from Cebu City to Santa Fe four times a week.

Hagnaya is the port town where RORO ferries depart for Santa Fe, with around six boats per day (P170, one hour) from 5am to 5.30pm. Returning back to the mainland, the last boat from Santa Fe to Hagnaya departs at 4.30pm. In bad weather, call the **Hagnaya ticket office** (☎435 2078) to check for cancellations.

Regular Ceres buses depart Hagnaya for Cebu City (P132, three hours) or Bogo (P12, 30 minutes), where you can get an onward connection. If you're heading to Malapascua, disembark at Bogo to catch a bus to Maya.

An overnight ferry between Cebu City and Santa Fe is another option.

From Bantayan town, a ferry bound for Cadiz (P220, four hours) on Negros departs every second morning at 10am. On alternate mornings, a smaller, faster bangka sails for Sagay (P250, three hours), also on Negros.

Chartering a boat to Malapascua is possible but it's safer, quicker and cheaper to head via mainland Cebu.

Malapascua Island

☎032 / POP 3500

While it's the world-class diving that attracts most visitors to the tiny and idyllic island of Malapascua, its lovely beaches and air of *joie de vivre* are what confirms its reputation as one of Cebu's most popular destinations. Located off the northern tip of the province, its tight island community, absence of cars and sporadic electricity supply give Malapascua a laid-back charm that keeps it grounded in the face of some rapid-fire development.

Diving with the thresher sharks is the main highlight, and it's one of the best places in the world to see these distinctive-tailed sharks.

If you are heading to Malapascua from Maya and miss the last boat, you can overnight there at **Abba Family Lodge** (☎437 2525; d with fan/air-con & shared bathroom P500/750; ❄), 100m from the pier.

Activities

The action at Malapascua is centred on diving, but nondivers aren't left entirely without options. A good three-hour **walk** will take you all around the coast of the island, with plenty of photo opportunities and including attractions such as the waterside cemetery with its sun-bleached graves, the lighthouse on the island's northwest coast and the 12m-high lookout up near Guimbitayan, which some foolhardy souls treat as a cliff jump. Bring water. The best beaches on Malapascua are located at the southern end of the island, where the resorts are situated.

Diving

The most popular dive off Malapascua is Monad Shoal, where you can see thresher sharks and manta rays. Your best chance to see them is at 'cleaning station', a plateau at a depth of 25m, 15 minutes by bangka, where the sharks congregate early morning to get their beauty scrub courtesy of the wrasses (cleaner fish) that await them. Be warned, however: sightings aren't guaranteed, due to either poor visibility or the sharks being a no-show.

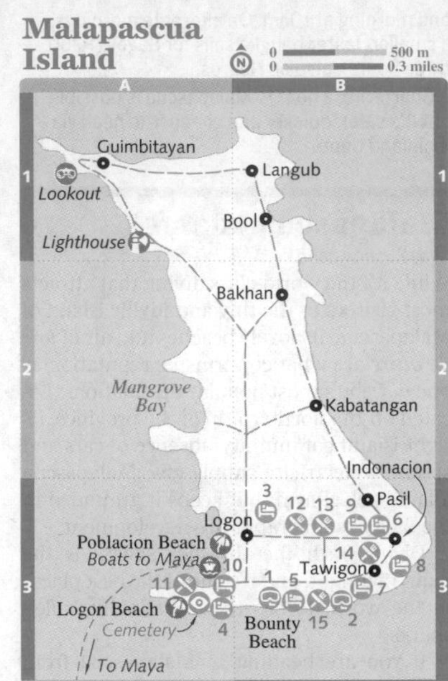

Malapascua Island

Activities, Courses & Tours
- Evolution Diving .... (see 6)
- Exotic Divers .... (see 8)
- 1 Sea Explorers B3
- 2 Thresher Shark Divers B3

Sleeping
- 3 Bebe's Lodging House B3
- 4 Blue Corals Resort A3
- 5 Cocobana Beach Resort B3
- 6 Evolution B3
- 7 Hippocampus Beach Resort B3
- 8 Malapascua Exotic Dive & Beach Resort B3
- 9 Mr Kwiz B3
- 10 White Sand Bungalows A3

Eating
- 11 Angelina A3
- 12 Ging-Ging's Garden Restaurant B3
- 13 La Isla Bonita B3
- 14 Purple Snapper B3
- 15 Sunsplash Resort B3

Dynamiting has mainly destroyed the closer reefs, but macrophotographers will love the area around **Gato Island**, a marine sanctuary and sea snake breeding ground (from February to September). There are also three **wreck dives** in the area, including a WWII wreck and the *Dona Marilyn* ferry, a passenger ferry that sank during a typhoon in 1988 killing 250 people, now a site of soft corals and abundant marine life.

Snorkelling equipment (around P200) is available from dive centres, with the most accessible spot being the house reef straight out front with some decent corals. Otherwise you can join a dive group to Calangaman Island.

There are numerous dive centres on the island, most offering standard rates – one dive US$25, equipment rental US$6 and an open-water diving certificate US$350.

With the influx of tourists to the island, several operators have signed up to an environmental code of conduct, which, among other things, aims to protect the thresher sharks. A P50 marine sanctuary protection fee is tacked on. If conservation is important to you, check the dive company has signed up.

Diving companies on Malapascua include **Evolution Diving** (☎0917 628 7333; www.evolution.com.ph), **Exotic Divers** (☎437 0983; www.malapascua.net; Malapascua Exotic Dive & Beach Resort), **Sea Explorers** (☎0917 640 1689; www.sea-explorers.com) and **Thresher Shark Divers** (☎0927 612 3359; www.malapascua-diving.com).

Island Hopping

It's easy to organise boat trips (around P800 half-day) around the islands, which will include snorkelling and dolphin watching. The nearby islands of **Carnassa** (one hour) and **Calangaman** (two hours) both have stunning beaches as well as excellent snorkelling, with prices around P3000 for full-day hire.

Sleeping

White Sand Bungalows BEACH RESORT **$**
(☎0927 318 7471; www.whitesand.dk; r from P900) The Danish-owned White Sand has its own spot across from wonderful Poblacion Beach, with very reasonably priced and comfortable nipa huts and a great relaxed beachy feel. A good choice for those wanting to plonk themselves on the sand with a good book.

Hippocampus Beach Resort BEACH RESORT **$$**
(☎437 0460; www.hippocampus-online.com; r with fan/air-con from P1500/2800; ❄📶) Its name

inspired by the Latin word for seahorse (in case you were wondering), Hippocampus has some large and very well designed terraces set back from Bounty Beach. It's fronted by a cute outdoor bar and restaurant.

Cocobana Beach Resort BEACH RESORT $$
(☎437 1040; www.cocobana.ch; s/d cottages incl breakfast with fan from P800/1000, with air-con from P2200/2400; ❄) Smack bang in the middle of Bounty Beach, Malapascua's original resort is a perennial favourite. It has comfy cottages, 24-hour electricity, a bar and a decent restaurant. Accommodation-dive packages are available through Sea Explorers.

Evolution BEACH RESORT $$
(☎0915 666 1584; r incl breakfast with fan/air-con P1600/2500; ❄📶) On the southeast edge of the beach, this small, laid-back English/Irish-run dive resort is doing great things. Staff are personable, rooms simple and comfy, while the Craic House restobar serves up quality food – the spicy tuna burger gets rave reviews. Rooms are limited, with preference given to those who dive here.

Malapascua Exotic Dive & Beach Resort BEACH RESORT $$
(☎437 0983; www.malapascua.net; r with fan P1200, with air-con P2400-4800; ❄) Located on the quiet easterly beach, Exotic is very much a self-contained resort, and as luxurious as it gets on Malapascua. Staff are friendly, laid-back and competent, and the rooms are good value for money, especially since you get hot water and a fridge. The attached dive shop is first class.

Blue Corals Resort BEACH RESORT $$
(☎437 1021; www.malapascuaisland.com.ph; d with fan/air-con from P1500/2800; ❄@📶) A prominent structure, tacked onto the rocky ridge that juts into the sea at the western extremity of Bounty Beach. East-facing rooms have breathtaking views. Has pricey internet (P100 per 30 minutes).

Mr Kwiz PENSION HOUSE $
(☎0906 620 5475; r P500) Good cheapie in the village, with basic concrete and very pink rooms. Is accessed via a small path running beside Evolution, 100m from the beach.

Bebe's Lodging House PENSION HOUSE $
(☎0916 756 6018; r without/with bathroom P300/500) On an island dominated by pricey beachside resorts, Bebe's offers a no-frills, family-run alternative in the village.

Eating & Drinking

Malapascua has a decent choice of eating, and most bars have happy hour between 5pm and 6pm.

TOP CHOICE **Angelina** ITALIAN $$$
(www.angelinabeach.com; meals P320-400; ❄📶) Classy Angelina boasts a romantic spot on a sandy cove at Poblacion Beach, with an authentic menu based on northern Italian recipes from Emilia-Romagna. As well as pizzas, it features handmade pasta and ravioli, or risotto with crab, shrimp and squid cooked in wine sauce (P355). Many ingredients are imported from Italy and there's an extensive wine list. Dine indoors or on the beach.

Ging-Ging's Garden Restaurant FILIPINO $
(meals P60-100) Offers the very best economy restaurant on the island with a good mix of Filipino and international dishes. The sweet and sour fish (P60) is a good deal.

La Isla Bonita INTERNATIONAL $$
(☎0926 294 3930; meals P200-280; ⏰8am-2pm & 6-10pm) In the humble surroundings of Logon village, suave little La Isla Bonita serves up a range of fresh, quality ingredients, with a good seafood selection, cooked in a variety of styles, but always with care.

Sunsplash Resort INTERNATIONAL $$
(☎0905 269 4234; www.sunsplash.info; meals P215-280) With its cushioned chill-out zones, drinking competitions and movie-projector screens, this restobar is geared for maximum carousal. Otherwise grab a chair at its beach bar. Or if that still doesn't suit you, keep on moving and jump on an awaiting boat to zip you out to the famous floating bar. The menu comprises hearty meals for the homesick, such as cordon bleu and kebab gyros.

Purple Snapper BURGERS $$
(www.purplesnapper.com; burgers P230) Purple Snapper knows what it takes to make a good burger, using New Zealand ground beef to serve up hits such as the ⅓-pounder mushroom burger.

Information

The island's electricity is supplied by a diesel-powered generator that operates from 6pm to 11pm, although some resorts have their own (noisy) generators.

There's no ATM on Malapascua, so cash up before you arrive; the closest ATM is at Bogo.

Several resorts have wi-fi and internet access; try Maldito's (per hour P60 or free if you eat there).

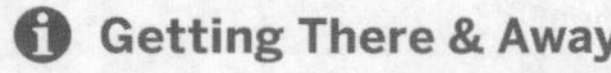

Getting There & Away

Transport to the island is via bangka from Maya (P80, 30 minutes). The boat leaves whenever it's full, which is usually, but not always, hourly from 6.30am to around 5.30pm. The last boat departing from Malapascua to Maya is at 2pm.

There are also bangka services to San Isidro on Leyte and Esperanza, Masbate.

Ceres buses from Maya to Cebu City (P163, four hours) depart hourly, or you can head to Bogo for onward bus connection (P40, one hour).

Moalboal

☎032 / POP 5211

Diving, drinking and dining (in that order) top the list of activities in the rambling dive colony of Moalboal (hard to pronounce – try mo-ahl-bo-ahl). About 90km from Cebu City, Moalboal proper is on the main road; the part that tourists mean when they say 'Moalboal' is actually **Panagsama Beach**, a cramped and rowdy resort village a short tricycle (P100) or *habal-habal* (P30) ride west of town.

While diving is the primary reason to visit Moalboal, if you were hoping to unwind with a lazy beach holiday, you can head to nearby **White Beach**, which unlike Panagsama has a decent beach. Popular with locals, it's subject to the usual flux of domestic tourist spots: relatively quiet during the week, it's overflowing on weekends and holidays. White Beach is a 20-minute tricycle (P150) ride from Panagsama, or a 15-minute tricycle (P100) or *habal-habal* (P50) ride from Moalboal.

Sights

Kawasan Falls WATERFALLS

(admission P10) Located 20km south of Moalboal, inland from Badian, the Kawasan Falls comprise a series of three waterfalls amid scenic forest; the largest cascades from 20m. A highlight of any visit here is a dip in its refreshing swimming holes, coloured a milky blue. While it's a little spoilt by the weekend crowds, as well as development with small restaurants and tables (an extortionate P300 to sit at), it remains a pretty spot. More adventurous souls can scramble beyond the third waterfall to more secluded spots, or otherwise arrange canyonning trips in Panagsama. To get here, take a bus (P11) to Badian market and then a tricycle (P30) to the start of the trail. It's a pleasant 20-minute walk along the banks of a river; a guide isn't necessary. There's a P50 parking fee if you have your own transport.

Naomi's Bottle Museum & Book Club BOOKSHOP

(☎0917 435 3910) Run by an ultrafriendly local couple, this quirky book exchange sets a wonderful example by recycling bottles to use both as decoration and to store old manuscripts as well as words of wisdom – which are presented as a small gift to all visitors, as well as similar items for sale.

Activities

Diving & Snorkelling

Tiny **Pescador Island** offers some of Cebu's most spectacular diving. With generally excellent visibility and depths of around 50m, the island's waters are usually teeming with fish. The stars of the show are the swirling mass schools of sardines, as well as the occasional cameo appearance from thresher sharks. It's accessed via an often-choppy 3km boat ride from Moalboal's Tongo Point diving spot.

Snorkelling is possible, too; the best spot is said to be on the island's southern side, while the house reef at White Beach also has some lovely corals and marine life. Otherwise head straight out until you reach the drop-off, about 30m out. Most resorts rent out snorkelling sets for around P250 per day.

The average price of a dive is US$25. An open-water certificate is around US$350. There is a reef conservation fee of P100 to dive at **Savedra Reef** and Pescador.

There are many diver operators in town, so it's a question of visiting a few and going with whoever you feel most comfortable with.

Nelson's Dive Shop (Ocean Safari; ☎474 3023, 0917 276 7969; www.ibara.ne.jp/~bitoon; Eve's Kiosk)

Neptune Diving (☎495 0643, 0917 455 6742; www.neptunediving.com)

Savedra Dive Centre (☎474 0014, 0917 321 1475; www.savedra.com)

Sea Explorers (☎in Cebu 234 0248; www.sea-explorers.com; Kasai Village Beach Resort)

Seaquest Dive Centre (☎474 0005; www.seaquestdivecenter.ph; Sumisid Lodge)

WOLFGANG DAFERT: FREEDIVER INSTRUCTOR

A self-described 'merman' of 16 years, the 37-year-old Austrian Wolfgang Dafert has been in the Philippines for over six years, and offers **freediving courses** (☎0928 263 4646; www.freediving-philippines.com) in Moalboal, which makes a great alternative to the usual diving.

What exactly is freediving? Freediving is diving without the use of heavy scuba equipment, just on a single breath of air. The silence is like a kind of meditation, and an added bonus is without the annoying bubbles you're able to get closer to the fish while freely enjoying being part of the ocean.

How do you do learn to do it? After two days of training, students will learn the right breathing and relaxation techniques while knowing how to deal with the urge to breathe. Everybody can learn to dive deeper and longer than you'd think is possible. For beginners, the urge to breathe is the first hurdle you have to overcome. In the course, you will learn the right relaxation techniques (similar to yoga) and how to 'transfer' this first breathing reflex into a relaxed sensation so you can still stay underwater longer. It's mind over matter, in that you learn and experience that you *can* hold your breath longer than your body is actually telling you.

What is your record depth and time spent underwater? Freediving down to 70m depth (as deep as a 23-storey building), while holding my breath for seven minutes and 10 seconds.

What's the best thing about diving in Moalboal? For fun freediving, it's the massive resident school of millions of sardines at Pescador island – a one-of-a-kind natural spectacle in itself. Uh...and let's not forget another air-breathing underwater creature – there are plenty of turtles in Moalboal!

Visayas Divers (☎474 3068; www.visayadivers.com; Quo Vadis Beach Resort)

Other Activities

Planet Action ADVENTURE TOURS

(☎0916 624 8253, 474 3016; www.action-philippines.com) Offering some of the most exhilarating adventure tours in the Visayas, Planet Action caters for beginners through to advanced actioneers, and includes all equipment and meals. A range of day excursions (from P2200) include canyonning, caving, mountain biking and horse riding, and it also rents mountain bikes (from P300 per day). Planet Action also offers excursions to Negros for a three-day hike up Mt Kanlaon volcano (all-inclusive P9500 per person).

Sleeping

PANAGSAMA BEACH

Most resorts are either affiliated with a dive company or otherwise have a centre onsite, so it's worth asking ahead about cheap package deals that combine diving with accommodation.

Quo Vadis Beach Resort BEACH RESORT $$

(☎474 0018; www.moalboal.com; d with fan/air-con from P850/900; ❄@📶🏊) Has solid nipa huts positioned amid lovely gardens, while the more expensive cottages (P2500) open right up to the beach, with stylish decor, polished floorboards and big bathrooms that make them the nicest in town. It's associated with Visaya Divers. Children under 12 stay for free.

Tipolo Beach Resort BEACH RESORT $$

(☎0916 653 7608; www.tipoloresort.com; d P1500; ❄@) Run by the folk from Planet Action, this small seaside resort has pleasant rooms with clean tiled floors, sturdy bamboo furniture and outdoor seating, along with mod cons like hot water, fridge and a safe. Its restaurant is renowned for hearty breakfasts and strong brewed coffee.

Moalboal Backpacker Lodge HOSTEL $

(☎0905 227 8096; www.moalboal-backpackerlodge.com; dm/s/d with fan from P220/350/450, 📶) A much welcome addition to the Panagsama traveller scene, this newish backpackers succeeds in giving budget visitors exactly what they need. With a dormitory, common kitchen and very reasonable dive packages, it's a blessing for those watching their pesos. Though just don't expect much assistance from staff. The rickety bamboo chill-out terrace is a good spot for a drink.

Sumisid Lodge BEACH RESORT $$

(☎474 0005; www.seaquestdivecenter.ph; s/d without air-con & bathroom P700/1000, s/d with air-con

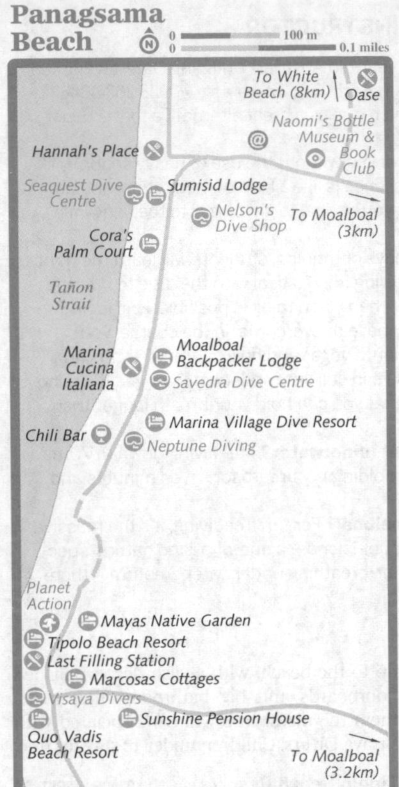

& bathroom P1800/2300;) At the beating heart of the bar district, Sumisid has rooms to suit all budgets, but somehow the cheapest rooms have the best views, if you can manage without air-con. It also has a lovely restaurant on a sandy beach. It's affiliated with Seaquest Dive Centre.

Sunshine Pension House PENSION HOUSE $
(0921 689 1865; www.sunshinepension.webs.com; d with fan P800;) An excellent position away from the crowds, rooms here are vibrant with colourful sea-themed murals and bright bedsheets, and hot-water bathrooms. It's away from the beach, but has a huge swimming pool, free internet and motorbikes for rent (P300 per day).

Mayas Native Garden BEACH RESORT $$
(0915 480 9610; www.mayasnativegarden.com; cottage with fan/air-con P800/1500, house P2500;) Has wonderfully simple thatched-roof cottages in a lush garden setting. The double-storey house is incredible value with all mod cons.

Cora's Palm Court PENSION HOUSE $
(474 3220; cora _abarquez@yahoo.com; r with fan/air-con from P400/1500;) Perched right on the waterfront, rooms here are stark white and bare bones, but nonetheless large and have lockable cupboards. Pricier rooms have kitchenettes and small fridges; long-term guests can negotiate a decent discount.

Marcosas Cottages BEACH RESORT $$
(474 0064; www.moalboal-cebu.com; d without/with kitchenette & sea view P1700/2150;) A mazelike compound of white thatched cottages set around a luxurious pool and manicured grass gives Marcosas that unmistakable resort feel. It's decent value for money and has the Blue Abyss dive shop.

Savedra Beach Bungalows BEACH RESORT $$
(474 0011; www.savedrabeachbungalows.com; r from P1500;) Rooms are generic, but comfortable, and balconies open directly to the water.

Marina Village Dive Resort BEACH RESORT $
(474 0034; www.marina-village-resort.com; r without/with air-con P600/1600;) Set in a neatly kept garden with Bermuda grass, the nipa huts with fan are fantastic value.

WHITE BEACH

Prices shift up a notch at White Beach; the extra dosh affords you a *real* beach.

Club Serena Resort BEACH RESORT $$$
(474 0050; www.clubserenaresort.com; r P3000-5600;) Luxurious and quirky in equal measure, Serena is a little gem right on the beach. Every structure, from the spacious octagonal bar-restaurant to the sprawling tree-house room, is designed with personal flair and fitted for maximum indulgence. It has the Aquaholics dive shop on-site.

Blue Orchid Resort BEACH RESORT $$
(474 0800, 0929 273 1128; www.blueorchidresort.com; r from P2500;) Mediterranean-inspired villas at Blue Orchid have a wonderful secluded location away from the rowdy beach crowd. And while it lacks a beach, it makes up for it with a small sandy platform complete with deckchairs and enticing polished-wood gazebos looking over sparkling turquoise waters to Negros. Large rooms have wooden poster beds and spacious blue-tiled showers with piping-hot water. The huge suite with jacuzzi is a great

spot for honeymooners. It has a professionally run dive shop.

Ravenala BEACH RESORT **$$$**
(☎253 5053; cottages with fan/air-con P3000/3500; ❄) Go for the fan-only rooms – smack, bang on the beach; the sea breeze and cooling properties of the rock walls make air-con less essential.

Asian Belgian Resort BEACH RESORT **$$**
(☎0917 744 7603; www.asian-belgian-resort.com; r with fan/air-con P1200/1800; ❄) The best budget option doesn't have a sandy beach, but has a good lookout over the water and a dive company.

BADIAN

TOP CHOICE **Badian Island Resort & Spa** BEACH RESORT **$$$**
(☎475 1102; www.badianhotel.com; r from US$150; ❄@🛜🏊) Those looking to spoil themselves in Moalboal should head straight to Badian Island, 20km south of Moalboal, for this luxurious resort that boasts some of the nicest rooms we've seen in the Philippines. The junior suites are outstanding value, while pool villas, which feature their own private salt-water infinity pools, are the ultimate in opulence.

Eating & Drinking

Most places to stay have restaurants, although there are plenty of other eateries worth a look.

There's a drinking spot to suit most tastes at Panagsama Beach, so bar hop till you find something you like. Nightlife is nonexistent on White Beach.

TOP CHOICE **Hannah's Place** INTERNATIONAL **$$**
(www.hannahs-place.com; meals from P250) A perfect location on the beach with a varied international and Filipino menu, and two-for-one beers from 5pm to 6pm.

Marina Cucina Italiana PIZZERIA **$**
(pizzas from P200; ⏲7am-3pm & 5-10pm) Here it's all about the ocean-side authentic thin-crust pizzas.

Oase GERMAN **$$**
(dishes from P190; ⏲2-10pm Wed-Sun) Classy and intimate German restaurant on the outskirts of Panagsama; has cheap beer.

Ravenala FILIPINO **$**
(dishes from P80) Lovely spot for a feed or a cold drink directly on the powdery sands of White Beach.

Chili Bar RESTOBAR **$**
(dishes from P80) A Panagsama institution, this seaside bar is the hang-out for dive instructors and has a lethal cocktail menu. Wednesday nights has a pool comp.

Last Filling Station CAFE **$$**
(meals from P180) Famous for its energy-boosting breakfasts, replete with yoghurt, muesli and baguettes. Also does decent strong brewed coffee.

ℹ Information

At the time of research there was no ATM in Moalboal, so cash up before you arrive. The closest ATM is at Carcar.

In Panagsama, get online at **Hotline Internet Cafe** (per hr P30).

ℹ Getting There & Away

Buses from Moalboal to Cebu City South Bus Station depart on the hour throughout the day (P107, 3½ hours) until 7.30pm. Squashy air-con vans (P100, 2½ hours) depart every 30 minutes until 5pm. A taxi will cost P2000.

Regular buses to Bato (P58, two hours) depart from the main street, from where you can catch another bus to Lilo-an (P15). Five daily ferries depart from Bato to Negros (P50, 25 minutes).

Argao

☎032 / POP 5853

Such incongruous attractions as Spanish colonial-era buildings and the endangered wrinkle-lipped bat make Argao a little special, but it's the brown-sand beaches of **Kawit**, **Mahawak** and **Lawis** that draw most of the guests.

Behind an unprepossessing facade on the highway, you'll find the friendly **Bamboo Paradise Beach Resort** (☎367 7271; s/d P1000/1500; ❄), with its pleasant courtyard, garden furniture, potted plants, throw rugs and sea views.

Argao is about 65km south of Cebu City, and plenty of Ceres and other buses stop here (P70, two hours).

Lite Shipping boats go from Argao to Loon (P110, two hours), on Bohol, two or three times daily. The last service leaves at around 3pm. There are also boats twice a week to Cabilao Island. To get either boat, you'll need to catch a Ceres bus to the port (P12), which is about 8km north of Argao proper.

Lilo-an & Sumilon Island

☎032 / POP 14,998

Lilo-an is a nondescript little village with wonderful views across the strait to Negros. Unless you plan to visit Sumilon Island, there's no great reason to hang around, with much better diving in Moalboal or Negros, but it can make a convenient overnight stop for those heading to Dumaguete. On the main road, there are a few dive centres that cater mainly to north Asian package tourists.

The best diving and white beaches are at the marine reserve on nearby Sumilon Island, one of the success stories of conservation in the Philippines. Visitors to the sanctuary are charged a P10 entrance fee and there is a further fee of P150 for diving. Dive shops from Negros also run trips here.

Sleeping & Eating

TOP CHOICE **Eden Resort** BEACH RESORT $$
(☎480 9321; http://eden.ph; r incl breakfast P2500;) Located high up the hill in Lilo-an, this Mediterranean-feeling resort has a magnificent setting perched on a cliff looking out to sea. Even if you're not staying here, it's worth popping in for a pizza and a swim in its luxurious infinity pool with amazing views.

Kingdom Resort BEACH RESORT $$
(☎480 9017; r from P1500;) South Korean dive resort at the bottom of the hill on the beach at Lilo-an, with upstairs rooms looking out to Negros.

Sumilon Bluewater Island Resort BEACH RESORT $$$
(☎481 0801; www.bluewater.com.ph/sumilon2; r P8760;) A luxury operation on Sumilon Island, Bluewater features white-sandbar beaches and rooms with Japanese touches, such as sliding screen doors. Ultimately it's overpriced and not overly private, sharing a porch with neighbouring rooms. There's free boat transfer for guests from the pier in Banlogan, 10km from Lilo-an. Nonguests can use facilities for P600.

Getting There & Away

Ferries to Negros depart from the new Lilo-an pier (P62, 30 minutes) hourly from 4am to 7.30pm, while bangkas depart from the old pier (P45, 40 minutes) hourly, arriving at Sibulan for Dumaguete.

In Oslob, 10km from Lilo-an, there's also a daily **Super Shuttle Ferry** (☎0933 968 2779) to Larena, Siquijor, at 10.30am (P200, one hour).

Ceres buses run all day from Lilo-an to Cebu City (P169, three hours) and Moalboal via Bato (P80, two hours).

The Sumilon Bluewater Island Resort pier is at Banlogan, 3km north of Mainit. Day trippers can charter a boat for the day through the resort for P600, inclusive of meal and facilities.

CAMOTES ISLANDS

☎032 / POP 78,058

Only a few hours by bangka from Cebu, the Camotes (kah-*maw*-tis) offer an authentic island life that many adventurous tourists crave. The group's two main islands, Poro and Pacijan, are connected by a mangrove-fringed land bridge that enables visitors to explore the two by motorcycle, the main mode of transport here. The best beaches and accommodation are on Pacijan. Visitors rarely make it to the third island, Ponson, which looks to Leyte rather than Cebu as its main link to the world.

Activities

There is good wall diving around Tulang Island, just north of Pacijan. Local authorities have succeeded in establishing marine sanctuaries in the reefs north and south of Poro Island, near Esperanza and Tudela. The two dive centres in the Camotes are low-key, one-man operations.

Ocean Deep DIVING
(☎0927 676 6641; www.oceandeep.biz) On Pacijan Island, affiliated with Mangodlong Paradise Beach Resort.

Flying Fish Resort DIVING
(☎0908 876 5427; www.camotesflyingfishresort.com) A small diving operation located on Poro Island.

Information

On Pacijan Island there's a **tourist information desk** (☎497 0296; www.travelcamotes.com) near the Municipal Hall in San Francisco, offering ferry information and maps of the Camotes (P100).

TFNG (per hr P15; ⏲8am-midnight) has internet near the Municipal Hall, while **Sel's Internet Cafe** (per hr P15; ⏲8.30am-8pm) is located at Poro pier.

There are no ATMs on the Camotes.

Camotes Islands

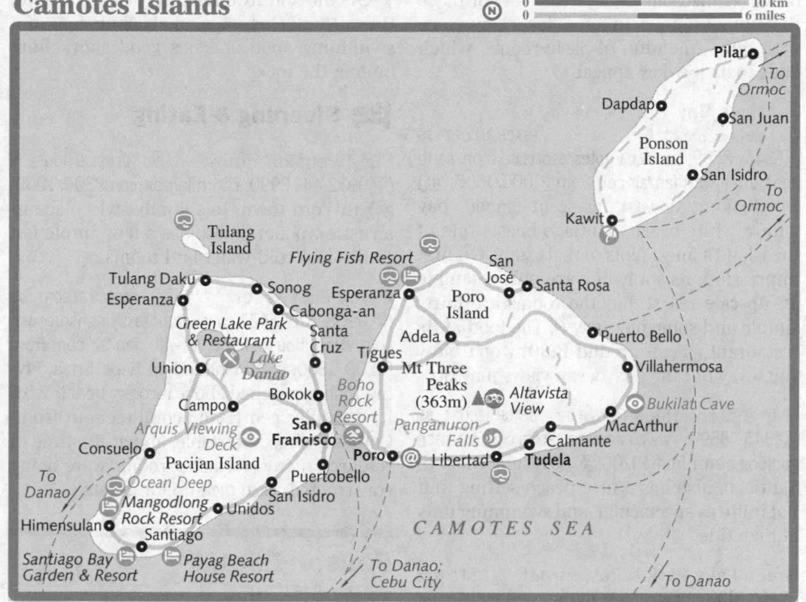

Getting There & Away

Golden Express departs Pier 1 at Cebu City at 5.30pm for Poro town (P380, two hours); the same ferry leaves Poro for Cebu City at 6am.

A faster and less painful way to get to the Camotes from Cebu is to leave from Danao, which has daily bangka services to both Consuelo and San Francisco piers (from P180) on Pacijan Island, and also to Poro Island (P200). First departure is at 5.30am, with regular services until midday, and a few late-afternoon services. Consuelo is the most convenient arrival point, closest to the best accommodation.

From the Camotes, there's a daily early-morning ferry to Ormoc on Leyte (P200, three hours) from Bokok wharf on Pacijan Island and Tudela on Poro

There are no ferries to Ponson from Cebu, but **Junmar** (0927 2128 666) runs a daily bangka service departing 1pm from Tudela on Poro Island to Pilar (P200, two hours). Otherwise you can charter a boat from Puerto Bello to Kawit (P50, 45 minutes). Ponson also has bangkas to Ormoc on Leyte.

Getting Around

The main means of travelling the Camotes is motorcycle. Prices are negotiable, but trips of 5km will cost around P40, up to 10km will cost P100 and over that (eg Poro town to Santiago) will cost around P200. Alternatively you can rent a motorbike from Mangodlong for P400 per day, with most sights well signed. Jeepney services are limed to meet the boats at outlying ports, such as Consuelo.

Pacijan Island

032 / POP 44,588

Pacijan has the only white-sand beaches on the Camotes around Santiago Bay, which is where the majority of hotels are located.

San Francisco, or 'San Fran', the main town on Pacijan Island, stands at one end of the long land bridge and mangrove forest that runs all the way across to Poro Island. San Fran has a lively market (to the left after the causeway, on the bay), a church and a pretty little town square.

A 30-minute motorbike ride from San Fran is **Esperanza**, Pacijan's second-largest town, which runs along a white-sand beach strewn with fishing boats. The road north from Esperanza takes you up to Tulang Daku, where you can ask a fisher to take you out to Camotes' best diving at **Tulang Island** (P500 return) or get the small public boat (P10 one way).

Sleeping & Eating

Payag Beach House Resort BEACH RESORT $
(233 1158; r with fan/air-con P700/1200;) Plonked directly on a private white-sand

beach, chilled-out Payag is the sort of place that suits Camotes to a tee. It's a tiny place with only a handful of basic rooms, which adds to its low-key appeal.

Santiago Bay Garden & Resort BEACH RESORT $$
(☎345 8599; www.camotesresorts.com.ph/santiago.htm; r with fan/air-con from P1000/1500; ❄) Overlooking a vast, crescent-shaped bay with a white beach, Santiago boasts one of the island's finest plots of real estate. On first impression, its sprawling grounds resemble an upscale resort, but the rooms are fairly simple and some have views. The food at its restaurant (meals around P180) won't blow you away but the nice ocean views may do.

Mangodlong Rock Resort BEACH RESORT $$
(☎345 8599; www.camotesresorts.com.ph/mangodlong.htm, r from P1700; ❄) Sister resort to Santiago, also has a nice beach setting, but not quite as spectacular, and swimming only at high tide.

Green Lake Park & Restaurant FILIPINO $
(meals P100; ⏲6am-late) On the road southeast of Union, follow the signs to this restaurant, where you can enjoy good Filipino cuisine on the banks of Lake Danao to the dulcet accompaniment of the karaoke machine.

Poro Island

☎032 / POP 21,529

Poro is the lesser of the two main islands. It lacks the beaches of Pacijan but if you have an off-road bike its forested hills have the better touring.

Poro is the main town on the island, an unassuming coastal settlement with a hint of the Spanish Mediterranean to it. Its main landmark is a Spanish church built in 1849.

Poro is the arrival point for those coming from Cebu City, but unless you have an early-morning ferry back to Cebu City there's no reason to stay here.

Beside a rough dirt road just beyond MacArthur is the well-hidden **Bukilat Cave** (admission P10). If you're up for the swim, it can be explored properly providing you can rustle up a guide and some torches (flashlights). Enquire at the tourist office in San Fran.

Just west of Tudela, a 1km walking trail takes you inland to **Panganuron Falls**, which tend to dry up in high summer (from March to May).

On the southwestern tip of Poro Island, **Boho Rock Resort** is an absolute gem of a swimming spot, and has good snorkelling among the rocks.

Sleeping & Eating

Big Z Pension House PENSION HOUSE $
(☎0932 441 2990; r with fan/air-con P300/1000; ❄) In Poro town, this family-style place in a rustic wooden house has a few simple fan rooms and cold-water bathrooms.

Flying Fish Resort BEACH RESORT $$
(☎0908 876 5427; www.camotesflyingfishresort.com; tree house P750, r with fan/air-con from P1200/1800; ❄) Isolated on Esperanza, Flying Fish is perched above a rocky beach with its own dive centre and coral reef out front. Cottages are comfortable, and at the time of research many sea-facing rooms were being constructed. Free pick-up for guests.

Ponson Island

☎032 / POP 11,941

The charm in visiting a place as remote as Ponson is the attention you'll get, which varies from warmly effusive to wryly amused. What it tells you is that very, very few travellers make it this far.

There are two main towns on Ponson: **Pilar** and **Kawit**. Kawit is the more picturesque of the two, with a lovely long, white-sand beach. There is no established place to stay in either town, although you can make enquiries about homestays at the respective barangay halls.

ROMBLON

☎042 / POP 264,400

Mysterious, overlooked and tricky to get to, the Romblon group of islands is a virtual Bermuda Triangle – and this is a large part of the islands' appeal. The old-world provincial capital of Romblon town is a charming base, and serves as a launching point for Sibuyan, one of the most biologically diverse places in the world. Travellers seeking to escape cabin fever in Boracay are well positioned to explore this road not taken, and those who brave the perils of irregular boat connections will be rewarded with the by-products of isolation: quiet and the urge to never leave.

Romblon is not technically part of the Visayas (it's lumped in an administrative district with Mindoro and Palawan), but it works best as part of a Visayan itinerary so we include it here. Romblon's fourth-largest island, Carabao Island, is covered in the Boracay section.

Getting There & Away

AIR

An airport near Tugdan on the east coast of Tablas is serviced almost daily by alternating Seair and Zest Air flights.

BOAT

Keep in mind that tropical storms often ground boats in the typhoon season (June to November), so be flexible if travelling during that time.

The most popular connections are from Caticlan (to Looc on Tablas island) and Batangas (to Odiongan on Tablas and Romblon town). Looc and Odiongan also have regular connections with Roxas, Mindoro. Sibuyan Island is connected to Roxas (Panay) and Mandaon (Masbate).

Romblon Shipping Lines' massive, comfortable MV *Mary the Queen* car/passenger ferry does a hopping route from Manila to Romblon town to Cajidiocan (Sibuyan) to Mandaon (Masbate), departing Manila every Tuesday at 5pm. That same boat does a separate route, departing Manila at 5pm on Fridays bound for Odiongan and Caticlan (Panay).

See individual Getting There & Away sections for more information.

Anchor Bay Aqua Sports on Romblon and Tablas Fun Center in Looc have speedboats for hire that can take you straight to/from Boracay in 20 minutes to one hour (per boat P12,000 to P22,500).

Companies serving Romblon:

Kalayaan Shipping (☎in Manila 02-710 3990)

Montenegro Shipping Lines (Odiongan pier)

Romblon Shipping Lines Inc (RSLI; ☎in Romblon town 0908 444 1175; www.romblonshippinglines.com)

Romblon

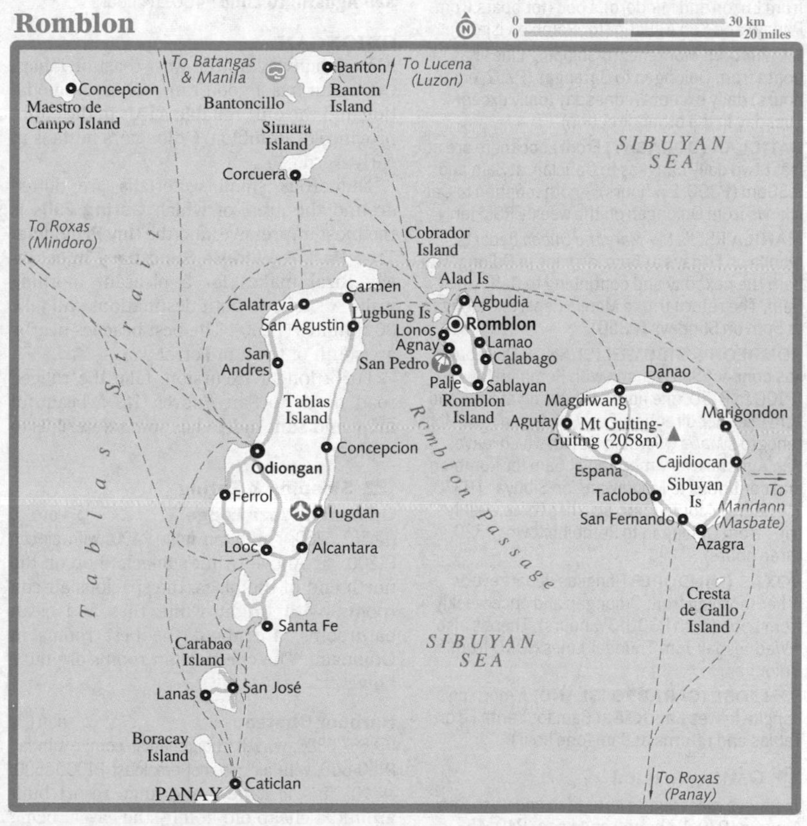

Tablas Island

☎042 / POP 151,059

Poor Tablas. Despite being the largest of the Romblon islands and the best connected to the outside world, it just gets no respect. Neighbouring Romblon and Sibuyan islands get all the accolades, while Tablas' largest town, Odiongan, struggles to shed its reputation as just a gritty port town.

In fact, Tablas is a gorgeous island in its own right, with loads of tourist potential. And as the main entry point to the province and closest of the three main islands to Boracay, it's well positioned to tap into that potential. A few entrepreneurs are finally starting to do just that, establishing resorts and adventure-tourism initiatives around Odiongan and, to the south, Looc, where the daily boats from Caticlan arrive.

Getting There & Away

The three main ports are Odiongan (for boats from Luzon and Mindoro), Looc (for boats from Panay) and San Agustin (for Romblon Island).

BATANGAS Montenegro Shipping Lines has boats from Odiongan to Batangas (P752, eight hours) daily except Wednesday (daily except Tuesday in the other direction).

CATICLAN (BORACAY) From Looc there are at least two daily bangkas to Caticlan, at 8am and 9.30am (P300, 2½ hours). Another option to Caticlan is from Odiongan on the weekly RSLI ferry.

MANILA RSLI's MV *Mary the Queen* departs Manila on Fridays at 5pm, arriving in Odiongan at 5am the next day and continuing to Caticlan at 6am. The return trip to Manila departs Odiongan at 5pm on Sundays (P850).

ROMBLON & SIBUYAN ISLANDS Daily bangkas connect San Agustin with Romblon town (P100 to P150, one hour), departing at 8am and 1pm in either direction. Early birds can take Montenegro's *Maria Querubin* RORO, which leaves San Agustin every morning at 6am for Romblon and continues to Magdiwang on Sibuyan (P370, 3½ hours). Montenegro also has three weekly trips from Odiongan to Romblon town (P320, three hours).

ROXAS (MINDORO) Bangkas depart every other morning from Odiongan and once weekly from Looc (both P300, 3½ hours). There's also a Wednesday 7am Thunder Lines RORO from Odiongan.

SAN JOSÉ (CARABAO ISLAND) A morning bangka leaves San José at 6am for Santa Fe on Tablas and returns at 9am (one hour).

Getting Around

Jeepneys meet flights in Tugdan and go to San Agustin (P70, 1¼ hours) and Looc (P40, 45 minutes). You can also hire a van at the airport to take you to San Agustin (P1500, 40 minutes) or Odiongan (P1200, 50 minutes).

Jeepneys connect the main towns on the island throughout the day but are fairly infrequent, with the exception of the more popular Looc–Odiongan route. There are more trips in the morning.

Jeepneys between Looc and Odiongan (P50, one hour) dry up at around 3.30pm. The last trips from San Agustin to Looc (P100, two hours) and Odiongan (P100, two hours) are around 2pm when the last ferries from Romblon arrive. Morning trips in the other direction should get you to the ferries on time.

By far the quickest way around the island is on the back of a motorcycle taxi, known as a 'single' in these parts.

Sample single fares and times:

Airport to Looc P50, 30 minutes
Airport to Odiongan P400, 1¼ hours
Airport to San Agustin P250, 45 minutes
Looc to Odiongan P120, 35 minutes
San Agustin to Looc P400, 1¼ hours

ODIONGAN

Almost halfway up the west coast of Tablas, Odiongan has a good range of accommodation and the only reliable ATMs in the entire province of Romblon. Odiongan's fiesta is in early April.

Numerous small waterfalls are dotted around the area, of which **Garing Falls** is the most impressive, and the tiny **Provincial Tree Park & Wildlife Sanctuary** in barangay Rizal makes for a pleasant morning walk. A single to both destinations will take 30 minutes (P250). The best beaches nearby are south of town in Ferrol.

For a longer excursion, take the rugged road north to San Andres. It's a beautiful drive and San Andres has some waterfalls to explore.

Sleeping & Eating

Odiongan Plaza Lodge HOTEL $
(☎567 5760; r with fan from P400, with air-con P1200; ❄) Above Lynne's Snack Shop on the north end of the plaza, the spacious air-con rooms, with bright white tiles and clean bathrooms, are about the best rooms in Odiongan. The cheaper fan rooms are tatty, however.

Harbour Chateau HOTEL $
(☎567 5386; www.harbourchateau.com; r with fan P150-600, with air-con incl breakfast P1000-1500; ❄📶) This is a new midrange resort built around a cheap old hotel – the caveat being

that the shabby old rooms are still in use. The newer rooms are more functional than anything, but big enough for three or four people. It's right on Poctoy Beach, towards the pier.

Rencios Resort RESORT $
(☎567 5834; doodsendaya@yahoo.com; r with fan/air-con P400/1200; ❄📶) Set out of town amid fish ponds and ornamental gardens, this distinctive resortlike place has a variety of clean and comfortable rooms with hot water. Loud karaoke is one annoyance.

Islands Gourmet Deli INTERNATIONAL $
(☎0919 483 8531; www.islandsgourmetdeli.com; Quezon St; meals P100-200; 📶) This should be your first stop if you're looking for a good meal and/or travel advice. The food is the best in town, there's good music and you can usually meet a few expats here. Owner Steve is an enthusiastic proponent of tourism in Tablas and can feed you ideas and help organise excursions. It's on the south edge of the centre on the main road to Looc.

Pearl's Cafe CAFE $
(☎567 6048; www.harbourchateau.com; Quezon St; ❄) The P50 Filipino breakfast alone is reason to come here. Pearl also slings a mean coffee, sells a few imported food products and runs a cheery two-room B&B from a second location down by the water (room including breakfast P1000). It's near Islands Gourmet Deli.

Information

Islands Gourmet Deli is the place to go for tips on travel around Tablas and Romblon in general. For money, there's a reliable Bank of the Philippine Islands (BPI) ATM near the plaza, and a less reliable Philippine National Bank (PNB) ATM on the corner of M Formilleza and JP Laurel Sts. There's a good **internet cafe** (Quezon St; per hr P30; ⏲24hr) opposite Islands Gourmet Deli.

LOOC

Looc (law-awk) is primarily the first stop on a journey from Boracay to Romblon and Sibuyan islands further east. A few beach resorts have opened up here in recent years if you want to linger.

Activities

Looc Bay Marine Refuge & Sanctuary SNORKELLING
(admission P100) Looc's main attraction is this 48-hectare coral reef protected area, 10 minutes by bangka from the town pier. The boat ride is included in the price of admission for groups of four or more; for smaller groups the boat is P300. Drop by the **KOICA office** (☎0918 500 9136) at the Looc Fish Port, a short walk from town, to make arrangements and rent snorkelling equipment (P50). Boats take you to the sanctuary's moored bamboo raft, from where you can snorkel amid giant clams. Don't touch the clams – they bite!

Buenavista Marine Sanctuary SNORKELLING
About 7km north of Looc (P100 by tricycle) is another marine sanctuary. It's only 2 hectares, but is located around an islet connected to the mainland by a bridge.

Festivals & Events

Fiesta Sa Dagat CULTURAL
Held in late April, the week-long Fiesta Sa Dagat (Festival of the Sea) includes a boat parade, boat races and a fishing competition.

Talabukon Festival CULTURAL
The Fiesta Sa Dagat coincides with the Talabukon Festival (the town fiesta), which celebrates the legend of the giant who defended the area from pirates by strangling them, giving the town its name Looc (literally, 'to strangle').

Sleeping & Eating

There are a few places to eat in town – try **Ashley's** (mains P75-130; ⏲7am-7pm), with a big picture menu of Filipino food and breakfasts (avoid the pizzas, however).

By the Sea Resort BEACH RESORT $$
(www.bythesearesort-tablas-island.com; r per person P3600; ❄@📶🏊) On top of stylish hillside cottages crawling up a hill above a private white-sand beach, this Italian-owned resort just south of Looc throws in heaps of extras like free transfers from Caticlan or Tugdan airport. Rates also include three meals a day, plus some drinks.

Tablas Fun Center BEACH RESORT $$
(☎0949 737 5543; www.tablasfun.com; r with fan/air-con P900/1300; ❄) The resort was just about to open when we passed through. Most of the sports are of the motorised variety (think swamp buggies and wave runners) but more fuel-efficient sports like sailing are on the menu, with the promise of kitesurfing to come. With a fleet of speedboats, it has big plans to woo Boracay visitors.

Angelique Inn GUESTHOUSE $
(☎0927 315 3638; r with fan/air-con P300/600; ❄) Overlooking the public stage on the plaza is

this cheerful venture run by the Gelindon family. The marble-floored rooms are bright and spacious, but bathrooms are shared. Be prepared to meet the whole clan.

Information

The Looc tourist office is at the southern corner of the town plaza, and there are a few internet cafes in town. For information, ask around for the Fiel sisters; you may be able to find one of them in the shop bearing the sign 'New Era', off the main plaza. One of them is a former mayor of Looc.

ALCANTARA

Alcantara, only 9km from Looc on the east coast of Tablas, is a small town with an OK beach. The jeepney from Looc to San Agustin passes through, making this an alternative overnight stop for tourists heading up to San Agustin.

Sleeping

Aglicay Beach Resort BEACH RESORT $$
(☎0915 425 6898; www.aglicaybeachresort.com; s/d from P900/1100; ❄) It's 4km from the highway along a dicey road, but guests are rewarded with a wide beach, pleasant holiday house–style bungalows and a palpable sense of seclusion – this is where you'd want to hole up if you're on the lam from the feds or trying to finish your novel. There's a small bar and restaurant, and staff can set you up with snorkelling equipment. Singles await by the highway to take you to the resort (P50, 10 minutes).

SAN AGUSTIN

San Agustin is a picturesque stop on the way to or from the island of Romblon. Although you would never plan on staying the night, you won't have a choice if you miss the last ferry at 1pm. If you get stuck here, there are several streetside barbecues and food stalls around the market.

Accommodation options in San Agustin are clustered on a street running perpendicular to the main road, a one-minute walk from the pier. None have permanent phone numbers; just walk in and choose.

Sleeping

Paksi Cove Resort BEACH RESORT $
(☎0946 145 6356; www.paksicoveresort.com; cottages P750-1000) Paksi has just a handful of cottages set on a secluded cove with its own beach in Calatrava, about 20 minutes by single (P30) from San Agustin. With a lush jungle backdrop, it's a great place to get away from it all.

Kamilla Lodge GUESTHOUSE $
(r without/with bathroom from P200/400) ❄) This cosy, friendly place in a striking modernist structure is the pick of the bunch.

Felnor Lodge & Restaurant GUESTHOUSE $
(s/d with shared bathroom from P200/300; ❄) Cheerful rooms – ask for one with a sea view. No restaurant, contrary to what the name implies.

August Inn GUESTHOUSE $
(s/d without bathroom P200/400, tr with bathroom P800; ❄) A few small tiled rooms on the 2nd floor of a bright pink building. The shared bathroom has a scoop shower.

Romblon Island

☎042 / POP 37,544

Tricky to reach and blessed with a charming town and an alternately rugged and sandy coastline, Romblon is an ideal destination for those with patience, time and a taste for beautiful remote places. Circumnavigating the island is practically a must – you'll ford streams and pass friendly villages, coconut-covered mountains, rice-terraced valleys, several lighthouses and oodles of roadside marble workshops. The ring road is rough in patches but is mostly sealed and generally rideable.

Sights & Activities

Beautiful historic **Romblon town**, surrounded by lush green hills, is a delight to approach by sea, and offers an even greater pleasure to those with time to wander its charming streets. The capital of the province of the same name boasts some 17th-century forts, fountains, churches, bridges and cemeteries that you can try to track down. For those without access to cable, a night walk through the **market** east of the plaza is better than TV.

Fort San Andres VIEWPOINT
For the best views in town, walk up the stairs to the ruins of this crumbling 17th-century fort overlooking the centre of town.

Island Hopping BOAT TOURS
Weather permitting, bangkas can be hired for day trips to the 'Tres Marias' – the nearby islands of **Lugbung**, **Alad** and **Cobrador**. Cobrador has OK snorkelling, and Lugbung

MARBLE ISLAND

Romblon Island is famous domestically for its grey marble, which graces the floors of churches and resorts all over the country, but especially in the Romblon area and in nearby Boracay. Ride around the island and you'll encounter dozens of quarries and workshops where tomorrow's Michelangelos can be seen carving Buddhas, life-sized lions, reclining nudes and commemorative portraits. The action is heaviest about 5km east of Romblon town near Lamao. Unfortunately, marble isn't the most practical souvenir to carry around, but it's remarkably cheap. A small mortar-and-pestle set or a penis ashtray costs a not-so-stiff P100 at the souvenir shops in the shopping centre on the main drag near the port in Romblon town.

has a good beach. Bring your own food. Figure on P500 for a one-way journey and P1000 to P2000 to make a day of it. The more adventurous can make the often rough crossing to the remote islands of **Banton**, **Sibale** and **Simara**. There is said to be great diving out here for expert divers with their own equipment. Completely isolated white-sand beaches, Spanish-era forts and – on Baton Island – ancient burial caves are the other attractions. It's at least P6000 to hire a bangka to these islands, or take the twice-weekly passenger bangka from Romblon to Banton Island (P300, 3½ hours).

Beaches BEACHES

Both **Tiambin Beach** and, a little closer to Romblon town, **Bon Bon Beach** are good for swimming and can be found by heading south on the west coast road (tricycle P100, jeepney P12). **San Pedro** also has a lovely beach, and OK reefs for snorkelling and diving.

Airsoft WAR GAMES

(☎0906 212 8143; per person per day P750) Airsoft is, apparently, the heir apparent to paintball. Carlos, a Filipino American who also runs the suave Stone Creek hotel, set it up and has a loyal cadre of local practitioners ready to line up against (or with) any tourists who want to give it a whirl. The playing fields are in the jungle a few kilometres out of town (they'll take you there).

Diving

The only dive centres on Romblon Island are the Three P Resort and Cabanbanan Beach Resort. North of Romblon Island is a **WWII Japanese wreck**, and on nearby Tablas Island the **Blue Hole** dive – the inside of an old volcano – is favoured by advanced divers.

Water Sports

Romblon's sheltered beaches and harbour are perfect to explore by paddle board. You can rent paddle boards (per half/full day P340/520) at **Anchor Bay Aqua Sports** (☎0918 247 9941; anchorbayromblon@yahoo.com), run by an Australian family 3km southwest of Romblon town centre. They also have windsurfers, a catamaran and a speedboat for waterskiing and wakeboarding. The Three P Resort also has paddle boards.

Sleeping

On smallish islands it's usually recommended to stay on beaches outside of town, but a dearth of good resorts around the island makes the town centre an attractive option. You'll also be close to the restaurants and well positioned to explore the island. Fiesta time in Romblon town runs for a week, around the second week of January; you may need to book accommodation well in advance at this time.

ROMBLON TOWN

Stone Creek House GUESTHOUSE $

(☎0906 212 8143; r with fan/air-con from P2000/3000, whole house P8500; ❄@☎) The only accommodation of any distinction in town is this stately stone townhouse that sleeps six. The design is smart and guests get the run of the common room, which has a big flat-screen TV with PlayStation. It's run by the team behind Airsoft, and they prefer to book out the whole house but may take individual bookings if you email in advance. Owner Carlos is dialled into the local travel scene.

Romblon Plaza Hotel HOTEL $

(☎507 2269; rphreservation@yahoo.com; Roxas St; r with fan/air-con from P650/1100; ❄@) This high-rise, adorned with plastic flowers and plants, is opposite the town basketball court. The rooms are big, clean and bright, and the pricier ones have excellent views, but the central location means it's noisy.

Blue Ridge Hotel HOTEL $
(0999 780 4631; Fetal Vero St; d P1000) A few minutes' walk from the town plaza, the Blue Ridge qualifies as upmarket in Romblon. The rooms are tidy and come with a few pieces of furniture tossed about haphazardly, but do not come with hot water.

D'Maeastro Inn LODGE $
(0949 930 277; d with fan/air-con P400/700;) This simple family-run wooden lodge looks over the harbour. It's on the bend in the road 300m south of Romblon Deli.

Muravian Hotel HOTEL $
(0919 970 5137; r with fan/air-con from P350/600;) Just behind the Rombon Plaza Hotel, it's simple in the extreme, but cheap.

AROUND THE ISLAND

San Pedro Beach Resort BEACH RESORT $
(0928 273 0515; minamingoa@yahoo.com; Ginablan; cottages P700) This well-managed resort refuge is set on a little white-sand beach in Ginablan, about 10km south of Romblon town. From the spotless bamboo cottages you can peer through the jungle canopy to the beach below, where there is good snorkelling at high tide. There's an affordable restaurant serving breakfast and lunch (order dinner in advance), as well as a library of discarded books to help you while away your days. From town, a tricycle to the resort costs around P150. If you're arriving from Romblon town under your own steam, you'll need good directions – signage is virtually nonexistent.

Cabanbanan Beach Resort BEACH RESORT $
(0910 283 7612, 0920 711 5451; www.romblon-isl.com; cottages P800-1000) Located on a spit of land only accessible by boat, there are several pleasant cottages here with luxurious hammocks, a restaurant and a PADI dive centre. The house reef is a fish sanctuary. Call in advance for free boat transfers from Romblon town to this paradise refuge, which does have 24-hour electricity.

Three P Holiday & Dive Resort NIPA HUTS $$
(0921 601 0252, 0939 368 9841; www.the-three-p.com; cottages P1000;) This relatively new dive operation has a few well-appointed nipa huts in a leafy compound on the beach about 6.5km southwest of Romblon town.

Buena Suerte Resort RESORT $
(507 2069; cottages P700;) This remotely situated resort seems to be closed as often as it's open, but escapists-from-all might check it out. Take the national road east out of town for 10km and look for the signposted turn-off in the small village of Tambac. You'll need all the *suerte* (luck) you can muster to brave the rough 1km track to the gate.

Eating & Drinking

The quality dining is a nice surprise – and a godsend if a typhoon has you stranded. Cheapskates are well catered for around the market and the plaza.

Romblon Deli & Coffee Shop INTERNATIONAL $$
(Mains P100-250; 6.30am-9pm) Front and centre on the waterfront near the ferry docks, this unassuming venture will surely be your first stop as you sort out what to do. Besides doubling as an information centre for all things Romblon, it has luxuriously fluffy banana pancakes, fantastic omelettes and other great breakfasts – including the notorious 'Feeling Shitty Breakfast' (two fags, a Coke and a coffee). It doesn't lose a step at lunch and dinner, producing things like beef tenderloin with blue-cheese sauce. Gin juice (P30) is another speciality (full cred for that).

Republika Bar & Restaurant INTERNATIONAL $$
(meals P150-220; 6am-9pm) A few doors down from the Romblon Deli is this excellent eatery featuring a creative and ever-changing menu. Got a craving for beef bourguignon or rib-eye steak? Perhaps sir or madam would like a genuine espresso? Take a seat outside for great people-watching.

Romblon Plaza Restaurant FILIPINO $$
(Roxas St; mains P150) The views from this bar and restaurant atop the Romblon Plaza Hotel make this the best spot for a sunset drink, although service is languid in the extreme.

Information

The post office and police office are in their usual place near the plaza, along with several **internet cafes** (per hr P20-35) with painfully slow connections. In the port area, **Bright & Bubbly** (8am-7pm) provides a laundry service.

Money

A PNB bank with an ATM is located opposite and up the street from Republika, but you should never rely on PNB, so bring cash.

ROMBLON BOAT CONNECTIONS

DESTINATION	BOAT TYPE	FARE (P)	DURATION (HR)	SCHEDULE
Batangas (via Odiongan)	RORO (Montenegro)	960	12	2pm Tue, Fri & Sun
Lucena (via San Agustin & Banton Island)	RORO (Kalayaan)	700	13	three weekly
Magdiwang (Sibuyan)	RORO (Montenegro, Kalayaan)	256	2¼	7am daily (Montenegro) plus 3 weekly (Kalayaan)
Mandaon (Masbate) via Cajidiocan	RORO (RSLI)	350	8	6am Wed
Manila	RORO (RSLI)	850	12	7pm Thu
San Agustin	Bangka, RORO (Montenegro)	100-150	1	daily 8am & 1pm (bangkas), 12.30pm (RORO)

Tourist Information

Romblon Deli & Coffee Shop (☎0929 304 0920, 0999 583 5064; dpkershaw@gmail.com) Proprietors David and Tess Kershaw hand out maps of the island (when in stock) and dispense advice. Want to do something? They'll know how to do it. They are also up on boat schedules and other minutiae that travellers rely on, and run a few tours of their own.

ℹ Getting There & Away

See the boxed text above for boat connections to and from Romblon town.

Additional bangkas make the trip from Romblon to Magdiwang on mornings when big ferries arrive from Batangas and Manila.

ℹ Getting Around

A circuit of the island by tricycle is pretty much impossible because the road is too steep in many parts. You're much better off hiring a single (with driver P700 not including petrol, without driver P300 to P500 per day). You should be OK driving solo but be careful in rainy conditions. Jeepneys go around most of the island but are irregular and thin out the further you go from Romblon town.

Sibuyan Island

☎042 / POP 35,249

Sibuyan Island is the Galapagos Islands of the region. In pristine isolation, having been cut off from all other land masses during the last ice age, the island, 60% covered by some of the densest forest found in the Philippines, is home to five unique mammal species – including the bizarre tube-nosed fruit bat. No other island of its size in the world is known to have as many unique species, and it is believed that more flora and fauna species will be discovered with further exploration. The island's natural resources are being protected and nurtured, and the area around massive Mt Guiting-Guiting (2058m) is protected. A more recent threat to Sibuyan's pristine environment has come from Manila-based nickel mining operations. Vigorous protests against potential extractions, led by the mayor of San Fernando, bore fruit in 2011 when the national government cancelled a firm's permit to explore for nickel at the foot of Mt Guiting-Guiting.

Technically there are entry points into Mt Guiting-Guiting Natural Park from the three municipalities of Magdiwang, Cajidiocan and San Fernando, but, as guides and permits are compulsory, visitors must first proceed to the Magdiwang visitors centre, where information and the necessary arrangements can be made.

ℹ Getting There & Away

Most travellers arrive on boats from Romblon town into Magdiwang's Ambulong port (2km from Magdiwang proper). Boats from Roxas, Panay, alight in San Fernando; boats from Masbate go to Cajidiocan.

LUCENA (LUZON) Kalayaan Shipping has a rickety-looking boat from Magdiwang to Lucena (P800, 17 hours, three weekly) via Romblon town, San Agustin and Banton Island.

MANDAON (MASBATE) There are bangkas from Cajidiocan to Mandaon, Masbate, on Tuesdays and Fridays at 9am (P350, four hours). The big RSLI ferry departs Wednesdays at 10am.

MANILA The RSLI ferry departs Cajidiocan for Manila at 3pm every Thursday (P920, 16 hours).

ROMBLON & TABLAS The best option to Romblon town is the daily Montenegro ferry at around 10am (P260, 2¼ hours), continuing on to San Agustin, Tablas. Additional bangkas make the trip on days when there are ferry departures from Romblon to Batangas and Manila.

ROXAS (PANAY) Bangka ferries to Roxas leave from San Fernando's Azagra port on Mondays, Wednesdays and Fridays (P300, five hours) and, on some days, from Cajidiocan. There's a 7am Thursday trip from Magdiwang to Roxas via San Fernando, returning back the way it came on Friday morning.

Getting Around

There are about three jeepneys daily between Magdiwang and Cajidiocan (P70, 1½ hours), and between Magdiwang and San Fernando (P100, two hours). Some of these are timed to meet ferries at the pier in Magdiwang. San Fernando and Cajidiocan are also linked by jeepneys (P55, one hour, three daily). Most trips are morning trips.

Most of Sibuyan's ring road is unpaved, so not perfect for motorbike travel, but you can still hire singles and tricycles to take you between the three main towns. Resorts hire out motorbikes (P600 per day) and mountain bikes.

MAGDIWANG

The entry point for most visitors and gateway to Mt Guiting-Guiting Natural Park, Magdiwang is a friendly, no-frills town lined with picture-perfect little houses on stilts decorated with flowering pot plants.

Sights

Cataja Falls WATERFALL

This three-tiered waterfall cascading into a refreshing swimming hole makes for a great half-day excursion. Walk (or ride) east out of town past the basketball court (leaving it on your right) and continue about 1km to a fork in the road. Take the right fork, then another quick right up a hill, and continue for another 2km or so to the first sign of civilisation – a cluster of nipa huts along the road. Leave your bike here if you have one, and ask around for a guide to take you through farms and forest to Cataja Falls (P100, 30 minutes).

Lambingan Falls WATERFALL

About 12km from Magdiwang (4km past the turn-off to Mt Guiting-Guiting Natural Park Visitors Centre) is this beautiful waterfall and swimming hole. Tricycles can take you here (P130, 25 minutes).

Sleeping & Eating

TOP CHOICE **Sanctuary Garden** MOUNTAIN RESORT $

(☎0920 217 4127; www.sanctuarygardenresort.com; camping/dm P50/200, r P500-1500; ❄) While it won't satisfy those who just have to be on the water, it will satisfy anyone who's a fan of comfort and style. There's a mix of elegant private cottages on stilts (some with balconies and mountain views) and budget rooms in a fragrant pinewood house. It's on a babbling brook near Mt Guiting-Guiting's main trailhead, and thus perfect for early-rising climbers. The owner, Edgar, can give you the skinny on the climb and on various DIY excursions.

Europhil Beach House BEACH RESORT $

(☎0939 768 4023; cottages P300-500) If you want to be on the water, this place has two cottages right on the beach. Affable host Wolfgang cooks some of the best food on the island, but get here early if you want to eat. It's about 1km south of town on the road to the pier.

Corran Guesthouse GUESTHOUSE $

(☎0920 530 8533; MH del Pilar St; s/d from P250/400; ❄) Still known by its old name, Vicky's, this homey guesthouse has timber-floored rooms on the 2nd floor with an immaculate shared bathroom. Vicky runs a catering business and cooks wonderful Filipino and Western meals, and is a fount of helpful travel information. It's opposite the school in town.

Bagumbahay Beach Resort BEACH RESORT $

(☎0918 234 7090; r with fan/air-con from P500/800; ❄) This is a quiet 15-room place with almost nonexistent service on a brown-sand beach in town. Meals are by request.

Rancher's GUESTHOUSE $

(☎0908 786 4006; José Rizal St; s P250, d with fan/air-con from P500/750; ❄) They put a little effort into style at this lodging house in the middle of town, but don't let the boutiquey sign fool you: it's still pretty basic.

MT GUITING-GUITING NATURAL PARK

This 15,000-plus-hectare natural park is one of the Philippines' natural treasures. A biologist's wonderland, the island has been cited as one of the centres of both plant and animal diversity in Asia and the Pacific. It's home to an estimated 700 plant species, some of which are only found on the island, 130 bird species and a long list of rare and endangered mammals and reptiles.

The climb up Mt Guiting-Guiting is one of the best in the Philippines. You do not need technical expertise, but you do need a guide. The most popular route, out of Magdiwang, brings you up to camp three on day one. You spend the night, then reach the summit before noon the next day. Then sleep another night at camp three, or try to make it all the way back to Magdiwang.

You need a permit (P200) to climb the mountain. First drop by the **Municipal Tourism Office** (0908 786 4006) in Magdiwang town centre to register and be briefed on the climb. It can help you get to the **Protected Areas Office** (7am-5pm), about 8km east of Magdiwang (P100 by tricycle from Magdiwang). Motorbikers be warned: the office is about 3km off the highway down a rutted, red-mud road; wipe-outs are almost a given if it's wet.

At the Protected Areas Office, pay your permit fee and secure a guide (per day P500) and porters (optional) – try to take care of this the day before you set out. The office has some ratty old tents for hire. For newer equipment try Sanctuary Garden. Mountaineering attire is recommended for assaults on the summit (including cold-weather gear and good shoes).

CAJIDIOCAN & AROUND

Cajidiocan (cah-ee-*d'yo*-can) is an alternative base to Magdiwang for trips into Mt Guiting-Guiting Natural Park. However, visitors should check in at Magdiwang first.

Around **Lakting Falls** you'll find pretty rainforest and cave pools you can swim in. They are a 20-minute walk from the main road. Ask Reiner (of Reiner's Place) or a local for directions. Reiner can also help you get a guide for longer walks, such as the four-hour trek along the Cambajao River.

On the town's main street you'll find the aptly named **Marble House** (0906 135 5758; s P250-800, d P500-1000;) – it has no signposting but you can't miss it. The rooms are well furnished and very cosy, with small LCD TVs. The shared bathroom is large and, of course, marble.

On the main road north of Marble House, **Mariposa** (meals P40-150) serves European comfort food in an attractive space with a grand wooden bar and satellite TV for sports.

About 3km towards San Fernando (P40 by tricycle), **Reiner's Place** (0906 278 5457; d incl breakfast P600; 7am-9pm) has wonderful marble-tiled rooms on the water in an area known as 'the German Village'; it's made up of only German and German-Filipino families.

SAN FERNANDO

This town, near the banks of the mighty Cantingas River, is one of the three entry points onto the island. Although it's a quiet town, caught almost off guard by visitors, the accommodation here is scenic and relaxed.

For a real getaway, private bangkas can take you to **Cresta de Gallo** (P1000, 40 minutes), a small white-coral sand island off the southern tip of Sibuyan. You can skip around the island in about half an hour and see little but your own footsteps. There is some OK snorkelling, but you will have to bring your own gear.

On the coastal side of town, **Sea Breeze Inn** (0921 211 6814; s/d from P250/500) is a family-run affair; bamboo huts with verandas face out to sea. There is a common kitchen, and an attached cafe.

The market area has three inexpensive eateries with irregular opening hours.

PANAY

Hedonists head for Panay's most sought-after destination: the long and luscious white-sand beach at Boracay. It's all that many visitors to the region, or for that matter the country, ever see. Despite offering the attractions of the Visayas in a microcosm, the rest of Panay keeps a low tourism profile, which makes its other parts appealingly low-key. These include tropical Guimaras Island – just a short commute from the lively regional capital of Iloilo City – and stunning World Heritage listed Spanish churches. A rugged coastline runs south and west, and a more domesticated one to the north and east. Inland, remote and little-explored mountains and waterfalls beckon active hikers. Adventure sports – particularly mountain biking, trekking, kayaking and rock climbing – can be arranged out of Iloilo.

The amazing Ati-Atihan Festival, held in Kalibo in January, is the Philippines' most famous fiesta. Much of Panay's festive tradition can be traced back to its indigenous tribal groups, namely the Ati and Ata, and communities of both groups remain on the mainland.

Getting There & Away

The main airports are in Iloilo in the south, and Caticlan (for Boracay) and Kalibo in the north. Kalibo has a few international connections and is a budget alternative for people heading to Boracay.

On the seas, car ferries to Caticlan from Roxas, Mindoro, and fastcraft to Iloilo from Bacolod, Negros, are the most popular boat connections. But you can reach a host of additional islands

Panay

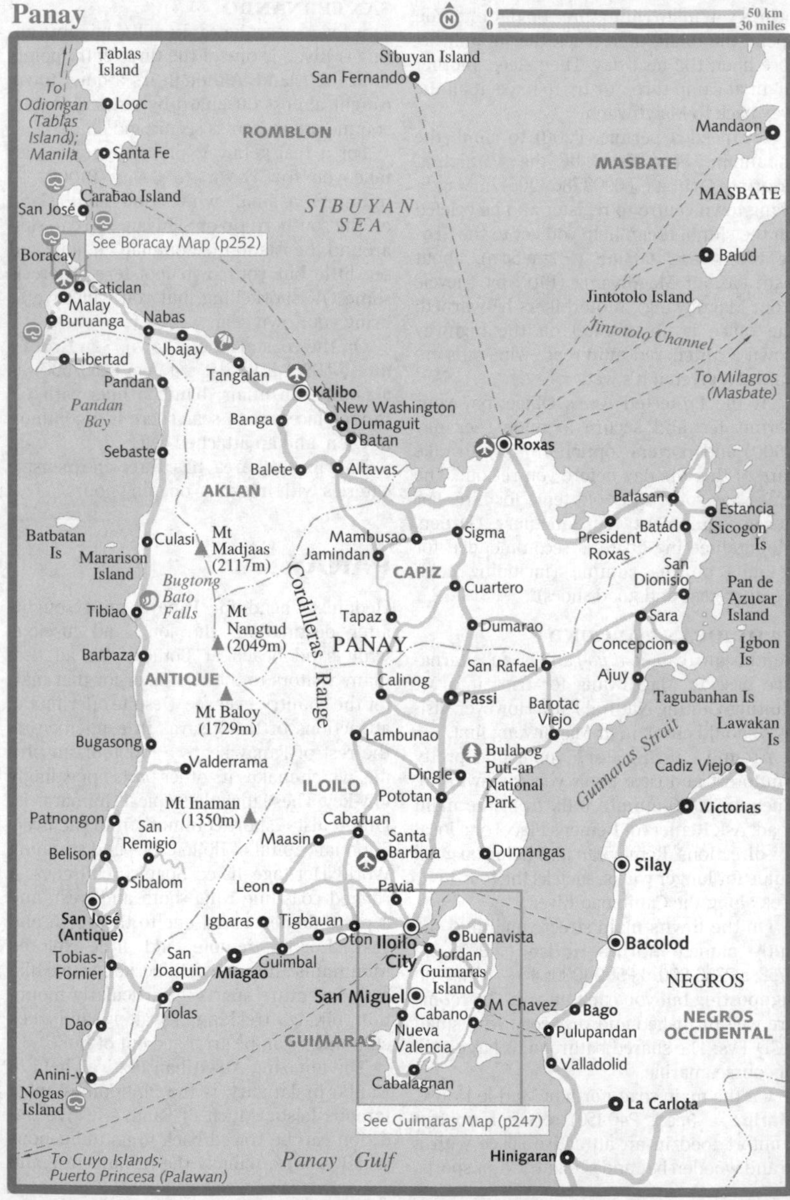

from the main ports of Caticlan, Kalibo, Roxas, Iloilo and Dumangas.

Iloilo

033 / POP 418,710

As regional centres go Iloilo (ee-lo-ee-lo) City is not too daunting. It's large enough to provide all the big-city comforts but small enough to maintain a down-to-earth provincial vibe, and the sizeable student population keeps the nightlife vibrant. For those planning to explore Panay, or combine a trip to Boracay with nearby Guimaras, Iloilo is an ideal base. 'Downtown' Iloilo is surrounded by three old suburbs: Molo, Lapaz (la-pass) and low-lying Jaro.

History

Iloilo, the last capital of the Spanish empire in Asia, was surrendered to the Filipino Revolutionary Army in 1898 after Manila had already fallen to invading American forces. The seat of government was temporarily transferred here, as the city's deep-water port had already made it an important centre of trade and commerce with Europe. Only a week later a 3000-strong American force shelled and took the city, thus marking the official beginning of the war of independence against the USA.

Sights

Museo Iloilo MUSEUM

(Bonifacio Dr; admission P25; 8-11am & 2-5pm Mon-Sat) Panay's main museum has a worthwhile display on the indigenous Ati (Negrito) people and a collection of old *pinya* (pineapple fibre) weavings, for which the area is famous. It also has treasure plucked from sunken ships, and jewellery unearthed from Spanish burial sites.

Lapaz & Jaro HISTORIC DISTRICTS

North of Iloilo City proper, over the Forbes Bridge (Bonifacio Dr), are the suburbs of Lapaz and Jaro. Both are home to a number of ancestral houses and impressive churches. Well worth a visit is Jaro's **Belfry Plaza**, dominated by the **Jaro Belfry**, a lonely old figure standing high and handsome on the edge of the square. Across the road is the huge **Jaro Metropolitan Cathedral**, the seat of the Catholic diocese in the western Visayas. An annual feast and fiesta is held here in honour of the church's patron saint, Señora de la Candelaria.

You can try asking permission to enter some of the ancestral houses, such as the opulent **Nelly Gardens Mansion** (Bonifacio Dr). The regional tourist office hands out a (mediocre) map with some of these houses marked. Plot your own walking tour or hire a pedicab to take you around. To get here, flag down a 'Jaro' jeepney from downtown or from the Forbes Bridge.

Molo HISTORIC DISTRICT

About 1km west of the centre is the area known as Molo. Once a separate town, it's now more or less part of Iloilo proper, but it retains its independence with a large, central plaza dominated by lovely **St Anne's Church**.

Activities

Iloilo has a welcoming community of adventurers ready and willing to take you scuba diving, rock climbing, mountaineering, mountain biking, kayaking and caving. Some of the most popular activities are rock climbing and caving in Bulabog Puti-An National Park, and scuba diving and mountain biking around Guimaras. For other activities, contact the folks at Panay Adventures who can arrange packages, put you in touch with guides or simply offer advice to independent adventurers.

Tours

Panay Adventures ADVENTURE TOURS

(321 4329, 0917 717 1348; panay_adventures@yahoo.com.ph) Anthropologist Daisy and partner Reuel arrange highly recommended tours around Guimaras and Panay for all tastes and budgets. Daisy is an anthropologist by training and one of the most popular excursions she offers is the Tribal Tour (per person P2500), which involves a visit to the various ethnolinguistic groups around Panay. For the more energetic, there are mountain-bike trips on Guimaras, and climbing and caving in Bulabog Puti-An National Park. Van and car hire are available.

Festivals & Events

Several outer suburbs and towns around Iloilo City proper have annual carabao (water buffalo) races. The most colourful is held on 4 May in Pavia, 5km north of Iloilo.

Dinagyang Festival CULTURAL

Celebrating the Santo Niño with outrageous costumes and dances, this three-day mardi

Iloilo City

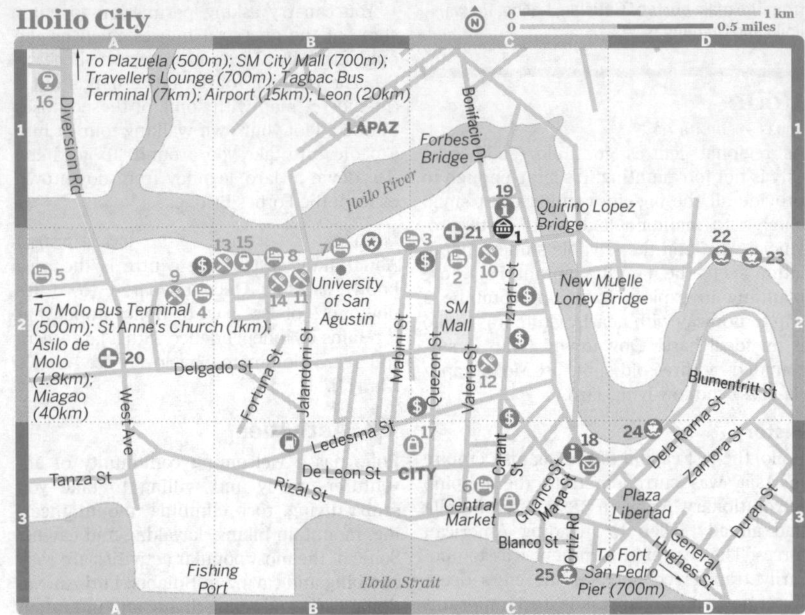

gras-style party takes place in the fourth week of January.

Paraw Regatta REGATTA

A race from Iloilo over to Guimaras in traditional sailing outriggers called *paraw*. Dating to the 16th century, this is a high-speed version of the trip supposedly taken by Panay's ancient Malay settlers on their journey to the island from Borneo. It's held in late February or early March depending on the weather.

Sleeping

There's a surfeit of good-value accommodation in Iloilo; much of it is conveniently located along the river on General Luna St, not far from the main eating and entertainment complex, Smallville.

TOP CHOICE **Smallville 21** HOTEL $$

(501 6821, 0917 301 0021; smallville21hotel@yahoo.com; Smallville complex; d P1500-3000) Stunning value, the new Smallville 21 has a super-stylish design, all the mod cons you could ask for and fluffy beds that invite entry via flying leap. Not much separates it from pricier Smallville neighbour Iloilo Business Hotel. If the festive location doesn't bother you, this is an easy top choice.

Highway 21 Hotel HOTEL $

(335 1839, 0917 722 4321; General Luna St; s/d from P750/875) With its lovely light-filled corridors, comfortable rooms and professional staff, this place is a steal. You can even store baggage if you want to spend a few nights in Guimaras or further afield. Rooms in the 'new wing' are bigger and flashier than those in the 'annex' and well worth the couple hundred extra pesos. Wi-fi costs P100 per day.

Pensionne del Carmen PENSION HOUSE $

(0926 578 2057; 24-26 General Luna St; s/d from P500/550, riverfront tr P700) It's essentially a homestay, and a brilliant one at that, quiet and right on the river and run by the nicest family you'll ever meet. It could even be too quiet – stay elsewhere if your game plan involves late-night shenanigans.

Iloilo Business Hotel HOTEL $$

(320 7972; www.iloilobusinesshotel.com; Smallville complex; r incl breakfast from P2800) Expert use of wood panelling in the well-appointed rooms gives this high-rise hotel some contemporary flair. You get a big buffet breakfast and a nice range of amenities for the price, plus a prime Smallville location.

Iloilo City

Sights
1 Museo Iloilo.....C2

Sleeping
2 Eros Travellers Pensionne.....C2
3 Family Pension House.....C2
4 Highway 21 Hotel.....A2
5 Hotel del Rio.....A2
Iloilo Business Hotel.....(see 16)
6 Iloilo Grand Hotel.....C3
7 Pensionne del Carmen.....B2
8 Riverside Inn.....B2
Smallville 21.....(see 16)

Eating
9 Al Dente.....A2
10 Atrium Shopping Mall.....C2
11 Bluejay Coffee & Delicatessen.....B2
12 Butot Balat.....C2
13 Coffee Break.....B2
Freska.....(see 16)
Robinson's Mall.....(see 17)
14 Vege Burger.....B2

Drinking
15 Mellow Mangrove.....B2
16 Smallville Complex.....A1

Entertainment
Aura.....(see 16)
Flow.....(see 16)
MO2 Ice.....(see 16)

Shopping
17 Robinson's Mall.....C3

Information
18 Bureau of Immigration.....C3
19 Department of Tourism.....C1
20 Iloilo Doctors' Hospital.....A2
21 St Paul's Hospital.....C2

Transport
22 Milagrosa Shipping.....D2
23 Montenegro Lines.....D2
24 Muelle Pier (Boats to Bacolod).....D3
25 Ortiz Boat Station (Boats to Guimaras).....C3

Hotel del Rio HOTEL $$
(☎335 1171; www.hoteldelrio.com.ph; MH del Pilar St; old/new r incl buffet breakfast from P2800/3400;) Another great choice at the upper-midrange, stay here if you want the amenities of a convention-style hotel in a more secluded location. The renovated top-whack rooms are as sleek as anything in town. Older rooms lack style but some come with partial river views and huge terraces.

Iloilo Grand Hotel HOTEL $
(☎335 1801; www.iloilograndhotel.com; Iznart St; s/d from P555/888;) The best of several faded downtown relics, the 110-room Grand brings to the table large rooms with desks and clean beds, but little else. Singles are smoky but good value. Ask for the promo rates and request a quiet room at the back. Wi-fi costs extra.

Family Pension House PENSION HOUSE $
(☎335 0070; familypension@yahoo.com; General Luna St; s P325, d without/with air-con from P450/675;) Rooms in this neoclassical building with polished floorboards are poorly maintained, and the budget rooms shoeboxes, but it's cheap and remains popular with backpackers.

Riverside Inn HOTEL $
(☎508 3488, 0922 838 0191; www.riverside-inn.net; General Luna St; s/d from P695/995;) Great-looking hotel for the price with one glaring issue: street noise. Rooms at the back are essential. Wi-fi costs extra.

Eros Travellers Pensionne PENSION HOUSE $
(☎337 1359; General Luna St; s/d from P490/570;) Motel-style cheapie with basic rooms set back from the street.

Eating & Drinking

Diversion Rd, between the river and SM City mall, is the restaurant strip – many of the best eateries are in Smallville and in the upscale Plazuela outdoor arcade near SM City. Closer to the centre, Atrium and Robinson's malls have food courts.

TOP CHOICE **Bluejay Coffee & Delicatessen** CAFE $$
(General Luna St; sandwiches/mains from P85/150; 10am-10pm;) If you don't care too much for Iloilo, you can seclude yourself in this dreamy cafe and be perfectly content. Combining the best elements of a Starbucks-style coffee shop and a German deli, it specialises in imported-meat sandwiches – think pastrami, roast beef, honey ham, smoked turkey – and carries a range of gourmet food products for demanding self-caterers. A smaller second branch on Iznart St opens at 8am and is the perfect spot for an air-conditioned, wi-fi-enabled breakfast.

Butot Balat FILIPINO $
(☎321 3752; Solis St; meals P150-250; ⏲10.30am-11pm) Sit in a thatched dining pavilion and munch on Ilonggo specialities such as *tira-un* (chicken in banana leaves) at this well-manicured garden restaurant downtown. Don't be put off by the unappetising name that translates as 'skin and bones', a reference to the use of marrow stock in Ilonggo cooking. Most dishes serve two to three.

Al Dente ITALIAN $$
(☎336 7813; 101 General Luna St; pastas P150-200; ⏲11am-11pm) One of three restaurants run by locally renowned chef Pauline Banusing, Al Dente serves up Italian classics with contemporary flair, including a mouth-watering mango cheesecake. It shares a kitchen and menu with its sister steakhouse, Pacific 101; unfortunately, it also shares a less-than-pretty communal toilet.

Freska FILIPINO $$
(☎321 3885; Smallville complex; mains P100-200; ⏲11am-3pm & 5pm-1am) Sharing a space with Maki sushi bar, this is another place managed by Pauline Banusing. The theme is traditional Ilonggo seafood, with snapper and shellfish taking pride of place on the menu.

Mellow Mangrove RESTOBAR $$
(General Luna St; mains P100-170; ⏲6pm-1am Mon-Sat) This tucked-away restaurant overlooking the river is popular with young couples on dates. Sizzling meat dishes dominate the menu and San Miguel costs P39. Wash that krappy-oke out of your hair – the music here is genuinely groovy.

Arevalo Beachside Barbecues SEAFOOD $$
(barangay Arevalo, Otom; meals P200-500) Seafood lovers should head 10km west out of town to the village of Arevalo, where several beachside seafood buffets await. If you've been to the beach barbecues in Roxas, you're in for a disappointment, but it's still a decent deal for seafood on the beach. Try **Tatoy's** for the best food (although it's on the wrong side of the road), or the popular **Breakthrough** for good atmosphere and incredibly indifferent service. Most 'Arevalo' jeepneys get you here.

Vege Burger VEGETARIAN $
(General Luna St; meals P50-75; ⏲9am-7pm; ✎) The eponymous products, made of coconut or banana blossoms, are small but cost just P25 so order a few of them. Other vego options are on the menu and there's a built-in coffee shop.

Coffee Break CAFE $
(General Luna St; ⏲24hr; 📶) Little Starbucks clone has the usual frappé and sandwich options.

☆ Entertainment

Smallville Complex CLUBS
(Diversion Rd) Iloilo's club scene isn't bad, and most of the action is here. **Flow** is king, while a host of contenders battle for its crown – namely **MO2 Ice** and **Aura**, which draws a younger crowd. Admission at all is free on weekdays and about P150 at weekends. Beer bars and live music abound in Smallville.

Shopping

Robinson's is the big downtown mall, while **SM City** beyond Smallville on Diversion Rd is where uptown mall rats hang. Both have the usual complement of movies, restaurants and other mall-like diversions.

Asilo de Molo SOUVENIRS
(☎338 0252; asilo_demolo@yahoo.com; ⏲9am-5pm Mon-Fri) Drop in here for wallets, T-shirts and wonderful embroidery woven by newly skilled women. It's on the site of a former girls' orphanage, 0.8km west of Molo Church on the way to the beach, easily reached by any 'Molo' jeepney.

Information

Internet Access

Internet cafes are all over town, including in the malls, and the going rate is around P30 per hour.

Medical Services

Iloilo Doctors' Hospital (☎337 7702; West Ave) Most modern hospital in town.

St Paul's Hospital (☎337 2741; General Luna St)

EAT YOUR WORDS

'You have to eat the local speciality!' insisted Edison N Molanida, Miagao's affable tourism officer. 'It's KBL. KBL for KBL!'

After being momentarily lost in translation, this turned out to stand for *kadyos, baboy, langka* (a tasty mix of black bean, pork and jackfruit), a dish that's a must for *kasal, bunyag* and *lutong* (weddings, christenings and funerals).

Money

ATMs are huddled in the malls and along central Iznart St.

Tourist Information

DOT (☎337 5411; deptour6@mozcom.com; Capitol Grounds, Bonifacio Dr; ⏰8am-5pm Mon-Sat)

Visas

BOI (☎509 9651; Customs House Bldg, 2nd flr, Aduana St)

 Getting There & Away

The big malls have ticketing offices open from 9am to 8pm daily.

Air

PAL, Airphil Express and Cebu Pacific each fly daily to Cebu City and Manila, with the latter two adding daily direct flights to Davao. Zest Air also flies to Manila.

Boat

Bacolod, Negros, is the main destination; if you have wheels, head to Dumangas, 20km north of Iloilo City, to catch a frequent RORO ferry to Bacolod (P80, two hours).

Tickets for long-haul operators **SuperFerry** (☎336 2110) and **Negros Navigation** (☎335 1966) can be bought at branches in SM City mall; for other companies, buy tickets at the piers.

BACOLOD From the central Muelle pier, Weesam Express, Supercat and Oceanjet tackle the rough crossing to Bacolod about 20 times per day from 6am to 5pm (P225 to P325, one hour). Only Oceanjet has open-air seating (P225). There's no need to reserve these in advance; just show up at the pier.

CEBU Trans-Asia (P710, 12 hours, six weekly) and Cokaliong (P550, 12 hours, three weekly) serve Cebu City from Iloilo.

GUIMARAS Bangka ferries to Jordan (P15, 15 to 20 minutes until dark) leave from two points: most commonly from Ortiz boat station, at the southern end of Ortiz St (take a Mandurriao jeepney); and also from a dock in front of the post office near the Muelle pier. You can take motorbikes on these boats.

MANILA From the Fort San Pedro Pier east of the Muelle Pier, Negros Navigation (two weekly) and SuperFerry (weekly) have ferries to Manila (from P1000, 20 hours).

MINDANAO Negros Navigation has a weekly boat to Cagayan de Oro (P1995, 14 hours, weekly) among other destinations in northern Mindanao. SuperFerry has a weekly boat to General Santos City (from P1300, 30 hours).

PALAWAN **Milagrosa Shipping** (☎337 3040) departs at 7pm Mondays and Thursdays, and **Montenegro Shipping Lines** (☎708 1322) departs Saturday mornings to Puerto Princesa (from P950, 25 to 30 hours) via the Cuyo Islands (12 hours). They depart from neighbouring piers on the north side of the Iloilo River (take the Lopez Bridge). The pricier Montenegro boat is faster, larger and more seaworthy.

Bus & Jeepney

The main destination outside Iloilo is Caticlan (for Boracay). If you miss the last service, get a bus to Kalibo, where you can change for Caticlan. A few speedy vans to Caticlan (P350, 4½ hours) leave in the morning from the main **Tagbac bus terminal**, about 7km north of the centre. Vans to Kalibo are more frequent.

Ordinary buses to Antique Province, including San José de Buenavista (P105, 2½ hours, every 30 minutes until 7pm), leave from the Molo bus terminal, 500m west of the centre. All go via Miagao. A few buses here head to Caticlan via Antique Province if you want a more scenic (but slower) trip.

The following destinations are served by Ceres buses from the Tagbac terminal.

Caticlan P313, six hours, every 30 minutes until 4pm

Estancia P156, three hours, frequent

Kalibo P150, 3½ hours, every 30 minutes until 6pm

Roxas P146, three hours, every 30 minutes until 6.30pm

Getting Around

To/From the Airport

The airport is 15km north of town in Santa Barbara. Airport shuttle buses (P70, 20 minutes) depart from the Travellers Lounge from 4am to 6pm. The schedule is a bit sporadic; get there at least two hours before your flight. You can also hail a Santa Barbara–bound jeepney on Diversion Rd. A taxi from Iloilo City centre will cost about P300.

Car

Hire cars, either self- or driver-driven, are readily available through your hotel. Figure on P2500 per day for an air-con van to cruise around the countryside, excluding petrol. Panay Adventures Tours rents cars and motorbikes, with optional tour guide thrown in.

Around Iloilo

BULABOG PUTI-AN NATIONAL PARK

About 33km north of Iloilo, this 854-hectare park is home to monkeys, endangered pythons, native orchids, old-growth forest, 18 species of bat and rare species of tarantulas and scorpions. There are about 35 **caves**

DON'T MISS

MIAGAO CHURCH

The relaxed coastal town of Miagao (mee-*yag*-ow), 40km west of Iloilo City, is the site of the elegant honey-coloured **Miagao Church** (officially known as Santo Tomas de Villanueva), one of four Philippine churches to have made Unesco's World Heritage list (in 1993). Built between 1787 and 1797, the church served as a fortress against Muslim raiders and over the years was damaged by fighting, fire and earthquakes; it was finally restored to its rococo glory in 1962. Its fabulous bas-relief sandstone facade depicts St Christopher strolling through a tropical forest of coconut palms and papaya trees with baby Jesus.

Old Spanish church lovers should check out the baroque specimens in the neighbouring towns of **Guimbal**, 8km east of Miagao, and, further east, **Tigbauan**, where the Stations of the Cross are represented in detailed mosaics around the inside walls.

within the park, eight of which are within 3km of the park entrance, plus several swimming holes.

Its particular attraction, though, is for climbers: some of the best **rock climbing** routes in the Philippines have been set up in the park by local enthusiasts. More advanced climbers can enjoy 50m routes and even help peg new ones if they wish. Beginners are also encouraged to come along for a lesson. **Panay Adventures Tours** (☎033-321 4329; 0917 717 1348; panay_adventures@yahoo.com.ph) in Iloilo can refer you to guides.

For simple hikes and caving, secure a guide (P150) at the ranger station near the park entrance. Technically you're supposed to secure a park permit (P100) before coming out here at the DOT office in Iloilo or at the **park office** (☎0909 500 9563) in Baratoc Viejo. However, if you arrive here on your own you should be able to pay at the ranger station.

The ranger station has two basic cottages where you can sleep (suggested donation P250). Mattresses are supplied, but not blankets. You can also pitch a tent among the mahoganies. There's plenty of drinking water, but bring your own food.

Getting There & Away

The park entrance is a rough tricycle (P150, 20 minutes) or single (P100, 10 minutes) ride from the town of Dingle. To get to Dingle, hop off the Iloilo–Kalibo bus in the town of Pototan or in the village of Tabugon, where public tricycles (P10 to P15) await by the National Hwy to shuttle passengers to Dingle. Slow and infrequent jeepneys direct to Dingle from the Tagbac terminal in Iloilo are another option.

The rock climbing area is 2km off the road linking Dingle with the National Hwy.

LA CONSOLACION

Within trekking distance of La Consolacion, a barangay of Miagao, are a wealth of natural attractions, including **Sinuhutan Cave**, **Danao Lake**, interesting rock formations and cool fern forests. Miagao's helpful **tourist office** (☎033-315 8050, ext 106; www.miagao.gov.ph) in the Municipal Hall has ideas for excursions in the area.

BUCARI

To escape the bustle and heat of the lowlands, head northwest out of Iloilo City to the mountains around the town of Leon. **Pineridge Bucari Mountain Resort** (☎0920 712 4912; r per person P1000) is a peaceful retreat nestled into these pine-covered mountains at about 500m above sea level. Accommodation is in large cottages with views of the surrounding valleys and forests. There are some hiking and mountain-bike trails in the immediate vicinity, or you can just chill. Day trippers are welcome. Call in advance if you want a meal (per person P300).

To get here from Iloilo take a jeepney to Leon from the public market in Jaro (40 minutes), then either arrange a pickup with the resort or take a tricycle, motorcycle taxi ('single') or occasional jeepney to Bucari (barangay Bacolod, 40 minutes).

Guimaras

☎033 / POP 151,238

Just a short boat ride from urban Iloilo City and Panay, Guimaras is an example of what a divide of only a few kilometres of water can mean in terms of development. But this gulf, both physical and mental, only heightens Guimaras' allure. The island's reputation rests squarely on the renown of its sweet mangoes, but it attracts visitors because of its winding scenic roads (perfect for mountain bikes and motorbikes) and beaches.

In August 2006 the island's beautiful southwest coast was afflicted by a devastating oil spill. Recovery was slow but these days you won't notice many residual effects, and swimming is safe in all resort areas.

San Miguel, the island's laid-back capital, is not much more than a wide main street. It has a ticketing office, bakeries and *sari-sari* (small neighbourhoods).

Sights

Guimaras Museum MUSEUM
(10am-5pm Mon-Sat) The small Guimaras Museum, near the Capitol Building in San Miguel, exhibits a jumble of old relics and knick-knacks. The staff are a good source of information on the island.

Navalas Church CHURCH
The time-ravaged Navalas Church is in Navalas, about 7km from Buenavista, at the northern end of the island. Built in the 17th century, the limestone church is fronted by some beautiful big trees and a squat roofless bell tower. Navalas is a P400 tricycle ride from Jordan. If you're up this way, head over to Navalas beach and check out the much-photographed summer retreat of the wealthy López family, **Roca Encantada** (Enchanted Rock), which lies just offshore.

Oro Verde Mango Plantation PLANTATION
(0905 952 8767) To see Guimaras' famous mangoes up close, try Oro Verde mango plantation, near Pina. Over 12,000 trees (some over 100 years old) are grown on the plantation, a busy place come harvest time in April and May. Contact the plantation to make an appointment to visit. It's 5km northwest of Guimaras Adventure Park.

Activities

Mountain Biking MOUNTAIN BIKING
A few resorts in Guimaras rent out OK **mountain bikes** (per day around P300), but be

Guimaras

warned that it's easy to get lost on the island. For a better bike, and trail guides, contact **Panay Adventures Tours** (☎321 4329, 0917 717 1348; panay_adventures@yahoo.com.ph; bike rental P700). Or in Guimaras find **Tommy** (☎0927 553 7575; bike rental P500), who can usually be found at his sometimes-working bar near Hoskyn Port in Jordan (ask around for Tommy's Place).

Island Hopping BOAT TOURS
The entire southern coast of Guimaras is speckled with dozens of islands, some rambling and inhabited, others not much bigger than a large sea turtle. You won't have much trouble finding a private strip of white sand here. The most accessible islands are off barangays San Antonio and Cabalagnan (Nueva Valencia) at the southern tip of Guimaras, where you can pay a boatman at the pier about P250 (one way) to take you out to the sizeable island of Panobolon or its smaller neighbours. Resorts are planned for some of these islands, but there should be plenty of beach to go around.

Off Navalas in the north of the island are the **Siete Pecados**, or the 'Islands of Seven Sins'. You can hire a bangka to explore them from one of the resorts in the area.

Guimaras Adventure Park ADVENTURE SPORTS
(☎0926 606 4538; vincecam08@yahoo.com; rappelling P150, paintball P200-300) A nearly 30-hectare plot of forested land on the way from San Miguel to Buenavista, Guimaras Adventure Park offers paintball, target shooting and rappelling. You can camp here too (tents P300). It's a P100 tricycle ride west of Jordan or northwest of San Miguel.

Festivals & Events

Manggahan Sa Guimaras Fiesta FOOD
(Mango Festival) The island's main festival honours the country's much-admired mangoes just after harvest time in April or May. A parade sees mango floats coast down the main drag in San Miguel, there's a mango-eating contest (about 13kg usually wins it) and the lawns in front of the Provincial Capitol Building in San Miguel become a giant carnival grounds.

Ang Pagtaltal Sa Guimaras RELIGIOUS
Jordan's Easter crucifixion ceremony draws good crowds to Guimaras every Good Friday. Unlike re-enactments in other parts of the country, the Guimaras presentation usually sees an amateur 'Christ' roped rather than nailed to his cross.

Sleeping

Note that you can't always turn up to the higher-end resorts on spec because access is difficult and often by boat. Try to make advance reservations and see if the resort can help you get there. There's not much in the way of true budget accommodation in Guimaras – mountain-bike guide Tommy rents a room for P400.

AROUND SAN MIGUEL

Valle Verde Mountain Spring Resort MOUNTAIN RESORT $
(☎0918 730 3446; valleverde_mtresort@yahoo.com.ph; d with fan P500-800, with air-con P1500; ❄≋) Valle Verde makes a refreshing tree-change from the usual run-of-the-mill beach resorts. Perched on one of the island's highest points, there are wonderful views of a jungle-covered valley with Lawi Bay in the distance. Turn off the highway 6km south of San Miguel and proceed 1km down a rough road (P100 by tricycle from San Miguel).

SOUTH COAST

Many of the resorts down here are near busy Alubihod Beach, but you'll find better value elsewhere.

Costa Aguada Island Resort BEACH RESORT $$
(☎0918 924 1237, in Manila 02-896 5422; www.costaaguadaislandresort.com; r with fan/air-con from P1700/2500; ≋) This resort on Inampulugan, a large island 30 minutes off the southeast coast, is another good place to feel a little like Robinson Crusoe. The 68 bamboo and nipa cottages are spacious and the open-air restaurant serves fresh seafood. Arrange a pick-up at Sabang port through the resort (P625).

Baras Beach Resort BEACH RESORT $
(☎0917 303 0282; www.baras.willig-web.com; d/q cottage from P950/1200) If WWIII is declared, this would be a fine place to hole up until it all blows over. Accessible only by boat, it has large, sturdy nipa huts perched on rocky outcrops over the water with direct views of picture-perfect sunsets. Add a bunch of good friends and a deck of cards to count out your dozy days and life starts looking pretty good. Facilities are bare bones, but who's gonna worry about air-con after the apocalypse? Pick-ups from Alubihod's Puyo wharf are P300.

La Puerta Al Paraizo BEACH RESORT $$
(☎0926 413 5970; lapuertaalparaizo@rocketmail.com; r with fan P1800, with air-con P2800-3800;) Brand-new La Puerta lays claim to mainland Guimaras' most fashionable digs to go with an enviable location on a limestone bluff over two private white beaches. We'd prefer less concrete and more verandas, but you can't argue with the fabulous views of the mushroomlike islands offshore. It's in San Roque – turn off the main highway about 6km south of Alubihod. The resort is 5km from the turn-off. A tricycle/multicab costs P500/700 from Jordan.

Kenyama Beach Resort BEACH RESORT $$
(☎394 0018, 0939 427 6433; http://kenyamaresort.jimdo.com; Guisi Beach, Dolores; cottages P700-1200, r with air-con from P2500;) The cottages are extremely basic here and not really liveable, but the air-con doubles, in the big main building with balconies overlooking the white sand of Guisi Beach, are big and comfortable. It's about 5.5km off the main highway; the turn-off is 3.5km south of Alubihod.

NORTH COAST

El Retiro BEACH RESORT $$
(☎328 0779, 0916 256 7556; www.elretirobeachpark.blogspot.com; r with fan/air-con incl breakfast from P1400/1700;) This is probably the best resort in the northern Buenavista area. It sits on a wide beach in view of the Lopez House and serves up acceptable, if not spectacular, cottages.

Kelapa Gading Beach Resort BEACH RESORT $$
(☎0917 302 7458; r with fan/air-con from P800/1500;) There are a couple of resorts on an OK beach in the township of East Valencia (Buenavista). None are particularly good value, but this one has a few affordable fan nipa huts to go with basic air-con rooms.

Information

The helpful **tourist office** (www.guimaras.gov.ph; 7.30am-5pm) at the pier in Jordan is worth a stop, even just as a refuge to keep the dozens of tricycle drivers at bay while sorting out plans. Transport rates for all island destinations are posted here. **White Star Internet** (per hr P20; 7am-9pm) is on San Miguel's main drag opposite the Provincial Capitol Compound.

Getting There & Away

There are bangkas and ferries between Iloilo and Jordan's Hoskyn Port every 15 minutes during daylight hours (P15, 15 minutes).

Bangkas run daily to the west-coast Negros town of Pulupandan (P60, 50 minutes) from the eastern Guimaras ports of Tumanda (Cabano) and M Chavez (two daily from each port).

Getting Around

At the pier in Jordan the tourist office can help you hire a tricycle or multicab to any resort. Public jeepneys link Jordan with San Miguel (P15), but aren't convenient for most resorts, which often lie several kilometres off the highway.

Mountain bikers are advised to go with a guide who can lead you to some off-road trails and single tracks.

Mountain bikers and motorbikers can find their way around the main roads reasonably enough with the crude free map handed out by the tourist office. A better map of Guimaras is on the back of EZ Map's Panay map.

Antique Province

For years this rugged province hugging Panay's west coast has been a somewhat forgotten entity, difficult to access and even more difficult to get around because of poor infrastructure and a soaring mountain range that effectively cuts it off from the rest of Panay. But as roads improve and as nearby Boracay continues to swell in popularity, Antique (an-*tee*-kay) Province's time may finally be about to arrive.

SAN JOSÉ DE BUENAVISTA

☎036 / POP 54,800

'San José Antique', as it's often called, is the provincial capital and your first port of call if you are coming over from Iloilo about 96km to the east. There's not much to draw travellers, so continue on to Tibiao if you can. If you're up for a scenic excursion, head south about 40km along the coast to Anini-y, which has sulphur hot springs and a marine sanctuary offshore around **Nogas Island**.

San José has Antique's only ATM machines and a few internet cafes on the main strip. If you need to stay a night, try **Centillon House 2000** (☎540 9403; http://centillionhouse.com; TA Fornier St; s/d incl breakfast P900/1300;) or **Adelaide Tourist and Travelers Inn** (☎540 9182; adelaideinn@gmail.com; Bantayan Rd; s/d from P700/900;). Both are slightly north of the town centre.

For eating, **Boondoc's** (mains P90-180; 11am-11pm), on a hill behind the main mall, has seafood and terrific views over the entire town.

Frequent Ceres buses go east to Iloilo (P105, 2½ hours) and to all points north.

TIBIAO

036 / POP 4000

Most of the action in Antique Province takes place in Tibiao, 75km north of San José, where the Tibiao River tempts kayakers and brooding Mt Madjaas (2117m) beckons mountaineers. You're only about 1½ hours (85km) from Caticlan here, so it has obvious potential as an adventure hotbed for travellers in the market for an excursion from Boracay.

Locals say Mt Madjaas is the most challenging climb in the Visayas. They might get some argument from Mt Kanlaon loyalists, but at least one route up this is beastly – a seven- or eight-hour grunt basically straight up. Easier routes do exist, and along the way you'll traverse old-growth forest and plenty of waterfalls. A guide is mandatory – secure one along with a permit (per day P150) from the **mayor's office** (277 8077) at the municipal hall in Culasi, the town north of Tibiao.

As the name implies, at **Tibiao Fish Spa & Katahum Tours** (0917 631 5777; http://katahum.com; fish spa P20 plus per min P2), you can let swarms of little fish nibble the bacteria off your feet here – it's the most affordable fish spa in the world, according to its founder, Flord Calawag, who helped crossbreed these fish himself using local freshwater species. But wait, there's more. Katahum Tours runs great tours to surrounding rivers, waterfalls and swimming holes, including white-water kayaking trips on the Tibiao (which maxes out at about Grade III) and tamer trips for beginners. One of the more unique tours involves going out with local fishermen at daybreak and hauling up the nets, which often contain huge tuna and Spanish mackerel.

The only accommodation is at the **University of Antique Hometel** (d with shared bathroom P600), on the quiet grounds of the local university, and it's great value. Book through Katahum Tours.

Regular buses between San José and Caticlan stop at Tibiao.

LIBERTAD

This rugged municipality, peppered with caves, mountains and coral reefs offshore, is practically in Boracay's backyard. Unfortunately, the roads leading here (from Caticlan 30km to the north, or from Pandan 21km to the east) are gruesome, so access remains difficult. It's smoother to hire a bangka.

Villa Tinigbas (0949 963 4103; www.tibas.com.au; barangay Tinigbas; r with shared bathroom P4500, with private bathroom P6500-8500;) is a new resort that is well positioned to take advantage of the numerous caving, hiking, diving and island-hopping opportunities in the area. Accommodation is in large villas that have one or two beds and floor space for up to 10 people. The owner is a conservation biologist involved in local conservation projects – ask about volunteer opportunities. He has a 24ft boat for island trips and can organise jungle walks and other adventures. It's 7km northwest of Libertad proper.

Infrequent buses serve Libertad from Caticlan (7.30am, 2pm and 4pm), San José and Kalibo. It's easier to just take a single from Caticlan (P300, 1¼ hours). Or disembark from the San José–Caticlan bus in Pandan and take a bus, jeepney, single or tricycle from there (about 45 minutes).

Caticlan

036

Caticlan is little more than a departure port for Boracay. Buses arriving here carry passengers straight to the wharf, and guides lead the throngs through the terminal and onto outrigger boats. If you get here after 10pm, you may have to charter a private boat to get to Boracay (difficult after 11pm), or sleep at one of the basic pension houses in town.

Getting There & Away

Air

Caticlan's small airport, about 500m from the port, services the ever-popular flights from Manila and Cebu.

Airphil Express, Cebu Pacific, **Seair** (D'Mall, Boracay) and **Zest Air** (D'Mall, Boracay) have frequent flights from Manila to Caticlan until 4.30pm or so, and Cebu Pacific (two daily) and Airphil Express (daily) also ply the Cebu to Caticlan route. Planes cannot land in Caticlan after dark so delays past 6.30pm result in planes being rerouted to Kalibo.

From Caticlan airport to Caticlan pier is a five-minute walk or a one-minute tricycle ride (P50).

Boat

For the Caticlan–Boracay boat service, see p264.

BOATS FROM CATICLAN

DESTINATION	BOAT TYPE	FARE (P)	DURATION (HR)	SCHEDULE
Carabao Island (Lanas)	Bangka	70	1	around 9am daily
Carabao Island (San José)	Bangka	70	45min	around 9am daily
Roxas (Mindoro)	RORO (Montenegro, Starlite)	400	4	daily (4am, 10am, 2pm, 6pm & 10pm)
Manila	RORO (RSLI)	900	17	noon Sun
Tablas Island (Looc)	Big bangka & RORO	300	2½	Two daily, mornings
Tablas Island (Odiongan)	RORO (RSLI)	300	3	noon Sun

Keep an eye out for the possible opening of a Caticlan–Bulalacao–Coron (Palawan) RORO route once the new ferry terminal in Bulalacao, Mindoro, is ready.

See the boxed text above for other destinations served by boat from Caticlan:

Montenegro Shipping Lines (☎288 7373; Caticlan Pier)

Romblon Shipping Lines (RSL; ☎288 3202, 0930 296 1837; www.romblonshippinglines.com; Caticlan Pier & Casa Pilar Resort, Boracay)

Starlite (☎288 7495; Caticlan Pier)

Bus & Jeepney

As soon as you exit the port at Caticlan, a throng of bus, van and jeepney drivers will converge upon you, yelling out destinations and signalling for you to follow.

ILOILO Ceres has hourly air-con buses to Iloilo, the last one departing at 4pm (P313, six hours). Speedier air-con vans (P350) usually depart in the morning only.

KALIBO Most Iloilo-bound buses go via Kalibo (P100, two hours), and there are frequent vans to Kalibo centre (P100, 1½ hours) and direct to Kalibo airport. A few jeepneys make this trip as well (P75, 2¼ hours). Chartering a van to Kalibo costs P1200 to P1500.

SAN JOSÉ (ANTIQUE) Ordinary Ceres buses depart roughly every two hours (P250, 3½ hours).

Boracay

☎036 / POP 12,000

With a postcard-perfect, 4km-long white beach and the country's best island nightlife, it's not hard to figure out why Boracay is the Philippines' top tourist draw. Overdevelopment has made some old-timers long for the halcyon days of no electricity, but the debate about whether it's better now or was better then won't worry you too much when you're digging your feet into the sand on White Beach and taking in the Philippines' most famous sunset. Parasails, seabirds, Frisbees and *paraw* (small bangka sailboats) cut across the technicolour horizon, while palm trees whisper in the breeze and reggae wafts through the air. Oh yeah, and you're in a beachfront bar that's generously serving you two-for-one cocktails. Yes, even 'developed' Boracay remains a master mixologist of that mellow island vibe.

Sights

White Beach BEACH

Glorious, powdered-sugary soft White Beach is the centre of the action in Boracay and the only sight most visitors see. Three out-of-service 'boat stations' orient visitors along its length. Until recently, these stations were where the bangkas from Caticlan arrived. Nowadays everyone arrives at a the purpose-built Cagban pier on the island's southern tip. People still complain about this arrangement, but White Beach is a better place because of it – less noise, less water pollution and fewer bangkas marring the sunset.

The complexion of White Beach changes as you stroll its length. The area south of Boat Station 3, known as Angol, most resembles the less-developed 'old Boracay' and contains most of the budget accommodation.

Boracay

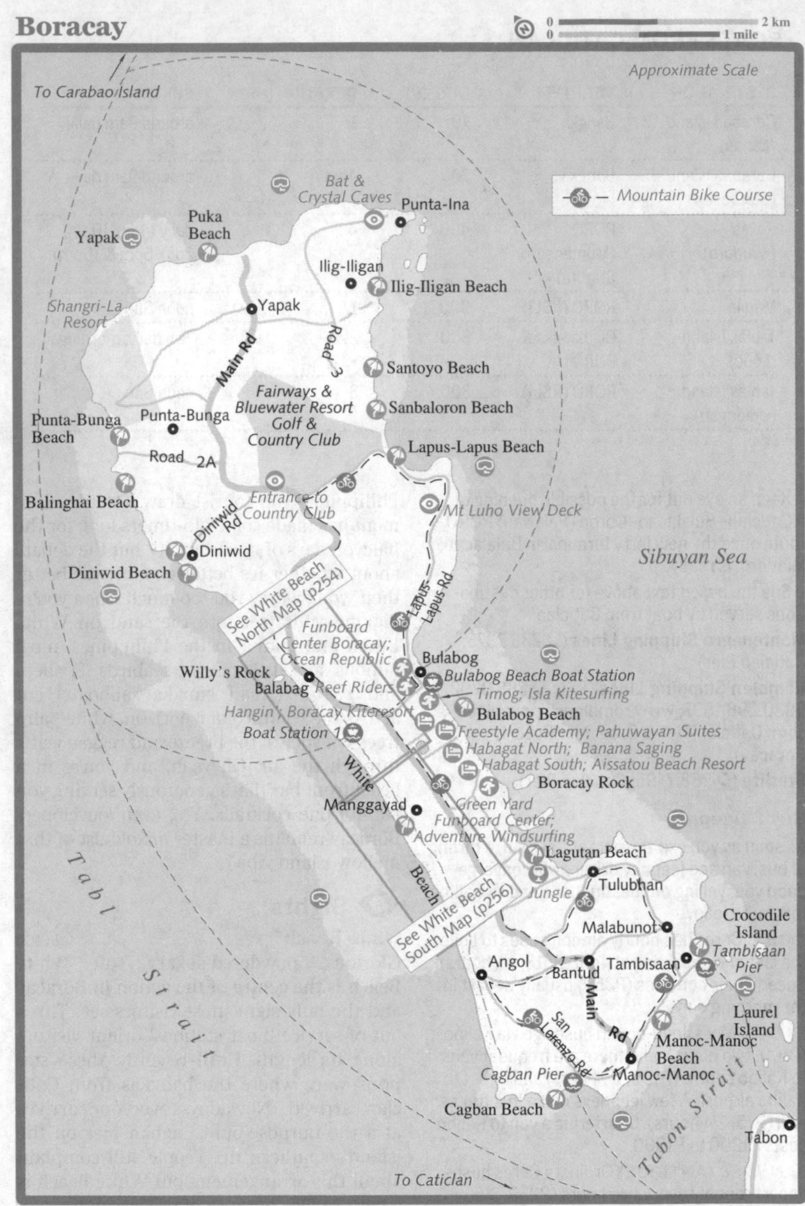

The stretch between Station 1 and Station 3 is busy and commercial. Most top-end accommodation is on an incredible stretch of beach north of Boat Station 1.

The beach is dominated by a sandy pedestrian highway – the White Beach path – where motorised vehicles are banned and it's almost compulsory to go barefoot. Vendors are thick along the path and you will quickly tire of being asked if you want sunglasses or a boat ride. Avoid this annoyance by walking along the beach instead.

Other Beaches BEACHES

Believe it or not, Boracay has other beaches that are almost as pretty as White Beach, if not quite so interminable. A scenic walk around the point from the north end of White Beach brings you to lovely, secluded-feeling **Diniwid Beach** (Map p252). On the north tip of the island, pretty **Puka Beach** (Map p252) is popular with buggy-riding Asian package tourists – walk to the extremes to find your own patch of sand. *Puka* are the tiny shells of the cone snail that make most of the necklaces, anklets and bracelets you'll see all over Boracay. A few simple eateries on Puka Beach keep the masses fed and hydrated. Other northern beaches are well off the package-tourist radar and you'll have them practically to yourself. Try to find hard-to-reach **Ilig-Iligan Beach** (Map p252), which looks onto a couple of scenic limestone islets that are swimming and snorkelling distance from the shore.

Mt Luho View Deck VIEWPOINT

(Map p252; Lapus-Lapus Rd; admission P60) Looming high above the east coast, this 'mountain' has stunning views across the island, though the steps up to it were apparently designed for nimble, long-legged giants. The cross-country road linking it with

GROWING PAINS

Just 7km long and only 1km wide at its midriff, Boracay is a speck in the sea compared with islands like Bali and Phuket, with which it's often compared. A recent maelstrom of hype – *Travel & Leisure* readers voted Boracay the No 4 island in the world in 2011 – has led to an explosion in the island's popularity among Westerners and Russians.

Meanwhile, Asian package tourists continue to descend en masse, driven by new wealth in China and the launch of direct flights to Kalibo from Taiwan and north Asia. Visitor arrivals are dominated by Taiwan, Korea and, to a lesser extent, China (the US is a distant fourth, followed by Russia and Australia). This is changing the character of the island, as more resorts cater exclusively to the Asian package tourist.

All of this raises the obvious question: is Boracay in danger of being loved to death? The obvious answer is yes. With capacity on White Beach just about maxed out, developers have set their sights on the relatively unspoiled rest of the island. A giant new Shangri-La resort occupies the once-remote northwestern tip of the island, while hulking new developments hog space along the east coast. Only the northeastern tip remains relatively untouched.

Boracay was struggling to avoid environmental catastrophe even before it suddenly became an international celebrity. The sewage system can't keep up with output and much of it ends up in surrounding waters. In the hottest months (March to May) proliferating green algae mars the shallow waters of White Beach. Waste management is a massive problem. Brownouts are frequent and environmental regulations are poorly enforced.

What does all of this mean for humble tourists who just want to get on with drinking worry-free *weng-weng* cocktails? By all means enjoy that *weng-weng*, but here are a few things you can do to lessen your impact.

» Spread the wealth. We're not saying don't visit Boracay, but build other destinations into your itinerary that are perhaps less fragile and more in need of tourist dollars.

» Steer clear of the large, all-inclusive resorts around the island. The rest of the Philippines is filled with places where you can find privacy and isolation without giving developers incentive to raze Boracay's last untouched corners.

» Reuse water bottles and throw your trash away (duh).

» Walk or utilise pedicabs along the White Beach path rather than taking noisy, smoke-belching tricycles. If you need to take a tricycle, take a public one (P8) rather than a private one (from P50).

» Don't smoke cigarettes on White Beach (it's against the law).

» Don't take home sand from White Beach as a souvenir.

The Boracay Yuppies, a group that focuses on green issues, has more tips. Look for them on Facebook.

White Beach North

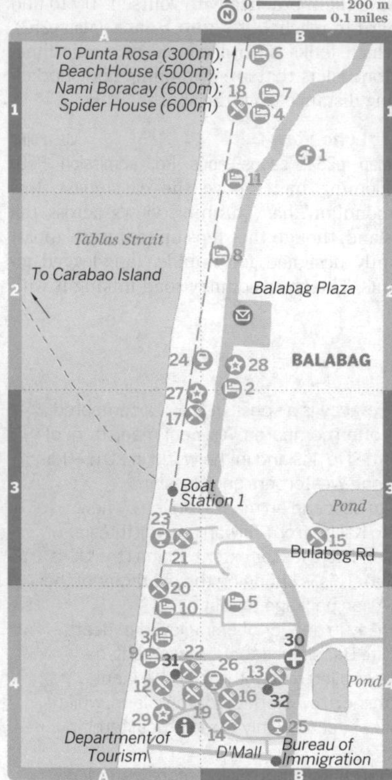

the main road is lush, green and forested; quite a contrast to the coast.

Activities

On Boracay you can try your hand at a stupendous array of sporting pursuits, including *paraw* rides, diving, kitesurfing, skimboarding, wakeboarding and parasailing. There's fishing too, but don't expect to catch much. Daily games of football, volleyball and ultimate Frisbee kick off in the late afternoon on White Beach. Yoga is offered in a few places, including Mandala Spa and 9am classes at True Food Indian restaurant at Station 2. If Boracay doesn't have your activity of choice, consider heading down to Tibiao in Antique Province, or take a bangka over to Romblon.

Sailing

Sunset *paraw* trips are a quintessential Boracay experience. The boats zip right along,

White Beach North

Activities, Courses & Tours

1 Boracay Horse Riding Stables ... B1
Tribal Adventures ... (see 10)

Sleeping

2 Boracay Beach Club ... B2
3 Boracay Beach Resort ... A4
4 Cottage Queen ... B1
5 Frendz Resort ... B4
6 Friday's ... B1
7 MR Holidays Hotel ... B1
8 Nigi Nigi Too ... B2
9 Red Coconut ... A4
10 Sandcastle's ... A4
11 Sea Wind ... B1

Eating

12 Aria Restaurant ... A4
13 Budget Mart ... B4
Crafty's ... (see 25)
14 Cyma ... B4
15 English Bakery ... B3
Friday's ... (see 6)
16 Heidiland ... B4
Jammers ... (see 12)
17 Jonah's Fruit Shake & Snack Bar ... A3
18 Kasbah ... B1
19 Lemon Cafe ... A4
20 Mañana Mexican ... A4
21 Real Coffee & Tea Cafe ... A3
22 Smoke ... A4

Drinking

23 Beach Bum Bar ... A3
Bom Bom ... (see 9)
24 Cocomangas Wine Bar ... B2
25 Crafty's ... B4
Exit Bar ... (see 9)
26 Rumbas ... B4

Entertainment

27 Club Paraw ... A3
28 Cocomangas Disco ... B2
29 Epic ... A4

Information

30 Boracay Lying-In & Diagnostic Center ... B4

Transport

31 Seair ... A4
32 Zest Air ... B4

and all that competition keeps the prices reasonable. Trips start at P700 per hour for up to five or six passengers, and you can usually haggle for lower.

Red Pirates BOAT TOURS
(Map p256; ☎288 5767; redpiratesboracay@hotmail.com) Red Pirates has a super-sized *paraw* (12-persons capacity) and does the standard cruises off White Beach (per hour P800) plus longer trips to secret spots around northern Panay and Carabao Island.

D'Boracay Sailing BOAT TOURS
(☎0906 308 8614; www.boracay-sailing.com) For something more upscale, this company hires out a 42ft luxury catamaran and organises two-hour sunset cruises including wine, beer and canapes (per person P3500).

Diving & Snorkelling

The scuba diving around Boracay pales in comparison to more renowned hot spots like Puerto Galera, but it's a great place to take a diver certification course. And there are some OK spots around for underwater breathers. Boracay's pride and joy, **Yapak**, off the northern tip, is a sheer soft-coral-covered wall running from 30m to 65m. Big-fish lovers adore this spot, though depth, currents and surface chop restrict it to advanced divers only. There are also drift dives and cave dives, and the protected (in the high season) side of the island offers calm, shallow reefs for beginners. One such reef is **Crocodile Island**, off the small beach at Tambisaan.

There are many, many dive centres on Boracay, and prices are set by the Boracay Association of Scuba-Diving Schools. Walk-in prices are P1600 per dive with full gear, and P20,000 for an open-water diving certificate. The high prices generally means the quality of equipment and instruction is high, and fly-by-night operations fail.

A few places offer attractive accommodation/diving packages, including the following longer-standing and/or well-known operators based at White Beach:

Aqualife Divers Academy DIVING
(Map p256; ☎288 3276; www.aqualifedivers.net; Station 3)

Blue Mango Dive Center DIVING
(☎288 5170; www.boracaydive.com; Angol)

Calypso Diving DIVING
(Map p256; ☎288 3206; www.calypso-boracay.com; Station 2)

Victory Divers DIVING
(Map p256; ☎288 3209; www.victorydivers.com)

White Beach Divers DIVING
(☎288 3809; www.whitebeachdivers.com; Angol)

Kitesurfing

During the height of the northeast monsoon *(amihan)*, which runs from December to March, consistent winds, shallow water and rapidly inflating but still decent prices (about US$450 for a 12-hour certification course) make Bulabog Beach on the east side of the island the perfect place to learn kitesurfing. The action shifts to White Beach during the less consistent May-to-October southwest monsoon *(habagat)*, when heavy onshore chop makes it more of an experts' exercise.

The following operate year-round. We list just their Bulabog location; all set up shop on White Beach in the off season.

Freestyle Academy (Map p252; ☎0915 559 3080; www.freestyle-boracay.com)

Habagat (Map p252; ☎288 5787; www.kiteboracay.com)

Hangin' (Map p252; ☎288 3766; www.kite-asia.com)

Isla Kitesurfing (Map p252; ☎288 5352; www.islakitesurfing.com)

Ocean Republic (Map p252; ☎288 4977; www.ocean-republic.com)

Timog (Map p252; ☎288 3302; www.timogkiteboarding.com)

Windsurfing

Boracay was an Asian windsurfing mecca long before kitesurfing was even invented, but now windsurfers are in the minority on Bulabog Beach. The season mirrors that of the kitesurfing season. Costs are P700 to P1300 per hour for board rental, and about P1300 per hour for lessons. Since 1988 Boracay has hosted the Boracay International Funboard Cup, held in January.

It's not hard to find a good-quality short or long board to rent in the high season. Try the following on Bulabog Beach:

Adventure Windsurfing (Map p252; ☎288 3182)

Funboard Center Boracay (Map p252; ☎288 3876; www.windsurfasia.com)

Green Yard Funboard Center (Map p252; ☎288 3663; www.boracaywindsurfing.com)

Reef Riders (Map p252; ☎260 2394; www.reefridersboracay.com)

Other Activities

Tribal Adventures ADVENTURE TOURS
(Map p254; ☎288 3207; www.tribaladventures.com; Sandcastles Resort, Station 2) Tribal Adventures offers a host of adventures on mountainous mainland Panay, including kayaking trips in Tibiao.

Fairways & Bluewater Resort Golf & Country Club GOLF
(Map p252; ☎288 3974; www.fairwaysandbluewater.com; weekday 18 holes incl cart, caddy & clubs P7330) It's quite pricey for the Philippines, but it's an undeniably stunning track with soaring tee boxes and sweeping views.

Boracay Horse Riding Stables HORSE RIDING
(Map p254; ☎288 3311; ⏰6am-6pm) Caters for all levels of experience (P575/1030 per one/two hours). The stables are off the main road, north of the post office.

Massage & Spa

There are almost as many spas on Boracay as there are hotels – and that's saying a lot. Freelance masseurs roam the length of the beach, massage-spa-yoga places are springing up like salutes to the sun, and many of the resorts also offer similar services. Expect to pay from P400 at the low end for a full-body massage – or *way* more at the high end.

Mandala Spa SPA
(Map p256; ☎288 5857; www.mandalaspa.com; ⏰10am-10pm) The leader of the pack, it's associated with the exclusive resort of the same name and lives up to its lofty standards. Treatments cost from P3000 for a facial to around P11,500 for the 'Princess Treatment' or a Mandala detox day.

Sleeping

We cover only the main accommodation areas here – White Beach; Diniwid Beach, which is just north (and practically an extension of) White Beach; and kitesurfer hang-out Bulabog Beach on the back side of the island.

Additional resorts are dotted around the island in more isolated spots. Many of them, such as the new Shangri-La Resort, are utterly private. But you'll pay a premium for such resorts on Boracay. If it's seclusion you seek, you'll find much better value (and be more secluded) in places like Romblon, Guimaras, Siquijor or southern Negros.

Rates everywhere drop 20% to 50% in the low season (June to October). Bargaining might bear fruit at any time of year.

ANGOL (SOUTH OF STATION 3)

You can still find good value on rooms in Angol, where some say the spirit of the 'Old Boracay' survives. There are really no drawbacks to staying down here. It's still an easy, pleasant walk to the busy central area of White Beach around D'Mall.

Walk-in guests are advised to check out a quiet colony of about 10 budget resorts located down a path behind the Arwana bar/resort. All are within a two-minute walk of the beach.

TOP CHOICE **Mandala Spa** LUXURY RESORT $$$
(Map p256; ☎288 5857; www.mandalaspa.com; r from US$305) There's nothing Old Boracay about this place. One of the most romantic resorts you'll find anywhere, it roosts hilltop on a rare plot of inland forest, close to the

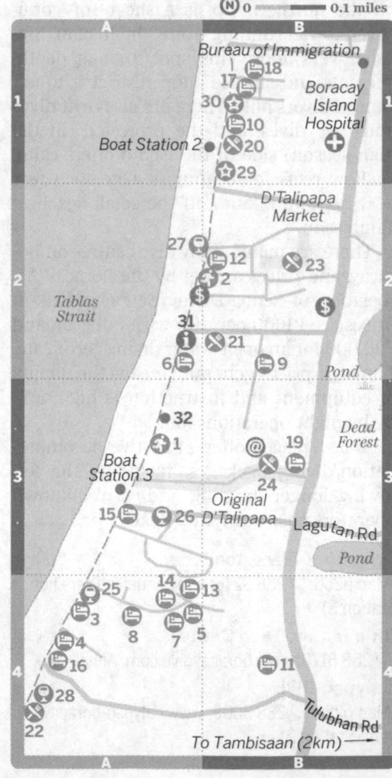

main road but somehow sealed off from its din. Mandala started as an upscale spa before raising the bar for other resorts in Boracay with a mix of healthy living, Zen-like ambience and ultracontemporary teak-and-bamboo cottages that come with amenities like DVD players and outdoor showers with stone walls. Rates include a daily massage and free morning yoga classes.

Ocean Breeze Inn BEACH RESORT $
(Map p256; www.oceanbreezeinn.info; r P900-1500; ❄) Probably the top value of the places behind Arwana. The best rooms are also the cheapest: the rattan-swathed standalone cottages in the garden. These complement the simple, well-appointed air-con concrete rooms. It doesn't serve food but there's free coffee.

Surfside Boracay BEACH RESORT $$$
(Map p256; ☎288 5006, 0920 951 1366; http://boracaysurfside.com; r incl breakfast from US$85; ❄📶) This Japanese-run resort has all the mod cons you could want – including magic microphones in most rooms! Tasteful Visayan arts and crafts and attractive locally sourced furniture adorn the rooms. The twin configuration of most rooms is a problem, and they could do more with the verandas. Great dive/accommodation packages available.

Dave's Straw Hat Inn BEACH RESORT $$
(Map p256; ☎288 5465, 0917 716 8647; www.davesstrawhatinn.com; walk-in r with fan/air-con from P1200/1800; ❄@📶) The air-con rooms here are comfy modern cottages with nipa roofs and private verandas, set in a leafy green garden. The fan rooms are less charming but still excellent value. Scores points for the breakfasts, especially the discus-sized pancakes.

Angol Point Beach Resort BEACH RESORT $$
(Map p256; ☎288 3107; cottage P2750; ❄📶) It has a loyal cadre of adherents who swear the old-school-vibe given off by this clutch

White Beach South

Activities, Courses & Tours

1 Aqualife Divers Academy A3
Blue Mango Dive Center .... (see 4)
Calypso Diving .... (see 6)
Mandala Spa .... (see 11)
Red Pirates .... (see 28)
2 Victory Divers B2
White Beach Divers .... (see 4)

Sleeping

3 Angol Point Beach Resort A4
4 Blue Mango Inn A4
5 Bora Bora Inn A4
6 Calypso Resort A2
7 Dave's Straw Hat Inn A4
8 Escurel A4
9 Jung's House Resort B2
10 Le Soleil de Boracay Hotel B1
11 Mandala Spa B4
12 Nigi Nigi Nu Noos B2
13 Ocean Breeze Inn A4
14 Orchids Resort A4
15 Sulu-Plaza A3
16 Surfside Boracay A4
17 Taj Guesthouse B1
18 Tans Guesthouse B1
19 Trafalgar Garden Cottages B3
Tree House Da Mario's .... (see 22)
Tree House Da Mario's .... (see 16)
White Beach Divers Hostel .... (see 4)

Eating

Bei Kurt und Madz .... (see 25)
Carinderia .... (see 3)
Cowboy Cucina .... (see 4)
20 Deparis B1
21 Dos Mestizos B2
22 Pizzeria Floremar A4
23 Plato D'Boracay B2
Summer Place .... (see 30)
24 Zest Boracay B3

Drinking

25 Arwana A4
26 Boracay Nutria Water A3
27 Charlh's Bar A2
Nigi Nigi Nu Noos .... (see 12)
28 Red Pirates A4

Entertainment

29 Juice B1
30 Summer Place B1

Information

31 Boracay Tourist Center A2
Filipino Travel Center .... (see 31)

Transport

32 RSLI A3

of nipa huts in a beachfront coconut field makes it the best resort on the island. For others, it's a bit spartan and lifeless. It has no restaurant, but it does disseminate free coffee.

Sulu-Plaza BEACH RESORT $$
(Map p256; ☎288 3400, 0917 474 5058; www.sulu-plaza.com; r P1600-2000; ❄📶) For a very reasonable price you get a stylish room filled with two bamboo chairs, comfy thick beds and attractive art, plus a beachfront location right at Boat Station 3.

White Beach Divers Hostel HOSTEL $
(Map p256; ☎288 3809; www.whitebeachdivers.com; r P500-600; 📶) A stellar deal, especially if you get the spacious bamboo loft at the back, which sleeps three. Other rooms are more basic. The owner has set up a small information booth out front and is a receptacle of knowledge about tours in Romblon and other areas in reach of Boracay.

Blue Mango Inn BEACH RESORT $$
(Map p256; ☎288 5170, 0906 205 1605; www.bluemangoinn.com; r incl breakfast P2000-4500; ❄@📶) The stylish cottages in the leafy back courtyard are probably your best bet here. Divers doing courses with Blue Mango Divers net big discounts on rooms, and it doesn't skimp on things like bottled water and shampoo like some resorts in this price range.

BORACAY BOOKING TIPS

» Some hotels give discounts to walk-in guests – ask before making that reservation. We list walk-in rates here if there's a discrepancy, and note it in the price details.

» About half of Boracay hotels charge credit-card users a 3% to 5% surcharge.

» Huge discounts on many of the hotels we list are often available on Agoda.com and other Asian booking sites.

» Always ask for a 'promo rate', especially in the low season (even if the rooms are already discounted substantially).

» Bargain hard always, but especially in the low season.

Orchids Resort BEACH RESORT $
(Map p256; ☎288 3313, 0917 242 0833; www.orchidsboracay.com; walk-in r P915-2000; ❄📶) Orchids has well-maintained rooms in an attractive dark-stained nipa complex, and a quiet little garden with, yes, orchids all over. The stand-alone cottages are particularly appealing. Unfortunately, rigid booking conditions make this mainly a walk-in option. Wi-fi is P50 per day.

Tree House Da Mario's BEACH RESORT $
(Map p256; ☎288 3601, 0918 661 9640; treehouse_damario@yahoo.com.ph; dm P200-300, d P1000-3500; ❄) Proprietor Mario offers a wide variety of rooms spread across two complexes. The four-bed dorm rooms, in the southernmost property behind Da Mario's tasty Italian restaurant, are the island's cheapest crash pads. The dorms at the other property are nicer but a tad pricier. Fancier rooms at both places seemed in need of a little TLC.

Bora Bora Inn BEACH RESORT $
(Map p256; ☎288 3186; r P800-1800; ❄) Among the cheapest – and furthest from the beach – of the Angol bunch, incongruously perched among a grove of pines.

Escurel BEACH RESORT $$
(Map p256; ☎288 3611, 0928-341 1911; s/d from P1300/1500; ❄@📶) For air-con rooms near the beach, you won't do much better.

CENTRAL WHITE BEACH (STATIONS 1–3)

If you stay here you are committed to being in the thick of things. The trappings of Boracay's success are everywhere: resorts, restaurants, bars, beach vendors, touts, masseuses, souvenir shops, transvestites and petty thieves. That said, most resorts are set well back from the beach so you can still get a decent night's sleep.

You'll pay a slight premium for staying on this stretch but there's a complex of budget resorts around Tans Guesthouse, roughly behind Summer Place, that pack in the local tourists. Foreigners usually prefer Angol.

TOP CHOICE **Calypso Resort** BEACH RESORT $$$
(Map p256; ☎288 2038; www.calypso-boracay.com; r P5040-8775; ❄@📶) The awesome views from the deluxe rooms are just the icing on a cake that already includes an inviting contemporary-meets-local design and superbly appointed rooms in a two-storey white concrete edifice at the back. The beds are astounding. You should be able to toler-

ate divers if you stay here, but you certainly don't need to be one.

Boracay Beach Resort BEACH RESORT **$$**
(Map p254; ☎288 3208; www.boracaybeachresort.com; cottages P2500-4165, ste P6800-11,400; ❄📶) The standard cottages are a super deal at this location, but it's worth upgrading to the deluxe cottages, which have fully tiled marble bathrooms, inviting linens, and large and well-furnished verandahs. Try asking for a free transfer from Caticlan.

Nigi Nigi Nu Noos BEACH RESORT **$$$**
(Map p256; ☎288 3101, 0923 701 2163; www.niginigi.com; walk-in r from P3000; ❄📶) The Balinese-style bamboo and nipa cottages, set in a lush garden, have huge rooms and balconies with benches; they're easily the most elegant rooms on this stretch of the beach if you're into the native look.

Le Soleil de Boracay Hotel BEACH RESORT **$$$**
(Map p256; ☎288 6209; www.lesoleil.com.ph; r incl buffet breakfast from P5400; ❄@📶🏊) This boutique-style hotel brings a little bit of the Mediterranean to Southeast Asia. It has several wings with several types of rooms, but all have detailed woodwork and colourful pillows and linens. We'd like to see nicer balcony furniture for this price.

Trafalgar Garden Cottages BUNGALOW **$**
(Map p256; ☎288 3711; trafalgarboracay@hotmail.com; Original D'Talipapa; r P650-1700; ❄) This leafy little village of budget rooms is close to the main road yet not as noisy as you might think. The P650 stand-alone cottages are as cheap as it gets on Boracay, and even have small porches with hammocks. It's just a short walk to the beach.

Frendz Resort BEACH RESORT **$$**
(Map p254; ☎288 3803; frendzresort@hotmail.com; dm P700, r P2800-3800; ❄@📶) Frendz' dorm rooms are a bit overpriced but much cosier than those at Tree House. Most private rooms are in well-kept native-style cottages. Aussie-managed and backpacker-friendly, with a restaurant, bar and pool table.

Sandcastle's APARTMENTS **$$$**
(Map p254; ☎288 3207, 0920 558 7188; www.boracaysandcastles.com; q from P7085; ❄@📶) For a pimped-out party palace, it's hard to beat Sandcastle's. The large studio apartments are truly swanky, with luxurious sofas and beds, and nicely appointed kitchens. The costlier beachfront rooms are just steps from the White Beach walking path; if your life feels too public, just close the blinds. Big discounts often available.

Jung's House Resort HOTEL **$**
(Map p256; ☎288 5420, 0917 320 5420; r with fan/air-con P800/1000; ❄) The Korean owner offers up the island's cheapest air-con rooms in this concrete building about 150m in from the beach. Rooms are surprisingly liveable for the price.

Red Coconut BEACH RESORT **$$$**
(Map p254; ☎288 3508; www.redcoconut.com.ph; d incl breakfast P4000-4750; ❄📶🏊) Good choice if you're looking for a big, central, beachfront resort around a pool.

Taj Guesthouse HOTEL **$$**
(Map p256; ☎288 4628; tajboracay@gmail.com; d/q P2000/2500; ❄📶) Probably the best choice of the nondescript hotels behind Summer Place. Check out the flashier annexe.

Tans Guesthouse HOTEL **$$**
(Map p256; ☎288 6878; http://tansguesthouseboracay.com; r from P1500; ❄📶) Like neighbour Taj, Tans has a wide variety of rooms spread over a couple of locations.

NORTH OF STATION 1

Any promotional photo of Boracay you've seen was probably taken at this heavenly stretch of White Beach. At low tide the expanse of white sand seems infinite, and the sunset *paraw* action – a Boracay trademark – is particularly intense. Naturally this is luxuryville, but you can still find good value amid the four-star resorts.

TOP CHOICE **Friday's** BEACH RESORT **$$$**
(Map p254; ☎288 6200; www.fridaysboracay.com; r incl breakfast P17,000-22,000; ❄@📶🏊) Standing proprietarily and elegantly on the finest stretch of White Beach, Friday's remains the quintessential Boracay beach resort. The cottages with private verandahs and hammocks look like tree houses, but inside they're anything but rustic, with DVD players, free wi-fi, bathrobes, slippers, and plush pillows and linen. A large, gorgeous nipa pavilion houses the fine restaurant.

TOP CHOICE **Punta Rosa** BOUTIQUE HOTEL **$$$**
(off Map p254; ☎288 6740, 0917 500 7878; www.puntarosa.com; d incl breakfast P4500-7600; ❄📶) Among Boracay's most stylish resorts, Punta Rosa is located just off the beach at the nearly deserted far northern end of White Beach. In-the-know Manila expats head here and

reap rewards like peace, quiet, cosy floor beds, flat-screen TVs, DVD players and lots of throw pillows in your room.

Boracay Beach Club BEACH RESORT $$$
(Map p254; ☎288 4853, 0910 777 8888; www.boracaybeachclub.com; s/ste incl breakfast from US$123/165; ❄📶) The 'BBC' is across the road from White Beach but don't let that deter you. It has a lovely pool area with plenty of shade and you are less than a minute's walk from the beach. Standard rooms are compact but ubercomfortable with not a hair out of place, and the suites are lavish.

Sea Wind BEACH RESORT $$$
(Map p254; ☎288 3091; www.seawindboracah.ph; r P8250-11,000; ❄@📶🏊) Sea Wind has long been the place where people settled when they didn't quite want to pay for Friday's. It doesn't have quite the flourish of Friday's, but it shares the same exquisite patch of sand. It's getting fancier as it expands – across the street are luxurious bungalows scattered around a lush hillside. Beachfront rooms aren't quite as swanky.

MR Holidays Hotel HOTEL $$$
(Map p254; ☎288 5360, 0917 893 2362; www.mrholidaysboracay.com; d P3000-5000; ❄) Midrange resorts are rare in these parts, but there's a grouping of them behind Kasbah restaurant and this is the best value of the lot. Rooms are snug but immaculate and have some style.

Nigi Nigi Too BEACH RESORT $$$
(Map p254; ☎288 3150; www.niginigitoo.com; cottage US$65-90, r US$90-140; @📶) Most rooms are in the concrete main house, but they are similar in style to the rooms at Nigi Nigi Nu Noos. Verandahs are done right at both Nigis.

Cottage Queen NIPA HUTS $$
(Map p254; ☎288 3062; r P1200) Great value for these parts, but it only has two simple cottages.

DINIWID BEACH

Continue north from White Beach along the narrow concrete path that hugs the point and you get to peaceful and quiet Diniwid Beach. It's a beautiful spot, highlighted by a strip of the softest white sand you'll find anywhere.

TOP CHOICE **Nami Boracay** BEACH RESORT $$$
(off Map p254; ☎288 6753; www.namiresorts.com; r incl breakfast P10,675-13,725; ❄📶) Perched above a fantastic beach like a deluxe tree house, Nami offers privacy and breathtaking views. The 12 luxury rooms have their own outdoor jacuzzis above the ocean, and the restaurant has a champagne brunch (P660) and an eclectic menu serving everything from Filipino and Asian fusion to burgers and goat's cheese filet mignon. Incredible.

Spider House BEACH RESORT $$$
(off Map p254; ☎0949 501 1099; www.spiderhouseresort.com; r from P3000; 📶) This is another one of those places you can't quite believe is in Boracay. Located on the rocky headland at Diniwid's north end, you might as well be at the end of the world. The rooms and common area are perched over a patch of choppy ocean. They are bamboo-y and have prime views. All are fan-cooled and some share bathrooms.

Beach House BEACH RESORT $$
(off Map p254; ☎288 3934, 0928 931 1075; cja1025@yahoo.com; d incl breakfast P2500-3500; ❄@🏊) The best midranger here, Beach House's rooms are clean and have style, but what really makes it is the front-and-centre location on Diniwid Beach. Shoot for a beachfront room.

BULABOG BEACH

Across Boracay's narrow middle from White Beach – just 10 minutes' walk from D'Mall – is the less-peopled Bulabog Beach. This is the kitesurfing beach, and the resorts here jack up rates in the December-to-March season, when stiff onshore winds keep the water and air flowing. Bulabog is stagnant and filled with bangkas during the low season, when the *habagat* winds blow offshore. The water here isn't very clean, as much of Boracay's sewage empties into this side of the island.

Aissatou Beach Resort BOUTIQUE HOTEL $$$
(Map p252; ☎288 5787, 0917 492 1537; www.kiteboracay.com; r from P3500; ❄📶) Behind Habagat's southern branch, the nine rooms here are impeccably maintained and generously fitted out with handcrafted furniture, imported toilets and locally commissioned art. They throw chaise lounges on the beach out front. One fuss: no restaurant.

Pahuwayan Suites BEACH RESORT $$$
(Map p252; ☎288 1449, 0949 750 4242; www.pahuwayan.com; r incl breakfast P3750-4250; ❄📶) Kitesurfers with an eye for style and some extra money to blow might consider this

nicely outfitted place behind Freestyle Academy. All the rooms have flat-screen TVs, awesome beds, fancy fixtures and semi-private patios done right. Top-floor rooms have prime ocean views.

Banana Saging BEACH RESORT $$
(Map p252; ☎288 6121; www.boracayguesthouse.com; r with fan/air-con from P1100/1500; ❄📶) Super deal behind Habagat's northern branch; rooms are clean and even have design flourishes like funky lights and sculptures.

Boracay Kiteresort BEACH RESORT $$
(Map p252; ☎288 3766; www.kite-asia.com; r with fan/air-con from P1200/1800; ❄📶) Above Hangin's popular bar, the fan rooms are fairly basic but work if you just want a place to crash, while pricier rooms have more flare.

Eating

White Beach path is one big fantastic food court – half the fun of dining is taking a walk at sunset and checking out the smells, menus and other people along the path. Many places tempt customers with generous set meals or dinner buffets (from around P200 per person). Scrutinise well before being seduced by the displays – much of the seafood lies out in the heat for hours on end.

You'll find the best deals on Filipino food near two wet markets: D'Palengke in the southeast corner of D'Mall (the busy pedestrian arcade at White Beach's midpoint); and D'Talipapa near Boat Station 2. Some of the best all-around restaurants are in D'Mall of all places. *Turo-turo* restaurants on the main road offer super-budget cuisine if that's how you roll.

All restaurants listed are beachfront unless otherwise noted.

ANGOL

TOP CHOICE **Cowboy Cucina** INTERNATIONAL $$
(Map p256; mains P180-600) As the name implies, the emphasis is on meat, and it does it well. Here you can experience the anomaly of digging your feet in the sand while gnawing on meaty ribs – the island's best, in this case (P325). There's also a kids' menu and a Sunday roast.

Bei Kurt und Madz INTERNATIONAL $$
(Map p256; mains P200-400; 📶) Has a blissfully long happy hour (2pm to 8pm) featuring P30 San Miguel and a diverse, affordable menu to satisfy both noodle lovers and meat-and-potatoes types. German sausages are the speciality here.

Michaella's Carinderia FILIPINO $
(Map p256; meals P75-110) This snack shack – on a loop in the path south of Boat Station 3 – has food as cheap as you'll find on the beach. Wash it down with P30 San Miguel.

Pizzeria Floremar PIZZERIA $$
(Map p256; pastas & pizzas P180) Da Mario's restaurant does fantastic pizza, great home-style pasta – probably the best in Boracay – and good salads.

CENTRAL WHITE BEACH

TOP CHOICE **Plato D'Boracay** SEAFOOD $$
(Map p256; D'Talipapa; seafood per kg P100-150) The lobster, prawns and other shellfish at this family-style seafood grill come straight from the adjoining D'Talipapa market (Talipapa means 'wet market' in Filipino). The prices, which substantially undercut the seafood barbecues on the beach, reflect the reduced transport costs.

Cyma GREEK $$$
(Map p254; ☎288 4283; D'Mall; mains P250-600; ⏰11am-11pm; 🍷) This Greek restaurant is known for grilled meat, appetisers such as flaming *saganaki* (fried salty cheese) and outstanding salads. Affordable gyros are available for thriftier diners. Service is slick and professional, and the Mediterranean-blue dining room makes you forget you're in D'Mall.

Dos Mestizos SPANISH $$$
(Map p256; ☎288 5786; mains from P300) Local restaurateurs favour this Spanish restaurant when they go out to eat. Authentic paella, bean soups and hearty stews make this quite a different taste sensation to most of the food on offer elsewhere. Order a *lechón* (P3250) to your crib and have a party.

Lemon Cafe INTERNATIONAL $$$
(Map p254; D'Mall; mains P300-550) Fresh is the key here, ranging across several culinary areas with good salads, creative sandwiches, classic eggs Benedict brunches and tasty laksa. The lunch box special – soup of the day, green salad, choice of sandwich or rice dish and dessert – is a snip at P450. Add 10% for service.

Aria Restaurant ITALIAN $$$
(Map p254; mains P360-600; ⏰11am-11.30pm) Aria has a prime people-watching location

on the beach path at D'Mall's entrance. It has a stylish and modern dining room and cooks fabulous Italian food – *tagliatelle con tartufu (*white truffle) comes to mind, as does the truly stunning cardamom *panna cotta*.

Crafty's INDIAN, THAI **$$**
(Map p254; Main Rd; dishes P200-300) Never mind what's on White Beach, truly the best Indian food on Boracay emerges from the kitchen of this rooftop bar looming over D'Mall. And yes, it's actually spicy. It also has some of the spicier Thai food around.

Deparis FRENCH, THAI **$$**
(Map p256; dishes P200-300) The French *je ne sais quoi* with food is on full display at Deparis, where a piece of steak and some fries on a white plate suddenly become a culinary revelation. The Thai dishes aren't bad either.

Real Coffee & Tea Cafe CAFE **$$**
(Map p254; breakfasts P100-200; ⌚7am-7pm; 🖉) Tucked just off the beach path, this old favourite has, believe it or not, real coffee and tea as well as yummy sandwiches, fresh fruit shakes, healthy breakfasts and homemade brownies. The name harkens back to a time, not so long ago, when you could only get Nescafé on Boracay.

Summer Place MONGOLIAN **$$**
(Map p256; all-you-can-eat Mongolian barbecue P250; ⌚5pm-late) This is one of the better Mongolian barbecues available on Boracay, keeping its ingredients fresh and quickly replenished. Take your spoils to the tables on the beach; the dining room gets hot. Later in the evening, this becomes a serious party place.

Smoke FILIPINO **$**
(Map p254; D'Mall; mains P100-120; ⌚9am-6am) Now with two branches on opposite ends of D'Mall, Smoke is Boracay's best value, with freshly cooked Filipino food, appetising coconut-milk curries and a P80 Filipino breakfast. The branch closest to the main road is open from 7am to 10pm.

Mañana Mexican MEXICAN **$$$**
(Map p254; mains P275-450; ⌚11am-11pm; 🖉) Eating Mexican food on the sand is never a bad thing. Serves classic burritos and tortillas, and mixes a mean mango margarita.

Zest Boracay FILIPINO **$$**
(Map p256; Original D'Talipapa; meals P150-200; ⌚8am-8pm) The setting won't appeal to all, but if you're looking for a clean budget eatery with Filipino staples and the full complement of breakfasts, look no further.

Jammers MEXICAN **$**
(Map p254; sandwiches P100-200) Delicious, quick and affordable fish sandwiches, tacos and burgers on a prime patch of real estate.

English Bakery BAKERY **$**
(Map p254; Bulabog Rd; breakfasts P100-200) Fresh-baked bread and on-the-run breakfasts like bacon, egg and cheese sandwiches (P130).

Heidiland DELI **$$**
(Map p254; D'Mall) Stocks beach picnic supplies like sandwiches, bread and gourmet imported food products.

Budget Mart SUPERMARKET **$**
(Map p254; D'Mall; ⌚7.30am-11.30pm) Best selection of groceries.

NORTH OF STATION 1

Friday's INTERNATIONAL **$$$**
(Map p254; dishes P370-640) If you're looking to splurge on a night of fine resort dining, Friday's is your choice for setting, food and general ambience. Target the Friday barbecue buffet.

Kasbah MIDDLE EASTERN **$$$**
(Map p254; mains P250-500) This posh resort strip is the last place you'd expect to find an unpretentious Moroccan restaurant like Kasbah. We're not complaining. The delectable *kemias* (appetisers) like hummus and *zaalaouk* (an eggplant and tomato dip) are most consistent. Postmeal, kick back and send wafts of hookah smoke skyward.

Jonah's Fruit Shakes FILIPINO **$$**
(Map p254; shakes around P80) Amid plenty of competition, Jonah's proudly boasts the best shakes on the island – the avocado and banana mix is sensational. Also has an extensive menu of Filipino faves.

Drinking

Evenings on White Beach kick off with one long happy hour, mostly starting around 4pm or 5pm and finishing at 7pm, 8pm or even 9pm. Many bars don't usually close down until between 1am and 3am or when the last customer stumbles home.

TOP CHOICE **Red Pirates** BEACH BAR **$$**
(Map p256; Angol) Way down at the south end of White Beach, this supremely mellow bar throws funky driftwood furniture onto the

SAVINGS IN A BOTTLE

Save the environment – and plenty of money – by refilling plastic water bottles at filling stations dotted along Boracay's main road. Closer to the beach, near Station 3, is **Boracay Nutria Water** (Map p256; 1L refill P7; ⌚6.30am-8pm).

sand and best captures the spirit of the 'Old Boracay'.

Nigi Nigi Nu Noos BEACH BAR $$
(Map p256; Station 2-3); ⌚happy hr 5-7pm) The legendary mason jars of Long Island iced tea (they're two-for-one during happy hour) more than capably kick-start any evening.

Exit Bar BEACH BAR
(Map p254; Station 2) Could be called 'Expat' Bar. As Boracay's expats are a colourful lot, that's not a bad thing.

Bom Bom BAR
(Map p254; Station 2) With nightly bongo-infused live music, Bom Bom practically defines cool and is the best spot to kill time between dinner and late-night dancing.

Crafty's BAR $$
(Map p254; Main Rd) You come to this breezy hideaway on top of Craft's Supermarket for the views, or to swap yarns (or sorrows) with the characters who always seem to be hanging around the bar.

Charlh's Bar BEACH BAR
(Map p256; Station 2-3) Another place with a crusty crowd of regulars. They often prop up an acoustic guitar player behind the bar to produce sweet rhythms.

Beach Bum Bar BEACH BAR $$
(Map p254; Station 1) Fire dancing is all the rage on Boracay, and this is probably the best place to kick back on the beach with a cocktail (two-for-one all night) and observe. It certainly has the most flamboyant lead dancer.

Arwana BEACH BAR $
(Map p256; ⌚happy hr 1-10pm) All-day happy hour means Boracay's cheapest San Miguel (P25) and P69 cocktails on demand.

Rumbas SPORTS BAR $
(Map p254; D'Mall) With a few big screens and a good range of channels, Rumbas is about the closest thing Boracay has to a sports bar.

☆ Entertainment

Follow thumping beats to find the discos; about five or six of them carry momentum into the wee hours, even in the low season. Live music is practically everywhere between about 6pm and 11pm.

Juice NIGHTCLUB $$
(Map p256; Station 2-3) The smallest, most down-to-earth and gay-friendly of the central beach discos, with equal numbers of people dancing and just hanging out by the bar.

Jungle BAR, CLUB $$
(Map p252; Lagutan Beach; admission varies) Isolated on a cove at the back side of the island, hippy, trippy Jungle bar is known for three-day full-moon parties and its notorious 'F*** you Archie' cocktail. Often quiet or dead; just as often raucous.

Epic NIGHTCLUB $$
(Map p254;Station 2) More flashy and uppity than its predecessor in this spot, Hey Jude's (RIP), but it remains the most popular of the beach discos, and does a good job keeping the sleaze away. Also popular for table football.

Summer Place NIGHTCLUB $$
(Map p256; admission varies) This seething disco goes off just about every night; it attracts a few more unsavoury elements than Epic.

Cocomangas BAR/DISCO
(Map p254) Attempting Cocomangas' 'Drink for Your Country' shooters challenge is a Boracay tradition. The snug, beachfront Cocomangas Wine Bar is a more mellow place to drink for your country than the somewhat sleazy disco across the street.

Club Paraw NIGHTCLUB
(Map p254) This large open-air club has met the considerable challenge of getting people to move north of Boat Station 1 to party.

ℹ Information

Internet Access

Internet (per hour P30 to P70) and wi-fi (usually free) access are everywhere.

Boracay Tourist Center (Map p256; Station 2-3; per hr P70; ⌚9am-10.30pm) Has fast connections.

Cybros (Station 3; per hr P20; ⌚8am-11pm)

Laundry

Laundry facilities are widespread along the main road around D'Mall (per kilo P35).

Medical Services

For serious ailments, diving boats can provide fast transport to the mainland and then patients are taken to Kalibo or flown to Manila.

Boracay Lying-In & Diagnostic Center (Map p254; ☎288 4448; D'Mall; ⊙24hr) The expats' private clinic of choice.

Money

BPI (D'Mall) and **Metrobank** (D'Mall) have user-friendly ATMs, and there are a few others along the main road and the beach path. Many resorts and the tourist centre also handle foreign exchange.

Post

There's an efficient and reliable postal counter at the tourist centre (although it charges a whopping almost 50% service fee for mailing each item), and a post office at the northern end of the Main Rd.

Tourist Information

Boracay Tourist Center (Map p256; Station 2-3; ⊙9am-11pm) This is a hive of tourist-related activity. From behind a long row of desks, staff offer postal and telephone services, general Boracay information, money changing (including Amex travellers cheques) and fast internet connection (P70 per hour).

Filipino Travel Center (Map p256; ☎288 3704/5; www.filipinotravel.com.ph; Station 2-3; ⊙9am-6pm) In the Boracay Tourist Center; helpful and professional, and offers ticketing services.

Visas

BOI (Map p254; ☎288 5267; Nirvana Resort, Main Rd; ⊙7.30am-5.30pm Mon & Tue) Easy Visa renewals.

Getting There & Away

Air

The swiftest way to Boracay from Manila is by air to Caticlan – but you won't be alone trying to book these flights during the high season. A cheaper alternative is the airport in Kalibo, from where it's an easy 1½ to two hours by road to Caticlan.

Boat

A fleet of pumpboats shuttles people back and forth between Caticlan and Boracay (P150, 15 minutes) every 15 minutes between 5am and

WORTH A TRIP

CARABAO ISLAND

From Puka Beach on the northern tip of Boracay, it almost seems as if you could swim to this lush island, known as 'Hambil' by locals (don't try it, the currents are deadly). Carabao is actually part of Romblon, but is much easier to visit from Boracay/Caticlan than from anywhere on Romblon. With its quiet streets, white beaches and stunning reefs offshore, it offers a chance to vacation from your vacation on Boracay.

The narrow streets of the island are so quiet that on a long walk past rice fields, over hills and through shady coconut and nipa stands, you may only pass an eponymous carabao. You can hire a motorbike or even a horse to get around, stopping off at beaches and visiting **Ngiriton Cave** to the north and **Angas Cave** to the south.

There are a few accommodation options on Carabao Island if you want to stay for more than a day. On a fine stretch of white beach near the boat landing in Lanas you'll find **Ivy's Vine** (☎0929 715 7881; www.carabao-island.com; dm P300, duplex cottages with fan/air-con P800/1200), which features a great double-storey bar and restaurant with a pool table, and a dive centre (the owners run White Beach Divers in Boracay). Lanas has a few more resorts that lie north of Ivy's.

Carabao is only 6km wide and less than 10km long. There's no ring road, but a road (paved in parts) does run along the entire east coast, and there's a paved road linking the main town, San José, with Lanas on the west coast.

The easiest way to get here is to hire a bangka at Boat Station 1 on Boracay's White Beach (or Bulabog Beach Boat Station in the low season). They ask about P2500 round trip for a small bangka.

A couple of big public bangkas depart from Caticlan to both Lanas and San José every morning (P70, 45 minutes to one hour), but the return trips are usually not until the next morning. Carabao Island locals who work on Boracay commute back home every afternoon from Boat Station 1 (high season) or Bulabog Beach (low season). You can hitch a ride for P60 and return any day on the early-morning commute. Don't try this journey in high winds, especially in a small bangka.

6pm, and then as the need arises between 7pm and 10pm. The fare is composed of a P75 environmental fee (which contributes to sustainable waste/sewage disposal on the island), a P50 terminal fee and P25 for the boat. All boats arrive at Boracay's Cagban Pier, where a queue of tricycles awaits to take you to your hotel. They cost P25 per person or P150 per tricycle (more if you are going north of Boat Station 1).

From June to November, brisk southwesterly winds mean you'll often be shuttled round the northern tip of Caticlan to Tabon, where the same fleet of boats will take you to Boracay's alternative pier at Tambisaan.

Getting Around

To get from one end of White Beach to the other, either walk, take a pedicab along the walking strip (P20 to P60) or flag down a tricycle along the main road. These cost only P8 provided you steer clear of the disingenuously named 'special trips' offered by stationary tricycles, which cost a not-so-special P40 to P60.

Kalibo

036 / POP 69,700

For travellers, Kalibo, the capital of Aklan Province, is primarily an alternative port of entry to Boracay and the site of the granddaddy of all Philippine festivals, the raucous Ati-Atihan Festival in January. At other times of the year it's a fairly typical loud and congested Philippine provincial city. Kalibo is thought to have been founded around 1250 by Malay settlers from Borneo. The local dialect is Aklano.

Sights & Activities

Heritage Arts & Crafts TEXTILES
(268 5270; heritagearts_craft@yahoo.com; Luis Barrios St; 9am-5pm Mon-Sat, by appt Sun) In addition to *pinya* weaving, this shop/workshop weaves abaca from banana seeds, which produces a stiff cloth, and also weaves a vine known as *nito* into stiff baskets and mats. You can observe weavers at work and there's a small shop selling good-quality products.

Bakhawan Eco-tourism Centre & Mangrove Park MANGROVES
(admission P15; 8am-5pm) Five minutes from town in New Buswang (P40 by tricycle), this 170-hectare park is the base for a mangrove reforestation project begun in the late 1980s. Visitors can check out intertidal ecology from an 850m bamboo boardwalk while enjoying birdsong and mud critters. It's a welcome green escape from the polluted city.

Festivals & Events

Ati-Atihan Festival CULTURAL
In January the fantastic Ati-Atihan Festival is held. The nation's biggest and best mardi gras, it most likely dates back to the days of the Borneo settlers. Described by its promoters as a mix of 'Catholic ritual, social activity, indigenous drama and tourist attraction', it's a week-long street party raging from sun-up to sundown, peaking on the third Sunday of January.

Sleeping

For Ati-Atihan you should book a hotel months in advance and expect to pay from two to five times the normal price.

TOP CHOICE **Ati-Atihan County Inn** HOSTEL $
(268 6116; D Maagma St; dm/d/tr/q P150/800/900/1200;) Not only is this Kalibo's best value, but it also abstains from raising its rates during the Ati-Atihan Festival. All rooms are bright, cheery, clean and air-conditioned, and the 16-bed fan dorm is immaculate. It even does the origami swan towel-folding thing popularised in Boracay.

Marzon Hotel HOTEL $$
(268 2188; www.marzonboracay.com; Quezon Ave Ext; d/tr/q P1500/2100/2800;) This extremely well appointed place would be P6000 in Boracay, but then again you don't have the beach. You do, however, have a 25m pool.

Kalibo Hotel HOTEL $$
(268 4765; bcombinn@hotmail.com; 467 N Roldan St; r P1050-1600;) The hotel formerly known as Beachcomber Inn is well located in the centre, yet not too loud. A friendly and professionally run midranger.

Garcia Legaspi Mansion HOTEL $
(262 5588; garcialegaspimansion@yahoo.com; 1016 Roxas Ave; r with fan/air-con from P500/P700;) The best thing about this place is the eccentric and in-the-know owner Gerwin. Rooms are well furnished and well maintained, but all overlook the noisy main street.

La Esperanza Hotel HOTEL $
(262 3989; laesperanzahotel@yahoo.com; Osmeña Ave; dm/d with fan P150, r with air-con P1000-3000;) Overpriced air-con rooms and

dorms that run a distant second to Ati-Atihan County Inn.

Bakhawan Inn HOTEL $
(☎262 7013; New Buswang; r P600-700; ❄) The location by the mangrove park is quiet, but it's annoyingly far from everything besides mangroves.

Eating & Drinking

Gaisano Mall has internet cafes, cinemas, shopping and a few fast-food joints.

TOP CHOICE Saylo FUSION $$
(☎268 6800; Quezon Ave Ext; mains P85-260; ❄) Kalibo's best restaurant calls itself 'hip and trendy'. No arguments here. The music is groovy and fine local art adorns the walls as punters tuck into the likes of black-ink pasta, goat in green curry and generously stuffed pita pockets. The hummus is a garlicky delight.

L@tte Cafe & Internet Station CAFE $
(Quezon Ave Ext; mains from P50; ⏲9.30am-10pm Mon-Sat; ❄📶) Hip and modern like its sister establishment next door, the Marzon Hotel, L@tte is a delightful refuge from Kalibo's urban mayhem. Internet is available at a bank of nice computers (per hour P30).

Kitty's Kitchen INTERNATIONAL $
(☎Rizal St; dishes P60-110; ⏲10am-9pm; ❄) An air-conditioned oasis in the centre, Kitty's has Mexican food and other Western surprises like bangers and mash, and Kansas City ribs.

Smokehauz RESTOBAR $$
(☎268 1461; Ramos St; ⏲to 3am) Nightly live music.

Abregana RESTOBAR $$
(☎262 1482; Martelino St; ⏲3pm-1am) Also has nightly live music.

Information

BOI (☎500 7601; Luis Barrios St; ⏲8am-5pm Wed-Fri) Handles visa renewals. Staff divide working hours between here and a separate office in the airport.

Kalibo Tourism Office (☎262 1020; 2nd fl, Municipal Hall, Burgos St) Moderately helpful staff can arrange *pinya* weaving tours and help you get a room if everything is booked out for Ati-Atihan.

Getting There & Around

Air

Travellers bound for Boracay can now fly straight to Kalibo from a handful of international

Kalibo

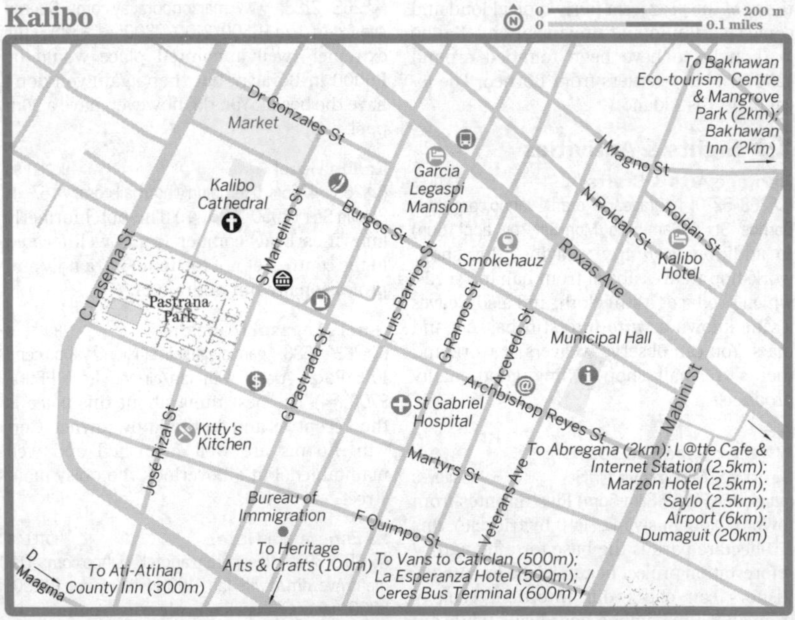

0 200 m
0 0.1 miles

To Bakhawan Eco-tourism Centre & Mangrove Park (2km); Bakhawan Inn (2km)
Dr Gonzales St
Market
J Magno St
Garcia Legaspi Mansion
Kalibo Cathedral
Burgos St
S Martelino St
N Roldan St
Roldan St
C Laserna St
Luis Barrios St
Smokehauz
Roxas Ave
Kalibo Hotel
Pastrana Park
G Ramos St
Acevedo St
Municipal Hall
G Pastrada St
Archbishop Reyes St
Mabini St
St Gabriel Hospital
José Rizal St
Kitty's Kitchen
To Abregana (2km); L@tte Cafe & Internet Station (2.5km); Marzon Hotel (2.5km); Saylo (2.5km); Airport (6km); Dumaguit (20km)
Martyrs St
Veterans Ave
Bureau of Immigration
F Quimpo St
To Heritage Arts & Crafts (100m)
D Maagma
To Ati-Atihan County Inn (300m)
To Vans to Caticlan (500m); La Esperanza Hotel (500m); Ceres Bus Terminal (600m)

PINYA KALIBO

Panay is the capital of *pinya* production in the Philippines, and the heart of the industry is in Kalibo. *Pinya* weaving is an 8th-century tradition that produces fine cloth from silk-like pineapple-leaf fibres. Once it's woven, it's sent elsewhere – often Laguna, near Manila – to be turned into embroidered placemats, handkerchiefs or *barong*. A *barong Tagalog* made of *pinya* is of the highest quality, worn only at weddings, inaugurations and other formal occasions. Through Heritage Arts & Crafts or the tourist office in Kalibo you can arrange tours of local pineapple plantations where they demonstrate the seven steps of *pinya* weaving.

destinations – namely Seoul, Shanghai, Taipei and Pusan – with Zest Air. Expect more destinations to be added.

Domestically, you'll save a nice chunk of change by flying to Kalibo instead of Caticlan if you're heading to Boracay. Regular flights from Manila to Kalibo on Airphil Express and Cebu Pacific are dirt cheap. The planes are larger too but, of course, this option involves a road connection that Caticlan doesn't.

Tricycles charge a flat P100 to take you into the centre of Kalibo, or you can walk 500m out to the highway and flag down a public tricycle or jeepney for P10.

Boat

From the nearby port of Dumaguit, Super Shuttle Ferry has three weekly ferries to Batangas (P750) via Odiongan (P455), and Moreta Shipping Lines serves Manila twice weekly (18 hours).

Bus & Van

From the **Ceres bus terminal** (Toting Reyes Ave) frequent buses go to Caticlan (P100, 1¾ hours), Iloilo (ordinary/air-con P186/216, four hours) and Roxas (ordinary P100, two hours).

Air-con vans meet all flights at Kalibo airport, taking passengers straight to Caticlan (P200, 1½ hours). Vans to Caticlan from town cost half that. Vans also serve Iloilo (P250, 3½ hours) and Roxas (P120, 1¾ hours). Vans depart from several points in the centre, the main cluster being near La Esperanza Hotel at the corner of Toting Reyes and Quezon Ave.

Roxas (Capiz)

036 / POP 147,700

Welcome to the self-described 'seafood capital of the Philippines'. Roxas, the busy capital of Capiz Province and commercial capital of northern Panay, ships out tonnes of processed sea critters daily. The city lies off the well-trod Boracay–Kalibo–Iloilo tourist route, so there's really not much reason you'd come here – except to eat delicious, incredibly cheap seafood, or perhaps as a springboard to Sibuyan Island in Romblon.

Sights & Activities

Baybay Beach BEACH

About 3km north of downtown Roxas is this 7km-long brown-sand beach lined with eateries and picnic shelters. Besides being the Philippines' top mecca for seafood shacks, the wide, flat beach is good for swimming and ideal for jogging. Watch fishermen unloading their catch at dawn and again at dusk.

Santa Monica Church & Bell CHURCH

This 1572 church in the town of Panay, a 20-minute jeepney or tricycle (P100) ride from Roxas, has the distinction of housing the largest bell in Asia. It's made entirely of coins from the Spanish period, and is more than 2m tall.

Mangrove Parks MANGROVES

Roxas has two mangrove parks where you can stroll along stilted bamboo walkways checking out the curious root formations and mud dwellers below. **Cadimahan** (admission P10) is between Baybay Beach and Culasi port, and offers two-hour tours on bamboo paddle boats (P500). **Culajao Mangrove Ecopark** (admission P20) hires out paddle boats and picnic nipa huts. It's east of Banica, about a 15-minute tricycle ride from Roxas.

Festivals & Events

Sinadya sa Halaran Festival CULTURAL

A colourful four-day event in early December celebrates the Immaculate Conception. It includes a solemn, candle-it fluvial parade on the Roxas River.

Sleeping

Baia Norte Beach Blub HOTEL $

(621 2165; Baybay Beach; d P880-1800;) When in Roxas you stay in the incredibly

noisy centre, or you can stay here on a yawning stretch of Baybay Beach. The choice should be easy. The characterless but clean rooms aren't completely immune to tricycle noise but at least the din is partially drowned out by breaking waves.

Roxas President's Inn HOTEL $$
(☎621 0208; www.roxaspresidentsinn.com; cnr Rizal & Lopez Jaena Sts; s/d from P980/1500;) A mix of old-world charm and modern amenities, this is the best place to stay in the centre. Rooms are a tad musty smelling, but are stylishly furnished. There are only two economy singles.

San Antonio Resort BEACH RESORT $$
(☎621 6638; d P1000-2340;) This big, bustling resort, popular with Filipino families, is a second Baybay Beach option. While it's not actually on the beach (it's across the road), it does have one humongous pool. Rooms are fairly spartan unless you upgrade.

Halaran Plaza Hotel LODGE $
(☎621 0649; P Gomez St; d with fan P500, with air-con P750-850;) An old-school wooden lodge in the centre, it's worn and noisy but has character and huge rooms.

Eating

TOP CHOICE **Baybay Seafood Buffets** SEAFOOD $$
(Baybay Beach; meals P150-300) The main reason to come to Roxas is to eat at one of the seafood shacks and eateries strung out along Baybay Beach. The best strategy is to walk along the beach road until you see something that strikes your fancy. At one nondescript shack we paid less than P200 for a huge plate of oysters, a plate of scallops and eight mouthwatering garlic butter shrimp. For something a little bigger and fancier, and not much more expensive, try **Coco Veranda** (10am-11pm), which has terrestrial offerings as well.

Cebrew CAFE $
(Gaisano Arcade, opposite Gaisano Mall, Arnaldo Blvd; drinks & snacks P50-100; 11.30am-2am;) A nice air-conditioned escape from the city. Come here for frappes, brownies, ice cream and, of course, free wi-fi.

Information

The widely distributed EZ Map Panay includes a Roxas city map that's much better than the one handed out for free by the tourist offices.

City Tourism Office (☎621 5316) On the northern bank of the river by the bridge.

Provincial Tourism Office (☎621 0042; Capitol Bldg) Good source of ideas for things to do around Capiz Province.

Getting There & Away

Air

The Roxas–Manila route is serviced daily by Cebu Pacific and Philippine Airlines. Offices are at the airport, a five-minute tricycle ride (P15) north of central Roxas.

Boat

From the large **Culasi Port** (☎522 3270), about 3km beyond (west of) Baybay Beach, there are near-daily bangka ferries to Sibuyan Island in Romblon – mostly to San Fernando (P300, five hours), but also to Cajidiocan and Magdiwang. The schedule for these fluctuates; call for details. Also from here, Negros Navigation and Moreta Shipping have a couple of boats a week to Manila.

To the east of town, the little **Banica pier** is the departure point for near-daily bangka to Masbate. Trips alternate to Mandaon, Milagros, Balud and Jintotolo, cost about P350, take four to six hours, and depart between 8.30am and 10am. There's also a boat to Palompon, Leyte, on Tuesdays and Fridays (P350, five hours).

Bus & Jeepney

Buses for Iloilo (P146, three hours) and Kalibo (ordinary P100, two hours) leave regularly from the Ceres Liner terminal on the southern end of Roxas Ave, opposite the Caltex service station. Air-con vans to Kalibo are also frequent (P120, 1¾ hours). Change in Kalibo for Caticlan.

NEGROS

POP 3.6 MILLION

With its rugged mountain interior, unspoilt beaches, underwater coral gardens, distinctive indigenous traditions and urban groove, the sheer overwhelming diversity of Negros is impossible to sum up in a single gesture. Despite this, Negros has somehow managed to fly under the tourist radar, and only now is it starting to get the recognition it deserves.

More people are stopping to absorb the good-time vibe of Dumaguete, the funky college town in the southeast, and enjoy its surrounding dive sites that rival anywhere else in the country for marine splendour. Up north, the stunning beach havens around Sipalay, or the forested hill stations of Mt Kanlaon, the 'living museums' of Silay and great food at Bacolod, reaffirm its reputation as a rising star of the Philippines.

For more than a century Negros was famed as the country's 'sugar bowl'. From the 1850s, the majority of arable land was turned over to sugar-cane plantations. In both the cities and the smaller towns, many historic buildings still stand testament to the fortunes made by the sugar barons. The 'Sugarlandia' phenomenon is still very evident in the north of the country, where convoys of trucks loaded with cane rumble endlessly down the highway, through a sea of silver-green cane fields.

Negros

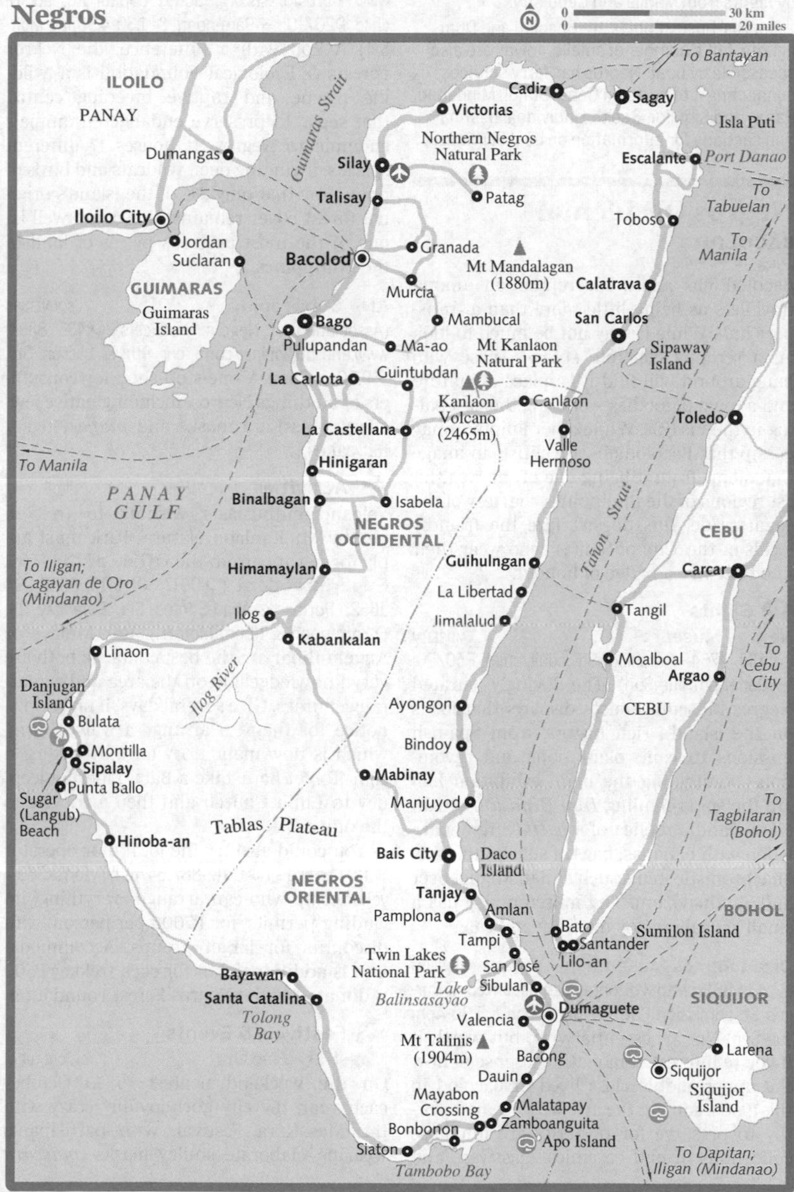

The island is divided into two provinces lying either side of a central mountain range: Negros Oriental (whose capital is Dumaguete) is to the east, and Negros Occidental (capital Bacolod) is to the west.

Getting There & Away

Bacolod and Dumaguete airports are serviced by flights from Manila and Cebu City.

Negros' busiest ports are Bacolod and Dumaguete, but a number of smaller towns are also accessible by boat. Negros has ferry services connecting it to ports on Cebu, Bohol, Mindanao, Panay and Siquijor. See the individual destination sections for information on boat services.

Negros Occidental

BACOLOD

034 / POP 499,497

Bacolod has an unfair reputation among travellers as being little more than a transport hub. While it may not be much to look at, a scrappy concrete sprawl, those who hang around will find it's a place of culture and a town of foodies – offering the best eating in the Visayas. While other Filipinos may gossip that Bacolodians are elitist, an image that stems from it being one of the wealthiest regions of the Philippines courtesy of the sugar trade, this doesn't faze the friendly locals of the 'City of Smiles' who wear their fine taste like a badge of honour.

Sights

Negros Museum MUSEUM
(433 4764; Gatuslao St; adult/child P50/20; 10am-8pm Tue-Sun) The lovingly curated Negros Museum houses displays that focus on the island's rich history, from Spanish missions to cane plantations and revolution. Dominating the main exhibition hall are the sugar-hauling *Iron Dinosaur* steam engine and a replica of a *batil* (cargo boat), laden with bananas, bags of sugar and a few anachronistic items such as San Miguel beer and Tanduay rum. The museum also has a small art gallery, toy museum and cafe.

Dizon Ramos Museum MUSEUM
(434 8512; http://dizonramosmuseum.com; Burgos St; admission P30; 10am-noon & 1.30-4pm Tue-Sun) Not an essential visit, but worth it if you're interested in getting a sense of how the upper-middle class lived in Bacolod in the 1950s. Among the artefacts deemed worthy to preserve for posterity are immense collections of naff ceramics, glassware and religious knick-knacks, as well the dining table set for Sunday dinner.

One block up from here is a magnificent **art-deco mansion** owned by GV & Sons.

Negros Forests & Ecological Foundation ZOO
(Biodiversity Conservation Center; 433 9234; www.negrosforests.org; South Capitol Rd; adult/child P20/10; 9am-noon & 1.30-4.30pm Mon-Sat) A zoo with a difference, the Negros Forests & Ecological Foundation is a 'wildlife rescue and captive breeding centre' that seeks to preserve endangered animals endemic to Negros. It houses 17 different species, including deer, wildcats and birds of prey. Now that only 3% of the island's original forest cover remains, this could well be one of the most precious pieces of land in the Philippines.

ANP Showroom SOUVENIRS
(Association of Negros Producers; 433 8833; www.anp-philippines.com; cnr 9th & Lacson Sts; 9.30am-7pm) A one-stop shop for consumers of all things Negros, including native jewellery, MassKara masks and *piaya* (sugary flat cakes).

Activities

Volcano enthusiasts wishing to trek in nearby Mt Kanlaon Natural Park must apply for permits from the **Office of the Park Superintendent** (0917 301 1410, 0939 894 3662; Porras & Abad-Santos Sts, Barangay 39; 8am-noon & 1-5pm Mon-Fri). Rex Mulave or Angelo Bibar are the best contacts; both are very knowledgeable on the area and can arrange guides. Give several days', if not weeks', notice for them to arrange a waiver form, which is now mandatory for all trekkers to sign. To get here, take a Bata–Libertad jeepney to Lupit Church and then a tricycle to the office.

You could also try the local tour operator **Billy Torres** (0917 887 6476; billytorres369@yahoo.com), who can arrange everything, including permits, for P7000 per person, with discounts for larger groups. Accommodation is additional, but for each trekker P500 is donated to the Negros Forest Foundation.

Festivals & Events

MassKara Festival CULTURAL
On the weekend nearest to 19 October each year, the city goes joyfully crazy with the MassKara Festival, with participants wearing elaborate smiley masks (*máscara*

is Spanish for mask) and dancing in the streets.

Sleeping

If you want to be close to the swankiest bars and restaurants, and as far from the dust and grime as you can get, the place to stay is uptown. On the other hand, downtown is a lot livelier (during the day at least) and has its share of good accommodation.

TOP CHOICE Suites at Calle Nueva BOUTIQUE HOTEL $$
(☎708 8000; www.thesuitesatcallenueva.com; 15 Nueva St; s/d incl breakfast from P800/1200; ❄📶) Undoubtedly the best value for money in town, this centrally located boutique hotel has tasteful rooms every bit as comfortable as a mini high-end hotel. Beds are new and comfy, couches are embellished with pillows, and rooms have plasma TV and sparkling bathrooms with modern fittings. The free cooked buffet breakfast will tide you over for most of the day.

11th Street Bed & Breakfast Inn GUESTHOUSE $
(☎433 9191; www.bb11st.webeden.co.uk; 11th St; s/d/tr incl breakfast with fan P400/500/600, with air-con P650/800/990; ❄📶) Enjoying a calm sidestreet location, yet still walking distance to all the action on Lacson St, this leafy pension feels like you're staying in a well-heeled family home. Rooms are no-frills, but immaculately clean.

Hotel Sea Breeze HOTEL $
(☎433 7370; San Juan St; r from P750; ❄📶) One of the original hotels in Bacolod, Sea Breeze provides a glimpse into the grandeur of the sugar plantation glory days. A grand wooden staircase leads past an old ballroom up to worn but functional rooms. There's a nice garden courtyard out back.

L'Fisher Hotel HOTEL $$
(☎433 3731; www.lfisherhotelbacolod.com; cnr 14th & Lacson Sts; r from P1195; ❄@📶🏊) Like the setting for an Agatha Christie mystery, L'Fisher is unselfconsciously theatrical with its opera-house atrium, potted ferns, taffeta-uniformed staff and obligatory piano player in the lobby. Rooms have all the comforts; its sister hotel **L'Fisher Chalet**, adjoined at the back, has less expensive rooms (from P1195) and a decadent rooftop infinity pool.

Pension Bacolod PENSION HOUSE $
(☎433 3377; 11th St; s/d with fan P150/200, with air-con P430/520; ❄📶) This well-run place in a quiet location offers excellent value for money with 76 reasonably sized, well-kept rooms. Little wonder that it's often fully booked, so reservations are recommended.

Check Inn HOTEL $
(☎432 3755; www.checkinn.com.ph; Luzuriaga St; s/d from P650/850; ❄@📶) With midrange comforts such as hot water and cable TV at budget prices, this slick downtown chain hotel is great value and runs like clockwork. There is free use of a gym.

Saltimboca Tourist Inn HOTEL $
(☎432 3617; r with fan with shared bathroom P430, with air-con from P700; ❄📶🏊) A mixed bag, gaudy Saltimboca has rooms that are a little dated, but nevertheless good value with a nice garden setting. It has a small pool, a res-

WORTH A TRIP

THE RUINS

Set on lovely manicured grounds surrounded by sugar plantations, the **Ruins** (☎476 4334; www.theruins.com.ph; admission P50; ⊙8.30am-8pm) is an early-20th-century mansion that provides an eerie glimpse into yesteryear. Only the skeletal frame of this grand Italianate building remains, destroyed by the US during WWII to prevent the advancing Japanese from using it as their headquarters. Rather fancifully called the Taj Mahal of Negros, the Ruins were likewise built on foundations of love: the sugar magnate Mariano Macson constructed the mansion as a monument to the memory of his Portuguese wife, Maria. Opened to the public in 2008, it now serves as a decadent **restaurant** (⊙11am-8pm) with a Mediterranean-Spanish-inspired menu. Try to visit at sunset, when the neoclassical columns and stately arches of the ruin provide fantastic photography opportunities.

Located 7km north of Bacolod, to get here catch a 'Bata' signed jeepney from Lacson St and ask to be dropped at the Ruins; from there it's a P15 tricycle ride. Otherwise it's a P200 taxi ride from Bacolod.

Bacolod

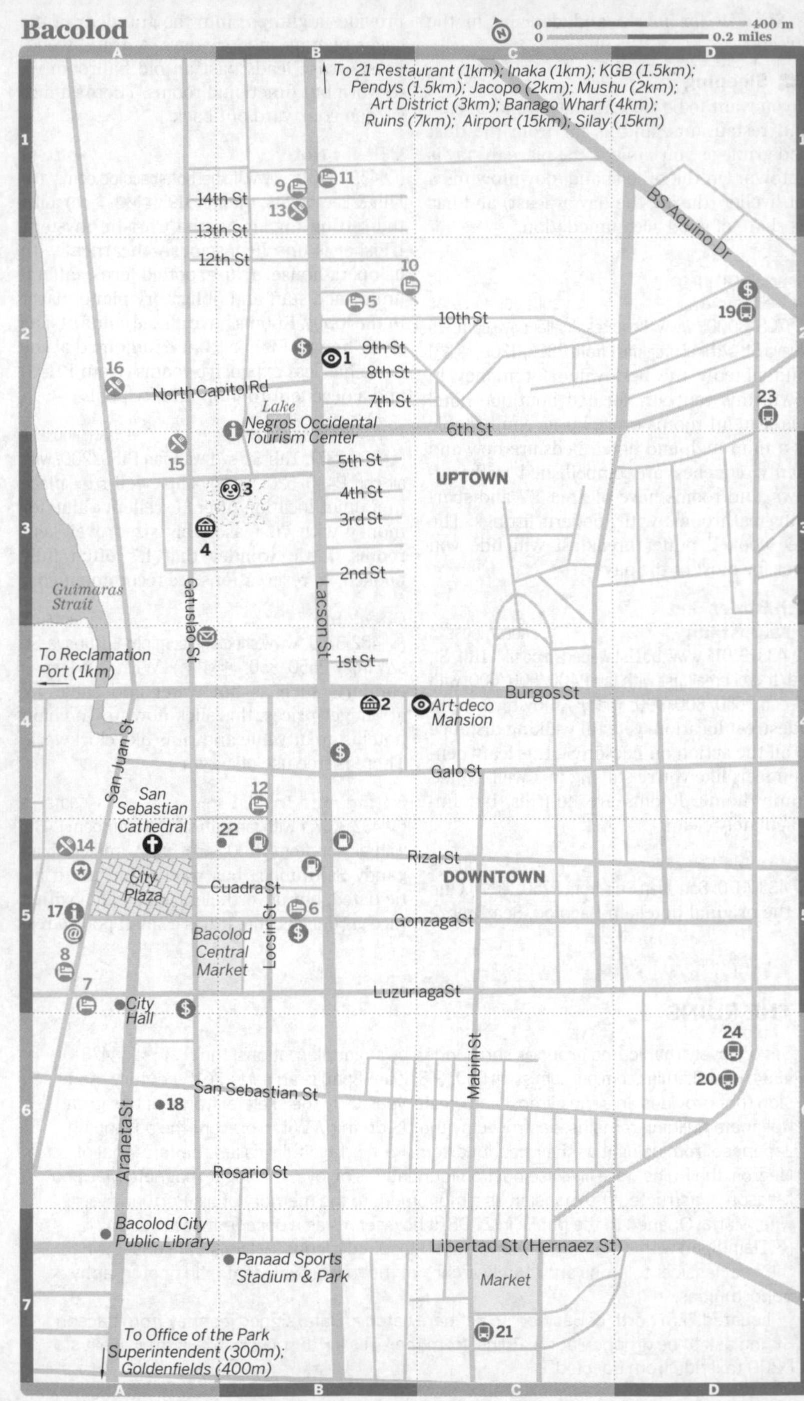

0 400 m
0 0.2 miles
To 21 Restaurant (1km); Inaka (1km); KGB (1.5km); Pendys (1.5km); Jacopo (2km); Mushu (2km); Art District (3km); Banago Wharf (4km); Ruins (7km); Airport (15km); Silay (15km)
BS Aquino Dr
14th St
13th St
12th St
10th St
9th St
8th St
7th St
6th St
North Capitol Rd
Lake
Negros Occidental Tourism Center
5th St
4th St
3rd St
2nd St
1st St
UPTOWN
Guimaras Strait
Gatusiao St
Lacson St
To Reclamation Port (1km)
Burgos St
Art-deco Mansion
Galo St
San Juan St
San Sebastian Cathedral
Rizal St
DOWNTOWN
City Plaza
Cuadra St
Gonzaga St
Bacolod Central Market
Locsin St
Luzuriaga St
City Hall
Mabini St
San Sebastian St
Araneta St
Rosario St
Bacolod City Public Library
Libertad St (Hernaez St)
Panaad Sports Stadium & Park
Market
To Office of the Park Superintendent (300m); Goldenfields (400m)

Bacolod

Sights

1 ANP Showroom....B2
2 Dizon Ramos Museum....B4
3 Negros Forests & Ecological Foundation....B3
4 Negros Museum....A3

Sleeping

5 11th Street Bed & Breakfast Inn....B2
6 Bascon Hotel....B5
7 Check Inn....A5
8 Hotel Sea Breeze....A5
9 L'Fisher Hotel....B1
10 Pension Bacolod....B2
11 Saltimboca Tourist Inn....B1
12 Suites at Calle Nueva....B4

Eating

13 Calea....B1
14 Manokan Country....A5
15 Organic Market....A3
16 Pala Pala....A2

Information

17 Tourist Information Office....A5

Transport

18 Aboitiz Express....A6
Cebu Pacific....(see 22)
19 Ceres Bus Liner North Terminal....D2
20 Ceres Bus Liner South Terminal....D6
21 Jeepneys for La Carlota, Ma-ao & Mambucal....C7
22 Negros Navigation & SuperFerry....B5
23 North Bus Station....D2
24 South Bus Station....D6

taurant and an ostentatious disco-bar with live music on Wednesday to Saturday nights.

Bascon Hotel HOTEL $
(435 4071; basconbacolod@gmail.com; Gonzaga St; s/d with fan P500/650, with air-con P650/750;) Established in 1965, judging by its decor not a lot has changed at this downtown hotel. Located up from the market, the area buzzes during the day but is quiet at night. Rooms have cable TV and hot water; check out a few, as some are nicer than others.

Eating

Bacolod has a great love of affair with food, so you will eat very well here. As well as popular streetfood precincts, uptown Lacson St has a great restaurant strip.

Sweet tooths will not want to miss out on the napoleons (pastry filled with custard cream) from **Pendys** (Lacson St), a Bacolod institution. **Calea** (Lacson St) is also very highly regarded for its cake and coffee.

Manokan Country FILIPINO $
(chicken P25-65) If you ask someone from Manila what Bacolod is most famous for, the answer will inevitably be chicken *inasal* (chicken marinated in lemon and soy, and barbecued on charcoal), and Manokan Country is *the* place to get it. It comprises a strip of basic open-air restaurants, where not a single part of the chicken goes to waste, from head to feet; select your choice of skewers. Plates of shucked oysters (P35 per plate) make for a popular appetiser, and an unbelievable bargain. Cheap, cold beer is the perfect accompaniment.

Aboys FILIPINO $$
(Goldenfields; meals P160-350; 10am-10pm Mon-Sat) A Goldenfields institution, south of town, ultrapopular Aboys specialises in Filipino cuisine. Select your meal from its display of juicy marinated meats and seafood; the tender grilled marlin belly is seriously amazing.

Inaka JAPANESE $$$
(Lacson St; meals P80-640; 10am-4pm & 6-10pm Tue-Sun) Tastefully decorated with modern art, Inaka has an authentic Japanese menu with a good sushi and sashimi selection. Vegetarians will want to try tofu steak with mushroom rice (P220).

Pala Pala SEAFOOD $$
(North Capitol Rd; 10am-late) A local favourite, head first to the adjoining fish market to choose your seafood dinner before picking any of the small hole-in-the-wall eateries that'll charcoal barbecue your fish, prawns or lobster. Cooking fees start from P50, and they have cheap beer.

Jacopo STEAKHOUSE $$
(Lacson St; meals P170-285) Smart and casual Jacopo is renowned for its tenderloin steak and succulent kebabs at very affordable prices. Upstairs has avant-garde decor with trippy lighting projected upon the walls. It's across from Robinson's Place mall.

21 Restaurant FILIPINO $$
(Lacson St; www.21restaurant.com; mains P185-360) Crisp white tablecloths, professional

waiters and appetising menu set the tone for this classy affair. The only thing out of whack are its very reasonable prices. Grilled squid stuffed with lemongrass is a delicious and healthy choice.

Organic Market CAFE $
(Gatuslao St; shakes P25; ⏲6am-6pm Mon-Sat) In a lot just behind the Provincial Building, this sunny and spacious cafeteria serves up healthy salads, snacks and shakes using organic produce from certified farms across Negros. Outside has stands selling organic fruit and veg.

Drinking & Entertainment

Uptown has the best bars for hanging out with arty locals, while Goldenfields entertainment precinct south of town is better for nightclubs and attracts a more seedy crowd.

KGB BAR
(23rd St; ⏲6pm-late) A popular hang-out for students, young professionals, artists and expats, KGB is one of the most relaxed bars in town. The front bar has trees protruding through a draped cloth ceiling, while at the rear are more seats and pool tables. Check out the great artwork on its walls.

Art District BARS
(Lacson St, Mandalagan) A new complex of bars, restaurants and galleries frequented by artists and a young student crowd, there are several options here that make it worth a trip, including **Gallery Orange** (⏲2-9pm Mon-Sat), which exhibits modern art by local Negrese artists. **Gypsy Bar Tea Room** gets raucous with a student-heavy crowd smoking sheesha and indulging in a scarily cheap drinks menu; a sign warns of the P250 fine for vomiting! The more chilled-out **Café Joint** (⏲4pm-late) is an outdoor bar that's a hang-out for creative types.

Mushu BAR
(cnr Lacson & 20th Sts) At super groovy Mushu you can enjoy sickly sweet house cocktails and watch local bands while eating excellent Chinese counter meals, such as salt-and-pepper crablets (P80).

Information

All tourism-related queries should be taken to the **Negros Occidental Tourism Center** (☎433 2515; www.negrosoccidentaltourism.com; Provincial Capitol Bldg), a vibrant team passionate about Bacolod and its surrounds. There's also a small **tourist information office** (☎433 7362; San Juan St) opposite the City Plaza with a few brochures.

There are plenty of ATMs. The **post office** (Gatuslao St) is near the intersection with Burgos St, while the **police station** (San Juan St) is opposite the City Plaza.

Wherever you are in town, internet cafes are never far away, especially if you're near the university area; there are also a few on the top floor of SM City. Rates are around P25 per hour.

Getting There & Away

AIR

PAL, Cebu Pacific and Airphil Express all have daily flights to both Cebu City and Manila. Zest Air also flies to Manila.

BOAT

The Bredco Port is a P15 tricycle ride from the City Plaza and services Manila and Iloilo on Panay. All fastcraft operators and **SuperFerry** (☎434 2531) have ticketing outlets at the port. SuperFerry and **Negros Navigation** (☎441 0652) have ticketing offices downtown.

ILOILO The most popular route is from Bacolod to Iloilo City by frequent fastcraft (see p245) for details. There are also many car ferries departing to Dumangas, about 20km northeast of Iloilo City.

MANILA SuperFerry has three services a week to Manila (from P1300, 19 hours), while Negros Navigation (P1100, 19 hours) runs to Manila four times a week, departing from Banago Wharf, 7km north of central Bacolod.

MINDANAO SuperFerry manages the Bacolod to Mindanao route with a Saturday service to Ozamis (from P1100, 18 hours) and Iligan (P1100, 14 hours), and a twice-weekly service to Zamboanga (from P1100, 17 hours). Negros Navigation has a Tuesday service to Cagayan de Oro (P1176, 17 hours) also from Bredco Port.

BUS & JEEPNEY

The main bus company is Ceres Bus Liner. For destinations north of Bacolod, phone the **North terminal** (☎433 4993); for destinations south of Bacolod (including San Carlos), phone the **South terminal** (☎434 2387).

Buses between Bacolod and Dumaguete (P310, six hours 45 minutes) go via Mabinay, departing every half-hour from 2.30am till 10.30pm from the South terminal.

Services to Cebu City depart from both terminals, but the quickest is from the north terminal, which has a ferry leg between San Carlos and Toledo (P535, eight hours). The bus from the South terminal goes via Mabinay (P507, nine hours), departing at 2.40am and 5.40pm.

Ceres and other smaller bus lines travel the coastal route between Bacolod and San Carlos (P140, four hours), stopping or terminating at towns along the way, including Cadiz (P80, 1½ hours) at 12.30am and 6.30am and Sagay (P80, 2½ hours), which have boat services to Bantayan Island. However, the fastest way to get to San Carlos is the scenic inland bus (P140, three hours) at 7.15am and 12.15pm.

Southbound bus stops include La Carlota (P43, one hour) every 45 minutes till 5pm, Ilog (P85, 2½ hours) and Sipalay (P169, 4½ hours), every 30 mins, till 8pm.

Ceres buses are fast and plentiful but if you can't find anything going your way, wander over to the secondary north and south bus stations that service the smaller bus lines and are within easy reach of the two Ceres terminals.

Many jeepneys service the short-haul routes. Jeepneys for La Carlota (P30, 1¼ hours), Ma-ao (P25, 30 minutes) and Mambucal (P25, 45 minutes) are stationed behind the market between Libertad St and Lizares Ave.

Getting Around

The airport is 15km from Bacolod, just east of Silay. A taxi to the city centre will cost around P300.

To get to the city centre by jeepney from the north or south bus stations, take a 'Shopping' jeepney to Lacson St. Both 'Bata' and 'Mandalagan' jeepneys run north–south along Lacson St to downtown.

A car with driver is about P1500 per day; you can organise this through the tourist offices and many hotels.

There are regular buses to Silay (P14, 30 minutes) from the north bus station.

LA CARLOTA

☎034 / POP 19,218

La Carlota lies about 45km south of Bacolod, at the base of Mt Kanlaon. The town's annual **Kabankalan Sinulog** is a wild street party held on the second Sunday in January, when dancers are daubed in black in imitation of the island's Negrito people. On the Sunday nearest 1 May, the city holds its annual **Pasalamat Festival**, a fun-filled mardi gras with dazzling native costumes and huge parade floats.

Jeepneys run to Bacolod (P30, one hour) or Guintubdan (P30, one hour) until about 5pm, departing from the market. After this time you'll have to settle for a tricycle to take you to Guintubdan (P300, 30 minutes) for the nearest accommodation. Contact the **mayor's office** (☎460 2582) for more information.

MT KANLAON NATURAL PARK

With its dense forest and hike up to the summit of an active volcano, the 24,388-hectare Mt Kanlaon Natural Park is one of the most popular treks in the Visayas. The central highlands are home to some critically endangered species of wildlife and birds, and also several species of orchid.

Activities

For keen hikers, **Mt Kanlaon** (2465m) is not a tricky or demanding climb, but because of the risks involved, hiking to the summit of the active volcano is a necessarily complicated business, with a lot of red tape to endure in the process.

There are three routes to the top, one of which can be done by fit climbers in a day. Most treks to the summit take from one to two days return, though some diehards are known to do it from Guintubdan in 10 hours (not recommended).

Whatever route you take, the best place to camp on the first night is Margaha Valley, the spectacular flat basin of the old (extinct) crater. The most rewarding part of the climb is the home stretch from Pagatpat Ridge to the summit, where, on a clear day, you can see Margaha Valley below, the smoking crater above and Bacolod in the distance. The hardest part of the climb is the long, steep incline leading up to Pagatpat Ridge itself.

Species that inhabit the region include wild boar, civet cat, leopard cat, spotted deer, hornbill, hawk eagle and the critically endangered bleeding-heart pigeon. If you're wanting to spot wildlife, you can tailor your trip to make this a focus, though sadly it's unlikely you'll see much.

HIKING MT KANLAON

If you wish to hike up the volcano, you *must* obtain a permit (P300) from the Bacolod-based **Office of the Park Superintendent** (☎0917 301 1410, 0939 894 3662; Porras & Abad-Santos Sts, Barangay 39, Bacolod; ⏲8am-noon & 1-5pm Mon-Fri). This is for your own safety, as well as for preservation of the park environment, and only a limited number of hikers are permitted to visit the park at any given time. The climbing season is March to May and October to December.

There are three entrance stations to the summit: Murcia, Guintubdan and Canlaon. Trekkers wanting to walk to the summit without joining an organised group will need to organise a guide (P500 per day, maximum nine trekkers per guide) with the park superintendent in Bacolod or through the **Department of Environment & Natural Resources** (DENR; ⏲6.30am-7pm Mon-Fri) office in Guintubdan. Porters cost an additional P1300 per day.

If hiking up a mountain of red tape is not your idea of adventure, a far easier way to arrange matters is to go as part of an organised group. **Dumaguete Outdoors** (☎035-226 2110; www.dumagueteoutdoors.com; 3 Noblefranca St, Dumaguete), **Harold's Mansion Tourist Inn** (☎035-225 8000; www.haroldsmansion.com; 205 Hibbard Ave, Dumaguete), **Planet Action** (☎0916 624 8253, 032-474 3016; www.action-philippines.com) in Moalboal or local **Billy Torres** (☎0917 887 6476; billytorres369@yahoo.com) can arrange trips and handle the necessary paperwork at a moment's notice.

The weather can be unpredictable, so bring a T-shirt, light waterproof jacket, light pants and climbing shoes, but prepare for a chilly night (thermals and a woollen hat are recommended).

Every few years sees some volcanic activity, or 'sneezing' as locals call it. There is daily monitoring for any threat of volcanic eruption, with no permits issued in such cases. The park superintendent will sometimes evacuate the mountain and enforce a clearance zone of 6km around its base. The last eruption occurred in August 1996, killing three hikers.

Sleeping & Eating

The resorts of Mt Kanlaon are scattered around its eastern flanks.

GUINTUBDAN

High on the slopes of Mt Kanlaon, the wonderfully cool ferny barangay of Guintubdan has two 'resorts' owned by La Carlota and Bago cities, respectively. The fact that there is any accommodation here at all makes Guintubdan an attractive place to be based for hikes to the summit. Self-sufficiency is the watchword for both resorts; staff can cook food but you might have to settle for rice and tinned meat. From either resort, guides can also take you on excellent day trips (P150) to any of the seven nearby waterfalls.

There are only a couple of jeepneys per day from Guintubdan to La Carlota (last one at 2.30pm), where you will need to change for Bacolod. Jeepneys stop at both resorts but the schedule is ad hoc, so just ask a local when they are likely to arrive.

Guintubdan Visitors Center GUESTHOUSE $
(☎/fax La Carlota mayor's office 034-460 2582; s/d from P400/800, camping for 6-person tent P150) This impressive stone building has basic clean rooms with cold-water bathrooms, and a communal area with magnificent views. Bring your own food and use the kitchen, or the staff can cook whatever is available.

Raphael Salas Nature Park GUESTHOUSE $
(☎034-461 0540; dm P100, r with private bathroom P300) A mere 200m up the road from Guintubdan Visitors Center, Raphael Salas offers more of the same. The accommodation is a little more spartan but the views are a little better, so take your pick. Set meals are P200.

MA-AO

There is a single resort in the forested hillsides around Ma-ao. To get there, catch a jeepney to Ma-ao from Bago (P20, 45 minutes) or Bacolod (P40, 1½ hours). From Ma-ao, the 30-minute tricycle ride to the resort will cost P200. The nearby Kipot Twin Falls (admission P20) make a nice side trip.

Buenos Aires Mountain Resort MOUNTAIN RESORT $
(☎034-461 0540; tourismbago@yahoo.com; dm P200, cottages from P800, r with air-con from P1200; ❄☒) Built in the 1930s, this hacienda-style mountain resort situated by a river is famous for having housed President Quezon when he hid from the Japanese during WWII. There is a restaurant on-site. Note that the 'hostel' rooms are actually more hotel-like than the cottages, which are comfortable but rustic. Be mindful of the mossy steps if you're carrying a heavy backpack. It's best visited on weekdays, when you can enjoy the quiet of the forest surrounds.

SILAY

☎034 / POP 24,524

Located 14km north of Bacolod, Silay was once the jewel in the crown of the Negros sugar boom. The town first tasted sweet success when a French resident planted sugar cane in the 1850s, and its pier swiftly became an international port of call. Silay's golden age was between 1880 and 1935, when its 31 recognised 'ancestral homes' were built. The haciendas of Silay were bastions of refinement and privilege, and in the early 1900s the town became *the* place for European musicians and artists to hang out. But it wasn't to last. The combination of growth in nearby Bacolod, damage wrought in WWII and the development of the sugar industry overseas resulted in a decline in Silay's cultural and industrial activity.

Sights & Activities

Seeking out traces of Silay's glorious golden age is a must for any heritage-architecture-loving visitor. Of Silay's ancestral buildings, the best preserved are three grand historical homes, two of which are museums, the other a private residence. No visit to Silay would be complete without sampling the delicacies of El Ideal Bakery, which is also one of the recognised 31 ancestral buildings.

Silay's tourist office has a useful free city map listing all ancestral buildings.

TOP CHOICE Hofileña Ancestral Home HISTORIC BUILDING

(☎495 4561; Cinco de Noviembre St; adult/child P40/20; ⏲by appointment) The stately Hofileña Ancestral Home contains one of the Philippines' finest art collections, as well as antiques belonging to one of Silay's principal families, the Hofileña family. The house is now owned by the charismatic and loquacious Ramon Hofileña, a tireless preserver of Negros Occidental's cultural heritage. If you book ahead, Ramon will proudly show you around his house, including his collection of paintings, ancient artefacts and collectables.

For almost 35 years, Ramon has run the **Annual Cultural Tour of Negros Occidental** (tours P700). The three one-day tours are scheduled in December, and take in attractions from the nearby region, including the famous Church of St Joseph the Worker at the Victorias Milling Company. With a few days' notice, Ramon can arrange architecture tours of Silay any time of the year.

Bernardino Jalandoni Ancestral House MUSEUM

(☎495 5093; Rizal St; adult/child incl tour P50/20; ⏲9am-5pm Tue-Sun) Built in 1908 and affectionately known as the 'Pink House', Bernardino Jalandoni Ancestral House is virtually unchanged from the days when it was home to the Jalandoni family. Now a museum, the polished hardwood floors, furniture and objets d'art on the 2nd level are the best preserved of the historical items. In the back room are old photos of beauty pageant winners from the 1940s and '50s, and a glass case filled with dozens of Ken and Barbie dolls in traditional Filipino costume, including the oddly appropriate General MacArthur Ken, re-enacting the (staged) Leyte landing, and Imelda Marcos Barbie, surrounded by dozens of shoes.

Balay Negrense Museum MUSEUM

(☎714 7676; Cinco de Noviembre St; adult/child P40/20; ⏲10am-6pm Tue-Sun) Also known as the Victor Gaston Ancestral Home, Balay Negrense Museum was built of balayong hardwood in 1898 and has the most photogenic exterior of any house in Silay. Victor's father, Yves Leopold Germain Gaston, is credited with being the first to cultivate sugar cane commercially in the region. The house has been painstakingly restored and furnished with period pieces donated by

Silay

Silay

Sights
1 Balay Negrense Museum....A3
2 Bernardino Jalandoni Ancestral House....B1
3 Church of San Diego....B2
4 Hofileña Ancestral Home....A2

Sleeping
5 Baldevia Pension House....B1

Eating
6 Café 1925....B3
7 El Ideal Bakery....B3

Transport
8 Buses and Jeepneys to Bacolod....B3
9 Buses and Jeepneys to San Carlos....B1

locals. The bevelled-glass windows and Chinese carved lattice work are original.

Church of San Diego CHURCH
On the main road through town, the silver-domed Church of San Diego was designed by the Italian architect Lucio Bernasconi. It was built in Romanesque style in 1927 and is topped by a crucifix that, when lit at night, is visible far out to sea.

Sleeping & Eating

Fortuna Pension House PENSION HOUSE $
(☎714 8166; fortuna_pension@yahoo.com; r with shared/private bathroom P750/1000; ❄@) Built in the 1950s, this three-storey wooden home set in farmlands offers a glimpse of hacienda living. There's a lovely loft room, but the drawback is the shared bathroom. Breakfast is the only meal available (P100). Fortuna is around 1km south of the city – turn left at José Locsin St, pass the City Health building and follow the signs. A tricycle will cost P15.

Baldevia Pension House PENSION HOUSE $
(☎495 0272; cnr Burgos & Rizal Sts; r with fan P450, with air-con P650-1400; ❄) Another ancestral house, this well-run establishment, in the stately building that dominates the main drag, has comfortable but spartan tiled rooms with spotless hot-water bathrooms. Fan rooms are often booked up.

TOP CHOICE **El Ideal Bakery** BAKERY $
(Rizal St; pies & cakes P25-40; ⏲6am-6.30pm) Just south of the public plaza, in one of the less prepossessing ancestral houses, is the home and birthplace of many of the delicacies for which Silay has become famous. The bakery was set up in 1935, during Silay's heyday, to provide snacks for the gamblers who couldn't drag themselves away from the table. Its dark, wooden interior retains this atmosphere. Some of the bakery's famous creations include *lumpia ubod* (spring rolls filled with pork, shrimp and the juicy tip of the coconut palm) and *piaya* (flat bread sprinkled with brown sugar and sesame seeds). Of the great selection of pies, cakes and sandwiches, our favourite was the old-school egg pie (custard tart). If you're just about to set off for Mt Kanlaon or Northern Negros Natural Park, this is the place to stock up on trekking treats.

Café 1925 CAFE $
(www.cafe1925.weebly.com; JP Ledesma St; ⏲9am-10pm Mon-Sat; 📶) Funky little cafe with friendly staff serving strong coffee, sirloin steak sandwiches (P90) and homemade mango cheese ice cream (P60).

Information

Silay's **tourist office** (☎495 5553; silaycity_tourism@yahoo.com; cnr Zamora & Gamboa Sts; ⏲8am-noon & 1-5pm Mon-Fri) is located in the public plaza, and can organise tours to nearby sugar plantations and permits to Northern Negros Natural Park.

Opposite the market, **Woofy.net** (Rizal St; per hr P15; ⏲8am-midnight) provides internet access.

There are several ATMs, with **Metrobank** (cnr Burgos & Rizal Sts) having the largest withdrawal limit.

Getting There & Away

Silay airport is approximately 10 minutes away from the city proper. A tricycle will cost P10 and taxi around P500.

Both buses and jeepneys travel between Silay and Bacolod (P14, 30 minutes). In Silay, all buses and jeepneys heading north and south stop along Rizal St.

From Silay, there are buses all day stopping at the coastal towns towards San Carlos (P130, three hours).

AROUND SILAY

The sugar plantations that surround Silay have their own colourful histories. To arrange a visit you'll need to arrange a tour through the Silay tourist office. Sadly, Victorias Milling Company was closed to tourists at the time of research, but enquire to see if things have changed.

Only a 15-minute ride by jeepney north of Silay, tours of the **Hawaiian Philippine Sugar Company** (☎034-495 2085; ⏲8am-noon & 1-5pm Mon-Fri Nov-Apr) can include watching the harvesting process (November to April), locomotive riding, handcart riding and even homestays (P300 per person).

About 32km east of Silay (P50 by jeepney, one hour), **Northern Negros Natural Park** (Patag National Park) was the site of a horrendous battle during WWII in which 6000 Japanese soldiers lost their lives. The park – which by some calculations is the largest remaining forested zone on Negros – is home to many rare species, especially birds. More than 90 species of birds have been recorded here, 37 of which are endemic to the park. These days, great hikes are possible from Patag village into the natural park, with several waterfall visits along the way. The Silay tourist office can organise a guide (P150 per person) and a **homestay** (per person P300).

The only other accommodation is in the old **Patag Hospital building** (per person with shared/private bathroom P80/100). Even if you wish to go it alone, you will require a permit (P10) from the Silay tourist office, which is for your security more than anything else. You'll need to write a letter stating dates and participants for the climb. Theoretically permits should be issued in no more than five minutes.

SAGAY

☎034 / POP 19,323

Sagay City is a combination of Old Sagay, on the coast, and New Sagay, on the National Hwy – 5.5km apart, it's P9 by tricycle between the two. But it's best known as the proud guardian of the 32,000-hectare **Sagay Marine Reserve**, established in 1999 to protect one of the only areas on Negros still teeming with marine life. The sanctuary is centred on **Carbin Reef** (P50 entry), about 15km northeast of Old Sagay (20 minutes by bangka). Also here is **Maca Reef**, where flocks of migratory birds are a common sight.

To organise a boat, ask at the **tourist office** (☎488 0649; www.sagay-city.com.ph; City Hall, New Sagay) or at the pier. A small boat will cost P1000 (maximum five people). Snorkelling equipment (P300) can be arranged at the tourist office; diving is discouraged due to the shallowness of the reef.

The tourist office can help organise accommodation in town. Belonging to the city government, the enormous **Balay Kauswagan** (☎488 0316; Municipal Hall, New Sagay; dm P200, tw with air-con & private bathroom P800; ❄🏊) is a characterless convention centre with OK rooms and a swimming pool, but no restaurant.

There is a daily 10am bangka to Bantayan town on Bantayan Island (P250, 2½ hours). Ceres buses run regularly to Cadiz (P16, 30 minutes) and Escalante (P9, 15 minutes).

ESCALANTE

☎034 / POP 14,569

Like neighbouring Sagay, Escalante is a city of two parts – with Old Escalante on the coast and New Escalante on the highway. City Hall, the town plaza, the bus terminal and Equitable PCI bank are all in New Escalante; the port of Danao, from where the boats to Cebu leave, is in Old Escalante. It's 7km between the two, and a tricycle will cost around P10 (15 minutes).

The helpful **tourist office** (☎454 0696; www.escalantecity.gov.ph; City Hall, New Escalante) can assist with accommodation and activities. It can also arrange guides (P1000 per day) for the nearby caves, some used by the Japanese as hideouts in WWII, or birdwatching at **Kalanggaman**.

The little **Isla Puti** (aka Enchanted Isle), a 20-minute bangka ride from Escalante (also approachable from Vito Port, Old Sagay), has some attractive white-sand beaches. Boats (good for 10 people; P600, 20 minutes) can be organised at Barcelona pier or through the town's tourist office. You can stay at **Jomabo Island Paradise Beach Resort** (☎0920 438 8963, in Bacolod 034-434 3972; www.jomabo.com; r & cottages P1500-3000).

In town, the best sleeping option is **Rodeway Inn** (☎454 0176; National Hwy, New Escalante; d with fan & shared bathroom P350, with air-con & private bathroom from P800; ❄📶), a friendly and efficient family-run operation with comfortable and secure accommodation. It's located opposite the pretty town plaza.

A daily ferry departs for Tabuelan (P200, two hours) on Cebu at 8am from Old Escalante's Danao Port. There are direct buses from Escalante to Bacolod (P85, two hours), and to Dumaguete via San Carlos (P107, five hours).

SAN CARLOS

☎034 / POP 33,614

San Carlos is the main port city connecting Negros to Cebu, with daily ferries heading to Toledo, on Cebu's west coast. The place is not overflowing with charm, but it's fine for an overnight stay. **Sipaway Island** is a 15-minute boat trip away, and has some nice beaches. Otherwise there are falls, caves and rice terraces in the area. Contact the **tourist office** (☎312 6558; http://sancarloscityinteractive.com) for more information.

Skyland Hotel & Restaurant (☎312 5589; Broce St; r with fan/air-con P475/625; ❄📶), halfway between the pier and the bus terminal, has hot water in spotless rooms. The restaurant food (mains P150) is well prepared.

ℹ Getting There & Away

M/V Lite Ferry (☎729 8040) has daily boats to Toledo (P190, 1½ hours) at 5am, 10am and 3.30pm. **Montenegro** (☎0922 890 2573) has a faster but pricier service (P225, 45 minutes) at 5am, 1pm and 3pm.

There are regular all-day buses from San Carlos' bus station (1km from the pier; P7 by tricycle) to Dumaguete (P107, four hours) and Bacolod (P155, four hours). To La Carlota, first catch a bus to the mountain town of Canlaon (P55, one hour), and from that terminal catch another across the tablelands of Mt Kanlaon to La Carlota (P81, 2¾ hours); it's one of the most scenic road trips in Negros.

SIPALAY

034 / POP 11,275

About 200km from both Bacolod and Dumaguete, the remote seaside town of Sipalay (si-*pah*-lie) is surrounded by spectacular beaches, secluded coves, scattered islets, dive reefs and waters teeming with marlin, trevally and tuna.

Beach lovers will head straight to the slice of paradise called **Sugar Beach** (Langub to the locals), while divers prefer the dedicated dive resorts of **Punta Ballo**. Both are located a few kilometres out of Sipalay.

Other than catching a bus, there's no reason to visit the sprawling town of Sipalay. The tiny **Sipalay Tourist Information Centre** (Poblacion Beach; www.sipalaycity.gov.ph; 8am-5pm daily Oct-May, Mon-Fri Jun-Sep) can assist with boat hire and accommodation. There's no ATM in Sipalay, with the closest 2½ hours away in Kabankalan.

Driftwood City Restaurant (0919 236 7055; Poblacion Beach; meals P120-170; 8am-late) serves up tasty pizzas by the sea, and can also organise boat service from Sipalay to Sugar Beach (around P300). Book ahead.

If for some reason you get stuck, **Sipalay Suites** (473 0350; www.sipalaysuites.com; r with fan/air-con from P700/1500;) has comfortable rooms.

Regular buses run between Sipalay and Bacolod (P169, 4½ hours). To get to Dumaguete involves three separate Ceres buses, all with regular services; firstly head to Hinoba-an (P32, 50 minutes), transfer to Bayawan (P77, 1½ hours) and then on to Dumaguete (P100, 2½ hours).

SUGAR BEACH

With just a handful of eclectic, home-spun resorts, a gorgeous stretch of beach and psychedelic sunsets, Sugar Beach remains one of Negros' best-kept secrets. Its beach is a lovely sweep of tanned sand that slopes at a perfect gradient into the sea – without a rock or weed in sight, it's ideal for swimming. The atmosphere is low key, so if you're looking for a beach party you're better off heading to Boracay.

Diving trips can be arranged through Takatuka Lodge.

Sleeping & Eating

All resorts are strung along the beach.

TOP CHOICE **Takatuka Lodge & Dive Resort** BEACH RESORT $$
(0920 679 2349; www.takatuka-lodge.com; d with fan & cold water P1050, with air-con & hot water P1550;) The amount of love and energy that has gone into the wacky German-owned Takatuka Lodge is in evidence *everywhere* you look in its restaurant, and its themed lodges are even wilder. All rooms are decked out in vibrant colour and design, with surreal touches. The Mad Mix room features quirky touches like an upside-down toilet as a showerhead, while you can live out your rock star fantasies in the Rockadelic room complete with Marshall amps, electric guitars and a gold record mounted on the wall. Light switches are creatively hidden, sometimes in naughty spots. The restaurant has the best food in Sipalay, with a huge varied menu, and the only operational dive centre on Sugar Beach.

Driftwood Village Resort BEACH RESORT $
(0920 900 3663; www.driftwood-village.com; dm P280, d with shared/private bathroom from P400/800;) The best choice for budget travellers, laid-back Driftwood offers a classic mellow beach vibe with hammocks and nipa huts scattered about its leafy grounds. The kitchen specialises in Thai tucker, but European classics are also available (dishes around P200).

Bermuda Resort BEACH RESORT $$
(0920 529 2582; www.bermuda-beach-resort.com; d from P850; @) All the cabins at this friendly little resort are fun and quirky – one has a double bed in the shape of a boat – with excellent private bathrooms. Staff can arrange trekking expeditions in the nearby countryside, and its classy restaurant serves European cuisine; try the garlic prawns.

Sulu Sunset Beach Resort BEACH RESORT $
(0919 716 7182; www.sulusunset.com; cottages without/with sea view from P450/1100; @) Eleven cute cottages ranging from drab and basic to semiluxurious with verandahs and hammocks.

Getting There & Away

To get here by land, ask the bus driver to let you off in barangay Montilla, 3km north of Sipalay, then catch a tricycle (P75) to barangay Nauhang, where paddle boats row you across a small tidal river for P15 per person; agree on a price beforehand to avoid being ripped off. Once across, walk around the point till you get to the long stretch of sand that is Sugar Beach. Note that during high tide, particularly in the rainy season you may need to get a motorised boat (P200) from the bridge in Nauhang, or otherwise call your resort to arrange to be picked up.

If you prebook, many resorts can organise boats from Sugar Beach to Sipalay for around P300.

PUNTA BALLO

Home to some of the best diving in Negros, Punta Ballo is situated 7km southwest of Sipalay on a promontory with a divine white beach of fine shell sand, and a backdrop of wooded hills. Swimming is only possible at high tide.

At last count there were well over 30 dive sites in the area, including three wrecks (one from WWII). Several resorts in Punta Ballo have on-site dive centres. Prices are fairly standard: one dive is US$25, equipment rental starts from US$5 and an open-water certificate is US$350.

Sleeping & Eating

TOP CHOICE Artistic Diving Beach Resort BEACH RESORT $
(☎0919 409 5594; www.artisticdiving.com; r with shared bathroom P500, with fan/air-con P1250/1590;) The original and still the best. Named after its owner (Arturo), Artistic has large, comfortable row cottages with private balconies, cable TV and hot-water bathrooms set in a well-tended garden by the beach. It serves a Swiss-influenced menu with homebaked bread, and good veggie curries. Dive-accommodation packages are available.

Easy Diving Beach Resort BEACH RESORT $$
(☎0917 300 0381; www.sipalay.com; fan/air-con bungalows from P1400/1800;) Located further along the beach, Easy Diving has pleasant Mediterranean-style bungalows, a nice beach and a well-set-up dive centre. Its main downside is the prickly management.

Getting There & Away

The turn-off for Punta Ballo is at the town plaza, on the left as you come into town. A 7km *habal-habal* (P50) or tricycle (p150) trip leads you to the resorts, which all look out to sea.

BULATA & DANJUGAN ISLAND

Twenty kilometres north of Sipalay lies the little town of Bulata. Turn off here and a long dirt track will lead you to the swish **Punta Bulata White Beach Resort** (☎433 5160; www.puntabulata.com; nipa bungalows from P2000, r from P3000;). Accommodation options range from Asiatic 'spa' rooms in a semicourtyard around a swimming pool to small nipa bungalows and large stilt houses. There's an elegant beachside restaurant with an impressive seafood menu.

Recently opened up to tourists, **Danjugan Island** (admission day trip incl lunch P1750, overnight incl admission for 1st/succeeding nights P3000/2000) is managed as a nature reserve by the Bacolod-based NGO **Philippine Reef & Rainforest Conservation Foundation** (PRRCF; ☎in Bacolod 034-441 1617, 0918 600 1589; www.prrcf.org). Located 3km west of Bulata, the 42-hectare island has pristine coral reefs, six lagoons, a primary limestone rainforest and mangroves. It's home to more than nine species of bat and 58 species of bird, including the endangered white-breasted eagle and the grey-headed fishing eagle. Basic accommodation with solar power and no running water can be arranged through the PRRCF. Prices include boat transfer, three meals and access to kayaks and snorkelling equipment. There's also a **dive centre** (per dive incl equipment P2000). Reservations three days in advance are recommended.

Day trips can also be arranged through Punta Bulata White Beach Resort for P1750 per person, which includes boat trip, lunch and snorkelling.

Negros Oriental

Negros Oriental is the more popular province of Negros. Everything is within easy reach of its picturesque provincial capital of Dumaguete, including some fantastic diving (particularly Apo Island), lovely nature treks, waterfalls and world-class caving.

There are good roads and virtually non-stop bus services around the coast, so visiting the myriad resorts and natural attractions of Negros Oriental is as simple and pleasurable as helping yourself to a buffet.

DUMAGUETE

☎035 / POP 116,392

A favourite among travellers, the university town of Dumaguete is far more hip and urbane than your average provincial capital. It's a confident place that really knows how to be a town, and its cosmopolitan harbourfront promenade is a great place for a stroll or to stop off at its upmarket seaside restaurants and bars. Even though there's not a lot to do here, it's an ideal base for nearby dive sites or forays into the wilds of Negros Oriental.

Sights & Activities

Two landmarks in town are the coral-stone **Bell Tower** (cnr Perdices & Teves Sts) near the public square, built between 1754 and 1776, and the large and lively **public market** on Real St.

Rizal Boulevard STREET

While Filipino cities aren't generally known for their beauty or charm, Dumaguete's scenic waterfront promenade along Rizal Blvd is an exception to the rule. Constructed in 1916, this attractive quarter-mile is lined with old-fashioned streetlamps, and is a peaceful spot to stroll, attracting families on picnics, powerwalkers and those content to sit on benches gazing out to the sea. Across from the promenade are a good selection of restaurants and bars.

Anthropology Museum & Centre for the Study of Philippine Living Culture MUSEUM

(admission P40; 8.30am-11.30am & 2-5pm Mon-Fri) Set in a historic building over three levels, displays include artefacts from Siquijor and bamboo spears from Negritos people. It's in the central university campus area; enter from Hibbard Ave, the extension of Perdices St, and head to the old building with the staircase at front.

Dumaguete

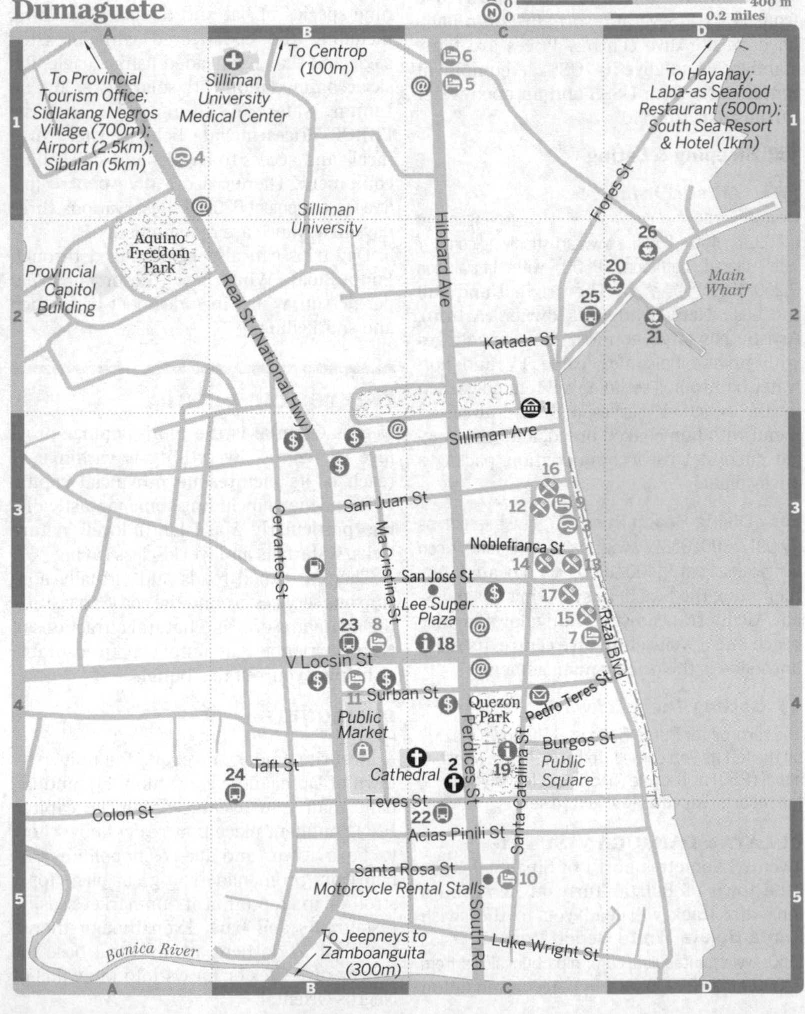

Centrop ZOO

(Center for Tropical Conservation Studies; ☎422 6002; Ipil St; adult/child P10/5; ⏰9am-5pm Mon-Sat) Opposite the hospital is this small zoo and research centre housing 16 species of indigenous mammals, reptiles and birds, including the critically endangered Negros bleeding-heart pigeon, Philippine spotted deer and the Visayan warty pig. Donations are appreciated.

Sidlakang Negros Village CULTURAL VILLAGE

(☎226 3105; Blanco Dr) On the same site as the provincial tourism office, this cultural expo centre promotes products and crafts from Negros Occidental, with most municipalities showcased in the village. Best time to visit is during a festival, as otherwise many of the pavilions are often closed, though the main ones are generally open year-round. To find it, take the National Hwy towards the airport and turn right at the side street opposite the Mercury Drugstore.

DIVING

Most of the resorts along the coast south of town have attached diving facilities. In Dumaguete itself there are three reliable dive centres.

Adventure Dive Shop DIVING

(☎422 1718; www.adventurediveshop.com; Rizal Blvd; ⏰11am-8pm Mon-Sat, 6-9pm Sun) A popular operation on the main strip.

Diveworx DIVING

(☎422 6715; National Hwy) Across from the Provincial Capitol Building.

Scuba Ventures DIVING

(☎0915 809 0544; www.dumaguetedive.com; Hibbard Ave) A good Filipino-run outfit, next door to Harold's Mansion Tourist Inn.

OTHER ACTIVITIES

Within easy striking distance of Dumaguete are a number of gorgeous waterfalls in the hinterlands of Valencia, the virgin forests of Twin Lakes National Park and the limestone caves of Mabinay, which are accessible with a guide. As well as Dumaguete Outdoors, Harold's Mansion Tourist Inn is a good place to arrange trekking and caving trips, among other tours.

Dumaguete Outdoors ADVENTURE SPORTS

(☎226 2110; www.dumagueteoutdoors.com; 3 Noblefranca St; ⏰9am-6pm Mon-Sat) A range of outdoor activities can be arranged here, including diving, canyonning and hiking

Dumaguete

Sights

1 Anthropology Museum & Centre for the Study of Philippine Living Culture ... C2
2 Bell Tower ... C4

Activities, Courses & Tours

3 Adventure Dive Shop ... C3
4 Diveworx ... A1
Dumaguete Outdoors ... (see 13)
Scuba Ventures ... (see 6)

Sleeping

5 Coco Grande Hotel ... C1
6 Harold's Mansion Tourist Inn ... C1
7 Honeycomb Tourist Inn ... C4
8 Hotel Palwa ... B4
9 La Residencia Al Mar ... C3
10 OK Pensionne House ... C5
11 Vintage Inn ... B4

Eating

12 Café Antonio ... C3
13 Casablanca ... C3
14 Jutsz Café ... C3
15 Mamia's ... C4
16 Persian Kebab Tandoori ... C3
17 Sans Rival Cakes ... C3

Drinking

Zanzibar ... (see 13)

Information

18 Bureau of Immigration Office ... C4
19 Dumaguete Tourism Office ... C4

Transport

Aleson Shipping ... (see 21)
20 Cokaliong Shipping ... D2
21 Delta Fast Ferry ... D2
George & Peter Lines ... (see 21)
22 Jeepneys to Dauin and Malatapay ... C5
23 Jeepneys to San José and Tampi ... B4
24 Jeepneys to Valencia ... B4
Montenegro Shipping Lines ... (see 21)
25 North Bus Terminal ... C2
26 Oceanjet ... D2
SuperFerry Office ... (see 21)

trips around the area, as well as caving at Mabinay and Bayawan. All equipment is provided. Those planning to climb Mt Kanlaon in Negros Occidental can avoid a lot of hassle and red tape by joining one of its regular trips.

Sleeping

TOP CHOICE Harold's Mansion Tourist Inn GUESTHOUSE $
(☎225 8000; www.haroldsmansion.com; 205 Hibbard Ave; dm/s/d incl breakfast with fan P250/350/500, s/d/f with air-con, hot water & cable TV P750/800/1125; ❄@📶) Hands down our favourite place in town for its fun atmosphere and professional management. Harold knows what makes backpackers tick, and offers clean, well-priced rooms from dorms to comfortable doubles, with free internet, breakfast and transport pick-up, and a social rooftop that's a great place to meet fellow travellers. As a genuine Dumaguete homeboy, Harold's a top source of information on activities in the 'hood, and tours can be arranged around Negros, including popular trips to Malatapay markets on Wednesday mornings. It's also a good place to arrange diving trips, and has a liveaboard boat based in Dauin. It's also taking the right steps with eco initiatives like slowly introducing solar heating and water-free urinals.

South Sea Resort & Hotel BEACH RESORT $$
(☎422 0113; www.southseahotel.wordpress.com; r with cold/hot water from P1000/1500; ❄📶🏊) It's out of the way, and hard to find down a maze of alleyways, but South Sea's seaside location makes the effort worthwhile. Rooms are classy and spacious, and great value. While there's no beach for swimming, its deluxe swimming pool makes up for it. The attached restaurant, Likha, is a tapas and vodka bar.

Coco Grande Hotel HOTEL $$
(☎422 0746; cocograndehotel@yahoo.com; Hibbard Ave; d incl breakfast from P1230; ❄📶) Sister hotel to the popular Coco Grove on Siquijor, this place is run by brisk, professional staff. The large and inviting rooms have stone and parquetry floors, a fridge, cable TV and wicker furniture. The artwork in its corridors brightens the place up.

Honeycomb Tourist Inn HOTEL $
(☎225 1181; www.honeycombtouristinn.com; Rizal Blvd; s/d incl breakfast from P800/1000; ❄📶) The rooms are dated and have drab motel carpet, but it remains great value for its location on Rizal Blvd. Staff are helpful, and the seafood restaurant is good. Book well ahead for sea-facing rooms.

Hotel Palwa HOTEL $$
(☎422 8995; www.hotelpalwa.com; V Locsin St; r incl breakfast from P969; ❄@📶) In the middle of the action, bright and cheerful Palwa has neat pastel-coloured rooms at great value, cable TV and hot water. The in-house travel agency can arrange tours of the area.

La Residencia Al Mar HOTEL $$
(☎422 0888; laresidenciaalmar@yahoo.com.ph; Rizal Blvd; r from P1790; ❄📶) An olde worlde reproduction of a Spanish hacienda, replete with oil paintings in the style of Fernando Amorsolo, a wide wooden staircase and pots overflowing with ferns. The rooms have solid wooden floors and naff colonial-style decor. Unless you go for the pricier, sea-facing rooms (P2300), you're probably better trying elsewhere. Has a good Japanese restaurant.

OK Pensionne House PENSION HOUSE $
(☎422 7731; Santa Rosa St; d with fan/air-con from P275/440; ❄) This massive, sprawling and slightly rundown place is just what it says it is: OK. It has an enormous variety of rooms – the more expensive (P550 and up) are a big step up from the cheapies in terms of quality.

Vintage Inn PENSION HOUSE $
(☎422 9106; Surban St; s/d with fan P300/400, with air-con from P400/600; ❄📶) A safe, clean and central budget option, opposite the market.

Eating

Barbecue stalls set up along Rizal Blvd in the evening, for a cheap and tasty option. Don't leave town without trying *silvanas* (cookies with crunchy cashew-meringue wafer filled with buttercream) from **Sans Rival Cakes** (San José St), the greatest thing *ever*.

Jutsz Café ITALIAN $$
(cnr Santa Catalina & Noblefranca Sts; mains P100-580; ⏰10am-10pm) Charming Italian restaurant which uses lovely fresh ingredients; try the shrimp and mushroom *pomodoro basilico* spaghetti with divine tomato and basil sauce. It also does half-sized meals.

Casablanca AUSTRIAN $$
(Rizal Blvd; mains P185-575) One of Dumaguete's most popular restaurants, Casablanca tries its hand at most cuisines but is known primarily for its hearty Austrian dishes. In a

lovely spot on the waterfront, it serves up crispy and succulent roast pork and Vienna schnitzel, with a delicious eggplant variation for vegetarians. Sesame-seared tuna with salsa makes a fine appetiser, and there's a good sandwich selection for lunch.

Mamia's INTERNATIONAL **$$**
(64 Rizal Blvd; mains P150-300;) Sophisticated boulevard dining at reasonable prices, featuring a healthy selection of seafood and imported Aussie steaks. There's a good local vibe, blissfully free of the sexpat brigade. Staff are cheerful and beer is cheap, and it has a popular attached cafe with proper coffee, toasted sandwiches and breakfasts.

Lab-as Seafood Restaurant SEAFOOD **$$**
(Flores St; meals around P250) In a rambling indoor-outdoor setting, Lab-as packs out on weekends and stays loud and lively until the wee hours. It's a popular choice for excellent fresh seafood and local vibe. You can't go wrong with marinated *maya maya* (red snapper) barbecued on charcoal. After dinner check out the live music at Hayahay next door.

Persian Kebab Tandoori INDIAN **$$**
(San Juan St; mains P95-350; 11am-11pm Mon-Sat) A classier-than-usual outlet of the Persian Palate chain, this Indian and Middle Eastern serves vegetarian samosas, falafel and curries.

Café Antonio CAFE **$**
(San Juan St; meals P40-80; 10am-11pm;) Upstairs in a historic Spanish-era building, this stylish student cafe serves great coffee, sandwiches and grilled meats. You can even sit yourself down to eat in a swing.

Drinking & Entertainment

An ever-so-slightly icky atmosphere descends on the bar area of Rizal Blvd after dark, so social animals should do as the locals do and head out to the hipper nightspots further afield.

Hayahay BAR
(4pm-late) This is a great place to go out for a drink or meal (it shares a kitchen with Lab-as next door). There is a different style of music every night; on Friday and Saturday the bands keep crooning until 4am.

Zanzibar BAR
(www.zanzibardumaguete.com; 2 San José St; 5pm-late) Popular with a young student crowd, intimate Zanzibar has dance music that pumps over two small levels.

Information

The **BOI** (225 4401; 38 V Locsin St; 8am-noon & 1-5pm Mon-Fri) is a good place to extend your visa minus the crowds, and it's usually issued on the same day. It's next to the Lu Pega Building.

Based at a new location, the **Provincial Tourism Office** (225 1825; www.negrostourism.com, www.negor.gov.ph; 8am-8pm) has exceptionally helpful staff with great info, and can arrange tours to the surrounding area, including dolphin-watching, Mabinay caves and Lake Balanan. It shares a site with the Sidlakang Negros Village. There's also the smaller but more central **Dumaguete Tourism Office** (422 3561; tourismdgte@gmail.com; Quezon Park; 8am-noon & 1-5pm Mon-Fri).

An excellent resource for anyone planning to hang around Dumaguete for a while is www.dumagueteinfo.com, which includes an active forum.

As you'd expect from a university city, there is no shortage of internet cafes. The cheaper ones charge P15 per hour.

There are several banks in town with ATMs, including branches of BPI, Chinabank, Metrobank and PNB. The main **post office** (cnr Santa Catalina & Pedro Teres Sts) is near Quezon Park. The best medical facilities are at **Silliman University Medical Center** (225 0841; V Aldecoa Rd; 24hr).

Getting There & Away

AIR

PAL and Cebu Pacific both have two flights daily between Dumaguete and Manila.

BOAT

After Cebu City, Dumaguete is the best connected port in the Visayas. The following companies have offices at the pier:

Aleson Shipping Lines (225 8169)
Cokaliong Shipping (225 3588; www.cokaliongshipping.com)
Delta Fast Ferry (420 0888)
George & Peter Lines (422 8431)
GL Shipping Lines (480 5534)
Montenegro Shipping Lines (422 3632)
Oceanjet (0923 7253 734; www.oceanjet.net)
Super Shuttle Ferry (0922 880 2518)
SuperFerry (225 0734; www.superferry.com.ph)

BOHOL Oceanjet has a morning and afternoon fastcraft service to Tagbilaran (P650, one hour 40 minutes).

CEBU Cokaliong Shipping and George & Peter Lines (from P300, 6½ hours) service the Cebu City to Dumaguete route, while Oceanjet (P970, four hours) has two daily fastcraft. The easiest way to get to the south of Cebu, particularly Moalboal, is to get a jeepney (10 minutes) to **Sibulan port** (☎035-419 8280) just north of Dumaguete and from there catch a regular fastcraft or bangka over to Lilo-an (P45, 20 minutes), with the first trip at 5.30am and last at 5.30pm.

LUZON SuperFerry has a weekly ferry to Manila (from P600, 27 hours) at 1.15pm Thursday, Cagayan de Oro (P1028, seven hours) on Sunday and Iligan City (P607, 6½ hours) on Wednesday.

MINDANAO George & Peter Lines, Cokaliong, Montenegro and Aleson Shipping Lines have daily boats to Dapitan (Zamboanga City; from P262, four hours).

SIQUIJOR Delta (P160, one hour) and GL Shipping (P120, one hour) have numerous trips to Siquijor town, while Oceanjet has one evening service at 7.40pm (P200, 45 minutes). Montenegro has one daily slow ferry to Larena (P136, two hours).

BUS & JEEPNEY

The **Ceres Bus Liner station** (South Rd) is a short tricycle ride south of town (P8). It services routes both north and south, including regular buses to Zamboanguita (P30, 45 minutes) and Bais City (P45, one hour). To get to Sipalay involves catching a bus to Bayawan (P100, two hours), transferring to Hinoba-an (P77, 1½ hours) and then another bus to Sipalay (P32, 50 minutes) – it's easier and quicker than it sounds, with buses departing regularly until 11.30pm. Buses also service Bacolod every 30 minutes until 7.30pm (P310, 6½ hours), and Cebu City, departing every two hours until 2.15pm, and a nightbus at 10.30pm (P270, five hours), which includes a ferry crossing.

There is a smaller bus terminal next to the pier that does short hauls north, including Bais City (P40, 1¼ hours), Mabinay (P80, 2½ hours), Manjuyod (P55, 1½ hours) and San José (for Twin Lakes; P30, 30 minutes). Jeepneys from the stand on the corner of Real and V Locsin Sts also head to San José. Jeepneys to Valencia leave from Colon St, a few blocks west of the public market. Jeepneys to Zamboanguita stopping at Dauin and Malatapay leave from near the Bell Tower on Teves St, as well as from Real St, about 1km south of the Banica River.

ℹ Getting Around

A tricycle into town from Dumaguete airport costs around P12. There are tricycles everywhere and they charge P8 for trips around town; for slightly longer trips you might want to offer P10 to P15.

On the corner of Santa Rosa and Perdices Sts are several motorcycle rental stalls. Bikes are P300 per day, or P1750 per week. It pays to compare prices and check brakes and headlights. Try **Kokoi's** (☎0906 659 7942).

TWIN LAKES NATIONAL PARK

About 20km northwest of Dumaguete, the twin crater lakes of **Balinsasayao** and **Danao** offer some of the most scenic hiking in the Visayas. The area is virgin forest and full of wildlife, from monkeys to rare orchids, and a great spot for birdwatching; with a guide, it's possible to hike to Casaroro Falls. It's the traditional home of the indigenous Bukidnon people, and if you're exceptionally lucky you might spy a Philippine spotted deer or a Visayan warty pig, two of the several endemic species threatened by illegal hunting and habitat loss.

Entry to the park is P100, payable at the checkpoint office – where guides (P300) and binoculars may be available, but it's better to arrange a guide from the provincial tourist office in Dumaguete. Keep going 900m beyond the gate to reach the first lake, where there are kayaks available for hire (per hour P100). There's also a pleasant restaurant overlooking the shimmering lake.

Arriving from Dumaguete, the entry point for the 15km scenic track to Twin Lakes is just before San José on the coastal road at kilometre marker 12.4 (you'll see the sign pointing inland). A *habal-habal* from here to the lake is P300 round trip. To get to the turn-off from Dumaguete, catch one of several daily buses from the north bus terminal (P18) or a jeepney from Real St.

BAIS CITY & AROUND

☎035 / POP 13,860

About 40km north of Dumaguete, Bais is one of the country's top spots for dolphin and whale watching. More species of cetaceans (including killer whales) have been seen in Tañon Strait's waters, separating Negros and Cebu, than anywhere else in the Visayas.

That said, whale sightings are actually very rare, especially outside of their March to October migration season, though spinner dolphins are quite common throughout the year. Bais City **tourist office** (☎402 8338; City Plaza) can organise a 10-seater boat for P3500. Boats depart from **Capiñahan wharf**, 4km from town (P25 by tricycle from the plaza), where you can also arrange boats for a similar price. The best time for sightings is 7am to 10am, or otherwise late afternoon. Trips last three to four hours, and the package includes visits to the white-sand bar at Manjuyod and birdwatching at the 250-hectare **Talabong Mangrove Forest and Bird Sanctuary**, which features a network of raised walkways through the mangrove forests. You can see herons and egrets among other species.

The best place to stay in Bais is the historical **La Planta Hotel** (402 8321; Mabini St; r from P1281;), with pleasant shady surrounds, large and bright doubles, and an atmospheric but overpriced restaurant.

Heading a further 8km north you'll reach **Manjuyod**, where you can arrange a visit to its exquisite white-sand bar, a narrow 7km stretch at low tide. Basic accommodation is available in **stilt cottages** (cottage P3800); at high tide the water rises just above the foundations, making the houses appear marooned in the middle of the ocean. Lighting is solar-powered and you'll need to bring your own supplies. The rate includes return boat transfer and can be arranged through the Manjuyod **tourist office** (404 1136; manjuyodtourismoffice@yahoo.com.ph).

At the junction on the road to Manjuyod, head left (inland) a further 20km to get to **Mabinay**, 87km from Dumaguete, home to a complex of over 400 caves. Guides and information are available from the very helpful **Bulwang Caves Information Centre** (0917 789 2445; entry per beginner/advanced cave P15/30), which can arrange guides (from P400) to the eight caves that are open to the public, ranging from beginner to extreme. The most popular and accessible (with lighting and a walkway) is **Crystal Cave**, an underground fantasy land of gleaming and sparkling crystal, milky white stalactites, and home to the big-eared horseshoe bat, tailless scorpion and black swifts. Spelunking is possible in the 8.7km-long **Odloman Cave**, the second largest in the Philippines. It involves a vertical entrance rappel and is only accessible during December to May; a subterranean river rages through it at other times. Serious cavers are advised to bring their own equipment, with limited helmets and flashlights available.

The information centre can also arrange trips to visit a nearby **Aeta village**, the Negrito ethnic group who are indigenous to Negros, with a darker appearance and curly hair. In the village there's thought to be fewer than 20 pure-blooded Aeta left.

If you're wanting to stay the night, **Econotel Guess Inn** (0918 510 3997; r from P500;) has a range of rooms (some featuring Jacuzzis and waterbeds!), 3km before the caves.

There are regular buses to Dumaguete (2½ hours, P110).

VALENCIA & AROUND

035 / POP 1280

Valencia is a clean and leafy town with stately tree-lined avenues and a large, grassed central square. It sits at the foot of **Mt Talinis** (1904m), whose twin peaks are also evocatively known as Cuernos de Negros (Horns of Negros). There are four trails to the peak, and guides can be arranged at the provincial tourist office in Dumaguete, or through **Dumaguete Outdoors** (035-226 2110; www.dumagueteoutdoors.com; 3 Noblefranca St, Dumaguete) or **Harold's Mansion Tourist Inn** (035-225 8000; www.haroldsmansion.com; 205 Hibbard Ave, Dumaguete).

Four kilometres from Valencia are the glorious, 30m **Casaroro Falls** (admission P15), which are most refreshing after the climb down the 335 steps to get to them. The best way to get to the falls – other than walking – is to hire a *habal-habal* from the market to take you to the steps (P150). Be warned: if you have your own bike, the last 500m of the ride are extremely rough and treacherous, so it's advisable to walk from where the paved road ends – which takes you through some picturesque hill villages.

On the road to Casaroro Falls is the newly opened **Harold's Ecolodge** (dm/r P200/500), of Harold's Mansion fame, with simple wooden bungalows that make a great spot for nature lovers and those wanting to trek Mt Talinis. The nearby videoke is a blight, but thankfully finishes up before dark.

Jeepneys run all day between Dumaguete and Valencia (P21, 30 minutes). A *habal-habal* from Dumaguete costs around P150.

DAUIN

035 / POP 3417

Dauin (dow-*in*) is the largest of the southern towns and known for its macro diving in the marine reserve of **Masaplod Norte**. There is a pleasant brown-sand beach and good snorkelling over the drop-off about 20m out from shore. There's also the sulphur **Baslay hot springs** (admission by donation), along a bumpy road 10km off the main highway, best accessed by motorcycle or *habal-habal*.

WORTH A TRIP

WWII IN VALENCIA

Housed in the private residence of Felix Constantino Cata-al on the outskirts of Valencia, the **Cata-al War Memorabilia Museum** (035-423 8078; entry by donation; 8am-5pm) boasts one of the finest collections of WWII memorabilia in the Philippines. The vast majority of the collection was found by Felix himself during his scavenges in the thick jungle of Mt Talinis, a site that saw fierce fighting. The area was one of the last strongholds of the Japanese, who had set up base here 25km from the shoreline, just beyond firing range from the US naval ships. Eventually US aircraft bombed the area for over a month, with some estimates of up to 10,000 people losing their lives.

Items on display include 'Big Mama' bomb casings, machine guns, pistols, antitank shells, medals, helmets, grenades, gas masks, uniforms, dog tags and personal items like a still-operational phonograph and green Coca Cola bottles. Among the most valuable pieces are samurai and officer ivory swords used by Japanese soldiers for *seppuku* (the samurai ritual of suicide by disembowelment). Sadly, Felix's discoveries have also included the remains of Japanese soldiers, which have been duly handed to the Japanese government.

Inspired by the mementos of his father, a WWII veteran who was taken prisoner of war and who still resides on the premises, Felix began collecting as a five year old, when heavy rains would unearth bullets, helmets and machine-gun magazines in the hills. But his efforts really started in 1983 after the Japanese had finished their search for missing soldiers. Of the historical finds, Felix claims there's still one granddaddy to come, as he is adamant that the area is home to much of Yamashita's treasure, a quasi-myth that the Japanese loot accumulated from Singapore was buried here.

In the peaceful hillside, a few kilometres out of Valencia, you'll find a **WWII shrine**, a small obelisk erected in 1977 to commemorate the Filipino, American and Japanese soldiers who died in battle.

Sleeping & Eating

Mike's Dauin Beach Resort BEACH RESORT $$
(0916 754 8823; www.mikes-beachresort.com; r from P2500;) Run by the owner of the Adventure Dive Shop in Dumaguete, Mike's is a popular choice with divers, with spacious and comfortable but overpriced rooms.

Pura Vida Beach & Dive Resort BEACH RESORT $$
(425 2284; www.pura-vida.ph; s/d incl breakfast from P2772/3234;) Affiliated with the Philippines-wide dive company Sea Explorers, this is a top-quality dive resort and health spa.

Atlantis Dive Resort BEACH RESORT $$$
(424 2327, 0917 562 0294; www.atlantishotel.com; s/d from P4770/5680;) With charming Spanish-style buildings and Mayan-inspired decor, Atlantis is a dive resort with character, and offers technical dive training.

Puerto Cita Beach Resort BEACH RESORT $
(0919 656 2244; www.puertocitas.com; r from P950;) There's no dive centre here, but the relaxed and pleasant garden bungalows are among the cheapest you'll get in Dauin.

MALATAPAY

035

Malatapay is best known by tourists for its huge and lively **market**, where every Wednesday morning villagers, fishers and Bukidnon tribespeople can be found loudly bartering their goods and feasting on *lechón* (spit-roasted whole pig).

Malatapay is also known for being the departure point for Apo Island, with boats leaving from the beach in front of the market.

If you want to stay here to access Apo Island dive sites, **Thalatta Resort** (426 1039; www.thalatta-beach.com; cottages incl breakfast P3000;) is a slick operation with cheesy Balinese-style nipa huts around a lovely infinity pool with ocean views. This place gets points for deriving some of its energy from thermal and photovoltaic solar panels, and is wheelchair accessible. It has a dive centre.

APO ISLAND

035 / POP 745

Rugged and volcanic, the minuscule 72-hectare island of Apo is fast becoming known for having some of the best diving and snorkelling in the Philippines. And if that's not enough for you, there are also some gorgeous white coral-sand beaches, great short walks and a friendly island community.

Electricity is available only in the mornings and evenings.

Activities

Other than the basic homestays, the handful of resorts on Apo all have dive companies.

During high tide in the mornings, just out front on the main beach, you're almost guaranteed to encounter massive green sea turtles feeding in the shallows, providing a memorable snorkelling experience.

Apo Island Marine Reserve & Fish Sanctuary DIVING

This 15,000-sq-metre protected area (part of the Negros Oriental Marine Conservation Park), situated in Negros' southeastern corner, is one of the most successful and best-run marine reserves in the Philippines. The reserve contains a vital marine breeding ground and is a favourite site among divers and snorkellers for its excellent visibility. You'll have to pay a general admission fee of P100 and then an additional snorkelling/diving fee of P50/300, which all goes towards the maintenance of the sanctuary.

Sleeping & Eating

There's limited lodging on Apo, so reservations are recommended (well in advance for the January and December peak season). There's a smattering of homestays that offer basic rooms for around P500.

TOP CHOICE **Liberty's Lodge** BEACH RESORT $$

(☎424 0888; www.apoisland.com; with full-board dm P800, s/d with shared bathroom from P1300/1950, with private bathroom from P1500/2150; @☜) Perched high above the beach and village, this is the place that most divers head for. Paul's Diving offers top instruction, which is one attraction, but the friendly, laid-back atmosphere and the wide range of well-designed rooms with balconies and excellent views are equally as memorable. Room prices include three meals, which makes it fantastic value.

Apo Island Beach Resort BEACH RESORT $$

(☎225 5490; www.apoislandresort.com; dm P800, cottages from P2500) Tucked away in a private rocky cove, this place claims the best white-sand beach and completes the package with a quiet resort atmosphere. The Spanish-mission rooms and cottages have fan and cold-water bathrooms. The simple menu has good Filipino food (dishes P175 to P210). It has its own dive centre. During high tide it's accessed via steps leading up past Liberty's.

Mario Scuba GUESTHOUSE $

(☎0906 361 7254; marspascobello@hotmail.com; r from P400) Small dive centre/homestay has sunny rooms, with the pricier ones (P1000) being top value, having massive rooms with polished floorboards and balcony.

Getting There & Away

Apo Island is about 25km south of Dumaguete. The departure point is from Malatapay Beach, where an afternoon bangka departs to Apo (P300, 30 minutes) around 3pm, though often later. Your other alternatives are to organise a ride with Liberty's Lodge for around P300, share a trip with others or hitch a ride with a dive company. If you're in a hurry, a special trip is P1000 one way for four people. Waterproof your valuables.

From Apo, there's a daily public bangka to Malatapay (P300), departing around 6.30am.

TAMBOBO BAY

☎035

At the southernmost point of Negros, gorgeous Tambobo Bay has the hideaway ambience of a pirate's cove. Popular with yachties who anchor in the safe waters at the mouth of two small rivers, the entrance to the bay has a few stretches of white beach with an evening view of spectacular sunsets.

Run by an entertaining English couple, Jamie and Nikki, **Kookoo's Nest** (☎0919 695 8085; www.kookoosnest.com.ph; huts with shared/private bathroom from P650/1000) is situated on a tiny white-sand cove, with five simple bamboo huts perched above the water's edge. The excellent restaurant and dive centre are equally simple and idyllic.

To get here, catch a *habal-habal* from Zamboanguita (P150), or arrange a pick-up service by Kookoo's Nest.

SIQUIJOR

☎035 / POP 87,695

For most Filipinos, Siquijor is a mysterious other-world of witchcraft and the unknown. True, this tiny island province is famous for its mountain-dwelling *mangkukulam* (healers) who brew traditional ointments for modern ailments, but these days Siquijor's most popular healing practice involves a cocktail and a deckchair at any number of its laid-back beach resorts. A sealed 72km coastal road circumnavigates the island, affording unobstructed ocean vistas and an opportunity to take in truly low-key village life.

Once a part of Bohol and then Negros Oriental, Siquijor didn't become an independent province until 1971, although economically and politically it still seems like a little sister to its larger neighbours. This appears unlikely to change as long as Siquijodnons continue to head to Cebu, Manila or abroad seeking work.

While it is less renowned than other Visayas locations, there are good dive sites, including Paliton Beach (with three submarine caves), Tubod, Salagdoong Beach (with plenty of coral and the odd mako shark), Sandugan and Tongo Point (with colourful reefs). Nearby Apo Island has a range of excellent dive sites, and there's a 30m wreck, a Japanese hospital boat, near the Larena pier. Just about everywhere on Siquijor is great for snorkelling – find the nearest beach and dive in. Like many beaches in the Visayas, swimming is only possible during high tide, and wearing flip-flops is recommended as protection against sea urchins.

Getting There & Away

Mid-Sea Express (www.midseaexpress.com) offers weekly flights to Siquijor from both Cebu City and Tagbilaran, Bohol; check the website for the latest schedule.

There are two ports on Siquijor, with ferries departing from either Siquijor town or Larena, though most travellers arrive in the former. Schedules can be sensitive to change, so be sure to check at the pier ahead of departure.

Services from Siquijor town:

NEGROS Several companies have regular ferries to Dumaguete, including GL Shipping Lines (P120, one hour 15 minutes) until 3.45pm, Delta Fast (P160, one hour) and Montenegro Shipping Lines (two hours) at 4pm. Ocean Jet has a 6am fastcraft (P200, 45 minutes).

From Larena:

BOHOL Lite Shipping heads to Tagbilaran (P180, three hours) en route to Cebu City, departing around 5pm. Palacio Shipping has three services a week to Tagbilaran at 9pm.

CEBU Cebu City is serviced by Lite Shipping three times a week via Tagbilaran (P290, 8½ hours), while Cokaliong Shipping has a weekly ferry (P280, seven hours) departing 11pm Monday. Super Shuttle Ferry has daily ferries to Oslob (two hours) in the south of Cebu at 6.30am and 2pm.

MINDANAO Lite Shipping services Plaridel, while Montenegro heads to Dapitan at 6am daily (P136).

NEGROS Delta Fast (P160) and Montenegro (P100) have an early-morning ferry to Dum-

Siquijor

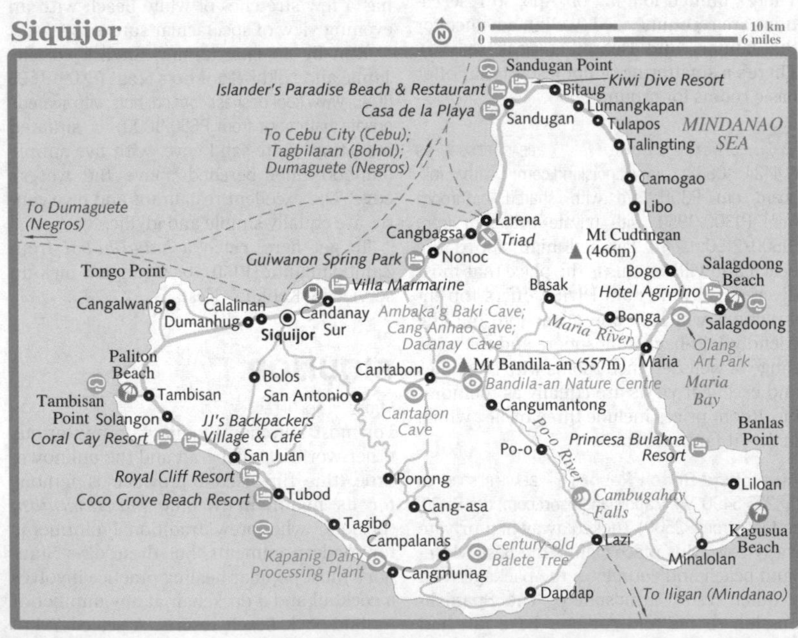

aguete (45 minutes) departing at 5.30am and 6am, respectively.

There's also a port at Lazi, with **Orlines Shipping** (☎482 0058) heading to Iligan, Mindanao, on Tuesday and Friday at 5pm.

Getting Around

A great way to explore the island is by bike or motorcycle. Compared with most other roadways in the Philippines, the 72km coastal ring road is practically devoid of traffic, so you can take your finger off the horn and afford to take in the view without fear of rear-ending the vehicle in front of you. With leisurely stops along the way, by car, motorcycle or tricycle a circular trip around the island takes the best part of a day. Prices are around P1500 per jeep (for three people) for guided day trips around the island, P750 for a multicab, P300 for a motorbike and P300 per day for mountain bikes. From the central market area of major towns, a *habal-habal* trip is approximately P60 per 10km. The road passes through the island's main towns and settlements, some glorious stretches of beach (especially on the east coast) and several spurs that provide access to the interior.

If you are relying on jeepneys to get around, get started early, as many stop for the day at around 3pm. Jeepneys travel around the coastal road from Larena to Lazi (P65), via Maria (P40), but don't get as far as Siquijor town. They also do the Larena–Maria leg via Basak.

Siquijor Town

☎035 / POP 1357

Other than a lively market selling fresh fish and the usual selection of small shops, there's not much going on in Siquijor town. There's a picturesque coral-stone **church** built in 1783 that you can climb up for a bird's-eye glimpse of the town.

The **Siquijor Provincial Tourism Office** (☎344 2088; www.siquijor.gov.ph; Provincial Capitol Bldg) is a short tricycle ride from the pier, though don't expect too much help. Internet access is available at **JJKs** (per hr P15; 8am-midnight) near Samyz Pizza Bar & Restaurant.

The only way to get from Siquijor town to Larena is by tricycle (P20, 15 minutes), or a very occasional passing pedicab. **Scandinavian** (☎0939 640 5132) has motorcycles for rent at the pier.

Sleeping

TOP CHOICE **Villa Marmarine** GUESTHOUSE $$
(☎480 9167; www.marmarine.jp/en; bungalow without bathroom P500, s/d from P1000/1400; @) Run by an irrepressibly cheerful Japanese couple who have poured their personalities into their business, Villa Marmarine features a Japanese-inspired design that makes it all hang together so well. Mezzanine levels, *furo* baths, wooden ceiling fans and self-contained kitchenettes are so well arranged you'll feel like reproducing it at home. It's on a great white-sand beach, complete with deckchairs, and also has an on-site dive centre. Other pluses: wheelchair accessibility, free use of laptops, free snorkelling gear and a tennis court. The only downside is that there's only one cheap room. It's 10 minutes east of Siquijor town by *habal-habal* (P30).

Swiss Stars Guesthouse GUESTHOUSE $
(☎480 5583; National Hwy; r with shared/private bathroom from P380/500; @) This is a good budget option just east of Siquijor town if you don't mind being off the beach, and also has an affordable restaurant.

Larena & Around

☎035 / POP 1790

In Larena there's a post office and an Allied Bank with an unreliable ATM. There is nowhere decent to stay in Larena proper, but it's easy enough to get a *habal-habal* from the port area to any of the surrounding resorts at any time of the day or night.

Sleeping

The following accommodation options are all in the vicinity of Sandugan Beach, 6km north of Larena. Kiwi Dive Resort is the only full-service dive centre in the area.

Kiwi Dive Resort BEACH RESORT $
(☎424 0534; http://kiwidiveresort.com; cottages with fan/air-con from P450/750; @) It's a lovely walk down a trellis-covered pathway from the simple and clean hillside rooms to the beach, sitting area and small bar with satellite TV. There's a dive centre, and motorbikes, mountain bikes, jeeps and kayaks are available for hire. Call to arrange a free pick-up from the piers.

Islander's Paradise Beach & Restaurant BEACH RESORT $
(☎377 2412; www.islandersparadisebeach.com; cottages with fan/air-con from P670/950; @) One of the oldest resorts on Siquijor, Islander's is a loose village of faux nipa cottages right on the water, perfect for admiring the incredible sunsets. To get there, go past the

THE SHAMANS OF SIQUIJOR

Long associated with tales of shamans, witchcraft and black magic, Siquijor is often tagged with the moniker 'the Mystique Island'. It's not a reputation that sits well with the governor of Siquijor, who is concerned that such an image deters Filipinos from visiting. So much so that a sign greets newly arrived visitors with the message: *'Siquijor is just perfect for relaxing and recuperating. Sorcery and black magic do not exist in this island – anyone who offer services for occult practices are fakes. Report immediately to Provincial Tourism Office.'*

The catch 22 is that it's this mysterious aspect of Siquijor that attracts many foreign visitors to the island.

Instead, the island promotes itself as a place for 'white magic', in reference to the 'folk healers' who reside in the mountains around San Antonio. Most of the island's healers are over the age of 70, a strong sign that the tradition is dying out with a lack of faith from younger generations – who generally scoff at any notion of witchcraft on the island. With that said, most locals have an anecdote to tell that involves a mystical occurrence of some sort or another; some uplifting, others not so.

While there isn't that much of a tourist trade in healing on Siquijor, if you do wish to see a *mangkukulam* (healer), ask a local to accompany you or speak with the staff at the **Coco Grove Beach Resort** (☎481 5008; www.cocogroveresort.com) near San Juan, who can give you the names of specific healers. Expect to pay about P500 for their services, which commonly involve a brief diagnostic examination and a smoky mix of herbs and curative oils. One of the most common healing practices is *bolo-bolo,* which involves a glass of water containing a black stone being blown through a straw, and hovering the glass over the patient's body until it becomes a browny colour, which identifies the ailments. Sceptics dismiss it as trickery, while others swear by it.

The best time to visit is during Holy Week, which sees a congregation of folk healers and shamans from all over the Philippines for the **Lenten Festival of Herbal Preparation** in San Antonio, attracting visitors from all over the world.

disturbing castle structure painted in camouflage (don't be afraid) and follow the slope down towards the beach.

Casa de la Playa BEACH RESORT **$$**
(☎484 1170; www.siquijorcasa.com; cottages P1300-2200; ❄📶) The surreal, Day-Glo theme is likely to eventually grow on you at this wacky place. Its lovely waterfront cottages take far less convincing, which are more like mini houses with their upmarket interiors. A very cool pagoda restaurant specialises in vegetarian cuisine.

Guiwanon Spring Park NIPA HUTS **$**
(☎0926 978 6012; cottages P300) Reminiscent of an Ewok village, simple treehouse bungalows here are accessed via a rickety wooden walkway that passes over mangroves. Run by a fishing cooperative, it's cheap and a bit of a novelty, but has a very inconvenient location.

✕ Eating

Triad FILIPINO **$**
(mains P90-250; ⏲10am-9pm) For something a little bit out of the ordinary, drop into the weird and wonderful Triad, perched on a hill above Larena like a beached UFO. The food here is nothing special, but you'll hardly notice with such an impressive view that takes in distant Cebu and Negros. A tricycle up here will cost P30.

Break Point RESTOBAR **$**
(mains P45-150; ⏲8am-midnight) A good spot to hang out with the locals, this outdoor restobar in Larena, is nice for a cold beer on a balmy evening and does a decent chilli squid.

Bandila-an Nature Centre & the Caves

Sitting atop Mt Bandila-an (557m), Siquijor's highest peak, is the Bandila-an Nature Centre, the start of a walk past natural springs, fluttering butterflies, birds and an enormous variety of floral species. Almost 10km from Siquijor town, it's a slow climb up the mountain road full of switchbacks, peering down into jungle ravines.

The nature centre itself is really nothing more than a desk and chair in an otherwise empty concrete room in the mountain village of Cantabon. Within a few kilometres of the office is a series of caves, including **Cang Anhao**, **Ambaka'g Baki**, **Dacanay** and **Cantabon Cave**; the latter is the most convenient and well known of the bunch. It's easy enough to find a guide (at the nature centre or through a resort) who can supply torches (a must) and safety helmets (an extra precaution). Tours should cost around P500 (up to three people, and includes equipment). Expect to get dirty and wet navigating your way through narrow vertical climbs, waist-deep water and high humidity.

The best road to Bandila-an Nature Centre and Cantabon from the main ring road heads up from Siquijor town from beside the Siquijor Central Elementary School. A rougher route (OK on a motorbike) can be taken from San Juan.

At the 6km mark you'll pass **San Antonio**, centre of the ceremonies during Holy Week and home to many of the island's healers.

San Juan & Around

☎035 / POP 760

A typical small Visayan town, San Juan is centred around a plaza and a landscaped enclosure known as Calipay's Spring Park. In town, **Shanemark** (☎0919 564 7725) rents motorbikes for P270 per day, and there's a small bookshop.

Divers not staying at a dive resort should head to **Siquijor Dive Safari** (☎481 5089; tatarelacion@yahoo.com), located just outside Coco Grove Beach Resort. It's run by the fun-loving Tata Relacion, who caters to the backpacker and student market.

South of San Juan is the stunning white-sand **Paliton Beach**. The water is clear as glass and there are wonderful views of Apo Island. Take the turn-off at the little church in Paliton village, near the island's westernmost point, and head along a dirt track for about 1km to get to the water; the main beach is a short walk along.

For a fun side trip, drop into the **Kapanig Dairy Processing Plant** (⌚8am-4pm Mon-Sat) at the tiny village of Cangmunag, 700m off the highway, halfway between San Juan and Lazi. This community microbusiness dispenses ultrafresh bottled milk, cheese and yoghurt. Flavoured varieties (P25) come in chocolate, mango or *ube* (purple yam), and frozen milkbar desserts (P3) are also available in the same flavours.

Further ahead is the beautiful **balete tree**, estimated to be 400 years old and believed by some to be enchanted. It's a good stopover for a quick dip in its springwater swimming area.

Sleeping & Eating

Some of the nicest accommodation and beaches are out this way.

TOP CHOICE **JJ's Backpackers Village & Café** BEACH RESORT $
(☎0918 670 0310; jiesa26@yahoo.com; tent/dm/d P150/300/400; @) Laid-back JJ's is a throwback to the carefree days when you could camp on a beach, cook your own food and enjoy yourself without any worries. Located on a well-maintained patch of beach, there are only a few rooms here but there are plans to expand; otherwise you're free to pitch a tent. Its cafe serves cheap and very tasty food, with the burgers and fruit shakes highly recommended. It also bakes its own bread and uses fresh milk. Each morning a fisherman stops by selling fish which you can cook for dinner. Cheap motorbike rental is also available.

Coco Grove Beach Resort BEACH RESORT $$
(☎481 5008; www.cocogroveresort.com; r from P2400; ❄📶🏊) An upmarket resort at Tubod, about 3km southeast of San Juan, Coco Grove has a well-deserved reputation for excellent service, good food and comfortable accommodation by the beach. With the luxury of access to **Tubod marine sanctuary** (P50 entry) straight out front, with astounding visibility, it has a highly regarded dive centre. Free use of kayaks.

Royal Cliff Resort BEACH RESORT $$
(☎481 5038; www.royal-cliff-resort.de.tf; huts Sep-Apr P980-1500, May-Aug P700-1000) A low-key resort with concrete duplex cottages; go for the more expensive stand-alone huts, which are large, homey and well decorated. Its restaurant has unbeatable sea views, and abundant beachside hammocks provide good sunset vantage points.

Coral Cay Resort BEACH RESORT $$
(☎481 5024; www.coralcayresort.com; r with fan P850, air-con cottages from P1700; ❄📶🏊) On a lovely stretch of beach at Solangon, about 3km northwest of San Juan, it features a mix of charming wood-floored beachfront

and garden cottages, and functional cheaper rooms in a low-slung building towards the back. The great beach bar has views of the sun setting over Apo Island. It's popular with an older expat crowd.

Castaways Beach Cafe HOSTEL $
(☎0939 617 6462; www.castawayscafe.com; r from P250) A new backpackers in San Juan, Castaways is on the water, but there's no beach and it lacks atmosphere.

Czars Place HOTEL $
(☎481 5012; r with fan/air-con P500/800; ❄) Known for its raucous Friday nights, Czars has live bands on its stage out back, and also has rooms; lacks beach access.

Lazi & Around

☎035 / POP 19,440

The quiet southeastern town of Lazi is bisected by the island's only major river, the Po-o (po-oh). The town is home to the impressive and stylishly time-worn, coral-stone and timber **San Isidro Labrador Church** built in 1884. Over the road is the oldest convent in the Philippines, a magnificent timber and stone villa, creaky with age and eerily serene. There's a small **museum** (admission P20; ⏲10am-4pm Tue-Sun) with historical photographs and churchy relics.

Just out of Lazi, turn left at the service station and amble up several kilometres to the refreshing **Cambugahay Falls** on the Po-o River. Above the falls, there's a paid parking bay on your left for your tricycle (P20) or motorbike (P10). Steps just across the road will take you down to this series of popular swimming spots. Never leave valuables unattended, as theft is a regular occurrence.

Between the towns of Lazi and Maria, **Kagusua Beach** is reached via the pretty village of Minalolan – look for the turn-off to the barangay of Nabutay and travel past the old limestone mine. A good road leads from the village down to Kagusua, where steep concrete steps take you down to a string of beautiful secluded coves. Ask the *habal-habal* driver to drop you at the turn-off so you can enjoy the lovely shaded walk (five minutes) to a perfect beach. Paddle around the edge of the rocks on either side to find even more secluded spots. This stretch of beach has apparently been sold to developers, meaning it could potentially get a whole lot less appealing.

Between Kagusua and Salagdoong is the large horseshoe-shaped Maria Bay, where you'll find **Princesa Bulakna Resort** (☎0905 292 0591; www.princesabulakna.com; cottages P1050-2600; ❄☒). It's built on a sheer flower-covered hillside that slopes down to a stunning beach and marine sanctuary. Cheaper A-frame cottages are sterile and austere, so it's worth upgrading to a nicer room.

Improbably promoted as the island's most picturesque beach, **Salagdoong**, a few kilometres past the town of Maria, does have white-sand coves, but it's overdeveloped with a big waterslide and popular with rowdy day trippers. The government-owned **Hotel Agripino** (☎0917 964 4873; r P800-1200; ❄☒) has some decent sea-facing rooms with balconies if you can handle the faux satin sheets.

A little further on is **Olang Art Park** (Galeria Cielomia; ☎0939 464 5180; escminnie@yahoo.com), a retreat for Filipino artists that's set over 3 hectares, with a small gallery of modern art. It remains very much a work in progress.

BOHOL

☎038 / POP 1.23 MILLION

Only a short flight from Manila or quick ferry journey from Cebu, the lush island province of Bohol offers independent travellers a wealth of options both on and off the beaten track. Bohol is promoted almost exclusively through iconic images of cute bug-eyed tarsiers and the majestic Chocolate Hills, and while both are fantastic highlights, in reality it's the diving on Panglao Island that brings in the crowds. Add a jungle interior, an adventure sport paradise, rice terraces and the pristine white beaches of Anda, and you get a more rounded picture of what Bohol really is about. The island has a distinct traveller atmosphere, and is largely free of the older sexpat brigade.

Boholanos still affectionately call their province the 'Republic of Bohol', in reference to the island's short-lived independence at the turn of the 19th century. It's an appropriate appellation – today's successors of the republic are fierce protectors of Bohol's distinctive cultural heritage.

ℹ Getting There & Away

AIR

There are many daily flights from Manila to Tagbilaran airport, as well as newly introduced flights to Cebu City.

Bohol

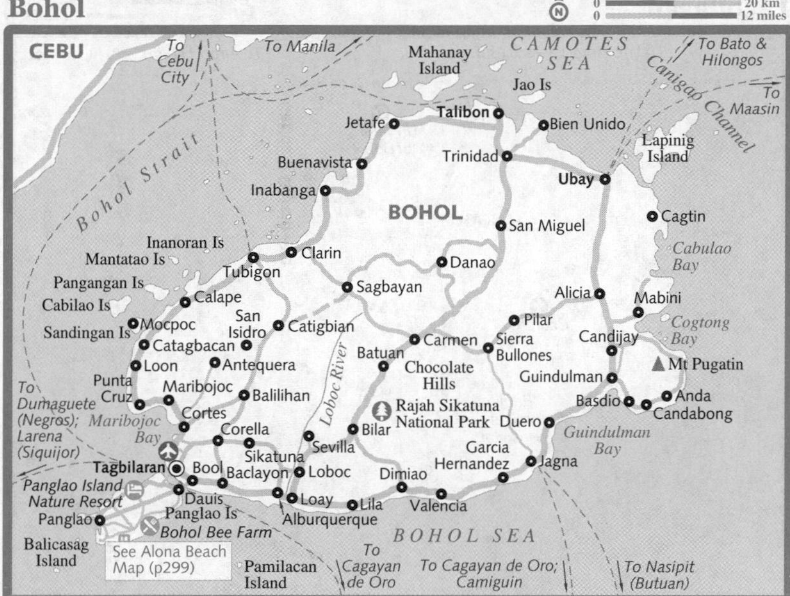

BOAT

Tagbilaran is Bohol's main port – other ports include Tubigon, Jagna, Ubay and Talibon. There are umpteen ways that you're able to travel here from Cebu City, as well as connections to Manila, Leyte, Mindanao, Siquijor and Negros.

Tagbilaran

☎038 / POP 92,297

Derived from two Visayan words meaning 'hidden shelter' *(tago bilaan)*, the name Tagbilaran is a reference either to its positioning on a calm, protected strait or its historical role as a sanctuary from Moro invaders. Today the town is overrun by legions of noisy tricycle taxis and there's nothing calming or protected about it. If your interests are divided between the watery and land-based kind, then this commercial city is a practical place to base yourself.

In the heart of town, have a look at the huge **St Joseph the Worker Cathedral**, built in 1767, burnt to the ground in 1798 and rebuilt and enlarged in 1855. Across the road is the **National Museum** (adult/child P10/5; ⌚9.30-11.30am & 1.30-4.30pm Sun-Fri) with a small but well-presented collection of artefacts discovered around Bohol.

Activities

There may not be much to do in Tagbilaran itself, but you'll find several creative tour start-ups that offer more adventurous travellers a chance to get beyond the Panglao/Chocolate Hills experience.

TOP CHOICE **Paddles & Ladles** KAYAKING

(Island Buzz; ☎0918 357 3818; paddles2ladles@gmail.com; 80-B Gallares St; trips from P1500) Departing from nearby Cortes at sunset, and run by the laid-back Buzzy, these memorable evening kayak trips set out to see the fireflies, which pulsate in the trees like Christmas lights. Grab a few beers for the leisurely paddle along the nipa-palm-lined Abatan River, free of the motorised karaoke boats that plague Loboc River. In harvesting season you'll stop en route to watch villagers weaving the walls and ceilings for nipa huts. The trip climaxes as night descends, revealing the sight of trees full of shimmering fireflies. Combined with the stillness of the night, it can be an immensely tranquil experience. Prices include dinner and transport to Cortes. Be sure to bring a towel and spare clothes, as you'll get wet. Also arranges longer sea-kayaking adventures.

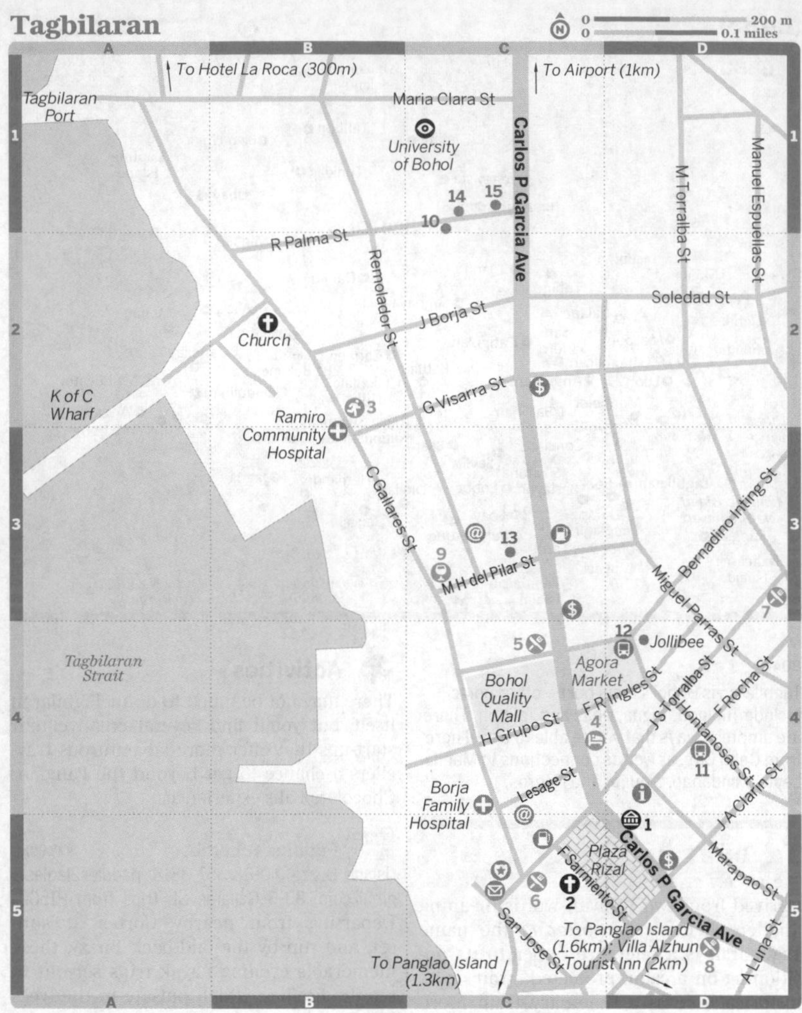

Barkada Tours ADVENTURE TOURS
(☎0920 901 2792; www.barkadatours.com; day trips incl meals from P1800) Off-the-beaten-track, environmentally responsible adventure tours ranked from 'couch potato' through to 'adventure-plus'. Trips can be tailored and are fully catered.

Festivals & Events

Bohol Fiesta CULTURAL
Tagbilaran is the headquarters of this giant festival celebrating St Joseph. The town's own fiesta kicks off the proceedings on 1 May, with lead-ups from 22 April.

Sandugo Festival CULTURAL
This festival, held in the first week of July, celebrates the March 1565 blood compact, where Spanish conquistador Miguel Lopez de Legazi and Boholano chieftain Rajah Sikatuna shared a cup of each other's blood as a peace treaty. It's followed by a string of other festivals (such as an arts and culture festival and an agricultural fair) that have turned the whole of July into one big party month.

Sleeping

For an authentic slice of Boholano life, contact **Process-Bohol** (☎416 0067; www.

Tagbilaran

Sights
1 National Museum D5
2 St Joseph the Worker Cathedral C5

Activities, Courses & Tours
3 Paddles & Ladles B2

Sleeping
4 Nisa Travelers Inn C4

Eating
5 Food Stalls C4
6 Garden Cafe C5
7 Gerarda's D3
8 Payag D5

Drinking
9 Martin's Music Restobar C3

Transport
10 Boysam Motor Rental C1
11 Bus for Panglao D4
12 Multicab for Dao Bus and Jeepney Terminal D4
13 Negros Navigation C3
14 Speed Motor Rental C1
15 Trans-Asia Shipping Lines C1

processbohol.org), a nonprofit community-run organisation that arranges cheap **homestays** (incl breakfast P350) with families. The fee helps struggling communities maintain a sustainable livelihood.

Nisa Travelers Inn PENSION HOUSE **$**
(☎411 3731; www.nisatravellersinn.com; Carlos P Garcia Ave; s/d incl breakfast with fan & shared bathroom P550/700, r with air-con & private bathroom P1100; ❄) You won't find cheaper or more central accommodation in Tagbilaran. Nisa Travelers Inn has a welcoming, traveller-friendly vibe, with clean rooms and 24-hour checkout. Discounts are generally available here, and they can also arrange tours.

Hotel La Roca HOTEL **$**
(☎411 3796; www.bohollaroca.com; Graham Ave; s/d from P875/950; ❄@) The first grand hotel in Tagbilaran, La Roca is now something of a faded beauty but still retains much of its charm. The standard rooms are large and terrific value. Don't be tempted by the much pricier deluxe, which is essentially the same as the standard room with the addition of breakfast.

Villa Alzhun Tourist Inn & Restaurant HOTEL **$$**
(☎412 3883; www.villa-alzhun.com; 162 VP Inting St, Mansasa; s/d from P1100/1500; ❄@) A lovely old-style villa, 2km south of town overlooking Tagbilaran Strait. Wood-floored rooms are heavy on the chintz but well kept. The restaurant out over the water has unbeatable sunset views.

Eating & Drinking

For late-night barbecue snacks, go to the row of **food stalls** (Bernadino Inting St) at the back of Bohol Quality Mall.

Gerarda's FILIPINO **$**
(JS Torralba St; meals P75-295; ⏲10am-10pm) In a historic family house with antiques, polished floorboards, sparkling cutlery and ambient jazz, sophisticated Gerarda's does fabulous Filipino food. Associated with Alison's Seafood Park chain, Gerarda's is so confident about the quality of its food that you don't have to pay if you don't like it. The seafood *kare kare* (fish and crab in peanut sauce) is a winner.

Payag FILIPINO **$**
(cnr Carlos P Garcia Ave & Matig-a St; meals P55-250) In a lovingly renovated Spanish-era home with a few quirky additions, everything on the menu is excellent (we checked), but the sizzling *gambas* (prawns) are to die for.

Garden Cafe AMERICAN **$**
(JS Torralba St; meals P75-200; ⏲6.30am-10.30pm) A fun cowboy-themed restaurant that employs deaf waiters and chefs. The menu – which includes a beginner's guide to sign language – is chock-full of good ol' Yankee fare, from fried chicken to onion rings and burgers. Upstairs, choose your order and dial it straight through to the kitchen from tableside phones as you enjoy the kitschy Wild West decor.

Martin's Music Restobar RESTOBAR **$$**
(cnr C Gallares & MH del Pilar Sts; meals P100-300; ⏲6pm-late) Upstairs bar that's popular with students for its regular live music.

Information

Internet Access

Many hotels have internet or wi-fi, but otherwise there are several internet cafes in the streets surrounding the University of Bohol.

Medical Services

Ramiro Community Hospital (☎411 3515; 63 C Gallares St)

Money

Most major banks have branches here with ATMs. **Metrobank** (Carlos P Garcia Ave) has the largest withdrawal limit.

Post

Main post office (JS Torralba St) Opposite the old city hall.

Tourist Information

Bohol Tourism Office (☎412 3666; www.bohol.gov.ph; ground fl, New Capitol Bldg, Marapao St; ⏰8am-6pm Mon-Fri) Wonderfully helpful and professional staff can provide maps, assist with travel information and accommodation, and book tours and transport. Contact the office via boholtourism@yahoo.com, rather than through the email address on its website (which is for provincial government info only). It also has a small branch at the airport and pier.

ℹ Getting There & Around

Air

The ticketing offices are at the airport, a few kilometres north of the city centre. There are also several travel agencies in town and most of the hotels can help with bookings.

PAL, Cebu Pacific, Airphil Express and Zest Air all have several daily flights between Manila and Tagbilaran. Mid-Sea Express has three flights a week to Cebu and Camiguin.

Boat

Apart from **Trans-Asia Shipping Lines** (☎411 3234; R Palma St), the following ferry ticket offices are all located at the pier:

Cokaliong Shipping (☎501 8598)

Lite Shipping (☎411 4724)

Negros Navigation (☎032-554 8777) Has an office at the pier and on MH del Pilar St.

Oceanjet (☎032-255 7560)

Palacio Shipping (☎0916 210 2927)

SuperCat (☎501 8380)

Weesam Express (☎501 8223)

CEBU Between SuperCat, Oceanjet and Weesam there are around eight fastcraft trips between Tagbilaran and Cebu (from P500, one hour 45 minutes) from 6.30am to 7.20pm. Several slower and larger crafts also service the route daily.

NEGROS Oceanjet leaves for Dumaguete (P680, two hours) daily at 8am and 5.45pm.

MANILA Negros Navigation sails from Tagbilaran to Manila (from P1499, 27 hours) on Sundays at 3pm.

MINDANAO Oceanjet has an 8am boat to Dapitan (P950, three hours 40 minutes). Trans-Asia has a boat for Cagayan de Oro (from P655, 10 hours) leaving at 7pm every Monday, Wednesday and Friday. Negros Navigation services Iligan (P744, seven hours), Ozamis (P744, 12 hours) and Dipolog (P944, 23½ hours). SuperFerry has a boat to Dipolog (P940, nine hours) early Sunday morning. Lite Shipping and Palacio head to Plaridel (P400, 11 hours) at around 6pm.

SIQUIJOR Oceanjet has a daily 5.45pm ferry to Siquijor town via Dumaguete (P800, three hours). Lite Shipping heads to Larena (P180, two hours) fives times a week at 6pm, while Palacio leaves at 7pm (P170, four hours).

Bus

See p301 for details on getting to Panglao Island. Buses to Panglao depart from the corner of Hontanosas and F Rocha Sts.

For other destinations, Tagbilaran's primary road-transport hub for buses and jeepneys is the **Dao Bus & Jeepney Terminal** beside the large Island City Mall. It's a P30 tricycle ride northeast of town, or a multicab from the northeast corner of the Agora Market (opposite Jollibee). Buses head to Loboc (P30, one hour), Carmen (P60, two hours), Anda (P100, four hours), Ubay (P120, five hours), Loon (P30, 45 minutes) and Tubigon (P50, 1½ hours), with the last services around 6pm.

V-hire vans also depart from Dao terminal, providing a much quicker though pricier and squashier option, and you may have to pay extra for your bag.

Car & Motorcycle

Hiring a car for the Chocolate Hills–Danao–Loboc–Tarsier Sanctuary day trip loop is a convenient means of getting around. **Lugod Rent A Car** (☎411 2244) is a reliable company, charging P3500 for eights hours (P200 per extra hour).

Motorbikes can be rented from **Boysam Motor Rental** (☎411 2594) or **Speed Motor Rental** (☎0906 507 7848), both on R Palma St, for P500 per day. Remember to test the horn, brakes and headlights, and insist on a helmet.

Panglao Island

☎038 / POP 62,083

Panglao Island is generally associated with **Alona Beach**, a congested strip of resorts and dive centres on the southern side of the island. Unless you're there for the diving, Alona has little to offer the independent traveller. With a few exceptions, accommodation is overpriced and nothing to write home about, but divers can score nifty package deals by combining dives with accommodation. While the underwater scene at Alona is exceptional, those craving a real off-the-beaten-track deserted beach experience – with the option of diving – should consider making the trip to Cabilao Island (p302) or Anda (p306) instead.

Just as you cross over the bridge to Panglao Island from the mainland, take a moment to look around the scenic village of **Dauis** and admire the magnificent 19th-century Lady of Assumption Cathedral and its adjacent rectory, which has recently been restored. There is a small **museum & gift shop** (⌚9am-6pm) that sells fine, locally crafted jewellery and also an array of coffee-table books on local culture.

Activities

Diving

Diving is what draws tourists to Panglao, with the island offering some of the finest spots in the Philippines, in particular the underwater paradise of Balicasag Island. Pamilacan Island is also very nice, but less visited as its corals are left to recover from dynamite fishing.

You can probably score the best deal by combining accommodation with diving. The average prices are one dive US$25, equipment rental US$6 and open-water diving certificates US$350.

Snorkellers can swim 75m straight out to enjoy the soft corals of Alona's house reef.

The following operators are based out of Panglao Island resorts:

Genesis Divers (☎502 9056; www.genesisdivers.com; Peter's House)

Philippine Islands Divers (☎502 9164; www.phildivers.com; Bohol Divers Resort)

Scuba World (☎502 9450; www.scubaworld.com.ph; Aquatica Beach Resort)

Sea Explorers (☎in Cebu 032-234 0248; www.sea-explorers.com; Alona Vida Beach Resort)

SeaQuest Divers (☎502 9069; www.seaquestdivecenter.net; Oasis Resort)

Tropical Divers (☎502 9031; www.tropicaldivers-alona.com; Alona Tropical)

Island Hopping

You can rent bangkas on Alona Beach for P3000 per half-day of island-hopping, and dolphin-watching and whale-watching expeditions, though there have been negative reports that this more resembles 'dolphin chasing' – so you might be better to organise this through Baclayon, 6km from Tagbilaran.

Swimming

If you're desperate for some quiet beach time, leave Alona behind and head to **Panglao Island Nature Resort**, which has a lovely private beach open to nonguests for P250 (P350 on weekends).

Swimmers can experience the refreshingly cold waters of **Hinagdanan Cave** (admission P15) at Bingag, on the island's northern coast, with its mixture of fresh and salt water.

At Alona the best swimming is at the far eastern end out front of Hennan Resort, where boats are prohibited to anchor less than 50m from shore.

Sleeping

ALONA BEACH

Just about all the beachside resorts either have dive centres or are closely affiliated with one, and most of them also have restaurants and bars. The multitude of resorts

Alona Beach

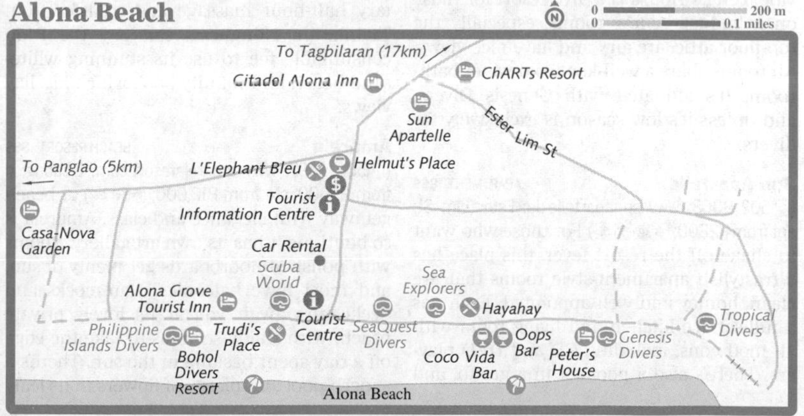

are so closely packed together that shopping around for food or diving deals is no problem.

TOP CHOICE ChARTs Resort BOUTIQUE HOTEL **$$**
(502 9095; www.charts-alona.com; d incl breakfast with fan P1500, r with air-con P2200-5000;) Art lovers will be smitten by this ultracreative resort on the road towards Alona Beach. Set around a dolphin-shaped pool, the gorgeous rooms evoke a Dalíesque Mediterranean-Asian atmosphere; there are no sharp edges and the stucco-textured walls highlight the fine varnished furniture. All artwork, both in and outside the rooms, is for sale, and there's an upstairs cafe that serves excellent coffee and meals.

Citadel Alona Inn PENSION HOUSE **$**
(502 9424; www.citadelalona.com; d with fan/air-con P600/800;) If you can live with a shared bathroom, this family-run operation on the road leading to Alona Beach is a super-value option. Rooms are small but comfortable and well decorated, and there's even a common kitchen area, which will suit long-termers.

Alona Grove Tourist Inn NIPA HUTS **$**
(502 4200; alongagrove@yahoo.com; hut without fan shared/private bathroom P600/700, with air-con P1300;) A chilled-out budget option just up from the beach with nipa huts scattered among its pleasant garden with manicured grass. Rents motorbikes for P500 per day.

Peter's House BEACH RESORT **$**
(502 9056; www.genesisdivers.com; r divers/nondivers from P500/850) A nipa-hut complex with a friendly and laid-back communal vibe, Peter's House is a dive resort for those on a budget. A few rooms, especially the top-floor attic, are airy and have nice views. All rooms share a well-kept cold-water bathroom. It's affiliated with Genesis Divers, and unless it's low season is exclusively for divers.

Sun Apartelle APARTMENT **$$$**
(502 9063; www.sunapartelle.de; Ester Lim St; apt from P2800;) For those who want to shake off the resort fever, this place has ultrastylish apartment-style rooms that are clean, homey and well appointed. Each has a full-service kitchen and living room with all mod cons, including CD and DVD players. There's also a pool set in a grotto, and a sunny restaurant. Prices drop by about a third for longer stays.

Bohol Divers Resort BEACH RESORT **$**
(502 9050; www.boholdiversresortph.com; r with fan from P500, with air-con, hot water & TV from P3000;) At the quiet end of the beach, this popular resort is set around a nice garden and freshwater swimming pool. There's a wide range of accommodation, from inexpensive concrete fan rooms to pricier villas. It's affiliated with Philippine Islands Divers.

Casa-Nova Garden BEACH RESORT **$**
(502 9101; s/d from P300/500;) True shoestring accommodation survives in Alona thanks to this cosy oasis. It's a bit out of the way, however. The turn-off is 700m beyond (west of) Helmut's Place.

AROUND THE ISLAND

There aren't any genuine budget options around Panglao, but most resorts will let nonguests access their beaches and facilities for a 'consumable' fee, meaning you are obliged to spend a certain amount of money on food or drinks.

Panglao Island Nature Resort BEACH RESORT **$$$**
(501 7288; www.panglaoisland.com; s/d incl breakfast & dinner from P7260/9740;) One of the more beautifully integrated resorts on the island, the cheaper rooms on this 14-hectare property have a holiday-house feel with sweeping ocean views, while the more upmarket bungalows have showers that look out onto a private garden, a spa bath built into the balcony and good feng shui indoors. A sea-view restaurant with a creative menu offers a good range of healthy salads (P220). Rates include a complimentary half-hour massage and transfer from Tagbilaran. Nonguests can pay the P450 consumable fee to use its stunning white-sand beach and infinity pool, which has bay views.

Amarela BEACH RESORT **$$$**
(502 9497; www.amarelaresort.com; Libaong; d from P7000, ste from P12,000;) A beach getaway with elegance and class, Amarela is so boutique it has its own art gallery. Rooms with polished floorboards get plenty of sun, and most have balconies. Hammocks and deckchairs await you at its lovely private beach, with shady sections to take the edge off a day spent basking in the sun. There's a superb pool and plenty of flowers in its leafy

grounds. It's located 4km outside of Alona Beach along the coastal road.

Bohol Bee Farm BOUTIQUE HOTEL $$
(http://boholbeefarm.com; r P2000-4000; ❄📶🏊) Scattered around an organic farm, rooms in the well-designed, rustic cottages have wooden floors and are painted in earthy colours, while the family rooms have cool mezzanines and balconies on the 2nd floor. Clamber down to the sea where there is a purpose-designed sunbathing deck. It's 7km east of Alona Beach along the same stretch of coast.

Eating & Drinking

On Alona Beach, generally the best food is at the restaurants away from the beach, while the beach is the best spot for a drink.

TOP CHOICE **L'Elephant Bleu** FRENCH $$
(www.lelephantbleu.com; mains P260-620; ⏰8am-midnight; 📶) The electric-blue VW parked out front makes for a stylish first impression, and the food at this casual French restaurant backs it up. The flambéed garlic prawns are exceptional, and traditionalists can bookend it with snails as a starter, and a perfectly made crème brûlée for dessert. There's also wine, cheese and great coffee. Cult movies are screened on Monday nights in its beer garden. Also has budget lodging.

Bohol Bee Farm ORGANIC $$
(http://boholbeefarm.com; mains P180-380; 📶) A great spot for a healthy lunch or light meal, this organic farm makes for a lovely excursion, located 7km from Alona. Try the squash muffins, lemongrass juice, herb pasta and spicy flower salad. Take a tour (departing every hour till 4pm) through the fecund garden to see where the food on your plate comes from. Carnivores don't despair, there's plenty for you too, such as the honey-glazed chicken on organic red rice.

Graziella ITALIAN $$
(meals P225-315) It might be rebadged with a new name (formerly Kamalig), yet people continue to come for its genuine Italian dishes. Italian wine is served by the glass (P110).

Trudi's Place FILIPINO $
(dishes from P90; ⏰6am-10pm) An ugly ice-cream cake of a restaurant, but good for cheap food. You can get Filipino and Western dishes and a decent selection of salads.

Hayahay PIZZA $$
(☎pizzas P190; ⏰7am-midnight) On the beach, Hayahay serves up pizzas, Thai and meat pies for homesick Aussies.

Helmut's Place BAR
(⏰10am-late) Away from the fuss, the emphasis in this friendly and slightly seedy bar is on drinking. Cocktails are dangerously cheap at P160.

Coco Vida Bar BAR
(⏰8am-late) The most buzzing bar on the beach when we visited.

Oops Bar BAR
(⏰8am-late) Saturday nights see Oops' beach bar's disco pumping.

Information

There's a BPI ATM in Alona Beach.

The privately owned **Tourist Information Centre** (☎502 9487; ⏰9am-9pm) is more a general store, but has internet (per hour P60), changes money, offers credit-card cash advances, sells ferry tickets and beach paraphernalia, and has a postal service and transport info. A smaller office down the same street has internet access.

Getting There & Around

From Tagbilaran, buses with 'Tawala Alona' signboards head to Alona Beach roughly hourly until 3pm from the corner of Hontanosas and F Rocha Sts (P25, 45 minutes). Buses also leave from here to Panglao town (P20, 30 minutes).

A simpler way to reach Alona (or elsewhere on Panglao) is to hire a tricycle from anywhere in Tagbilaran (P200, 30 to 45 minutes) or a *habal-habal* (P100 one way). You can find drivers hanging around the corner of FR Ingles St and Carlos P Garcia Ave in Tagbilaran, or outside the information office at Alona Beach. Taxis from Tagbilaran are quicker and cost around P350.

Prices for car and van drivers out front of the 'tourist centre' are around P500 to Tagbilaran, P3000 to Anda, P2200 to Loboc, P1800 to Loon and P1500 to Corella.

Balicasag Island

One of the premier diving spots in the Philippines, Balicasag, about 6km southwest of Panglao, is ringed by a pristine reef that has been declared a marine sanctuary. It drops away to impressive submarine cliffs as deep as 50m. Soft and hard corals can be found around the cliffs, as can trevally, barracuda, wrasse and the very occasional whale shark from December to March.

Balicasag Island Dive Resort (in Cebu City 032-211 440; ptabidr@bohol-online.com; dm per person P800-1000, duplex cottages P2500;), run by the Philippine Tourism Authority, has air-con duplex nipa cottages with private bathrooms and verandahs. It has friendly staff, a good restaurant and a coral-sand island all to itself. The dormitories here can sleep up to eight people, though smaller groups may be required to pay for the empty beds.

Balicasag is a 45-minute boat ride from Alona Beach, and is visited mainly by dive companies, but otherwise ring ahead for the resort to arrange your pick-up. If visiting for the day, a return boat trip from Panglao will cost around P2000.

Cabilao Island

038 / POP 4203

Legend has it that idyllic Cabilao is inhabited by the dreaded dog-shaped Balikaka monster that sporadically attacks livestock. In reality Cabilao is so chilled out, the only sounds to break the perfect calm are church bells and the odd rooster. There are limited beaches here, so Cabilao is a destination that attracts primarily divers, but otherwise it can make a great spot if you want to slow things right down.

Like Balicasag and Pamilacan Islands to the south, the waters off Cabilao contain an impressively rich dive site, with two community-run **marine sanctuaries** (diving fee P50). Though home to seven species of shark, the area is also full of microlife, including the high-profile pygmy seahorse *(Hippocampus bargibanti)*, which, at only 8mm long, may be easier to spot in a diving magazine than in the wild, where it's camouflaged among the surrounding red coral.

The celebrity seahorse is found on the house reef, but there is diving, for beginners to advanced, all around the island. The island's top reef is off the northwestern point, near the lighthouse. Highly regarded **Sea Explorers** (416 0463; www.sea-explorers.com) has one of its five Visayan dive centres on Cabilao.

In addition to diving, a feature of Cabilao Island is its **church**, which has what is claimed to be the country's biggest stone staircase.

Sleeping

There are four sleeping options on Cabilao, three of which are on the northwestern side of the island. Most have dive centres. Electricity on the island is limited.

TOP CHOICE **Cabilao Beach Club** BEACH RESORT $$
(416 0463; www.cabilao.com; r with fan P2800;) Affectionately known as 'CBC', the Swiss-managed Cabilao Beach Club sits alone on the northeastern tip of the island, with sophisticated and spotless clean thatched cottages with modern tiled bathrooms. The restaurant has therapeutic ocean views and Sea Explorers is on-site. Rates are halved in low season.

Polaris Resort BEACH RESORT $$
(505 4118; www.polaris-dive.com; r with fan/air-con from P2100/3000, tree house P2100;) Has decent large rooms in concrete cottages as well as two 'tree houses' up on stilts. It's a good family option; kids will love the Disneyland-esque artificial rock pools and hillocks. Extra ticks for partially using solar energy. There is an attached PADI dive centre. Nearby is a sandbar that at low tide is good for swimming and snorkelling.

Getting There & Away

To get to Cabilao Island you must head several kilometres north of Loon to Mocpoc (a good 20 minutes on a bumpy road; bus or jeepney P10, *habal-habal* P50). Loon is 27km from Tagbilaran (bus or jeepney P30, 45 minutes). From Mocpoc, to head to the northeast of Cabilao to access Cabilao Beach Club, it's a 20-minute bangka ride (P20) to Cambaquiz pier, but you'll have to wait until the boat is full or else pay for the empty seats (P140). From the pier at Cambaquiz it's a five-minute walk to Cabilao Beach Club. To access the resorts on the northwest of the island, take a bangka to Talisay (P20), from where you can get a *habal-habal* to Polaris Resort or Estrella for P50. A boat from Mocpoc directly to the resorts will cost around P500. From either Panglao or Mactan islands, it can take two to three hours.

There are also boats from Cabilao to Cebu, heading to Argao (P120, two hours) on Monday and Saturday at 8am. Otherwise there are daily morning and afternoon boats to Argao (P110, two hours) from Catagbacan, 8km northof Loon.

Bohol Interior

038

TARSIER SANCTUARY

In barangay Canapnapan, between the towns of Corella and Sikatuna, you can visit the **Philippine Tarsier Sanctuary** (0927 541 2290; www.tarsierfoundation.org; admission

P50; ⌚9am-4pm). This simultaneously crazy and cuddly looking little primate can fit in the palm of your hand yet leap 5m, rotate its head almost 360 degrees and move its ears in the direction of sound. It has huge imploring eyes, 150 times bigger than a human's in relation to its body size.

The tarsier is not only one of the world's smallest primates and the oldest surviving member of the primate group at 45 million years old, it is also an endangered species. The main threats to its survival are habitat destruction, introduced species, hunting and the pet trade. While also found in Samar, Leyte and parts of Mindanao, Bohol is the province that is doing the most to promote awareness of the tarsier and attempting to ensure its survival; it's also the most likely place visitors are going to see one of these guys.

The visitors centre includes information boards, a captive breeding program, wildlife sanctuary and hiking trail. Check out the framed photograph of former First Lady Amelita Ramos presenting a tarsier to Prince Charles in 1997. The tarsier was dubbed 'Datu Charles' (Chief Charles) and its eventual fate is unknown. The breeding areas are off limits, but a small patch of forest beside the centre allows for guided walks and discreet viewing of several mature tarsiers.

To get here from Tagbilaran, catch a bus to Sikatuna (P25, one hour) from the Dao terminal and ask to be dropped off at the sanctuary. From Nuts Huts lodging north of Loboc, the sanctuary is a 30- to 45-minute motorbike ride, or you can take a jeepney from Loboc (P25, 45 minutes).

LOBOC

☎038 / POP 16,299

Floating restaurants blasting the tunes of Frank Sinatra and other oldies cruise a stretch of the Loboc River north of the town of the same name. Even this incongruous soundtrack doesn't diminish the appeal of Loboc, poking out from the jungle underbrush and home to the **San Pedro Church** (c 1602), the oldest on Bohol. Cruises take you upriver to the **Tontonan Falls** and the Visayas' oldest hydroelectric plant. Nearby is the **Loboc Eco-Tourism Adventure Park** (☎537 9292), with a 500m zipline (P350) running over a gorge.

In late May to June, Loboc hosts the **Balibong Kingking Festival**, which honours Our Lady of Guadalupe.

Nuts Huts (☎0920 846 1559; www.nutshuts.com; dm P300, nipa huts from P700) is a popular lodging ensconced in the jungle on the edge of the Loboc River, 2km north of Loboc town. The stilted nipa huts are hidden at the bottom of the steep hill at a lovely spot along the river. All have balconies and sweeping views, though they're very basic, for roughing it in the jungle. Meals are served in the wonderful dining room/lounge area, where a wall of jungle on the opposite bank of the river completely fills the view. Make use of guided treks to the nearby caves (expect to get wet) or Rajah Sikatuna National Park, or simply lounge in the hammocks and take it easy. It also has a wood-heated herbal sauna.

To get to Nuts Huts from Tagbilaran, catch a Carmen-bound bus and get off at the Nuts Huts sign about 3km beyond Loboc. From there, it's around a 15-minute walk along a rutted dirt path. It's preferable to take a bus to Loboc and then a shuttle boat up the Loboc River from the Sarimanok landing north of Loboc centre (per person P200, minimum two people). You can also take a *habal-habal* (P50) straight to Nuts Huts from Loboc.

Loboc is about 24km from Tagbilaran, accessed by bus or jeepney (P30, one hour).

CHOCOLATE HILLS

One of Bohol's premier tourist attractions, and certainly most hyped, are the iconic Chocolate Hills, a series of majestic grassy hillocks that span far into the horizon. Straddling three municipalities, the largest and most visited concentration is 5km south of Carmen at the Chocolate Hills Complex. The hills get their name from the lawnlike vegetation that roasts to chocolate brown in the dry season (December to May), and are best viewed during a hazy dusk or dawn. Romantics might want to believe the legend that they are the solidified teardrops of a lovelorn giant. Scientists, on the other hand, say that the 1268 near identical hills, with sizes ranging from 40m to 120m, are the result of the uplifting of ancient coral-reef deposits, followed by erosion and weathering.

At the Chocolate Hills drop-off point, which is on the main road, at the base of the **Chocolate Hills Main Viewpoint** (admission P50), motorbikes can whisk you up the hill (P20 one way), where the views are compromised by kiosks selling kitschy souvenirs. Of course, you can also walk up the hill (20 to 30 minutes). The same bikers will take you to and from Carmen for P20 (one way), or arrange fun motorbike tours (P250) along winding roads to the main viewing sites, as well as to lesser-known spots, such as the **Eight Sisters Hillocks**.

The nearby town of Carmen is home to Fatima Hills. Pilgrims climb the steps up to the **Our Lady of Fatima statue** here every year on 13 May.

The **Chocolate Hills Complex Hotel** (☎0919 680 0492; r P1200; ❄📶✉) is a convenient place to stay to view the hills at dawn or dusk, and all up very good value. Ask for a room with a view.

ℹ Getting There & Away

The best way to get to the Chocolate Hills is to hire your own motorbike in Tagbilaran or Loboc; it's a scenic ride and north of Loboc it's virtually traffic-free. Combine your ride with a visit to the Tarsier Sanctuary or even Danao.

From Tagbilaran there are regular buses from the Dao terminal to Carmen (P60, two hours). Most hotels in Tagbilaran can organise a hire car to take you to and from the Chocolate Hills. The average price for a standard air-con sedan with driver is P2000.

From Nuts Huts, the Chocolate Hills are a 45-minute motorbike ride, or you can flag down a Carmen-bound bus.

From Carmen there are also buses to and from Talibon (P62, two hours) and Tubigon (P50, 1½ hours).

DANAO

☎038 / POP 17,716

Set among mountainous jungle with spectacular gorges, caves and raging rivers, **Danao Adventure Park** (☎412 2338, 0939 431 4306; www.eatdanao.com; Suislide P350) is a giant adventure playground designed for adrenaline junkies. Rappelling, caving, rock climbing, kayaking and tubing are all highly recommended, but it's the thrill-seeking activities that it's most well known for. The 'Suislide' zipline will have you soaring across a 500m gorge like Superman, or you can take the 'Plunge' with a breathtaking 75m free fall into the valley, supposedly the largest in the world.

The brainchild of Danao's entrepreneurial mayor, the park has transformed the region from one of Bohol's poorest municipalities into one of the hottest new destinations, and employs many of the villagers here. Keep an eye out for the rockin' house band that belts out '60s rock'n'roll (covers and originals), comprising disadvantaged locals.

At time of research the park was in the process of starting up **scenic flights** over the Chocolate Hills, and the dune buggy looked like it'd be a ridiculous amount of fun. There are **rooms** (camping incl tent P225, r with fan/air-con P600/1000) here if you plan on hanging around.

Located 72km from Tagbilaran, to get here take a bus to Danao (P85, 2½ hours) and then a *habal-habal* (P40, 15 minutes) to the park.

BILAR

☎038

A popular stopover for day trippers, the **Simply Butterflies Conservation Center** (☎535 9400; www.simplybutterfliesproject.com; adult/child incl guide P30/5; ⌚7.30am-5pm) houses a smallish exhibit of butterflies. Guided tours point out some interesting titbits, and the centre also offers **night safaris** (per person P900; ⌚5.30-7.30pm) close to Rajah Sikatuna National Park to spot tarsiers. While you'd be very, very lucky to see one in the wild, it's a nice experience to walk through their natural habitat, also home to owls, frogmouths, bats, civet cats and fireflies.

Bilar also has **Logarita Spring** (admission P10; ⌚Sat-Thu), a public swimming hole overlooking rice fields.

The town is about 40km east of Tagbilaran, served by regular buses (P40, 1½ hours).

ANTEQUERA

☎038 / POP 1669

Just out of Antequera (ahn-tee-*care*-ah), about 20km from Tagbilaran (bus or jeepney P30), are **Mag-aso** and **Inambacan Falls**, the largest falls on the island, as well as some of Bohol's best caves. Cave guides can be tracked down in Antequera itself, or through one of the adventure tour groups in Tagbilaran.

BACLAYON

☎038 / POP 2178

About 6km from Tagbilaran by (bus or jeepney P8), Baclayon was founded by a pair of Spanish Jesuit priests in 1596. Magnificent coral-stone **Baclayon Church** was constructed much later in 1727. It also has a **museum** (admission P25) with a collection of religious artefacts.

Baclayon is the best spot to arrange trips to Pamilacan Island for whale- and dolphin-watching tours.

It also has wonderful **heritage houses**, saved from demolishment by the Baclayon Ancestral Home Organisation, which can arrange walking tours to its 67 Spanish colonial houses, dating back to 1853. It also offers homestays in the ancestral houses.

CAGED CRITTERS

Despite long-term grassroots efforts to crack down on the practice, more and more tarsiers are being captured in the wild to be put on display in cages for the admiration of tourists or as curios to liven up shop corners. To make matters worse, their keepers often let you place one of these critically endangered creatures on your shoulder for a photograph. Even with the gentlest handling, their small and delicate bones are easily broken. Kept in captivity, tarsiers will not live more than 12 months, and they've been known to commit suicide while in captivity. The very existence of this destructive industry generates demand, as dead animals need to be constantly replaced with live specimens.

Thankfully there have been improvements. In May 2011 the governor of Bohol, in liaison with the Department of Environment & Natural Resources (DENR), negotiated the release of hundreds of caged tarsiers. However, the DENR's role in this matter is a confused one. While they enforce the release of caged tarsiers, they likewise issue 'wildlife farm' permits that allows tarsiers to be displayed for commercial purposes, and have come under heavy criticism from NGOs like the Philippines Tarsier Foundation (PTFI).

If you do see a caged tarsier *anywhere*, you are encouraged to report it to the **DENR** (☎in Cebu 032-346 9177; r7@denr.gov.ph) and also to notify the **Protected Areas & Wildlife Bureau** (☎in Manila 02-928-1178; cites@pawb.gov.ph) for good measure.

You'll be doing the entire species a favour if you reserve your viewing for the Philippine Tarsier Sanctuary, which comes closest to replicating the tarsiers' natural habitat.

For more information, get in touch with the helpful **tourist office** (☎540 9474; www.baclayontourism.com) located at the port.

Pamilacan Island

☎038 / POP 1189

The tiny island of Pamilacan, about 23km east of Balicasag, is cetacean central, home to whales and dolphins. Since the 1992 ban on capturing these creatures, Pamilicanons, descendants of three generations of whalers, have had to find other ways to earn a living. There are now no fewer than three community-based outfits that organise expeditions and employ former whalers. All use old converted whaling boats and local crews. The trip includes a full day on the water and transfers from Baclayon (on Bohol) or Panglao; boats hold four to six people. Whale sightings are relatively rare, but the best time for spotting them is from February to July; dolphins are common year-round. Try **Pamilacan Island Dolphin & Whale Watching Tours** (PIDWWT; ☎540 9279; http://whales.bohol.ph; Baclayon public market; group of 4 from P1500).

Pamilacan is also good for diving, with its marine sanctuary home to manta rays and soft corals, and continues to slowly recover from dynamiting.

There are several accommodation options on Pamilacan, all providing basic meals. Electricity goes off after 10pm, but so do the karaoke machines, so rest is guaranteed. **Nita's Nipa Huts** (☎0921 320 6497; r with full-board, fan & shared bathroom P600) is the cheapest and most well-established option; the double rooms with views on the water's edge are the best positioned. Nita can organise snorkelling or a night-time squid-fishing trip for visitors, and arranges a pick-up from Panglao for P2000.

Pamilacan is the domain of Baclayon **tourist office** (☎540 9474; www.baclayontourism.com), so get in touch with them for more information.

You can arrange a boat between Pamilacan and Baclayon (one way/return P1500/2000, 45 minutes) or if you're lucky there'll be a public boat (P100) if there are enough people around; Wednesdays are your best bet, with it being market day. Boats from Alona Beach will take you to Pamilacan for around P2500.

Bohol's Coastal Road

TUBIGON

☎038 / POP 2769

The ramshackle fishing town of Tubigon (to-bee-gon), in the middle of Bohol's lush northwestern coast, is well served by daily fastcraft to and from Cebu City, though otherwise there's not a lot on offer here for travellers.

Tinangnan Beach Resort & Lodging House (☎0908 172 5115; r with fan & shared bathroom P250) is set upon stilts and has a rickety bamboo floor over intertidal mangroves. It's a five-minute tricycle ride (P20) north from the central bus and market area.

Jadestar (345 3745) and **MV Start Crafts** (0922 381 0116) among others offer plentiful daily ferries to and from Cebu City (from P150, one to two hours). Tickets are purchased near the market.

Buses to Tagbilaran (P50, 1½ hours) go via Loon (P30, one hour), or otherwise there are faster vans (P90, one hour). If you're heading straight for the Chocolate Hills from Tubigon, buses inland leave regularly for Carmen (P50, 1½ hours).

BUENAVISTA

038 / POP 844

Buenavista has a friendly, picturesque **market** on a mangrove inlet. Here, or at the river crossing 3km south on the main road, you can buy the local delicacy – urchin gonads.

For something even more special, you can go on a **Cambuhat Village Ecotour**, a cruise up the mangrove-lined Daet River from Buenavista to the village of Cambuhat, where you'll see an oyster farm and raffia weaving. Call the Buenavista **tourist office** (513 9188) for more information.

The area south of Buenavista, near the town of Inabanga, is known for its traditional healers.

TALIBON

038 / POP 4693

Talibon, on the north coast, is one of Bohol's busiest centres. Its long pier has regular boats to and from Cebu, as well as to Jao (pronounced 'how') Island nearby (P15, 15 minutes); however, there's no accommodation on Jao. All transport leaves from the market on the main street before the pier. Contact the **mayor's office** (515 0051) for further tourist information.

Talibon Pension House (0918 927 4280; r with fan/air-con from P250/500;) is probably the best accommodation in town.

Regular ferries head to Cebu City (from P240, three to four hours), including **Golden Star Fastcraft** (032-318 5591) and **VG Shipping** (032-238 7635; vgshipping@yahoo.com), departing 10am and 10pm daily.

Buses depart to Tagbilaran (P110, four hours) and Carmen (P62, two hours) for the Chocolate Hills.

BIEN UNIDO

038 / POP 23,412

Bien Unido offers the only diving in the north of Bohol. The town's mayor has taken the impressive initiative to combat illegal fishing and dynamiting by sinking 5m religious statues of the Santa Maria and Santo Niño to thwart religious locals from further damaging the Danajon Double Barrier Reef. The statues make for an interesting underwater spectacle, and marine life is expected to regenerate within a short time.

Accommodation is available at **Bien Unido Double Barrier Reef Dive Camp** (d P1300;) near Jao Island, which is a 10-minute boat trip from Bien Unido. As well as diving, the camp can arrange kayaking and island hopping.

For more information, visit www.bienunido.com, or contact the **mayor's office** (517 2391).

UBAY

038 / POP 3698

At the opposite end of Bohol to Tagbilaran, the remote town of Ubay has a lively market on the sea, just near the pier. There are plenty of cheap Filipino eateries on the water's edge, and Ubay also offers uncharted tourism territory around nearby **Lapinig Island**. There is a tiny **lodging house** (s with fan P75) a short distance from the pier gates.

Ferries and bangkas run to Southern Leyte – with boats to Bato (P250, two hours) from 8.30am until 1pm. Super Shuttle Ferry has a daily 12.30pm ferry to Maasin (P250, three hours), while **Leopard** (0922 892 9899) heads to Hilongos (P150) at 9am.

Buses run between Ubay and Talibon (P120, four hours).

ANDA

038 / POP 1412

Dubbed the 'cradle of Boholano civilisation' for its significant prehistoric sites, the stunning Anda peninsula on the southeast corner of Bohol still seems to belong to a forgotten time. From Anda town, almost 3km of untouched empty white-sand beach stretches west along the coastline. This is where all the resorts are situated; a gentle breeze blowing off the water keeps things cool, even in the hot season. Peace and privacy are the order of the day, so a word of warning to the gregarious: if you like to be surrounded by activity, you might find Anda a little *too* chilled. For a party atmosphere, head to Alona Beach on Panglao Island instead, but don't expect the beaches to be as idyllic.

There's no ATM in Anda, with the closest one in Tagbilaran. The municipal of Anda may ask for a P50 entry, which supposedly goes to keeping the beach clean.

Sights & Activities

People come to Anda for its stunning, relaxed beaches that'll likely make you want to abandon your best-laid plans. Most resorts have private patches of white-sanded beach; otherwise, the majestic **Anda Long Beach** is the widest beach, but its popularity with day trippers takes away some of its charm.

There's also some good diving on the stunning **Basdio Reef**, which can be arranged through one of the dive centres at the resorts.

If you want more than beach attractions, there are underground pools, limestone caves and some prehistoric rock paintings to explore. For more information and to arrange guides, contact Arvin Rubillos at the **tourist office** (☎528 2009).

Sleeping & Eating

Most accommodation on the beach is pricey, but there are some cheaper pensions found in the town of Anda itself. The best is probably the **Transient Lodge** (☎0927 383 3734; per person P600), named for the sign that reads 'We accept transient lodgers'.

Flower Beach Resort BEACH RESORT **$$**
(☎0918 579 6166; www.flower-beach.com; r from P1900; ❄@🛜) Run by an ultrafriendly couple, this well-designed resort boasts a great spot on a tiny but luxurious cove of white sand. The 'ocean-side' huts, overlooking a perfect swimming beach, have no air-con, but with the constant sea breeze this is not an issue. For P200 more you get air-con, a fridge and hot water, but no beach view. Motorcycle rental is available. There's a full-service dive centre that takes advantage of the 14km offshore reef.

Anda White Beach Resort BEACH RESORT **$$$**
(☎0915 541 0507, 0918 691 1011; www.andabeachresort.com; r P4100; ❄🏊) With its large, motel-style rooms (cable TV, DVD players, hot water) and infinity pool with ocean view, this is the most luxurious place that humble Anda has to offer. It's also got a fantastic beach. The restaurant menu includes such decadent surprises as 'king prawns with a touch of white wine' and the well-stocked bar offers mixed drinks for P190. Nonguests can use the swimming pool for P150, and there is an attached dive centre.

Dapdap BEACH RESORT **$**
(☎528 2011; www.boholdapdapresort.com; fan nipa huts P900, air-con nipa huts P1500-3200; ❄) Filipino-owned Dapdap is a good-value option, but a bit samey as far as beach resorts go. The beach here is nice, and the restaurant has a large menu that often runs out of stock. Ask for a discount.

Getting There & Away

There's an occasional direct bus or van from Tagbilaran to Anda (P140, three hours); otherwise, catch a bus to the junction town of Guindulman (P100), then a tricycle to Anda (P150).

JAGNA

☎038 / POP 32,034

Other than to catch a ferry to Mindanao, there's no reason to hang around this dusty market town, notable for its sizeable Muslim population.

Super Shuttle Ferry (☎0939 850 2987) has a daily service to Camiguin (P425, 3½ hours) at 1pm, while **Ocean Jet** (☎0922 857 5500) departs at 9.30am (P550, two hours). Super Shuttle also heads to Cagayan de Oro (P650, seven hours), as does **Cebu Ferries** (☎411 3651).

To Tagbilaran, there are regular vans (P100, one hour) and buses (P60, two hours) until 6pm.

LEYTE

For students and historians of the Pacific and WWII, the word 'Leyte' conjures up images of bloody naval battles and the site of MacArthur's famous return. For Filipinos it's equally associated with the rags-to-riches rise of Imelda Marcos and the nostalgic, romanticised portrait she painted of her birthplace after she made good in the capital. For travellers, Southern Leyte, wrapped around the deep-water Sogod Bay, is one of the Philippines' many diving hot spots; there are sites with rich reefs and drop-offs. Wall and cave diving is possible at Lungsodaan in Padre Burgos. The Cebuano-speaking Leyteños live in the south, and their Waray-speaking neighbours live in the cattle ranching country of northern Leyte.

Getting There & Away

AIR

Tacloban has daily flights to Manila and Cebu.

BOAT

Leyte is well linked to neighbouring islands via ferry, including Cebu City from Ormoc, Maasin and Hilongos; and to Manila, Bohol and Camotes as well as Surigao on Mindanao from Southern Leyte.

Leyte

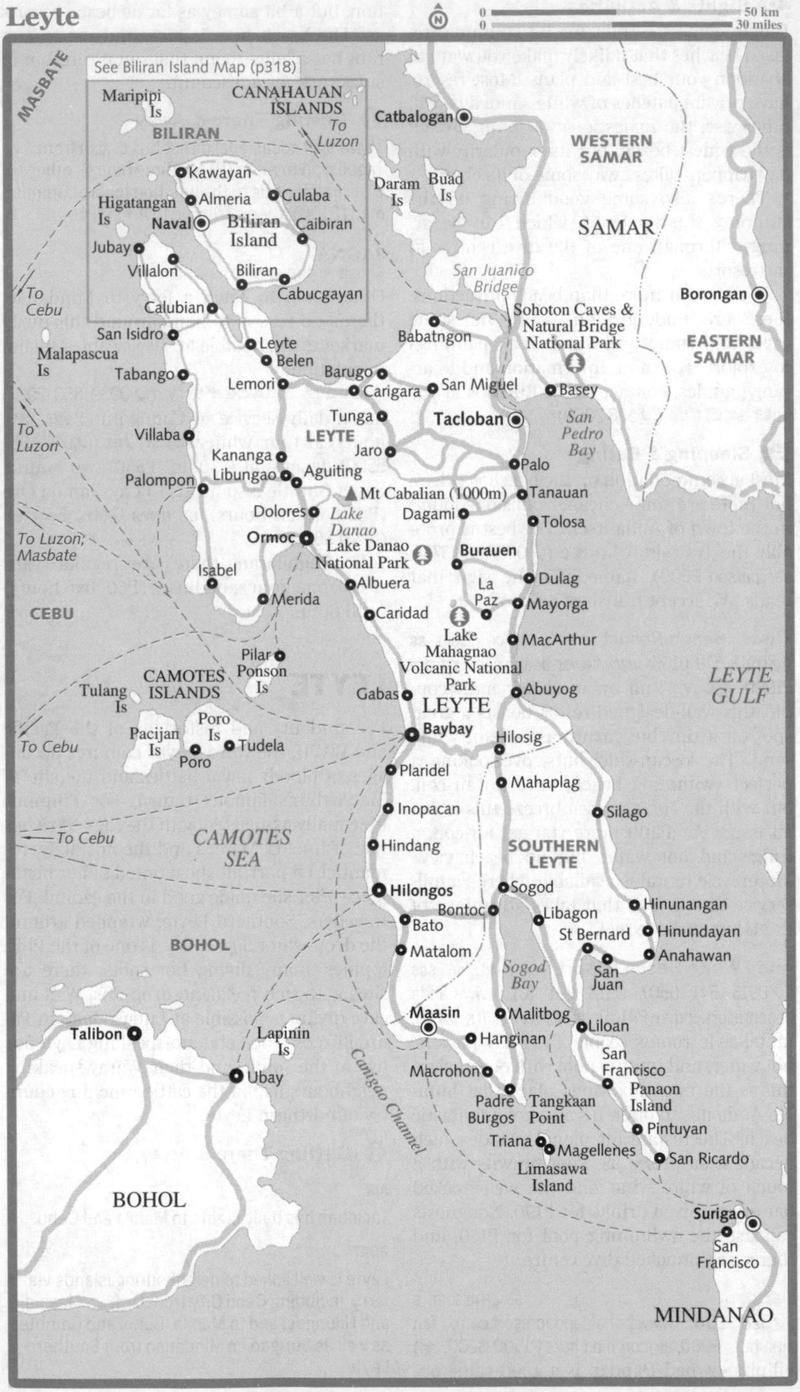

0 — 50 km
0 — 30 miles

See Biliran Island Map (p318)

MASBATE
Maripipi Is
CANAHAUAN ISLANDS
To Luzon
BILIRAN
Kawayan
Higatangan Is
Almeria
Culaba
Naval
Biliran Island
Caibiran
Jubay
Villalon
Biliran
Cabucgayan
To Cebu
Calubian
San Isidro
Malapascua Is
Leyte
Belen
Tabango
Lemori
Barugo
Carigara
San Miguel
To Luzon
Villaba
Tunga
LEYTE
Jaro
Kananga
Libungao
Aguiting
Palompon
Mt Cabalian (1000m)
Dolores
Lake Danao
To Luzon, Masbate
Ormoc
Lake Danao National Park
Isabel
Albuera
Merida
CEBU
Caridad
Pilar
Ponson Is
CAMOTES ISLANDS
Tulang Is
Poro Is
To Cebu
Pacijan Is
Poro
Tudela
To Cebu
CAMOTES SEA
BOHOL
Talibon
Lapinin Is
Ubay
BOHOL
Catbalogan
WESTERN SAMAR
Daram Is
Buad Is
SAMAR
San Juanico Bridge
Borongan
Sohoton Caves & Natural Bridge National Park
Babatngon
EASTERN SAMAR
Basey
Tacloban
San Pedro Bay
Palo
Tanauan
Dagami
Tolosa
Burauen
Dulag
La Paz
Mayorga
Lake Mahagnao Volcanic National Park
MacArthur
LEYTE GULF
Gabas
Abuyog
LEYTE
Baybay
Hilosig
Plaridel
Mahaplag
Inopacan
Silago
Hindang
SOUTHERN LEYTE
Hilongos
Sogod
Hinunangan
Bontoc
Libagon
Bato
St Bernard
Hinundayan
Matalom
San Juan
Anahawan
Sogod Bay
Maasin
Malitbog
Liloan
Hanginan
San Francisco
Canigao Channel
Macrohon
Panaon Island
Padre Burgos
Tangkaan Point
Pintuyan
Triana
Magellenes
San Ricardo
Limasawa Island
Surigao
San Francisco
MINDANAO

BUS

There are frequent bus services between Leyte, Biliran and Samar, and daily connections with Luzon and Mindanao. Regular buses leave from Tacloban and Ormoc for Manila via Samar. **Philtranco** (www.philtranco.com.ph) runs from Tacloban and Ormoc to Davao on Mindanao, via Surigao, in the afternoon – departure times fluctuate.

There are air-con van services between several of the larger towns on Leyte, Biliran and Samar.

Northern Leyte

It may not have diving to offer but the northern province has plenty of other natural sights, WWII history and modern towns that link it to Manila.

TACLOBAN

053 / POP 217,200

While it's the political capital of Leyte, this bustling city – its streetscape knitted together with the grey spaghetti of electric cables – is also the geographic and commercial centre of both Leyte and Samar. Tacloban is a relatively cosmopolitan outpost with great food, good accommodation, a decent bookshop and efficient transport links. Activity centres on the busy wharf area and market in the middle of town, and the waterfront promenade.

Tacloban's most famous daughter is Imelda Romualdez Marcos, whose family home is at Tolosa, a little way south. The family's influence in the town is evident in street names and various public buildings.

Historically, Tacloban is better known as the place to which General MacArthur returned with US liberating forces on 20 October 1944 (actually, he landed at Palo, a few kilometres outside the city). This date is celebrated annually, and there are WWII memorials around the town, including moulded reliefs on outer walls of the Capitol Building that commemorate the landing.

Sights & Activities

Santo Niño Shrine & Heritage Center NOTABLE BUILDING

(admission for up to 6 people incl tour P180; 8am-5pm) Built to Imelda Marcos and her family's specifications, yet bizarrely never slept in, this palatial mansion is every bit as ostentatious as her legendary shoe collection. It houses a varied display of antiques and objets d'art, with each room dedicated to a Filipino province, as well as a diorama of Imelda in the midst of one beneficial act or another. Upstairs has rooms for each of the family members, while on the ground floor is a gaudy church dedicated to Santo Niño. To get here take a jeepney from Rizal Ave.

FREE **MacArthur Memorabilia Rooms** HISTORIC SITE

(cnr Justice Romualdez & Santo Niño Sts; 8.30am-noon & 1-5pm Mon-Fri) WWII buffs will want to visit the MacArthur memorabilia rooms on the 2nd floor of the College Assurance Plan (CAP) building. Housed in rooms that MacArthur used in the (now decaying) grandeur of the 1910 Price Mansion, this is a charming mini museum featuring photographs and other titbits. Outside is a statue of MacArthur and Filipino president Sergio Osmeña, which captures the moment when power was handed back to the Filipino government. On weekends, you can ask the watchman downstairs to let you in.

Bukid Outdoor Shop ADVENTURE SPORTS

(0918 905 0079; 206 Burgos St; 9am-7.30pm, climbing wall 1-7pm Mon-Sat) You'll find a group of outdoor enthusiasts with information and local contacts for activities, including kayaking, mountain biking, hiking and climbing at Bukid Outdoor Shop. It's also got an indoor rock-climbing centre on-site (P50), and is a good source of information on skimboarding in Tanauan, the skimboarding capital of the Philippines, just south of Palo.

Festivals & Events

Late June is all about festivals in Tacloban, and makes for a great time to visit with various fiestas during the week; you'll need to book accommodation well ahead.

Pintados-Kasadyaan CULTURAL

The 'painted' festival, held on 27 June, celebrates the traditional tattooing practised here before the Spanish arrived; nowadays water-based paints are used for the festival's body decoration.

Sangyaw CULTURAL

Mardi gras Leyte-style, with colourful floats and dancing troupes through the streets of Tacloban on 29 June.

Sleeping

It's highly advisable to book well ahead in late June, as people descend on Tacloban for the festive season.

Hotel Alejandro HOTEL $$

(321 7033; http://alejandro.tacloban.biz; Patermo St; d from P1100;) This three-storey

hotel built around the classic 1930s home of Alejandro Montejo looks like a regal colonial villa. The rooms are nothing special but the common areas of the old building – especially the verandah on the 2nd floor – make up for this. A newer annexe houses a small rooftop pool and terrace, and the permanent photo exhibition along the walls traces Tacloban's domestic and war history.

Welcome House Pension PENSION HOUSE **$**
(☎321 2739; 161 Santo Niño St; r with fan & shared bathroom P350, with air-con & bathroom P600; ❄📶) Set around a quiet garden courtyard, these budget rooms are simple and clean as a whistle. Out of the chaos of the town centre, it's close to the restaurant and internet strips of Burgos St and Ave Veteranos.

Rosvenil Pensione PENSION HOUSE **$**
(☎321 2676; 302 Burgos St; r with shared/private bathroom from P600/650; ❄📶) A good budget choice, built around a rambling 1940s wooden house in which the original family still lives. In the old building are clean basic rooms; the newer, more sizeable and comfortable rooms are in a beautiful three-storey building with wrought-iron railings and a balcony. There's even a garden to sit in.

Hotel La Rica HOTEL **$**
(☎325 3337; Zamora St; r from P750; ❄📶) Decent rooms to suit a range of requirements. Light high-ceilinged rooms above the street are comfortable but noisy during the day; towards the back it's quieter and darker. When choosing a room, beware of the karaoke bar on the top floor.

Manhattan Inn HOTEL **$**
(☎321 4170; Zamora St; s/d from P710/1060; ❄📶) Good-value downtown hotel with fairly run-of-the-mill rooms, but they're quiet and some look down upon the market and water.

Leyte Park Hotel HOTEL **$$**
(☎325 6000; www.leyteparkhotel.com.ph; r P1400-15,000; ❄📶🏊) This crumbling behemoth,

Tacloban

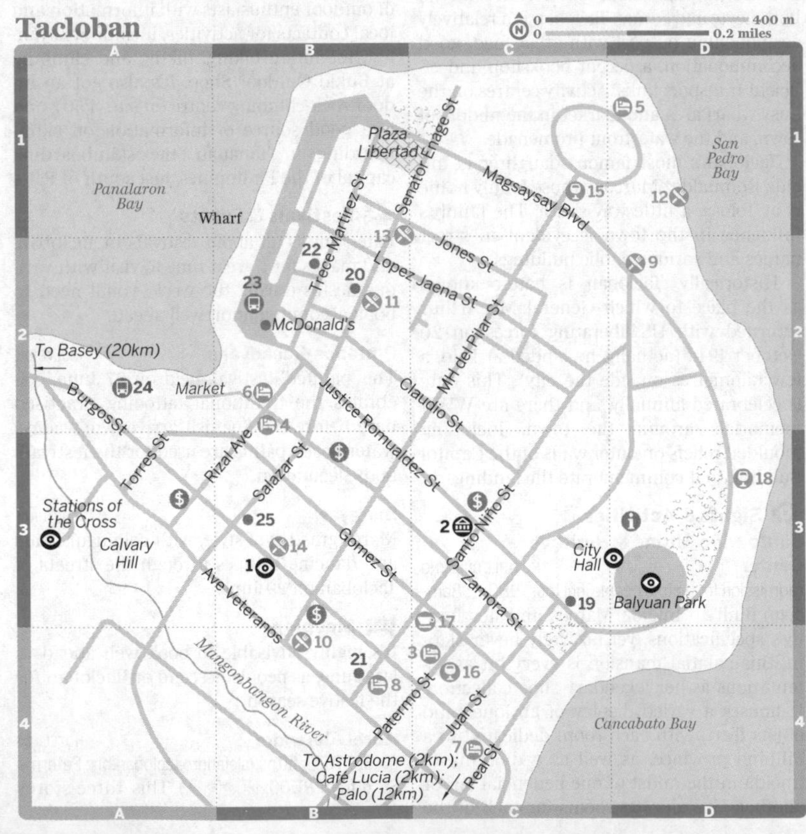

once the premier resort in Tacloban, was still undergoing much-needed renovation when we visited; the unrenovated rooms are very tired, in extreme contrast to the elegant new villas with individual infinity pools. Nothing can detract from the fabulous waterfront location though, with a good-sized pool (nonguests P100) and views across the ocean from the coffee shop.

Eating & Drinking

A boom in the restaurant scene in Tacloban over the last few years is continuing, giving it the greatest variety of eating options in Leyte or Samar. Some stylish restaurants are around the Astrodome and Leyte Park, while **barbecue stands** can be found along Magsaysay Blvd.

Those wanting to get out of town for some fresh country air can venture to **Rafael Farms** (☎325 0729; Babatngon), with a lovely garden setting in the mountains and good-value four-course banquets (P250). It's located in Babatngon, a 30-minute drive from Tacloban.

Ochó Seafood & Grill SEAFOOD $$
(Senator Enage St; dishes from P100; ⏰10am-11pm; ❄📶) A unanimous favourite with locals, Ochó is a rowdy affair with a glimpse of suave. Select your fish, squid or shellfish from the display and get them to cook it however you like it. Or try one of the enormous soups, thick enough for a meal for two. Vegos are also catered for, and can choose the cooking style for tofu and green vegies.

Socsargen Grill GRILL $
(dishes from P100; ⏰6am-11.30pm) Part of the Rosvenil Pensione, this casual and popular open-air restaurant does fish raw (sashimi) or barbecued (*lapu-lapu* – grouper) and sizzling *gambas*.

Giuseppe's ITALIAN $$
(173 Ave Veteranos, dishes P100-475; ⏰10.30am-10.30pm; ❄) A long-standing Tacloban eatery, brick-walled Giuseppe's is decorated like an Italian bistro and serves pastas and pizzas.

Stereo Sushi JAPANESE $$
(Senator Enage St; mains P150-450; ⏰4-11pm; ❄) Stylish Japanese joint run by hip young owners, offering a good sushi selection, and live music on Saturday nights.

Café Lucia CAFE $$
(Real St; dishes from P120; ⏰2pm-midnight; 📶) Just past the Astrodome, Lucia is popular with a younger crowd plugged into their laptops, here for the free wi-fi. They're also here to enjoy its lovely, grassy spot on the water and good coffee. It also does decent pastas.

San Pedro Bay Seafood Restaurant RESTOBAR $
(mains P100-200; ⏰10am-11pm) The breezy, waterfront San Pedro Bay Seafood Restaurant, on the grounds of the Leyte Park Hotel, is justifiably popular among expats.

Sunzibar MEXICAN $$
(Burgos St; dishes from P100; ⏰10.30am-10pm Mon-Sat) Stylish, minimalist hole-in-the-wall eatery popular for decent Mexican, with good chicken fajitas.

Tacloban

Sights
1 Bukid Outdoor Shop B3
2 MacArthur Memorabilia Rooms C3

Sleeping
3 Hotel Alejandro C4
4 Hotel La Rica B2
5 Leyte Park Hotel D1
6 Manhattan Inn B2
7 Rosvenil Pensione C4
8 Welcome House Pension B4

Eating
9 Barbecue Stands D2
10 Giuseppe's B4
11 Ochó Seafood & Grill B2
12 San Pedro Bay Seafood Restaurant D1
Socsargen Grill .... (see 7)
13 Stereo Sushi B1
14 Sunzibar B3

Drinking
15 Club 65 Hundred C1
Elements .... (see 15)
16 Julio's Buffet & Jazz Joint C4
17 Libro C3
18 Lion's Den D3
Na ning .... (see 15)

Information
19 Bureau of Immigration Office C3

Transport
20 Cebu Pacific B2
21 Duptours B4
22 Grand Tours B2
23 Jeepneys to Palo B2
24 Old Bus & Jeepney Terminal A2
25 Van Vans B3

Julio's Buffet & Jazz Joint BAR

(Patermo St; ❄) This little place near Hotel Alejandro is a drinks-with-live-jazz venue. It just falls short of its potential, though some nights are livelier than others. It's worth popping your head in Thursday to Sunday, with music starting around 9pm.

Libro CAFE

(cnr Santo Niño & Gomez Sts; ⏲noon-8pm Mon-Thu, to 10pm Fri & Sat) A fantastic secondhand bookstore that serves real coffee (P38), sandwiches on ciabatta bread (from P50) and a great selection of cakes.

Club 65Hundred DRINKING PRECINCT

(Magsaysay Blvd) A precinct of upmarket restaurants, bars and discos, where Tacloban's beautiful people come out to play. **Na ning** is the pick of the bars, with its ice-blasted beers, while **Elements** (⏲10pm-late Thu-Sat) is one of the leading clubs in town.

Lion's Den RESTOBAR

On the waterfront, a good local place for an evening beer as the sun goes down.

ℹ Information

Pick up a copy of **8 Magazine** (P88), a quarterly glossy magazine with latest happenings, available from various bars and bookstores.

Internet cafes abound, while Metrobank and BDO have ATMs.

BOI (Justice Romualdez St; ⏲8am-noon & 1-5pm) Handles same-day visa extensions if you arrive in the morning. It's in an unlikely-looking wooden shack at the back of a government compound.

Regional Tourist Office (☎321 2048; www.visitmyphilippines.com; dotreg8@yahoo.com; Kanhurao Hill) Exceptionally helpful, it can provide you with an abundance of information for both Leyte and Samar.

ℹ Getting There & Away

AIR

Tacloban is well connected to Manila, with no fewer than 12 flights per day; Cebu Pacific, PAL, Airphil Express and Zest Air all fly to Manila daily.

There are also daily flights to Cebu City, serviced by Cebu Pacific, Airphil Express and PAL.

The airport is about 10km south of the centre of town. A jeepney will cost P30, or P200 for a taxi. Tricycles are theoretically not permitted to head to the airport.

BUS, VAN & JEEPNEY

Regular daily buses, vans and jeepneys from other parts of Leyte and Samar use the New Bus Terminal at Abucay, about 2km west of the city. Frequent multicabs run between there and downtown.

To get to Padre Burgos you can take a bus or van to Sogod (P100, four hours), from where there's regular onward transport to Padre Burgos until around 4pm.

Long-distance buses also leave from here to Manila (from P900, 22 hours), with several departures daily.

Some local jeepneys and buses, such as the service to Basey (for Sohoton Caves & Natural Bridge National Park), still use the old terminal by the market in town – this may change.

Almost all destinations are also serviced by much more comfortable and quicker air-con vans for only slightly more pesos. **Duptours** (☎523 8107; cnr Ave Veteranos & Santo Niño St), **Van Vans** (☎325 8293; Salazar St) and **Grand Tours** (☎325 4640; cnr Trece Martirez & A Mabini Sts) all have vans servicing most parts of Leyte, including Ormoc (P120, two hours) and Maasin (P220, 3½ hours), as well as Naval (P130, 2½ hours) on Biliran and a few Samar destinations, including Catbalogan (P120, 2½ hours) and Guiuan (P130, three hours).

SOHOTON CAVES & NATURAL BRIDGE NATIONAL PARK

Although this national park is on Samar, it is easiest to access it from Tacloban, which is why it's included here. The journey upriver to the park from **Basey**, the access town, is half its charm, with the wide swath of water flanked by palms and higgledy-piggledy villages of bamboo houses on stilts. Upstream the river narrows and limestone outcrops appear and extend upwards until the boat is travelling through a small gorge. The park itself contains a series of **caves** under limestone outcrops, with enormous, sparkling stalactites and stalagmites. Ten minutes further upstream and a 300m walk through the forest, there's a wide **swimming hole** under the arch of the limestone natural bridge that gives the park its name. Surrounded by forest, it's a quiet, steamy green outpost where local villagers are actively engaged in managing the park and guiding visitors. Kayaking trips are available.

Heavy rain can cause flash floods and the park is often closed during the wettest months of December to February.

It's easy enough to arrange trips and guides in Basey at the **Municipal Tourism Information Office** (☎055-276 1471; Basey pier; ⏲8am-5pm Mon-Fri, to 1pm Sat & Sun), where staff will organise the round trip, which takes between four and five hours – an hour each way by boat, and then a couple of hours in the park. Boats do not leave Basey after 1pm.

Costs are complicated but go something like this: a trip for between one and six people costs around P2000 and includes the pumpboat (P1500) and a guide (P350), who joins at Sohoton and supplies a couple of hurricane lamps (P300). There's also an individual entry fee of P200 and the mayor's permit fee of P50. Trips can also be arranged at the tourist office in Tacloban.

If you miss the last transport, you can stay at **Distrajo's Lodge** (☎055-276 1191; per person from P250), a friendly, family-run rabbit-warren of a guesthouse opposite the pier. You'll see fine mats around town – Basey is justly famous for the quality of its weavings.

To get to Basey, take a bus or jeepney (P50, 1½ hours) from the market in Tacloban, which will take you across the steep San Juanico Bridge into Samar. To allow for the unexpected, you're probably wise to leave Tacloban by 8am if you're day tripping. Take a packed lunch – there's no food or water available beyond Basey. Minivans (P30) run regularly back to Tacloban from Basey pier until 4pm.

ORMOC

☎053 / POP 177,520

The hillsides surrounding Ormoc Bay make a scenic backdrop for those arriving by boat, but otherwise it's a typical busy port town. Its saving grace is its breezy waterfront promenade with some great restaurants and bars. Ormoc's size makes it an eminently walkable city and it's easy to find your way around.

Ormoc was a centre of WWII activity, with some of the bloodiest battles on Philippine soil taking place over several days in 1944 between the allied US and Filipino forces and the retreating Japanese. The bay is literally littered with American and Japanese shipwrecks, and while there are no commercial dive operators here, serious divers with deep and/or technical diving experience can contact long-term resident diver **Rob Lalumiere** (☎0918 907 2265; rob.lalumiere@yahoo.com) for information on diving the wrecks.

Sleeping

Ormoc Villa Hotel HOTEL $$
(☎255 5006; www.ormocvillahotel.com; Obrero St; r from P1830; ❄📶🏊) A prettily landscaped garden and pool (nonguests P100) make this an oasis in the city. Rooms are large and comfortable, and the restaurant serves a good selection of food (sandwiches from P110).

Hotel Don Felipe HOTEL $
(☎255 2460; hdfelipe@yahoo.com; I Larrazabal St; s/d with fan P400/480, with air-con P650/850, new Bldg P1100/1400; ❄@📶) A massive edifice on the waterfront, with rooms in the main building – some featuring balconies over the water – that are well kept. Annexe rooms are small, dark and a bit grungy.

Sabin Resort Hotel HOTEL $$
(☎561 4499; Bantigue; r from P1850; ❄📶🏊) This green and lush place on the sea is a few minutes out of town. Rooms are big and bright with balconies; some front the bay. There are pretty gardens and an enormous pool (nonguests P100).

IALodge HOTEL $
(☎561 0088; ialodgereservations@gmail.com; cnr Bonifacio & Burgos Sts; r from P700; ❄📶) The sister hotel to Ormoc Villa, it's a big step down

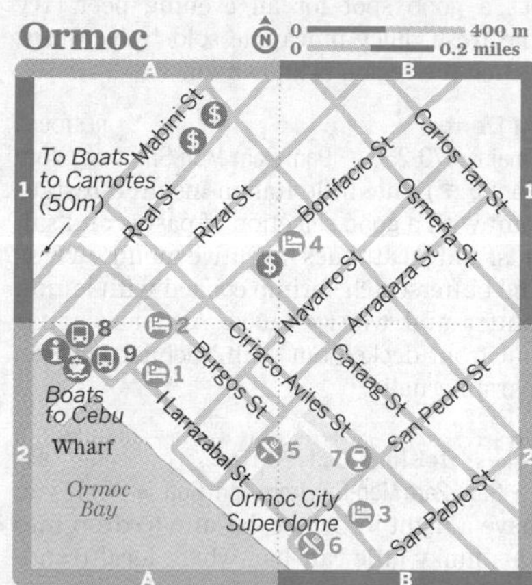

Ormoc

Sleeping
1 Hotel Don Felipe A2
2 IALodge A2
3 Ormoc Villa Hotel B2
4 Pongos Hotel B1

Eating
5 Al Dentre A2
6 Barbecue Stalls B2

Drinking
7 Bebidas Coffee Bar B2

Transport
8 Jeepney Station A2
9 Public Transport Station A2

in quality but is much cheaper and has a handy central location. Rooms are comfortable and staff are friendly.

Pongos Hotel HOTEL $
(☎255 2540; pongoshotel@yahoo.com; Bonifacio St; r with fan P350, with air-con from P600; ❄📶) A hotel with a split personality. Very ordinary rooms in the old part are fading, while the rooms in the newer buildings are big with cool, tiled floors and are worth paying a bit extra for.

Eating & Drinking

Ormoc has a buzzing eating precinct ranging from street food to plush restaurants and bars. Head for the waterfront and enjoy the views and occasional breeze. A cluster of eating places fills the promenade beyond the Superdome. Opposite is a host of barbecue stalls that come to life from sunset onwards; it's a good spot for an evening beer. Try the fresh, juicy pineapple sold by vendors, which the region is known for.

Al Dentre RESTOBAR
(mains P70-250; ⌚9am-2am Mon-Sat, from 4pm Sun; ❄📶) Cute little Italian-inspired restaurant with a good selection of pastas and salads, and an at times inventive menu such as the butterscotch shrimp cooked with lemon butter and whisky sauce. Also has a bar out front decked out with Michael Jackson paraphernalia.

TOP CHOICE **Bebidas Coffee Bar** BAR
(⌚9am-2am Mon-Sat, from 4pm Sun; ❄📶) If you have a night in Ormoc, be sure to drop into this funky little cafe-bar, where local trendies drop in for a good coffee or dangerously cheap cocktails – mixed by experts behind the bar.

Information

Ormoc bristles with internet cafes. **Metrobank** (Real St) and **BPI** (Lopez Jaena St) have ATMs and change US dollars.

The helpful tourism officer, Ira Bantasan, can be found in the **Ormoc City Tourism Office** (☎255 8356; www.ormoc.gov.ph/tourism; Ebony St; ⌚8am-noon & 1-5pm) in its new location outside the port.

Getting There & Away

BOAT

SuperCat (☎561 9818) and **Weesam Express** (☎561 0080) have daily fastcraft that ply the Ormoc–Cebu City route (from P675, 2½ hours). Slower boats to Cebu include Cebu Ferries at 1.30pm Monday to Thursday and Lite Shipping at 10pm daily except Friday (P400, four hours).

There are also morning and afternoon pumpboats to Camotes (from P140, four hours).

From Palompon, **Super Shuttle Ferry** (☎0915 513 1510) has a daily noon ferry to Bogo (P250, 2½ hours) on Cebu, which is convenient for those heading to Malapascua.

BUS & JEEPNEY

There are regular buses to and from Tacloban (P98, three hours), Maasin (P130, four hours) and Naval (P90, 2½ hours) on Biliran Island. You can also take regular transport northwest to Palompon (P80, 2½ hours) and San Isidro (P90, three hours).

At the main bus station you'll also find air-con vans that ply the same routes, offering a quicker service for slightly more.

AROUND ORMOC

A good day trip from Ormoc is to **Lake Danao Natural Park** (permit P45), a beautiful body of fresh water in the hills 18km from town. You can swim and picnic for the day, or overnight in a basic lodge (room P300) or campground. A jeepney or multicab (P35) usually makes the 45-minute trip up around 10am and returns late afternoon. A multicab for the day will cost about P1000.

The **Leyte Mountain Trail** is a ruggedly beautiful 45km trekking trail that takes in rainforest, lakes and waterfalls. But sadly it's rarely visited due to being unmaintained, with no infrastructure en route, and the occasional NPA skirmishes out bush make the tourism department wary of publicising it. Keen hikers can expect to take four to seven days to walk the trail. A guide is essential – contact **Aileen Suarez** (☎255 4369, 0918 925 5801) of the Ormoc Mountaineering Club for information and advice.

Southern Leyte

Offering some of the best diving in the country, the laid-back southern province is where the majority of visitors spend their time in Leyte.

MAASIN & AROUND

☎053 / POP 79,730

Maasin (mah-*ah*-sin), the bustling provincial capital of Southern Leyte, is sandwiched in picturesque fashion between the ocean and hills behind. It's a suitable base for hiking in the region and is also the most convenient place if you're staying in Padre Burgos. It has a beautiful old **church**, built in 1700.

DON'T MISS

I SHALL RETURN: THE LEYTE LANDING

When US forces were forced to make a hasty retreat from the Philippines in December 1941, relinquishing control to the invading Japanese, in his speech upon departing General MacArthur uttered the famous words of defiance, 'I shall return.' The Philippines endured three brutal years of occupation, but on 20 October 1944, MacArthur was true to his word and fulfilled his vow to return and liberate the Philippines. Famous footage shows MacArthur wading knee-deep ashore accompanied by a group of high-ranking soldiers, including the future Filipino president Sergio Osmeña. His return speech began with the stirring words, 'People of the Philippines, I have returned.'

The scene is immortalised at the landing site of Red Beach, 1km from Palo, at the **Leyte Landing Memorial**, with the inspiring larger-than-life-sized bronze-cast figures of MacArthur and his cohort walking in the water, complete with Ray-Bans.

There's also a **rock garden** where many international tributes were set in stone in 1994 to commemorate the 50th anniversary of the Leyte landing.

You can also visit **Guinhangdan Hill**, known in WWII as Hill 522, the scene of fierce fighting. The beautiful 16th-century church was turned into a hospital from October 1944 to March 1945.

The township of Palo is 12km from Tacloban. To get here, take a Palo-bound jeepney (P15) signed 'Via Government Centre' from near McDonald's on the waterfront in Tacloban. Ask the driver to drop you off at the Red Beach roundabout, about 1km before Palo township. Tricycles (P20) are available to travel the short distance between each site.

For those who want to stay here, at the time of research the plush-looking **LKY MacArthur Resort** was in the process of opening up, just beyond the Red Beach monument on a stunning part of the coast.

Activities

Few people explore the area around Maasin, even though there are several good hikes, and caves and waterfalls to explore. Some hikes can be done solo, others need a guide, and all require a degree of patience, stamina and travel discomfort. Solo options include hikes to **Guinsohoton Falls** and **Cagnituan Cave**. Guides are needed for hikes to **Lake Danao** – a crater lake at 1000m on lush Mt Cabalian – where you can thankfully collapse and camp after a three-hour bus ride and two-hour hike up. Another option is **Uwan-uwanan gorge and falls** – a flatter hike of an hour or so through the gorge, spray-cooled by waterfalls as you go. For further information and to arrange a guide, contact Nedgar at the Provincial Planning Development Office (PPDO).

Sleeping & Eating

Villa Romana Hotel HOTEL $$
(☎381 0639; villaromana_hotel@yahoo.com.ph; s/d incl breakfast from P950/1350; ❄@📶) Slap bang on the water and overlooking the pier, this smart hotel is the best sleeping and eating option in town. Rooms are elegant and well furnished, and the downstairs waterfront restaurant, Kinamot, is justly popular, with good seafood and other dishes – the simple grilled prawns and garlic rice (P135) is a winner.

Ampil Pensionne PENSION HOUSE $
(☎570 8084; T Oppus St; s/d without bathroom P200/300, r with bathroom P400-800; ❄📶) A great budget option in town, this place has rooms set off the street around a small courtyard, so it's relatively quiet.

Information

There is internet access aplenty in town. **Metrobank** (T Oppus St) has an ATM, while Candy's Supermarket or Southern Comfort up the road will change US dollars cash for good rates, but only when the owner is there.

Nedgar Garvez in the **PPDO** (☎570 8300; Provincial Capitol Bldg; 🕗8am-noon & 1-5pm Mon-Fri) is the local tourism officer, and can be contacted on ☎0915 879 4923 or nvg4663@gmail.com. There's also a smaller **City Tourism Office** (☎570 8097; maasin_cipto@yahoo.com) in town.

Getting There & Away

Regular buses run to Ormoc (P130, four hours), Padre Burgos (P30, one hour) and Tacloban (P180, five hours). There are also regular buses to Liloan (P100, four hours), the ferry port for

Mindanao. You can also get to Padre Burgos by jeepney (P30), finishing up at 6pm.

Air-con vans depart to Ormoc (P150, 3½ hours) and Tacloban (P220, four hours).

Cokaliong has three ferries a week to Cebu City (P320, six hours), leaving at midnight, and a twice-weekly service to Surigao (P300, four hours). Super Shuttle Ferry has a daily evening ferry to Ubay on Bohol (P250, three hours).

There are also several daily boats from Bato to Ubay (P245, three hours) on Bohol, and further north Roble Shipping has a daily service from Hilongos to Cebu City.

PADRE BURGOS & AROUND

☎053 / POP 10,200

Laid-back Padre Burgos straggles for about 3km in a lazy green line along the edge of the lovely **Sogod Bay**. It's considered to be one of the premier diving spots in the Philippines for its pristine hard and soft coral reefs, deep wall, cave and current dives, and the abundance and variety of its big fish, particularly for its population of whale sharks.

There's an internet cafe near the pier but no ATM – Maasin or Sogod are the closest places to get money.

Sights & Activities

Whale Sharks WILDLIFE

A floating population of whale sharks, known locally as *tiki-tiki,* sometimes move through Sogod Bay annually between about January and April, but are a bonus rather than a guaranteed wildlife experience.

Coral Cay Conservation CONSERVATION GROUP

(www.coralcay.org) Check out the website of this international organisation to see why a program of working with local communities in this area to preserve and conserve the reefs is so important. It accepts only volunteers arranged well in advance.

Limasawa Island ISLAND

If you have time to spare, head to sleepy Limasawa Island, a place of historical and religious significance in the Philippines. It's where the Spanish first celebrated mass on 31 March 1521, thereby starting the Christianisation of the country.

A five-minute walk to the left from the pier leads to the first **mass site**. Beside it, a hot and steamy walk up 450 steps takes you to the **commemorative cross** – where you can gaze at gorgeous views out across the ocean to Mindanao, Bohol and mainland Leyte. The island also has beautiful small coves that are ideal for swimming and snorkelling.

A pumpboat makes the journey to and from Padre Burgos (P50, one hour) daily at 1pm and lands at barangay Magellanes, though double check where the boat is heading. If you come by public boat (rather than as part of a dive-boat day trip), you'll likely need to stay overnight; there's no commercial accommodation but the mayor (ask around for him) will arrange for you to stay somewhere. Chartering a bangka will cost anywhere from P600 to P1000 return.

Dive Resorts DIVING

There are several dive resorts here to look after Padre Burgos' predominantly diving visitors, charging between P1500 and P2000 per dive, including gear. They can also organise dive trips to the islands of Limasawa and Panaon, with seats for snorkelling or beachcombing nondivers when there's space.

Tangkaan Point, to the south of town, offers good offshore snorkelling.

Sleeping & Eating

Peter's Dive Resort BEACH RESORT $

(☎573 0015; www.whaleofadive.com; r with fan/air-con from P400/1300; ❄📶🏊) Peter's is just off the road on a pebble beach with a variety of rooms catering to all budgets. Several inexpensive rooms with shared bathroom are in the main building, and larger, more comfortable cottages on the water have private bathrooms. Try to get a room with a balcony. There's a utilitarian restaurant with a good selection of Filipino and international dishes. Rooms are slightly more expensive for nondivers.

Southern Leyte Dive Resort BEACH RESORT $$

(☎572 4011; www.leyte-divers.com; San Roque; r P850-2650; ❄) The oldest and prettiest of the dive resorts, the nine cottages here – bamboo with fans, or comfortable modern air-con – are off the main road and front a sandy beach. It's a family-run place, with a sundowner platform, and hammocks and potted plants everywhere. Excellent food in the garden restaurant (dishes from P100) includes sashimi, pasta, salad and German sausages.

Sogod Bay Scuba Resort BEACH RESORT $$

(☎573 0131; www.sogodbayscubaresort.com; r/beachfront cottage P1100/1500; ❄@) Offers simple, clean and bright rooms overlooking the bay, or cheaper rooms in a concrete building 200m up the road, away from the water. The restaurant (dishes from P100) offers a good selection of food with a view.

Padre Burgos Castle BEACH RESORT **$$$**
(0927 548 8598; www.padreburgoscastle.com; Tangkaan; s/d P3600/4500;) A few kilometres out of Padre Burgos, this boutique hotel is built on a cliff face overlooking Tangkaan beach and makes for a wonderful option for nondivers. Its unique design features a weird sci-fi tower jutting out from the roof, and its rooms are lovely with comfy beds and stylish fittings. The restaurant opens up to an inviting pool, and there's a private coral-sand beach, a short climb down the stairs. It can also arrange diving with one of the Padre Burgos centres.

Getting There & Away

Regular jeepneys and buses travel to Padre Burgos from Maasin (P30, one hour), where you can get connecting buses for onward travel. There's also regular transport to Sogod, a good place to connect to other parts of Leyte.

SOGOD & AROUND

053

The busy little town of Sogod, at the mouth of Sogod Bay, has a picturesque forest backdrop and trekking opportunities at nearby caves and waterfalls; contact the tourist officer, **Robe Estillore** (0921 291 8027; carlstone75@yahoo.com) for more information. Metrobank has an ATM, and may be your last chance to get money for a while.

Regis Bed n' Breakfast (382 2776; Veloso St; d with fan/air-con P250/400;) offers clean, quiet and secure rooms in its very pink building.

Sogod is a major transport hub – you can connect here to buses west to Maasin (P70, two hours), north to Tacloban (P100, four hours) and south to Liloan (P60, one hour) for boats to Mindanao.

The nearby town of Agas-Agas has a **zipline** (P280) that rather terrifyingly passes over the tallest bridge in the Philippines, at 89m, before continuing through the valley.

LILOAN & AROUND

053

On the remote southern island of Panaon, Liloan is a tiny ramshackle port town clinging to the shores of Sogod Bay. The only reason to visit is to catch a ferry to Lipata, near Surigao on Mindanao (P300, 3½ hours), departing daily in the early and late afternoon. If you're unfortunate enough to need to stay here, **Ofelia's Lodge** (s/d P150/250) near the market is the only place to go.

Green and rustic Panaon Island is a patchwork of alternating small fishing villages, white bays and some great diving. **Napantao Reef** off San Francisco is highly regarded and a popular site with the Coral Cay Conservation group (see p326). While in **Pintuyan**, you can arrange snorkelling in nearby Son-ok, which can be a wonderful spot to see whale sharks. The local **tourist office** (587 2015) can arrange these whale-shark tours for P1400, which is inclusive for three people, boat rental, guide and conservation fee. For further information, get in touch with tourism officer **Moncher Bardos** (0916 952 3354; moncher64bardos@yahoo.com), and be sure to call ahead to check if the whale sharks are about.

Pintuyan Beach Resort (www.pintuyan.com; r incl full board €45) is the best place to stay and can arrange diving equipment. Otherwise there's the cheap **La Guerta Lodge** (0926 142 6986; r with fan/air-con P150/350). There are buses to Sogod (P90, 2½ hours) for onward transport.

Car ferries to Lipata depart from a new RORO ferry terminal in Benit, San Ricardo (P120, 1½ hours, four daily); this is a quicker and cheaper option than Liloan. From Benit, a *habal-habal* (P100) is the best way to get to Pintuyan.

HINUNAGAN & AROUND

053

To the northeast of Liloan, a scenic and relatively quiet coastal road winds through rice fields towards Tacloban. A good place to break the journey and ease bus-shaken limbs is Hinunagan. The town is nothing special but there are nearby caves and waterfalls to hike or horse ride to; to organise guides or further information, contact the helpful **municipal tourist office** (0999 442 1086; pedrofauste@yahoo.com) located near the church.

Pretty **Tahusan Beach**, 4km south of town, is one of the finest in Leyte, and while the beach isn't picture-perfect white, alternating from a honey-brown (April to October) to black (December to March), it's a great stretch of soft sand that's perfect for swimming.

Doña Marta Boutique Hotel (0920 981 6581; www.donamartahotel.com; r incl breakfast from P2000;) is the best place to stay at Tahusan, with a few individually styled (and rather dainty) rooms set in a pleasant garden on the beach. Free breakfasts are gourmet, comprising bacon, eggs and avocado on toast with brewed coffee and fresh fruit.

Otherwise there's the cheaper **Morgana Beach Resort** (☎0927 998 3846; malulanja cino@yahoo.com; r P800-1800; ❄), also on the beach, with good-value rooms arranged around a building designed like a ship. Come during the week to avoid the beachside karaoke.

TOP CHOICE **Rosita's Native Restaurant** (☎0917 501 0131; mains from P80; 📶) serves some of the best food we've eaten in Leyte, featuring an attractive and comfortable bamboo decor with a fantastic, massive menu centred on fresh seafood – the massive grilled prawns with butter and garlic are sensational, as is the crab in coconut milk. There are also lots of vegetable dishes (from P40) to gladden the heart and boost the vitamin intake. The cheap cocktails have a similar effect.

It's worth visiting the nearby offshore islands of **San Pedro** and **San Pablo**, both with white coral sand, snorkelling and swimming. San Pedro has simple accommodation at **Vista Resort** (☎0919 379 0333; r P250), and the scrap-metal remains of a Japanese WWII fighter, visible at low tide. Both islands are best accessed from Canipaan barangay with public bangkas (P20) departing when full. Otherwise you can charter a boat for P1000 return.

From Hinunagan there are hourly buses to Tacloban (P140, three hours) till 2pm and Sogod (P80, three hours) until 4pm.

BILIRAN ISLAND

☎053 / POP 150,000

Tourism is slowly, slowly taking off on this quiet island province, with plenty to keep you busy for a few days while enjoying being away from the crowds. It has waterfalls, rice terraces and several sandy white beaches on

Biliran Island

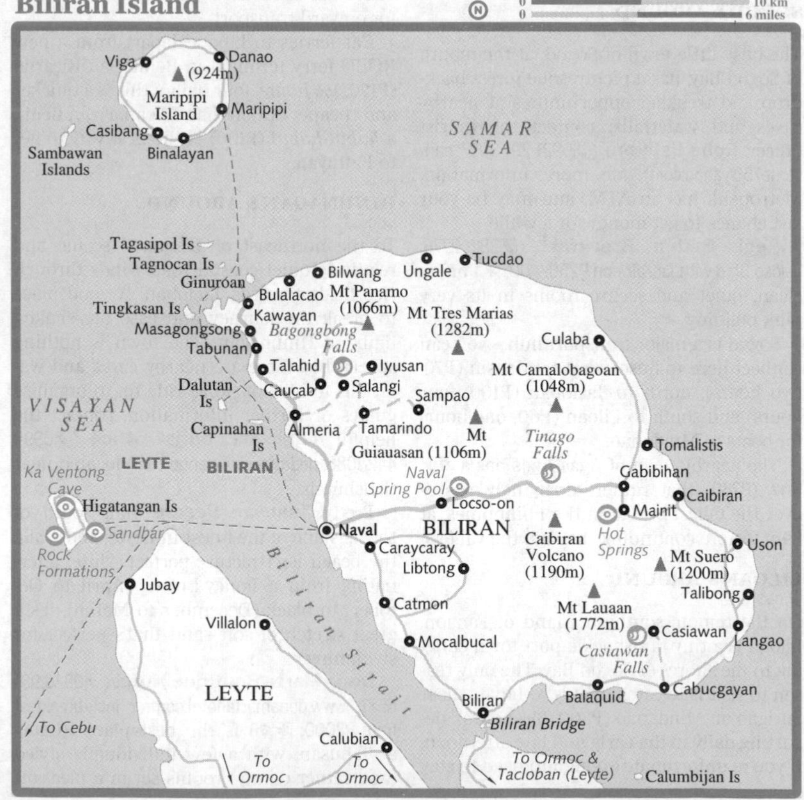

offshore islands, as well as trekking to an active volcano.

Biliran, about 32km long and 8km wide, became a province separate from Leyte in 1992; a short bridge connects the two. The island is lush and it can rain any time, with the most rainfall in December and the least in April. Most people are subsistence farmers or fishers who generally speak Cebuano on the west coast and Waray-Waray on the east.

Getting There & Away

You can get to Biliran from Cebu, Leyte, Luzon and Samar.

BOAT

Roble Shipping travels to and from Cebu and Naval (P450, 9½ hours) at 8.30pm Tuesdays and Sundays, while Super Shuttle Ferry departs at 8pm Thursday (P430). It can be faster to get the boat to Ormoc, and then a bus to Naval. Ticketing offices for both ferries are away from the pier in town.

BUS

There are regular bus services from Naval to Ormoc (P90, three hours) and to Tacloban (P120, three hours). Air-con minivans run between Naval and Tacloban (P130, 2½ hours) and Ormoc (P130, two hours) every 30 minutes till 5pm.

For those with stamina, buses leave Naval at 5.45pm for Manila (P1300, 24 hours).

All buses and jeepneys arrive and depart from a terminal near the *embarcadero* (waterway landing).

Getting Around

Buses and jeepneys make regular daily trips from Naval north to Kawayan (P25, 30 minutes) and southeast to Cabucgayan (P50, one hour) via Biliran town. Motorised and pedal tricycles operate in the towns. The flat fee for short local trips is P6.

Public transport does not run along the coast road between Kawayan and Caibiran, or along the cross-country road between Naval and Gabibihan. You can hire a motorcycle with driver to travel these stretches for around P1000 per day.

Naval

053 / POP 44,300

Naval (nah-*bahl*), the provincial capital, is stretched along a road from a handful of government buildings to the low-rise harbour area. There's little to do here but it makes a handy base for day trips around the island. Staff at the **Provincial Tourism Council** (500 9627, 0906 470 7040; http://tourism.biliranisland.com; 8am-noon & 1-5pm Mon-Fri) are housed in a building to the right of the main Capitol Building, where the 2nd floor is given over to a small selection of local artefacts and photos. Ask for Jun Dacillo. Naval has many internet cafes, and there's an ATM at Metrobank.

Sleeping & Eating

Most eateries in town are on P Inocentes St, the main street of Naval, which leads from the market, jetty and terminal area.

Marvin's James Seaside Inn HOTEL $
(500 9171; r P600-1500;) On the water, friendly Marvin's is a mustard-yellow, three-storey modern building 2km north of town (tricycle P10). Rooms are clean and comfortable, and have private bathrooms and cable TV – go for light and breezy rooms 12B or 17, with full sea views and almost-private balconies. There's a homey indoor lounge sitting and dining area (with good food), and the annexe across the street has a nice pool (nonguests P20).

Biliran Garden Resort HOTEL $$
(500 9233; r from P1500;) A prettily landscaped complex with a country-club feel to it, this 17-room resort is 3km inland from Naval (P15 by tricycle) on the banks of a small river in barangay Lomboy. Rooms are good value: big, clean and light with decent-sized bathrooms. There's also a swimming pool (nonguests P50) but it loses points for its dismal on-site mini zoo.

D'Jan Dell's Cabin PENSION HOUSE $
(500 9338; P Inocentes St; d with fan/air-con from P300/500;) Located in town, this place is basic and noisy, but clean and welcoming.

North of Naval

This pretty stretch of coast is the only part of the island that is easy to explore by public transport.

Located a few kilometres beyond Almeria is **Agta beach**, the best-known beach on the mainland, though it's fairly mediocre compared to most in the Visayas. The best place to stay is **VRC Resort** (0916 466 5809; www.agtabeach.com; s/d with fan P300/400, r with air-con from P600;), which has several swimming pools and a selection of decent-value rooms, all of which are busy with karaoke-loving locals on the weekend. Go for the bungalow on the hill with sea views.

It's a good base for visiting **Dalutan**, an island with white sand and good snorkelling just offshore. You can hire a bangka for around P700 return.

Bagongbong Falls are a two-hour hike from Caucab, where the barangay captain will help you find a guide (P150).

The **rice terraces** of Sampao, Iyusan and Salangi are each about 5km off the main road; you'll need to walk in unless you charter a motorbike. While they can't compare in scale to the Banaue terraces, they're pretty and worth seeing if you're not going up to northern Luzon.

A little further offshore is pretty, barely developed **Maripipi Island**, with its lovely Candol Beach. A motorcycle (P100) can take you around the 23km island in an hour or so, or walk the round-island road. You can stay at **Napo Beach Resort** (☎0921 347 6620; www.beachresortmaripipi.com; r with fan/aircon from P800/1800; ❄≋) or otherwise homestays with local residences can be arranged (ask for Judith Daviola's home).

To the west, the uninhabited **Sambawan Islands** have white sand and are good for snorkelling

A daily passenger boat leaves from Naval to Maripipi (P60, 1½ hours) midmorning, returning the following day; it's easier to hire a bangka (one way P1000, 30 minutes) in Kawayan.

East & South of Naval

Situated off the cross-country road, **Naval Spring Pool** at Locso-on and, a few kilometres further, **Tinago Falls** have some basic infrastructure for visitors, with relatively easy access. There's a short walk into Tinago, and, if the water's not flowing too fast, there are two big swimming holes at its base.

Located nearby is **Caibiran Volcano**, which last erupted in 1939; it can be climbed in a steady 1½ hours. Check with the Provincial Tourism Council in Naval for directions to these places as they are not signposted; you will need to hire a guide, which can be arranged in Caibiran at barangay Pulang Yuta.

The sulphuric **Mainit hot springs** are a series of small cascades with sitting pools, exposed on a riverbank beside rice fields. On the east coast, and reputed to have exceptionally sweet water, **Tomalistis Falls** pour from a cliff face and are accessible only at low tide (or otherwise by boat) – though the flow has lessened as villagers divert the water for domestic use. **Casiawan Falls** (cah-shaw-won) can put on a good show depending on the amount of recent rainfall, and remains appealingly undeveloped. They're a 20-minute drive on a track off the south coast road at Cabucgayan, and then another 10 minutes by foot.

West of Naval

Due west of Naval is **Higatangan Island**, where a shifting white sandbar is good for swimming and snorkelling, and you can walk to the **Ka Ventong Cave**, renowned for the snakes that call it home. On the western side of the island, accessible by boat only, is a series of interesting rock formations with small sandy bays between them. Former President Marcos, along with fellow resistance members, reportedly took refuge on the island in WWII, and Marcos Hill is named in his memory.

A couple of small and simple resorts provide accommodation, including **Higatangan Island Beach Resort** (☎0999 512 8006; www.higatanganislandresort.com; r from P800; ❄). There's an 11am bangka from Naval (P50, 45 minutes) daily, and the boats leave in the other direction at 7am, so overnighting is a must if you're using public transport. A one-way charter costs around P1500.

SAMAR

Samar is a ruggedly beautiful island. Its wild coastline and wide views stretch almost all the way to the tip of southern Luzon in the north and to within shouting distance of northern Mindanao in the south. The heavily forested interior, full of cave systems and waterfalls, is beginning to be explored by local adventure entrepreneurs, and experienced surfers can head to the little-visited east coast. It's possible to fly into Catarman in the north, where there is a mass of little-explored offshore islands, or to Calbayog on the more developed west coast.

History

Magellan first set foot in the Philippines here in 1521, on the island of Homonhon in the south. During the Philippine-American war, Samar was the scene of some of the bloodiest battles. Tales of brutal combat wove their way into US Marine Corps folklore, and for years after the war American

Samar

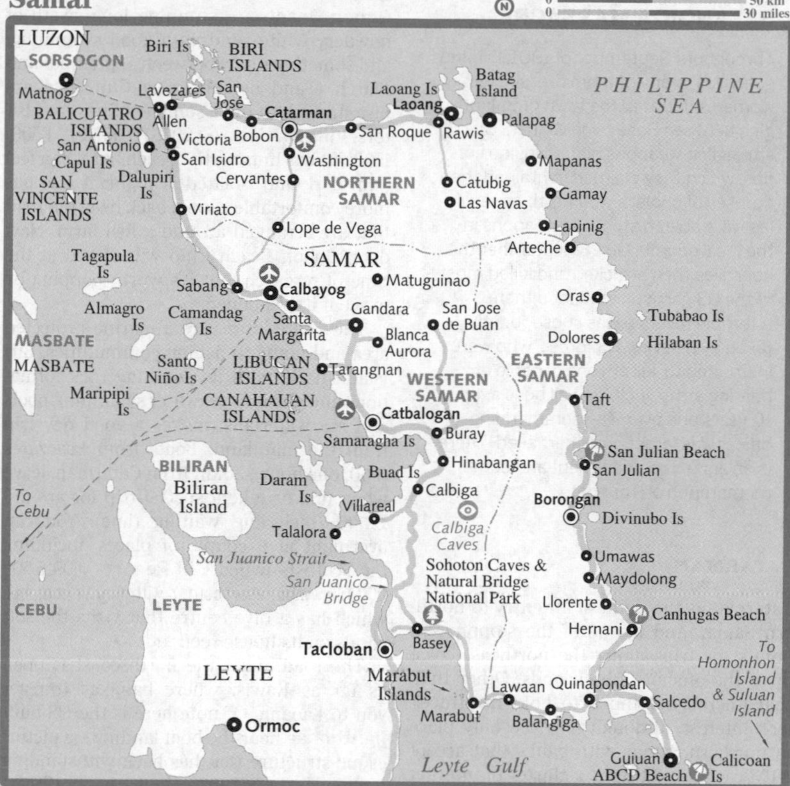

veterans of the campaign were toasted in mess halls by their fellow marines with, 'Stand, gentlemen, he served on Samar.'

Getting There & Away

AIR

Samar is well connected to Manila with daily flights from Calbayog (one hour, 20 minutes) and Catarman (one hour).

BOAT

Boats from Calbayog and Catbalogan head to Cebu City. There are regular boats from Allen to Matnog on Luzon.

BUS & VAN

There are many buses and vans to Tacloban, Leyte, from Catarman, Guiuan, Calbayog, Borongan and Catbalogan. An efficient fleet of vans also link these towns to one another.

Philtranco (☎02-851 8078) and **Eagle Star** (☎02-913 1510) have daily services to Manila from most major towns in Samar.

Northern Samar

The beautiful and little-visited north coast of Samar seems to be on a slow-but-sure track to becoming a low-key tourism destination. An enthusiastic band of entrepreneurial expats, supported by locals, is creating small (and some not-so-small) resorts and opportunities for tours of the north's myriad islands. The attractions here include fabulous rock formations and swimming holes, snorkelling, diving and surfing sites, picture-perfect white-sand beaches, and seafood from some of the cleanest parts of the ocean you'll find.

Parts of the northeast of Samar are a refuge for small groups of the New People's Army (NPA), who continue to skirmish with government forces. Foreigners have not been targeted and any action tends to occur in the remote hinterlands.

BALANGIGA MASSACRE

Throughout September of 1901, Filipino guerrillas, many of them dressed as women, infiltrated the town of Balangiga between Basey and Guiuan. By smuggling weapons hidden inside coffins, which they claimed contained the corpses of cholera victims, the guerrillas were able to stockpile weapons in the local church. On 28 September the guerrillas then attacked and killed most of the US garrison stationed there.

A terrible revenge was subsequently taken by relieving US forces, who were instructed to 'kill anyone capable of bearing arms', including all boys aged 10 years and over. The commanding officer was later court-martialled. There is an annual re-enactment and commemoration on that date.

CATARMAN

☎055 / POP 81,000

Catarman is the point of air entry to northern Samar, and is one of the stopping-off points for trips along the northeast coast or to the offshore Biri Islands. Other than that, there's not much to hold the traveller's interest, although it is the only place in northern Samar with banks that accept ATM cards, and there's a cluster of internet cafes around the corner of Magsaysay and Annunciacion Sts. The handful of pensions in town includes the clean and cheerful **SaSa Pension** (☎251 8515; www.sasapensionhouse.multiply.com; Jacinto St; r with fan & shared bathroom P375, with air-con from P775; ❄📶), with rooms that cover most budgets. Eat at **Michz** – the restaurant, not the fast-food outlet – which, surprisingly, has good pesto pasta (P85), or the **Nest**. Located 6km east of town is the **UEP White Beach Resort** (☎0912 651 1134; www.uepwhitebeach.webs.com; r from P800; ❄🍴), with standard rooms along a lovely stretch of beach. It's owned by the local university and gets occasional surf from October to December.

ℹ Getting There & Away

Airphil Express and PAL have daily flights between Catarman and Manila, while Cebu Pacific and Zest Air have four weekly flights. The airport is 2km from town (P20 by tricycle). There are jeepneys to Allen (P60, one hour), while Grand Tours vans head to Calbayog (P100, 1½ hours) via the cross-country road.

AROUND CATARMAN

Bobon Beach – a stunning long swath of powdery white sand with good swimming, and sometimes surf between September and March – and neighbouring **San José** are just starting to offer some facilities for visitors. **Villa Alabado** (☎0926 717 9630; r P500-1200; ❄) has huts on the beach but it can feel a bit dark and isolated at night; it also has more comfortable rooms back near the road that are arranged around a fish farm. Next door, Bobon Beach Club was closed at the time of research, but it's worth popping by to see if it's reopened.

The **Biri Islands** are a marine protected area and home to fishing communities. Biri Island itself, with its stunning rock formations and glorious seawater swimming pools and sea waterfalls, makes a good day trip from the mainland. Boats from Lavezares (P50, one hour), 30km from Catarman, leave when full, or take a special trip for around P1500 (including waiting time). You can overnight at a couple of places, including the Scottish-owned **Biri Resort** (☎0915 509 0604; www.biriresort.com; r with fan/air-con; ❄), which has a dive centre that visits the soft corals on its house reef.

The road along the north coast is open as far as Rawis, where bangkas transfer you to Laoang. Of note here is the US-built **lighthouse** near the boat landing – a picturesque structure that has been withstanding typhoons since 1907. Along the northeast coast is an undeveloped area of surf beaches and rock formations; the rough coastal track makes for good mountain biking.

ALLEN

☎055POP 22,330

This small port town services the ferry route between northern Samar and southern Luzon. If you can't make the boat connections and need to stay overnight here, by far the best option is **Wayang Wayang Resort** (☎0917 804 7585; barangay Jubasan; r P750-1950; ❄), 4km south of town with a surprisingly comfortable complex of large nipa huts on the water. Staff are friendly, and there's a restaurant and individual bamboo huts, good for eating or watching the sunset. Splash out for the nicer rooms with splendid sea views, balconies and bathtubs.

Many el cheapo lodges line the road near the old Dup Dup pier, with **Christ Ians Lodge** (☎0949 479 9779; r from P250; 🍴) being the best of the bunch along Buenos Aires beach.

A word of advice: if it's getting late, stay the night in Allen and catch a morning boat. You do not want to be benighted in Matnog where the ferries arrive – trust us on this one.

RORO ferries from Allen to Matnog (P120, one hour 15 minutes) are serviced by **168 Shipping** (☎0918 619 1446) and Santa Clara, departing every few hours.

There's a bus to Tacloban (P350, seven hours) at 9am. Otherwise, your best bet is to get a van to Calbayog (P100, 1½ hours) through **Grand Tours** (☎9209 694 485), from where you can arrange onward transport to Tacloban; buses in Calbayog usually finish around 4pm.

Jeepneys run to Catarman (P60, one hour) up until 5pm.

BALICUATRO ISLANDS

This group of islands is just below the northwestern point of Samar. The largest island, **Dalupiri** (more commonly known as San Antonio), has good beaches and clear water, and is close to the mainland. Such is its appeal, it's the kind of place where it's easy to get stranded longer than you planned.

There are several chilled-out accommodation options on the beachfront. Electricity is off from 6am to midday each day, so rooms can be hot if there is no breeze.

The Swedish-owned **Crystal Sand Beach Resort** (☎0929 197 1843; www.crystalsandbeachresort.weebly.com; bungalows with fan P500, r with air-con P750; ❄📶) is up from the village centre with a great location 500m off a marine sanctuary. There's no diving here but it can arrange snorkelling equipment. The main rooms are ugly pink concrete, but simple bungalows are better suited to its beach location. It can arrange trips to Seven Islands, where it's building some huts.

Other options include the prettily landscaped and well-established **Haven of Fun** (☎0917 327 6594; www.havenoffunbeachresort.com; r with fan/air-con P600/1200; ❄), just a walk from the pier, or the laid-back **Puro Beach Resort** (☎0916 545 0468; r with fan/air-con P500/800; ❄).

Public boats leave for San Antonio (P30, 30 minutes) several times daily from Victoria (P15 tricycle trip from Allen) and less frequently from Dup Dup pier in Allen; to return, stand on the beach and flag down a passing passenger boat. A special trip will cost around P300.

The forested island of **Capul**, to the west, has an even slower pace of life. It was a galleon staging post during Spanish days – the name probably comes from Acapulco, where the ships were headed – and has a lighthouse and ruined fort which you can just glimpse upon arrival, where sentries once combed the horizon for Moro pirates. There's also a picturesque Spanish-era church, which is one of the oldest in Samar.

Chilled out **Capul Island Beach Resort** (☎0921 672 6524; www.perfectplaces.com/vacation-rentals/33125.htm; r with fan/air-con P500/1000; ❄) has decent rooms on a lovely beach, though occasionally rubbish washes ashore. There's only electricity from 4pm till midnight. There's a kitchen but no restaurant, so you'll have to buy your food at the market, a 30-minute walk or P10 *habal-habal* ride.

A public boat leaves Capul at 6.30am daily, and returns from Allen (P70, one hour) around 11am. You'll need to stay overnight, or take a special trip back (P500).

Beyond Capul Island are the **San Vicente Islands**, including Seven Islands with their amazing crystal-clear water, soft corals and beaches with fine, pinkish sand. You'll need to charter a boat; Crystal Sand Beach Resort on Dalupiri makes trips here.

Western Samar

Adventure tourism is coming into its own along Samar's west coast, with opportunities for hiking, caving and mountain biking in the interior.

CALBAYOG

☎055 / POP 147,200

As far as travellers are concerned, Calbayog is a convenient entry point for those flying in or out from Manila. It's a dusty and sleepy town, but otherwise a pleasant enough place.

Stay at **Eduardo's Hotel** (☎209 2407; Pajarito St; d with fan/air-con from P400/500, ♣🅱), where rooms vary in size, quality and noise quotient, but are all clean and comfortable. It's walking distance from plenty of internet cafes, is next door to Metrobank's ATM, and just around the corner is **Carlos & Carmelo's**, a popular pizza and burger joint. If you're looking to stay in comfort, the high-end **Ciriaco Hotel** (☎209 6521; www.ciriacohotel.com; r incl breakfast from P4800; ❄📶🏊) is the plushest hotel on Samar, located 5km out of town along the highway. It offers free hotel transfer.

Getting There & Away

Airphil Express and PAL fly daily between Calbayog and Manila, while Cebu Pacific and Zest Air have four flights a week. The airport is 10km out of town, and a tricycle will cost P100.

Local buses and jeepneys depart from the Capoocan bus terminal north of Rosales Bridge, 2km from the town centre. Buses to Tacloban (P180, four hours) run until 4pm.

Grand Tours has regular vans between Calbayog and Catarman (P100, 1½ hours), and Allen (P100, 1½ hours).

Cokaliong Shipping has ferries to Cebu City (from P690, 11 hours) departing Calbayog at 7pm on Tuesday, Thursday and Saturday, while Palacio leaves on the same days at 6.30pm (P780, 12 hours).

There is a boat from Calbayog to Masbate (P250, six hours) Mondays and Fridays, departing from the small boat landing on the road to the main port.

CATBALOGAN & AROUND

☎055 / POP 84,180

The provincial capital of western Samar, Catbalogan serves as a great base to explore the surrounding network of extraordinary caves and subterranean rivers that lay hidden beneath lush jungle and gorges in the region – which has done wonders in putting Samar on the tourist map. The town itself has a laid-back feel with a friendly atmosphere, and has the best variety of accommodation on the island.

There are no real sights but in **Pita Park** near the port there is a memorial to the terrible 1987 *Doña Paz* ferry disaster; most of the 5000 or so victims were from Catbalogan and elsewhere on Samar.

Internet cafes abound in town, and BDO and Metrobank have ATMs.

Activities

To visit the underground sights, you'll need to get in touch with **Trexplore** (☎251 2301, 0919 294 3865; www.trexplore.blogspot.com; Abesamis Store, Allen Ave; ⏰8am-8pm), the only outfit qualified to lead trips to caves, rivers and gorges all over Samar. It's a one-person operation run by the energetic, entrepreneurial and engaging Joni A Bonifacio, and can tailor trips to just about any specifications, but you should make arrangements well in advance. It has an attached shop which sells a range of quality outdoor clothing, shoes and equipment.

One of the most popular day trips is to the recently discovered **Jiabong cave**, comprising four caves that feature a staggering variation of underground scenery, from river systems, waterfalls, sandy beaches, natural swimming pools and mud baths to majestic white calcium sulphate stalactites. At times you'll forget you're deep underground.

To the north, trips run to the gorgeous **Bangon**, **Mawacat** and **Larik falls**, and the **Guinogo-an cave** system.

To the south, **Calbiga Cave**, the Philippines' biggest karst formation and, at 2970 hectares, one of the largest in Asia, is an adventurer's playground. It was only first systematically explored in 1987, and the main cave, **Langun-Gobingob**, has a chamber the size of three football fields.

All these attractions require a combination of driving, hiking and – depending on your skills and interest – fairly serious caving, along with camping and swimming. Jiabong is the only really feasible day trip from Catbalogan. Costs start from around P3000 per person, with discounts for larger groups, and include food, transport, equipment and a CD of photos taken by Joni during the day.

Sleeping & Eating

TOP CHOICE Summers Garden Pension House PENSION HOUSE $
(☎251 5135; r incl breakfast from P900; ❄📶) An excellent choice for those looking for more homey accommodation, this large, immaculately kept house has wooden floors, a sunny patio and a garden in the front yard. The four rooms are all large and airy, and the elderly owners are charming. Breakfast is a big cook-up of bacon and eggs.

Fortune Hotel HOTEL $
(☎251 2147; 555 Del Rosario St; r with fan/air-con from P390/700; ❄📶) A reliable and longstanding hotel, the Fortune has a wide range of rooms in terms of price, size and conveniences. Go for rooms off the busy main road. It also has a bustling restaurant on the ground floor serving up Chinese and Filipino meals (dishes P50).

New Maqueda Bay Hotel HOTEL $$
(☎251 2386; r from P950; ❄📶) A few kilometres south of the centre of town, the once relatively splendid Maqueda has undermaintained rooms with bathrooms – some with balconies that sit out over the water. The draw here is the sea-view restaurant with picture windows, perfect for taking in the fantastic sunsets.

First Choice Hotel HOTEL $
(☎251 2688; hotelfirstchoice@yahoo.com; Del Rosario St; s/d with fan P300/400, r with air-con P950-1500; ❄📶) It's facade may have the dreariness of your stereotypical cheap motel, and the obscene pink colour scheme does it no favours, but rooms here are cheap, clean and decent value.

Flaming Hat FILIPINO $$
(meals P60-210; ⏰10am-9.30pm; ❄📶) By far the best eating option in town, this smart restaurant is the place locals head to for special occasions. The menu has a good selection of Filipino dishes and pizzas, but the garlic pepper shrimp or grilled pork belly are standouts. Cocktails are astonishingly cheap (P45), though you'll likely get an interesting interpretation of the original.

Balay Balay RESTOBAR $
(⏰9am-late) It's a little out of the way, near the New Maqueda Bay Hotel, but this outdoor bar on the water is a great spot to enjoy a beer with a sunset.

ℹ Getting There & Away

The best way of getting around is with the air-con vans that provide an efficient and regular service. **Duptours** (☎543 9127), **Van Vans** (☎543 9118) and **Grand Tours** (☎0920 908 6185) all head to Tacloban (P100, two hours), while Van Vans and Grand Tours also head to Calbayog (P90, 1½ hours). From Calbayog, there are connecting vans onwards to Allen and Catarman.

There are also frequent buses to the above destinations, but they're much slower and a similar price. They continue further north to Allen (P180, six hours) and Catarman (P180, six hours). There are daily bus services to Borongan (P140, three to four hours). Buray, a 30-minute jeepney ride (P25) south of Catbalogan, has more services to the east coast than from Catbalogan.

Philtranco and Eagle Star buses to Manila (P1120, 18 hours) leave fairly regularly from the bus station near the wharf.

Roble Shipping Lines runs to and from Cebu City (P650, 12 hours) once a week, departing Catbalogan at 8pm Friday evening.

Eastern & Southern Samar

A visit to Samar's east and south coasts offers plenty of wilderness experience and relaxed beachside pleasures, along with the added attraction of oodles of WWII history. Traditionally this coastline has been battered by passing typhoons, though changing weather patterns have seen fewer big storms make landfall, instead bypassing en route to Bicol.

There are some great surf spots along the southeast coast, with Calicoan Island and Borongan the best known.

BORONGAN

☎053 / POP 59,350

While Borongan itself is a fairly unremarkable, industrious town, surfers will want to check out the area for its reef and beach breaks, most notably Bato and Baybay beaches, and the surrounding islands. It gets swell intermittently throughout the year, though it's really only for the experienced, hardy and patient. The most scenic part of town is the boulevard around Baybay Beach, which has a nice stretch of honey-brown sand. The surrounding area comprises forested, mountainous country and little villages that seem unfazed by the outside world. It's possible to arrange hikes to waterfalls.

Borongan is also the jumping-off point for the island of **Divinubo**, a pretty spot 10 minutes offshore, with a lighthouse built by the Americans in 1906. Divinubo has good snorkelling, caves and forested slopes. To get here, take a tricycle to Lalawigan, where you can wait for a boat to fill up (P12) or charter a special trip (P500, 30 minutes). Alternatively, at low tide it's sometimes possible to walk all the way across from Borongan.

For more information, contact the **tourist office** (☎0917 426 9167; turismoborongan@gmail.com) opposite City Hall, which has a good selection of brochures.

There are several internet cafes in Borongan on the blocks around the Eagle Star bus terminal. Metrobank has an ATM.

🛏 Sleeping & Eating

Barbecue stands set up in the early evening along Baybay Beach.

Pebbles & Tides BEACH RESORT $$
(☎560 9104; www.pebbles101.bravehost.com; huts P950; ❄) Enjoying a waterfront location on Bato Beach, basic huts are comfortable enough and have their own verandah. While the beach itself is scrappy, its gets some good waves, making it a good option for surfers. It also serves some of the best food in town.

Domsowir Hotel HOTEL $
(☎261 2133; r with fan/air-con P125/455; ❄📶) The ageing Domsowir is centrally – if noisily – located on the riverbank. The beer's renowned as the coldest in town.

Hotel Dona Vicenta HOTEL $$
(☎261 3586; hoteldonavicenta@yahoo.com; r P980-3070;) Your typical business hotel, Dona Vicenta has large, comfortable rooms, but the atmosphere suffers somewhat from the constant background music from the neighbouring Uptown Mall. An adjoining pool is a welcome facility, especially as it's a bit away from the beach.

Phenpoint Grill FILIPINO $
(mains P70-200) Pleasant open-air eatery up the road from Baybay Beach, serving cheap and tasty Filipino dishes and sandwiches. Try the *lapu-lapu* (red grouper) with garlic sauce (P95). Also has a branch near the capitol building.

Getting There & Away

Eagle Star runs a direct service between Borongan and Catbalogan (P170, four to five hours), or take a jeepney to Buray and connect there to Catbalogan. Otherwise you can jump on a Manila-bound bus that passes through Catbalogan. Air-con minivans go to Tacloban (P190, five hours) via Basey, as do public buses. Buses also run to Guiuan (P120, three hours).

GUIUAN

☎053 / POP 43,460

The literal and metaphorical end of the bumpy road to the southeastern tip of Samar, Guiuan (ghee-won) is slowly turning itself into a low-key tourist destination. There's no beach here, but accommodation looks out to a luxurious, sparkling bay that makes for a great spot to base yourself for a day or two. There are plenty of nearby islands, including Calicoan Island – best known for its surfing. Once the airport gets up and running, which has been a long time in the making (basically since WWII, when it was constructed), it's likely to firm Guiuan as one of Samar's most popular destinations.

Guiuan's interesting history spans the period from the days of the first colonisers to those of the final liberators, with Magellan's landing site on the offshore island of Homonhon and the remnants of a massive US army base onshore.

The **tourist office** (TIPC; ☎0927 458 1175; ⏰9am-noon & 1-7pm) can provide information on the surrounding region, and doubles as a souvenir store.

There' s a PNB with an ATM in town (expect long queues), but it's unreliable; we recommended bringing enough cash with you.

Sights & Activities

In town is an impressive 16th-century **church** with fabulous carved Spanish doors and a sturdy watchtower.

Weather Station LOOKOUT
Walk up to the weather station for wide sweeping views across the Pacific Ocean and Leyte Gulf. During WWII, the US military transformed the area into a launching pad for attacks on Japan, and it was once the largest PT (patrol boat) base in the world, with as many as 300 boats and 150,000 troops stationed here, including a young future-President Kennedy. The 2km **runway** is still serviceable and has become the walking/jogging/cycling centre of town. A simple and moving **memorial** donated by a Japanese veteran is located at Dumpao Beach.

Pearl Island ISLAND
Go across the bay (P400 to P500 including waiting time, 30 minutes) to Pearl Island, which provides protection for giant clams and offers good snorkelling.

Sleeping & Eating

There are only a handful of places to stay, with by far the best options along the water a couple of kilometres from town (P10 by tricycle).

Tanghay View Lodge BEACH RESORT $
(☎0915 416 8067; www.tanghaylodge.multiply.com; r P250-1300;) Managed for many years by gregarious Susan Tan, there is accommodation here to suit most budgets. Leading the pack are comfortable air-con rooms with private bathrooms; struggling behind are small rooms with shared bathrooms that are clean as a pin but hot and steamy. Painted bright blue and white, the lodge has an appealing restaurant with a mix of pavilions and decking on the edge of the water. Try its speciality, conch in a gingery stir-fry (P90). Half-day tours (around P400) can be organised, combining the town's attractions, caves and nearby Calicoan Island.

Misty Blue Boathouse BEACH RESORT $
(☎0920 471 9526; mistyblueboathouse@hotmail.com; r with fan/air-con P500/1000;) Run by a burly, ultrafriendly Australian, this laidback resort has all the fundamentals covered with its seaside location, inviting pool, open-air restaurant serving wood-fired pizzas and even a floating bar. The pick of the rooms are the cheapest ones with fan that open to superb water views. Check out the beast of

a jet ski, that can be used to zip guests to nearby islands with great swimming.

Getting There & Away

At the time of research, the runway had just been relaid, as Guiuan airport awaited its first scheduled flight – though with these things, it's wise to not hold your breath.

Several buses and jeepneys leave for Tacloban (P130, 4½ hours) and Borongan (P120, three hours); the last of each departs at 3pm.

Air-con minivans (P120, 2½ hours) also make the run to Tacloban (P130, three hours). If you're heading for Borongan, a good alternative is to get a van to the junction 45 minutes from town (P50) – where the road forks north to Borongan (P100) and west to Tacloban – and wait there for a minivan. The last van from Guiuan leaves at 2pm. Otherwise, the fastest way is to jump on a bus heading to Manila that also departs from Guiuan.

CALICOAN ISLAND

About 16km by road from Guiuan, sleepy Calicoan Island is known primarily as a surfing destination, but people also come for its quiet beaches and lazy island vibe.

The best waves are at **ABCD Beach**, named after both the four reef breaks along this coast, and also after 'Advance Base Construction Depot', which is one for the WWII buffs. It has great left- and right-handed reef breaks between May and October. There's a strong current and rip, not suited for beginners. Surfers should get in touch with local surf guru **Jun Jun** (☎0906 451 9719), president of Guiuan surf club. He can arrange surfboards and bodyboards (per day P500), as well as lessons (per day P1000). If you get stuck for accommodation he can also organise a place to stay. He's also a good contact for other surf spots along Samar's southeast coast.

There's good swimming (if the surf's not up) at 3km-long **Ngolos Beach** to the north of ABCD. WWII historians will also want to see the remains of **Navy 3149 Base**. The west coast of the island has some amazing white-sand beaches and swimming.

At the southern tip of the island is the fishing village of **Sulangan**. Pilgrims from all over come to visit the church with its shrine of patron saint of miracles, San Antonio de Padua.

The best-value accommodation is at **Calicoan Villa** (☎0917 206 9602; www.calicoanvilla.com; r with fan/air-con from P1000/2500; ❄@≋),

THE WHITE RUSSIANS OF TUBABAO

For such an obscure little island, **Tubabao** had a surprisingly eventful decade during and after WWII. Firstly serving as a significant US base during the war, in 1949 it saw the arrival of 5500 Russian refugees who were fleeing persecution from Communist China. Having settled in Harbin in 1917, after escaping bolshevism in the USSR, the anticommunist 'White Russians' once again found themselves on the run. Accepting the offer of refugee status by the Filipino government, they were sent to the almost uninhabited island of Tubabao.

It was far from the tropical holiday experience that visitors are here for today. Accommodation comprised old US army tents, with very poor, overcrowded conditions coupled with disease, oppressive weather and a lack of basic necessities that made it very much a refugee camp. Wooden churches of various denominations were constructed, and the movie house and ice-cream parlour provided some degree of normalcy to their lives.

After two years on the island, in 1951 most refugees were granted asylum to America, Australia and France, with the remaining Russians evacuated in December 1951 after a massive typhoon destroyed all the buildings on the island, leaving Tubabao to return once again to its slumber.

Today Tubabao is comprised of a number of relaxed fishing villages, with only very minuscule remains of the Russian camp to be seen – no more than the concrete flooring of the movie house, church, mess hall and power station. The bridge that once connected Tubabao to the mainland was also destroyed, and it's now accessed by small boats that depart from a landing next to Misty Blue Boathouse.

Even though there's *very* little to see on this sleepy island, if you're not pressed for time it can make for an interesting hour or two wandering about. Get in touch with **Cesar** (☎0920 268 7510), a barangay captain on Tubabao, who can lead you to some of the sites. In Guiuan, a small photo exhibition of the camp is located next door to the tourist office, bizarrely in the back of the police lockup.

with simple A-framed bungalows looking out to stunning views of ABCD Beach. There are more upmarket rooms in the main building. It has a good pool and surfboards for hire (per day P500), and a generally all-round good feel to the place.

Otherwise there's the plush **Calicoan Surf Camp** (☎0917 628 6615; www.calicoansurfcamp.com; r incl breakfast from P6700; ❄☒), which is neither a camp nor is it surf-oriented, but rather an exclusive resort on gorgeous grounds with an ocean-viewing boardwalk and wonderful infinity pool. Rooms are in thatched-roof batak-style huts with very comfortable interiors.

Infrequent multicabs and jeepneys run between Guiuan and Calicoan (P30), or hire a tricycle (P300). The last jeepney back to Guiuan is around 2pm.

HOMONHON ISLAND & SULUAN ISLAND

The island of Homonhon is where Magellan first landed in the Philippines on 16 March 1521. The island has blowholes, white-sand beaches and a freshwater cascade and creek. You can get a public bangka from Guiuan (P20, two hours), though this is unpredictable and depends on the tide and weather – May to July is usually the most clement period.

An hour beyond Homonhon, the same travel constraints apply to Suluan, which has a derelict **lighthouse**. The 500 steps up to it are good exercise and the reward is a fantastic view across the islands of Leyte Gulf and the Pacific Ocean. There are also **coastal caves** that are accessible at low tide. If you plan to stay overnight on Suluan, the barangay captain will find you a room.

An option is to hire a boat in Guiuan, set off early, and visit both islands in a day trip (around P6000). Take local advice and be prepared to be delayed.

MARABUT ISLANDS

This pretty cluster of tiny jagged limestone islands adds interest to the already scenic stretch of coastline between Basey and Marabut; the views here are vaguely reminiscent of Vietnam's Halong Bay, but in miniature.

The **Marabut Marine Park** (☎276 5206; www.caluwayanresort.com; r from P1600; ☒) is a good jumping-off point to explore the rocky outcrops, with sea kayaks for hire to paddle the few hundred metres out to shore. There's also **Caluwayan Palm Island** (☎276 5206; www.caluwayanresort.com; r from P1600; ☒), with relatively pricey rooms; it fronts the islets and rents out paddle boats (P100 per hour).

From Marabut, local buses ply the route every hour or so between Tacloban (P30, 1½ hours) and Guiuan (P100, three hours).

SOHOTON CAVES & NATURAL BRIDGE NATIONAL PARK

This is Samar's premier natural attraction, a protected area of caves and forest, and home to at least six of Samar's endemic birds. Access is via Basey, which, given its proximity to Leyte, is usually visited from Tacloban. For further information, see p312.

Mindanao & Sulu

Includes »

Best Places to Eat

- Night Café (p335)
- Kawayan (p353)
- Claude's Café (p358)
- Alavar Seafood House (p367)

Best Places to Stay

- Camiguin Action Geckos Resort (p345)
- Sagana Beach Resort (p353)
- Ponce Suites (p355)
- Chema's by the Sea Resort (p360)

Why Go?

Despite boasting jaw-dropping beaches, killer surf, rugged mountain ranges and indigenous cultures living very much as they have for centuries, Mindanao remains off the tourism industry's radar. Of course, the conflict that has ebbed and flowed now for several generations bears much of the responsibility. That's not to say there isn't urbanisation – much of the northern coastline has been paved over, and the southern city of Davao is cosmopolitan and sophisticated – just that much of what has been lost elsewhere in the Philippines is alive in Mindanao.

Though it's big and bulky, because of its varied ethnographic make-up, competing land claims and highly prized abundant natural resources, Mindanao can seem undersized. Since the 1950s Muslims have been the minority and are the majority in only four of the 21 provinces, where 14,000 sq km are given over to the Autonomous Region in Muslim Mindanao (ARMM), an area that includes islands stretching towards Malaysia and Indonesia.

When to Go

Cagayan De Oro

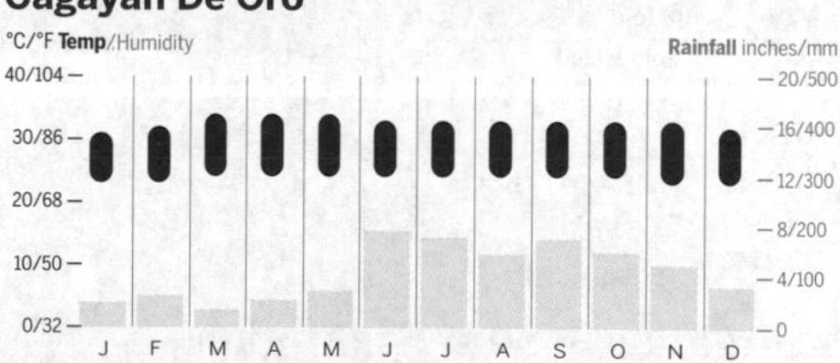

Jun-Sep The driest season on the eastern seaboard.

Nov-Mar The wettest season on the eastern seaboard.

Nov-Apr The driest season for most of the island.

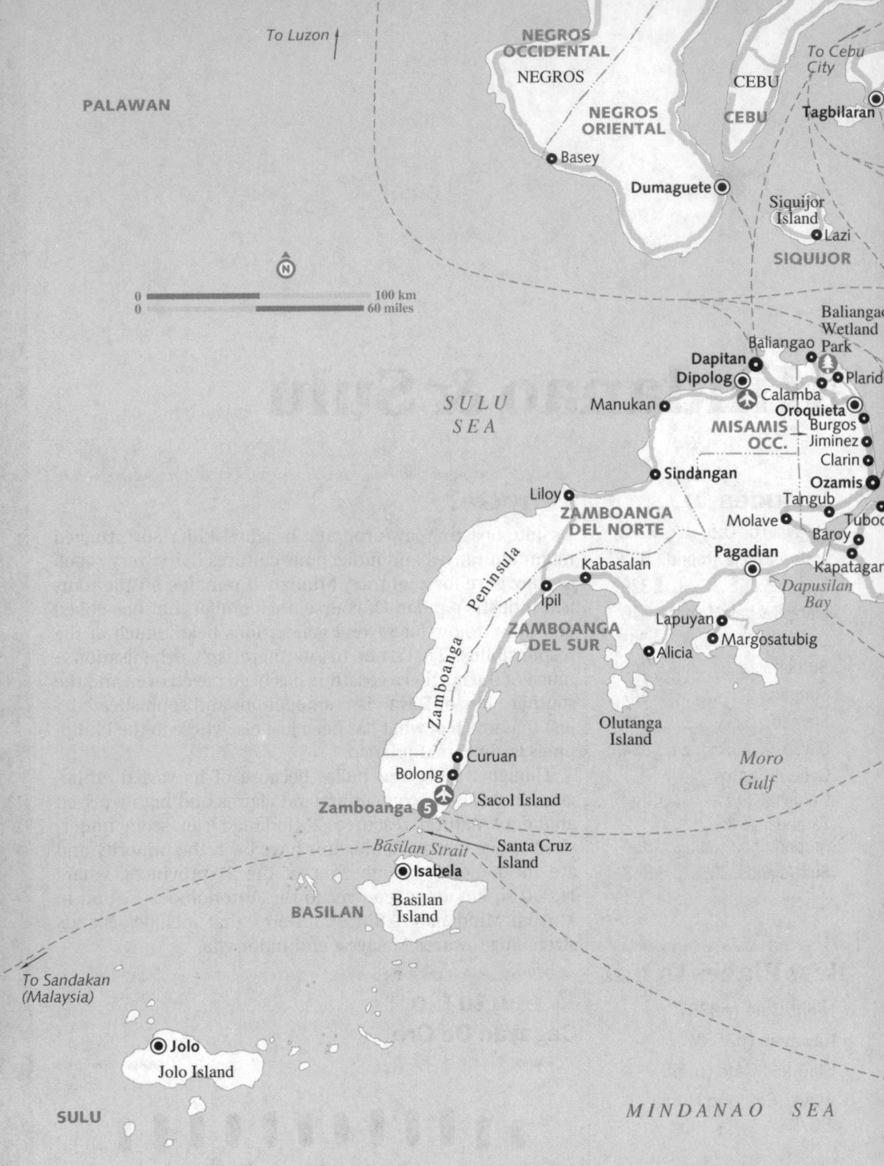

Mindanao & Sulu Highlights

1. Hop from natural springs to waterfalls around lush **Camiguin** (p341)
2. Catch a wave at **Cloud Nine** (p352), the surf break on Siargao
3. Roll through white water on the **Cagayan de Oro River** (p338)

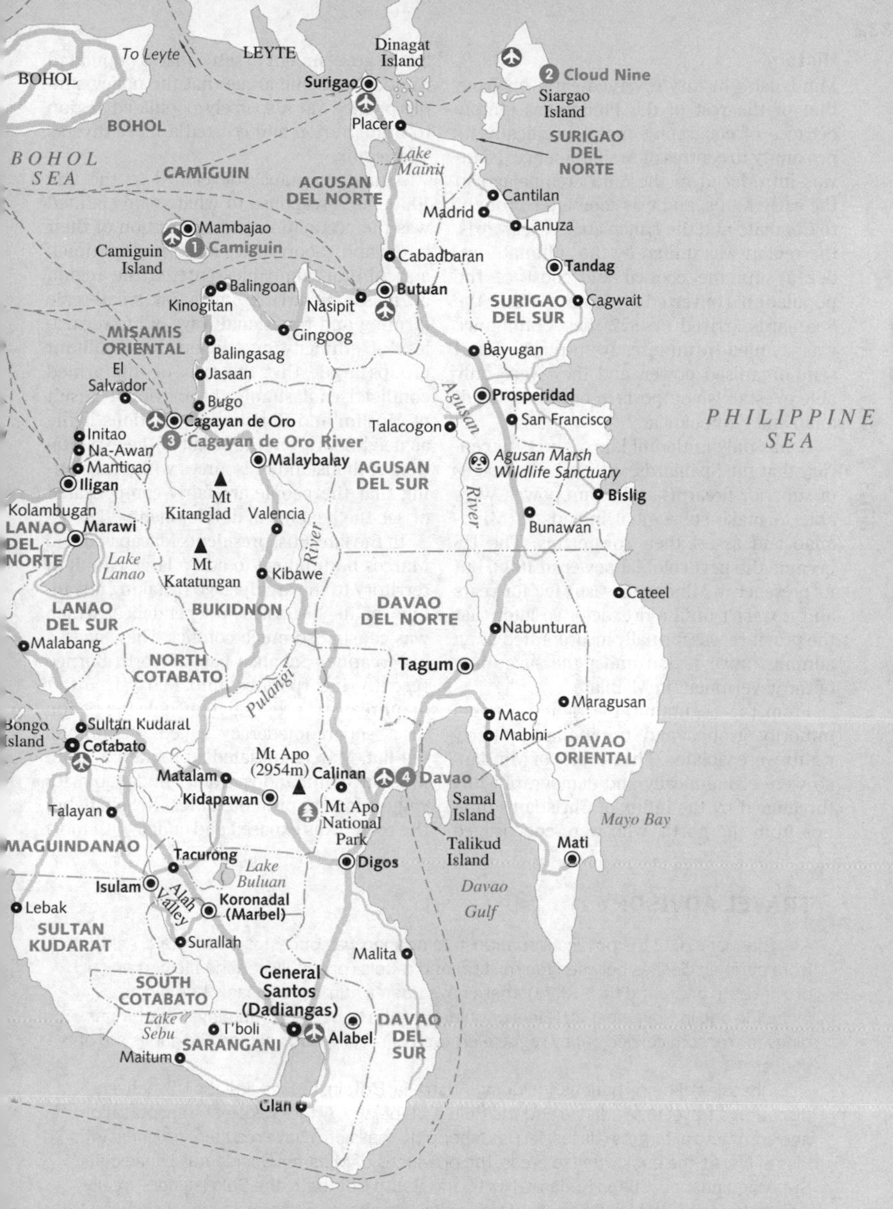

4 Bar-hop from one buzzing compound to the next in cosmopolitan **Davao** (p359)

5 Take in the island's history and ethnic diversity in **Zamboanga** (p365)

History

Mindanao's history diverged early on from that of the rest of the Philippines simply because of geography, more specifically its proximity to centres of Arab influence. Islam was introduced in the Sulu archipelago in the early 1300s, and was soon after brought to Cotabato and the Lanao area. Afterwards, the region was united by the sultanate under a supreme council and most of the population converted to Islam. When the Spaniards arrived in 1527, their dominance was stymied by an already entrenched and semi-organised power, and they were only able to establish outposts in northern Mindanao and Zamboanga.

It was only in the middle of the 19th century that the Spaniards, with the advantages of superior firearms and steam power, were able to make substantial inroads in Mindanao and assert their sovereignty. The US became the next colonial power in 1898, but its presence in Mindanao wasn't felt for years and it wasn't until a decade or so later that the province was formally incorporated as an administrative region under the suzerainty of the government in Manila.

From the beginning, the rights of tribal minority groups and traditional property rights were violated. The peoples of Mindanao were economically and demographically threatened by the influx of Christian Filipinos from the north, who were encouraged by the government to settle in less populated Mindanao. Some argue that the policy simply opened up a sparsely populated region to immigration and created a more diverse ethnic mix.

Armed resistance developed in the late 1960s as a response to what some claimed was the occupation and annexation of their homeland. Soon after, large multinational agricultural companies entered the region en masse, invariably impacting small-scale farming and traditional ways of life regardless of ethnicity or religion. Less militant groups argue that the crux of this armed conflict is not simply the inevitable result of Muslim and Christian populations living as neighbours, but the result of the exploitation of the island's resources without ensuring that the people are fairly compensated or see the benefits of development.

In the late '60s, presidents Macapagal and Marcos both hoped to add a large chunk of territory to the archipelago by taking advantage of its historical independence, which was causing so much conflict. They made a bid to annex Sabah, a part of North Borneo recently incorporated into Malaysia. After an unrealistic proposal to include the region in a superconfederacy called Maphilindo fell flat, Marcos initiated a program to train Muslim commandos from Mindanao with vague plans to promote unrest in Sabah, but the secret was exposed and ended with most

TRAVEL ADVISORY

As of January 2012 the political situation in Mindanao was once again uncertain. Aside from periodic clashes between the military and rebels (primarily confined to certain provinces in or around the ARMM), there have been a number of deadly bombings, including one in November 2011 in a popular pension house in Zamboanga City. Kidnappings for ransom carried out by rogue elements of rebel groups and armed gangs are of concern.

Embassies of many nations, including Australia, Britain, France and the US, actively discourage travel to Mindanao and the Sulu archipelago. Attacks against transportation and commercial targets (buses, ferries, shopping malls etc) have resulted in significant loss of life. As the book when to press, the provinces of Miasmis Occidental, Lanao del Sur, Maguindanao, Sultan Kudarat, North and South Cotabato, the Sulu Islands – really any part of the ARMM – were considered risky; you should exercise caution if planning to travel to Marawi in Lanao del Norte. Check with your embassy, or better yet with Filipinos who know specific parts of Mindanao well, before venturing into any potentially dangerous areas.

All these caveats aside, as long as you rely on local knowledge, stay away from specific hot spots and err on the side of caution when choosing where and how to travel, you should be fine. Northern Mindanao, including Cagayan de Oro and the islands of Siargao and Camiguin, is peaceful and has generally been excluded from the troubles elsewhere. Davao, the business and commercial capital of Mindanao, is also perfectly safe to visit.

of the guerrilla recruits being killed under mysterious circumstances.

In 1976 an agreement was struck between one of the rebel groups, the Moro Islamic National Liberation Front (MNLF), and the government established the ARMM; in 1996 the MNLF was legitimised as a political group by Manila. Other groups didn't agree that limited autonomy within a federalised system was adequate, when for all practical purposes most significant issues are resolved in Manila; as a result a breakaway group, the Moro Islamic Liberation Front (MILF), was established in 1978. The most radical of the groups is the Abu Sayyaf, a small group of former MILF members dissatisfied with the drift towards compromise; it continues to call for a separate Islamic state in the southern Philippines. The government also claims that Jemaah Islamiyah, an Indonesia-based organisation, has infiltrated Abu Sayyaf (estimated 300 members) and other separatist groups, and is using remote parts of Mindanao to train dozens of recruits.

Successive government regimes have tried to assert their control through different means; Marcos tried through a combination of military action and amnesty offers, but it was talks between Cory Aquino and Nur Misuari, the founder of the MNLF, that finally led to a reduction in violence in the late 1980s. Unfortunately, most of the outstanding issues were never resolved and in the late 1990s and early 2000s the violence resumed.

In August of 2005 Zaldy Ampatuan was elected the new governor of the ARMM, which made him the first leader not to be a member of a rebel group. It was enough to provide the optimistic with hope that the conflict could be brought to an end. However, in early August 2008, before the Memorandum of Agreement on Ancestral Domain (MoA-AD) was signed by the Arroyo administration, the Philippines Supreme Court ruled it unconstitutional. One of the primary sticking points was the MILF's desire for an independent court system. The agreement called for a separate Muslim homeland and would have recognised the 11,000-strong Moro Islamic Liberation Front (MILF) as a juridical entity.

The MILF immediately responded with a series of deadly guerrilla attacks across a large swath of the island. The Philippine army in turn launched massive air and ground assaults against suspected rebel camps; more than 400 people were killed and an estimated 7,500,000 civilians displaced in some of the most intense fighting in decades. Peace talks were suspended and the Arroyo administration ordered the primary commanders of the August attacks be handed over but the opposition refused. After seven years, Malaysia pulled its peacekeeping force out of Mindanao.

Observers claim that the Aquino government has a better chance for peace than previous administrations in part because older rebels are weary of the fighting that has claimed their entire adult lives. The president has been willing to engage in face-to-face peace talks in Malaysia with Al Haj Murad Ebrahim, the leader of the MILF. However, there was another upsurge in violence beginning in October 2011 when 19 government soldiers were killed in clashes in Basilan 550 miles south of Manila. Dissatisfied with the MILF's willingness to continue negotiations with the government after 14 years of talks, a small breakaway group organised a series of attacks and skirmished with government troops in Zamboanga Sibugay province. Aquino has resisted calls for all-out war though air and ground assaults continued late into the year. Thousands of civilians have been displaced from their homes in the worst fighting since 2008.

The Maguindanao massacre (see p406), one of the most shocking incidents of violence in the last several years, however, was motivated more by clan and political power struggles.

It's estimated that since the late 1960s more than 160,000 people have died as a result of the conflict between government troops and rebel groups.

THE 2011 FLOODS

Flash floods triggered by Tropical Storm Washi devastated parts of northern Mindanao including Cagayan de Oro and Iligan in mid-December 2011. At the time of publication over 1000 people were confirmed dead with many more missing. As this book was researched prior to this disaster, you may need to double-check some information before heading to Mindanao.

Getting There & Away

There are regular daily flights from Manila to Butuan, Cagayan de Oro, Cotabato, Davao, Dipolog, General Santos, Surigao and Zamboanga City; from Cebu to Camiguin, Davao, General Santos, Siargao and Zamboanga City; and from Iloilo City on Panay to Davao. Silk Air flies to Singapore from Davao.

You can get to Mindanao by boat from Bohol, Cebu, Leyte, Luzon, Manila, Negros, Palawan, Panay and Siquijor in the Philippines, and directly from Indonesia. Transport schedules and prices listed in this chapter should be taken as guidelines only.

Getting Around

Most of Mindanao is easily traversed by relatively comfortable air-con buses, and the highway linking Cagayan de Oro and Butuan with Davao provides an inexpensive and convenient way to reach the south. Most people choose not to travel overland on the Zamboanga Peninsula and fly (or less commonly take a boat) to Zamboanga City.

A railway system, initially linking Cagayan de Oro and Cotabato, might forever remain in the planning stages.

NORTHERN MINDANAO

The coastline from Cagayan de Oro to Surigao and the offshore islands off the far northeastern tip is a region apart from the rest of Mindanao. Though largely spared from the violence elsewhere, it's often inaccurately stigmatised simply by dint of association. The vibrant university town of Cagayan is both a gateway to the region and a base for adventures in the surrounding Bukidnon Province. Volcanic Camiguin Island is seventh heaven for outdoor lovers and Siargao is one of the best places in the Philippines to hang ten.

Cagayan de Oro

088 / POP 554,000

Like university towns the world over, the energy and promise of youth endows otherwise ordinary places with a jolt of joie de vivre. Anyone over the age of 18 can feel like a fuddy-duddy walking the crowded, student-laden downtown streets of Cagayan de Oro (the 'Oro' refers to the gold discovered by the Spanish in the river here).

Much of Cagayan's relatively robust economy centres on the Del Monte pineapple processing plant north of town. Nestlé and Pepsi also make their corporate homes in the Philippines here. Popular with Korean tourists who come for English lessons, the relatively cool climate and golf, the city is also the base for a number of outdoor adventures including rafting, hiking, rock climbing and caving.

Sights

Museum of Three Cultures MUSEUM
(Corrales St; admission P100; 9am-noon & 2-6pm Mon-Fri, 9am-noon Sat) The three galleries here have an interesting mix of photos, ceramics, art and artefacts, including several huge ceremonial M'ranao swords and a full-scale *pangao*, a four-poster bed meant to accommodate the sultan's entire family. It's housed in a building of classrooms on the grounds of Capitol University, a short walk from Gaisano Mall north of the city centre.

Sleeping

Victoria Suites HOTEL $
(857 4447, 0917 707 4009; www.victoriasuitesonline.com; Tirso Neri St; s/d incl breakfast P650/850;) The two four-storey Romanesque pillars and awnings on this centrally located hotel's facade make it easy to spot. Inside, it's less grand, the minimal furnishings echoing private rooms in a hospital. That said, there's security, a coffee shop, an in-house masseuse and shiny tile floors.

Nature's Pensionne HOTEL
(857 1900; T Chavez St; r P580-870;) Ideally located only a few blocks from Divisoria, it's a professionally run operation and rooms in the newer 'business class' wing come with good-quality TVs and modern bathrooms; the older building's rooms have flimsy wooden walls.

Grand City Hotel HOTEL $$
(857 1900; Apolinar Velez St; r from P980;) Sharing a parking lot with Nature's Pensionne, its sister hotel next door, Grand City has a fancier lobby and elevator, but other than faux-wood floors and large queen-sized beds, rooms don't reflect the step up in price. Wi-fi is available for P100 per four hours.

Dynasty Court Hotel HOTEL $$
(272 4516; www.dynastycourthotel.com; cnr Tiano Brothers & Hayes Sts; r/ste from P1600/3000;) A four-star lobby and two-star rooms make this large hotel a mixed bag – the standard rooms with curtains but no windows are as much a metaphor as a design flaw, though the deluxe and suite rooms are

better maintained and include a large buffet breakfast.

Mallberry Suites HOTEL $$
(☎855 7999; www.mallberrysuites.net; Florentino St; r from P1800; ❄≋) A short stroll to the Limketkai Complex and Robinson's supermarket, the aptly named Mallberry is a seven-storey business hotel. Several restaurants and a bar add some edge to the corporate sensibility; however, there's no warmth in the plain and ordinary rooms.

Ridgeview Chalets BUNGALOW $$
(☎858 7930; www.ridgeviewchalets-cdo.com; Xavier Estates, Airport Rd; chalets P1850; ❄☰≋) Part of a high-end residential subdivision with panoramic views, a pool and extensive grounds out near the airport. The building exteriors have the chalet look but this ends at the door; rooms are carpeted and have chintzy bed covers and furnishings.

Marigold Hotel HOTEL $$
(☎856 4320; www.marigoldhotel.net; cnr Luna & Velez Sts; r incl breakfast P1300; ❄☰) Occupying the 4th and 5th floor of a nondescript building on the primary – and noisy – north-south thoroughfare, the Marigold won't win any awards for style. The rooms have a certain hospital-like efficiency and one guest per room gets a free massage upon request, plus a free Marigold umbrella or cap!

Pearlmont Inn HOTEL $$
(☎856 2653; www.pearlmontinn.com; Limketkai Dr; r from P1400; ❄) Only a short walk from the restaurants at Limketkai, the Pearlmont has a somewhat garish colonnaded facade and brightly lit lobby and coffee shop. Standard rooms lack warmth and light.

VIP Hotel HOTEL $$
(☎856 2505; www.theviphotel.com.ph; Apolinar Velez St; r incl breakfast from P1950; ❄☰) Somewhat barren rooms with furniture in need of an upgrade mean the six-storey VIP is not great value. Does have professional staff and a lobby restaurant.

Maxandrea Hotel HOTEL $$
(☎857 2244; www.maxandrea.com; JR Borja St; r P2100; ❄☰) An eight-storey business-class hotel halfway between Divisoria and Limketkai. Service can be spotty; make sure you get a room with windows and natural light.

Hotel Ramon HOTEL $
(☎857 4804; cnr Tirso Neri & Burgos Sts; r from P500; ❄☰) A sleepily staffed concrete block on the western edge of Divisoria; river views are blocked by dense foliage.

Parkview Hotel HOTEL $
(☎857 1197; cnr Tirso Neri & General Capistrano Sts; r with/without bathroom P575/330; ❄☰) Overlooks Divisoria and has wi-fi in the lobby.

Wilshire Inn HOTEL $
(☎720 762; cnr Aguinaldo & Yacapin Sts; s/d P450/P500; ❄☰) Not bad value, though some rooms have a musty smell.

Eating

The **Rosario Arcade** in front of the Limketkai Complex, a few kilometres northeast of Divisoria (Golden Friendship Park), is Cagayan's culinary and entertainment centre. A variety of international cuisines are represented, including Thai (Siam Thai Cuisine), Japanese (Ramen Tei) and Mediterranean (La Vetta); **Kagay-anon** (mains P275) for highly praised Filipino fare and **Bigby's** (mains P325) sort of generic international menu can also be recommended. For pastries and gelato, head to cheerful-looking **Missy Bon Bon** (gelato P55).

Every Friday and Saturday night, Divisoria is closed to everything but foot traffic and turns into an open-air dinner theatre, with a good chunk of Cagayan sampling food and drink along with musical accompaniment – locals refer to it as '**Night Café**'. A culinary Sunday-night market is held near the Paseo del Rio rotunda, the future site of a large hotel project south of the centre.

Any night of the week, street vendors hawk *isaw* (chicken intestines) for P5 a skewer and the questionably appetising *proven* (or proben, a fried mix of parts from the chicken's digestive system). Also look out for the region's speciality *kinilaw*, which is spiced with *tabon tabon*, a fruit native to northern Mindanao. Cagayan foodies claim their city's *lechon baboy* (roasted pig), stuffed with lemongrass and other herbs and spices, is the tastiest in Mindanao.

Some of the best seafood is served at a handful of restaurants; **Panagatan** (mains P200) is the most highly recommended, perched on stilts over the water around 10km west of the city on the highway to Iligan.

Karachi Restaurant INDIAN, PAKISTANI $
(Hayes St; mains P100; ⌚8.30am-10pm) A bare-bones restaurant providing a welcome shot of spicy Indian and Pakistani fare. The appetisers alone, especially the crispy samosas

Cagayan de Oro

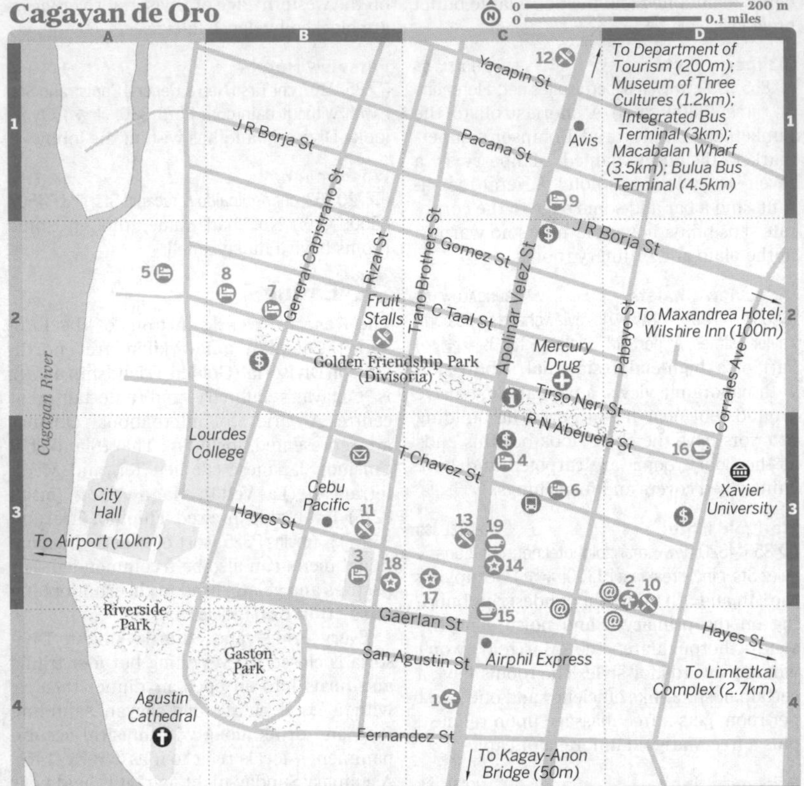

(P15), are enough to stave off hunger while waiting and waiting for generous meat and vegie dishes.

Cocina de Oro FILIPINO, MEDITERRANEAN **$$**
(mains P180; ⏲10am-11pm) Located just before the Limketkai Complex, this large restaurant has a split personality, at least as far as menus go. One is Filipino, including a handful of ostrich dishes, its speciality; the other menu is for Zorba's, which has Mediterranean classics.

Sentro 1850 FILIPINO, INTERNATIONAL **$$**
(50 Apolinar Velez St; mains from P180; ⏲10am-11pm) Serves a varied menu of Filipino, seafood and international dishes, such as baby back ribs, burgers (P120) and locally caught seafood in a relatively modern and stylish setting.

Butcher's Best Barbeque BARBECUE **$**
(Hayes St; meat skewers P15) Diners enjoy super-cheap skewers of barbecued meat and rice. Strictly utilitarian seating inside and out. Near the corner of Corrales Ave.

Malt Café & Art Lounge INTERNATIONAL **$$**
(Apolinar Velez St; mains P180; wi-fi) Casual modern spot with above-average sandwiches, pasta and salads.

Robinson's SUPERMARKET **$**
(⏲9am-8pm Sun-Thu, to 9pm Fri & Sat) For self-catering, this large, fully stocked grocery is part of the Limketkai Complex.

Drinking & Entertainment

Club Mojo (Hayes St; ⏲9pm-2am) and **Pulse** (Tiano Brothers St; ⏲7pm-3am) are around the corner from one another and have live music most nights of the week (nominal cover charges). On the 2nd floor of the former is **Rolf's Sports Bar**, a generic version with several TVs and billiards. DJs spin at **Tilt** (cnr Apolinar Velez & Hayes Sts; ⏲8pm-late) a few blocks away.

Cagayan de Oro

Activities, Courses & Tours

1	CDO Bugsay River Rafting	C4
2	Viajero Outdoor Centre	D3

Sleeping

3	Dynasty Court Hotel	B3
4	Grand City Hotel	C3
5	Hotel Ramon	A2
6	Nature's Pensionne	C3
7	Parkview Hotel	B2
8	Victoria Suites	B2
9	VIP Hotel	C1

Eating

10	Butcher's Best Barbeque	D3
11	Karachi Restaurant	B3
12	Malt Café & Art Lounge	C1
13	Sentro 1850	C3

Drinking

14	Bo's Coffee Club	C3
15	Kiwi Swirl	C4
16	Park Cafe	D3
	Rolf's Sports Bar	(see 17)

Entertainment

17	Club Mojo	C3
18	Pulse	B3
19	Tilt	C3

Transport

	Philippine Airlines	(see 8)

Coffee-house culture is big in Cagayan, which is not surprising given its large university population. There are several branches of **Bo's Coffee Club** (Apolinar Velez St; 7am-midnight; wi-fi) and **Coffee Works** (Limketkai Complex; wi-fi). More homey and personal is **Kiwi Swirl** (cnr Apolinar Velez & Gaerlan Sts; sandwiches P85; 9.30am-9pm; wi-fi), formerly Gazebo Café; in addition to frozen yoghurt and coffee drinks, it serves spaghetti and sandwiches. Popular with students is the outdoor **Park Cafe** (Corrales Ave; 24hr), right at the eastern end of Divisoria.

The Limketkai Complex and Gaisano Mall have cinemas.

Information

All the major banks are here and have ATMs. Several are located along Divisoria and Apolinar Velez St. There's a Citibank in the Limketkai Complex.

There are more than a dozen internet cafes in the blocks south of Divisoria; a handful are on Hayes St between Apolinar Velez St and Corrales Ave.

Bureau of Immigration (BOI; 272 6517; Room 205, BPI Bldg, Sergio Osmeña St; 8am-5pm Mon-Fri)

City Tourism Office (857 3165; Divisoria Park & Apolinar Velez St; 8am-noon & 1-5pm Mon-Fri, 9am-10pm Sat) Pick up flyers for info on hotels and transportation schedules; not much English spoken.

Department of Tourism Region 10 Office (DOT; 856 4048; dotr10@_nmyahoo.com; Gregorio Pelaez Sports Center, Apolinar Velez St; 8.30am-5.30pm Mon-Fri) A large office with enthusiastic and helpful staff; info on city and region.

Limbros Travel & Tours (856 2334; Rosario Arcade, Limketkai Complex) Books ferries, and domestic and international airline tickets.

Oro Laundry Station (Hayes St; 8am-7pm Mon-Sat) Charges P25 per kilogram.

Getting There & Away

Air

There are daily flights to Cagayan from Manila (1½ hours) with **Airphil Express** (857 1124; cnr Velez & Gaerlan Sts), **Cebu Pacific** (856 6661; cnr Rizal & Hayes Sts) and **Philippine Airlines** (857 2295; Tirso Neri St). Airphil Express and Cebu Pacific fly daily to Cebu (45 minutes) and the latter also flies to Davao (50 minutes).

From 2012 all domestic flights are scheduled to begin operating out of the new Laguindingan International Airport, with longer runways, 30km west of the city and 55km east of Iligan.

Boat

You can get to Macabalan pier by jeepney; a taxi will cost about P80.

Between Manila and Cagayan, SuperFerry has four weekly trips (P2250, 35 hours), while Negros Navigation (P650, Wednesday and Saturday) and Sulpicio Lines go twice weekly.

Several companies, including SuperFerry, Trans Asia and Negros Navigation, connect to Cebu City (about 10 hours) several days a week; the latter goes to Iloilo on Panay (P1995, 14 hours, weekly). Cebu Ferries and Super Shuttle Ferry go to Jagna on Bohol (P650, seven hours) several days a week, and Trans Asia also services Tagbilaran (P655, 10 hours, three weekly).

Bus

Eastbound and southbound buses leave 24 hours from the Integrated Bus Terminal at the Agora fruit and vegetable wholesale market. Aircon buses stop running in the early evening. For Surigao (departure point for boats to Siargao), you must transfer to another bus in Butuan.

Westbound buses depart from the terminal a few kilometres northwest of the city centre in barangay Bulua. In general, buses leave every 30 minutes to an hour.

DESTINATION	FARE (P)	DURATION (HR)
Balingoan	145	1¾
Butuan	325	4¼
Davao	600	6
Iligan	145	2

Taxi

A taxi to Balingoan (P3000) or Iligan (P1500) isn't such an extravagance for groups of three.

Getting Around

The old airport is 10km west of town and it will cost you P150 to get there by taxi. From this airport to town (P200 to P300) is a different proposition; taxi drivers can be aggressive and it isn't uncommon for them to try to increase the fare after it's been agreed upon. Jeepneys to the downtown area available outside the airport's front gate, though inexpensive, involve two transfers; take one marked SM City, then transfer to a Cogon-bound one and finally hop on one labelled Divisoria.

Jeepneys to many points, including the pier, Cugman (for Malasag Eco-Tourism Village) and the Limketkai Complex, pass by in front of Nature's Pensionne.

Rather than taking multiple taxis to sights around the city, which can add up, renting a car is a convenient and economical option for groups of two or more. **Avis** (☎857 1492; www.avis.com.ph; RT DeLeon Plaza, cnr Yacapin & Apolinar Velez Sts) has an office in town and it's possible to return the car in Davao. Rates average around P2700 per day (petrol not included); chauffeur-driven cars and vans are also available.

Around Cagayan de Oro

Cagayan is the gateway to outdoor adventures including rafting only an hour's drive south of the city in Bukidnon Province. Evolving from a few intrepid and resourceful pioneers cobbling together makeshift rafts, today there are several professional and environmentally aware outfits catering to large groups of visitors.

Rafting is good year-round – during the dry season, from January to May, the water is clearer and the runs more technical, while in June and July the water is faster if brown and murky.

Sights & Activities

The standard three-hour rafting trip (P700 to P900) takes you through a dozen Class I to III rapids; several Class IV rapids are part of an alternative longer trip (P1000 to P1500, six hours). Much of the trip is spent floating past bucolic scenery, and enthusiastic guides and excited first-timers add to the fun. A grilled lunch (P150) is available at the exit point. Six companies are officially registered, including highly recommended **Kagay CDO Rafting** (☎856 3972; www.cdorafting-map.com) and **CDO Bugsay River Rafting** (☎309 1991; www.bugsayrafting.com; Apolinar Velez St, Cagayan de Oro).

Malasag Eco-Tourism Village VILLAGE
(☎855 6183; admission P30) Set in acres of botanical gardens with a small wildlife collection of butterflies, birds and deer, the Malasag Eco-Tourism Village is a theme park of sorts, featuring tribal houses, a museum and an education centre. There are camping, cottages (from P500), a swimming pool (P50) and a good restaurant. Take a jeepney to Cugman and get off at Malasag, then take a motorcycle (P50) up the hill to the village. A taxi will cost about P250 one way.

Del Monte PLANTATION
(☎855 5976; ⌚8am-1pm Sat) Whatever your level of fruity passion, the sight of pineapples as far as the eye can see is pretty surreal. The pineapple plantations, all 95 sq km of them, are about 35km north and east of Cagayan, on the Bukidnon plateau at Camp Phillips (where General Douglas MacArthur fled after the battle of Corregidor Island in 1942). Jeepneys run to Camp Phillips but the plantations lie behind the complex, a clubhouse and golf course, so it's best to hire someone to drive you. A special return trip by taxi will cost around P750. The easiest thing to do is to arrange a car and driver with one of the rafting companies.

Del Monte also offers free tours of its pineapple processing factory at Bugo, approximately 15km east of Cagayan. Call a day or so in advance to book.

Makahambus Cave CAVE
Just a few metres before Makahambus Adventure Park is the cave where Filipino soldiers and their families sought refuge during the Philippines-American war; take a torch (flashlight). There's a **viewing deck** over the river. From here you can walk down the steps to the bottom of the gorge. Most

CLIMBING & SPELUNKING

A close-knit and dedicated group of outdoor adventurers call Cagayan de Oro home. One of the hubs of this community is the husband and wife who run the one-stop shop **Viajero Outdoor Centre** (857 1799, 0917 708 1568; www.viajerocdo.com; 137 Hayes St, Cagayan de Oro). Eric and Reina Bontuyan can arrange, teach and guide mountain treks, rock climbing and spelunking trips in the area.

Consider a hike to the top of Mt Kitanglad (2899m), the fourth-highest peak in the country, or to Mt Sumagaya (2248m) for spectacular panoramic views. Mt Balatukan (2400m) is the most strenuous, in part because of the lack of shade. The Talaandig, an indigenous group living in Bukidnon Province, are the mountains' caretakers and ritually sacrifice three chickens (P500) for every group of climbers.

A sample fee, for guiding alone, is P2000 for a two-day, one-night expedition. The best months for climbing these summits are from February to May (December and January are less ideal but doable), as otherwise you'll likely experience lots of rain and slippery slopes. Night-time wind chill temperatures can get downright frosty, especially in the 'summer months', and cold-weather clothes and gear are necessary. Check out www.pinoymountaineer for more information.

The largest caves are found in the Palaopao range, some 25 million years old. Paiyak Cave is the burial site for local indigenous people whose dead are placed in clay pots, whereas Sumalsag Cave is a more active trip involving wading and swimming.

people visit while at the adventure park as part of a rafting tour.

Makahambus Adventure Park ADVENTURE PARK
(0916 234 6776; sky bridge, zipline & rappelling P500; 8am-5pm) This is a common stop for rafters, since it's on the way to the river. There's a 120ft-long sky bridge tethered over 40m above the jungle, a zipline and rappelling on offer. Rafting companies offer the sky bridge and zipline at a discount (P200) as part of a package.

Mapawa Nature Park ADVENTURE PARK
(272 5265; admission P40; 9am-5pm Tue-Fri, from 7.30am Sat & Sun) Only a few kilometres from Malasag, this nature park has a zipline and natural water slide and pools – a canyoning package is P1000.

Malaybalay & Around

088 / POP 144,000 / ELEV 857M

Sitting on a plateau at the top of Mindanao, Malaybalay is the capital of Bukidnon, a topographically dramatic province. From Overview, on top of the hill in Quezon south of Valencia, you can see all the way to Cotabato on a clear day. (There's a **sculpture park** here with gigantic representations of the tribal groups that call the region home – Bukidnon, Higgonon, Matissalug and Umayammon.)

Driving up to Malaybalay from Cagayan, you'll see the impressive 3000m Mt Kitanglad in the distance; it's one of the highest mountains in the Philippines and still a habitat of the Philippine eagle. Much of the area has been deforested to make way for huge banana, carrot, pineapple and sugar cane plantations; virtually all of this produce is exported. Hiking to one of the more than 20 **waterfalls** in the area around the Bukidnon–Davao Hwy, commonly referred to as BuDa, is possible with some help from locals or guides from Cagayan de Oro.

About 40 minutes north of Malaybalay is the **Impalutao Reforestation Centre**, which offers hiking in one of the only untouched forests in the region. Artificial pools fed by springs, waterfalls and rivers throughout the reserve offer some cool places to swim. Take a bus from Cagayan to Malaybalay, but ask the conductor to let you know where to get off. From Malaybalay's public market there are regular jeepneys (20 minutes).

Just north of Valencia (south of Malaybalay), off the highway, is the pyramid-shaped **Monastery of the Transfiguration**, worth a visit if only for the gorgeous drive into the hills. You will need to hire a motorcycle to take you, as there is no public transport.

From mid-February to late March, Malaybalay is the setting for the annual **Kaamulan Festival**, celebrating the dances, songs, stories and delicacies of the area's different tribal groups.

On the highway in Malaybalay is the **Pine Hills Hotel** (☎221 3211; r from P900; ❄) and restaurant; at the lower end of the spectrum there's **Haus Malibu** (☎221 2714; Bonifacio Dr; r P200-700; ❄).

Iligan

☎063 / POP 308,000

Although it's promoted as the 'City of Magnificent Waterfalls', the inevitable first impression you have of Iligan is of a sprawling industrial park with countless cement and food-processing factories. Hydroelectric power (supplies 95% of Mindanao's needs) harnessed from the water of Lake Lanao in the hills above the city has meant Iligan has outstripped its neighbours in terms of development, though it still lags in terms of charm.

Sights & Activities

If you need assistance or ideas, Pat Noel from the **Iligan Tourism Office** (☎0919 320 9944; www.iligan.gov.ph) can act as a guide or simply provide travel advice.

President Gloria Macapagal-Arroyo's Childhood Summer Home NOTABLE BUILDING
Directly in front of Timoga Springs, along the main highway, this is only really interesting to political buffs. Perhaps most curious are the family photos of her from child to sultry adult (she's lying down on her side wearing a slinky gown in one large painting).

Timoga Springs POOLS
The super-cold Timoga Springs are refreshing on a hot day; plenty of food stalls surround these developed pools complete with slides.

Tinago Falls WATERFALL
(admission P10) Hidden deep in a mountain, Tinago Falls is the most spectacular of Iligan's waterfalls; you can drive to the start of the very steep stairway (365 steps) down. During the wet season, it's a loud violent cascade, but no matter what time of year, you can swim in the pool at the base (life vests are provided). There's even a jerry-rigged bamboo version of Niagara Falls' Maid of the Mist to take you into the spray.

Maria Cristina Falls WATERFALL
(admission P30) Even though the twin Maria Cristina Falls are being harnessed for their hydroelectric power, you can climb to the top of an observation tower for excellent views (there's a small zipline, eatery and crocodile park at the base).

Sleeping & Eating

Pinakurat, a chopped wild boar dish, is an Iligan speciality (hunting banned except in Muslim areas).

Rene's Diner & Pension House HOTEL $
(☎223 8441; r with fan/air-con P350/480; ❄📶) While Iligan is easily reachable by bus from Cagayan de Oro, the most convenient option if you want to spend the night is Rene's, directly on the main road, a few minutes west of the centre.

Corporate Inn Boutique Hotel HOTEL $
(☎221 4456; corpor8inn@yahoo.com; 5 Sparrow St, Isabel Village; s/d incl breakfast from P750/1050; ❄) Quieter but more out of the way, this is a more personable place than the unfortunate name implies, especially the outdoor sitting area. A handful of restaurants are within walking distance.

Cheradel Suites HOTEL $$
(☎0917 459 6773; Jeffery Rd; r incl breakfast from P1590; ❄📶🏊) The somewhat kitschy top-end choice in Iligan is about five minutes east of town. It's near the post office and Landbank.

Gloria's Ihaw Ihaw FILIPINO $
(mains P100) Across the street along the waterfront from Timoga Springs is Gloria's Ihaw Ihaw, serving delicious *kinilaw,* grilled fish and chicken.

Shopping

If you're after Islamic crafts, try **Jolo Iligan Trading** (Quezon Ave) or the **central market** (⏰5am-7pm) for weavings, traditional batiks and brassware.

Marawi & Lake Lanao

☎063 / POP 177,000

Marawi (officially known as the 'Islamic City of Marawi') sits prettily in a bowl of hills on Lake Lanao's northern shore. Considered the Islamic centre of the Philippines – there are functioning sharia courts and over 90% of its population is Muslim – daily rhythms here follow the beat of religious worship. The city's residents have preserved aspects of their traditional royal-heavy system of government, replete with a sultan, queen, *datu* (pre-Hispanic tribal chieftain) and princess. Leaders are mostly focused on social rather than administrative issues, and mediate conflicts between families – the downside to strong family ties, feuds can sometimes produce bad blood and violent reprisals that last for generations.

A road around the circumference of Lake Lanao, the second-largest lake in the Philippines and one of the deepest, means all the communities are easily accessible by road. Maranao or M'ranao, originally 'Maranaw', is the term used to refer to the people of Lanao, and is derived from the two words *taw* and *ranaw*, and literally means 'man of the lake'. The lake is the source of the Agus River that flows near Iligan, powering the hydroelectric power plants. Two intricately designed mosques are on the shore of the lake in the town of Bacolod.

Places to visit include the **Aga Khan Museum** (⏲9am-noon & 1-4pm) and the imposing **King Faisal Mosque** at the Mindanao State University (MSU) campus on the eastern edge of the city; the **palitan** (market) for carved wooden chests, fabrics and brassware crafted in Tugaya township across the lake; **Dayawan weaving village** outside the city proper; and in barangay Tokah, the ceremonial wooden **Torongan** buildings built on rocks, an example of how early Maranao royalty lived. If you're fortunate enough to visit during a festival or other public ceremony, you'll have a chance to hear *kulintang*, a musical genre similar to Indonesian gamelan.

The only proper hotel in town is the **Marawi Resort Hotel** (☎0917 716 6379; marawiresorthotel@yahoo.com; cottages P1300; ❄≋), located on the sprawling grounds of the MSU campus overlooking the lake. There's a restaurant, a golf course, a nice pool and good views of the lake.

SAFETY & SECURITY

This area has seen its fair share of violence; however, the threat of kidnapping for ransom is the most relevant danger to keep in mind. The region is best visited with a guide arranged from the Iligan or Cagayan de Oro tourism offices who knows the lay of the land. A handful of armed guards are usually part of the package and might unnerve some enough to reconsider.

Jeepneys and buses both run regularly between Iligan and Marawi (P50, one hour). A return trip by taxi from Iligan (if you can find a driver to take you), with a couple of hours' waiting time, will cost you around P2000. Alternatively, there are buses from Cagayan de Oro to Marawi (P250, 3½ hours) via Iligan.

Camiguin

☎088 / POP 70,000

Relatively unspoiled and of an ideal size for exploration, Camiguin (cah-mee-*geen*) can be singled out for its imposing silhouette – drop it down next to Hawaii or Maui and it wouldn't look out of place. With over 20 cinder cones 100m-plus high, Camiguin has more volcanoes per square kilometre than any other island on earth. Because it's uncorrupted by large-scale tourism – the 10km waters of Gingoog Bay separating the island from the mainland are partly responsible – those who do come here tend to feel proprietorial about this little jewel and guard news of its treasures like a secret. Besides the usual diving, snorkelling, sandy beaches, waterfalls and hot and cold springs, Camiguin offers the chance for jungle trekking, volcano climbing, rappelling and anything else the masochistic endurance athlete can dream up.

Mambajao (mah-bow-ha), the capital of Camiguin, is about half an hour's ride from the port at Benoni. There are shops, a market, government buildings and a few places to overnight, but most visitors stay closer to the northern beaches.

Sights & Activities

The waters surrounding Camiguin are good for diving, especially for beginners who can see interesting rock formations in shallow waters, a result of the lava flow from Hibok-Hibok's previous eruptions. There are over 10 sites of note especially good for beginners; the best diving is probably off White Island and Mantigue Island. If you're already a diver, expect to pay about P2800 for two boat dives including equipment. Snorkelling equipment is rented out for P200 (mask and snorkel), plus another P200 for fins and booties.

Climbing, trekking, mountain biking, horse riding, fishing, rappelling and any other action adventure can be booked through Camiguin Action Geckos or Johnny's Dive N

Camiguin

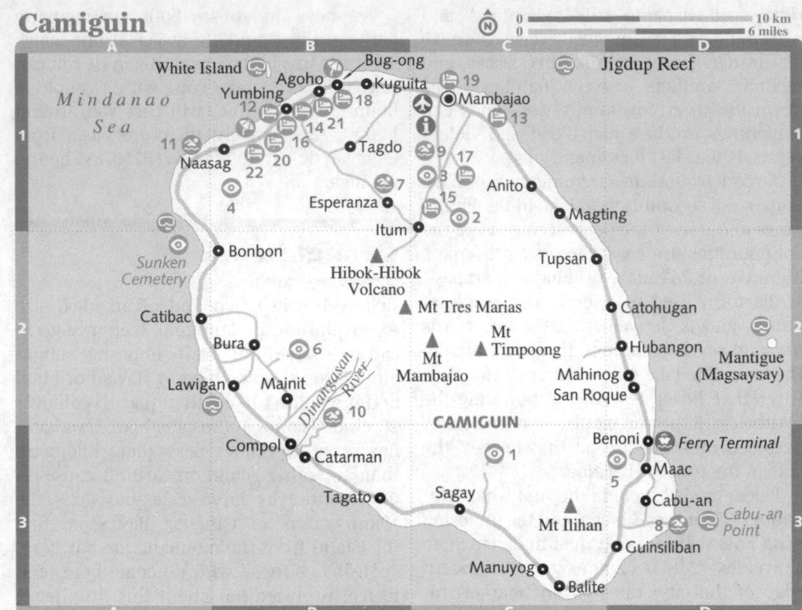

Fun, or through your accommodation. Trips up Hibok-Hibok or a trek across the island cost around P1660 per person. Excursions can be tailored to any specifications, from beginner to experienced.

Camiguin Action Geckos OUTDOOR ADVENTURE
(☎387 9146; www.camiguinaction.com) Diving and other activities can be arranged through Camiguin Action Geckos, at the resort of the same name.

Johnny's Dive N Fun DIVING
(☎387 9588; www.johnnysdive.com) This outfit has offices at Caves Dive Resort and Paras Beach Resort.

Free Diving DIVING
(www.freediving-philippines.com) If you want to go deep old-school style, free diving is now being taught by a German instructor based at Camiguin Action Geckos for four weeks every May. Groups of four or more might be able to arrange customised courses at other times.

BENONI TO MAMBAJAO

Mantigue Island DIVING, SNORKELLING
Between Benoni and Mambajao you'll see Mantigue Island – sometimes called Magsaysay – offshore. A few fishing families live here and a marine sanctuary means there's still some good coral in the cordoned area and stretches of a pretty white-sand beach. A return trip to the island from the village of Mahinog will cost P550. It's also a popular dive site; the island usage fees – entrance (P20), environmental fee (P30), plus P120 for divers (P80 for snorkellers) – are usually included in most dive packages.

Hibok-Hibok Volcano HIKING
Hibok-Hibok volcano (1320m), which last erupted in 1951 (when nearly 600 people were killed as a result), provides a dramatic spark – no pun intended – to the island's interior. Housed in a new building about 525m off the main road is the **Philippine Institute of Volcanology & Seismology (Philvolcs) Station**, which monitors the volcano's activity. A hired motorcycle or multicab will take you there to see the lacklustre equipment and memorabilia of past eruptions. It's possible to climb the volcano, but be warned that it's a demanding three-plus-hour steep, rocky climb and you should be reasonably fit (only possible in dry weather). Most resorts can provide guides (P1500, plus admission P500 per person); aim to leave around daybreak if you want to get up and down in a day. From the peak it's possible to see Bohol, Cebu and Negros on a clear day.

Camiguin

Sights

1 Binangawan Falls C3
2 Katibawasan Falls C1
3 Philippine Institute of Volcanology & Seismology (Philvolcs) Station C1
4 Stations of the Cross B1
5 Taguines Lagoon D3
6 Tuwasan Falls B2

Activities, Courses & Tours

7 Ardent Hot Springs B1
Camiguin Action Geckos .... (see 14)
8 Cantaan Kabila White Beach Giant Clam Sanctuary D3
Johnny's Dive N Fun .... (see 16)
9 Saii Springs C1
10 Santo Niño Cold Spring B2
11 Tangub Hot Spring A1

Sleeping

12 Agohay Resort B1
13 Bahay-Bakasyunan sa Camiguin C1
14 Camiguin Action Geckos Resort B1
15 Camiguin Highland Resort C1
16 Caves Dive Resort B1
17 Enigmata Treehouse Ecolodge C1
18 Jasmine by the Sea B1
19 Mambajao C1
20 Paras Beach Resort B1
Puesta del Sol .... (see 22)
21 Seascape B1
22 Secret Cove Beach Resort B1

Eating

Luna Ristorante .... (see 20)
Mambajao .... (see 19)
Puesta del Sol .... (see 22)

Ardent Hot Springs HOT SPRINGS

(admission P30; 24hr) Head out late in the afternoon when the air temperature has cooled down for the lukewarm to hot waters. The big pool is emptied for cleaning on Wednesday and takes the best part of the day to refill. The springs are in a lush but developed setting and get very busy on weekends.

Katibawasan Falls WATERFALL

(admission P25) A beautiful clear stream of water dropping more than 70m to a plunge pool where you can swim and picnic. The few souvenir kiosks and concrete walkway means it doesn't feel like a natural refuge. A special trip by jeepney or multicab from Mambajao will cost about P300 return; from the resorts around Agoho it's about P350 return.

FREE **Saii Springs** COLD SPRINGS

Around 4km-plus (the final 1km is walked) inland from the church in Mambajao is this concrete pool fed with cold spring water.

Taguines Lagoon LAGOON

Just south of Benoni is the artificial Taguines Lagoon, used primarily as a fish-breeding area.

NORTH COAST TO GUINSILIBAN

Kuguita, **Bug-ong**, **Agoho** and **Yumbing** are the most developed of the northern beaches, and where much of the accommodation is located. However, because of erosion, a great deal of the actual beach between Agoho and Yumbing has gone missing. In fact, a number of sea walls have had to be erected to protect seafront properties. Where the beach does still exist, it's of the dark and coarse variety, a result of the island's volcanic activity.

Tuwasan Falls WATERFALL

About 10km further along the island road from Bonbon is Catarman (the town was destroyed by the 1871 eruption of nearby Mt Vulcan Daan), near which is the little-visited and unspoiled Tuwasan Falls. The road here is mostly paved and a tricycle or motorbike can take you to the start of the path. From there it's about a 15-minute hike down a steep and narrow trail to the falls, walking twice through the river (not possible after heavy rain as the river is too high). The falls thunder into a pool, which may be too rough to plunge into; or simply scamper over boulders and plunge into pools, making your own private canyoning tour! There's a cold-water pool in **Bura** on the way to the falls.

Cantaan Kabila White Beach Giant Glam Sanctuary BEACH

Some of the best-preserved coral around Camiguin, as well as giant clams, can be found in the waters just off this small white-sand beach halfway between Benoni and Guinsiliban in barangay Cantaan. The family that owns the property maintains the site and charges for a guide (P150), entrance (P50) and environmental fee (P25), and can rent a mask and snorkel for P250. You can observe clams being bred in tanks for free.

Binangawan Falls WATERFALL

This, the shortest of the falls at 15m or so, is one of the most difficult to reach and only advisable with a guide arranged through your accommodation or the tourism office (P1500). The turn-off is just past the village of Sagay; from here it's another 5km or so up until the road begins to deteriorate and then another few kilometres at a steep pitch along a rough rocky path. Actually reaching the falls involves plenty of walking; bring water and protection from the elements.

Tangub Hot Spring HOT SPRING

Water temperatures at the Tangub Hot Spring fluctuate with the tides, from cold to warm to hot, depending on the source; a volcanic spring below the sea bed provides the hot water at this completely undeveloped site around 12km west of Mambajao.

White Island BEACH

(admission P20) Uninhabited White Island (Medano Island), a pure, white-sand bar a few hundred metres offshore, is accessible by boats (P400) that now only leave from a spot next to Paras Beach Resort. If you visit at any time but the early morning, the sun can be brutally intense. The shape of the island is constantly evolving, fighting a constant battle against the tide, erosion and occasional sand theft.

Santo Niño Cold Spring COLD SPRING

(admission P20; ⏲24hr) Close to Catarman and several kilometres off the highway along a paved road.

Stations of the Cross VIEWPOINT

Just before Bonbon you'll pass the Old Camiguin Volcano, whose slopes have been turned into a steep and beautiful Stations of the Cross. There are great views from the top and a bunch of souvenir stalls selling cheap T-shirts and the like clustered at the bottom of the steps.

Sunken Cemetery LANDMARK

Between the hillside and Bonbon you'll see an enormous white cross floating on a pontoon in the bay, marking the spot of the Sunken Cemetery, which slipped into the sea following the earthquake of 1871; it's now a snorkelling and diving spot.

The same earthquake destroyed the 17th-century **Spanish church** in Bonbon; its quiet ruins still stand, with grazing cattle nearby and a makeshift altar inside.

Spanish Watchtower HISTORIC SITE

In Guinsiliban, behind the elementary school by the pier, are the remains of this centuries-old sight which used to guard against possible Moro attacks from the mainland. A pretty shrine is maintained here.

Festivals & Events

Lanzones Festival CULTURAL

Camiguin is widely recognised for having the sweetest *lanzones* (small yellow fruit that taste like a mix of lemons and lychees) in the archipelago. The Lanzones Festival, the annual paean to this delicacy, is celebrated around the third week of October. Gluttony is encouraged during a week of parades, pageants and dancing.

Panaad RELIGIOUS

During Holy Week, the Panaad involves a 64km walk around the island, an expression of devotees' penitence and commitment. Stations of the Cross are placed on the route, ending with 'Tabo' on Easter Sunday in Mambajao.

Sleeping & Eating

MAMBAJAO & AROUND

Mambajao has several simple eateries, groceries and market stalls; stop by **Vjandeap Bakery** for the island's speciality pastries. The Rooftop Hotel has the best restaurant.

Bahay-Bakasyunan sa Camiguin HOTEL $$

(☎088 387 1057; www.bahay-bakasyunan.com; r incl breakfast from P2750; ❄@📶🏊) The class act of Camiguin, this resort extends all the way from the highway to the water, shaded by a towering grove of coconuts. Stylish and modern A-frame cottages (from P4000) face older bamboo bungalows across a manicured lawn that runs down to a seaside pool and restaurant.

Enigmata Treehouse Ecolodge HOSTEL $

(☎0918 230 4184; http://camiguinecolodge.com; dm/ste from P200/800; @🏊) Alternative-eco meets alternative-art at this treehouse-cum-lodge. Everywhere you look there are branches and bottles and fabrics – not surprisingly, privacy isn't a priority, but communal living is. It's located up a hill off the main road (look for the large tribal Tarzan statue) about 2km southeast of Mambajao;

phone before turning up. As it is, you're pretty much left to your own devices.

Camiguin Highland Resort HOTEL $$
(☎0920 953 3295; www.camiguinhighlandresort.com; r from P2300; ❄@≋) Resembling a nouveau-riche suburban McMansion, this fish-out-of-water resort is perched halfway up a mountain. Apart from the lush surroundings, it's a completely artificial creation, but worthwhile scenery is only a minute or two away on foot or horseback. There's a good restaurant, a coffee shop, a pool and a spa bath.

Rooftop Hotel & Restaurant HOTEL $$
(☎0918 589 8915; www.camiguinrooftophotel.com; cnr Neriz & Rizal Sts, Mambajao; r from P2000; ❄ᯤ) Each of the seven individually and curiously themed rooms on the 3rd floor has high ceilings and homey touches. The ground-floor **restaurant** (mains P170; ⊙6am-11pm) qualifies as the finest dining in Mambajao, serving up pizzas (P250), burgers, sandwiches and Filipino standards. There's a billiards table and movies are sometimes screened on the 2nd floor.

GV Hotel HOTEL $
(☎387 1041; Burgos St, Mambajao; r without/with air-con P330/530; ❄) Offers basic accommodation in Mambajao.

Camiguin Island Grill FILIPINO $
(mains P130) For inexpensive barbecue chicken (P60) and grilled fish and prawns; out on the highway east of Mambajao.

J&A Fishpen SEAFOOD $
(mains P170) Seafood comes straight from the pens on the Benoni lagoon this restaurant overlooks.

NORTHERN BEACHES

TOP CHOICE Camiguin Action Geckos Resort BEACH RESORT $
(☎387 9146; www.camiguinaction.com; r without bathroom P600, cottages with bathroom from P1800) Every island in the Philippines should have a place just like this. 'Rustic sophistication' says it all – you'll find perfectly constructed, spacious, hard-wood cottages with verandahs combined with touches of class and taste. For more value, try one of the small but appealing 'travellers' rooms' upstairs from the open-air restaurant. Every type of outdoor activity possible can be organised here, and there's a full-service dive shop on the premises. To top it all off, it sits on one of the widest stretches of beach around.

Caves Dive Resort BEACH RESORT $$
(☎0918 807 6888; www.cavesdiveresort.com; Agoho; r without bathroom P700, cottages with fan/air-con incl breakfast from P1500/2500; ❄ᯤ) This resort, located on a fairly wide stretch of sand, has a bit of a split personality. The once-charming main beachfront building with a restaurant and basic bamboo rooms is rundown, while the concrete garden cottages towards the back of the property are well kept. One of Johnny's Dive N Fun shops is here.

Agohay Resort HOTEL $
(0928 410 4994; agohayvillaforte@yahoo.com; Agoho; dm P200, r with fan/air-con P800/1200) This large property leads from an enormous native-style dorm pavilion down to a beachfront restaurant. Besides two large rooms that can sleep six, there's one smaller, overdecorated room worth a stay for the outdoor shower area landscaped with rocks and plants. Well managed only when owners on property.

Seascape BUNGALOW $
(☎0910 920 6152; Bug-ong; cottages/r P500/700) Hemmed in by a neighbouring McMansion and a seawall instead of beach, Seascape seems alternately laid-back or abandoned – you can wander the overgrown property undisturbed or unhelped. On the plus side are two large bamboo rooms with seaside balconies; there are several other poorly maintained bungalows set back in the yard. The restaurant is good for a sunset drink.

Puesta del Sol HOTEL $$
(☎0915 334 8608; ww.puestadelsol-camiguin.com; Yumbing; r P2000; ≋) A quiet little compound with a postage-stamp-sized pool and equally small beach surrounded by large concrete walls. Only two rooms with especially nice bathrooms and a small restaurant.

Secret Cove Beach Resort HOTEL $$
(☎387 9084; www.secretcovecamiguin.net; Yumbing; r P1400; ❄) Personable owners, excellent food and a well-stocked bar at this compact and tranquil spot. Some of the rooms, however, lack natural light and could use some attention.

Jasmine by the Sea HOTEL $
(☎387 9015; melindawidmer@yahoo.com; Bug-ong; r with fan P800) Only four small basic

rooms line one side of a pleasant open-air bar-restaurant, which serves good Western and Filipino food.

Paras Beach Resort BEACH RESORT **$$**
(☎0926 944 3606; www.parasbeachresort.com; r from P2250; ❄📶🏊) Typical at resorts of this kind, popular only with large Filipino groups and families, in lieu of a beach there's a pool, and in lieu of quiet there's loud music. The furnishings and decor in some rooms have been upgraded nicely while others languish. The complex also offers billiards, a bar, restaurant and water sports.

Luna Ristorante ITALIAN **$$**
(mains P200; ⏱7am-midnight; 📶) Located on the main road in Yumbing, right after the turn-off for the Paras Beach Resort. It does excellent brick-oven pizza, especially a seafood version, and you can spend the afternoon outside in the concrete gazebo.

Puesta del Sol MEXICAN **$$**
(mains P185) When the owners are here at this restaurant next to Secret Cove it's well managed and pleasant.

 Information

Philippine National Bank (PNB) and Landbank in Mambajao have unreliable ATMs; don't count on being able to use them with foreign cards. PNB changes US dollars but only accepts crisp bills $5 and above (travellers report difficulty changing euros). A better option is the **All in One Island** store, on the road between the Rooftop Hotel & Restaurant and church, which changes US dollars and euros at good rates.

There are two internet cafes on Rizal St.

Fun Trips Travel & Tours (☎387 0380; www.funtripstravelcamiguin.com; B Aranas St, Mambajao) One of the only independent operations, primarily a travel agency. All of the hotels can arrange island tours and a variety of day trips.

Tourist office (☎387 1097; www.camiguin.gov.ph; Provincial Capitol Bldg; ⏱8am-5pm Mon-Fri) Part of a complex of government buildings up a hill just southwest of Mambajao.

 Getting There & Away

Air

Fly Avia Tour (☎in Cebu 032-495 2268, 0910 805 9846; www.flyaviatour.com) Runs charter flights to Cebu (per person P4000, minimum two) and other destinations. The airport is a few kilometres west of Mambajao.

Mid-Sea Express (☎0927 634 4632; www.midseaexpress.com) Operates thrice-weekly flights to Cebu (P1950); the schedule is fluid.

Boat

Ferries cross from Benoni, 18km south of Mambujao, to Balingoan on the mainland roughly hourly from 4am until 3.30pm (P170, one hour). Departures from Balingoan to Benoni are from 4.30am to 6pm. Oceanjet has a fast ferry to Balingoan at 8.30am (P250, 30 minutes).

From the Balbagon pier near Mambajao, Super Shuttle Ferry has a daily 8am car ferry (P425, 3½ hours) to Jagna and a Sunday-evening car ferry to Cebu (P880, 11 hours). Oceanjet has a daily fast-craft ferry from Benoni to Jagna (P550, two hours) at 2.20pm.

There's no longer a daily fastcraft service to Cagayan de Oro; however, Oceanjet or another company might take over this route.

 Getting Around

The road around the island is 64km long, so it's possible to make the circuit in a few hours. For ease of travel and access to places that jeepneys don't go, the best option is to rent a motorcycle (P300 to P500); less thrilling but convenient is to hire a multicab that can comfortably seat six (P1500) and take you around for a day.

Air-con minivans, jeepneys, motorellas (the local term for motorised tricycles) and multicabs meet arriving boats in Benoni to transport passengers to Mambajao (P25, 40 minutes). A special ride to Mambajao costs P100 to P150 ; to the resorts north of Mambajao you'll pay P250. From Mambajao, hop on a 'westbound' tricycle for the majority of resorts.

Balingoan

POP 9000

About halfway between Cagayan de Oro and Butuan, Balingoan is the main jumping-off point to Camiguin. Boats (P170, one hour) run about every hour from 4.30am to 6pm. Ocean Jet has a fast ferry (P250, 30 minutes), though its departure time from Balingoan was up in the air at the time of reseach.

Regular buses run between Balingoan and Cagayan de Oro (P145, 1¾ hours), and Butuan (P350, 2¼ hours). It's a short walk from the Balingoan bus terminal to the pier.

Butuan

☎085 / POP 298,000

Historical and archaeological interest aside, this city sprawled along the banks of the Agusan River, 9km south of the coast, is a typical provincial city in every way – traffic-clogged streets and fractured footpaths make walking a challenge. It is, however, a logical stop, even for a night, if you're travelling between the islands of Camiguin and Siargao. A major port to some degree since at least the 4th century, Butuan is widely recognised as the earliest known place of settlement and sea trade in the Philippines.

Towards the airport is the **Balangay Shrine Museum** (admission free; ⌚8.30am-4.30pm Mon-Sat) at barangay Libertad, home to the remains of a *balangay* (seagoing outrigger boat) dating from 321, one of the oldest known artefacts in the Philippines. (The word 'barangay' in fact derives from *balangay,* as the boats were big enough to move whole communities of settlers in one journey.) Unearthed only a few metres away are several coffins dating to the 13th and 14th centuries. A tricycle (per hour P100) will take you to the site, which is uninspiring in and of itself; the ride out here through several small communities is worthwhile.

Like Limasawa in Leyte, Butuan claims the honour of the first Mass (8 April 1521) held by Magellan on Philippine soil at nearby **Magallanes**, north of the city at the mouth of the Agusan River where it empties into Butuan Bay; a memorial marks the spot.

Sleeping

VCDU Prince Hotel HOTEL $

(☎342 7267; Montilla Blvd; www.vcduprincehotel.com.ph; s/d P800/P1000; ❄📶) A no-brainer if you have a night in the city, this centrally located high-rise offers the best value even if rooms are minuscule.

Almont City Hotel HOTEL $$

(☎342 5263; www.almont.com.ph; San José St, Rizal Park; r incl breakfast from P1500; ❄📶) A more upscale, contemporary and even more centrally located choice on the northern side of Rizal Park.

Butuan Luxury Hotel HOTEL $

(☎342 5366; Villanueva St; s/d P800/1100; ❄📶) One of the better budget choices is this inaccurately named hotel; on the plus side, rooms are clean and some get good natural light.

Eating

There are a handful of fast-food joints in the Rizal Park area, as well as in Gaisano Mall, the biggest mall in the city, and also a few kilometres west of the centre on JC Aquino St.

Margie's Kitchen CAFE $$

(1342 Sentro Bldg, JC Aquino St; mains from P150; ⌚10am-1am; 📶) Looks like an upscale university coffee house and has an eclectic menu, but the drinks and desserts are the real draw.

Weegols Grill Haus FILIPINO $$

(Montilla Blvd; mains P160) A Butuan institution, serving up roasted chicken, soups and other meat dishes.

Rosarios CHINESE, FILIPINO $$

(JC Aquino St; mains from P170) Serves tasty Chinese, Filipino and seafood dishes in an almost antiseptically clean restaurant. Specials include bird's nest with dried scallops and assorted hotpots (P225 for four to six people).

Getting There & Away

Air

The airport, 10km west of the city centre, is reachable by taxi (P200) or tricycle (P150). Airphil Express, Cebu Pacific and PAL have several flights a day from Manila, and Cebu Pacific has direct flights to Cebu.

Boat

Butuan's main port area is at Nasipit, about 24km west of town. Jeepneys run between Nasipit and Butuan (30 minutes).

SuperFerry has boats running twice a week between Manila and Nasipit (P1800, 20 hours), Jagna (P750, seven hours) on Bohol and Cebu (P900, 10 hours).

Bus

The bus terminal is 3.5km north of the city centre; few taxis but plenty of tricycles wait to ferry you into town. The last bus of the day for Davao leaves at around 2.30pm; however, ordinary buses leave periodically 24 hours. In general, buses leave every 30 minutes to an hour. Duration figures and prices are for air-con buses.

DESTINATION	FARE (P)	DURATION (HR)
Balingoan	195	2¼
Cagayan de Oro	325	4½
Davao	500	7¼
Surigao	195	3

Surigao

☎086 / POP 132,000

For those heading to Siargao Island, this fairly nondescript city, the capital of Surigao del Norte Province, is usually a necessary overnight stop. The town plaza is the centre of activity, hosting everything from impromptu chess matches to first dates, while the long waterfront boulevard is a strictly functional expanse. Attractions in the area include **Silop Cave**, 7km away, with its 12 entrances leading to a big central chamber; **Day-asin**, a floating village, 5km from the city; and **Mati**, to the south, where the Mamanwas people have created a 'village' to showcase their culture. There are also several beaches nearby, including **Mabua Pebble Beach**, where you can spend a few hours waiting for your outbound flight.

Though it's much larger than Siargao and closer to the mainland, the island of **Dinagat** (nah-gat) sees few visitors, primarily because accommodation is limited. However, the rugged and wild coastline certainly warrants more attention. The island is home to several fishing communities and the northwest coast is especially picturesque, featuring jungle-clad karst formations jutting out of turquoise waters. During Holy Week, pilgrims visit the twin lakes of **Bababu** on an islet near Basilia, believing the waters have curative powers. Three daily bangkas (P100, four hours) leave at 8am, 10am and noon from in front of the Tavern Hotel for San José on Dinagat.

Sleeping

EY Tourist Pension HOTEL $$
(☎826 5440, 0921 425 1846; Navarro St; s/d from P780/900;) The hotel of choice of Siargao expats. Sure, it has the mirrored-glass facade of a Chinese office building and the lobby's plastic ambience screams massage parlour, but the small carpeted rooms with hot and cold shower and cable TV are the best value in Surigao.

Tavern Hotel HOTEL $$
(☎826 8566; www.surigaoislands.com/tavernhotel; Borromeo St; r incl breakfast from P1500;) The most upscale place in Surigao and the only hotel to take advantage of the city's waterfront location. More sophisticated sea-view rooms in the newer annex are worth the price. In addition there's a bar (open 5pm to 1am) with live music most nights of the week and an outdoor coffee shop (open 6am to 1am).

Metro Pension Plaza HOTEL $
(☎231 9899; Navarro St; s/d P500/700;) Regardless of whether you're alone, definitely opt for the larger rooms with matrimonial beds, otherwise the dim rooms feel gloomy.

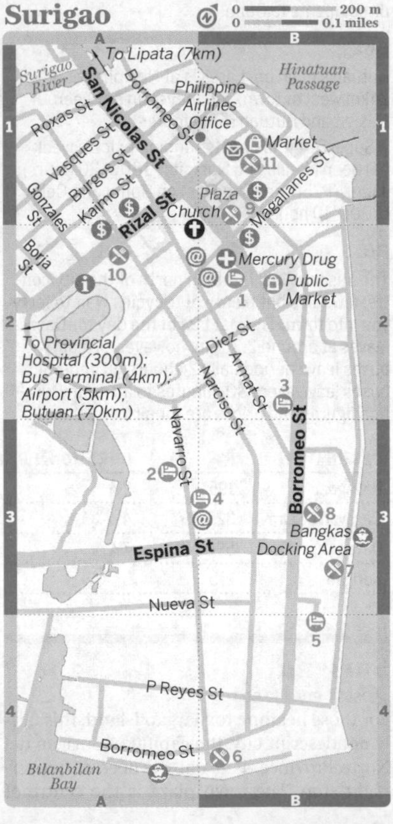

Surigao

Sleeping
1 Dexter Pension House B2
2 EY Tourist Pension A3
3 Lemondee Hotel B2
4 Metro Pension Plaza B3
5 Tavern Hotel B4

Eating
6 Barbecue Stalls B4
7 Calda's B3
8 Frank Lloyd Jazz Bar B3
9 Fruit Stalls B1
10 Island's Seafood Restaurant A2
11 Mario's Garden Grill & Restaurant B1
Red Table Dim Sum .... (see 11)

Drinking
BG & C Coffeehouse .... (see 11)
Rab's Book Café .... (see 11)

FOLLOWING THE WAVES TO THE NEXT BREAK

A few dedicated foreigners who swear by the surf at Cloud Nine on Siargao – speak to Wilmar of **Hippie's Surf Shop** (☎0928 744 0495; www.surfshopsiargao.com) for information – report equally great breaks around **Lanuza**, but you need to set aside several days simply to get there and back. November and December are the best months for surfing and you can arrange a homestay with Jerry Erizara, currently the vice-mayor of Lanuza (his number often changes, so ask around). A rickety bus or jeepney from Surigao takes around five hours; if coming from Siargao, you can take the daily 6am boat from Dapa to Socorro on Bucas Grande Island (one hour) and from there transfer to another boat to Cantilan (two hours) on the Mindanao mainland; grab a tricycle to the terminal and hop on a jeepney marked 'Tandag' south to Lanuza (30 minutes).

The showers are cold and the toilets seat-free, but the cable TVs are top-notch.

Lemondee Hotel HOTEL $
(☎232 7334; Borromeo St; s/d P500/650; ❄📶) The aged furniture and tiny bathrooms here are sure to disappoint compared to the promising-looking yellow-and-blue facade.

Dexter Pension House PENSION HOUSE $
(☎232 7526; cnr San Nicolas & Magallanes Sts; s/d from P200/350; ❄) This is passable for low-maintenance types.

Eating

The restaurant at the Tavern Hotel is fairly ordinary. Fast-food restaurants are clustered on the southwest side of the plaza; an appetising row of fruit stalls lines the east side. Masses of barbecue stalls can be found on Borromeo St around the pier.

Island's Seafood Restaurant SEAFOOD, FILIPINO $
(Rizal St; mains P160; ❄📶) A small, bustling, modern place serving up seafood by weight (*lapu-lapu;* grouper; P80 per 100g) and standard meat and chicken dishes.

Calda's PIZZERIA $
(Borromeo St; pizza P180; 🕙9am-midnight) Massive thin-crust pizzas served up next to the Dunkin Donuts fronting the wharf just behind the Tavern Hotel.

Mario's Garden Grill & Restaurant FILIPINO $
(Borromeo St; barbecue P30; 🕙9am-midnight) An outdoor barbecue with live music next door to City Hall.

Frank Lloyd Jazz Bar FILIPINO $$
(Borromeo St; dishes P160; 🕙8am-late) Looks abandoned during the day but is more welcoming at night when there's often music.

Lined up next to one another on the driveway to Mario's are three modern places for food and drinks: **BG & C Coffeehouse** (🕙8am-11pm; 📶), a Starbucks equivalent; **Red Table Dim Sum** (dishes P50); and **Rab's Book Café** (mains P150; 📶), which serves tacos, burritos and more in a living-roomlike setting with unpleasant fluorescent lighting.

Information

There are several banks with ATMs (stock up on cash before heading to Siargao) around the plaza and a few internet cafes scattered around town.

For information about travel elsewhere in the region, the provincial **Surigao del Norte Provincial Tourism Office** (☎231 9271; Rizal St) is located by the city grandstand. There's a **BOI** (☎826 8263; Narcisco St) office for visa extensions.

Getting There & Away

Air

Airphil Express, PAL and Cebu Pacific have daily flights to Manila; the latter also has several flights a week to Cebu. The arrivals and departures coincide with boat transfers to Siargao, though connections are tight. Catch a taxi or tricycle (P30) to the airport, 5km west of the town centre.

Boat

CEBU Cebu Ferries has departures Monday, Wednesday and Friday at 11pm. Cokaliong Shipping has trips daily except Sunday at 7pm.

DINAGAT Bangkas (P100) for San José on the island of Dinagat leave at 8am, 10am and noon from the area in front of the Tavern Hotel.

LEYTE Car ferries ('ROROs') serving the Southern Leyte towns of San Ricardo (P100, 1½ hours, at 4am, 8am, 4pm and 8pm) and Liloan (P300, 3½ hours, at 6.30am, 11am, 1pm, 6pm and midnight) leave from the pier in Lipata, around 8km west of Surigao.

BUSES FROM SURIGAO

DESTINATION	FARE (P)	DURATION (HR)	FREQUENCY
Butuan	195	2¾	every half-hour or so; last air-con at 7pm
Davao	500	7	hourly
Tandag	200 (ordinary)	6	when full

MANILA SuperFerry services Manila (31 hours) several days a week at 11am.

SIARGAO Speedy, super-sized bangkas to Dapa on Siargao (P200, 2¼ hours) leave at 6am and 11am from the long wharf in front of the Tavern Hotel, as does a slightly larger and slower boat (P200, three hours, 11.30am). In bad weather, opt for the daily RORO (P250, four hours, noon), which uses the **main pier** (Borromeo St), 2km south of the plaza.

If your destination on Siargao is Burgos in the north instead of Cloud Nine, take the noon bangka (P200) to Santa Monica from **Punta Bilang Bilang**, a short walk southwest from the main pier.

Bus

The bus terminal is about 4km out of town towards the airport; a tricycle costs P30. For Cagayan de Oro, you must change buses in Butuan. See the table above for bus details.

Siargao

Initially drawn to Siargao (shar-gao) by good year-round waves and a tranquillity lost in other equally Philippine beautiful islands, a small group of passionate Aussie, American and European surfers are still living the good ol' days. There's no trussed-up tourist scene, only laid-back resorts happily making do with the tourists who find them – and it's a self-selected group. Besides surfers looking for the next challenge on their international *wanderjahr,* low-key do-it-yourself types do well here. There are rock pools, mangrove swamps, offshore islands with strange rock formations and wildlife, waterfalls, forests and hammock sitting, usually the coda to any day.

The port is in the main township of **Dapa**. On arrival you'll probably want to head straight over towards one of the resorts located along the dirt road between General Luna (known locally as GL) and 'Cloud Nine'. **Mem's** (☎0919 419 3285; r P600; ❄), right by the pier, is an acceptable place to bed for the night if you want convenience for an early-morning ferry.

Activities

Surfing is year-round, but generally considered best from August to November, when there are some big swells as a result of typhoon winds. The period from December to April has some strong crosswinds, while from May to July the surf tends to be lighter. Surfboard rental can be arranged at resorts around the island. Booties are highly recommended to protect your feet, since the break is along a reef, albeit a 'soft' one.

Siargao is also one of the few places in the country with organised **deep-sea fishing** (day trip for up to three people P5000); by all accounts it's top-notch. Reeling in a 130kg sailfish isn't uncommon – mahi-mahi and Spanish mackerel are also on the menu. The fishing's generally good year-round, although seas can be rough December through February. Contact **Junior Gonzalez** (☎0920 772 8875), who also offers accommodation at his home in Pilar.

Deep caves, such as the Blue Cathedral, and strong currents mean that diving here is for the experienced only. To arrange trips, contact **Driftwood Surf & Dive** (☎0928 302 2992; www.surfdriftwood.com) or **Siargao Divers** (☎0927 733 4805; www.siargaodivers.com).

Festivals & Events

The **Siargao Cup** surfing competition, one of the largest international sporting events in the country, is held around Cloud Nine in late September or early October. The **Filipino National Cup**, another competitive surfing event, is generally held the week before.

Information

Room rates increase during surfing tournaments and Holy Week, wherever you are on the island. The two banks in Dapa – Green Bank and Cantilan Bank – should not be relied upon for cash withdrawals (some report Green Bank accepting foreign Visa cards). Both Dapa and General Luna each have at least one internet cafe; Ocean 101

Resort in Cloud Nine has one open to nonguests and most resorts have wi-fi and a stand-alone computer for those without their own.

Getting There & Away

AIR

Cebu Pacific has twice-weekly direct flights between Cebu and Siargao's Sayak airport near Del Carmen. Another option is to fly from Manila to Surigao. A few *habal-habal* (motorcycle taxis) wait outside the airport's gates for arrivals; however, it might be more convenient to arrange transport in advance with your accommodation.

BOAT

For information on boats to Surigao, see p349. The schedule to Surigao is 5.30am and 11am for the fast bangka, 5.45am for the bigger bangka and 6am for the RORO. The early-morning departures allow you to connect to Manila flights in Surigao or travel by bus to Davao in a single day; however, it means leaving Cloud Nine extremely early. Arrange a motorcycle to Dapa through your accommodation.

Bangkas to Socorro on Bucas Grande leave from the municipal wharf next to the main one.

Getting Around

Jeepneys run from Dapa to GL (one hour); a better option is to hop on a *habal-habal* (P150 to P200, 30 minutes), motorcycles large enough to seat more than one passenger with bags and usually jerry-rigged with a canopy to guard against the elements. To tour the island on your own, the going rate for motorcycle hire is around P300 for half a day to P800 for the day.

GENERAL LUNA & AROUND

POP 13,400

Several blocks of dirt roads, dilapidated buildings and a few eateries ending in a public beach lined with a row of *sari-sari* (neighbourhood) stores: that's General Luna, and to the visitor who stays at one of the resorts on Cloud Nine, it might as well be the big city. There are several surfing breaks south of GL reached by bangka, including a few around offshore islands. A river perfect for swimming during high tide is near the village of Union, between GL and Cloud Nine.

WEATHER

Unlike other parts of Mindanao, and Manila for that matter, the wet season on Siargao coincides with the northeast *amihan*, roughly from December to March. The dry season, when the *habagat* winds blow from the southwest, is from June to September.

Sleeping

Patrick's and Cherinicole Resort are the only two places listed here in GL proper. The others are about halfway between GL and Cloud Nine on a narrow sandy beach, unfortunately not suited for swimming

Kalinaw Resort BEACH RESORT **$$$**
(0921 320 0442; www.kalinawresort.com; villas for 2 incl breakfast from P5200; wi-fi) Photos of this French-owned resort could make the centrefold of any contemporary design magazine. Creative and whimsical bathrooms are the highlight, but minimalism reigns throughout, including in the attached restaurant that does the best brick-oven pizza on the island

Island Dream Resort BEACH RESORT **$$$**
(0939 891 4538; www.islandreamsiargao.com; cottages P4000; air-con, wi-fi, pool) You might want to camp out in the bathroom for hours on end in these villas. They're equal in size to the bedrooms, with stone floors, windows to the ceiling and tubs a honeymoon couple would love. Each has their own large porch and surrounds a well-manicured lawn and pool with an open-air restaurant-lounge fronting the road.

Siargao Inn Beach Resort BUNGALOW **$$**
(0917 714 4110; www.siargao-inn.com; r with fan/air-con P1800/2500; air-con, wi-fi) Owned and operated by a young friendly couple, one of whom is a top surfer who can school you on the basics, this laid-back place has a number of cottages with nipa roofs and mahogany floors and walls; the bedding and design are pleasantly simple, and there's a beachside restaurant-bar.

Patrick's on the Beach BUNGALOW **$$**
(0918 481 6483; www.patrickonthebeach.com; r with fan/air-con from P1200/2100; @ wi-fi) Small nipa-hut cottages and a restaurant line a fairly cramped beachfront area; however, the tree house cottage (P1800) fronting the beach is unique.

Cherinicole Resort BEACH RESORT **$$**
(0918 244 4407; www.cherinicolebeachresort.com; r with fan/air-con P1000/1500; air-con, pool) Next door to Patrick's, it draws Filipino families and groups. The rooms that surround a small pool are below-average places to bed for the night.

Surigao & Around

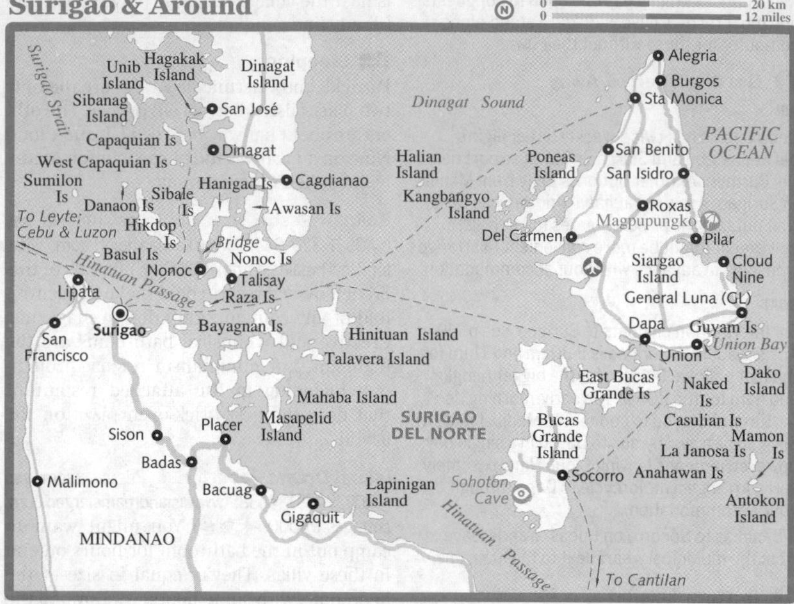

Eating & Drinking

All of the resorts have restaurants and most welcome nonguests. Marydales and Jabiness (*ha*-be-ness), both in town, are basic eateries. Any new bar, however humble a hole-in-the-wall, is liable to spur excitement in GL, as nightlife is limited; as one local expat wag put it, 'We'll go to the opening of an envelope.'

Dajon Restaurant Grill & Bar FILIPINO, INTERNATIONAL
(mains P180) Heading out of GL on the road to Dapa, Dajon is a full-service restaurant.

Wave Cave BAR
(⌚8am-late) On the dirt road heading west out of GL towards the village of Malinau, Wave Cave has an open-air 2nd floor with a pool table and porch; there's beer (P40), shots (P80) and snack food.

Nine Bar BAR
Owned by a couple of Swedish guys, Nine Bar is an expat favourite on the road between GL and Cloud Nine.

CLOUD NINE

Solidly ensconced in the international surfing circuit (if it's April it's Fiji, December, Costa Rica etc), the surf break at Cloud Nine is unmistakably marked by the rickety wood pavilion running out into the water (tip: walk where you see nails in the joists, otherwise you just might create a new hole to fall through). Billabong and Quiksilver are the only technical words you'll need to know – it's a friendly and open surfing community, with plenty of up-and-coming local Filipinos welcoming foreigners and beginners alike. There are several other breaks for the experienced, accessible by bangka, including **Rock Island**, visible from the Cloud Nine beach, and at least a dozen good beaches are within an hour by boat or road.

All the resorts here can help organise day tours and boat trips as well as arrange surf lessons (P500 per hour, including equipment) and board rental (P300 per half-day). Or stop by **Hippie's Surf Shop** (☎0928 744 0495; www.surfshopsiargao.com) just before the Ocean 101 Beach Resort; Hippie also teaches yoga classes (P200) every Monday, Wednesday and Friday at 9.30am.

Sleeping & Eating

Private homes and more basic cottages are available for short- and long-term rental; simply ask around in GL or at any of the listed resorts.

TOP CHOICE **Sagana Beach Resort** BEACH RESORT $$$

(☎0919 809 5769; www.cloud9surf.com; per person incl 3 meals P3300;) This low-key, high-end resort occupies prime beachfront real estate steps away from the Cloud Nine pavilion. Each of the Balinese-inspired cottages features dark-wood floors, porches with hammocks and large bathrooms. Owners Jerry and Susan Deegan are warm and knowledgeable about virtually everything happening on the island. Meals, dinners especially, are worth the price alone. There's a small saltwater pool to cool off in. Generally closed December through February.

Next door at the **Bones Sports Pub**, a few tables are set up around a nipa hut on the beach and a TV is tuned to international sporting events.

Ocean 101 Beach Resort HOTEL $

(☎0910 848 0893; www.ocean101cloud9.com; r P660-1100;) This is where the majority of budget-conscious surfers end up. Built on a seawall just a short walk north of the Cloud Nine break, Ocean 101 has two main buildings and a simple eatery fronting a well-trimmed lawn. Less expensive concrete rooms with little character lead out towards the road; newer and nicer rooms with high ceilings, big bathrooms and balconies with views are in front.

Boardwalk at Cloud 9 HOTEL $$

(☎0939 164 1268; www.surfingsiargao.com; r from P1350;) The absolutely prime real estate directly in front of the Cloud 9 pavilion and attractive open-air restaurant make the Boardwalk popular. Rooms are spacious, if generic, standard hotel-type. A few cheaper basic rooms are in a small native-style building in back. Staff can teach stand-up paddle boarding and kitesurfing, and help arrange every other type of water sport.

Kawayan Resort COTTAGE $$$

(☎0920 364 0663; www.kawayansiargaoresort.com; r P4500;) Just behind the highly recommended restaurant of the same name are a few beautifully crafted, sophisticated wood cottages, with stone-lined outdoor showers and toilets with palm fronds and trees poking through. It's on the opposite side of the road as the beach in a leafy garden.

Kawayan Resort has the best **restaurant** (mains P250; ⏰6am-2pm & 6-11pm) on Siargao. French-, Basque-, Moroccan- and Filipino-inspired cuisine – Moroccan tagine (P450) is the speciality – is served in a sumptuously furnished all-wood dining area.

Kesa Cloud 9 Resort HOTEL $$

(☎0921 281 2960; www.cloud9philippines.com; r with fan & shared bathroom P1200, r with air-con & private bathroom P2200;) Kesa has a great location next door to the Boardwalk, but it's less service oriented than the other accommodation. Choose from the blandly modern if comfortable rooms in the main building or small nipa hut cottages towards the rear of the resort.

Point 303 HOTEL $

(☎0946 261 4316; r P600) Owned by Ocean 101 Beach Resort and directly across the street from Sagana Resort, the 14 rooms here are basic and clean; upstairs have hot showers. A small skateboard bowl filled with water masquerades as a pool.

ℹ Getting There & Away

It's easy to get a *habal-habal* from the pier at Dapa to GL (P150 to P200, 20 minutes) or the nearby resorts, or to Cloud Nine (P250, 30 minutes), though the road turns to dirt past GL. Tricycles cost nearly the same but are much slower.

BURGOS & AROUND

Approaching the lovely little town of Burgos from the south, it's worth stopping for a minute to exhale at the top of the rise in the road, taking in the view of the crescent-shaped beach and light blue waters below. It's quite an inspiring sight. The waves here, involving long paddles out and reef breaks (six within 1km), are good for experienced surfers year-round. Contact freelance guide **Raul Cursat** (☎0912 240 5563) for island hopping or inland expeditions to a number of caves. Locals might be willing to let you tag along on fishing trips.

Bohemian Bungalows (☎0916 391 0195; www.bohemianbungalows.com; r P750) has a room on the 2nd floor of a small charming house; a rondavel guesthouse was being built during our visit. Just a little further north are a handful of cottages at **Marco's at Burgos** (☎0917 391 2238; www.marcos-at-burgos.com; r with fan/air-con P900/1200;). A few kilometres south of Burgos in barangay Pacifico is **Surf & Sail Camp Resort** (☎0919 379 6244; jafesurfandsail.com; r with fan & shared bathroom/air-con & private bathroom P500/2000;), a large octagonal-shaped house with a restaurant, beachfront property and nearby surf breaks.

Van or tricycle transfers to any of these spots from Dapa will run around P2000. Two daily 5am bangkas (P500) leave from nearby Santa Monica for Surigao on the mainland.

On the road to Burgos from Cloud Nine or Dapa you pass through barangay **Pilar**, which is largely built on stilts over mangrove flats; **Blue Cathedral** is a dive site off the coast. Not far north of Pilar is **Magpupungko**, a beach with a number of crystal-clear swimming holes at low tide; it's only a half-hour boat ride (per boat P800) from Cloud Nine, and is crowded with locals on weekends.

ISLANDS NEAR SIARGAO

Just off the southern section of Siargao is the tiny white-sand-and-palm islet of **Guyam** (Gilligan's Island); the bigger **Dako** with its beautiful beach, snorkelling and diving; and **Naked Island**. A half-day trip by bangka to all three runs to around P1500.

South of Siargao, **Bucas Grande** is worth visiting for the Sohoton Cave and Lagoon, not to be confused with the park of the same name in southern Samar. This inland lake with all kinds of weird marine creatures and nonstinging jellyfish has Chocolate Hills-like mounds rising like the humps of an underwater monster and is accessible only during low tide. An all-day trip from GL or Cloud Nine, arranged through one of the resorts, costs around P2000.

There are surf breaks around **La Janosa** and **Mamon Islands**, and it's possible to paddle a surfboard between the two. You can spend the night in one of the very primitive cottages on La Janosa. To get here, hire a bangka from the pier at GL. Prices depend on distance and time, but expect to pay around P1500 per person.

On the island of **Kangbangyo** you can take a boat to the mangrove swamps of Caob, one of the largest in the Philippines, and look for crocodiles – a bangka from Del Carmen, a town on the western side of mainland Siargao, will cost around P300, depending on how deep you want to go into the mangroves.

SOUTHERN MINDANAO

The area around Davao is ripe for adventures, from climbing Mt Apo and hiking opportunities in the Compostela Valley to exploring the long coastline, both north and south of the city, not to mention several offshore islands. It sees few foreign travellers, but does get more than its fair share of weekending Davaoeños.

Davao

☎082 / POP 1,360,000

This sprawling city – the second largest in the world in terms of land area – is the beating heart of Mindanao. It's the culinary, cultural, economic and commercial capital of the south. Mt Apo, which looms majestically in the distance, symbolises the typical Davaoeños dual citizenship as both an urbanite and someone deeply rooted to the land outside the city. Locals who leave for Manila and Cebu return years later realising Davao (dah-*bow,* and sometimes spelt 'Dabaw') has more than enough action to keep them satisfied, and yet it's only a short drive or boat ride to forested slopes and white-sand beaches.

Able to hold out against the invading Spaniards until the mid-19th century, the city is an interesting mix of Muslim, Chinese, tribal and even Japanese influences – the latter because of early abaca-processing warehouses in the area and less happily because of WWII. Predominantly Christian, the city has seen its share of hard times, especially in the 1980s when there was guerrilla fighting in the streets.

While much of the land outside the city has been turned over to massive plantations growing export quantities of pineapples, bananas and citrus, there are plenty of opportunities for off-road adventures.

Sights & Activities

Some key streets are confusingly referred to by both old and new names. The city sprawls along the Davao Gulf to the south and is bounded by the Davao River to the west.

For **diving**, see Samal Island (p360). For information on outdoor activities, including diving off Samal Island, white-water rafting and hiking, contact **Pet Pet Decastro** (☎0917 701 8314; punta_del_sol@yahoo.com) or stop by **Edge Outdoor Shop** (Wheels N More Compound, JP Laurel Ave), owned by Erwin 'Pastor' Emata, who made one of the fastest ascents of Everest in 2007. If you're planning on **rafting** the Davao River west of the city, expect to spend some time in the water, especially in rapids that resemble washing machines after heavy rains. The best time to go for thrills is June or anytime in the wet season.

FREE **Museo Dabawenyo Museum** MUSEUM
(cnr A Pichon & CM Recto Sts; ⌚9am-noon & 1-6pm Mon-Sat) An excellent museum with two floors of well-designed galleries exploring the complex patchwork of indigenous tribal groups, religions and ethnicities of Davao and Mindanao as a whole. Especially interesting are the photographic exhibitions documenting both the Japanese and American occupations of the city.

Davao Crocodile Park ZOO
(☎286 1054; www.davaocrocodilepark.com; admission P300; ⌚8am-6pm Mon-Thu, to 9pm Fri & Sat, to 7pm Sun) Around 5km north of the city centre is this large complex of facilities spread out along the Davao River. A combination conservation centre and zoo, there are croc 'shows', including feeding sessions, tightrope walking, a cultural show and excellent riverfront restaurant serving up crocodile four ways – sizzling, pasta, omelette and plain old steak – as well as other meats (including ostrich) and seafood. Also runs a zipline (P300) in the hills nearby with panoramic views.

People's Park PARK
(admission free; ⌚5-8am & 1-10pm Mon-Thu & Sun, to 11pm Fri & Sat) A family-friendly expanse of green space, koi ponds, paved walking paths and larger-than-life-sized sculptures of native peoples of Mindanao, all designed by the prolific artist Kublai Millan.

Dabaw Museum MUSEUM
(admission P20; ⌚9am-5pm Mon-Sat) This museum, next to the Waterfront Insular Hotel northeast of downtown, has a good collection of tribal weavings and artefacts from most of the Mindanao tribes.

FREE **Long Hua Temple** TEMPLE
(Cabaguio St; ⌚7.30am-4.30pm) A huge Chinese Buddhist temple with beautiful wooden floors and carved walls and doors about 2.5km north of the city centre.

From here, walking back towards the city for a couple of hundred metres, you'll see a sign on a small side street on the right to the **Taoist Temple**, with its fantastic red pagoda. Ring a bell on the gate if you want to go inside.

Davao Wildwater Adventures RAFTING
(☎221 7823, 0920 954 6898; www.psdgroupph.com; per person P2000) This highly recommended professional outfit can be found on the same premises as the Crocodile Park. Overnight camping and rafting trips are in the planning stage.

Festivals & Events

Kadayawan sa Dabaw Festival CULTURAL
Much more than a simple harvest celebration, this festival held in the third week of August showcases tribal cultures, agriculture and crafts with street parades, performances and fantastic displays of fruit and flowers.

Sleeping

TOP CHOICE **Ponce Suites** HOTEL $
(☎227 9070, 0929 810 5699; www.poncesuites.net; cnr 3 & 4 Rds, Doña Vicente Village, Bajada; s/d from P595/700; ❄📶) Practically every inch of this mother-and-son-run hotel, inside and out, is covered with art – sculptures, poetry, photographs and paintings – all of it by the incredibly prolific Kublai Millan, who has transformed an otherwise ordinary building into a funky and personalised vision of hospitality. Sure the rooms are run-of-the-mill motel quality, but the Gaudi-esque rooftop restaurant is the whimsical highlight of the Ponce Suites.

Hotel Galleria HOTEL $$
(☎221 2480; hotelgalleriadvo@yahoo.com; General Duterte St; s/d P900/1300; ❄📶🏊) Something of a refuge in the crowded city centre, this professionally managed hotel's rooms surround an inner courtyard with a small pool. The rooms are modern and clean; they're not especially spacious, but there's also a lobby cafe to hang out in.

Las Casitas HOTEL $$
(☎222 3001; 185 J Rizal St; s/d with air-con incl dinner from P900/1100; ❄📶) Sporting a small comfortable lobby and downstairs coffee shop, this centrally located hotel is not a bad base. The elevator, unusual in this price range, is a blessing; however, the brightly painted rooms aren't furnished as nicely as you'd expect and noise can be a problem in some rooms.

Manor Hotel HOTEL $
(☎221 2511; www.manorhoteldavao.com; A Pichon St; s/d P850/1200; ❄) The pleasant ground-floor coffee shop is a bonus at this small, professionally run downtown place. The Manor Hotel has cosy – read, small – and efficient rooms with modern bathrooms

Davao

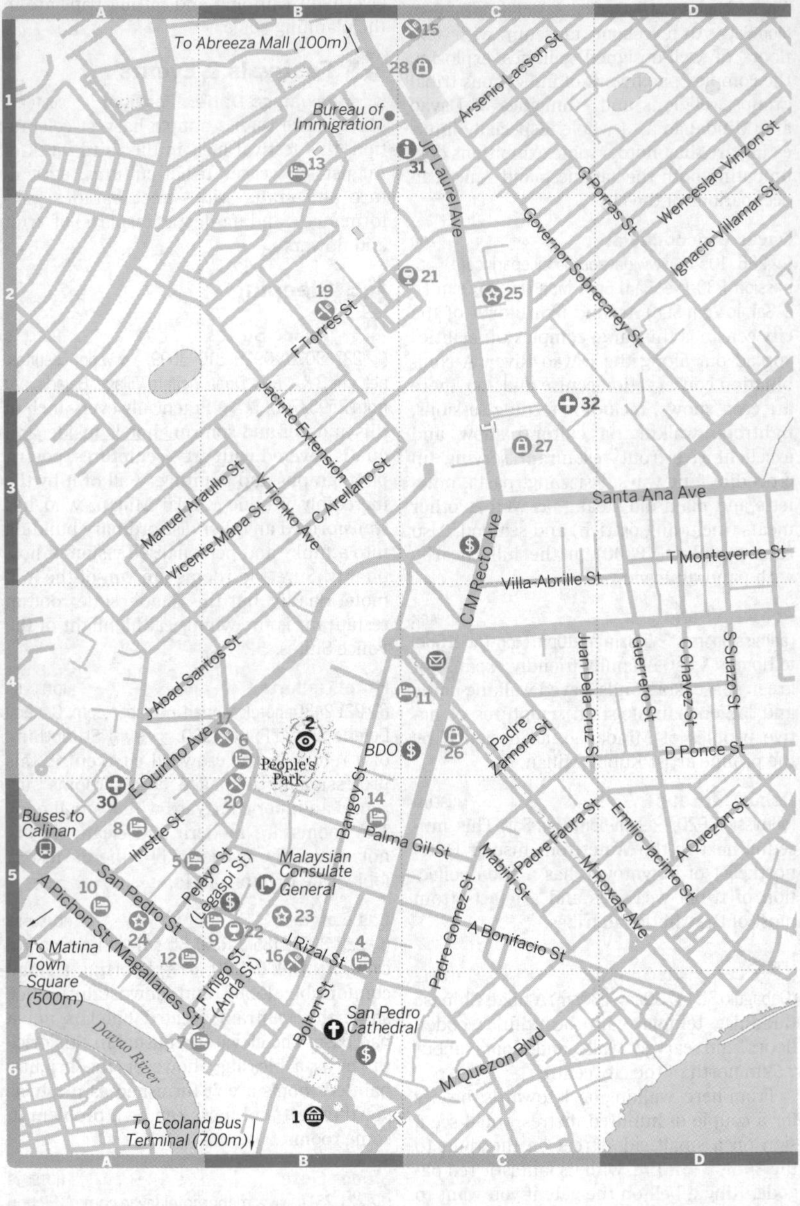

and TVs; some rooms have more light than others.

My Hotel HOTEL **$$**
(☎222 2021; www.myhoteldavao.com; San Pedro St; s/d P800/1000; ❄📶) A colourfully painted high-rise with sparkling clean floors and large modern rooms; street-facing ones get good light.

Aljem's Inn 2 HOTEL **$**
(☎300 8255; 49 J Rizal St; s/d incl breakfast P750/875; ❄📶) Better than **Aljem's Inn 1** (☎227 9629; A Pichon St; s/d P600/730; ❄), which

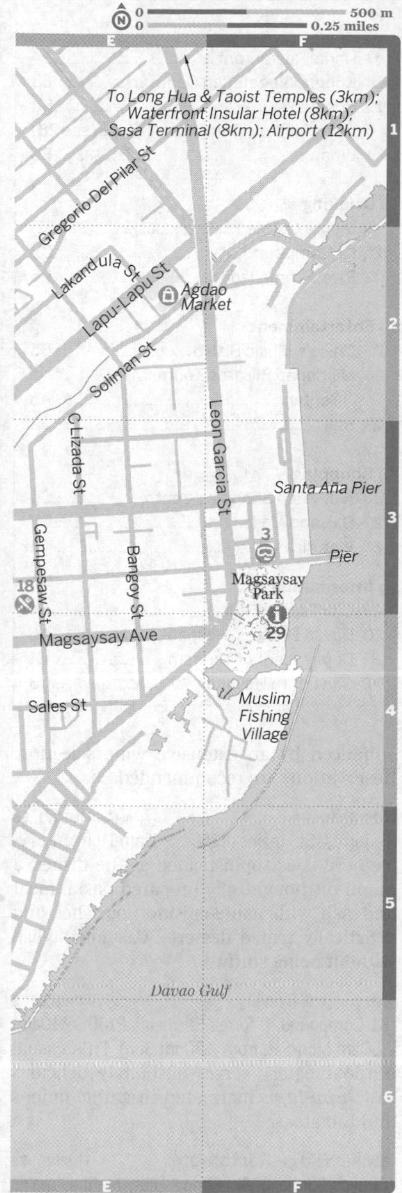

adjoins the Manor Hotel, though both are clean and well run. No 2 has some character in the form of wooden floors and tiled rooms.

Casa Leticia HOTEL **$$**
(☎224 0501; www.casaleticia.com; J Camus St; s/d P2400/2600; ❄@📶) It's all business at this convenient choice opposite People's Park, which isn't necessarily a bad thing. Decorated with wicker furniture and outdated patterns, the rooms, especially the extra-narrow studios, aren't for everyone.

Marco Polo Hotel LUXURY HOTEL **$$$**
(☎221 0888; www.davao.marcopolohotels.com; CM Recto Ave; r from P4800; ❄@📶🏊) The city's most luxurious hotel couldn't be more centrally located. Has several recommended restaurants.

Royal Mandaya Hotel HOTEL **$$**
(☎225 8888; Palma Gil St; www.theroyalmandayahotel.com; r incl breakfast from P3000; ❄@📶🏊) Large convention-style hotel in the centre of old downtown, with a nice restaurant.

Waterfront Insular Hotel HOTEL **$$$**
(☎233 2881; www.waterfronthotels.net; r from P3600; ❄@) If you want more breathing room, try this sprawling complex with gardens and a small private beach, 8km northeast of the city centre.

Grand Menseng Hotel HOTEL **$$**
(☎221 9040; www.grandmenseng.com; A Pichon St; s/d incl breakfast from P1500/1800; ❄@📶🏊) A Chinese-style hotel – booked with conventioneers, families and businesspeople – with upgraded rooms. The rooftop pool is often marred by loud music.

Bagobo House Hotel HOTEL **$$**
(☎222 4444; General Duterte St; s/d incl breakfast P1000/1300; ❄📶) In the centre of old downtown with clean rooms and a ground-floor restaurant.

Eating

Davaoeños take pride in their diverse culinary scene, easily the best in Mindanao.

The Davao durian, iconic symbol of the city, is definitely an acquired taste. During its acquisition you might lose your interest in acquiring it. The season runs from September to December – the rest of the year, try durian ice cream or durian cappuccino (available at Blugre Coffee) as a substitute.

On **F Torres St**, off JP Laurel Ave, there are easily more than a dozen restaurants (a culinary school too), as well as a handful of coffee shops, bars and nightclubs. A number of international cuisines are represented including Italian, Thai, Chinese and Japanese.

Another restaurant hub can be found in the **Victoria Plaza Compound**, an unassuming stretch of low-slung buildings behind the mall of the same name. More

Davao

than a dozen quality restaurants, including several large seafood, Chinese, Korean and Filipino, are here.

Banoks (J Camus St; mains P70) and **Whaw** (Legazpi St; mains P70) are two open-air barbecue joints on the same stretch of pavement across from People's Park. Pork and fish are the specialities, but other grilled meats are also on the menu.

The eateries around Santa Aña Pier and the Muslim Fishing Village are lively – especially in the early evening – and cheap places for fish.

Akiko Japanese Restaurant JAPANESE **$$**
(Victoria Plaza Compound; mains P250) One of the best options at the Victoria Plaza Compound, this Japanese eatery serves some of the freshest sashimi and sushi this side of the tuna market in Gensan.

Claude's Cafe INTERNATIONAL **$$$**
(☎222 4287; 29 J Rizal St; dishes P250) Relocated to a beautifully restored whitewashed colonial-era home, Claude's is still one of the best restaurants in Davao. Carefully prepared steaks, fish and pasta dishes are enhanced by an extensive wine selection. Reservations are recommended.

Ronaldo's ITALIAN, FILIPINO **$$**
(F Torres St; mains P250; ⊙11am-11pm) Service here is as sophisticated as the dishes, a menu of thoughtfully prepared pasta, meat and fish with haute-cuisine flourishes and artistically plated desserts. Casually stylish without being stuffy.

Barbeque Boss BARBECUE **$**
(K1 Compound, F Torres St; mains P100; ⊙10am-2.30am Mon-Sat, from 2.30pm Sun) This casual outdoor eatery serves absolutely delicious raw *lapu-lapu* marinated in garlic, onions and tomatoes.

Jack's Ridge Restaurant FILIPINO **$$**
(Cuayco-Santiago St, Shrine Hills, Matina; mains P200) For a breath of fresh air and sparkling views, head to this spot on a hilltop overlooking the city west of the centre (taxi P100). It has an extensive menu and a bar.

Hanoi Restaurant VIETNAMESE **$$**
(J Camus St; mains P200) Stylish Hanoi serves tasty Vietnamese cuisine; some dishes are

dumbed-down versions to appeal to standard tastes, like Chinese restaurants in America. Shares a kitchen and the building with a Japanese restaurant called Tsuru.

Kong-Ai Vegetarian Centrum VEGETARIAN $
(Gempesaw St; mains P60; ⏲10am-7pm; ☑) A basic Chinatown eatery serving cafeteria-style vegie meals popular with local shop workers.

Drinking & Entertainment

Matina Town Sq (MTS) and clusters of F Torres St including the **K1 Compound** are chock-a-block with bars, coffee shops and restaurants, many with live music. Every Tuesday and Thursday night there's a free outdoor show of indigenous music and dance at MTS, and there's other live music every night around 9pm; the stage fronts a half-dozen outdoor barbecue joints. Also, in MTS is **Kanto Jazz Blues**, a nice bar with singer-songwriter-type performers, and **Studio Onnie**, a stand-up comedy spot.

Rizal Promenade, an enclosed arcade with several bars and KTV spots, is a focus of nightlife in the older centre of the city.

A handful of bars serve 'frozen beer', a Davao speciality – it's cooled to five degrees below zero (holding the frosted bottle can be painful). Most of the top-end hotels here offer live music and dancing on weekends. Everything shuts down at 2am – the city-wide curfew.

Coffee houses are big business in Davao. You'll find several at MTS and in the K1 Compound, and there's a handful near Victoria Plaza and in the city centre south of People's Park.

Starr NIGHTCLUB
(Wheels N More Compound, JP Laurel Ave) The soundtrack is usually techno and house music at this club just down the street from Victoria Plaza. It's popular with university students and well-to-do postgrads.

Chico's Music Bistro LIVE MUSIC
(Paseo de Habana, 29 J Rizal St) In an old colonial building, this bar has live blues and jazz most nights of the week.

Mindanao Billiards Tournament Center SPORTS
(San Pedro St) For tension-filled competitive billiards.

Shopping

Abreeza Mall, not far north of downtown and **Victoria Plaza**, is the new and decidedly fancy kid on the block as far as malls go; **Gaisano Mall** is most centrally located, and SM is not far south of downtown. All four have cinemas.

Aldevinco Shopping Centre HANDICRAFTS
(CM Recto Ave) If you're looking for handicrafts, shop around this rabbit warren of stalls with textiles, batik, weavings, carvings and so on. Take your time and bargain – almost every day is a slow day for vendors. The stallholders are also keen to change euros and US dollars.

Information

All of the major banks have branches here, all with ATMs. Citibank has two branches (Rizal St and JP Laurel Ave).

Internet cafes are clustered in the streets south of People's Park and on CM Recto Ave near the Marco Polo Hotel. Of course, there's at least one internet cafe in each mall.

BOI (☎228 6477; JP Laurel Ave, Bajada; ⏲8am-5pm Mon-Fri) Directly across the street from Victoria Plaza.

City Tourist Office (☎222 1958; www.davaotourism.com; ⏲8am-5pm Mon-Fri) Towards the rear of Magsaysay Park. General information and contact details for people and agencies handling hiking, diving and other activities.

Davao Doctors' Hospital (☎224 0616; E Quirino Ave)

DOT Region XII Office (☎225 1940; www.discoverdavao.com; Room 512, Landco Corporate Center Bldg, JP Laurel Ave)

Indonesian Consulate (☎299 2930; General Ecoland Subdivision)

Laundry Talk (☎0920 576 6233; JTL Plaza, Surveyor St, Doña Vicente Village, Bajada; per kilo P20)

Malaysian Consulate (☎221 4050; 3rd fl, Florantine Bldg, A Bonifacio St)

Getting There & Away

Air

The airport is 12km north of the city centre; a taxi is P150. From the city, jeepneys heading for Sasa go towards the airport; you'll then need to take a tricycle to the airport terminal.

Silk Air (☎221 1039; www.silkair.com) and **Tiger Airways** (02-884 1524; www.tigerairways.com) fly to Singapore from Davao several days a week.

PAL, Airphil Express and Cebu Pacific fly several times a day to Manila; the latter two also fly to Cebu, Zamboanga City (one hour) and Iloilo City regularly. The terminal fee is P200.

Boat

Big interisland boats use the terminal at Sasa, by the Caltex tanks 8km north of town. This is also where boats to Paradise Island Beach Resort on Samal Island leave from. Jeepneys run here, or take a taxi for about P85.

Other boats to Samal and Talikud Islands go from Santa Aña Pier in town.

Bus

All long-distance bus transport is based at the Ecoland terminal, 2km south of the city centre.

Buses to Calinan for the Philippine Eagle Research Center leave from a small terminal on the corner of San Pedro and E Quirino Sts. Buses generally leave every 30 minutes to an hour.

DESTINATION	FARE (P)	DURATION
Butuan	500	7¼
Cagayan de Oro	500	6
General Santos	275	3½
Surigao	500	7

Getting Around

Jeepneys and tricycles clog the streets, sometimes making walking a more efficient option. A taxi to the Ecoland bus terminal will cost about P75, a jeepney about P12.

If you want to rent a car to explore the area on your own, Avis has offices in the Apo View and Marco Polo hotels.

Around Davao

SAMAL ISLAND

082

Ignore the official name, the Island Garden City of Samal (Igacos): this island just across the bay from Davao is simply referred to as Samal. Much like New Yorkers heading to the Hamptons or the Jersey Shore on weekends, Davaoeños flock to this island's 116km of beaches. Of course, not all of this beachfront is picture perfect – in fact, the majority of the resorts on the west coast face unsightly refineries and shipping terminals just across the busy channel. The east side of the island is quieter and more unspoiled.

Sights & Activities

All of the resorts charge day fees (P50 to P75) for use of their beach and pools if they've got one – even if you eat at their restaurants.

A bumpy road, only partly paved, runs along the west coast, best navigated on the back of a motorcycle. You can rent a motorbike for around P600 for the day.

Monfort Bat Cave CAVE
(admission P40; 8am-5pm) In barangay Tambo, around 11km north of Babak, is the Monfort Bat Cave, home to the largest colony of Geoffroy's Rousette fruit bats in the world. A knowledgeable guide will walk you around the five openings where an estimated 2.5 million of these nocturnal and smelly creatures flutter and hang (no smoking since the guano is like gunpowder). It's best to visit at dusk just before they wake in search of food, mostly overripe bananas and mangoes.

Carabao Divers DIVING
(300 1092; www.cdc.e-davao.com; Hermanos Bldg, Santa Aña Pier, Davao) If you just want to escape the city for a day, there are snorkelling and dozens of diving opportunities around the island, including two Japanese wrecks just off Pearl Farm beach and several good wall dives with healthy coral. Carabao Divers in Davao can be recommended (two dives including equipment P1400); several of the resorts also offer diving.

Hagimit Falls WATERFALL
(6am-6pm) Near San Jose in barangay Cawag, Hagimit Falls has a seemingly endless number of small falls and pools you can navigate through in your own private cascading tour. This is a very developed site with concrete paths and picnic huts, not a place to commune with nature.

Sleeping

Much of the western coastline from the Babak pier south to Peñaplata is chock-a-block with resorts (there's even a condo complex), many of which are crowded and noisy, especially on weekends. Some beaches are pleasantly wide, some extremely narrow, especially during high tide. All the resorts offer day passes for around P150 and some will let you sleep outdoors in the picnic huts (P220) for a few hundred pesos.

Pearl Farm Beach Resort BEACH RESORT $$$
(221 9970; www.pearlfarmresort.com; r incl breakfast from P5000;) For true world-class luxury, head to Pearl Farm, where you'll find five-star versions of stilt houses; if these or the hilltop villas aren't exclusive enough, more bungalows are located on the resort's own small offshore island.

Chema's by the Sea Resort BEACH RESORT $$$
(286 1352, 0917 814 0814; d/q cottage P3800/4500;) The relatively intimate

Chema's has large, beautifully furnished upscale native-style cottages with Balinese influences. The property is on a leafy hillside leading down to an infinity pool and beach with a wonderful patio and lounge area.

Maxima Resort BUNGALOW **$$**
(☎300 8636, 0923 659 3725; www.davaocrocodilepark.com; dm P500, cottages with fan/air-con P1800/4000; ❄) Water sports reign, including two giant tarpaulin slides, snorkelling and diving, at this full-service complex perched on a forested hillside with a handful of simple cottages. If you're in a group, it's worth considering the fully furnished four-bedroom house (P15,000) perched over the water nearby. It has its own pier, kayak and complimentary use of scuba tanks.

Paradise Island Park & Beach Resort BEACH RESORT **$$**
(☎233 0251; www.paradiseislanddavao.com; cottages with fan/air-con from P2300/2900; ❄@📶👪) This long-lasting Samal stalwart is its own mini Boracay. It's a huge immaculately landscaped complex with its own zoo and a sandy beachfront strip lined with shops, eating and activity areas; every water sport is available, only a pool is missing. Most of the 76 rooms are nicely furnished cottages with porches and their very own private fenced-in garden.

Bluejazz Resort BEACH RESORT **$$**
(☎302 8411; www.bluejaz.net; dm P770, r from P2000; ❄📶🏊) Several enormous ageing water slides are the centrepiece for this spread-out compound in need of a landscaper's attention. An eclectic mix of native and modern-style cottages.

Bluewaters Resort BEACH RESORT **$$**
(☎303 2618; www.ebluwaters.com; r with fan/air-con P1200/1500; ❄🏊) Next to Chema's, this resort has a handful of cottages and nondescript 'apartment' rooms, plus a nice infinity pool (day guests pay P50).

ℹ Getting There & Away

Bangkas go regularly to Samal (P10, 10 minutes, frequent from 5am to 11pm) from the big Caltex tanks near Davao's Sasa pier; walk through the village market to reach the departure point. Most of the resorts organise transfers for their guests from different piers around Davao. The Island City Express (P40, every 15 minutes) runs from the Ecoland terminal in Davao to the Sasa pier and then continues dropping passengers off on Samal.

A motorbike from the pier on Samal to your resort will run anywhere from P20 to P150 depending on the distance.

TALIKUD ISLAND

☎082

This little island to the southwest of Samal offers a real refuge for those looking to escape. Other than a few low-key resorts, there's not much here. A handful of good dive sites are off the west coast and there's a chance of spotting dugongs.

The enterprising can camp out on a beach with the permission of the property's caretaker. **Isla Reta** (☎234 7903; cottages P700), on the eastern side of the island facing Samal, has several basic bamboo cottages and a fish sanctuary just offshore. Simple meals can be provided and it's the closest accommodation to the pier in Santa Cruz. If you're in a big group you can rent the whole exquisite property of **Leticia's by the Sea** (☎0917 702 5427; per night P10,000; ❄), also on the eastern side (the same owners as Casa Leticia in Davao). On the southern coast of the island is the more upscale **Pacific Little Secret** (☎0917 747 7637; r incl 3 meals P4000), comprising two beautiful breezy houses with plenty of patio space fronting the water and beautiful views. **Babu Santa** (☎0918 726 1466) has basic cottages on a white-sand beach on Talikud's northwestern tip.

Boats run to Talikud (P30, one hour) hourly from 6am to early afternoon from Santa Aña Pier in Davao. The tiny township and jetty at Santa Cruz are a couple of hundred metres from Isla Reta, though most boats will drop you off at the resort.

PHILIPPINE EAGLE RESEARCH & NATURE CENTER

To view one of the largest eagles in the world (in terms of wing span), head to the **Philippine Eagle Research & Nature Center** (☎082-224 3021; www.philippineeagle.org; admission P50, ⌚8am-5pm), which is dedicated to conserving these endangered birds. Around 35 Philippine eagles (also known as monkey-eating eagles) are here, 20 of which were bred through artificial insemination. The camp is set in a pocket of native forest near Malagos, 36km north of Davao. There are enough wild birds flitting around to keep even the least avid birdwatcher happy – other species of eagles and animals also call the centre home. You can watch an informative video about eagles in the wild – there are about 500 in the Philippines – and the threats they are facing through deforestation and hunting.

The average eagle lifespan in the wild is 20 years, but it's much longer at the centre.

Volunteer guides are around at weekends to answer questions. Plan to get here at opening time to beat the crowds. To stay overnight in the area, try the collection of cottages at **Malagos Garden Resort** (☎301 1375; www.malagos.com; barangay Malagos; tents per person P250, dm P350, q from P2400; ❄), set in a beautifully landscaped property with gardens, walking paths, a bird park and a butterfly sanctuary; tents are provided for those interested in camping.

Getting There & Away

From Davao, catch a jeepney to Calinan (45 minutes) in front of Ateneo University across from the Marco Polo Hotel or on Roxas St between Quezon and Burgos Sts. Buses leave from the Annil Terminal at the corner of Quirino and San Pedro Extension. In Calinan, take a jeepney, motorcycle or tricycle to Malagos (10 minutes). A taxi from Davao runs around P600 one way.

MT APO & AROUND

☎082

Literally the 'grandfather' of all mountains, Mt Apo is a volcano that has never blown its top and, at 2954m, is the highest peak in the Philippines. Most mornings it is clearly visible towering above Davao. Local tribes believe deities reside near the summit and worship it as a sacred mountain, but it's the environmental stress caused by too much human traffic that makes permission sometimes difficult to obtain. The situation is fluid and should be sussed out at the tourist office in Davao (which can provide a list of reputable guides), Crocodile Park or in Kidapawan, 110km from Davao and the closest municipality to the starting point for hikes

WORTH A TRIP

OFF THE BEATEN TRACK AROUND DAVAO

» **Mati** Around a three-hour drive east and then south from Davao is Mati, in Davao Oriental, and nearby **Dahican Beach**, especially good for kayaking, windsurfing, surfing and snorkelling. The waters around Mati are also blessed with several white-sand islands and vibrant marine life including manta rays, sharks, turtles, dolphins and dugongs.

» **Glan** In Sarangani Province, south of General Santos, Glan has a white-sand beach bordering a bay; camping is allowed and there are several resorts along the waterfront.

» **Cateel** A long drive north from Mati along a road reminiscent of Hwy 101 in California brings you to Cateel, one of the oldest Spanish settlements in the Philippines. The 4km **Long Beach** is entirely undeveloped and good for surfing and skimboarding. East of Cateel is **Aliwag Falls** and to the south an impressively bio-diverse **mangrove reserve**.

» **Mainit Hot Springs** These sulphuric springs near Maco on the eastern side of the Davao Gulf can soothe tired bones. Further north from here, the **Toyozu Inland Resort** (cottages P750) in Nabunturan, the capital of Compostela Valley, has spas filled with water from a nearby spring. A small 1.5m-high mini volcano provides the heat – it's still growing.

» **Waterfalls** There are over two dozen waterfalls near Maragusan (640m), 83km southeast of Nabunturan. The two most worth visiting are Marangig Falls and Tagbibinta. A nice place to stay is **Haven's Peak** (☎0926 719 7558; www.thehavenspeak.com; dm/cottages P350/1400), with absolutely stunning views of the surrounding countryside.

» **White Water** Inner tubing (P200) down the Sibulan River outside Santa Cruz, between Davao and Digos, is better than any roller coaster. It's a fairly do-it-yourself affair; you have to show up on your own or arrange a guide in Davao. Air-con buses leave from the Ecoland terminal in Davao almost every half-hour, starting in the early morning. Ask to be dropped at the Sibulan Crossing; from there it's around 100m to the tubing staging area.

» **Dugong Watching** One of the few chances to see these gentle beasts in their natural habitat is around Malita, south of Digos. Two watchtowers have been built to make spying this usually elusive mammal easier. May and June are the best months because of improved visibility in the water.

to the summit. Coffee is grown on the mountain's slopes, the same latitude as Ethiopia.

The **hikes** take in primeval forests, rushing waterfalls and the possibility of spotting endangered plant and animal species, such as the carnivorous pitcher plants and the Philippine eagle. *Vanda Sandariana,* more commonly known as waling-waling, considered the mother of all commercial orchid plants, is endemic. Since the climb is strenuous and the path almost impossible to follow on your own, you'll have to visit one of the tourist offices anyway to hire a guide. There's no other reason to be in Kidapawan except to arrange treks up the mountain; the office of the **Kidapawan Tourism Council** (278 7053) is in the City Hall on the north side of the plaza. Experienced climbers recommend allowing a minimum of four days, and you'll need warm clothes and sleeping gear, since temperatures drop at night near the peak. Hiking permits cost P500, guides and porters around P400 and P300 per day respectively; food and equipment aren't included. The best time to go is from March to August when there's less chance of rain.

Most people actually begin their climb after a jeepney ride to **Ilomavis** and Lake Agko (1193m), where they stay overnight and arrange porters before heading for Lake Venado (2182m) and the summit.

For the longest zipline (P300) in Southeast Asia, stop at Camp Sabros near Kapatagan, on the southern slopes of Mt Apo – it's long enough to feel like you are flying over pine trees below. **Tudaya Falls**, one of the highest in the Philippines at 300ft, is nearby.

Nearby are Lake Mirror and Hillside, both part of **Mt Apo Highland Resort** (0918 959 1641; www.davaocrocodilepark.com; tent per person P300, cottage P2000;). Camping is a good option at both, and air mattresses and tents are available for rent. The restaurant at Hillside has a great view of Mt Apo and a reflection of the mountain in the water at Lake Mirror.

Also not far from here, at the foot of Mt Talomo, is the **Eden Nature Park Resort** (0918 930 7590; www.edennaturepark.com.ph; tents P800, r/cottages from P1300/4000;). A once-denuded slope, the victim of overzealous logging, has been transformed into a lush forest with hiking trails, sports fields, playgrounds and a 20-second-long zipline. A shuttle service operates from the park's main office in Matina Town Sq in Davao.

Getting There & Away

From Davao, take a bus from the Ecoland bus terminal to Kidapawan (P80, two hours, every 30 minutes). To jump-off points for the trek, take a jeepney from Kidapawan to Ilomavis (P55, one hour), 17km away.

General Santos (Dadiangas)

083 / POP 529,500

Known to locals as 'Gensan', to fishmongers as the 'Tuna Capital of the Philippines' and to sports fans as the hometown of Manny Pacquiao (aka Pacman), General Santos is the southernmost city in the Philippines. Formerly Dadiangas, the city was renamed in 1965 in honour of General Paulino Santos who, with accompanying Christian Visayans and Tagalogs, established a settlement here in 1939. These days it's a typically congested city, notable mostly for the huge ships that dock at the port here on Sarangani Bay, loading up freshly caught tuna for the journey to dinner tables all over Asia.

Prior to the city's establishment, the area was inhabited mostly by Maguindanao Muslims and B'laan tribespeople, and this history is showcased at the **Museum of Muslim & Tribal Culture** at the MSU campus, near the airport. There's also a small **museum of memorabilia** about General Santos (the person) at the Notre Dame Dadiangas College (NDDC). Both museums are open during school hours.

Gensan is really worth a detour during the **Tuna Festival**, held in the first week of September, and the **Kalilangan Festival**, celebrated in the last week of February and commemorating the founding of Gensan in 1939 with traditional dance, arts, cooking and handicrafts.

A better choice than staying in the city, the **Dolores Tropicana Resort Hotel** (380 7328; www.doloreshotels.rdgropu.com.ph; Tambler; r P1300;) is a large complex with a pleasant open-air restaurant and beachside cottages with views of Sarangani Bay right out their front doors. Generally considered the top business-class hotel in the city, **East Asia Royale Hotel** (553 4119; www.eastasiaroyalehotel.com; r P2500; @) is within walking distance of Gaisano Mall and houses a coffee shop, a restaurant and a happening bar. Directly across the street from the public market and only a block from the bay front, the **Amigotel Hotel &**

Suites (☎552 4574; www.amigotelgensan.com; cnr Santiago Blvd & Cagampang St; dm P250, r from P325; ❄📶), formerly the Anchor Hotel, has fairly chintzy rooms though there's a rooftop restaurant.

All of the following are recommended places to try tuna and *opah,* also known as moonfish, the specialities of Gensan: **Grab-A-Crab** (Laurel St; mains P250) for Chinese-style; **Manokan sa Negros** (Pioneer Ave; mains P150) for barbecue-style; and **Mi-Mosho-Be** (J Catolico St; mains P200) for Japanese interpretations. Head to **Kambingan sa Depot** (KSD; Acharon Blvd; mains from P50) directly across the street from several large oil depots for an early lunch (many dishes sell out early) of goat meat in a variety of ways, including goat balls soup – which some consider to be the Filipino Viagra.

 Getting There & Away

Air

Tambler airport is 12km west of the city centre; a taxi should cost around P125. Cebu Pacific, Airphil Express and PAL fly daily from Manila to General Santos (two hours). Cebu Pacific has flights to Cebu (1½ hours).

Boat

Makar Pier is 2km west of town. SuperFerry has boats bound for Manila (54 hours) via Zamboanga and Iloilo (30 hours), on Panay, several days a week; it also runs weekly trips to Zamboanga City (12 hours).

Bus

There are regular bus services running between General Santos and Davao (3½ hours), Cagayan de Oro (eight to 10 hours) and Butuan (eight to 10 hours).

The integrated bus and jeepney terminal is at Bula-ong on the western edge of town, about 1km from the town centre.

Lake Sebu

ELEV 300M

The watery bottom of a beautiful bowl, Lake Sebu is surrounded on all sides by hills and forests, interrupted by the spokes of bamboo fish traps and the occasional dugout canoe slowly skimming its placid surface. However, a large church on top of a hill overlooking the lake and several other modern concrete buildings somewhat mar the undeveloped lakefront and pristine views.

Saturdays are the best time to visit, when tribespeople from surrounding communities descend on the town for the weekly **market**. Stop by the **T'boli Museum** (⏲7am-5pm), really nothing more than a small native-style house selling locally made handicrafts; there are many roadside souvenir stalls selling the same weavings and brassware items. You can hire a boat (P350, one hour) for a swing around the lake and hike to nearby **Seven Falls** or **Trangikini Falls**. A motorcycle will take you to within half an hour's walk of each waterfall.

The annual **Lem-Lunay Festival**, celebrating T'boli culture, takes place in the second week of November, culminating in horse fights – the sport of royalty in local culture – where two stallions fight over a mare in heat.

Punta Isla (☎0919 485 2910; www.puntaislaresort.webs.com; r P750) is the best of the bungalow resorts overlooking the lake.

Koronadal (Marbel), only a one-hour bus ride from Cotabato or General Santos, is the junction for trips to Lake Sebu.

Cotabato

☎064 / POP 259,000

This city of the Maguindanao people lies on the Rio Grande de Mindanao, often called the Pulangi River. 'Maguindanao' is a compilation of the local words for kin, country and lake, so literally they are 'people of the lake country'. Islam is the oldest religion here, introduced in 1475, with Christianity a comparatively recent arrival, brought in by Jesuits in 1871. Cotabato has a reputation as being lawless and unsafe, considered unjust by locals, that owes much simply to its location in the middle of the ARMM.

Head up **Piedro Colina Hill** for good views; at the foot of the hill lie **Kutawato Caves**, bizarrely right in the middle of a busy intersection; inside are saltwater pools, an underground river and bats. However, the water is mostly dirty and can't be recommended.

The low-slung **Cotabato City Hall** has an impressive facade of mostly Islamic influence. A couple of kilometres out of town you'll find the Regional Autonomous Government Centre, which houses a **museum** (admission free; ⏲9am-4pm) and is the seat of government for the ARMM. Remember that Friday is a day of prayer for Muslims, so all government offices close early.

The best time to visit is in mid-June for mammoth dance parades of the **Araw ng**

Kutabato Festival or in mid-December during the **Shariff Kabungsuan Festival** commemorating the arrival of Islam in the region with riverine parades of decorated boats.

Estosan Garden Hotel (☎421 6777; Governor Gutierrez Blvd; r from P2000; ❄@≋) is generally considered the nicest hotel in town and certainly one of the largest; it's located a couple of kilometres from the city centre, next to the Regional Autonomous Government Centre.

Getting There & Away

Airphil Express, Cebu Pacific and PAL have daily flights to and from Manila (1½ hours). The airport is around 10km south of town.

Interisland boats and boats to Zamboanga (several times weekly) leave from Polloc Pier, 30km away.

Regular buses run daily between Davao and Cotabato (P220, five hours). There are no direct buses from General Santos; you have to take a bus to Tacurong (45 minutes) and then a minivan to Cotabato (1½ hours).

ZAMBOANGA PENINSULA

Zamboanga & Around

☎062 / POP 774,000

When the sun sets in the Philippines, this city, whose otherwise banal skyline is punctuated by several minarets, is one of the last places to see it go. While Zamboanga City is geographically the end of the line, historically it's been a first step, from Islam's arrival to the islands in the 1400s to waves of migrants from the Sulu archipelago. Even though the city is 70% Muslim, most women don't wear headscarves and modern fashions are as strong here as elsewhere. The most commonly spoken language is Chabacano, a Spanish-Creole mix made up of Malay grammar and unconjugated Spanish verbs. The possible origin of the city's exotic-sounding name is threefold: it may come from the 16th-century Malay word *jambangan,* meaning 'land of flowers'; from *sambaongan,* a 'docking point', identified on an early Spanish map; or from *sabuan,* the wooden pole used by local tribespeople to navigate their *vintas* (wooden boats with traditional brilliantly coloured angular cloth sails) over the coastal flats.

Often in foreign newspapers' datelines for reports of violence anywhere in Mindanao, Zamboanga has seen its share of the conflict over the years. The Philippine Army's Southern Command (Southcom) is headquartered here, along with a contingent of US Special Forces soldiers.

Sights

Rio Hondo VILLAGE

East of Fort Pilar is the Muslim stilt village of Rio Hondo; its mosque is a clear landmark visible from the ramparts of the fort. The village is built out over the edge of the water, and the houses are joined by footbridges. The tourist office doesn't recommend wandering around Rio Hondo without an escort, and the footpaths can be tricky to navigate. Contact **Gammar Hassan** (☎0906 457 1563), a former barangay official.

Taluksangay VILLAGE

Muslim and Christian communities live together peacefully in this settlement about 18km northeast of Zamboanga City. Like

FORT PILAR

At the southeastern end of town near the waterfront is this solid and squat building, partially restored to maintain its historic character. Its chequered past is worth noting: founded by the Spaniards in 1635; attacked by the Dutch in 1646; deserted in 1663; reconstructed in 1666; rebuilt in 1719; stormed by 3000 Moros in 1720; cannonaded by the British in 1798; abandoned by the Spaniards in 1898; occupied by the US in 1899; seized by the Japanese in 1942; and, finally, claimed by the Philippines in 1946.

Inside is a **museum** (admission free; ⊙8.30am-noon & 1.30-5pm Sun-Fri) with several impressive galleries, including an exhibition of 18th- and 19th-century prints and another with contemporary paintings. The **marine exhibit**, where you can learn about underwater ecosystems, includes some sophisticated displays. Across the inner courtyard of the fort is a terrific **ethnographic gallery** concentrating on the boat-dwelling Sama Dilaut (otherwise known as the Badjao, or sea gypsies) of the Sulu archipelago. Walk around the **ramparts** for 360-degree views of Zamboanga City and the busy ocean.

Rio Hondo, it's built partially out over the water; a mosque with red minarets built in 1885, the oldest on the Zamboanga Peninsula, dominates the skyline. The same sort of unwritten rules for visitors as Rio Hondo apply here; wear appropriate clothing and ask if you want to take photos. Jeepneys go to Taluksangay (35 minutes), or alternatively you can hire a taxi to take you there and back for around P150.

Santa Cruz Island ISLAND

Great Santa Cruz Island is around 7km off the Zamboanga waterfront, and is home to only a few dozen families from the Samal tribe. Visitors come to see the 2km-long pinkish beach, coloured from finely crushed red coral. You can swim here, but it's on a busy shipping channel and currents are strong. Several bangka are licensed to transport visitors to Santa Cruz; the round-trip fare should cost about P2500 for up to six people. Boats leave from the waterfront between the Lantaka Hotel and Fort Pilar in Zamboanga.

Festivals & Events

The city's main festival, **Fiesta de Nuestra Señora Virgen del Pilar**, takes place from 10 to 12 October. Although a Christian festival, a time for parades, dances, markets and food fairs, it's enjoyed by the whole community. It also has a big **regatta** that brings *vintas* out on the water.

Sleeping

Lantaka Hotel HOTEL $$

(☎991 2033; Valderoza St; s/d from P950/1200;) This venerable Zamboanga institution occupies a long swath of waterfront complete with a pool, an outdoor bar and several small nipa huts for lounging. The existing rooms are large and a little musty; sea-view rooms have small balconies with metal chairs. The old-school restaurant

serves standard Filipino and generic international dishes.

Marcian Business Hotel HOTEL $$
(☎991 0005; www.marcianhotel.com; Mayor Cesar Climaco Ave; r from P1000; ❄📶) Gleaming tile floors, spacious bathrooms with top-of-the-line shower heads, and beautifully designed boutique-style rooms make this the best midrange choice in the city. Located at one of the busiest intersections, the Marcian is a refuge from the noise and smog.

Grand Astoria Hotel HOTEL $$
(☎991 2510; www.grand.astoria.phil.com; Mayor Jaldon St; s/d from P850/1200; ❄@📶) This efficiently run midrange institution is often booked by groups attending seminars, conventions, weddings and the like. Room decor is nothing special, but staff are quick to rectify any problems. Airline ticketing offices and a restaurant on the ground floor.

Eating

There is a food court and several fast-food joints in the **Mindpro City Mall** and **Southway Mall**.

Mr Bean's Café CAFE $$
(Catribo Complex, Buenavista St; mains P150; 📶) Inside the Catribo Complex, a strip mall with several bars and restaurants, Mr Bean's serves good pizza.

La Vista Del Mar SEAFOOD $$
(mains P175) The best outdoor seafood restaurant is just past the Yakan Weaving Village (taxi P100) west of the city.

Zamboanga

Sights
1 Fort Pilar....D4

Sleeping
2 Grand Astoria Hotel....B2
3 Lantaka Hotel....C4
4 Marcian Business Hotel....B3

Eating
5 Catribo Complex....A2
6 Hai-San Restaurant....A2
7 Mindpro City Mall....B2
Mr Bean's Café....(see 5)
8 Southway Mall....B3

Transport
9 Aleson Shipping Lines....C1
Zamboanga Travel & Tours....(see 3)

TOP CHOICE **Alavar Seafood House** SEAFOOD $$
(barangay Tetuan; mains P200) Seafood, of course, is the speciality here – choose the species, size and cooking method from a menu of delicacies. What sets Alavar apart is the beautiful trellis-covered backyard. Enjoy a lantern-lit dinner serenaded by the loud squawking from an aviary of exotic birds. It's a P30 tricycle ride northeast of the city centre.

Mano-Mano na Greenfield FILIPINO $
(Governor Ramos St, barangay Santa Maria; mains from P70) Housed in a large flashy version of the native-style outdoor pavilion, Mano-Mano specialises in grilled pork spareribs and baby back ribs. About 1km north of the Edwin Andrews Air Base.

Hai-san Restaurant SEAFOOD $$
(San José Rd; meals P200) The just-caught seafood on display is a menagerie of that day's catch. Choose the specimen and style, and enjoy; almost everything is priced by weight.

Hana Sono JAPANESE $$
(Governor Camins Rd; sushi P140) Modern place in the basement of the Garden Orchid Hotel.

Shopping

About 7km out of Zamboanga, heading west, the **Yakan Weaving Village** is really no more than a collection of six or seven stalls selling some high-quality Yakan weavings, such as table runners and place mats, a little brassware and lots of ordinary mass-produced batik. Yakan are the indigenous people of nearby Basilan Island, and their woven designs are characterised by bright colours and geometric designs.

Information

The PNB and Bank of the Philippine Islands (BPI) around the plaza area and the Metrobank on La Purisma St have ATMs.

There are internet cafes scattered around the city centre east of Mayor Jaldon St and north of Plaza Pershing.

BOI (☎991 2234; 2nd fl, Radja Bldg, Airport Rd)

City Tourism Office (☎992 3007; Valderoza St; ⏰8am-noon & 1-5pm Mon-Sat) Next to the Lantaka Hotel; a second **office** (☎992 3007) is a block from Plaza Rizal.

Zamboanga Travel & Tours (☎991 2033; Lantaka Hotel) The personable Paciencia Tan Mañalac can provide everything from an oral history of the city to day tours and airline tickets.

GETTING TO MALAYSIA

Aleson Shipping Lines (991 2687; Veterans Ave) operates boats to Sandakan in Malaysia. Boats (economy/cabin P2900/3300) leave Zamboanga on Monday and Thursday in the early afternoon and arrive around 20 hours later. They depart Sandakan on Tuesday and Friday in the early evening.

Getting There & Away

Few travellers venture to Zamboanga overland and most arrive by plane. However, for the intrepid and patient who want to travel throughout northern Mindanao before visiting the city, it's possible to get either a fast ferry (four hours) or bus (eight hours) in the town of Pagadian in the far north of Zamboanga del Sur.

Philippine Airlines, Cebu Pacific and SuperFerry all have offices in a building attached to the Lantaka Hotel.

Air

PAL, Airphil Express and Cebu Pacific fly between Manila and Zamboanga (1½ hours) several times daily; the latter two also fly to Cebu (one hour) and Davao several times a week (one hour), and to Jolo and Tawi-Tawi in the Sulu archipelago.

Boat

SuperFerry has weekly runs to Cebu (14 hours), Davao (10 hours), General Santos (12 hours) and Iloilo (12 hours); also twice-weekly boats to Manila (48 hours). Smaller boats also run daily to Cotabato. Negros Navigation boats leave for Manila (32 hours) once weekly, going via Iloilo on Panay.

Smaller boats also run daily to from here to Cotabato.

Bus

If you travel by road, travel only during the daytime. Buses to Zamboanga run several times daily until late morning from Dipolog (eight hours) and Pagadian (seven hours). The terminal is near the Santa Cruz market on the outskirts of town.

Getting Around

The airport is 2km from the centre of Zamboanga. Walk out of the arrivals hall and catch a public tricycle, or take a special trip for P40. Taxis cost around P150. From town you can take a jeepney marked 'Canelar-Airport'.

SULU ISLANDS

Despite the mellifluous-sounding name, the 500 or so islands of the Sulu archipelago, stretching some 300km from Basilan to Borneo, have become synonymous with the conflict between government troops and Muslim separatist groups. The archipelago is divided into two provinces: Sulu, with its capital of Jolo (ho-*lo*), and Tawi-Tawi, with Bongao as its capital. It is further subdivided into the Jolo, Tawi-Tawi, Tapul, Tapiantana, Pangutaran and Sibutu groups of islands. Basilan, though the largest island in the archipelago, is administratively part of the Zamboanga Peninsula.

The rather isolated Cagayan de Tawi-Tawi Group lies off the coast of Borneo, midway between Palawan and the Sulu archipelago. These are still dangerous waters for sailors, less because of the elements than because of pirates and smugglers. Smaller passenger

Sulu Islands

vessels as well as cargo boats are regularly plundered in these seas.

About 94% of the archipelago's population is Muslim, and this area is part of the ARMM. However, culturally the region is dominated by the Tausugs, or 'people of the current'. In and around Tawi-Tawi, the Samal people live in stilt houses by the coast. Terminology for the people of the region can be confusing. Sama is a generic term covering four distinct groups of people sharing the Sama language, who inhabit the islands south of the Jolo Group. The Sama Laut, meaning 'sea Sama' and often referred to in English as 'sea gypsies', are generally referred to as Badjao, though they themselves do not use this term.

There are still communities of Badjao living on boats in the southern part of the archipelago, but many now live on permanent sites, either in stilt houses or on their boats at moorings. Although most Badjao are Muslim, animist beliefs and practices are still observed. Sitangkai, in the Sibutu Group, is known as the 'Venice of the Philippines', as many Badjao floating communities have settled there.

Getting There & Away

All scheduled access to the Sulu archipelago is from Zamboanga. Airphil Express and Cebu Pacific fly to Tawi-Tawi and Jolo daily.

Weesam Express has several trips a week to Jolo (P600, three hours); twice weekly, the boat stops in Jolo, then Bongao (P1200, 7½ hours), although at the time of research it was uncertain whether these would continue; check ahead.

Palawan

Includes »

Best Places to Eat

» Fresh grilled fish on a bangka cruising through the Bacuit Archipelago (p394)

» Kalui (p377)

» Beachfront restaurants in El Nido (p392)

» Badjao Seafront Restaurant (p377)

Best Places to Stay

» Nipa hut in a remote fishing village (p386)

» Sangat Island Reserve (p399)

» Flower Island Beach Resort (p388)

» Daluyon Resort (p382)

» Krystal Lodge (p397)

Why Go?

Nothing defines Palawan more than the water around it. With seascapes the equal of any in Southeast Asia, and wildlife terrestrial and aquatic, the Philippines' most sparsely populated region is also the most beguiling. Because of its silhouette – a long sliver stretching 650km all the way to Borneo – there's a certain liberating logic to travel here.

Centrally located Puerto Princesa (Puerto) is the culinary capital and primary gateway to nearby rural and oceanfront tranquillity. The majority of travellers go north, without question the highlight. Skimming along in bangkas around a maze of uninhabited islands feels somewhat post-apocalyptic.

The coastline serves as an alternative highway ferrying travellers between fishing villages and tourist-friendly towns. In the south where the topography is more rugged, it's possible to explore jungle-clad mountains though facilities are decidedly rustic. Diving and island-hopping snorkelling trips in the Bacuit archipelago and Calamianes group manage to captivate both those seeking adventure and those wanting to unwind.

When to Go

Puerto Princesa

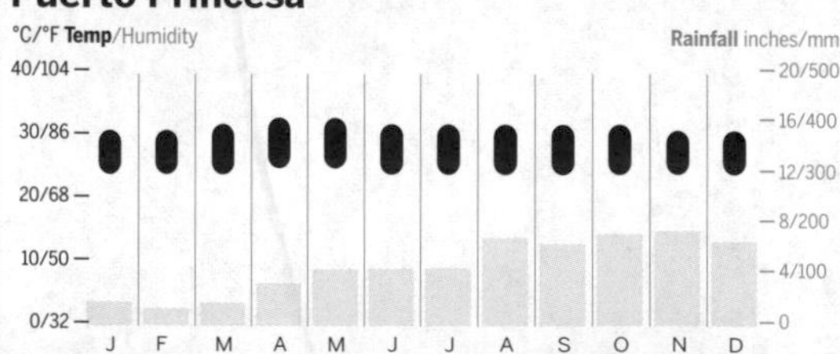

Mar-early May The best time for sea travel.

May-Oct The southwest monsoon, with heavy rain at least in the afternoon.

Nov-Feb Cooler and drier, a popular time to go.

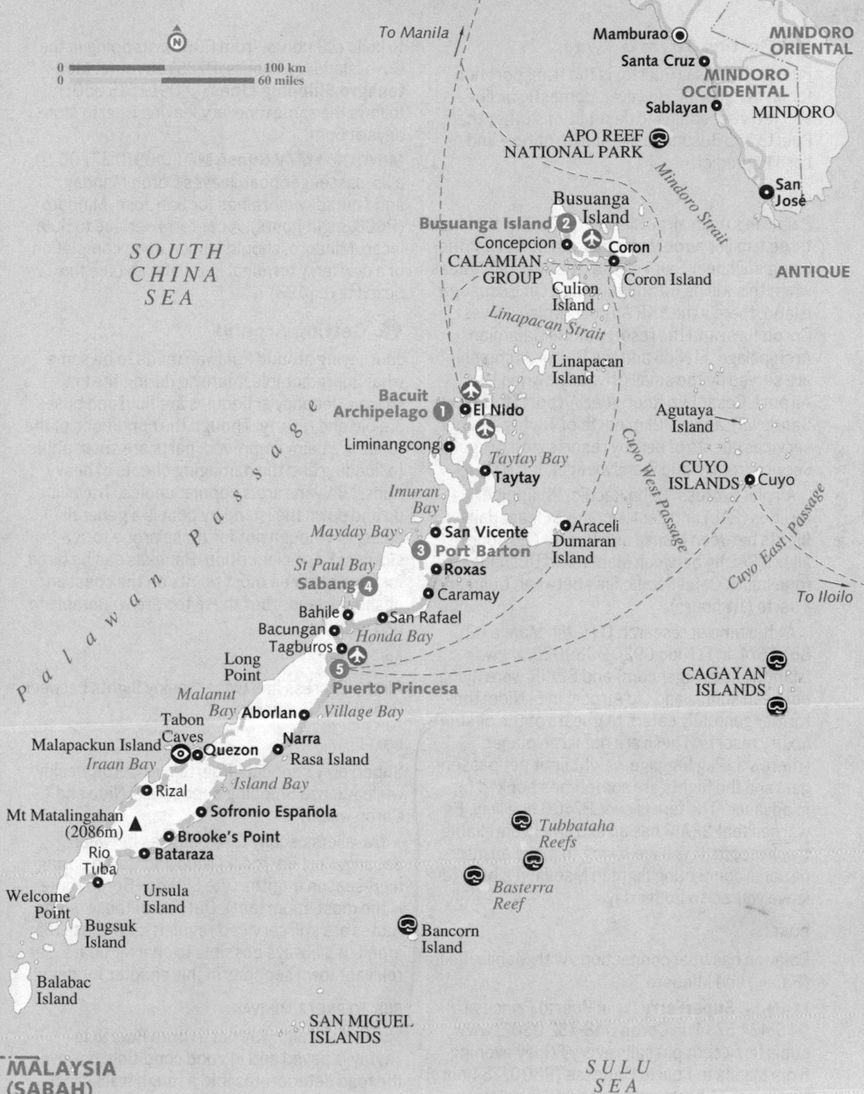

Palawan Highlights

1. Snorkel your way in and out of lagoons – nature's aquariums – in the **Bacuit Archipelago** (p394)
2. Wriggle through the portholes of WWII-era wrecks while diving around **Busuanga Island** (p396)
3. Move to the slow village pace, from hammock to beach and back again, in **Port Barton** (p385)
4. Make the most of a day in **Sabang** (p381), from floating through the cavernous darkness of the underground river to chilling on the beach at sunset
5. Breeze through the countryside outside **Puerto Princesa** (p373) on a motorcycle

Getting There & Away

Puerto Princesa (Puerto) is the transport hub for all of Palawan. However, domestic airline and ferry schedules to destinations other than Puerto and Busuanga are fluid in nature and hard to predict.

AIR

Palawan's main airport is in Puerto, but there are three smaller airports further north and another being built near San Vicente (it's anyone's guess when this will be up and running). On Busuanga Island, there's the YKR Airport, which serves Coron town and the resorts of the Calamian Archipelago. El Nido and the Bacuit Archipelago are served by the small privately owned Lio Airport. Cesar Lim Rodriguez Airport (formerly Sandoval), about 30km north of Taytay, mainly services guests of nearby resorts with irregular service from Island Transvoyager, Inc (ITI).

Airphil Express, Cebu Pacific, Philippine Airlines (PAL) and Zest Air offer at least daily flights between Manila and Puerto (1¼ hours); all but PAL fly between Manila and Busuanga (one hour). Cebu Pacific flies between Cebu and Puerto (1½ hours).

At the time of research **ITI** (☎in Manila 02-851 5674, in El Nido 0920 908 1025; www.islandtransvoyager.com) and SEAIR were flying between Manila and Lio Airport in El Nido; the former generally caters to guests of the offshore luxury resorts. These are not large planes (there's a 12kg luggage weight limit per passenger) and the flights are sometimes booked far in advance. The fare is over P7400 one way. Be warned that SEAIR has an extremely unreliable track record. If you are trying to make an international connecting flight in Manila, it's best to leave yourself a buffer day.

BOAT

Palawan has boat connections with Manila, Iloilo (Panay) and Mindoro.

MANILA **SuperFerry** (☎in Puerto Princesa 048-434 5734, in Coron 048-732 0302; www.superferry.com.ph) sails every Friday evening from Manila to Puerto Princesa (P800, 28 hours) via Coron. The return trip departs Puerto on Sunday mornings around 9am. **Atienza Shipping Lines** (☎in Coron 0919 377 9751, in El Nido 0918 566 6786) operates an unreliable El Nido–Coron–Manila trip. Departure from El Nido is Friday at midnight; it arrives in Coron Saturday morning and departs Coron Saturday afternoon at 4pm. The return trip departs Manila on Tuesdays and departs Coron on Wednesdays at 10pm. Because this is a cargo ship that accepts passengers, it's only an option for the extremely hardy or masochistic.

ILOILO (PANAY) **Milagrosa Shipping** (☎in Puerto Princesa 048-433 4806) sails twice a week (3pm Thursday and Sunday) from Puerto to Iloilo (30 hours, from P950), stopping in the Cuyo Islands (13 hours, P725) en route. **Montenegro Shipping Lines** (☎0919 516 6501) follows the same itinerary leaving Puerto Mondays at 6pm.

MINDORO **M/V Bunso MP** (☎0910 371 0621), a 25-passenger boat, leaves Coron Monday and Thursday mornings for San Jose, Mindoro (P600, eight hours). A car-ferry service to Bulalacao, Mindoro, should launch upon completion of a new ferry terminal in Bulalacao (see the boxed text, p193).

Getting Around

Journeying around Palawan tends to be somewhat unpredictable, more so during the low season. Jeepney schedules are fluid and buses are old and rickety. Though the conditions of the roads are being improved, parts are susceptible to flooding and the damaging effects of heavy rains. Minivans are a popular choice. Travelling up and down the island by boat is a generally pleasant (though not for those prone to sea sickness) if pricier option. Bangkas can be hired for trips between most points on the coast and offshore islands, but these too are vulnerable to bad weather.

AIR

Airphil Express has twice-weekly flights between Puerto and Busuanga.

BOAT

SuperFerry connects Puerto and Coron weekly, while Atienza Shipping connects El Nido and Coron weekly.

Travellers usually take bangkas between Sabang, Port Barton, El Nido and Coron during high-season months (the El Nido–Coron route is the most important). Outside of these, some routes are still serviced regularly; for those that aren't, it's always possible to charter boats. See relevant town sections in this chapter for details.

BUS, JEEPNEY & MINIVAN

Much of the highway north from Puerto to Taytay is paved and in good condition; however, the road deteriorates into a rough track from Taytay to El Nido. Southern Palawan is generally worse than the north in terms of road conditions.

Puerto is the transport hub. Jeepney/bus hybrids (overgrown jeepneys with the seats facing forward) leave from the terminal north of the city to virtually every destination in Palawan. A handful of bus companies operates along the major routes, though these are ageing beasts. Public minivans, generally the fastest and most comfortable option, ply important routes; most noteworthy is the one between Puerto and El Nido. If you are travelling in a group or willing to part with extra cash, you can hire a private van to almost any location.

CENTRAL PALAWAN

The geographical midpoint of the island is a logical place to begin your explorations. Only a short drive from Puerto Princesa, the fairly urbanised capital of the province, are bucolic pastoral scenes and island hopping. To the north is Sabang, with an alluring beach and subterranean river tour.

Puerto Princesa & Around

☎048 / POP 210,500

The capital of Palawan is more than simply the jumping-off point for excursions elsewhere on the island. 'Puerto', as locals call it, has a thriving restaurant scene, and day trips abound, offering everything from island-hopping to remote beaches to drives through stunning countryside. However, though cleaner than other Filipino cities, owing to an admirable and strictly enforced no-littering law, it's no tropical paradise. Despite the fact that it's hyped as the ecocapital of the country, tricycle traffic jams and concrete buildings abound.

Sights & Activities

Several sights within the vicinity of Puerto are often visited as part of a day-long 'city tour', which caters primarily to Filipinos from Manila; each sight in itself isn't especially thrilling, so renting a motorbike doing a version of the tour on your own is a recommended option. Acrobatic long-snouted spinner dolphins and gentle giant whale sharks can be seen in the waters around Puerto.

For serious divers, Puerto Princesa is the jumping-off point for liveaboards to the remote Tubbataha Reefs (see p379).

PUERTO PRINCESA

Palawan Museum MUSEUM

(Mendoza Park; admission P20; ⏲9am-noon & 1.30-5pm Mon-Sat) Housed in the old City Hall building adjacent to Mendoza Park, this

Central Palawan

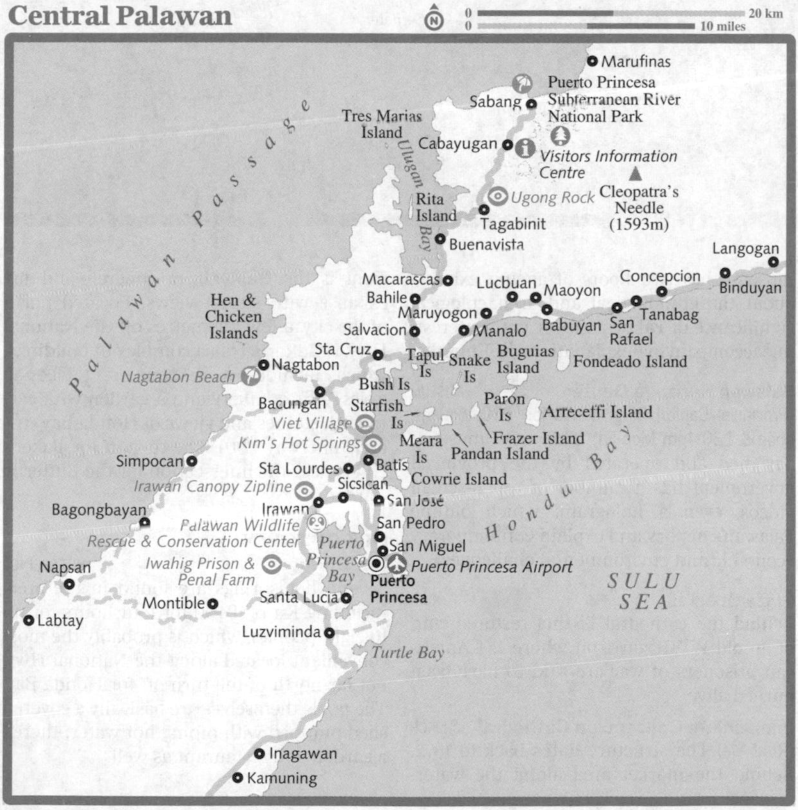

Puerto Princesa

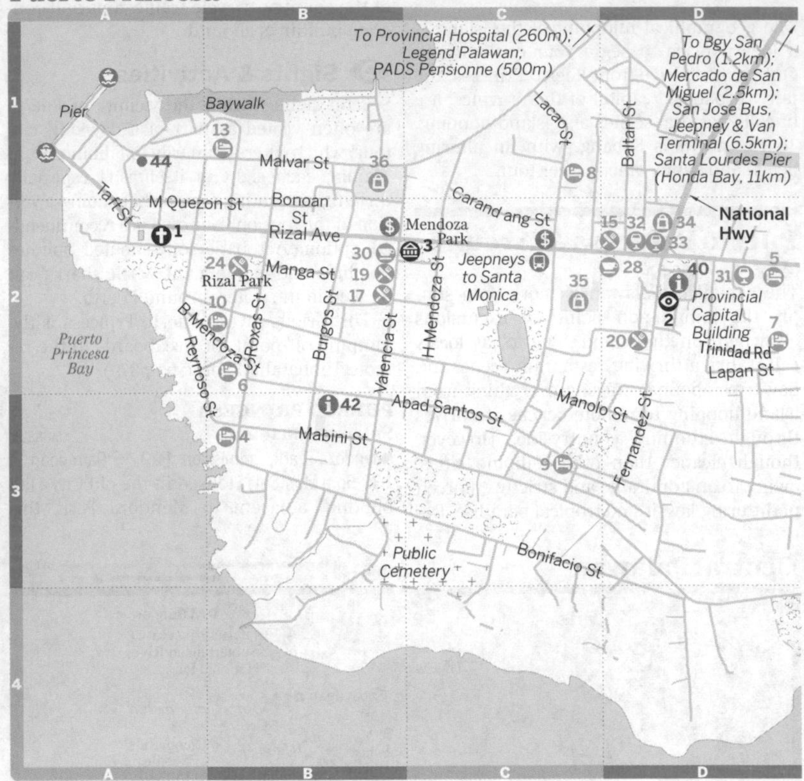

museum has two floors of ageing exhibits about the ethnological and archaeological significance of Palawan, most with interesting accompanying explanations in English.

Palawan Heritage Center MUSEUM
(Provincial Capitol Bldg; admission P30; ⌚9am-noon & 1.30-4pm Mon-Fri) This new museum designed and operated by the provincial government has a number of touch-screen videos, even a hologram, which outline Palawan's history and explain contemporary economic and environmental challenges.

Plaza Cuartel RUIN
Behind the cathedral is this restored ruin of an old WWII garrison where 154 American prisoners of war are said to have been burned alive.

Immaculate Concepcion Cathedral CHURCH
(Rizal Ave) The structure dates back to 1872. Behind the market area along the waterfront is the **Baywalk**, a concrete-and-dirt expanse with sunset views. Located north of the city, a few kilometres off the National Hwy, is **Baker's Hill**, a complex of buildings, which includes a **restaurant** (⌚Tue-Sat; mains P175), a bakery and a garden with cartoonish statues and views of Honda Bay (tricycle one way P80). The turnoff for Baker's Hill is near the intersection for the Butterfly Garden.

OUT OF TOWN

Hot Springs HOT SPRINGS
Several hot springs are found in the area, including Kim's (P400 for four hours for up to eight people), which is probably the most convenient located along the National Hwy, not far north of the turn-off for Honda Bay. The pools themselves are basically a covered shed pumped with piping hot water; there's a garden and restaurant as well.

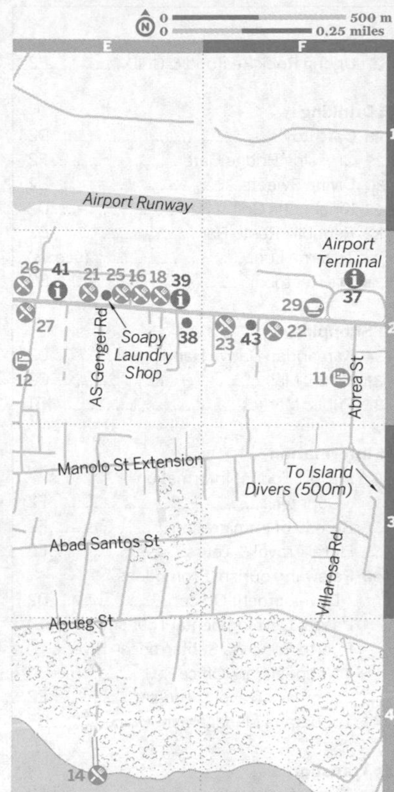

Palawan Wildlife Rescue & Conservation Center WILDLIFE RESERVE

(Crocodile Farming Institute; admission P40; ⌚8.30-11.30am & 1.30-4.30pm Mon-Sat) This wildlife reserve is a complex of concrete buildings and outdoor pens that houses hundreds of crocs, from newly hatched to scary behemoths. Guided tours leave every 30 minutes. Towards the back, in a densely forested area, other animals and birds eke out an existence in neglected aviaries and cages.

Palawan Butterfly Garden GARDEN

(27 Bunk House Rd, Santa Monica; admission P50; ⌚8am-5pm) An outdoor space near Santa Monica village where you can see different species of fluttering butterflies. Before entering, you can watch a short video that explains the life cycle of these delicate creatures.

Iwahig Prison & Penal Farm SITE

Around 5km past the Conservation Centre, the sign for this penal colony is an incongruent sight considering the beautiful countryside and dramatic mountain skyline in the background. Visitors are welcome to enter the extensive grounds (photography is discouraged), where prisoners, wearing differently coloured T-shirts depending on whether they are minimum, medium or maximum inmates, live, work and roam freely. It's mostly about the scenery.

Viet Village VILLAGE

A little further north of the hot springs is Viet Village, which, other than a restaurant serving highly praised *chaolong* (beef noodle soup), is now a ghost town; blowing tumbleweed wouldn't be out of place here. A thriving community of Vietnamese refugees who arrived in 1979 once called these weed-filled streets home.

Nagtabon Beach BEACH

This beach, on the northern side of the isthmus, has several hundred metres of white sand and shallow water good for swimming. Jeepneys from San Jose terminal leave around noon; the road is rough once it leaves the highway.

Festivals & Events

The **Baragatan Festival**, celebrated the third week in June, is held on the grounds of the Provincial Capitol Building. Palaweños from all over come together for dancing, singing, eating and drinking; vendors sell traditional handicrafts and culinary specialties.

Irawan Canopy Zipline ADVENTURE TOUR

(☎434 1132; from P200 to P650) Here you'll find few ziplines of different lengths in a protected forest area along the Irawan River, just near the Conservation Center. It has a nice cafe, and the booking office in Puerto is at the Lotus Garden Restaurant on Rizal Ave.

Sleeping

TOP CHOICE **Pagdayon Traveler's Inn** INN $

(☎434 9102, 0909 211 3677; Pagdayon Rd; r P900; ❄📶) This place is best described as modestly upscale native. Tile-floored rooms have small TVs, large closets and individual balconies, and the owners and staff are quietly professional and efficient. It's just down a narrow dirt road near the airport.

Casa Linda Inn INN $$

(☎433 2606, 0917 241 3144; casalindainn@gmail.com; Trinidad Rd; s/d with air-con P950/1100; ❄📶)

Puerto Princesa

Sights
1 Immaculate Concepcion Cathedral A2
2 Palawan Heritage Center D2
3 Palawan Museum C2
Plaza Cuartel ..... (see 1)

Sleeping
4 Ancieto's Pension B3
5 Badjao Inn D2
6 Banwa Art House B2
7 Casa Linda Inn D2
8 Hotel Fleuris C1
9 La Charica Inn C3
10 Manny's Guest House B2
11 Mercedes B&B F2
12 Pagdayon Traveler's Inn E2
13 Puerto Pension B1

Eating
14 Badjao Seafront Restaurant E4
15 Balinsasayaw D2
16 Bilao at Palayok E2
17 Bruno's Swiss Food B2
18 Bulwagang Princesa Garden Chaolong House E2
19 Café Nori B2
20 Ima's Vegetarian D2
21 Kalui E2
22 La Terrase F2
23 Lou Chaolong Hauz F2
24 Neva's Place B2
25 Sari's Baryo E2
26 Tio Rods Resto Bar & Lounge E2
27 Ugong Rock Seafood & Grill E2

Drinking
28 Café Itoy's D2
29 Crossing Bridge Café F2
30 Divine Sweets B2
31 Kinabuchs Grill & Bar D2
32 Republik Resto Bar D2
Taverna Luna ..... (see 18)
33 Tiki Restobar D2

Shopping
34 Kamantian Native Handicrafts D2
35 NCCC Mall C2
36 Public Market B1

Information
37 Airport Tourist Information Counter F2
38 Bureau of Immigration E2
39 Floral Travel & Tours E2
40 Palawan Tourism Promotions & Development Office D2
Pasyar Developmental Tourism ..... (see 38)
Puerto Princesa Subterranean River National Park Office ..... (see 5)
41 Sanctuary Travel & Tours E2
42 Tubbataha Management Office B3

Transport
43 Airphil Express F2
44 Negros Navigation A1
PAL ..... (see 43)

The meticulously maintained garden courtyard and pergola makes Casa Linda feel like a country refuge. The surrounding wood-floored rooms are clean and simply furnished, though thinly panelled walls mean noise can be a nuisance. There's a restaurant on-site, convenient for early morning pre-trip breakfasts.

Puerto Pension HOTEL $$
(☎433 2969, 0915 406 8568; www.puertopension.com; 35 Malvar St; r with shared/private bathroom from P900/1500; ❄📶) An impressive-looking four-storey wood-and-bamboo building, located not far from the town pier, with sweeping views of the bay from the top-floor restaurant. Everything is here, including wall-mounted TVs and fans – but there's only just enough room to slide around the bed. Breakfast is included with some rooms.

Banwa Art House PENSION HOUSE $
(☎434 8963, 0946 345 7853; www.banwa.com; Liwanag St; dm P350, r with/without bathroom P750/550; @📶) After a renovation and expansion, this groovy backpackers' spot, hidden behind a fence in a cramped residential part of town, is nicer inside than you might expect. A chilled, artsy back porch and lounge area is the highlight, and the rooms (two dorm rooms are gender-segregated) are clean and warm, though less than ideal for couples seeking privacy.

Hotel Centro HOTEL $$$
(☎434 1111; www.hotelcentro.ph; National Hwy, Barangay San Pedro; r incl breakfast from P5500; ❄📶🏊) Combining business class and resort luxury, Centro is now the most high-end option in Puerto. While its facade looks something like a corporate office, the outdoor

pool is the nicest around. It also features the usual bells and whistles like a gym and spa. It's on the National Highway, north of town.

Badjao Inn HOTEL $
(☎433 2761; badjao_inn@yahoo.com; 350 Rizal Ave; r with fan/air-con P500/1000; ❄@) Given the exterior of the Badjao looks like a '70s-era strip mall, the leafy and pleasant interior garden courtyard, complete with a sophisticated nipa-hut restaurant, is a revelation. Some of the rooms, such as the large, older fan rooms in front, are echo chambers of street noise; further back are more modern, concrete, air-con rooms

Hotel Fleuris HOTEL $$$
(☎434 4338; www.fleuris.com; Lacao St; s/d from P3000/3700; ❄@) Near Rizal Ave, though far enough away for a quiet night's sleep, the Fleuris is a business-class hotel with a few flourishes, including a piano bar and coffee shop. There's an outdoor pool, which is nice but for the fact it's next to the driveway and parking lot.

Legend Palawan HOTEL $$$
(☎434 4270; www.legendpalawan.com.ph; Malvar St; s/d from P4500/5100; ❄@) The Legend echoes big-city-hotel aesthetics found the world over in its grand, open-air, multi-storey atrium lobby. The large standard rooms are substandard for the price, but the comfort level rises if you go deluxe. Tiny dimensions aside, rooms in **PADS Pensionne** (r from P2200; ❄@), the next-door annex, have boutique amenities like wall-mounted flat-screen TVs.

Ancieto's Pension PENSION HOUSE $
(☎0927 205 9782; arc_tess@yahoo.com.ph; 71 Reynoso St; s/d with fan & shared bathroom P250/400; ❄) The highlight of this place is its roof-deck garden with a kitchen for guests' use, and views of the bay. Most of the rooms are basic; more expensive ones have private bathrooms and air-con.

Manny's Guest House PENSION HOUSE $
(☎0912 872 1294; www.mannysguesthouse.com; 2 B Mendoza St; r with shared bathroom & fan/air-con P400/650;) An old and charming wooden home with a kitchen for guests' use.

Palo Alto Bed & Breakfast B&B $$
(☎434 2159; www.paloalto.ph; Kawayanan St, Barangay San Pedro; r incl breakfast from P1500; ❄) This place has flat-screen TVs and two viewing decks for soaking up the breezes and views.

Mercedes B&B HOTEL $$
(☎0916 714 5220; www.mercedesb&b.com; Abrea St; r from P1200; ❄) A handful of nicely furnished modern rooms that front a mostly barren yard.

La Charica Inn HOTEL $$
(☎434 2088; www.lacharicainn.com; 126 Abad Santos St; s/d incl breakfast P950/1350; ❄) A narrow, somewhat tacky exterior conceals comfortable, modern rooms.

Eating

Puerto is easily the best place to eat in Palawan. In terms of sheer number of restaurants there's no competition, but the city also surprises in terms of variety. A slew of restaurants is located on Rizal Ave between the airport and the National Hwy, within walking distance of a number of hotels.

The city has a number of **chaolong restaurants** (dishes P40 to P45), small informal eateries serving up a tasty beef (or pork or chicken) noodle soup with a side of French bread. The restaurants are a lingering reminder of the Vietnamese community that once called Puerto home (see Viet Village, p375). **Lou Chaolong Hauz** (8am-4am) and **Bulwagang Princesa Garden Chaolong House** (24 hr) are near one another on Rizal Ave out towards the airport.

TOP CHOICE **Kalui** FILIPINO $$
(☎433 2580; 369 Rizal Ave; mains from P195; 11am-2pm & 6-11pm Mon-Sat) Kalui has a lovely Balinese ambience – wooden floors, colourful paintings, sculptures and masks adorn the walls, and there's a general air of sophistication. Choose from a few varieties of seafood, all served with vegies, plus there's a delightful fruit-mix dessert, served in a hollowed-out coconut. Reservations are recommended, especially for dinner and groups.

Badjao Seafront Restaurant FILIPINO, SEAFOOD $$
(☎433 9912; Abueg Sr Rd, Barangay Bagong Sikat; mains P195; 11am-10pm) This restaurant, perched over the water at the end of a raised boardwalk, is fairly high class in terms of table settings, but it's the sea and mountain views that raise it above the ordinary. A long lunch gnawing on whole grilled fish and other seafood is a nice way to spend an afternoon. Service is slow when busy.

WORTH A TRIP

HONDA BAY

Compared with the islands in the Bacuit Archipelago, Honda Bay may be a poor stepchild; however, this is a bit of an unfair comparison and a day spent **snorkelling** and **island-hopping** is almost a prerequisite if you're in the area for more than a night.

A regular tour allows you to visit three islands, usually **Pandan Island**, **Cowrie Island** and the aptly named **Snake Island**, a winding strip of white sand that changes shape with the tides. Package tours are available from travel agencies (see p380) and hotels in Puerto, and cost around P1100, which includes snorkelling, transport and lunch, and usually lasts from 8am to 4pm. To do it yourself, make your way to Santa Lourdes pier, 11km north from Puerto Princesa city centre (a multicab or tricycle will cost you P100), and ask around – a boat for up to six people should be around P1500. For the return trip to Puerto be prepared to wait as transport can be scarce. Keep in mind that other than a shack on Snake Island selling a handful of provisions and grilled fish, there are no restaurants or stores. Cowrie, Pandan and Starfish Islands charge nominal entrance fees.

The only established place to spend the night in the islands is on Arreceffi Island, at the luxurious **Dos Palmas Arreceffi Island Resort** (☎in Manila 02-637 4226; www.dospalmas.com.ph; full board per person from P11,000; ❄📶🏊). Choose from wood-floored cottages perched over the water, or larger, concrete beachside villas. There's a luxury spa, an infinity pool and fully functioning dive centre. It's a 50-minute bangka ride from Santa Lourdes pier and day trippers can use the facilities for P500.

Ugong Rock Seafood & Grill SEAFOOD $$
(Rizal Ave; mains P175; ⏰10am-2pm & 5pm-midnight) Choose your protein from the trays on display (crabs, prawns, lobster, mussels, squid and at least two types of fish), the method of cooking, and a sauce, and a short time later you'll be feasting on your creation. It's best to share a variety of dishes in a group.

Ima's Vegetarian VEGETARIAN $
(Fernandez St; mains P75; ⏰11am-9pm Sun-Thu, to 3pm Fri; 🌶) Ima's is run by a warm, softly spoken couple dedicated to healthy living through better eating. The bean burrito or tofu burger and other rice and veg dishes are sans additives and preservatives.

Neva's Place PIZZERIA $
(Manga St; mains P70, pizza P140-245) Some Puerto residents say Neva's has the best pizza in town; plus it has other choices, like chicken, pork and pasta, to round out the menu. There's a large dining area on the 2nd floor.

La Terrase FILIPINO, FRENCH $$
(Rizal Ave; mains P250; ⏰11am-midnight) This is a sophisticated open-air dining room with a small menu of pasta, seafood and grilled meats. Attention is paid to organic and locally sourced ingredients.

Bruno's Swiss Food EUROPEAN $$
(Valencia St; mains P550; ⏰Mon-Sat) For those craving Swiss, Polish and German sausage, and European beers and wines.

Tio Rods Resto Bar & Lounge FILIPINO $$
(Rizal Ave; mains P200; ⏰6am-midnight) Sleek two-storey place that serves seafood by weight, plus organic goat curry and good breakfasts.

Café Nori FILIPINO, JAPANESE $
(Valencia St; mains P100) A small place, between Divine Sweets and Bruno's Swiss Food, with a few Japanese dishes like chicken *katsu* and maki rolls as well as noodles and sandwiches.

Near one another on Rizal Ave are **Sari's Baryo** (mains P140), **Balinsasayaw** (mains P140) and **Bilao at Palayok** (mains P140); all serve a variety of Filipino favourites and grilled fish. The latter eatery, with a small pond, waterfall and soft music, is probably the most pleasant.

Two good choices in the Mercado de San Miguel, a few kilometres north of Rizal along the National Hwy, are **Gypsy's Lair** (mains P120; ⏰8am-11pm Sun-Thu, 9am-midnight Fri & Sat; 📶), a postage stamp–sized bohemian-style restaurant with Filipino and Mexican fare as well as live acoustic music on weekend nights, and **Sky Box** (mains P180; ⏰10.30am-

2am), which features a stylish outdoor bar and eclectic menu, including thin-crust pizza, burgers and BBQ ribs.

Drinking & Entertainment

A number of informal bars and karaoke shacks, along with a few restaurants good for drinks, are lined up along the road between the airport and National Hwy. There are a few good coffee shops with excellent pastries, as well as more substantial menus, including **Café Itoy's** (Rizal Ave; ⏰6am-11pm; 📶) and **Divine Sweets** (Valencia St; mains P150; ⏰7am-10pm; 📶).

TOP CHOICE **Kinabuchs Grill & Bar** RESTOBAR
(Rizal Ave; ⏰5pm-2am) This is where a good chunk of Puerto seems to go at night. It's a large open-air property with several billiard tables, big-screen TVs and an extensive menu (mains from P100), though most people come for the cheap beer and lively atmosphere. Adventurous eaters can try the *tamilok*, basically a woodworm that's said to taste like an oyster.

Crossing Bridge Café CAFE
(Rizal Ave; ⏰7am-11pm) Just outside the airport entrance, perfect for an iced coffee or cookies-and-cream frappucino while waiting for your flight.

Republik Resto Bar (mains P160) and **Tiki Resto Bar** (mains P160), located next to one another near the junction of Rizal Ave and the National Hwy, are happening outdoor night spots with live music and substantial food and drink menus. The former has a daily stand-up comedy spot at 10pm, however, jokes are in Tagalog. **Taverna Luna** (Rizal Ave), sandwiched between restaurants further out towards the airport, also has live music from 8pm to 1am.

Shopping

A few handicraft shops on Rizal Ave between the airport and AS Gengel Rd sell mainly generic imitation native masks and statues of the type found everywhere from Nairobi to Bangkok. A Robinson's megamall, the first mall in all of Palawan, complete with restaurants and cinema, was going up on the National Hwy about 5km north of Rizal Ave at the time of writing.

Kamantian Native Handicrafts HANDICRAFTS
(National Hwy) In terms of quality, this place has a somewhat higher-than-average selection of crafts.

Public Market MARKET
(Burgos St; ⏰9am-5pm) Piles of tropical fruit, colourful vegetables and fish stacked like sardines make up the colourful tableau here.

NCCC Mall MALL
(Lacao St; ⏰9am-7pm) An ageing, humble concrete block containing a supermarket, pharmacy and department store.

TUBBATAHA REEFS

A 10- to 12-hour boat ride from Puerto Princesa, Palawan, are the **Tubbataha Reefs**, a marine protected reserve often compared to the Galapagos Islands. The park is a natural wonderland with hundreds of species of seabirds and fish, including mantas, whale sharks and the full gamut of pelagic marine life.

In the mid-'80s fishermen from Cagayancillo, the closest inhabited islands to the north, began using dynamite and cyanide to catch fish on the reefs. Soon after, unregulated dive boats and increased commercial fishing prompted the government to declare it a national park, and it was declared a Unesco World Heritage Site in 1993. The World Wildlife Fund (WWF) has been an active partner in helping to provide technical expertise and management experience.

The season for visiting Tubbataha runs from March through June. The only way to visit is on one of the half-dozen or so live-aboards operating from Puerto Princesa. The average cost for a week-long trip is US$1200 to US$1500. **Cruise Island Adventure Inc** (☎in Manila 02-813 2909; www.expeditionfleet.com) based in Manila and **Queen Anne Divers** (www.queenannedivers.com.ph) and **Moonshadow** (www.moonshadow.ch) based in Puerto can be recommended. Tubbataha live-aboard vessels usually offer 'transition trips' at reduced prices when moving from and returning to their home ports, usually in early March and early June.

Drop by the Tubbataha Management Office in Puerto Princesa for more information on Tubbataha (p380).

Information

Internet Access

Several internet cafes are located along Rizal Ave, between the airport terminal and Jollibee restaurant.

Laundry

Soapy Laundry Shop (Rizal Ave; ⏲8am-8pm Mon-Sat, 1-8pm Sun; laundry per kg P28)

Medical Services

Palawan Adventist Hospital (☎433 2156; National Hwy, Barangay San Pedro)

Provincial Hospital (☎433 2621; Malvar St)

Salvador P Socrates Government Center (Kilusang ligtas malaria; ☎434 6346; PEO Rd, Barangay Bancao-Bancao) For malaria issues only; can perform blood tests.

Money

Important note: in all of Palawan only Puerto and Coron town on the far-north island of Busuanga have ATMs. Plan appropriately. There are several banks along Rizal Ave.

Tourist Information

Bureau of Immigration (☎433 2248; 2nd fl, Servando Bldg, Rizal Ave)

City Tourism Office (☎434 4211; www.visitpuertoprincesa.com; Puerto Princesa Airport; ⏲7am-6pm) Just outside the airport terminal to the right. Also has a desk in the terminal with staff to answer questions.

Palawan Tourism Promotions & Development Office (☎433 2968; www.palawan.gov.ph; ground fl, Provincial Capital Bldg, Rizal Ave; ⏲8am-noon & 1-5pm Mon-Fri) Extremely helpful and knowledgeable staff can answer questions about Puerto and other destinations in Palawan.

Puerto Princesa Subterranean River National Park Office (☎434 2509; www.puerto-undergroundriver.com; Badjao Inn, 350 Rizal Ave) Where to apply for standard permits or for those for longer underground river trips.

Tubbataha Management Office (☎434 5759, 0929 597 8529; www.tubbatahareef.org; 41 Abad Santos St) For more information on trips to Tubbataha, see the boxed text, p379.

Travel Agencies

Floral Travel & Tours (☎434 2540; floral_travel@yahoo.com; Rizal Ave)

Island Divers Ventures (☎433 2917; www.islanddivers.ph; Manalo Ext, Barangay Bancao-Bancao) Offers diving in and around Honda Bay.

Pasyar Developmental Tourism (☎723 1075, 0926 437 5224; www.pasyarpalawan.tripod.com; Rizal Ave) Dedicated to conservation and community-based tourism. Can tailor itineraries to your needs, from half-day trips to nearby San Carols River mangroves, to a week-long 'waterfalls adventure' as well as an 'old growth forest trekking tour' which involves tagging along with enforcement officers on the look-out for illegal loggers south near Quezon.

Sanctuary Travel & Tours (☎434 7673; sanctuarytours@yahoo.com; Rizal Ave)

Getting There & Away

For details on air and boat connections see p372.

Bus & Jeepney

All public buses, jeepneys and vans operate from the San José terminal, 7km north of Puerto city centre (tricycle is P40 per person or P100 if alone) off the National Hwy (there is a signpost that reads 'New Public Market'). Once you get there, simply ask around for the first bus or jeepney headed to your intended destination. See the table below for some sample bus routes.

The majority of departures are from 7am to 9am. There are other departures, some even late

BUSES FROM PUERTO PRINCESA

DESTINATION	COST	DURATION (HR)	FREQUENCY
Brooke's Point	P200	4	Six daily 6am-5pm
El Nido	Bus P380/ Minivan P600	Bus 9/Minivan 5	5am, 7am, 9am
Port Barton	P250	3½	8am, 9.30am
Quezon	P200	3	Hourly,7am-5pm
Roxas	P120	2½	Several, most in morning
Sabang	Bus P200/ Minivan P300	2¼	7am, 9am, noon
Taytay	P250	4½	Several, most in morning

UNDERGROUND RIVER ADVICE

You must purchase a **permit** (adult/child P200/P50) to visit the subterranean river at the office in Puerto or the **Tourist Information & Assistance Center** (☎723 0904; ⏲8am-4pm) at the pier in Sabang. The office here also arranges boat transport to the river (round trip for six people P700, 15 minutes). Permits (P400 per person) for longer trips (more than 4km, three hours) can be arranged a minimum of two days in advance at the office in Puerto.

Because most boats are reserved by tour groups it's best to show up first thing in the morning to guarantee seats, especially if there's a few of you (you pay around P100 per person).

Sometimes boat trips are cancelled due to rain and rough seas so when there's inclement weather we suggest contacting the office in Puerto in advance to save you a disappointing trip out to the river.

A final note: when looking up, keep your mouth shut – bats and swiftlets flutter above and are responsible for the guano that 'perfumes' the cave.

into the afternoon; however, it's best to show up as early as possible since jeepneys and vans don't leave until full – be prepared to wait and wait... Note that routes, operators, departure times and fares change all the time.

Car & Motorcycle

If you've got the cash, hiring a car or van and a driver is a good way to get around, and with a big enough group it can be a reasonable option – try **Tourister Rent a Car Travel & Tours** (☎0906 449 9991; ARL Bldg, Rizal Ave) or any of the travel agencies listed on p380. For El Nido (six hours) it's around P10,000 for a six-person van and driver.

Getting Around

The fixed rate for a tricycle from the airport to any destination in central Puerto is P50. Or you can simply walk out the driveway to Rizal Ave and flag one down for the standard fare (P8 for every 2km).

A day spent riding a motorbike through the countryside around Puerto is a day well spent. A number of places along Rizal Ave near the airport advertise rentals and charge between P250 and P550 per day.

Sabang & Around

☎048

A wide beach dramatically framed by mountains and warm calm waters, Sabang certainly has more to offer than simply its most famous attraction. The dubious campaign to vote Sabang's underground river one of the 'seven wonders of the world' notwithstanding, the river is worth seeing if in the area. Perhaps the closest thing we can compare it to is a bumper-boat ride through a theme-park haunted house, albeit one punctuated with the sounds of dripping water and fluttering birds, rather than screams and loud noises. After the hordes of day trippers who occupy the few beachside picnic huts are ferried back to Puerto, it's impossible not to feel as if they were intruders in your own little piece of paradise.

Sights & Activities

Puerto Princesa Subterranean River National Park BOAT TOUR

(formerly St Paul Subterranean River; www.puerto-undergroundriver.com) While the subterranean river is actually over 8km in length, standard tours only take you about 1.5km into the river (the round trip is 45 minutes; beyond this point, navigation becomes difficult). The limestone cave that the river passes through is one of the longest navigable river-traversed tunnels in the world. In 2010 a team of Italian spelunkers discovered the million-year-old fossilised remains of a dugong (sea cow) on a part of the cave wall not currently open to the public.

The boat from Sabang pier drops you off on a beach near the entrance to the cave (a few crab-eating monkeys and monitor lizards roam the area); from there you walk five minutes to the actual entrance and are assigned a boat for the trip into the cave. This second boat fare is included in your permit fee (p381 for details). Along the way, your guide, with the help of a spotlight, will point out various features of the caves (this usually means one-liners and double entendres like 'we call that formation Sharon Stone' rather than geological facts).

Beach BEACH

The beach in front of Sabang is quite nice and the warm, calm waters are perfect for swimming; another white-sand beach lies just across the Poyuy-Poyuy River. There are sand flies in the afternoon, so take precautions and consider swimming rather than sunbathing.

Jungle Trail HIKING

After visiting the cave, energetic souls might want to return to Sabang on foot over the 5km-long Jungle Trail. Starting from the ranger station near the subterranean river, the Jungle Trail initially climbs very steeply over some overgrown limestone karsts before dividing into two paths. The right fork is the Jungle Trail (there's another ranger station where you can rest), and the left is the Monkey Trail (which at the time of writing had been closed indefinitely after being damaged in a storm). You can also walk the Jungle trail in the opposite direction from Sabang to the subterranean river, but keep in mind that the trail officially closes at 3pm, that you need to purchase your park permit from the information office in Sabang, and that the trail's not well marked.

Poyuy-Poyuy River BOAT TOUR

(P150; ⏲8am-4pm) This community-driven project involves paddling with a guide a few kilometres up the mangrove-lined, brackish Poyuy-Poyuy River. The trip takes less than an hour and is best done in the early morning when the birdlife (parrots, hornbills, herons etc) is more active. Otherwise, you might spot a few baby pythons and mangrove snakes. From January through May the water is clear and you can see to the bottom. Walk through Mary's Beach Resort at the northern end of the beach and follow the overgrown path to the small office along the river.

Ugong Rock HIKE

Around 20km from Sabang near barangay Tagabinet is the trailhead for the 7km hike to Ugong Rock, a karst formation with commanding views of the surrounding countryside. Ropes and wooden bridges allow you to explore the somewhat tricky path through strangely shaped tunnels and chambers – guides (P100) and permits (P100) are issued at the trailhead. It's possible to camp out overnight in an area village but you must bring your own tent. The nearby zip-line wasn't in operation when we visited. A round-trip tricycle to the trailhead costs P700.

A few **snorkelling** spots are near Sabang, including Panganan Cave (P1500 for the boat trip) and **fishing** expeditions can be arranged with local boatmen or Daluyon Resort (p382).

Sleeping & Eating

Note that other than the two high-end resorts, there is no hot water in Sabang and electricity runs only from 6pm to 10pm. All of the accommodations listed here serve food and there are a couple of simple restaurants near the pier.

Daluyon Resort BEACH RESORT **$$$**

(☎433 6379; www.daluyonresort.com; r incl breakfast from P3900; ❄📶🏊) The Daluyon goes to show that luxury doesn't have to damage the aesthetic vibe of a beautiful locale, though you can't miss the two-storey thatched-roof cottages that peek out from behind towering palm trees. Inside, the rooms are all contemporary high end, from the flat-screen TVs to bathroom fixtures. The Daluyon easily has the best **restaurant** (mains P220) in Sabang.

Dab Dab Resort NIPA HUTS **$**

(☎0949 469 9421; cottages with/without bathroom P700/400) This resort, on the far side of the pier down a small dirt path, is an appealing haven. There's no beach here, only a rocky shoreline, but the four hardwood cottages with nipa roofs are much nicer than those on the beach. Each is equipped with a private porch and hammock; meals can be provided in the equally attractive restaurant and lounge area.

Sheridan Beach Resort BEACH RESORT **$$$**

(☎434 1449; www.sheridanbeachresort.com; r incl breakfast P7000; ❄🏊@📶) This contemporary, somewhat generic resort, the newest addition to Sabang's beachfront, wouldn't be out of place in Boracay. An air of exclusivity, although not in itself a bad thing, feels a little out of place here. The only downside to the tastefully designed rooms is that they either face each other in an outdoor corridor or they face the large pool, rather than the beach.

Mary's Beach Resort NIPA HUTS **$**

(☎0910 384 1705; cottages with/without bathroom P500/350) These no-frills cramped cottages are a popular choice, primarily because of their location at the very northern end of the beach where there's little foot traffic.

Blue Bamboo Cottages NIPA HUTS **$**
(☎0910 582 2589; cottages P300) These charmingly dilapidated all-bamboo cottages, located around 50m past Dab Dab, have their own porches, some with hammocks, private toilets and shared showers.

Taraw Lodge & Restaurant NIPA HUTS **$**
(☎0905 335 6235; cottages with/without bathroom P1000/500) These cottages are basic, especially the ones with common bathrooms. The restaurant gets extremely busy with groups at lunchtime.

Tribal Beach Resort Lodge & Restaurant HOTEL **$**
(☎0929 523 2553; tribalbeachresort@yahoo.com; P500) Five basic rooms. Next to Mary's Beach Resort, on the far northern end of the beach.

Getting There & Away

Boat

During high season (November to May), bangkas chug from Sabang up to El Nido (P2000, seven hours) almost daily, with drop-offs in Port Barton (P1200, 3½ hours). It's also easy to charter a boat on your own, which you'll have to do in the low/wet season (June to October); typical asking prices for six-passenger boats are P9000 for Port Barton and P12,000 for El Nido. Assuming good weather, the trip to Port Barton is a pleasant and convenient choice; the long passage to El Nido can be trying.

Bus, Jeepney & Van

The turn-off to Sabang along the main highway is in Salvacion, from where it's a scenic 35km drive over a winding, mostly sealed road.

Most travel agencies, guesthouses and hotels in Puerto offer all-inclusive tours to the subterranean river and this is how the majority of day trippers arrive. Otherwise, the most comfortable transport option is the minivans that leave from Puerto's San José bus terminal at 7am, 2pm and 4pm daily (P300, two hours). They leave Sabang to return to Puerto at approximately the same times.

There are two or three other departures a day that use a combination of jeepneys and buses (P200, three hours), and leave Puerto's San José bus terminal at 7am, 9am and noon; on the return trip, these leave Sabang at 7am, 10am, noon and 2pm. (Note that these are approximate times only.)

From Sabang, to reach Port Barton or El Nido by road you can take a jeepney (P80), van (P120) or tricycle (P1000) to Salvacion (45 minutes) and wait for a passing bus, jeepney or van heading to Roxas, Taytay or El Nido (four hours); for Port Barton, you then need to get off at the highway junction at San José and hop on a tricycle or motorbike (P400, one hour). It's possible to arrange a private van for Port Barton (P5000, three hours) and El Nido (P7000, five hours). Ask for Ed Garcia (☎0926 689 9812).

SOUTHERN PALAWAN

Few people head south of Puerto, partly because of the relative lack of facilities that cater to tourists. For those with reserves of endurance, who seek an adventurous alternative to more famous attractions elsewhere, the south, which is populated by indigenous tribal groups and Muslim communities, is rough but potentially rewarding travel.

Narra

☎048 / POP 62,000

This town is generally considered the rice granary of Palawan, a boast not often made on tourist brochures. The daily market is worth a stop and there are a few beaches in the area including **Isla Areana**, and the nearby offshore **Rasa Island** is home to a cockatoo colony. **Estrella Falls** is good for a picnic and **Victoria Mountain** (1709m), one of the highest peaks on the island, can be climbed, however, a local guide is necessary.

The nicest place to base yourself is the **Crystal Paradise Resort Spa & Winery** (☎0919 457 3042; www.crystalparadiseresort.com; 1 Sea Rd, Barangay Antipuluan; r incl breakfast from P4800; ❄≋), nestled in a cove around 7km from Narra. Besides the motel-style rooms with so-called native art, there's a villa with its own infinity pool; it's of arguable value

MALARIA WARNING

Malaria (chloroquine resistant) is considered endemic in southern Palawan and periodically a concern in rural areas elsewhere (dengue fever is more common). Antimalarial medication is recommended for anyone choosing to travel in this region; several types are available at Mercury Drug and other pharmacies in Puerto. To reduce your chances of contracting the disease, you should also bring insect repellent, wear long pants and long sleeves at night and use a mosquito net when possible.

though considering the price. The resort produces its own wine from mangoes, pineapples, bananas and other fruit.

Minivans connect Puerto and Narra (P160).

Quezon

☎048 / POP 51,000

This is the nearest major town to **Tabon Caves**, an extensive network of more than 200 caves honeycombed into Lipum Point. These caves have yielded remnants of prehistory in the form of crude burial grounds; human remains estimated to be 47,000 years old have been found here. The caves, a half-hour boat ride from Quezon, are fascinating for both their anthropological significance and the striking scenery.

The easiest way to arrange a trip to the caves is to visit the Quezon branch of the **Tabon Museum** (admission free; ⏰8am-noon & 1-5pm Mon-Fri), which is signposted off the main road into Quezon just before the town – ask for the tourism officer **Mabel Campilan** (☎0918 400 9645). A guide and boat (P1200) will be provided, otherwise you can probably find a person with a boat who will act as a guide for around P800 (it's about a half-hour boat ride in each direction, and then a walk up to the caves). Be sure to wear comfortable clothes, walking shoes and mosquito repellent. The museum itself contains Tagbanua ceramics, ritual paraphernalia and other archaeological finds from the area.

Near Quezon on Malanut Bay, the **Tabon Village Resort** (☎0910 239 8381; cottages with/without bathroom from P500/250) has several simple, ageing cottages in a garden setting and can arrange a boat trip to offshore islands. A less appealing but adequate option is the **Zambrano Pension House** (☎0921 612 1767; r P400; ❄), with a restaurant and bar on the premises.

Charing Bus Lines runs services hourly to Quezon from Puerto (P200, four to five hours).

Rizal

POP 35,500

This extremely remote town on the western side of the island is a base for explorations into the surrounding mountains, including **Mt Matalingahan** (2086m), the highest in Palawan.

The Tao't Bato people live around a six- to eight-hour trek from the town proper. They have no script or alphabet and they follow animistic beliefs; during the wet season they live on platforms in caves nestled into the mountains, and for the remainder of the year they practise slash and burn agriculture on the steep slopes. Otherwise, they sustain themselves through subsistence foraging and hunting. If you're interested in learning more, go to the municipal hall in Rizal and ask for freelance guide **Anthony Bojie Lorenzo** (☎0919 403 4435; bojielorenzo@gmail.com); he can arrange a guide and help supply camping equipment for the trip.

Castelar Store & Lodging Inn (☎0921 504 4108; r P500) has very basic fan rooms. Charing Bus Lines has three trips a day from Puerto (5am, 9am and 1pm, five to six hours).

Brooke's Point

POP 56,000

Relatively large by southern Palawan standards, Brooke's Point is just about the end of the road. It's the last major town on the southeast coast of Palawan, and a gateway to even sketchier areas to the south; as it's home to smugglers and modern-day pirates, locals here tend to be less welcoming than elsewhere. There are nevertheless opportunities for hiking, including to Mt Matalingahan (though it's easier done from Rizal) and numerous waterfalls and beaches in the area; ask for **Agnes Onda** (☎0908 736 4118), the tourism officer in town, to help arrange guides and supplies.

Mt Maruyog Farms & Gardens (☎0917 700 0867; www.maruyogresort.com; Tubtub, Brooke's Point; cottages with fan/air-con P500/P950; ❄🏊) offers nicely furnished bamboo, wicker and wood cottages in a beautifully landscaped garden. There's a tree house, restaurant and pool. **Silayan Lodge** (☎0918 386 1262; r P350) near the public market has basic fan rooms.

NORTHERN PALAWAN

Many travellers make a beeline for this region and find it difficult to move on. Endowed with a bending and twisting coastline lined with secluded coves and beaches and labyrinthine offshore islands, it's seventh heaven for beachcombers and under-

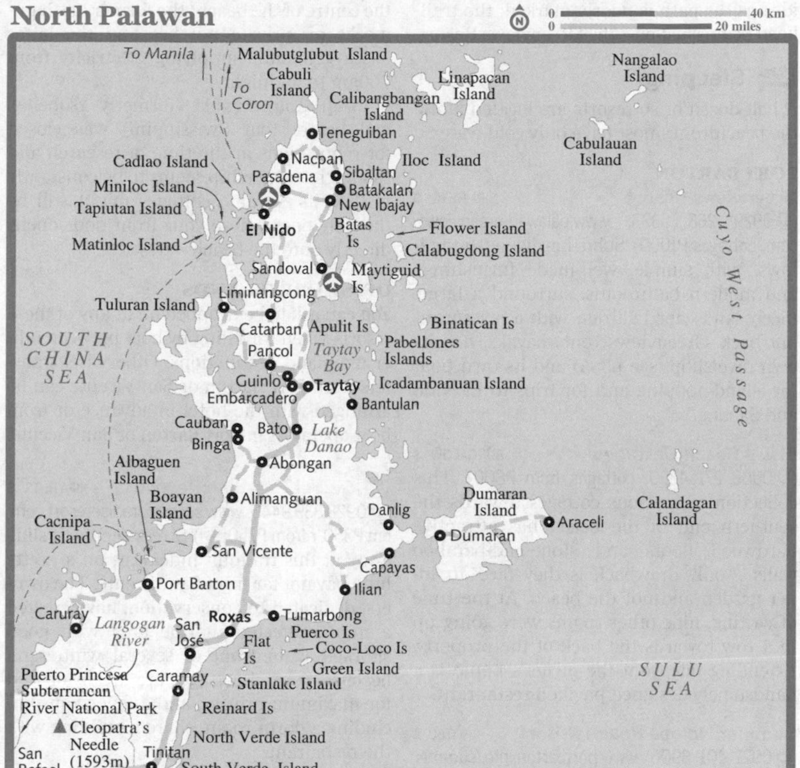

water adventurers alike. El Nido and Coron Town are the primary gateways to the area.

Port Barton & Around

POP 4400

Essentially a one-road town where the jungle drops precipitously into the bay, Port Barton offers simple pleasures. It's the kind of place where, after just a few strolls down the beach, you don't want to share the tranquillity with outsiders. Several islands with good beaches and snorkelling aren't far offshore, as are rows and rows of buoys, the sign of working pearl farms. Jellyfish can be a problem for swimmers at the town beach.

Sights & Activities

Island-hopping snorkelling trips (half-/full-day for up to four people P700/P1400) are the equal of similar trips in Honda Bay. Friendly local boatman **Jensen Gabco** (☎0921 626 9191) can be recommended.

Scuba Diving DIVING

There are several wreck and reef dives in the area. **Easy Dive** (☎0918 402 7041; www.palawaneasydive.com), located in a ramshackle house at the southern end of the beach, and **Sea Dog Diving** (☎0920 841 4650; www.seadogdivingpalawn.com), at Greenviews Resort (it also has a shop in El Nido), offer two boat dives including equipment and lunch for around P2800.

Long Beach BEACH

One of the longest undeveloped (for now) beaches in the country is the 14km white-sand Long Beach on the mainland near San Vicente.

Pamuayan Falls WATERFALL

Cool off here after the 4km walk from town. Hiring a guide for P50 to P100 isn't a bad idea as the path is poorly marked; the trailhead begins just past the Greenviews Resort.

Sleeping

A half-dozen or so resorts are located along the beachfront; most have only cold water.

PORT BARTON

Greenviews Resort NIPA HUTS $
(☎0929 268 5333; www.palawan-greenviews.com; cottages P1000) Solid hardwood bungalows, with simple, well-made furnishings and modern bathrooms, surround a large, nicely landscaped garden with a restaurant out back. Greenviews rents kayaks, has its own dive shop (see p385) and its own boat for island-hopping and for trips to El Nido and Sabang.

Elsa's Beach Cottages BUNGALOW $
(☎0908 271 4390; cottages from P800) This collection of spacious cottages towards the southern end of the beach has attractive hardwood floors and stone-and-bamboo walls – only drawback is they face an inner garden and not the beach. At the time of writing, nine other rooms were going up in a row towards the back of the property. Extending out from the owner's home is a handsomely designed pavilion restaurant.

Summer Homes Beach Resort HOTEL $
(☎0921 401 6906; www.portbarton.info/summerhomes; r P550, cottages P1200; ❄@📶) Located roughly in the middle of the beach, the rooms in this low-slung building behind the open-air restaurant feel more appropriate for Puerto since unlike its neighbours, Summer Homes has spurned the native look. The stand-alone cottages have ocean-view porches; these are the only rooms with hot water. A generator powers the resort's fans throughout the day.

Villa Marguerita APARTMENT $
(☎0919 488 0146; www.villamarguerita.com; r with shared/private bathroom P600/1200) A large native-style house with ample beachfront grounds meant for large groups, however, you can book individual rooms.

El Dorado Sunset Cottages BUNGALOW $
(☎0920 329 9049; r P400-800) On the road just before Greenviews, nine clean cottages behind a beachfront bar.

Malaika (☎0919 378 5497; cottages P1200) and **Ausan** (☎0930 957 2801; cottages P500) have two large attractive cottages each towards the centre of the beach; the former has hammocks on private porches and the latter has a generator supplying electricity from 7.30am to midnight.

Deep Gold Resort (formerly Ysobelle's and before that Swissippini) was closed for renovations at the time of research and though its ownership seems to be constantly in flux, its A-frame cottages might still be the only ones where your front door opens directly onto the beach.

OFFSHORE ISLANDS

You can ask to be dropped off at any of these resorts when travelling by boat between other mainland destinations. Otherwise, transfers from Port Barton or San Vicente can be arranged with the hotel in advance or from boat operators in Port Barton or San Vicente.

Secret Paradise Resort NIPA HUTS $
(☎0928 339 9446; www.secretparadiseresort.com; dm P350, r from P750; 📶) Stress seems to slide away at this tranquil hideaway, on a pretty little bay not far from San Vicente. The owners, dedicated to conservation, have created a mini protected marine area with good snorkelling in front of several white-sand beaches. Several cottages are ideally spaced for maximum privacy, and a few rooms, including a dorm room, share a building with the restaurant.

Coconut Garden Island Resort BEACH RESORT $
(☎0918 370 2395; www.coconutgarden.palawan.net; s/d P850/900, cottage P1200) Located on the route to Port Barton from Sabang by boat, this resort occupies a truly lovely white-sand beach on Cacnipa Island. Several buildings, including a restaurant, a handful of cottages and a row of rooms, are built up along a rise – all with ocean views and outdoor sitting areas.

Blue Cove Tropical Island Resort BEACH RESORT $$
(☎0908 562 0879; www.bluecoveresort.com; cottages from P950) On Albaguen Island, a half-hour bangka ride from Port Barton, the Blue Cove has a few bamboo bungalows, including one built on the water A truly charming beachside restaurant and bar also serves lunching day-trippers.

Eating

All of the resorts have their own restaurants and are open to nonguests.

Jambalaya Cajun Café INTERNATIONAL $$
(mains P180; ⌚7am-9pm; @) It's moving to an as yet undisclosed location, but no matter where it ends up you can expect a homey and quirky vibe courtesy of the welcoming Irish-Filipina couple in charge. Jambalaya (the Cajun version of paella), and gumbo (P70), a New Orleans dish, are the specialities; milkshakes and imported coffee are also on the menu. In addition, there's a book exchange and board games – hanging out is encouraged.

Bamboo House Restaurant FILIPINO, SEAFOOD $$
(mains P150) Near the Caltex station, Bamboo House is a friendly, family-run place with several tablecloth-clad picnic tables and a few small nipa huts in the yard. Seafood dishes, such as the fish curry, are especially good.

Information

The town has electricity from around 6pm to midnight. Jambalaya and Summer Homes have internet access though only during the hours when there's power; the latter has wi-fi (free for guests or patrons of restaurant who order a minimum of P150 worth of food or drink). There's no bank; a few resorts accept Visa and MasterCard.

A **Tourist Assistance Center** (☎0910 672 1641; ⌚8am-5pm) of limited utility has its headquarters on the 2nd floor of a wooden structure in the middle of the beach, near the Caltex station; set prices for various boat trips are posted.

Getting There & Away

Boat

During the November to May high season, it's possible to be dropped off in Port Barton on the regular scheduled boats between El Nido (P1500, five hours) and Sabang (P1200, 3½ hours). However, these boats are not allowed to pick up passengers, so if you want to leave Port Barton on one of these boats, you can be picked up on nearby Cacnipa Island. It's also easy to charter a boat on your own (ask at the Tourist Assistance Center) or join up with a group already doing the same; however, you might have to wait several days, at least during the low season. An association of sorts fixes and controls the prices for most of the island-hopping and longer trips. To Sabang, a small boat that holds four people is P3500; on a larger boat that can hold up to eight, the rate is P6000. To El Nido, a small/large boat is around P6000/12,000.

From Port Barton there are boats to San Vicente (P100, 45 minutes), a town along the mainland coast to the north. These generally leave daily at 8am during the high season, and depending on demand during the low season. You can also charter one yourself (P1200).

Bus & Jeepney

The 22km roadway between Port Barton and the highway at San José is rough and rocky. Several days of rainy weather only worsens potholes and muddy ditches. However, in good weather the trip is uneventful and the bus is a scenic and thrifty mode of transport.

A jeepney (an oversized one with forward-facing seats) runs daily from Port Barton to Puerto (P200, five hours, departs around 9am). It leaves from the waiting shed near the Bamboo House Restaurant. A hire van to Puerto for four people costs between P5000 and P6000.

Between Port Barton and Roxas, there is one jeepney a day (P150, 1½ hours, departing from the waiting shed between 8am and 9am), with the same schedule in the other direction.

It's also possible to 'charter' a motorcycle or tricycle (P400, one hour) to or from the highway junction at San José; you can also ride the regular morning jeepney (P100, one hour). From here, catch onward transport (buses and vans) north to Taytay and El Nido, or south to Sabang (you'll have to transfer again at the junction at Salvacion) and Puerto.

Taytay & Around

☎048 / POP 62,000

Formerly the capital of Palawan, today Taytay (*tye*-tye), a sleepy coastal town and primarily a way station for travellers, is distinguished by an impressive relic of the area's colonial history. Built on the very edge of town, the thick walls of **Santa Isabel Fort** (Kutang Santa Isabel) guarded against attacks from Moro pirates. On the right by the entrance is a marker indicating that it was first erected by the Augustinian Recollects (an order of Catholic priests) in 1667. Inside the enclosure is a well-maintained grassy garden and sweeping views of the bay.

More than a 20-minute drive south of town is **Lake Danao** (Manguao), the largest freshwater lake in Palawan. There are some trails for walking or mountain biking, and wildlife, including monkeys, monitor lizards and rare birds, abounds. Dugongs and elusive Irrawady dolphins can be spotted in the **Malampaya Sound**.

Sleeping

TAYTAY

Casa Rosa HOTEL $$
(☎0916 653 3311; www.casarosataytay.com; r without bathroom P350, cottages with bathroom P1000;

❄) Located on a hill behind the town hall, with sweeping views of the bay, this is the place to stay if you're stuck for a night in Taytay. Five cottages and two rooms – the former with terracotta floors and spacious bathrooms, are especially recommended – and a nice little **restaurant** (mains P145).

OFFSHORE ISLANDS

Room rates for Flower Island and Apulit Island include transfers from Taytay's airport or pier. Another option for all three resorts is by boat from Batakalan, a tiny fishing village about a 45-minute rough tricycle ride directly east of El Nido. There's one daily jeepney from El Nido (P90, 1½ hours), or a tricycle can be hired for P750.

TOP CHOICE Flower Island Beach Resort BEACH RESORT **$$$**
(☎0918 924 8895; www.flowerisland-resort.com; fan/air-con cottages incl all meals per person P4500/6100; ❄) Warning: leaving this idyllic low-key resort can induce severe depression. You might never have it so good again – the staff are warm and friendly, the native-style cottages such a perfect mix of modern comforts and rustic charm, and the small beach is of the whitest sand. Guests can also bed down in the five-story hilltop tower which has aerial views of the sea. Tours of the pearl farm factory nearby, which is owned by the same people as the resort, are fascinating. Affiliated with the Save Palawan Seas Foundation (see p442).

Apulit Island Resort BEACH RESORT **$$$**
(☎in Manila 02-844 6688; www.elnidoresorts.com; cottages per person incl all meals from P10,000; ❄📶) Rows of deluxe cabanas built directly over the water, which at night is illuminated by spotlights, turning it a translucent green, make this newly renovated resort an exclusive retreat. The offshore island nature reserve means there's nearby coral and marine life, perfect for snorkelling, and a range of other water-based activities.

Dilis Beach Island Resort BEACH RESORT **$$**
(☎0910 231 6392; per person incl meals from P1500) Located on Icadambanuan Island, at the south end of Taytay Bay, Dilis is a little offshore paradise. It has two cottages that front a white-sand beach, and two other modern rooms in a house set at the top of a hill. Food is especially good for such a modest operation. Bangkas can be hired in Taytay for around P1000 one way (the trip takes about one hour).

Getting There & Away

Air

ITI flies daily from Manila to Taytay's Cesar Lim Rodriguez Airport, located at the northern end of Taytay Bay, about 30km from town over a rough road.

Boat

For boats to and from El Nido (P2500, three hours) and other west-coast towns, you must use the pier at Embarcadero (also known as Agpay), an 8km tricycle ride (P150) from town.

Bus & Jeepney

Buses, jeepneys and vans travel frequently between Puerto and Taytay (P220, five to six hours, up to eight departures daily in each direction) on their way to and from El Nido (P150, 1½ hours) further north. The majority pass through in the morning. The road between these two towns is paved in parts and is a rough combination of gravel and dirt in others.

El Nido

☎048 / POP 5600

The ordinariness of El Nido only heightens the contrast between the mundane and the sublime, much like towns the world over that are the gateways to beautiful sights. Spanish for 'the nest', El Nido is the base for exploring the fabulous Bacuit Archipelago (p394). The town is sandwiched between towering limestone karst cliffs and Bacuit Bay, and is cluttered with buildings that creep onto the beach. Centre stage, however, is the looming Cadlao Island just offshore.

Taking a room in town means being close to restaurants and beachside bars, but also closer to the everyday sights and sounds; otherwise, you can stay in one of the nearby communities, or splash some cash for accommodation in the archipelago itself.

Sights & Activities

The most popular activity in El Nido is **island-hopping** and **snorkelling** in the Bacuit Archipelago. There are now standard itineraries advertised by seemingly every shopfront and hotel; those that don't can certainly arrange matters regardless. Prices are also standard, although some charge extra for snorkelling gear, and all include lunch (grilled fish, rice, salad, fruit and coffee). Tour A, which takes in various lagoons and beaches, is P700; Tour B, covering Snake Island, caves and Pinabuyutan Island, is P800; and Tour C, heading to Tapiutan Island, Matinloc Island and Secret Beach, is P900. The tour operated through El Nido Boutique & Art Café (p393) is especially recommended.

Stop by **Tao Philippines** (www.taophilippines; Serena St) and see the boxed text on p392 for information on highly recommended overnight island-hopping tours.

Every person entering the Bacuit Archipelago must now pay a P200 Eco-Tourism Development Fee (ETDF) meant to fund conservation projects; the small ticket is valid for 10 days and can be purchased from most hotels or boat operators.

For scuba divers, there are nearly two dozen **dive sites** in the area, from shallow reefs to deep wall and drift dives, making it a popular destination for PADI certification courses; the average cost for two boat dives with equipment is P2800. Several dive centres operate in town, including **El Nido Marine Club** (☎0916 668 2748; www.elnidomarineclub.com; Hama St), **Sea Dog Divers** (☎0916 777 6917; www.seadogdivingpalawan.com; Serena St) and **Submariner Diving Center** (☎0905 484 1764; ronny.oliwka@hotmail.com; Hama St). The especially recommended **Palawan Divers** (☎0916 552 1938; www.palawandivers.com.ph) also runs trips from El Nido to Coron.

Although often overlooked, the inland area around El Nido offers several interesting trips for the active and adventurous. **El Nido Boutique & Art Café** (☎0917 560 4020; www.elnidoboutiqueandartcafe.com; Serena St; ⏲transport info desk 7am-8pm; 📶) is a one-stop-shop for **hiking**, **mountain-biking** and **cliff-climbing** trips; half-day **treks** to Cadlao Island are popular. **Tuba Tours** (Hama St) can help arrange both island hopping and climbing.

Calilan Beach, around 20km north of town, is a beautiful, undeveloped stretch of sand near a small fishing village. Several kilometers after you've turned off the main road heading north from El Nido you will pass by a house signposted **Nagkalit-kalit Waterfalls**; from here it's a 45-minute walk through several rivers (wear waterproof shoes) to the small pool at the base of the falls, which you can swim in. Ask at the house for a guide (P300), who you'll need to find the falls.

The Makinit hotspring, basically a very hard-to-find swampy creek with water scalding to the touch, is not worth a visit.

Stop by Pittstop Motorbike Rentals (p394) for do-it-yourself information on reaching all the sights in this area.

Sleeping

Most of El Nido's beachfront hotel space is a claustrophobic hodgepodge of small buildings and construction sites. The east end tends to be quieter; the further west you go, the narrower the beach becomes and the more bangkas you find blocking your way. Hot water is uncommon, while electricity runs from around 2pm to 6am and several hotels and pension houses have generators for backup.

If you want to escape the tourist scene, consider places in quiet Caalan Beach (accessible from the walkway at the eastern end of El Nido beach, or another nearby narrow path for pedestrians and skilled motorcyclists) or Corong Corong, a waterfront village a few kilometres south of El Nido (tricycle ride from town P15); note, though, that its sandy beach, covered with overhanging palm trees, is about the width of a beach towel.

Alternatively, you can stay in one of the top-end resorts in the bay (p394).

EL NIDO

Entalulua Beach Cottages HOTEL $$
(☎0920 906 6550; www.entalula.com; r with fan/air-con P1000/1700; ❄) Entalulua has what are perhaps the finest of the beachfront standalone cottages, with private porches and nice bathrooms behind sliding doors. Ten other rooms are in a two-storey building set back from the beach that also doubles as the owner's home.

Rosanna's Beach Cottages HOTEL $$
(☎0920 605 4831; www.rosannas.multiply.com; Hama St; r with fan/air-con from P1500/2000; ❄📶) Rosanna's has four doubles in one building, as well as two cottages, all with private beachfront porches. Hardwood floors and walls are an upgrade from the flimsy bamboo found elsewhere; some have hot showers and include breakfast. Across the street, a modern annex with six rooms is especially good for groups or families.

La Salagane HOTEL $$
(☎0916 648 6994; www.lasalagane.com; Serena St; r incl breakfast from P1500; ❄📶) La Salagane is

El Nido

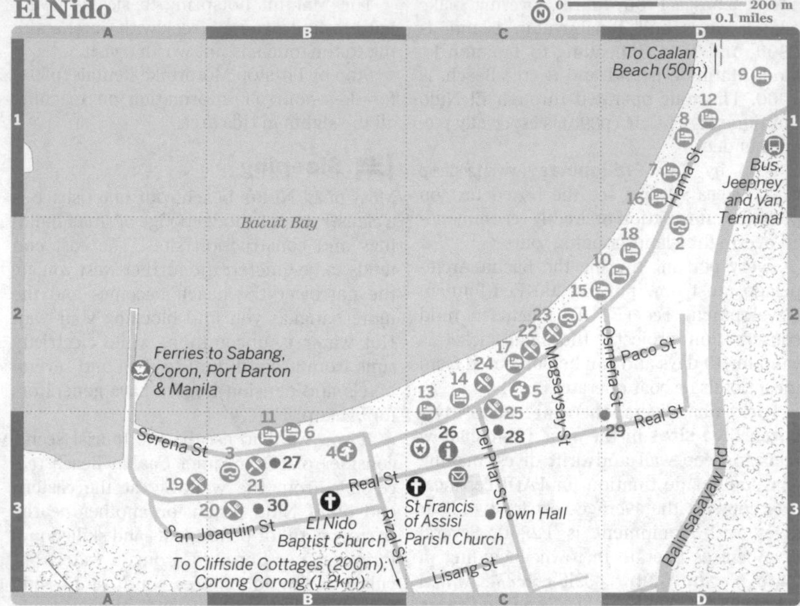

at the cramped end of town with no beach; however, its warm and inviting rooms have porches and hot water. An atmospheric waterfront restaurant serves French fare and seafood. The owner also has a place of the same name on Caalan Beach.

Alternative PENSION HOUSE **$**
(☎0917 595 5952; beckygordon8@yahoo.com; Serena St; dm P200, d with/without bathroom P800/500) One of the few places sandwiched in the western side of town. The dark ground floor is a stark contrast to the bright and open 2nd floor, which features funky lounging areas perched over the beach. Good-value breakfasts and healthy juices and shakes are available in the restaurant.

Marina Garden Beach Resort HOTEL **$$**
(☎0917 624 7722; www.mgelnido.com; Hama St; cottages from P700, r incl breakfast P2000; ❄📶) Located in the middle of the beach, Marina Garden's sandy grounds are roomy for El Nido, with enough space for a game of volleyball. The 'country villa' rooms in the low-slung concrete building are about as country as downtown Manila; they are of the standard, modern, hotel type. The few wooden cottages, remnants of an older incarnation, are in bad condition.

Chislyk Cottages BUNGALOW **$**
(☎0919 879 9333; ana.bacsa@yahoo.com; cottages P500) Several small bamboo cottages share an almost stamp-sized beachfront; however, each does have its own porch, complete with several wooden lounge chairs.

El Nido Garden Beach Resort HOTEL **$$$**
(☎0915 489 9009, 723 0127; www.elnidogardenresort.com; r P5300; ❄📶🏊) Because it's located at the far eastern end of El Nido, where there's a seawall instead of sand, this resort has improvised its own unique beach. Bungalows are built of concrete, stone and wood, and have high-end touches in the bathrooms. All surround a nicely landscaped garden and pool.

Ogie's Beach Pension HOTEL **$**
(☎0916 707 0393; www.ogspensionne.weebly.com; Hama St; r with fan/air-con incl breakfast from P800/1600; ❄📶) Situated right in the middle of the beach, from the outside Ogie's looks like a small vacant office building, so the clean, tile-floored rooms are a pleasant surprise. Eschewing the beach bungalow style, it's mostly concrete throughout, including the 2nd-floor sitting area with ocean views where breakfast is served.

El Nido

Activities, Courses & Tours

- El Nido Boutique & Art Café .... (see 21)
- 1 El Nido Marine Club C2
- 2 Palawan Divers D2
- 3 Sea Dog Divers B3
- Submariner Diving Center .... (see 22)
- 4 Tao Philippines B3
- 5 Tuba Tours C2

Sleeping

- 6 Alternative B3
- 7 Chislyk Cottages D1
- 8 El Nido Beach Hotel D1
- 9 El Nido Garden Beach Resort D1
- 10 Entalula Beach Cottages D2
- 11 La Salagane B3
- 12 Lally & Abet Beach Cottages D1
- 13 Marina Garden Beach Resort C2
- 14 Ogie's Beach Pension C2
- 15 Rico's Cottages C2
- 16 Rosanna's Beach Cottages D1
- 17 Rovic's Pension House C2
- 18 Tandikan Cottages D2

Eating

- 19 Balay Tubay A3
- 20 Blue Azul Restaurant B3
- 21 El Nido Boutique & Art Café B3
- 22 Habibi Restaurant & Shisha Café C2
- 23 Pukka Restobar C2
- Ric Sons .... (see 14)
- 24 Sea Slugs C2
- 25 Squido's Restaurant C2

Information

- 26 City Tourism Office C3
- El Nido Boutique & Art Café .... (see 21)
- 27 El Taraw Ticketing Agency B3

Transport

- 28 Pittstop Motorbike Rentals C3
- 29 Ten Knots Travel Office D3
- 30 Win Eulen Joy Liner Booking Office B3

Lally & Abet Beach Cottages HOTEL $$
(☎0928 502 9841; www.lallyandabet.com; Hama St; r with fan/air-con incl breakfast P1300/2000; ❄📶) Lally & Abet's long-running operation on the far northern end of the beach has spacious grounds, attractive porches and a restaurant. Interiors, however, are basic considering the price.

Tandikan Cottages COTTAGES $
(☎0920 318 4882; tandikan_elnido@yahoo.com; Hama St; cottages P800) These are basic and somewhat cramped thatched-roofed cabins.

El Nido Beach Hotel HOTEL $$$
(☎723 0887; www.elnidobeachhotel.com; Hama St; r P3500; ❄📶) Occupying a long stretch of sand on the eastern edge of the beach, you can't miss this two-storey, modern hotel.

Rovic's Pension House HOTEL $
(☎0928 520 2655; www.rovicspensionelnido.multiply.com; Hama St; r with fan/air-con P1300/1500; ❄📶) The small rooms themselves are nice; however, because they're lined up in an interior hallway natural light is scarce.

Rico's Cottages COTTAGES $
(☎0929 467 1632; Hama St; r P600) Two-storey building on the beach, with old wood-floored rooms and toilets without seats. On the plus side, there are porches with good views.

Cliffside Cottages COTTAGES $
(☎0919 785 6625; Rizal St; r from P500) Aside from their location under the cliffs, which offer a dramatic backdrop, relative quiet and some morning shade, these are basic, poorly maintained cottages; only some toilets have seats.

CAALAN BEACH

Makulay Lodge & Villas APARTMENT $$
(☎0917 257 3851; makulayelnido@yahoo.com; r/apt from P1000/2700; 📶) Occupying a small rise, immediately after you round the corner from town, Makulay offers convenience, privacy and wonderful views from the hilltop apartments. The more utilitarian ground-floor rooms have their own kitchens and open onto a small outdoor sitting area.

Kalinga Beach Resort BUNGALOW $
(☎0921 570 0021; r P800) Nicely constructed bungalows with individual porches and fans.

La Salangane APARTMENT $$
(☎0916 648 6994; www.lasalangane.com; apt P2500) Four large rooms with full kitchens in a mahogany house.

WATER WORLD

Perhaps the highlight of any trip to northern Palawan is a multiday bangka boat trip zigzagging through the Bacuit Archipelago, Linapacan, Culion and the Calamianes. Such a trip offers a rare opportunity to experience and interact with people and communities in the area, unmediated by the mass tourism industry. Travellers can stay in beachside nipa huts or in remote fishing villages, chowing down on freshly caught fish in the evenings. Spot some seaweed while snorkelling and voila, it's a side dish at dinner.

Tao Philippines (www.taophilippines.com; offices in El Nido & Coron Town), a socially conscious company that runs education and nutrition programs in northern Palawan, operates these increasingly popular Coron to El Nido expeditions, which depart on Sundays between mid-October and mid-June. All-inclusive costs average P3800 per person per day.

Golden Monkey Cottages BUNGALOW **$$**
(☎0929 206 4352; www.goldenmonkeyelnido.com; P1500) Beachfront cottages with high ceilings. There are a number of monkeys in a large cage on the premises.

CORONG CORONG & AROUND

Greenviews Resort BUNGALOW **$$**
(☎0921 586 1422; www.palawan-greenviews.com; Corong Corong; r with fan from P1000, cottages from P1700; ❄📶) Like its sister property in Port Barton, Greenviews looks like it was put together by highly skilled woodcarvers and craftsmen. From the hardwood floors, to the room furniture, to the wonderfully designed benches in the 2nd-storey restaurant, everything is a cut above the quality found elsewhere.

Island Front Cottages BUNGALOW **$$**
(☎0939 275 7801; www.islandfrontcottages.com; Corong Corong; r with fan/air-con incl breakfast P1500/2000; ❄) Somehow these overly decorated, colourful bamboo rooms, set in a cramped, wild garden, find a way to charm, with a mishmash of colours and carved wooden knick-knacks. Though it's on the beach there's little space for more than a bath towel.

Dolarog Beach Resort BEACH RESORT **$$$**
(☎0919 867 4360; www.dolarog.com; r/cottage per person incl breakfast & dinner P3500/5000; ❄📶) Although it's technically on the Palawan mainland, Dolarog Beach Resort is really only accessible by a half-hour bangka ride from town. Lining a small white-sand beach is a variety of fan and air-con cottages with hardwood floors and charming porches. A modern, low-slung building has several 'garden rooms', though these have less character.

Las Cabanas Beach Resort BUNGALOW **$$$**
(☎0917 887 8808; www.lascabanasresort.com; r per person incl three meals P4900) Five large cottages, spread out in a large nicely landscaped garden, front an out-of-the-way beach. With luggage it's best accessed by boat; otherwise it can be reached by following the footpath off the main road about 3km south of town and then walking a few hundred metres along the beach. It's right before turning the corner for Dolarog.

Four Seasons Beach Resort HOTEL **$$**
(☎0921 281 4057; www.elnidofourseasonsresort.com; r P2600; ❄📶🏊) Popular because of its narrow oceanfront pool and lounging area. Otherwise, the Four Seasons has standard, somewhat unremarkable rooms.

Eating & Drinking

A number of stand-alone restaurants catering specifically to foreigners are found along Hama St; these serve a mess of samplings from generic international and Filipino menus.

Of the hotels, La Salagane and the Alternative have the best restaurants.

Sea Slugs (an unfortunate name but it does get the speed of service about right) and **Ric Sons** are great places to spend an evening when the sun goes down, the tiki torches are lit and the duelling acoustic guitar performances begin. The food – the standard pasta, chicken and fish – however, doesn't live up to the ambience. A little further east is **Pukka Restobar**, which is the best value of the bunch, especially for breakfast.

El Nido Boutique & Art Café INTERNATIONAL **$$**
(Serena St; mains P220; ⏰6.30am-11pm; 📶) Sometimes this seems like the epicentre of

El Nido tourism. The large 2nd-storey dining room is a warm and relaxed place to eat and drink, serving salads, pizzas and especially good breakfasts. It has a bar and live music five nights a week.

Balay Tubay FILIPINO, INTERNATIONAL **$$**
(Real St; mains P120; ⏰5pm-2am) This place is the Filipino equivalent of a small downtown club for singer-songwriters. There's live music most nights from 8pm to midnight, when the owner plays bongo drums and sings back-up harmony. It has an extensive menu of grilled and sizzling seafood along with more generic fare.

Squido's Restaurant INTERNATIONAL **$$**
(Hama St; mains P150) Reminiscent of traveller spots in southern Thailand, Sqido's has a widescreen TV that is never turned off, and one of the most varied menus in El Nido.

Habibi Restaurant & Shisha Café INTERNATIONAL **$$**
(mains P180; 📶) A stylish lounge on the 2nd floor that overlooks the beach; pasta, pizza and delicious frozen coffee drinks are on the menu, as is flavoured shisha (P350).

Blue Azul Restaurant INTERNATIONAL **$**
(Real St; mains P140; ⏰6am-10pm; 📶) Falafel, shwarma and pad thai are just a few of the offerings found here.

ℹ Information

Keep in mind that there are no banks or ATMs in El Nido. Many hotels and restaurants offer wi-fi and there are several internet cafes along Hama and Serena Sts.

City Tourism office (☎0915 558 2896; www.elnidotourism; Real St; ⏰8am-8pm) In town; useful only for basic questions.

El Nido Boutique & Art Café (☎0917 560 4020; www.elnidoboutiqueandartcafe.com; Serena St; ⏰transport info desk 7am-8pm; 📶) A one-stop shop for all your travelling needs. Located near the pier, it will change money and make cash advances on credit cards (8% commission on advances, requires passport). It can handle ITI and other airline bookings, and help with onward boat transport (5% commission on some bookings). Importantly, it offers every imaginable water and land tour in the area. Also a book exchange, clothing and souvenir store, and internet cafe (per hour P100); wi-fi for customers.

El Taraw Ticketing Agency (☎0918 648 6765; boyet_dandal@yahoo.com; Serena St;) Can book all airlines.

ℹ Getting There & Away

Air

Considering that El Nido is one of the Philippines' prime tourist destinations, it's surprisingly difficult to reach by air. At the time of research, only SEAIR and ITI were flying into El Nido's Lio Airport, 7km north of town (a tricycle there will cost P150). It should be noted, however, that SEAIR is notoriously unreliable and can't be recommended for this route.

The El Nido Boutique & Art Café handles ITI tickets and reservations.

Boat

The most important boat service for visitors to northern Palawan is the El Nido–Coron connection. Oversized motorised bangka boats (M/Bca *Overcomer*, M/Bca *Welia*, M/Bca *Jessabel* and M/Bca *Joe* operate different days of the week) leave daily in good weather at around 7.30am (P2200 including lunch, coffee and soft drinks, seven to eight hours), though delays are common. Some of the boats are kept in dry dock for short periods during the low season so don't assume daily departures in that part of the year.

Atienza Shipping Lines' weekly El Nido–Manila boat (see p383) goes via Coron.

A bangka for hire costs around P15,000 to Coron.

There are infrequent boats to Sabang (P2000, seven hours) with drop-offs in Port Barton (P1500, 4½ hours). A private bangka to Port Barton will cost P6000/7500 for a six-/eight-person boat and P8500/13,000 to Sabang.

Bus, Jeepney & Van

These days the majority of visitors to El Nido arrive on minivans from Puerto (P600, five-plus hours, depart 5am, 7am, 7.30am, 9am, 11am and 1pm). Contact **Win Eulen Joy Liner** (☎0919 716 2210), **Fort Wally** (☎0917 276 2875) or El Nido Boutique & Art Café in advance to book a seat. Win Eulen Joy Liner also operates slower and less comfortable buses, as does **Sweety Bus Liner** to Puerto (P380, eight hours) with stops in Taytay (P150, 1½ hours) and Roxas (P200, six hours); there are three departures per day, at 5am, 7am and 9am. Privately hired vans to Puerto (P8,000 to P10,000, six hours) are another option.

There's one daily jeepney to Batakalan pier (P60, one hour, departs noon), from where you can arrange a pick-up to one of the off-island resorts on the eastern side of Palawan near Taytay. A tricycle costs around P750.

Buses, jeepneys and vans depart from the 'terminal' – basically a clearing in the dirt – across from the El Nido Garden Beach Resort.

Getting Around

Pittstop Motorbike Rentals (☎0919 874 7178; Del Pilar St) has meticulously maintained bikes (P700 excluding petrol) and Arnaud, the owner, can provide suggested itineraries, directions and advice. Four-wheel-drive jeeps, also available for rental, are a good option for those wanting to explore the Palawan mainland at their leisure.

Bacuit Archipelago

The crystalline waters of Bacuit Bay are a fantasyscape of jagged limestone islands, mesmerising from any vantage point, whether from under water, from the air or lying on a beach. Easily the rival of southern Thailand or Halong Bay in Vietnam, the islands hide so many white-sand beaches, lagoons and coves that you'll be overwhelmed.

MINILOC ISLAND

Miniloc Island is perhaps the most interesting of the islands of the archipelago. The real attractions here are **Big Lagoon** and **Small Lagoon**, two of the more photographed sights in all of Palawan.

Big Lagoon is entered by an extremely shallow channel (you may have to swim into the lagoon and leave the boat outside). Inside, surrounded by jungle-clad karst walls, is an enormous natural swimming hole.

To enter Small Lagoon, you can swim through a hole in a rock wall or paddle through in a kayak at low tide – be sure to leave before the tide changes, otherwise you might not be able to squeeze back through. Inside is a wonderful hidden world, complete with a small cave that you can swim into and explore.

MATINLOC & TAPIUTAN ISLANDS

Like the back of a half-submerged stegosaurus, Matinloc Island snakes some 8km along the western edge of the Bacuit Archipelago. Along with neighbouring Tapiutan Island, it forms narrow **Tapiutan Strait**, the walls of which offer some of the best snorkelling in the archipelago. Likewise, there is some excellent snorkelling and some good beaches on the eastern side of Matinloc.

The adventurous will surely want to check out tiny **Secret Beach**, which can only be entered by swimming through a keyhole slot in the western wall of Matinloc. But be warned, the entrance is lined with extremely jagged rocks and coral – *do not* even think of swimming through if there are any waves around as an accident could well be fatal.

CADLAO ISLAND

Cadlao Island is like a mini-Tahiti miraculously relocated to the Bacuit Archipelago. In addition to being a wonderful piece of eye candy for those staying on the beach in El Nido, it's also home to lovely **Cadlao Lagoon** (also known as Ubugun Cove). This lagoon offers some good snorkelling in the shallow coral gardens that lie off the beach at the head of the bay.

OTHER ISLANDS & BEACHES

Every island in the archipelago has secret spots that await the adventurous explorer. **Pangalusian Island** has some first-class snorkelling. Tiny **Pinasil Island** holds **Cathedral Cave**, an aptly named cavern with soaring limestone columns and wall-climbing monitor lizards, which call to mind the gargoyles of an actual cathedral. If you plan on exploring the cave, be sure to bring shoes and be careful walking on the sharp rocks. **Dilumacad Island** (Helicopter Island) has a fine beach on its eastern shore, which is topped only by the wonderful **Seven Commandos Beach** on the Palawan mainland. **Snake Island**, connected to the mainland by a narrow, winding strip of sand during low tide, offers striking panoramic views from the top.

Of course, there are many more beaches, bays and coral gardens in the archipelago. Our best advice is to pack a lunch, some snorkelling equipment, plenty of sunscreen, and find your own secret spot.

Sleeping

Miniloc Island Resort (☎in Manila 02-894 5644; www.elnidoresorts.com; cottage per person US$220; ❄📶) and **Lagen Island Resort** (r per person US$190-215, cottage per person US$285; ❄🏊@📶) are two premier sister resorts on private islands, with crystal-clear waters just offshore and idyllic settings in the Bacuit Bay. Miniloc, located in a sheltered cove, has native cottages and a more laid-back feel compared to Lagen's luxurious rooms and more exclusive feel. Both have bungalows perched over the water as well as other accommodation options. **Ten Knots Travel Office** (☎0917 207 2742; Real St, El Nido) in El Nido books these resorts.

Rates include transfers to and from El Nido airport. The owners of Miniloc and Lagen resorts were building another luxury retreat on Pangalusian Island at the time of writing.

Bacuit Archipelago

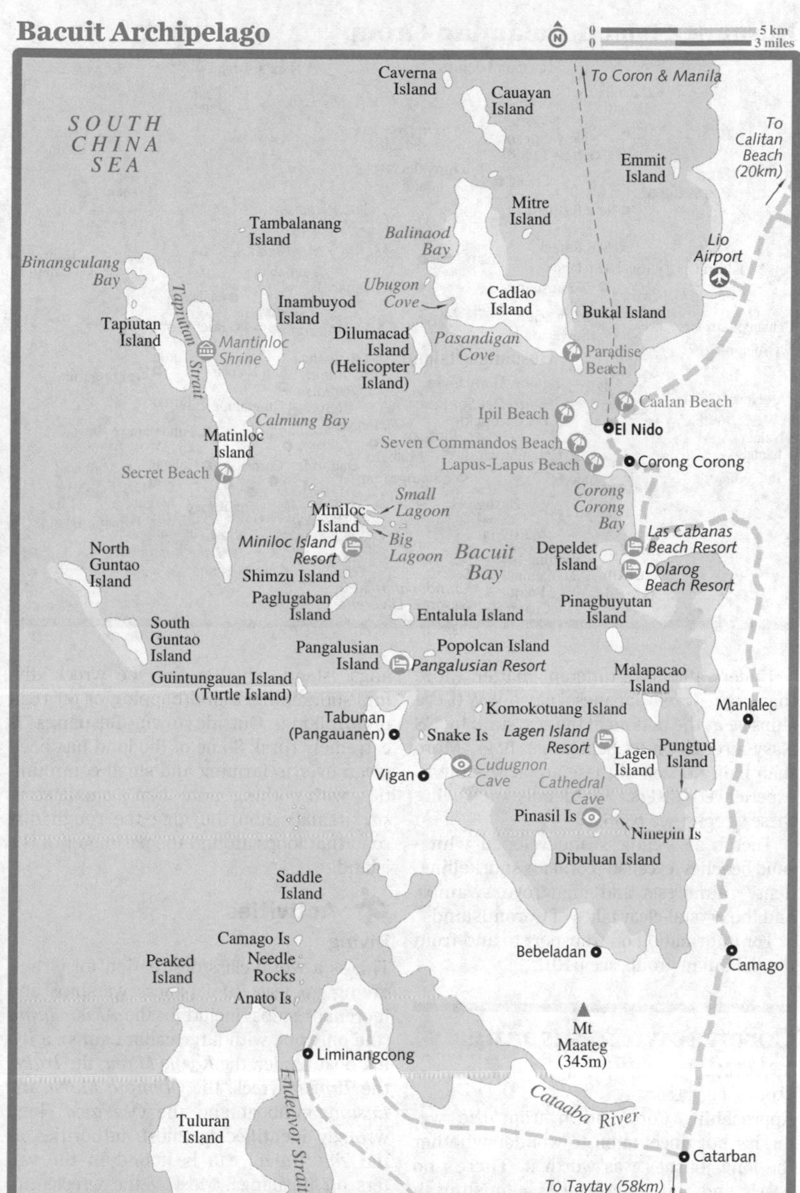

CALAMIAN GROUP

This group of islands in the far north of Palawan has a frontier edge. Heading north to Busuanga Island, where Coron Town, the largest settlement in the Calamian group, is located, you'll pass through Linapacan Island, Culion Island, and other small islands where groups of huts hug the foreshore of beautiful beaches. Otherwise, you'll find nothing – no roads, and not even any lights after the sun goes down.

Busuanga Island/Calamian Group

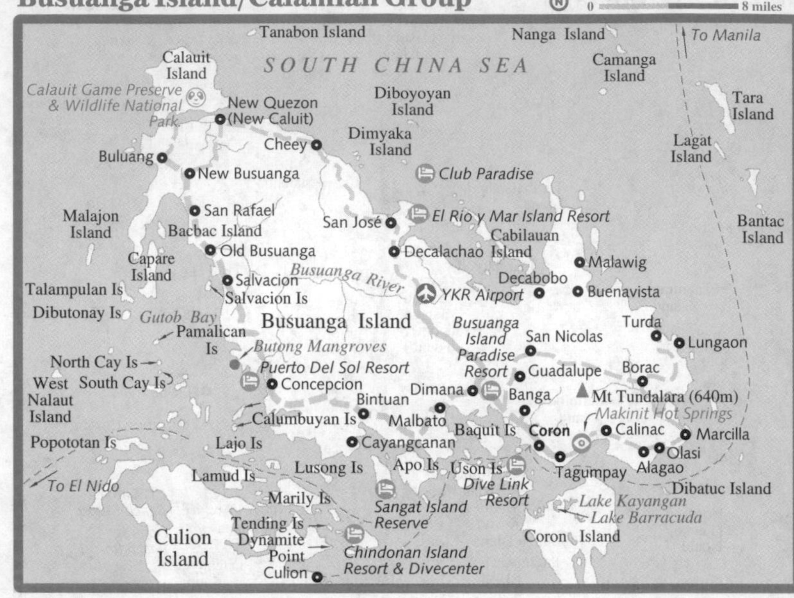

Underwater it's a different matter. More than two dozen Japanese navy WWII-era ships lie at the bottom of the sea, sunk by US Navy aircraft on 24 September 1944. More than half a dozen of these are accessible to experienced divers. For details on diving these wrecks, see p396.

There's also endless undeveloped white-sand beaches, excellent coral for snorkelling, dense rainforests and mangrove swamps, and the crystal-clear lakes of Coron Island.

For information on transport to and from the Calamian group, see p401.

Coron Town & Busuanga Island

048 / POP 10,000

Approaching Coron Town from the water, it's not uncommon to wonder whether the long journey was worth it. There's no beach and the waterfront is a mishmash of half-done buildings, ramshackle houses and the massive empty expanse of a misguided landfill project. This, the commercial and population centre of the Calamian group and main town on Busuanga Island, shouldn't be judged by appearances alone. It's best thought of as a gateway and base for other adventures on and around Busuanga Island, whether they be wreck diving, snorkelling, island hopping or off-road motorbiking. Outside town, Busuanga is extremely rural. Some of the land has been given over to farming and small communities, with nothing more than a single *sari-sari* (small shop) hugging the rough dirt road that loops around the perimeter of the island.

Activities

Diving

This is a world-class destination for **wreck diving**. At least 10 Japanese warships and merchant ships, including the *Akisushima* (the only one with large calibre guns), a flying boat tender, the *Kogyo Maru,* the *Irako,* the *Tangat* wreck, the *Olympia Maru,* the *Lusong* gunboat and the *Okikawa* (long wrongly identified by most authorities as the *Tae Maru*), can be found in the waters off Busuanga. Most of the wrecks are at least 45-minute to two-hour boat rides from Coron Town. The depths at which the wrecks are found vary from shallow to quite deep, so there are diving opportunities for beginners and experienced divers. The best wreck dives for beginners are the *Lusong* (also easily snorkelled) and *East Tangat,* at 9m and 22m, respectively.

Lake Barracuda on Coron Island is a popular dive site, less for what's visible than for the sensation of shifting temperatures underwater.

Dive operators mostly charge between P2200 and P2800 for two dives including equipment.

Discovery Divers (Map p398; ☎0920 901 2414; www.ddivers.com), based on nearby Decanituan Island (aka Discovery Island), maintains a shop at the end of a pier off Coastal Rd in town and at Puerto del Sol Resort.

Sea Dive (Map p398; ☎550 9207, 0918 400 0448; www.seadiveresort.com) is part of the hotel complex of the same name, and is experienced with big groups, while **DiveCal** (Map p398; ☎0918 285 2060; www.divecal.com) is associated with Dive Link Resort.

Other operators include **Coron Divers** (Map p398; ☎0918 653 9854; www.corondivers.com.ph; National Hwy) and **Rock Steady Dive Center** (Map p398; ☎0919 624 0034; www.rocksteadydivecenter.com).

Other Activities

Even if you're here to dive it's worth spending a day or two on a bangka (per day four/six people around P1500/2500) exploring nearby islands. The cost of a boat doesn't include admission fees for sights on Coron Island or snorkelling gear (which is generally P250). Virtually every hotel and resort can arrange a trip, as can several tour companies in town; otherwise, walk down to the pier behind the central market where boats congregate (the boat association lists prices on a board here).

Often included in bangka day trips to Coron Island is the opportunity to have a soak in the soothing-to-scalding waters of **Makinit Hot Springs** (Map p396; admission P150; ⏲6am-10pm). The springs are located 5km east of town, and are easily accessible by tricycle from Coron Town (round trip P300).

Snorkelling at the small protected sanctuary of **Siete Pecados** (admission P100), not far offshore from Makinit Hot Springs, is a reminder of what has been destroyed elsewhere – the coral here is a wonderland of colours and shapes.

One of the more interesting areas in which to **kayak** is near Butong (Map p396), a mangrove area that cuts through a small peninsula north of the town of Concepcion on Busuanga Island.

Hiking to the top of 640m **Mt Tundalara** (Map p396), the highest point in northern Palawan, is an endurance test, especially in the midday heat. It takes around 2½ hours. To get to the trailhead, take a tricycle to Mabingtungan, around 3km north of Coron Town.

Tours

Calamianes Expeditions Eco Tour (Map p398; ☎0919 305 4363; www.corongaleri.com.ph; San Augustin St) rents tents (per night P200), mountain bikes, kayaks as well as arranges day and overnight trips.

Run by Betan Pe (just ask for him around town), **Showtime Adventures** (☎0927 372 8846; www.showtimeadventuretours.com) offers overnight island-hopping and kayaking trips.

See the boxed text, p392, for information on the highly recommended multiday Coron–El Nido expeditions run by **Tao Philippines** (Map p398; www.taophilippines.com; National Hwy).

Another recommended tour operator is **Tribal Adventure Tours** (Map p398; ☎0920 558 7188; www.tribaladventures.com; National Hwy).

Sleeping

There are many decent places to stay right in Coron Town and, at the time of writing, a hotel building boom was well underway, though whether there's enough tourists to sustain them all is an open question. Otherwise, you can stay on one of the islands; some are only minutes away, while others are more substantial commutes.

CORON TOWN

TOP CHOICE **Sea Dive Resort** HOTEL $
(Map p398; ☎0920 945 8714; www.seadiveresort.com; r with fan & shared bathroom P400, r with fan/air-con from P800/900; ❄📶) There's no more convenient address in Coron Town than this multistorey building that juts into the bay. The higher up you go, the nicer the rooms become, though all of them are simple and clean, and have modern bathrooms with hot water. Noise from your neighbours is the only downside. A large, open-air restaurant is on the 1st floor and there's a nice bar out the back. The dive shop here is a hive of activity.

TOP CHOICE **Krystal Lodge** BUNGALOW $
(Map p398; ☎0949 333 0429; pretty_kryz23@yahoo.com; s/d P400/800, cottages P1200; 📶) Bunk down like locals in these all-bamboo

Coron Town

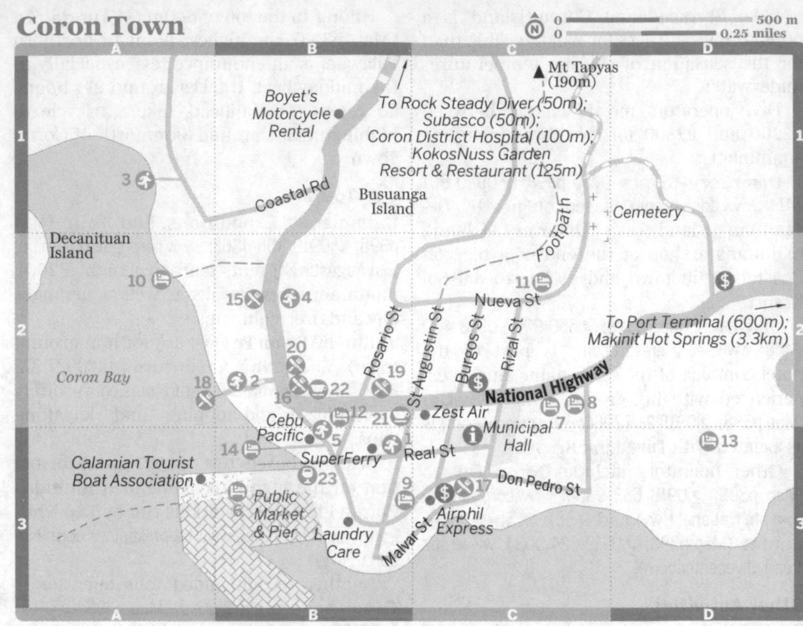

bungalows perched over the water. It's worth the extra pesos for fantastically charming cottages with their very own bars and sitting areas. The super-friendly proprietor even arranges a projector for outdoor movie nights, and breakfast is available.

KokosNuss Garden Resort & Restaurant BUNGALOW $$
(Off Map p398; ☎0919 776 9544; www.kokosnuss.info; National Hwy; r with fan & shared/private bathroom P450/1500, cottages with air-con P1700; ❄📶) This leafy compound, a 20-minute walk from town, has a variety of rooms that surround a slightly overgrown garden with plenty of shade. Rooms range from modern rondavel cottages with bright, painted murals to fan-cooled A-frame rooms in a bamboo structure.

Darayonan Lodge HOTEL $$
(Map p398; ☎0908 773 2964; www.darayonan.com; 132 National Hwy; s/d with fan P700/1000, s/d with air-con incl breakfast P1000/1350; ❄🏊📶) The cheaper bamboo rooms here definitely have character, while slightly more expensive deluxe and 'business' rooms are more generic; the building out back is quieter. The courtyard garden restaurant is an extremely attractive place for a meal.

Princess of Coron Austrian Resort HOTEL $$
(Map p398; ☎0919 236 1430; www.philippinen-urlaub.at; 6 Nueva St; r from P1500; ❄📶🏊) This hotel blends into a hillside above town about as seamlessly as you'd expect an Austrian resort would. The white stucco main building has large rooms with gleaming tiled floors and spacious bathrooms. A couple of A-frame cottages in the front are good for families; kids can cool off in the small pool.

Coron Village Lodge HOTEL $
(Map p398; ☎425 2231; www.coronvillagelodge.com; National Hwy; r from P850; ❄) Utilitarian and clean rooms, a leafy outdoor garden, and a nice bar and restaurant.

Island's View Inn HOTEL $$
(Map p398; ☎0906 255 0468; islandsviewinn@yahoo.com; Don Pedro St; r incl breakfast P1800; ❄📶) Rooms here are sparkling new, with flat-screen TVs, hot water and a 3rd-floor outdoor restaurant and lounge area.

Coron Gateway Hotel HOTEL $$$
(Map p398; ☎in Manila 02-887 7107; www.corongateway.com; Market Pier; r from P3900; ❄📶) Most luxurious accommodation and largest building in town, located out near the landfill.

Coron Town

Activities, Courses & Tours

1	Calamianes Expeditions Eco Tour	B3
2	Coron Divers	B2
3	Discovery Divers	A1
4	DiveCal	B2
	Sea Dive	(see 14)
5	Tao Philippines	B3
	Tribal Adventure Tours	(see 4)

Sleeping

6	Coron Gateway Hotel	B3
7	Coron Village Lodge	C2
8	Darayonan Lodge	C2
9	Island's View Inn	B3
10	Krystal Lodge	A2
11	Princess of Coron Austrian Resort	C2
12	Ralph's Pension House	B2
13	Saragpunta	D3
14	Sea Dive Resort	B3

Eating

15	Amphibi-ko	B2
16	Bistro Coron	B2
17	Kawayanan Grill Station	C3
18	La Sirenetta	A2
19	Mannekon Pis Restobar	B2
20	Marcilla Noodles	B2

Drinking

21	B.O.G. Coffee	B2
22	Dad's Coronzy Coffee & Tea	B2
23	Kookie Bar	B3

Ralph's Pension House PENSION HOUSE **$$**
(Map p398; ☎0921 631 5449; www.ralphspensionhouse.webs.com; National Hwy; r P1400; ❄☜) Somewhat tackily furnished rooms abutting the owner's living space; the property also has a verandah, a courtyard and a rooftop for lounging.

BUSUANGA ISLAND

Puerto del Sol Resort RESORT **$$$**
(Map p396; ☎0908 889 0866; www.puertodelsolresort.com; cottage P4600; ☜) The Puerto de Sol is a Mediterranean-style resort perched on a hillside with views of the bay. It's close to several wrecks, as well as inland activities like horseback riding and hiking. The white stucco cottages and large windows add to the light-filled atmosphere. Discovery Divers has a shop here.

Busuanga Island Paradise Resort BUNGALOW **$$$**
(Map p396; ☎0918 368 8904; www.busuangaislandparadise.com; Km 12, Coron-Busuanga Hwy; r from P3500; ❄☜≋) This place is remotely located, 12km east of Coron Town, in a forest where there's no beach or water in sight, other than a pool. Nevertheless, it brings resort chic to the hinterlands in the form of top-notch bungalows – think finished wood with contemporary trimmings.

El Rio y Mar Island Resort BEACH RESORT **$$$**
(Map p396; ☎in Manila 02-833 4964; www.elrioymar.com; r P7000; ❄☜≋) Hugging the shore of a beautiful white-sand beach north of the airport, El Rio y Mar is only accessible via a short boat ride. The wood-floor native-style cottages are superior to the bland, more modern rooms. There's a restaurant, a spa and a dive shop on the premises, and kayaking and windsurfing are also offered.

Pier House Lodging HOTEL **$$**
(☎0918 271 1956; www.pierhouselodging.com; Concepcion, r from P1600) Pier House is a white-stucco lodging house in Concepcion, that has a bar, a restaurant and large tile-floor rooms. It can feel deserted in low season.

Ann & Mike's Bar & Restaurant NIPA HUTS **$**
(☎0929 582 4020; r with shared bathroom P500) Ann & Mike's is across the pathway from Pier House, and has two good-looking nipa cottages and a pleasant little eatery.

Busuanga's northern coastline is largely undeveloped in part due to rough roads; however, at the time of writing, a collection of beachfront bungalows, the **Cashew Grove Beach Resort** (☎0949 869 4420; www.cashewgrove.com), was being constructed near the village of Cheey.

OTHER ISLANDS

Most of these resorts' room rates include transfers from the Busuanga airport or Coron Town, but it's worth confirming. Sangat and Chindonan are close to a good number of wrecks suitable for diving.

TOP CHOICE **Sangat Island Reserve** BEACH RESORT **$$$**
(Map p396; ☎0920 954 4328; www.sangat.com.ph; cottages per person incl 3 meals from P4000; ☜) Pulling up at the beach here feels like discovering the cool kid's secret hideout. Less than 40 minutes by speedboat from Coron

ANCESTRAL DOMAINS

Passed in 1997, the National Commission on Indigenous People (NCIP; also known as the Indigenous People's Act) is meant to enable tribal groups throughout the Philippines to re-acquire title to their land. Unsurprisingly, it's a long, complicated process, and most islands aren't officially titled as a result. Coron Island, however, was issued the very first, and Caluit Island was also returned to the Tagbanua. What then happens to the land is up to the whole community, with many choosing to lease land to non-Tagbanua for 25-year periods.

Tagbanua advocacy group **Saragpunta** (☎0919 886 1157, 0909 596 8936; saragpunta@yahoo.com) offers accommodation, both on a tribally owned island as well as in Coron Town. A night spent on **Tending Island** (☎0918 280 3257; P600 incl 3 meals), where a school educates students ferried in from elsewhere in the Calamianes Group, is a highlight of the area for some; you're welcome to deliver a lesson plan or lead the kids in song, and you'll have celebrity status for the day. Lodging – mattresses on a bamboo platform with pillows, blankets and mosquito nets – is perfectly comfortable, if basic. To get there, pay your way to Culion Town where pre-arranged pick-up is free, or hire a bangka from Coron Town for P1000 (1¼ hours).

Otherwise, if you're interested in supporting the organisation but don't want to head out to Tending Island, Saragpunta has a large native-style building next to its headquarters in Coron Town (see Map p398), with several basic rooms – it'll cost you P200 for a mattress on a bamboo platform, and an outdoor bathroom and shower. It can be a little difficult to find, but look for a two-storey shop with the sign 'Diamond Center' on the National Hwy, just before the St Augustine Academy. Follow the dirt road past here and around to the right for 100m or so. A small **shop** (National Hwy) next to the BPI bank sells Tagbanua handicrafts and souvenirs.

Town, and perfect for R&R or action, Sangat has a full-service dive centre, kayaks and jet skis. Several native-style bungalows front a nice white-sand beach and two others are perched atop small hills tucked into the encroaching jungle; the large villa around the corner, accessed via a footbridge, has an outdoor shower in a rock cave.

Club Paradise BEACH RESORT **$$$**
(Map p396; ☎in Manila 02-838 4956; www.clubparadisepalawan.com; per person incl 3 meals P5500-8500; ❄📶🏊) This resort on Dimyaka Island, north of Busuanga, lives up to its name. A true four-star resort, evident in everything from the beautiful variety of cottages (basically a high-end designer's version of the Filipino hut) to the sumptuous buffet meals. It's possible to arrange diving and snorkelling trips to Apo Reef, which is only two to three hours away.

Chindonan Island Resort & Divecenter BUNGALOW **$$$**
(Map p396; ☎0929 312 1594; www.chindonan.com; cottage/r per person incl breakfast & dinner P3600/2400; 📶) A few spacious modern stucco rooms are perched halfway up a hilltop on an island between Culion Town and Sangat – two native-style nipa huts are also available. The bar and restaurant are on the pier.

Discovery Resort RESORT **$$**
(Map p398; ☎0918 398 7125; www.divers.com; Decanituan Island; r with fan/air-con from P1000/1500; ❄@) Catering to divers, this modest resort is on Decanituan Island, only a 10-minute bangka ride from Coron Town. The wood-floored bungalows with tiled terraces have nice sunset views, and there's a bar and restaurant on the premises.

Dive Link Resort RESORT **$$**
(Map p396; ☎0918 926 1545; www.divelink.com.ph; Uson Island; r from P2000; 📶🏊) Only a 10-minute boat ride from Coron Town, Dive Link has no beach, but the renovated blue and yellow bungalows surround a pool often occupied by beginner divers.

Eating & Drinking

Most of the places to stay, including all the resorts located offshore or elsewhere on Busuanga, have their own restaurants. The one at Sea Dive Resort is the best in town, as much for its great location and social vibe as for the well-rounded menu.

Bistro Coron INTERNATIONAL **$$**
(Map p398; Don Pedro St; mains P170; ⏰8am-11pm) This place has an extensive menu including specials such as a version of *setoise*

(soup with shrimp, fried diced bread and fish chunks), and Hungarian, Italian and Swiss sausages.

La Sirenetta FILIPINO, INTERNATIONAL **$$**
(Map p398; mains P250) Easy to spot from the water, the four pillars at the end of a long pier, in the shape of the eponymous sirens, bring a little Vegas kitsch to town. An eclectic menu with European flavours; it's also good for sunset drinks.

Kawayanan Grill Station FILIPINO **$$**
(Map p398; Don Pedro St; mains P150; 📶) Usual Filipino fare – plus boiled goat innards – in outdoor nipa huts.

Amphibi-ko JAPANESE **$$**
(Map p398; National Hwy; ⏲11am-10pm; mains P140) Only a few tables and a few menu items, including sushi.

Manneken Pis Restobar FILIPINO, INTERNATIONAL **$$**
(Map p398; National Hwy; ⏲8am-8pm; mains P250) Pizza and porterhouse steaks are on the menu at this place, decked out with modern decor.

Marcilla Noodles VIETNAMESE **$**
(Map p398; National Hwy; mains P45) Modest eatery serving beef and pork *chaolong* (noodle soup).

Two comfortable and modern coffeehouses are **Dad's Coronzy Coffee & Tea** (Map p398; National Hwy; ⏲6am-10pm; 📶) and **BOG Coffee** (Map p398; cnr National Hwy & St Augustin St; ⏲2pm-10pm, closed Sun; 📶).

Subasco (off Map p398; National Hwy), on the way north out of town, has live music and karaoke, and the 2nd floor of **Kookie Bar** (Map p398; cnr National Hwy & Real St) is a good drinking spot near the market.

ℹ Information

BPI (National Hwy) and **Allied Savings Bank** (cnr Don Pedro & Burgos Sts) accept foreign ATM cards. The majority of hotels offer wi-fi access and there are a couple of internet cafes on the National Hwy near St Augustin St.

Coron District Hospital (Map p398; National Hwy)

Laundry Care (Don Pedro St; per kg P40; ⏲9.30am-noon &1.30-7pm)

Municipal Tourism Office (Map p398; ☎0919 354 0655; tourism_coron2010@yahoo.com.ph; Municipal Hall, cnr Real & Burgos Sts) Extremely helpful local tourism office.

ℹ Getting There & Away

Air

Busuanga Island, Coron Town and the rest of the Calamian Group are connected to Manila by **Airphil Express** (Map p398; Don Pedro St), **Cebu Pacific** (Map p398; ☎0929 898 1111; Don Pedro St) and **Zest Air** (Map p398; ☎0920 654 9484; National Hwy), which operate out of the YKR airport on the north side of Busuanga Island around 25km from Coron Town. Cancellations and delays because of bad weather aren't uncommon.

It's a half-hour (P150) minivan ride between the airport and Coron Town; vans meet incoming flights. In the other direction, most depart two hours before flights from in front of airline offices or hotels that offer transfers.

Boat

A few medium-sized bangka boats leave for El Nido from behind the market near the Coron Gateway Hotel (motorised bangka *Jessabel* picks up and drops off at Sea Dive Resort) nearly every day if the weather is good (P2200 including lunch, seven hours). Otherwise, you can hire a boat any day for around P15,000 for up to six people. See p393 for more information. Atienza Shipping Lines' Manila–El Nido cargo/passenger boat stops in Coron (see p383).

INLAND ISLAND ROADS

Exploring the Busuanga countryside on a motorbike is an exhilarating journey past small villages, forests and lush farmland, where smiling locals, including groups of curious schoolchildren, greet you with warm waves. Heading west out of Coron Town, the road deteriorates after the junction for the airport road north, and this calls for some off-road experience and confidence to navigate plank bridges, rocks and gravel. Coron Town to Concepcion is a reasonable goal for a half-day journey. The loop from the airport north to San José, northwest to Cheey and then to New Busuanga, before heading back southeast, should really only be tried in a 4WD vehicle. Several places rent motorbikes including **Boyet's Motorcycle Rental** (Map p398; ☎0928 292 9884; National Hwy) which charges P600 to P800 for the day.

See p383 for details on ferries to/from Manila, Mindoro and Puerto Princesa. The port terminal is around 1.5km east of the town centre.

Getting Around

At the time of writing, the local tourist boat association was in the process of trying to fix and apply higher fares than those listed in this book. Sample fares include P2500 for Malcapuya Island and P3000 for Calumbuyan Island. Tour companies, as well as hotels, generally offer lower fares.

A daily boat goes to Culion Town (P180, 1½ hours, noon).

A jeepney to Salvacion leaves Coron at 11am daily (P80, 1½ hours).

Minivans are also available for tours around Busuanga. A sample round-trip fare is P2500 for Concepcion.

Coron Island

This island, only a 20-minute bangka ride from Coron Town, has an imposing, mysterious skyline that wouldn't be out of place in a *King Kong* film. Flying over Coron, you see that what lies inland, on the other side of the fortresslike, jungle-clad, rocky escarpments, is inaccessible terrain pockmarked with lakes, two of which, **Lake Kayangan** (admission P250) and **Lake Barracuda** (admission P100), are Coron's primary attractions.

Accessible by a steep 10-minute climb, the crystal-clear waters of Lake Kayangan are nestled into the mountain walls. Underwater is like a moonscape; there's a wooden walkway and platform to stash your things under if you go for a swim. Don't expect privacy or quiet, though, as the lagoon where bangkas unload passengers looks like a mall parking lot at noon.

Lake Barracuda is of more interest to divers for its unique layers of fresh, salt and brackish water and dramatic temperature shifts, which can reach as high as 38°C. It's accessible by a short climb over a jagged, rocky wall that ends directly in the water.

Other common stops are **Banol Beach** (admission P100), a small sandy area with shelter from the sun, and **Twin Lagoons** (admission P50). Remember to carry enough small bills, as all fees are collected as you dock at each site.

The entire island is considered the ancestral domain of the Tagbanua, who are primarily fishermen and gatherers of the very lucrative *balinsasayaw* (bird's nests). Concerned about the impact of tourism, the Tagbanua have limited access to a handful of sights (there's talk of possibly imposing a single island-wide admission fee).

Culion Island & Around

Culion Island, one of the largest in the Calamian group, has excellent snorkelling around **Dynamite Point** on the northeastern tip. **Malcapuya Island**, about halfway down off the eastern side has a nice beach; nearby **Banana Island** also has a pretty beach on the eastern side and good snorkelling on the west. A full-day boat tour from Coron Town out this way should run between P3000 and P3500. At the time of writing, a high-end resort was going up on the northern tip of nearby Bulalacao Island.

In Culion Town you can visit the **Culion Museum & Archives** (admission P250; ⏲9am-noon & 1-4pm Mon-Fri) located on the hospital grounds. A half-hour film and several large rooms filled with photos and artefacts tell the poignant and little-known story of the leper colony that was opened here in 1906, once one of the largest in the world. The interior of the **La Immaculada Concepcion Church**, formerly a Spanish fort built in the mid-1700s, is worth a peek, and a hike up to where the eagle symbol is carved into the hills (created in 1926 by leper patients as a tribute to Philippine health services) offers panoramic views of town and the nearby islands.

Easily the nicest place in town is the modern **Hotel Maya** (☎0939 254 2744; www.islaculionhotelmaya.com; s/d P550/1100; ❄📶), owned and operated by enthusiastic students of Ateneo-Loyola College. **Tabing Dagat Lodging House & Restaurant** (☎0908 563 1590; www.tabingdagatlodge.multiply.com; r with fan/air-con P590/790; ❄) has light-filled rooms with small balconies in Barangay Balulua.

The town only has electricity between noon and midnight. There's a daily boat (P180, 1½ hours, 7.30am) from Culion Town to Coron Town.

Other Islands

Many islands are being eyed by Filipino and foreign developers alike as possible sites of future resorts and campsites. Some have already been purchased.

Almost directly west of Busuanga's Concepcion is **Calumbuyan Island**; the north-

UNDERWATER JEWELS

Rows of buoys float on the ocean's surface lined up like markers on a slalom course. Only a few metres below in wire baskets tethered to ropes hang dozens of oysters, a small percentage of which, in three or four years' time, might produce a shiny little pellet that will end up in jewellery stores in Hong Kong, New York and Paris.

Pearls, one of the earliest known gems – mentioned in ancient texts, including Hinduism's foundational epics, Chinese dictionaries of 30 centuries ago and the New Testament – come from oysters. However, the days of Steinbeckian free-diving characters are mostly over (that being said, the largest pearl ever found, the Pearl of Allah, weighing in at over 4kg, was discovered in the waters around Palawan in 1934). This is an industry reliant on lab technicians, marine biologists and the most up-to-date aquaculture science.

Called 'South Sea Pearls' (Indonesia, Malaysia, Vietnam and Australia are other producers), these gold- or champagne-tinged gems are generally considered to be finer compared to freshwater pearls grown in riverine conditions the world over. Only after nearly 10 years of experimentation and study did Filipino producers establish a successful process using the Pinctada maxima oyster. The mother or receiving oyster is implanted with a piece of mantle tissue from the donor oyster – the distinctive color comes from this piece. But ironically, the future pearl itself forms around a foreign object implanted by highly trained technicians in the gonad or reproductive organism of the mother oyster. In this case, they use a pellet (which already looks like a pearl minus the lustre, sheen and irregular shape and size) manufactured from the shell of freshwater oysters from Mississippi, USA (buying these accounts for 30% or more of production costs). After four years of cultivation and care the oysters are considered ready to be harvested.

Pearl farming is generally considered to have a positive impact on the health of fisheries, in part because the gun-toting security patrolling the waters for thieves also deters fishermen using illegal methods like dynamite and cyanide. However, those who make their living in the scuba industry around Busuanga Island in the Calamian Islands in northern Palawan claim that natural waste products from all the farmed oysters muddies the waters, decreasing visibility as well as corroding the metal of all the WWII-era wrecks that make it an outstanding diving destination.

Still, as Jacques Branellec, co-owner of Jewelmer, the largest pearl producer in the Philippines (and owner of the Flower Island Beach Resort, see p388) explains, 'What we do is equivalent to wine growing, in that it's a balancing act between uncontrollable natural forces like typhoons and rising water temperatures and a rigorously applied method.' The water, leased for 25 years from the government, has to be free from pollution, the right temperature, have an abundance of the right type of plankton and just enough current. An overall warming of water temperatures – a high of 35°C, nearly four degrees warmer than the previous high, was recorded in 2010 in Palawan – both destroys coral reefs and the cultivation of the oysters that require colder temps to flourish. Branellec points out that the industry is reliant on healthy seas and that the same environmental trends threatening fisheries and coral reefs worldwide could one day mean the end of cultured South Sea Pearls.

east side has one of the best reefs (admission P100) for snorkelling in the area. The caretaker who protects the site can provide coffee, as well as permission to spend the night (P400, this includes admission) sleeping in a basic hut, a hammock or tents you bring on your own.

A good snorkelling and diving spot is the reef near the southwestern tip of **Lusong Island**; the shallowest wreck, the *Lusong* gunboat, found off the southern edge, is also prime snorkelling territory.

A white sandy beach and magnificent sunsets make a trip out to **North Cay Island** worth the hassle; the reef on the north side is well preserved. It's possible to stop here as part of an island-hopping trip, but if you have the foresight and time, arrange an overnight stay in the island's caretaker home; bring your own supplies, other than fish, which can be provided.

Just off the northwestern tip of Busuanga is **Calauit Island**, home to the **Calauit Game Preserve & Wildlife National Park** (Map p396; ☎0921 215 5482; admission per person P350, 2hr guided tour P1000). Megafauna commonly seen on safari in Kenya, such as giraffe, zebra, impala etc, can be viewed in their, um, adopted habitat thanks to Ferdinand Marcos' efforts in 1976 to help save African wildlife, alongside several species endemic to Palawan (an alternative explanation offered is that Marcos' son Bong Bong wanted animals to shoot).

Whether arranged as an organised tour or done independently, it's a gruelling day-long journey. Boats from Macalachao, 7km north of Bululang on Busuanga, can be hired for P350 round trip (10 minutes each way). It's possible to spend the night just outside the park in a basic room for P250, or to camp with your own tent. The waters off Caluit Island are also a habitat for the dugong, commonly known as seacows, an endangered species and the only herbivorous mammal; it's rare, however, to spot them.

Understand the Philippines

population per sq km

USA | UK | PHILIPPINES

≈ 30 people

The Philippines Today

A New Era?

The first decade of the 21st century was a tumultuous one in Philippine politics. It began with an impeachment trial that saw millions of Filipinos take to the streets to oust President Joseph Estrada over corruption allegations – the country's second 'People Power' revolution in 15 years. Estrada gave way to his vice president, Gloria Macapagal-Arroyo, whose nearly 10 years in office were also dogged by scandals, including one concerning alleged improprieties in her 2004 re-election.

As we went to press, Arroyo had just been arrested on charges that she tampered with the results of subsequent congressional elections in 2007.

In the 2010 presidential elections, the country found the fresh face it was looking for in the form of Benigno Aquino III, the squeaky-clean son of Corazon Aquino, hero of the first People Power revolution in 1986. Riding a wave of national grief after his mother's death in 2009, Aquino emerged from a pack of candidates and won in a landslide victory.

The early returns on Aquino's first six-year term have been positive. Analysts have lauded his willingness to tackle corruption and interest groups. But two crucial issues promise to test Aquino's political will: the 'Maguindanao Massacre' trial, and the Reproductive Health Bill.

» President Benigno Aquino is the son of 11th president Corazon Aquino

» The previous (14th) president, Gloria Arroyo, is the daughter of 9th president Diosdado Macapagal

» 12th President Fidel Ramos is Ferdinand Marcos' second cousin

The Maguindanao Massacres & the Media

It was the election-related crime that shocked the world: in the run-up to the 2010 gubernatorial elections in Maguindanao, Mindanao, 58 people were gunned down at a campaign event for an opposition candidate. Thirty-four of the victims were members of the media.

The alleged perpetrators were associated with the region's dominant Ampatuan clan, led by patriarch and incumbent governor (at the time)

Faux Pas

» Don't lose your temper – Filipinos will think you're *loco loco* (crazy).

» When engaged in karaoke (and trust us, you will be), don't insult the guy who sounds like a chicken getting strangled, lest it be taken the wrong way.

» Abstain from grabbing that last morsel on the communal food platter – your hosts might think you're a pauper.

» Don't complain about neighbours getting cozy with you on jeepneys– space is meant to be shared.

Top Films

» **Imelda** (2004) Fascinating look into the psyche of Imelda Marcos.

» **Kubrador** (2006) Top actress Gina Pareño stars in this film about an illegal numbers game.

» **Serbis** (2008) Critically acclaimed film about a family-run porn-movie house in Angeles.

belief systems

(% of population)

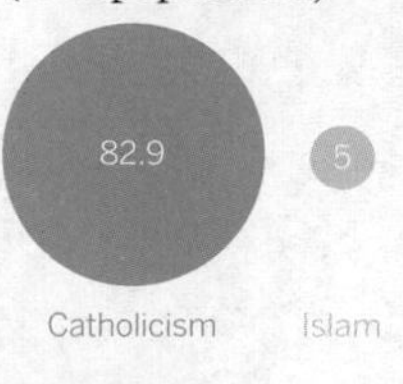

if Philippines were 100 people

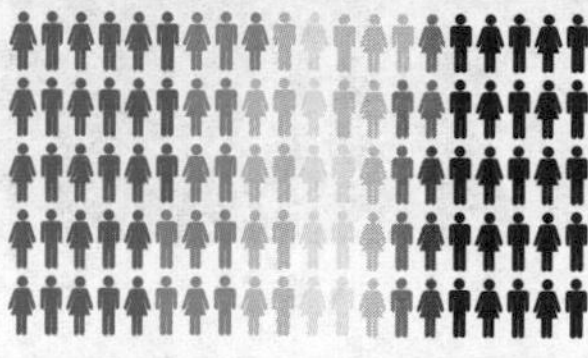

Andal Ampatuan Sr. His son, Andal Jr, who was running to replace him, is alleged to have masterminded the slaughter.

A conviction in such a high-profile case is far from certain in the Philippines, where clans like the Ampatuans tend to operate with impunity. President Aquino has vowed to achieve justice in the case. Ultimately, the success of his presidency may rest on doing just that.

Despite – or perhaps because of – the Philippines' vocal free press, the killing of journalists is common. The country ranked third in the Committee to Protect Journalists' 2011 'impunity index', which measures the prevalence of unsolved journalist murders – one more reason the trial is being closely watched.

» Population growth rate: 1.9%

» Median age: 22.9

» Life expectancy: 71.7

» Literacy rate: 92.6%

» Unemployment rate: 7.3%

100 Million & Counting

The Philippines' population surpassed 100 million in 2011, up from just 76.5 million in 2000. The exploding population is hampering efforts to reduce poverty. While GDP has exhibited steady growth since the 1990s, in real terms it has lagged behind population growth, so per capita income has remained stagnant. Meanwhile, the percentage of people living on less than US$2 a day has remained around 40%.

Over the years the powerful Catholic Church has successfully lobbied against stricter family-planning policies that might defuse the population bomb. But in 2008, Congress introduced the Reproductive Health Bill – a national family-planning program that encourages contraceptives and birth-control pills.

The controversial bill failed to pass during Arroyo's last two years in office. President Aquino has come out in support of the bill, and all eyes are on its fate for 2012, when the Senate could finally send it to the president for approval.

World Ranking

» Population: 12th

» Physical Size: 79th

» Number of Catholics: 3rd

» Most biodiversity: Top 17

» Health expenditures (% of GDP): 169th

» Journalists killed since 1992: 2nd

Top Books

» **Pacific Rims: Beermen Ballin' in Flip-Flops and the Philippines' Unlikely Love Affair with Basketball** (Rafe Bartholomew) As riotous as the title implies.

» **Playing with Water – Passion and Solitude on a Philippine Island** (James Hamilton-Paterson) This timeless account of life on a remote islet sheds much light on Philippine culture.

History

Ancient Filipinos stuck to their own islands and social groups until the 16th century, when Ferdinand Magellan claimed the islands for Spain and began the bloody process of Christianisation. The Filipinos' waning acceptance of Spanish rule evaporated after the Spaniards executed national hero José Rizal in 1896. They revolted and won, only to have the Americans take over, whereupon they revolted again and lost. WWII brought much bloodshed, but out of the war's ashes rose an independent republic, albeit one that would soon elect hardliner Ferdinand Marcos as president. Marcos' declaration of martial law in 1972 and the 1986 'People Power' revolution that led to his overthrow are the two defining moments of modern Filipino history. Since 'People Power' the country has remained democratic, but its fortunes have improved little in the post-Marcos era.

The 1904 World's Fair: The Filipino Experience is a page-turning account by Jose D Fermin of the 1100 Filipinos who were taken to the St Louis World's Fair in the US and displayed under zoolike conditions as examples of colonial triumph.

A History of Being 'Different'

It's often said that 400 years of Spanish and, later, American colonisation are what make the Philippines 'different' from the rest of Asia. In fact the Philippine archipelago was different long before the Spanish arrived and turned it into Asia's only predominantly Christian country.

The islands' first colonisers arrived by boat from the north, south and west, establishing a loose network of settlements that had little contact with each other. Thus, from early on the idea of a Philippine 'identity' was a tenuous one. Indeed, the early Philippines had several identities depending on which island you plopped down on. If you were to arrive in North Luzon 1000 years ago, you would have confronted the Ifugao tending to their spectacular rice terraces, which still wow tourists today around Banaue (see p142). It is thought the ancestors of the Ifugao were part of a wave that arrived some 15,000 years ago from China and Vietnam.

If you arrived 1000 years ago in southern Luzon or the Visayan lowlands, you would have encountered mostly animists of Malay origin,

TIMELINE

45,000 BC

'Tabon Man', the oldest discovered inhabitant of the 7000 islands, leaves a bit of his skull in a cave on Palawan, shedding light on the Philippines' deep, dark pre-history.

AD 100–200

The Chinese become the first foreigners to trade with the islands, which they call Mai. Thus begins a long history of Chinese economic and cultural influence in the Philippines.

AD 100–1000

Malays in outrigger *balangay* boats arrive in several waves, becoming the islands' dominant ethnic group. The archipelago's eight main languages derive from various Malay tongues spoken by these immigrants.

while in the southern regions of Mindanao and Sulu, Islam would already be spreading by way of immigrants from Brunei. Meanwhile, the archipelago's original inhabitants, the Negritos (also called Aeta, Dumagat or Ati), were sprinkled all over the place, much as they are today.

Rarely sedentary, the disparate communities of the Philippines roamed around hunting, gathering, fishing and growing a few basic crops such as rice. They formed small 'barangays' – named after the *balangay* boats in which the Malays arrived – under the leadership of a *datu* (chief). These simple barangays represented the highest form of political unit. The 'country', if you could call it that, possessed neither a centralised government nor a common culture or religion.

Into this diverse jumble strode the Spanish, with the singular mission to unite the Philippine islands around Christianity. Remarkably, they would largely succeed, and over the next several centuries a semblance of a unified Filipino identity, bearing traces of both Spanish and traditional culture, began to emerge. Chinese immigration waves and, later, American occupation would continue to mould the Filipino character before the country finally became independent in 1946.

Catholicism Arrives

In the early 16th century, Islam was beginning to spread throughout the region. Barangays as far north as Manila had been converted, and all signs pointed to the archipelago adopting Islam on a wide scale. But on 16 March 1521 Portuguese explorer Ferdinand Magellan changed the

READING LIST

Since the US military left their Philippine bases in 1992, there has been a treasure trove of books published about the unique relationship between the US and the Philippines. Our top five:

» *In Our Image: America's Empire in the Philippines,* by Stanley Karnow. Definitive work on America's role in the Philippines.

» *Benevolent Assimilation: The American Conquest of the Philippines 1899–1903,* by Stuart Creighton Miller. Eye-opening account of the Philippine-American War and how the US media treated that war.

» *America's Boy: A Century of United States Colonialism in the Philippines,* by James Paterson-Hamilton. Absorbing look at Marcos' symbiotic relationship with the US.

» *By Sword and Fire: The Destruction of Manila in World War II,* by Alphonso Aluit. Blow-by-blow account of the battle that flattened Manila, and America's role in it.

» *Retribution: The Battle for Japan,* by Max Hastings. Critically acclaimed WWII tome devotes much ink to the Philippines campaign and skewers MacArthur.

1100
Traders from China, India, Japan, Vietnam, Cambodia, Thailand and other countries are regularly trading with Philippine islands. The Chinese establish trading posts along the Luzon coast.

1521
Ferdinand Magellan lands at Samar and claims the country for the Spanish, but soon after is murdered by Chief Lapu-Lapu on Mactan Island off Cebu.

1565
Legazpi lands in Cebu and forces the local chieftain to sign an agreement making every Filipino answerable to Spanish law. Within 10 years Spain controls most of the Philippines.

1700
The galleon trade shuttling Chinese goods between the Philippines and Acapulco, Mexico, is in full swing, enriching Manila and earning it the moniker Pearl of the Orient.

course of Filipino history by landing at Samar and claiming the islands for Spain. Magellan set about giving the islanders a crash course in Catholicism and winning over various tribal chiefs. Having nearly accomplished his goal, Magellan was killed in battle against one of the last holdouts, Chief Lapu-Lapu of Mactan Island off Cebu.

The Fall of Joseph Estrada is a highly readable account by Amando Dovonila of the rise and crash of the actor who tried to be president during the late 1990s.

Determined to press its claim after conceding the more strategically important Moluccas (Spice Islands) to Portugal, Spain sent four more expeditions to the Philippines: Ruy Lopez de Villalobos, commander of the fourth expedition, renamed the islands after the heir to the Spanish throne, Philip, Charles I's son. Philip, as King Philip II, ordered a fresh fleet led by Miguel Lopez de Legazpi to sail from Mexico to the islands in 1564 with strict orders to colonise and Catholicise. In 1565 Legazpi returned to the scene of Magellan's death at Cebu and overran the local tribe. An agreement was signed by Legazpi and Tupas, the defeated *datu,* which made every Filipino answerable to Spanish law.

Legazpi, his soldiers and a band of Augustinian monks wasted no time in establishing a settlement where Cebu City now stands; Fort San Pedro is a surviving relic of the era. Legazpi soon discovered that his pact with Tupas was meaningless because the chief had no authority over the islands' myriad other tribes. So Legazpi went about conquering them one by one.

After beating the local people into submission, Legazpi established a vital stronghold on Panay (near present-day Roxas) in 1569. The dominoes fell easily after that, the big prize being Manila, which he wrested from Muslim chief Rajah Sulayman in 1571. Legazpi hastily proclaimed Manila the capital of Las Islas Filipinas and built what was eventually to become Fort Santiago on Sulayman's former *kuta* (fort).

The new colony was run by a Spanish governor who reported to Mexico. But outside of Manila real power rested with the Catholic friars – the *friarocracia* (friarocracy). The friars attempted to move people from barangays into larger, more centralised *pueblos* (towns). They built imposing stone churches in the centre of each *pueblo;* dozens of these still stand and a few, such as Paoay Church (p118), are Unesco World Heritage sites. The friars acted as sole rulers over what were essentially rural fiefdoms.

A Country of Our Own takes the controversial view that the Philippines will never be a strong nation because it has never had a unified soul, but author David C Martinez offers some possible solutions.

The Philippine Revolution

As Spain grew weaker, and as the friars grew ever more repressive, the natives started to resist. Several minor peasant revolts marked the end of the 19th century. Poorly funded and helplessly localised, they were easily quashed. But in the 19th century the face of the resistance would change as a wealthy class of European-educated mestizos (Filipinos of mixed Spanish or Chinese blood) with nationalist tendencies began to emerge. Known as *ilustrados,* the greatest and best-known of the lot was Dr José

1762

Great Britain occupies Manila for two years before being chased out. The incident demonstrates the weakness of the Spanish regime and marks the start of a united, nationalist Filipino spirit.

1815

The last Spanish galleon sails between Manila and Acapulco, marking the end of Manila's lucrative monopoly on global trade with Mexico, and hence much of South America.

1850

The sugar and tobacco industries thrive, creating a class of wealthy mestizos. The *ilustrados,* who studied abroad and brought ideas about independence back to the Philippines, emerge from this class.

» Cane cutters, the Visayas

Rizal, doctor of medicine, poet, novelist, sculptor, painter, linguist, naturalist and fencing enthusiast.

Executed by the Spanish in 1896, Rizal epitomised the Filipinos' dignified struggle for personal and national freedom. 'I am most anxious for liberties for our country', he wrote just before facing the Spanish firing squad. 'But I place as a prior condition the education of the people so that our country may have an individuality of its own and make itself worthy of liberties'.

By killing such figures, the Spanish were creating martyrs. Andres Bonifacio led an aggressive movement known as the Katipunan, or KKK, that secretly built a revolutionary government in Manila, with a network of equally clandestine provincial councils. Complete with passwords, masks and coloured sashes denoting rank, the Katipunan's membership (both men and women) peaked at an estimated 30,000 in mid-1896. In August, the Spanish got wind of the coming revolution (from a woman's confession to a Spanish friar, according to some accounts) and the Katipunan leaders were forced to flee the capital.

Depleted, frustrated and poorly armed, the Katipuneros took stock in nearby Balintawak, a barangay of Caloocan, and voted to launch the revolution regardless. With the cry 'Mabuhay ang Pilipinas!' (Long live the Philippines!), the Philippine Revolution lurched into life following the incident that is now known as the Cry of Balintawak.

After 18 months of bloodshed, most of it Filipino blood, a Spanish-Filipino peace pact was signed and the revolutionary leader General Emilio Aguinaldo agreed to go into exile in Hong Kong in December 1897. Predictably, the pact's demands satisfied nobody. Promises of reform by the Spanish were broken, as were promises by the Filipinos to stop their revolutionary plotting.

Meanwhile, another of Spain's colonial trouble spots – Cuba – was playing host to an ominous dispute between Spain and the USA over sugar. To save face, Spain declared war on the USA; as a colony of Spain, the Philippines was drawn into the conflict. Soon after, an American fleet under Commodore George Dewey sailed into Manila Bay and routed the Spanish ships. Keen to gain Filipino support, Dewey welcomed the return of exiled revolutionary General Aguinaldo and oversaw the Philippine Revolution mark II, which installed Aguinaldo as president of the first Philippine republic. The Philippine flag was flown for the first time during Aguinaldo's proclamation of Philippine Independence in Cavite on 12 June 1898.

Inside the Palace Really by Beth Day Romulo documents the rise and fall of the Marcoses – a couple made for drama.

The Philippines has been the world's major supplier of pineapples since the 1980s, when most production was moved from Hawaii due to labour costs.

The Philippine-American War

With the signing of the Treaty of Paris in 1898, the Spanish-American War ended and the USA effectively bought the Philippines, along with Guam and Puerto Rico, for US$20 million. A fierce debate raged in the US over what to do with its newly acquired territory halfway across the

1871
Army-appointed Spanish King Amadeo I appoints hardliner General Rafael de Izquierdo as governor of the Philippines in an effort to stamp out rising nationalist sentiment in the archipelago.

1872
Izquierdo's execution of Padre José Burgos and two other popular Filipino priests on suspicion of harbouring mutinous intentions reawakens the nationalist spirit spawned during the British occupation 100 years earlier.

1892
José Rizal returns home one year after his *El Filibusterismo*, which skewered the Spanish, is published. He forms La Liga Filipina, a social reform movement, and is banished to Mindanao.

1899
William Grayson, an American army private from Nebraska on night patrol near Manila, fires the first shot in the Philippine-American War. The shot kills a drunk Filipino noncombatant.

world. Hawks on the right clamoured to hold onto the islands for strategic and 'humanitarian' reasons, while 'anti-imperialist' liberals attacked the subjugation of a foreign peoples as morally wrong and warned that the battle to occupy the Philippines would drag on for years (about which they were correct). The themes of the home-front debate, and the ensuing drawn-out guerrilla war, would have parallels to the Vietnam and Iraq wars many decades later.

US President William J McKinley originally opposed colonisation before caving in to hawks in his Republican party and agreeing to take over the islands. Echoing the imperialists, McKinley opined that because Filipinos 'were unfit for self-government', he had no choice but to take over the islands and 'civilise' them.

The American military practised for the Vietnam War in the Philippines in the 1950s under the command of General Edward Landsdale, the model for Graham Greene's *The Quiet American*.

Drunk with their first small taste of independence, the Filipinos led by Aguinaldo had other ideas. They set up a makeshift capital in Malolos, outside Manila, in open defiance of the Americans. The Americans, in turn, antagonised the Filipinos. War broke out in February 1899.

The expected swift American victory didn't materialise, as the guerrilla campaign launched by Aguinaldo and rebels like Gregorio del Pilar and Apolinario Mabini proved remarkably effective at neutralising American military superiority. Aguinaldo was captured in March 1901, but still the war dragged on. As it did, and as casualties on both sides mounted, the American public grew more opposed to the war. Resentment peaked in September 1901 in the aftermath of the Balangiga Massacre (see p322). It was only on 4 July 1902 that the US finally declared victory in the campaign, although pockets of guerrilla resistance continued to dog the Americans for several more years. Some 200,000 Filipino civilians, 20,000 Filipino soldiers and more than 4000 American soldiers died in the war from combat or disease.

The American Era

The Americans quickly set about healing the significant wounds their victory had wrought. Even before they had officially won the war, they began instituting reforms aimed at improving the Filipinos' lot, the most important of which was a complete overhaul of the education system. Whereas the Spanish had attempted to keep Filipinos illiterate and ignorant of Spanish, the Americans imported hundreds of teachers to the country to teach reading, writing, arithmetic – and English. Within 35 years the literacy rate among Filipinos had risen from a miniscule percentage to almost 50%, and 27% of the population could speak English. The comprehensive education system arguably remains the single most important legacy of the American colonial period to this day.

The Spanish documentary *Returning to the Siege of Baler* (2008) recounts how 50 Spaniards holed up in Baler's church held out for 11 months against 800 Filipinos during the Philippine Revolution.

Besides schools, the Americans built bridges, roads and sewage systems. They brought the recalcitrant Moros in Mindanao to heel and

1901

The Americans capture revolutionary leader General Emilio Aguinaldo, who later urges his countrymen to accept US rule. His countrymen don't listen, and the war drags on another 1½ years.

1904

Head-hunting North Luzon Igorot tribesmen comprising a 'living exhibit' at the St Louis World's Fair steal the show with their loincloths and appetite for dog meat.

1935

Manuel L Quezon, a wealthy mestizo, wins the first national presidential election, marking the establishment of the Philippine Commonwealth. True Philippine independence would have to wait until after the war.

1942

75,000 American and Filipino troops surrender to Japan at Bataan – the largest surrender of troops in US history. The Bataan Death March ensues, and one month later Corregidor falls.

Christianised the Cordillera tribes of the north – two groups the Spanish had tried and failed to influence. And they instituted an American-style political system that gradually gave more and more power to Filipinos. The Americans also made a gesture considered unprecedented in the history of imperialism: they openly promised the Filipinos eventual independence.

Critics describe American benevolence during this period as a thinly veiled carrot disguising America's true goal of establishing economic hegemony over the islands. Whatever the motive, the US endorsed the Commonwealth of the Philippines in 1935, along with the drafting of a US-style constitution and the first national election. On paper at least, democracy and freedom had at last come to the Philippines. Unfortunately, WWII would ensure that they would be short-lived.

THE BIRTH OF PEOPLE POWER

People Power was born in the streets of Manila in February 1986. As the whole world watched, millions of Filipinos, armed only with courage and religious faith, poured out onto the streets to defy the military might of the Marcos regime.

Despite Marcos' unpopularity in the mid-1980s, People Power might never have happened were it not for the assassination of immensely popular opposition figure Ninoy Aquino. With his death, Filipinos felt they had lost their hope for a peaceful return to democracy. Some two million mourners followed Ninoy's funeral cortege as it slowly wound its way through the streets of Manila for over 12 hours.

The decline and fall of the Marcos dictatorship came swiftly after that. By 1986, even the USA, which had backed Marcos all those years against communism in Southeast Asia, began to withdraw its support. In the face of mounting criticism abroad and rising unrest at home, Marcos called for snap elections on 7 February 1986. Corazon 'Cory' Aquino, Ninoy's widow, became the (reluctant at first) standard bearer of the opposition at the instigation of the Roman Catholic Church. Marcos came out the winner of the election, but the people knew Cory had been cheated, and they were no longer to be silenced.

On 26 February a massive sea of humanity gathered around Camp Aguinaldo and Camp Crame, along Epifanio de los Santos Ave, better known as EDSA, where two of Marcos' former ministers, Juan Ponce Enrile and Fidel Ramos, had taken refuge after defecting to the side of the people. They sang, chanted, prayed, shared food and drink, both among themselves and with government troops, who refused to fire into crowds and eventually went over to the side of the people. By nightfall the restless crowds were threatening to storm the palace. At this point the US stepped in and advised Marcos to 'let go'. Hurriedly the Marcoses boarded a US aircraft and flew to Hawaii and into exile.

The Filipino people had staged the world's first successful bloodless revolution, inspiring others to do the same across the world.

1945

In battles to retake the Philippines, Manila is destroyed and 150,000 civilians killed. Many are the victims of doomed Japanese troops. The Pearl of the Orient would never be the same.

1946

Japanese General Tomoyuki Yamashita, whose orders to abandon Manila were defied by his subordinates, is tried as a war criminal and hanged by order of MacArthur.

1969

Ferdinand Marcos becomes the first Philippine president to win two terms in office, even as resentment over Marcos' increasingly heavy-handed rule and the Philippines' involvement in Vietnam simmers.

1972

As resentment of Marcos rises, the embattled president imposes martial law and jails thousands of teachers, journalists, union leaders and opposition leaders, including Benigno 'Ninoy' Aquino Jr.

The Destruction of Manila

When Japan bombed Hawaii's Pearl Harbor in 1941, other forces attacked Clark Field, where General Douglas MacArthur was caught napping, despite many hours' warning, setting off a string of events that would lead to the Japanese occupying the Philippines from 1942 to 1945.

'Jihadists in Paradise' is a riveting *Atlantic Monthly* article by Mark Bowden about Abu Sayyaf rebels' seizure of a Palawan resort and subsequent 18-month detainment of two American missionaries.

In 1944 MacArthur honoured his now-famous pledge to return, landing at Leyte, determined to dislodge the Japanese. The main battle ground in this onslaught was Manila, where defenceless residents suffered horrifically in the ensuing crossfire during February 1945. By the time MacArthur marched into the city, the combination of Japanese atrocities and American shelling had killed at least 150,000 civilians, and a city that had been one of the finest in Asia was destroyed.

A fierce debate rages to this day about who was to blame for the destruction of Manila. The vast majority of civilian casualties resulted from US artillery fire. But many argue that by failing to abandon Manila and declare it an open city, the Japanese gave MacArthur little choice but to bring the fight to Manila. Whatever the truth, Manila belongs in a category with Warsaw, Hiroshima and Hamburg as cities that suffered the most damage in WWII.

The Marcos Era

In 1965 Ferdinand Marcos, a dashing former lawyer from a prominent Ilocos political family was elected the Philippines' fourth post-WWII president under the seductive slogan 'This nation can be great again'. At first it indeed was a new era, and Marcos and his even more charismatic wife Imelda went about trying to bring back some of Manila's pre-war energy. Imelda drove projects such as the Cultural Center of the Philippines. By 1970, widespread poverty, rising inflation, pitiful public funding and blatant corruption triggered a wave of protests in Manila. When several demonstrators were killed by police outside the presidential Malacañang Palace, Marcos' image as a political saviour died with them.

Imelda Marcos ran unsuccessfully for president in both 1992 and 1998 while still under investigation for some 900 counts of corruption and other crimes. She ran successfully for Congress in 1995 and again at the age of 80 in 2010.

Citing the rise of leftist student groups and the NPA, Marcos imposed martial law on the entire country in 1972. Normally a constitutional last resort designed to protect the masses, martial law was declared by Marcos to keep himself in power (the constitution prevented him from running for a third term) and to protect his foreign business interests. Under martial law, a curfew was imposed, the media was silenced or taken over by the military, international travel was banned and thousands of antigovernment suspects were rounded up and put into military camps. An estimated 50,000 of Marcos' opponents were jailed, exiled or killed. Marcos would not lift martial law until 1981. His downfall five years later is well documented (see the boxed text, p413).

1980

Ninoy Aquino is released from custody to undergo a triple bypass operation in the United States. He will remain in exile for more than three years.

1981

Martial law is lifted on the eve of a visit by Pope John Paul II, who criticises Marcos' human rights record. Shortly after, a rigged election hands Marcos another six-year term.

1983

Aquino is shot dead at Manila's airport as he disembarks from a flight returning him from exile in the USA. Two million mourners pour onto the streets to accompany Aquino's funeral cortege.

1986

The bloodless EDSA I Revolution, popularly known as People Power, chases Marcos from the Philippines. Ninoy's widow, Corazon, who had lost the presidential election to Marcos days earlier, becomes president.

Ferdinand Marcos died in exile in 1989 and his shoe-happy wife, Imelda, soon returned to the Philippines. Despite evidence that she and Ferdinand helped themselves to billions of dollars from the treasury, Imelda continues to live freely in Makati and was even elected to parliament in 2010.

Terror in Manila February 1945, by Antonio Pérez de Olaguer, is an unflinching account of Japanese atrocities during the battle for Manila. It's based on oral histories by Spanish survivors.

The Moro Problem

Muslim dissent emanating out of Mindanao has been the one constant in the Philippines' roughly 450 years of history as a loosely united territory. After Legazpi landed in Cebu in 1565, he discovered that Muslim missionaries from Malacca had been living in Mindoro and Luzon for decades. Legazpi managed to dislodge Muslim chiefs from Maynilad (now Manila) and other central settlements with relative ease. But the southern territories would prove more difficult to conquer, and over the next 400 years a religious war would smoulder in Mindanao.

The country's largest separatist Muslim group is the 12,500-strong Moro Islamic Liberation Front (MILF), but the group that grabs all the headlines is Abu Sayyaf, which was responsible for a highly publicised kidnapping in 2001 that became the basis of the acclaimed *Atlantic Monthly* piece 'Jihadists in Paradise'.

The MILF signed a ceasefire with the government in 2001, but periodic violence and bombings continued to occur in Mindanao's predominantly Muslim Autonomous Region in Muslim Mindanao (ARMM) until the until the ceasefire collapsed in August 2008. Fighting intensified and continued until a truce was signed about a year later. Peace negotiations resumed in Malaysia in late 2009, but had borne little fruit at the time of research. See p332 for a comprehensive history of this conflict.

1989

A coup attempt against Cory Aquino sees hundreds of foreigners taken hostage in rebel-seized condos and hotels in Makati. Alleged US involvement in suppressing the siege stokes rising anti-American sentiment.

1991

Mt Pinatubo erupts, rendering the American military base at Clark unusable. The Philippine Senate votes to end the US military presence at Philippine bases permanently.

SEONG JOON CHO/LONELY PLANET IMAGES ©

» Mt Pinatubo

1999

As all-out war rages with the Moro Islamic Liberation Front (MILF), President Estrada signs the controversial Visiting Forces Agreement, which allows American troops back to train Filipino forces.

Culture

The Filipino

It's impossible to deny it: Filipinos have a zest for life that may be unrivalled on our planet. The national symbol, the jeepney, is an apt metaphor for the nation. Splashed with colour, laden with religious icons and festooned with sanguine scribblings, the jeepney flaunts the fact that, at heart, it's a dilapidated pile of scrap metal. Like the jeepney, Filipinos face their often dim prospects in life with a laugh and a wink. Whatever happens ... 'so be it'.

Mindanao artist Kublai Ponce-Millan's nine statues of indigenous Filipinos playing musical instruments in St Peter's Sq, Vatican City, was the first time a non-Italian artist was allowed to participate in the Vatican's annual nativity scene display.

This fatalism has a name: *bahala na,* a phrase that expresses the idea that all things shall pass and in the meantime life is to be lived. *Bahala na* helps shape the carefree, welcoming nature of the Filipino people. But it also has more than a little to do with the country's reputation as the 'Sick Man of Asia' – a reference to its steady economic fall from grace over the last 40 years or so.

Family and religion are the two most important forces in Filipino society. The close-knit Filipino family unit extends to distant cousins, multiple godparents, and one's *barkada* (gang of friends). Almost without exception, all members of one's kinship group are afforded the utmost loyalty; respect for elders is paramount.

Filipino families, especially poor ones, tend to be large. It's not uncommon for a dozen family members to live together in a tiny apartment, shanty or nipa hut. Because of this, personal space is not the issue for Filipinos that it is for Westerners. Foreign visitors to Philippine resorts are often amazed – or appalled – when a family of 10 takes up residence in the room next door, complete with pets, videoke machine and cooking equipment.

The most basic political unit, the barangay, is merely an extension of the family-based community unit that defined the social structure in pre-Hispanic times. The idea of working together for the common good, virtually nonexistent at the national level, is alive and well at the barangay level, where it's known as *bayanihan.* Originally a rural entity, the barangay today is no less relevant in urban shanty towns, where a healthy cooperative spirit is essential for survival.

Set in Israel, *Paper Dolls* (2006) documents the lives of transvestite Filipino Overseas Foreign Workers (OFWs) who work as caregivers by day and perform in Tel Aviv nightclubs by night.

Filipinos may be overwhelmingly Catholic, but they can sin with the best of them. Drinking is a popular pastime (cheap local brandy is the favourite poison), adultery and prostitution are rampant, and grudges are often settled with bullets.

To the chagrin of the Catholic Church, Filipinos are also a superstitious lot. In urban areas, faith healers, psychics, fortune-tellers, tribal shamans, self-help books and evangelical crusaders can all help cast away ill-fortune. In the hinterland, some people believe that caves and forests are inhabited by spirits, ghosts and *aswang.*

Filipinos are remarkably tolerant of, well, just about everybody, and that includes you, the traveller. Travellers of any race, creed or sexual orientation are uniformly received with the utmost warmth and courtesy.

The last vital thread in the fabric of Filipino society is the overseas worker. At any given time well more than a million Filipinos are working abroad. Combined they send home more than US$15 billion a year, according to official figures (the real figure is likely much higher). The Overseas Filipino Worker (OFW) – the nurse in Canada, the construction worker in Qatar, the entertainer in Japan, the cleaner in Singapore – has become a national hero.

Women in the Philippines

The Philippines has elected two female presidents in the last 20 years, and plenty of other women have held positions of power since the country became independent in 1946. Many credit 18th-century revolutionary leader Gabriela Silang with paving the way for the future success of women in the Philippines. Like Cory Aquino, who helped topple the Marcos regime, Silang was the widow of an assassinated dissident who took over a resistance movement against the Spanish upon the death of her husband (see p111).

But not all Filipinas reach such lofty heights. Poorer women in many households are expected to fulfil most of the child-rearing, cooking and household duties, in addition to being primary breadwinners. While men are allowed – even expected – to have a *querida* (mistress), women guilty of marital transgressions are often beaten or abandoned by their husbands.

Domestic violence is a serious problem that occurs in the Philippines. About 12 cases of domestic abuse are reported to the police every day, but that's most probably only a small percentage of actual cases, as many victims are too embarrassed to report incidents of abuse. Bantay Banay (www.lihokpilipina.com), a grassroots women's support organisation, has established community watch groups that aid victims of domestic violence in more than 50 cities across the country.

Arts

Music

Filipinos are best known for their ubiquitous cover bands and their love of karaoke, but they need not be in imitation mode to show off their innate musical talent.

One phenomenon that increasingly unites Filipinos is its burgeoning pop music scene, known as OPM (Original Pinoy Music). The term encompasses a wide spectrum of rock ('Pinoy rock'), folk and New Age genres – plus a subgenre that includes all three.

Embodying the latter subgenre is Kalayo, which plays a sometimes-frantic fusion of tribal styles and modern jam-band rock. The 11-piece band uses a plethora of bamboo reed pipes, flutes and percussion instruments, and sings in dialects as diverse as Visayan, French and Bicol. Grace Nono is another artist squarely in the New Age jungle milieu, but she's a whole lot more mellow. She croons deeply spiritual lyrics in a strangely melodic tribal squawk.

Moving toward the Pinoy rock mainstream, the eponymous band fronted by the singer Bamboo dominates the air waves. The slightly grungy rockers weigh in with a heady mixture of political invective and ballads laden with angst-ridden garage rock. Even more popular is the sometimes sweet, sometimes surly diva Kitchie Nadal, who regularly tours internationally. Rounding out the big three is the agreeable Rivermaya, formerly fronted by Bamboo. Its 2005 hit 'You'll Be Safe Here' made minor waves internationally. All of the above sing in both Filipino and English.

The heyday of Pinoy rock was 30 years ago, when blues-rock outfits like the Juan de la Cruz Band, Anakbayan and Maria Cafra ruled the

The range of literature on Mindanao includes Jose Y Delisay's *Soledad's Sister*, the short-story collection *Very Short Stories for Harried Readers*, and *Children of the Ever-Changing Moon*, an anthology of essays about the Moro experience.

Eye of the Fish is an interesting collection of essays by Manila-born, New York–raised journalist Luis H Fracia that is a good introduction to the various issues facing the Philippines and its people today.

Aswang – mythical vampire-like figures who eat unborn children – have been the subject of at least one American cult horror flick. Any rural Filipino will tell you in a matter-of-fact manner about the many *aswang* living in their local forests.

roost. These '70s bands looked and sounded the part, with long hair, bandanas and endless, soulful electric-guitar riffs. The Juan de la Cruz Band is credited with inventing Pinoy rock by busting out lyrics in Tagalog – the first big act to do so. From those humble origins evolved Eraserheads, the country's first modest international success. This four-man band, known as the Philippines' Beatles, rose to prominence in the early '90s with catchy guitar-heavy alternative rock. There's also the Philippines' U2 – The Dawn, a vaguely New Age '80s band – and the Philippines' Elvis, '60s actor-singer Eddie Mesa.

Ghosts of Manila (1994) by James Hamilton-Paterson is a chilling yet entertaining 'docufiction' of life, death and the corrupt chains binding Filipinos in the city's slums.

Folk music has solid roots in the Philippines. Freddie Aguilar's 'Anak', a song about parent-child relations, propelled him to fame at the beginning of the People Power revolution in the 1980s. Joey Ayala and his sister, Cynthia Alexander, play progressive folk infused with tribal elements. Aguilar plays regularly at Ka Freddie's House in Malate (Manila), while Alexander and Ayala play regularly at Conspiracy Bar in Quezon City, which they co-own.

Dating from the late 19th century, the *kundiman* genre, with its bittersweet themes of love, fate and death, remains one of the best-loved modes of musical expression in the Philippines. Traditional musical instruments used in *kundiman* include the *kudyapi*, a hauntingly melodic lute, and the *kulintang*, a row of small gongs mounted on a *langkungan*, a resonating platform.

One Filipino performer who has won international acclaim is Lea Salonga, the original *Miss Saigon*. Cecile Licad has likewise built herself a name globally, principally in Japan, the USA and Europe, as an interpreter of the piano music of Chopin and Schumann.

Architecture

Long before the Spanish arrived, the simple, utilitarian nipa hut defined Filipino architecture. The most basic nipa hut is made of wood and bamboo, with a roof of palm thatch – cool and breezy in hot weather and easily repaired if damaged by typhoons.

The 'yo-yo', which means 'come back' in Tagalog, was invented by a Filipino-American. The original yo-yo was a studded weapon attached to 20ft ropes.

YO-YO

The Spanish brought new forms of architecture, such as the *bahay na bato* (stone house) and squat, fortresslike 'earthquake-baroque' churches. But the basic design of the nipa hut endured. By the 19th century, Filipinos of means were building hybrid residences that mixed Spanish and Asian styles with elements of the nipa hut. These composite structures, distinguishable by their capiz-shell windows and huge upstairs *sala* (living room), remain the most elegant and distinctive architectural specimens the Philippines has to offer. The Spanish colonial city of Vigan is the best place to view them, although you will sometimes stumble across fine examples in the most remote barangays.

The American era was characterised by neoclassical architecture, evident in many of Manila's government buildings. During the 1930s, local architects introduced novel forms of Art Deco to the urban landscape, such as the Metropolitan Theater in Manila. The 1970s saw the emergence of the massive ferro-concrete creations of Leandro Locsin, who designed the Cultural Center of the Philippines and the Central Bank of the Philippines. Today the contemporary urban landscape is dominated by tinted-glass high-rises such as the corporate buildings along Ayala Ave in Makati and the residential towers of Fort Bonifacio.

Theatre

Filipino theatre evolved from marathon chants and epic legends, such as the Unesco-recognised Ifugao *hudhud*, sung in the rice fields around Kiangan in North Luzon to alleviate boredom while planting and harvesting. In the 17th century the Spaniards introduced *sinakulos* – passion plays depicting the life and death of Christ – to convert the locals to Christianity. Other early forms of theatre were the *moro-moro,* which glorified the Christian struggle against Muslims in the 19th century, and a light, localised musical form known as *zarzuela,* which was used to protest American occupation at the outset of the 20th century.

When the Americans arrived, English became the language of the national theatrical scene. The journalist, novelist and playwright Nick Joaquin wrote his signature work, *Portrait of a Young Artist as a Filipino,* in 1951. Other important playwrights of the 20th century were Rolando Tinio, whose Filipino adaptations of English-language classics such as Shakespeare's tragedies remain unparalleled in their field; and Rene Villanueva, best known for his children's books but also highly regarded as a playwright.

Contemporary playwrights blend tradition with the issues of the day. The Philippine Educational Theater Association (PETA; www.petatheater.com) has an excellent development program for up-and-coming playwrights. Relatively recent productions include Nick Pichay's modern adaptation of the *hudhud,* and Floy Quintos' satirical *Fluid,* which skewers Manila's social-climber-laced arts scene.

Po-on is an easy introduction to Filipino author F Sionil Jose, with all the tropes of Filipino literature: evil Spanish priests, heroic *ilustrados,* passive resistance and armed struggle. It's the first in a five-part series.

Painting & Sculpture

The most recognisable form of artwork in the Philippines is centuries old and, in fact, wasn't conceived as artwork: the *bulol,* the sacred wood figures carved by the Ifugao, have for centuries been used to guard rice fields. The names of the sculptors were rarely recorded, but elder Ifugao can often identify the sculptor of original *bulol* based on the statue's style. Reproductions of these powerful statues flood souvenir shops across the country.

Modern Filipino sculpture is epitomised by Guillermo Tolentino's neoclassical masterpiece in Caloocan City, the resplendent *Monumento,* honouring the revolutionary hero Andres Bonifacio. Another name visitors may notice is Jose Mendoza, whose sculptures adorn the streets of Makati.

ARNEL PINEDA'S JOURNEY

He was just a small-town boy, as his favourite band once put it, working on the not-so-lonely cover-band circuit in Quezon City, Manila, as lead singer for a band called Zoo. Arnel Pineda didn't reckon on achieving more or less fame than any of the zillion other Filipino cover-band singers that keep the crowds entertained in the bars and lounges of hotels from Bahrain to Beijing. One thing was for sure, though: Arnel Pineda could imitate the throaty wail of Journey's lead singer Steve Perry like nobody's business.

In 2006 something happened that made few waves in the international rock scene, but would change Pineda's life forever. The ageing rockers of Journey were forced to drop lead singer Steve Augeri, who was losing his voice but had never *really* sounded like Perry anyway. The next year, after another lead singer didn't work out, the band stumbled across some clips of Pineda on YouTube. Incredulous, they invited him to LA for an audition.

When Pineda applied for his visa, the story goes, nobody at the US embassy believed his ostensible 'purpose for travel' – auditioning to be lead singer of Journey. So they asked him to sing a few bars of 'Wheels in the Sky.' He nailed it, they issued the visa, and he was on his way to rock 'n' roll infamy.

The band introduced Pineda as their new lead singer in early 2008, turning 90 million Filipinos into Journey fans overnight. Filipinos love a good rags-to-riches story to affirm their hope that things can always get better. Pineda, a one-time homeless kid on the streets of Manila, has done more than give Filipinos a good story – he has given them something to be proud of.

Painting in the Spanish era was dominated by the two unchallenged masters of Filipino art: Juan Luna and Felix Resurreccion Hidalgo. Luna's vast *Spoliarium* and Hidalgo's *Antigone* stunned European art circles when they won gold and silver medals at the prestigious 1884 Madrid Exposition.

The early 20th century saw the rise of the masters Fabian de la Rosa and Fernando Amorsolo. De la Rosa's work is distinguished by disciplined composition and brushwork, while Amorsolo painted quintessential rural Philippine scenes and subjects in a free-flowing, impressionist style.

Vicente Manansala, Arturo Luz, Anita Magsaysay Ho, Fernando Zobel and Hernando Ocampo were among the great Filipino modernists who emerged after WWII. Zobel toyed with cubism before becoming the country's foremost abstractionist. The brilliant ethnic-Chinese painter Ang Kiukok, who studied under Manansala, opened eyes with his violent cubist paintings of fighting cocks, stray dogs and tormented lovers.

The contemporary Filipino art scene is ever abuzz. The conceptual artist David Cortez Medalla, based in Britain, has pioneered avant-garde art movements such as minimalism and performance art. In addition to being well received internationally, artist-with-a-conscience Benedicto Cabrera ('Bencab') has dedicated considerable effort to the development of contemporary art, and created Tam-awan village, an artists retreat in Baguio (p121).

Suggested Websites

» **Filipiniana.net** (www.filipiniana.net) Publishes the complete works of Rizal

» **NCCA** (www.ncca.gov.ph) Outstanding website on arts and ethnic groups

» **The Bontoc Igorot** (www.gutenberg.org/files/3308/3308-h /3308-h.htm) Delightfully dated ethnography primer

Dance

Filipino dance is as rich and varied as the islands themselves. The national folk dance is the *tinikling,* which involves a boy and a girl hopping between bamboo poles, held just above the ground and struck together in time to music or hand-clapping. Some say this dance was inspired by the flitting of birds between grass stems or a heron hopping through the rice paddies. A version of the *tinikling* is the breathtaking *singkil,* where two dancers representing a Muslim princess and her lady-in-waiting weave in and out of four poles struck together at increasing speed.

The mountain people of North Luzon are famed for vigorous hunting dances such as the *tag-gam* and victory dances such as *balangbang*. Down south, an old favourite is the graceful *pangalay,* a courtship dance from the Sulu islands in which women in flowing robes vie for a man's affection.

Two of the best known and most successful Filipino folk-dance troupes are the Bayanihan National Folk Dance Company, which first wowed the world in 1958 at the Brussels Universal Exposition, and the Ramon Obusan Folkloric Group, founded in 1972. Both are resident companies of the Cultural Center of the Philippines.

KARAOKE

Many Westerners would sooner have their wisdom teeth removed without anaesthetic than spend an evening listening to inebriated amateurs pay homage to Celine Dion and Julio Iglesias. But when Filipinos want to unwind, they often do it with karaoke – or 'videoke' as it's known throughout the Philippines.

Filipinos are unabashed about belting out a tune, whenever and wherever, alone or in company. They pursue the craft without a hint of irony, which means that criticising or making fun of someone's performance is decidedly taboo, and may even provoke violence.

With all that videoke going on it can be awfully hard to find peace and quiet in certain tourist hot spots. If loud, unmelodious singing grates like fingernails on a blackboard, stick to resorts run by foreigners, which tend to be less videoke-friendly.

Many Filipino ballet talents have won international recognition abroad, among them Maniya Barredo, former prima ballerina of the Atlanta Ballet, and Lisa Macuja, who played Giselle with the Kirov Ballet in Russia. Macuja now runs her own ballet company, Ballet Manila.

To the M'ranano people of Mindanao, the *sarimanok* (rooster) is symbol of good fortune; it breaks the silence, a link between night and day or the unseen and seen.

Sport

Sport in the Philippines is dominated by one man: lightweight boxer Manny Pacquiao, widely considered the best pound-for-pound prizefighter in the world. Pacquiao, who emerged from poverty in Mindanao to win title belts in five different weight classes, is a tremendous source of national pride for Filipinos. He ran successfully for Philippine congress in 2010, but continues to dominate opponents in the rings.

An even quirkier national hero takes the form of stocky, bespectacled Efren 'Bata' ('The Kid') Reyes, one of the world's best nine-ball billiards players. The other big sport, besides cockfighting, is basketball. Most midsized towns have at least one concrete court with a corrugated-iron roof, and you'll find at least a crude interpretation of a court in even the poorest, most remote barangays. The overwhelmingly popular Philippine Basketball Association (PBA) draws many former US college stars.

Manila's privileged prefer playing polo, or golfing at one of the many world-class courses around Manila.

Did You Know?

The Philippines has no jury system.

Cockfighting

Cockfighting is to the Philippines what baseball is to the USA or rugby is to New Zealand. You'll see cockfights on TV but the only way to truly understand the Filipino passion for the sport is to see it for yourself.

Before each fight, the noise level rises to a crescendo as bets are screamed out to middlemen in a scene reminiscent of a stock exchange. A hush falls over the crowd as the clash begins. The birds, fitted with lethal three-inch ankle blades, wander around aimlessly for a few moments before being reminded by their handlers that there's an adversary in the vicinity. The actual fight, once it finally begins, is short and brutal. The winner is whisked away to a team of waiting surgeons, who stitch up any gaping wounds and dose the bird with antibiotics. The loser usually makes his way into the cooking pot.

Western tourists complain about the practice, but they don't get much sympathy from Filipinos, who just smile and wonder what all the fuss is about.

If you want to see a cockfight, check the schedule at the main cockpit in any given provincial city – Sundays tend to be the most boisterous. In Manila, your best bet is the **Pasay City Cockpit** (Map p58; Libertad St, Pasay).

Food & Drink

Kain na tayo – 'let's eat'. It's the Filipino invitation to eat, and if you travel in the Philippines you will hear it over and over and over again. The phrase reveals two essential aspects of Filipino people: one, that they are hospitable, and two, that they love to, well, eat. Filipinos are constantly eating. Three meals a day just isn't enough, so they've added two *meryenda*. The term literally means 'snack', but don't let that fool you – the afternoon *meryenda* can include something as filling as *bihon* (fried rice sticks) or *goto* (Filipino congee) plus *bibingka* (fluffy rice cakes topped with cheese).

Asia Recipe's Filipino section at www.asiarecipe.com/philippines.html offers a comprehensive listing of Filipino recipes, along with some fascinating essays on Philippine cuisine in the light of traditional customs and folklore.

Filipino food has a somewhat poor reputation in both the West, where Filipino restaurants are rare, and Asia, where the cuisine is considered unimaginative and unrefined. This perplexes Filipinos, who are convinced their home-cooked comfort food is the greatest thing in the world. In truth, indigenous (Pinoy) food is neither as bad as its international reputation, nor as delicious as locals would have you believe. Of course, it all depends on your tastebuds.

The usual complaints about Filipino food are that it's too heavy, too salty and – especially – too sweet. Sugar is added in abundance to everything, from the hamburgers at Jollibee to locally rendered Thai food. But if you know what to order, or know a good cook, you'll find delights aplenty emerging from Filipino kitchens.

The Food of the Philippines by Filipino food guru Reynaldo Alejandro is an excellent introduction to Filipino cooking.

Staples & Specialities

Much of the Philippines' poor culinary reputation rests on the back of one food: *balút,* a boiled duck egg containing a partially developed embryo, sometimes with tiny feathers. Fortunately, most national staples are a lot more palatable than *balút*. If there were a national dish, it would undoubtedly be *adobo* – pork, chicken or just about any meat stewed in vinegar and garlic. It's delicious done right, but can be awfully salty and greasy if done wrong. Other dishes you'll find with striking regularity include *sinigáng* (any meat or seafood boiled in a sour, tamarind-flavoured soup), *kare-kare* (oxtail and vegetables cooked in peanut sauce), *crispy pata* (deep-fried pork hock or knuckles) and *pancit* (stir-fried noodles). *Ihaw-ihaw* eateries, serving *inihaw* (grilled meat or fish), are everywhere. *Lechón* (suckling pig roasted on a spit) is de rigueur at Filipino celebrations. Common appetisers include *lumpia* (small spring rolls, usually vegetarian) and the truly delicious *kinilaw* (Filipino-style ceviche).

Go to www.filipinorecipe.com for an excellent range of recipes for Filipino dishes, as well as a good food glossary and a Filipino cooking forum.

Then there's the ubiquitous Filipino breakfast – rice (preferably garlic rice) with a fried egg on top, with *tapa* (salty beef strips), *tocino* (honey-cured pork), *bangús* (milkfish) or *longganiza* (sausages) on the side. For dessert, try *halo-halo,* a glass packed with fruit preserves, sweet corn, young coconut and various tropical delights topped with milky crushed ice, a dollop of crème caramel and scoop of ice cream.

Filipino food tends to be long on meat and short on greens. There is only one common vegetarian dish: *pinakbét,* a tasty melange of pumpkin, string beans, eggplant, okra and other vegies, seasoned with garlic, onions, ginger, tomatoes, shrimp paste and, sometimes, coconut milk; if you don't eat shrimp paste, ask for it not to be used.

Different regions of the Philippines have their own specialities and render staples such as *longganiza, lechón* and even *balút* in different ways. Of the regional cuisines, the spicy food of Bicol is probably most amenable to Western palettes (see boxed text, p162), while Filipinos consider Pampanga province in central Luzon the country's food capital.

Filipino Cuisine by Gerry Gelle and Michael O'Shaughnessy is a comprehensive overview of Filipino dishes and cooking.

Fruits & Vegetables

If you find you aren't getting enough fruits and greens in the Philippines (and many do), buy them at outdoor fruit stands, street markets or, in bigger cities, supermarkets. Fruits and vegetables come in an astonishing variety, and anything grown domestically is dirt cheap.

Exotic tropical fruits such as durian, mangosteens, rambutans, jackfruit and longans, which will be familiar to those who have travelled elsewhere in Southeast Asia, are grown seasonally here. Walnut-sized *lanzones,* similar to longans but more sour, are a local speciality. *Santol* look like oranges, but have white pulp with the texture of wet fur. The Davao area is known for growing the country's best tropical fruit, including delicious mangosteens, stinky durian and succulent pomelos.

Despite importing only 10% of its rice, the Philippines is the world's largest rice importer.

Temperate vegetables such as lettuce, carrots and broccoli are grown at high altitudes and sold in markets nationwide. Somewhat exotic vegetables grown locally include *kamote* (sweet potatoes), *ube* (purple yam), *ampalaya* (a bitter gourd) and *sayote* (chayote).

Lastly, the Philippines really, truly does have the best mangoes in the world. Period.

The Philippine mango was listed as the world's sweetest fruit by the *Guinness Book of Records* in 1955.

Drinks

Nonalcoholic Drinks

You shouldn't have trouble drinking tap water in most of the Philippines. Still, to be safe stick to boiled or bottled water, which is cheap (except in restaurants). Many restaurants try to push expensive bottled water on you; if you don't want it, request 'service' water.

Tea is served in Chinese restaurants; elsewhere, soft drinks rule. *Buko* juice, said to be good for staving off dehydration, is young coconut juice with bits of translucent coconut meat floating in it. It's usually sold in the nut, but you'd best stick to the type that comes in presealed cups or bottles. *Guayabano* (soursop) juice is sweet and refreshing. The popular little local citrus known as *calamansi* or *kalamansi* is used to make a refreshing cordial or added to black tea. Wondrous curative powers are ascribed to it, so take a sip...

Alcoholic Drinks

At around P30 a bottle, San Miguel ('San Mig') pale pilsner and light beer enjoys a virtual monopoly on the local brew market, although pricier imports do provide some competition in Manila. With the exception of meek rival Beer Na Beer, most domestic beers you see on store shelves are San Miguel products, including the wildly popular Red Horse 'extra strong' (alcohol content 7%, chance of bad karaoke post–Red Horse 100%).

Palatable brandies, whiskies and gins are produced domestically. Tanduay Rum (P40 to P80 for a 500mL bottle) is a perfectly drinkable travelling companion – and a handy antiseptic! Rural concoctions include *basi,* a sweet, portlike wine made from sugar cane juice. *Tuba* is a strong palm wine extracted from coconut flowers; in its roughly distilled form it's called *lambanog*. Local firewater packs a punch – your stomach (if not your head) will thank you in the morning if you partake of the *pulutan* (small snacks) always served with alcohol.

Celebrations

Each village, town and city in the Philippines has its own fiesta, usually celebrated on the feast day of its patron saint, as determined by the Catholic calendar. Historically every household was expected to prepare food and serve it to anybody who appeared at the door. Nowadays, food is still prepared but on a greatly diminished scale, and only people who have been invited show up at the buffet table. The fare on such occasions varies regionally, but generally consists of pork, beef and chicken dishes, sometimes with some fish and seafood thrown in.

Kaldereta (beef or sometimes goat-meat stew), *igado* (stir-fried pork liver), fried chicken and, of course, *lechón* are some of the dishes you can expect to find at a fiesta. Sweet rice cakes, usually local delicacies, are served as dessert. Birthdays and other private parties are usually celebrated with a big plate of *pancit,* though nowadays this has been widely replaced by spaghetti, the local version of which will strike most Westerners as being unduly sweet. A birthday cake and ice cream are a must, especially at children's parties.

Dingras, in the province of Ilocos Norte, holds the world record for the largest cassava cake (a form of *bibingka* – fluffy rice cakes topped with cheese), at a whopping 100m.

Where to Eat & Drink

The basic Filipino eatery is a *turu-turò* (literally 'point point'), where customers can order by pointing at the precooked food on display, but Filipino restaurants come in many guises, from small roadside canteens to huge enterprises. Ordinary restaurants and food stalls might be alright for a while, but it's definitely worth trying well-prepared, authentic Filipino cuisine from a popular chain such as Gerry's, Dencio's or Max's.

Unlike the rest of Southeast Asia, where street vendors sell complete meals, in the Philippines food carts tend to offer nothing more substantial than *meryenda*. Fish or squid balls are popular, usually fried in boiling oil and served on skewers. Mobile vendors may also sell *balút* (carried in a basket) and a sweet bean-curd snack known locally as *taho.*

Some cities boast special outdoor food markets where clusters of vendors serve regional and national specialities; notable examples are in Vigan, Legaspi, Dumaguete and Cagayan de Oro.

TRAVEL YOUR TASTE BUDS

The Philippines is a good place for culinary daredevils. Start off with the obvious one: *balút,* or 'eggs with legs' as it's also known. The WOW Philippines tourism website offers the following instructions for eating *balút:* 'Lightly tap on the wider end of this boiled duck egg and gently peel off some of the shell. Season with a little rock salt and enjoy sipping out the flavourful soup. Once done, peel off more of the shell to reveal a yolk at hard-boiled consistency, and a nearly developed duck embryo.'

Once you've crossed *balút* off your list, other exotic foods won't seem quite so exotic. *Aso* or *asusena* (dog meat) is said to be tastier than any other red meat, though we can only report this based on hearsay. It's immensely popular in the Cordillera Mountains of North Luzon, as is 'Soup No 5' (bull-ball soup).

In some provinces, people will cook anything under the sun *adobo*-style – rat, cat, bat, frog, cricket, *bayawak* (monitor lizard), you name it. To work up the courage to consume any of these, down a few shots of *lambanog* (roughly distilled palm wine). Beetles, fried or floating in soup, and steamed tree-ant nests are two other gastronomic specialities found in the Philippines, though these have become harder to find of late.

In comparison, *sisig* – sizzling grilled bits of pig jowl – seems downright tame. We mention it because it's a favourite Filipino bar snack and it really is tasty, though it won't do your cholesterol level any favours. *Sisig* is the cousin of *bopis* – pig's lungs, chopped and fried.

Vegetarians & Vegans

If you're vegetarian or vegan, you'll have a hard time in the meat-mad Philippines, and may want to consider bringing some food from home. It's hard to find soy-based products outside of big cities, where Chinese merchants and restaurants sell tofu, soy milk etc. Beans in general don't figure prominently on the menu in the Philippines, thus, getting adequate protein can be tricky. If you feel this is going to be a problem, then it's wise to stock up on these products before leaving Manila or Cebu.

Most places, even *turu-turò* offer some version of stir-fried vegetables, but many vegetables are cooked with (or simply include) bits of meat. Meat stock is commonly used in kitchens, and it's nigh-impossible to ask a chef to change their cooking methods, especially in villages. In larger towns you'll find small shops that sell bread, cereals and milk, and in bigger cities like Manila, Cebu or Puerto Princesa you'll find well-stocked supermarkets. Again, if you're setting off for the hinterlands or small islands, stock up before hitting the road. All that said, if you eat fish and eggs, you'll have no problem in the Philippines, and steamed rice is always an option!

HALO-HALO

The eclectic Filipino dessert *halo-halo* is appropriately translated as 'mix-mix'.

Habits & Customs

An everyday meal in the Philippines is a fairly informal occasion, though it can take on the trappings of a formal Western-style dinner in the houses of the rich. Generally Filipinos eat with a fork and a spoon (no knife) – many visitors find this a little hard to get used to. When eating, most Filipinos sit in Western-style chairs around a table.

Eat Your Words

Names of dishes often describe the way they are cooked, so it's worth remembering that *adobo* is stewed in vinegar and garlic, *sinigáng* is sour soup, *ginataan* means cooked in coconut milk, *kilawin* or *kinilaw* is raw or vinegared seafood, *pangat* includes tomatoes in a light broth and *inihaw* is grilled meat or fish (*ihaw-ihaw* denotes eateries that specialise in grilled food). The word for 'spicy' is *maangháng*.

For other Filipino words and phrases, see the Language chapter (p455).

Useful Phrases

I'm a vegetarian.	Akó ay bedyetaryan.
I don't eat meat.	Hindî akó kumakain ng karné.
What's good?	Anong masarap?
Please bring...	Pakidalá ang...
How much?	Magkano?
Is a service charge included?	Kasama na ba ang serbisyo sa tsit?
Until what time are you open?	Hanggang anong oras kayo bukas?

Basics

Bread	tinapay
Breakfast	almusál/agahan
Butter	mantikilya
Coconut milk	gatâ
Coffee	kapé
Dinner	hapunan
Eggs	itlóg

Fork	tinidór
Glass	baso
Knife	kutsilyo
Lunch	tanghalian
Plate	plato
Rice (cooked)	kanin
Rice (uncooked)	bigás
Serviette/napkin	serbilyeta
Snack	meryenda
Spoon	kutsara
Sugar	asukal

Meat & Poultry

Beef	(karnéng) baka
Chicken	manók
Duck	pato
Goat meat	(karnéng) kambíng
Ham	hamón
Meat	kárné
Pork	(karnéng) baboy
Venison	(karnéng) usá

Seafood

Catfish	hitò
Clams	tulyá
Crabs	alimango (large, thick shelled), alimasag (spotted, thin shelled), talangkâ (small river crabs)
Fish	isdâ
Lobster	uláng
Grouper	lapu-lapu
Milkfish	bangús
Mussels	tahóng
Oysters	talabá
Shrimp	hipon
Squid	pusit
Prawns	sugpo

Vegetables

Bean sprouts	togè
Beans	bataw
Bitter melon	ampalayá
Cabbage	repolyo
Cassava/manioc	kamoteng kahoy
Chilli leaves	dahon ng siling

Eggplant	talóng
Okra	okra
Potatoes	patatas
Spinach-like vegetable	kangkóng
Sweet potatoes	kamote
Tomatoes	kamatis
Vegetables	gulay

Fruit

Avocado	abokado
Banana	saging
Fruit	frutas or prutas
Grapefruit	suhà
Lime	dayap
Lime (local)	calamansi
Mango	manggá
Orange (local)	dalandán
Papaya/pawpaw	papaya
Pineapple	pinyá
Plum (local)	sinigwélas
Star apple	kaimitò
Watermelon	pakwán

Spices & Condiments

Fish paste	bagoong
Fish sauce	patís
Garlic	bawang
Ginger	luya
Pepper	pamintá
Salt	asín
Shrimp paste	bagoong alamáng
Small hot chilli	siling labuyò
Soy sauce	toyò
Sugar	asukal
Vinegar	sukà

Drinks

Beer	serbesa
Boiled water	pinakuluáng tubig
Cocoa	kokwa
Coffee	kapé
Cold water	malamíg na tubig
(Cup of) Tea	(isáng) tsaá
Hot water	mainit na tubig
Juice	juice

Lemonade	limonada
Mineral water	míneral water
Orange drink	orens juice
Soft drink	sopdrink
Water	tubig
With/without ice	may/waláng yelo
With/without milk	may/waláng gatas
With/without sugar	may/waláng asukal

Menu Decoder

adobo	often called the national dish; chicken, pork or a mixture of both, marinated in vinegar and garlic and stewed until tender
adobong pusít	squid or cuttlefish cooked adobo-style
arróz caldo	Spanish-style thick rice soup with chicken, garlic, ginger and onions
aso	dog; eaten with relish (or just plain) by North Luzon's hill tribes
balút	boiled duck egg containing a partially formed embryo
calamares	crispy fried squid
crispy pata	deep-fried pork hock or knuckles
goto	rice porridge made with pork or beef innards
halo-halo	various fruit preserves served in shaved ice and milk
lechón	spit-roast whole pig served with liver sauce
lechón kawali	crispy fried pork
lomi	type of noodle dish
lumpia	spring rolls filled with meat and/or vegetables
mami	noodle soup; similar to *mee* in Malaysia or Indonesia
menudo	pork bits sautéed with garlic and onion and usually garnished with sliced hot dog
pancit bihon	thick- or thin-noodle soup
pinakbét	mixed vegetable stew
pochero	hotpot of beef, chicken, pork, Spanish sausage and vegetables, principally cabbage
rellenong bangus	fried stuffed milkfish
tapsilog	a modern compound combining three words: *tapa* (dried beef), *sinangag* (garlic fried rice) and *itlog* (fried egg); usually eaten for breakfast
tocino	cured pork made with saltpetre

Environment

The Philippines is in an uphill battle to preserve the epic array of flora and fauna that make it one of the world's top biodiversity 'hotspots'. Deforestation, overfishing and wonton pollution have already decimated many of the country's fragile seascapes and rainforests. The clock is ticking on what little remains. In recent years the country has made some progress in the realm of conservation. No-fish zones and marine sanctuaries have been declared. Forests and species have been given protected status. As in many poor countries, however, root problems such as population growth, poverty and public indifference to the nation's myriad environmental challenges offset what progress is made.

The message to tourists who want to enjoy the Philippines' natural treasures is clear: see them while you still can.

The cuddly looking Palawan bearcat is neither bear nor cat, but a species of viverridae related to the civet.

The Land

An assemblage of 7107 islands stretching some 1900km from the tip of Batanes to the Sulu archipelago, the Philippines stubbornly defies geographic generalisation. The typical island boasts a jungle-clad, mountainous interior and a sandy coastline flanked by aquamarine waters and the requisite coral reef.

There are variations, of course; some islands consist of little more than a slick of white sand, the snout of a submerged volcano or an imposing wall of stratified limestone emerging from the depths and shooting straight up to the heavens. The latter formation is typical of the Philippines' most awe-inspiring natural site, Palawan's Bacuit Archipelago.

Check out Conservation International's biodiversity hotspot information on the Philippines at www.biodiversityhotspots.org/xp/Hotspots/philippines.

The Philippines' many mountains, volcanoes, coral reefs, limestone caves and even its world-famous beaches owe their existence to the country's location on the Pacific Ocean's Ring of Fire. The prettiest volcano is highly active Mt Mayon, whose perfectly symmetrical cone graces many a postcard. The tallest mountain is Mindanao's Mt Apo, one of four peaks higher than 2900m.

Underground, meanwhile, angry subterranean forces have sculpted some of Asia's longest and largest caves, such as Palawan's Subterannean River.

Man too has played a part in shaping the country's geographic beauty, creating the spectacular rice terraces of North Luzon.

Wildlife

Millennia of geographical isolation from the rest of Southeast Asia has resulted in the evolution of thousands of species found nowhere else on earth, leading biologists to dub the archipelago 'Galapagos times 10'.

The world's biggest pearl was found by a Filipino diver in the waters off Palawan in 1934. It weighed over 6kg and was valued at US$42 million.

The country is home to approximately 13,500 species of plant; only four countries boast more. Scientists estimate that 30% to 40% of those species are found only in the Philippines.

The country's fauna likewise exhibits remarkable endemism; the islands are home to at least 111 mammals that are found nowhere else in

USEFUL WEBSITES

The following websites contain information related to the environmental concerns facing the Philippines. Some are Philippines-specific, others address the problems in a worldwide context.

» **Coral Cay Conservation** (www.coralcay.org) Works to protect coral reefs and other tropical forests.

» **Haribon Foundation** (www.haribon.org.ph) One of the forerunners of the Philippine environmental movement, it's mission is to protect the country's biodiversity. Active in preserving habitats of endangered species and other areas.

» **Negros Forests & Ecological Foundation Inc** (www.negrosforests.org) Works to protect various Philippine habitats, focusing on Negros.

» **One Ocean** (www.oneocean.org) Works to protect and manage Philippine coastal areas.

» **Protected Areas & Wildlife Bureau** (www.pawb.gov.ph) Among other things, this great site has primers on government programs to protect the *tamaraw*, cloud rat, *pawikan* and the Philippine owl, raptor, cockatoo and crocodile.

the world – even notorious animal haven Madagascar has fewer endemic species of mammal. Despite this, the Philippines is not particularly well known for spotting terrestrial wildlife, as its critters tend to be quite small and/or elusive.

The waters and skies are as diverse as the land. The country's 500 species of coral rank it second in the world in terms of coral diversity. Some 600 species of bird call the Philippines home. Close to 200 of those are found only in the Philippines – only much larger Indonesia and Brazil have more endemic varieties.

Animals

The country's most iconic mammal is the lovable, palm-sized tarsier, a primate found mainly on the island of Bohol. You are highly unlikely to spot these nocturnal creatures in the wild, but can responsibly view them at the Tarsier Sanctuary (p302). Contrary to popular belief, the tarsier is not the world's smallest primate. That distinction belongs to the pygmy mouse lemur of Madagascar. However, the Philippines can still proudly lay claim to the world's smallest hoofed mammal – the rare Philippine mouse deer of Palawan.

Other endangered terrestrial mammals you might be lucky enough to spot include the Philippine crocodile in Sierra Madre Natural Park (p147); indigenous water buffalo, known as the *tamaraw,* in Mindoro's Mt Iglit-Baco National Park (p195); and any of the eight species of fruit bat (flying fox) that dwell in caves across the country.

A 21ft-long crocodile, one of the largest in the world, was captured in 2011 near Bunawan, Mindanao.

Lizard sightings are more common. Geckos are ubiquitous, and there's a wide variety of venomous and nonvenomous snakes, including pythons and sea snakes. More elusive scaled beasts include the rare sailfin dragon and the flying lizard – discovered by national hero José Rizal while he was exiled in Dapitan on Mindanao.

Moving to the seas, divers and snorkellers flock to the country to see whale sharks, thresher sharks and myriad other fish. Less well known are dugong (known locally as *duyong*), a type of sea cow once found in great numbers in Philippine waters but now relatively rare. Two places where you can spot them if you're lucky are in Malita, Mindanao, and in the waters off the north tip of Busuanga Island in northern Palawan. There are a few places around the country where you might spot whales if your timing is right. However, you're more likely to spot dolphins.

The national bird is the endangered Philippine eagle, also known as the monkey-eating eagle or *haribon,* said to be the world's largest eagle; only several hundred survive in the wild, mostly in the rainforests of Mindanao, Samar, Leyte and in the Sierra Madre Mountains of North Luzon. The **Philippine Eagle Foundation** (www.philippineeagle.org) works to save this majestic bird.

Further south, the Sulu hornbill of Sulu, Jolo and Tawi-Tawi is an amazing and elusive mountain-dwelling bird. The Palawan peacock pheasant is a remarkable bird: the males of this species have a metallic blue crest, long white eyebrows and large metallic blue or purple 'eyes' on the tail. Nearing endangered status, these ground-dwellers are found only in the deepest forests of Palawan.

Plants

While the pretty yellow-flowered *nara* is the national tree of the Philippines, the unofficial national plant must surely be the nipa palm, which lends its name and leaves (used as wall and roof material) to the traditional nipa hut found all over the country.

The national flower of the Philippines is the highly aromatic *sampaguita,* a variety of jasmine. The orchid could also stake a claim as the country's national flower, with some 900 stunning endemic species, including the *waling waling (Vanda sanderiana)* of Mindanao and the red-spotted star orchid *(Renanthera mautiana).*

The Philippines' 24mm *Hippocampus bargibanti* recently lost the title of world's smallest seahorse to a newly discovered rival in Indonesia: the 16mm *Hippocampus denise.*

Ecotourism

With its natural wonders facing a litany of environmental threats, the Philippines is ripe for an ecotourism revolution. Underwater, the revolution has begun: the growth of scuba diving has led to the creation of protected marine reserves, while in Donsol former dynamite fishermen now earn their crust bringing tourists to snorkel with whale sharks.

Alas, there have been few such successes on land, where logging interests thwart forest-protection efforts and tourism officials seem oblivious to the country's potential as an adventure-tourism Mecca. Only a few enterprising individuals offer the spelunking, jungle-trekking, rappelling, kayaking and mountain-bike tours for which the country is tailor-made.

National Parks

Better management of the country's national parks is needed before any terrestrial ecotourism revolution occurs. It is estimated that only seven of the Philippines' national parks would actually satisfy international criteria for a true national park. In most Philippine national parks there are human habitations, sometimes extensive. Only a select few parks have features such as park offices, trail maps, legitimate camp sites or any facilities at all. Parks that do have modest facilities include Mt Pulag National Park in North Luzon (p130), Mt Kanlaon National Park on Negros (p275), Mt Isarog National Park in Southeast Luzon (p161), and the spectacularly diverse Mt Guiting Guiting Natural Park (p238) on Sibuyan Island in Romblon.

Of the Philippines' six species of cloud rat, two are critically endangered and one may be extinct. Cloud rats are a nocturnal rodent found only in the Philippines.

OIL RICH

The $US4.5 billion deepwater Malampaya pipeline carries natural gas from drilling platforms northwest of the tip of mainland Palawan through the Linapacan Strait to power plants on Luzon. In operation since 2001, it's the largest single foreign investment in the country's history: an estimated US$800 million flows from the private oil companies to the government. A large chunk of that is earmarked for the Palawan government, but much of it is thought to end up in the pockets of politicians.

In most other protected areas you're pretty much on your own. Take the country's largest protected area, 476,588-hectare Northern Sierra Madre Natural Park (p147) in Luzon, for example. The park contains roughly half of the Philippines' remaining primary forest, but a lack of established trails and maps means you'll need serious backcountry navigation experience, jungle survival skills and/or an excellent local guide to enjoy it.

The situation is slightly better at the town and provincial level, where a few renegade local governments (such as the city of Alaminos, near Hundred Islands National Park) have put their weight behind the establishment of marine and wildlife reserves, and have actively campaigned against illegal fishing and destructive mining, logging and energy projects in protected areas. Between 1997 and 2008 the number of marine protected areas in the country doubled, to more than 1150. Environmentally aware Palawan has more than 60 marine protected areas. Improved protection has led to a marked increase in marine life and the gradual rehabilitation of coastal parks such as Hundred Islands National Park and Apo Reef Natural Park.

Think twice before ordering live fish for dinner in Philippine restaurants – many are caught using cyanide or other destructive fishing methods.

Environmental Issues

Land

Conservation International has singled the Philippines out as one of the world's top conservation priorities because of grave threats to its forests and wildlife. Before 1900, about two-thirds of the Philippines was covered with dense primary rainforest. Now, it is estimated that less than a quarter of the Philippines is forested, and only a small percentage of this area is true primary forest. Deforestation continues at an extremely high rate; the country's forests could be extinct by 2100 at current levels of deforestation.

Environmentalists have noted that much of what's left of Philippine forests is too high up for loggers to be bothered with, or it's scrappy secondary forest yet to be eaten up by the ravenous Integrated Forest Management Agreements that have allowed most of the damage (an astonishing 75% of Philippine forest is classified as production forest).

This unfortunate situation has been caused by unregulated logging, massive farming expansion and a migrating lowland population. Throughout the 20th century, indigenous people's claims on upland regions were ignored and rich resources were plundered by a powerful elite. Poor lowland communities headed for the hills, often to jobs clearing land, and the indigenous residents were pushed onto less and less fertile land.

The Mindanao Trench in the Philippine Sea, at 10,497m, is the second deepest spot under the world's oceans.

The battle to save what's left of the upland forests has begun with indigenous land-rights claims and new conservation policies, but both domestic and foreign corporations continue to lobby the government to allow widespread logging and, especially, mining. President Gloria Macapagal Arroyo was happy to oblige during her term: between 2006 and 2009, investment in the mining sector more than doubled. It remains to be seen whether her predecessor, Benigno Aquino III, will be more stingy in handing out mining permits.

The government claims that adequate safeguards are in place to prevent displacement of indigenous communities, widespread environmental devastation and serious accidents such as the Marcopper accident at Santa Cruz, Marinduque, that have dogged past mining projects. Only time will tell if the mining companies will comply with the rules.

Sea

With a coastal ecosystem that stretches for almost 20,000km, the Philippines is one of the earliest victims of rising global ocean levels and temperatures.

Centuries-old coral is dying almost overnight. The World Bank recently estimated that only about 1% of Philippine coral reefs remains pristine, while more than 50% is unhealthy. Snorkellers and divers in tourist haunts around Puerto Galera (Mindoro) and Boracay (Panay) can now see for themselves what a coral graveyard looks like.

One of the main culprits has been increased sea temperatures brought about by global warming, which scientists say have caused massive coral bleaching. El Niño has also taken its toll on Philippine reefs, as have coral-destroying crown-of-thorns (COT) starfish, which are proliferating as overfishing reduces populations of its predators, such as the Napoleon wrasse. The COT problem has driven environmental and local diver groups to organise starfish collections in the hope of saving reefs in areas such as Puerto Galera and Padre Burgos (Leyte).

Another major threat to the reefs is poverty, which continues to force fishing communities to employ destructive fishing methods like dynamite, cyanide and chlorine fishing. Cyanide stuns fish so they can be caught live and sold for a higher price, but at the same time it kills the coral. Dynamite fishing kills both fish and coral outright. For a fascinating look at the cultural and economic forces at play behind dynamite fishing, read James Hamilton-Paterson's *Playing With Water*.

The golden spotted monitor lizard, discovered in North Luzon's Northern Sierra Madre Natural Park, made the International Institute for Species Exploration's coveted Top Ten Newly Discovered Species list for 2011.

Survival Guide

Directory A–Z

Accommodation

Budget Ranges

» In this book a hotel qualifies as 'budget' (one '$' symbol) if it has double rooms for less than P1000 and/or dorm beds for no more than P500 per bed.

» 'Midrange' ('two '$' symbols) is P1000 to P3000 (for the cheapest double room).

» 'Top end' ($$$) is anything over P3000.

On the Cheap

» Breaking down the budget category, in this book rooms in the P200 to P450 range are generally fan-cooled with a shared bathroom.

» Rooms in the P500 to P700 range usually have fan and private bathroom. Anything higher should have both air-conditioning and a private bathroom. Those prices are a shade higher in Manila and in trendy resort areas such as Boracay and Alona Beach.

Seasonal Price Fluctuations

» This book lists high-season (November to May) rates.

» Prices in resort areas go down by up to 50% in the low season, but may double, triple or even quadruple during the 'super peak' periods of Holy Week (Easter), around New Year and, in some areas, around Chinese New Year.

Booking Ahead

As the Philippines becomes more popular, it's becoming more difficult to just walk in and find a room in certain smaller resort areas and touristy towns like Vigan. Booking ahead is a good idea in the high season, essential in 'super peak' season and entirely optional during the low season. That said, if you don't book ahead, even in the high season, don't worry about it – you'll always find something eventually.

Deposits

Many resorts, especially at the top end, require a deposit – often 100%! Annoyingly, they rarely accept credit-card deposits, forcing you to wire or direct-deposit the money into a Manila bank account. More annoying still, 50% to 100% of your deposit is usually nonrefundable if you cancel less than two weeks before you're scheduled to arrive.

Circumvent this draconian practice by choosing another resort. If you must visit, consider just showing up without a reservation. Call the resort a few days ahead to see if they have vacancies. If they do, chances are you'll be able to walk in with little problem (if you try this, have a backup resort in mind just in case).

Discounts & Promo Rates

A few potential money-saving tips for booking hotels in the Philippines:

Promo rates Especially during off-peak periods, hotels often offer 'promo rates' that they won't tell you about unless you ask. So always ask if there's a promo rate.

Walking in In many resort areas, the 'walk-in' (ie no reservation) rate is substantially cheaper than the reser-

WELLNESS CENTRES

Wellness centres, which take you in for a week or more of exercise, vegan meals, massages and (usually) alcohol-free living, are increasing in popularity in the Philippines. Good ones include the Farm at San Benito (p89) outside Manila; the private island–based **Malapacao Resort** (www.malapacao.com) in Palawan; and Boracay's Mandala Spa (p256). An enticing Philippines itinerary could be to spend a week or more partying in a resort town, followed by a week of detox in a wellness centre.

PRACTICALITIES

» **Magazines & Webzines** The once glossy, now online *Newsbreak* is the best of the lot. It's connected to the **Philippine Centre for Investigative Journalism** (www.pcij.org). A variety of international magazines and newspapers are also widely available.

» **Newspapers** The Philippines has a vocal and vibrant press, with about 20 major national and regional English-language newspapers to go along with scores of regional publications. The best of the broadsheets are the *Philippine Daily Inquirer*, *Business World* and *Business Mirror*. These national papers can be found in newspaper stands all over the country. Other big national dailies with plenty of international and sports news as well as local content include the *Philippine Star* and the *Manila Bulletin*.

» **Radio** Manila rock/pop stations worth listening to are Jam 88.3 and – for Filipino Rock – Win Radio 107.5.

» **TV** About seven major channels broadcast from Manila, sometimes in English, sometimes in Tagalog. Most midrange hotels have cable TV with access to between 20 and 120 channels, including some obscure regional channels, a couple of Filipino and international movie channels, and the big global news and sports channels such as BBC and ESPN.

» **Weights & Measures** The Philippines is metric, but inches, feet and yards (for textiles) are common in everyday use for measuring things. Weights are normally quoted in kilograms and distances in kilometres.

vation rate. Conversely, in some hotels the reservation rate is actually cheaper than the walk-in rate. It always helps to ask.

Websites Some of the popular Asian online booking sites, such as Agoda.com, offer massive discounts on rooms in the Philippines, especially in Manila, Cebu and Boracay.

Activities

Scuba diving (p25) is the most popular adventure activity in the Philippines, but you can also snorkel, surf, trek, kitesurf and spelunk your way around the archipelago. Information on these activities can be found in the individual chapters. See the wonderful website www.pinoymountaineer.com for comprehensive profiles of treks not covered in this book.

Popular outdoor activities covered in less detail in this book:

Birdwatching See www.birdwatch.ph.

Cycling and mountain biking See www.bugoybikers.com.

Deep-sea fishing The Philippines' waters teem with sailfish, tuna, trevally, wahoo, mahi-mahi and other sportfish, but few organised operators run tours. The only operator we found was in Siargao (p350). Elsewhere you may be able to find a fisherman to take you out in his bangka (outrigger). Sipalay in Negros Occidental and Santa Ana on Luzon's northeast tip are particularly fertile fishing waters.

Golf There are several world-class courses in the Manila area. Although many of them are private, you can usually talk your way onto them if you're keen. The Fairways & Bluewater course on Boracay has some truly stunning views and is open to the public.

Kayaking If you have your own kayak and are into first descents, there are remote, virtually unexplored rivers all over the big islands, especially North Luzon and Mindanao. For kayaking tips, contact Raft Sagada (p132).

Rock climbing See www.climbphilippines.com.

White-water rafting The best white water is on the upper Chico River in North Luzon (p138), but it's seasonal (September to December), expensive and hard to get to.

Business Hours

Opening hours throughout the book are only listed if they differ to those listed here.

Banks 9am-4pm Mon-Fri (most ATMs operate 24 hours)

Bars 6pm to late

Embassies & consulates 9am-1pm Mon-Fri

Post offices 9am-5pm Mon-Sat

Public & private offices 8am or 9am-5pm or 6pm, with a lunch break noon-1pm, Mon-Fri

Restaurants 7am or 8am-10pm or 11pm

Shopping malls 10am-9.30pm

Supermarkets 9am-7pm or 8pm

Children

» Filipinos are simply crazy about kids, and are rather fond of parents, too – you and your offspring will be the focus of many conversations, and your children won't lack for playful company.

» You can buy disposable nappies (diapers) and infant formula in most towns and all cities, but be sure to stock up on such things before heading off the beaten track.

» Many hotels and resorts offer family rooms, and can provide cots on request.

» Discreet breastfeeding in public is acceptable in all areas except some conservative Muslim areas in the south.

» It is almost impossible to arrange a taxi with a child seat.

» Many restaurants can provide a high chair upon request.

» See Lonely Planet's *Travel with Children* for further useful advice about travel with kids.

Customs Regulations

» Firearms and pornography are forbidden.

» You can bring up to 2L of alcohol and up to 400 cigarettes (or two tins of tobacco) into the country without paying duty.

» Foreign currency of more than US$10,000 and local currency of more than P10,000 must be declared upon entry or exit.

Discount Cards

» A 20% discount on domestic flights is offered by Philippine Airlines (PAL), Asian Spirit, Cebu Pacific and SEAIR for passengers who are 60 years of age or over.

» Shipping lines will usually offer a similar discount for senior citizens, and sometimes for students with a valid student ID.

Electricity

Embassies & Consulates

The **Philippines Department of Foreign Affairs** (DFA; www.dfa.gov.ph) website lists all Philippine embassies and consulates abroad, and all foreign embassies and consulates in the Philippines.

In addition to the following countries, most Asian countries requiring their citizens to have visas for entry have embassies in Manila, including Cambodia, China, India, Laos, Myanmar and Vietnam.

Australia (Map p62; ☎02-757 8100/8102; www.australia.com.ph; 23rd fl, Tower 2, RCBC Plaza, 6819 Ayala Ave, Makati, Manila)

Canada Cebu City (☎032-254 4749; 45-L Andres Abellana St); Manila (Map p62; ☎02-857 9000; www.dfait-maeci.gc.ca/manila; Levels 6-8, Tower 2, RCBC Plaza, 6819 Ayala Ave, Makati)

France (Map p62; ☎02-857 6900; www.ambafrance-ph.org; 16th fl, Pacific Star Bldg, cnr Gil Puyat Ave & Makati Ave, Makati, Manila)

Germany Cebu City (☎032-236 1318; Ford's Inn Hotel, AS Fortuna St); Manila (Map p62; ☎02-702 3000; www.manila.diplo.de; 25th fl, Tower 2, RCBC Plaza, 6819 Ayala Ave, Makati, Manila)

Netherlands Cebu City (☎032-346 1823; Metaphil Building, Tipolo, Mandaue); Manila (Map p62; ☎02-786 6666; http://philippines.nlembassy.org; 26th fl, Equitable PCI Bank Tower, 8751 Paseo de Roxas, Makati, Manila)

New Zealand (Map p62; ☎02-891 5358-67; www.nzembassy.com; 23rd fl, BPI Buendia Centre, Sen Gil Puyat Ave, Makati, Manila)

UK Cebu City (☎032-346 0525; 4 Palmera St, Villa Terrace, Greenhills Rd, Casuntingan, Mandaue); Manila (☎02-858 2200; http://ukinthephilippines.fco.gov.uk; 120 Upper McKinley Rd, McKinley Hill, Fort Bonifacio)

USA (☎02-301 2000; http://manila.usembassy.gov; 1201 Roxas Blvd, Ermita, Manila)

Food

See p422 for more on eating in the Philippines. In this book the budget breakdown is as follows:

Budget ($) Average price for a main dish (entree for US travellers) less than P120

Midrange ($$) P120 to P250

Top end ($$$) More than P250

Gay & Lesbian Travellers

» *Bakla* (gay men) and *binalaki* or *tomboy* (lesbians) are almost universally accepted in the Philippines.

» There are well-established gay centres in major cities, but foreigners should be wary of hustlers and police harassment.

» Remedios Circle in Malate, Manila, is the site of a June gay-pride parade and the centre for nightlife.

» Online gay and lesbian resources for the Philippines include **Utopia Asian Gay & Lesbian Resources** (www.utopia-asia.com).

Insurance

» A travel-insurance policy to cover theft, loss and medical problems is a good idea.

» Some policies specifically exclude 'dangerous activities', which can include scuba-diving, motorcycling and even trekking.

» Check that the policy covers ambulances and an emergency flight home. See the Health chapter (p449) for more on health insurance.

» Worldwide travel insurance is available at www.lonelyplanet.com/bookings. You can buy, extend and claim online anytime – even if you're already on the road.

Internet Access

» Internet access isn't a problem in most of the Philippines; any reasonably sized town will have at least one internet cafe. Even many of the smallest towns and islands have internet access.

» Bank on P25 per hour for internet access, double or triple that in very remote or particularly touristy areas.

» Connections are generally fast and efficient, but get slower as you get further from civilisation.

» Plenty of hotels and resorts have computers for guests to use and wi-fi is popular in hotels and coffee shops in large cities and touristy areas.

» The @ symbol in this book indicates that a hotel has an internet-enabled computer for guests to use. The wi-fi symbol indicates that a hotel (or other establishment) has wi-fi – either in the rooms, or in the hotel lobby/restaurant area. Wi-fi is free of charge unless otherwise indicated.

» If you have an internet-enabled mobile phone you can get online through the regular wireless networks of both Philippine mobile-phone providers, Smart and Globe Telecom. You can also hook your laptop up to Smart or Globe 3G networks. Get set up at any Smart or Globe wireless centre; most shopping malls in Manila and elsewhere have one.

Legal Matters

» Drugs are risky – being caught with marijuana for personal use can mean jail time.

» Should you find yourself in trouble, your first recourse is your embassy, so make a point of writing down the phone number.

» Small bribes remain a common way of getting out of traffic infractions.

Maps

» For a map of the entire country, the best of the lot is probably Nelles Verlag's 1:1,500,000 scale *Philippines*, which is available internationally.

» For local travel, E-Z Maps (published by United Tourist Promotions) and **Accu-Map** (www.accu-map.com) produces excellent maps covering most major islands, large cities and tourist areas. They are widely available at hotels, airports, bookshops and gas stations. These are essential tools if you plan to do any driving.

» To buy highly detailed topographical maps of virtually any region contact the government's mapping agency, **Namria** (☎02-810 4831; Lawton Ave, Fort Bonifacio, Makati).

Money

» The unit of currency is the peso (P), divided into 100 centavos.

» Banknotes come in denominations of 20, 50, 100, 200, 500 and 1000 pesos.

» The most common coins are 1, 5 and 10 pesos.

ATMs

» Getting crisp P500 and P1000 peso bills out of the myriad ATM machines that line the streets of any decent-sized provincial city usually isn't a problem.

» Where a region covered in this chapter does not have ATMs (such as most of Palawan), it is noted in that section.

» The Maestro-Cirrus network is most readily accepted, followed by Visa/Plus cards, then by American Express (Amex).

» The most prevalent ATMs that accept most Western bank cards belong to Banco de Oro (BDO), Bank of the Philippine Islands (BPI) and Metrobank.

» Most ATMs charge P200 per withdrawal and have a P10,000-per-transaction withdrawal limit; the HSBC ATMs in Manila and Cebu let you take out P40,000 per transaction.

Cash

» Emergency cash in US dollars is a good thing to have in case you get stuck in an area with no working ATM. Other currencies, such as the euro or UK pound, are more difficult to change outside of the bigger cities.

» 'Sorry, no change' becomes a very familiar line in the provinces. Stock up on P20, P50 and P100 notes at every opportunity.

Credit Cards

» Major credit cards are accepted by many hotels, restaurants and businesses.

» Outside of Manila, businesses sometimes charge a bit extra (about 4%) for credit-card transactions.

» Most Philippine banks will let you take a cash advance on your card.

Tipping

» A 10% service charge is generally included in the price at restaurants, but leaving an extra P20 per person is always appreciated (perhaps P40 to P50 per person if service is not included).

» At minimum, round up taxi fares (for example, from P164 to P170), but consider tipping more (say P20 to P50).

Travellers Cheques

» We don't recommend taking travellers cheques as banks seem to have a vendetta against them.

» Without exception you will need your passport and the original receipts, and you may find that banks and moneychangers will only change cheques between 9am and 10am, or only at limited branches.

» Your best chance is with Amex US-dollar cheques – other companies and denominations may not be changeable. The best places to cash Amex cheques are at its branch in Makati.

Photography

» It's good form to ask people for permission before taking their photo, especially among the mountain tribes in North Luzon and Mindanao.

» Check out *Lonely Planet's Guide to Travel Photography* for further tips.

Public Holidays

Government offices and banks are closed on public holidays, although most shops and malls stay open. Maundy Thursday and Good Friday are the only days when the entire country closes down – even most public transport stops running, and some airlines ground their planes.

New Year's Day 1 January

People Power Day 25 February

Maundy Thursday Varies; around March or April

Good Friday Varies; the day after Maundy Thursday

Araw ng Kagitingan (Bataan Day) 9 April

Labour Day 1 May

Independence Day 12 June

Ninoy Aquino Day 21 August

National Heroes Day Last Sunday in August

All Saints' Day 1 November

End of Ramadan Varies; depends on Islamic calendar

Bonifacio Day 30 November

Christmas Day 25 December

Rizal Day 30 December

New Year's Eve 31 December

Muslim Holy Days

Most Muslim holy days are observed only in the Muslim parts of Mindanao, though some are now also national holidays.

Hari Raya Haji Varies; depends on Islamic calendar

Hijra New Year Varies; depends on Islamic calendar

Maulod En Nabi (Prophet's Birthday) Varies; depends on Islamic calendar

Ramadan Varies; depends on Islamic calendar

Hari Raya Puasa (Feast of the Breaking of the Fast) Begins on the last evening of Ramadan and may last for three days.

Safe Travel

» The Philippines certainly has more than its share of dangers. Typhoons, earthquakes, volcano eruptions, landslides and other natural disasters can wreak havoc with your travel plans – or worse if you happen to be in the wrong place at the wrong time.

» Keep an eye on the news and be prepared to alter travel plans to avoid trouble spots.

» Mindanao (the central and southwest regions in particular) and the Sulu Archipelago are the scenes of clashes between the army on one side and Muslim separatist groups on the other (see p332).

» Manila in particular is known for a few common scams (see p76).

Telephone

» The Philippine Long Distance Telephone Company (PLDT) operates the Philippines' fixed-line network. Local calls cost almost nothing, and long-distance domestic calls are also very reasonable.

» International calls can be made from many hotels (for a hefty price) or from any PLDT office. PLDT offers flat rates of US$0.40 per minute for international calls (operator-assisted calls are much more expensive).

Dialling Codes

» For domestic long-distance calls or calls to mobile numbers dial ☎0 followed by the city code (or mobile prefix) and then the seven-digit number.

» Useful dialing codes from land lines:

Philippines country code ☎63

International dialling code ☎00

PLDT directory ☎187 nationwide

International operator ☎108

Domestic operator ☎109

Mobile Phones

» Roaming with your home phone shouldn't be a problem (provided it's GSM enabled), but it's expensive. A better strategy is to purchase a local prepaid SIM card, which costs as little as P40 and comes preloaded with about the same amount of text credits. They are readily available at convenience stores, *sari-sari* stores and phone kiosks in shopping centres.

» The two companies with the best national coverage are **Globe** (www.globe.com.ph) and **Smart** (www.smart.com.ph)

» Text messages on both networks cost P1 to P2 per message, while local calls cost P7.50 per minute (less if calling within a mobile network).

» International text messages cost P15, and international calls cost US$0.40 per minute.

» Many remote provincial villages lack landlines but are connected to one or both of the Philippines' two main mobile networks.

» Philippine mobile-phone numbers begin with ☎09. If a number listed in this book has 10 digits and begins with ☎09, assume it's a mobile number.

Phonecards

» Prepaid phonecards are widely available from hotels, *sari-sari* stores and phone kiosks, and are usually in denominations of P100 or P200.

» PLDT cards such as 'Budget' (for international calls), 'Pwede' and 'Touch' cards can be used to make calls from any PLDT landline or from card-operated PLDT phones located in hotel foyers, commercial centres and shopping malls. Calls to the US using the Budget card cost only P3 per minute; other international destinations cost slightly more. 'Pwede' and 'Touch' cards allow dirt-cheap domestic calls from any PLDT landline or payphone.

Time

The Philippines is eight hours ahead of Greenwich Mean Time/Universal Time Coordinated (GMT/UTC), meaning when it's noon in Manila, it's 11pm the previous night in New York (midnight during daylight savings); 4am the same day in London; 1pm the same day in Tokyo; and 2pm the same day in Sydney (3pm during daylight savings).

Toilets

» Toilets are commonly called a 'CR', an abbreviation of the delightfully euphemistic 'comfort room'.

» Public toilets are virtually nonexistent, so aim for one of the ubiquitous fast-food restaurants should you need a room of comfort.

» In Filipino, men are *lalake* and women are *babae*.

» Filipino men will often avail themselves of the nearest outdoor wall – hence the signs scrawled in many places: 'Bawal Ang Umihi Dito!' ('No Pissing Here!').

Tourist Information

» The official organ of Philippine tourism is the **Philippine Department of Tourism** (DOT; www.visitmyphilippines.com).

» The main DOT centre is in Manila and you'll find regional DOT offices – varying in usefulness from the mildly helpful to the completely useless – in popular destinations throughout the Philippines. Most DOT offices should at least be capable of setting you up with accommodation. The better ones can also help find guides or hire vehicles, while a few actually run adventure tours, such as whale-shark tours in Donsol, spelunking in Tuguegarao (North Luzon) and diving at Apo Reef through the tourist office in Sablayan (Mindoro Occidental).

Travellers With Disabilities

» Steps up to hotels, tiny cramped toilets and narrow doors are the norm outside of four-star hotels in Manila, Cebu and a handful of larger provincial cities.

» Lifts are often out of order, and boarding any form of rural transport is likely to be fraught with difficulty.

» On the other hand, most Filipinos are more than willing to lend a helping hand, and the cost of hiring a taxi for a day, and possibly an assistant as well, is not excessive.

Visas

» Citizens of nearly all countries will receive a 21-day visa free of charge upon their arrival.

» If you overstay your visa you face fines, and airport immigration officials may not let you pass through immigration.

» Your passport must be valid for at least six months beyond the period you intend to stay.

Visa Extensions

» To renew your 21-day visa to 59 days or beyond you must apply for an extension from any **Bureau of Immigration** (BOI; www.immigration.gov.ph) office. Most regional hubs and touristy areas like Boracay have BOI offices. Popular ones are listed in this book, or hit the 'Subport Offices' link on the BOI website for a full list of regional BOI offices.

» To extend a 21-day visa to 59 days costs P3030. Longer extensions are possible, with correspondingly higher fees; see the BOI website for exact fees.

» The visa renewal process is generally painless, with one notable exception: the massive BOI office in Manila. You can pay a travel agent about P1000 to go to the Manila BOI office for you. If you insist on going it alone, bring proof of identity and expect long lines.

» It's best to apply for a visa extension before your 21-day visa expires. Applying after it expires carries an additional P1010 fine. It may or may not be possible to extend retroactively (and pay at least the P1010 fine) upon departure at the airport, but we wouldn't chance it.

» A better option is to secure a three-month visa before you arrive in the Philippines. These cost US$30 to US$45 depending on where you apply. Multiple-entry visas valid for up to six or 12 months are also available.

Onward Tickets

» You must have a ticket for onward travel to enter the Philippines if you plan to receive a 21-day visa on arrival.

» While Philippine immigration inspectors rarely ask to see an onward ticket, most airlines will refuse entry on flights headed to the Philippines without proof of onward travel. A photocopy of your onward ticket will not suffice; you need to show the actual ticket or e-ticket. If you do not have one, the airline will make you purchase a one-way ticket out of the Philippines, departing within 21 days from your date of arrival. When you get to Manila, you are free to exchange this ticket – for a hefty fee, of course.

» If you're applying for a longer-term visa through a Philippine embassy or consulate abroad, you should also have proof of onward travel, although in this case a photocopy of your itinerary from your travel agent may suffice (call the embassy to clarify).

Volunteering

The Philippines has loads of 'voluntourism' opportunities, including the following:

Center for Education, Research and Volunteering Philippines (CERV; ☎0918 938 7030; http://cervphilippines.blogspot.com) Offers volunteer opportunities in metro Manila and Romblon.

Gawad Kalinga (www.gk1world.com/ph, volunteers@gk1world.com) GK's mission is building not just homes but entire communities for the poor and homeless. Volunteers can build houses, teach children or get involved in a host of other activities.

Habitat for Humanity (☎02-846 2177; www.habitat.org.ph) Builds houses for the poor all over the country, concentrating on disaster-affected areas.

Hands On Manila (☎02-386 6521; www.handsonmanila.org) This organisation is always looking for volunteers to help with disaster assistance and other projects throughout the Philippines.

Process Bohol (www.processbohol.org) Has volunteer opportunities in ecological and social-development projects in Bohol and Southern Leyte.

Springboard Foundation (☎02-821 5440; www.springboard-foundation.org) Not a volunteer organisation, per se, but has ties to many charity organisations doing volunteer work in the Philippines.

Volunteer for the Visayas (☎053-325 2462; www.visayans.org) Runs various volunteer programs around Tacloban, Leyte.

World Wide Opportunities on Organic Farms (http://wwoof.ph) There are several WWOOF sites in the Philippines, including the Julia Campbell Agroforest Memorial Park (p144) and the Enca Farm (p127), both in North Luzon.

To get involved with species-conservation and biodiversity and projects contact the following:

Coral Cay Conservation (www.coralcay.org)

Haribon Foundation (www.haribon.org.ph)

Save Palawan Seas Foundation (www.projectseventhousand.org.ph) NGO dedicated to educating local fishermen in Palawan about the dangers of destructive fishing and agricultural practices. Owned by one of largest pearl producers in the Philippines.

WWF Philippines (www.wwf.org.ph)

Transport

GETTING THERE & AWAY

Most people enter the Philippines via one of the three main international airports:

» **Manila** Ninoy Aquino International Airport (NAIA), by far the most popular and best connected to the rest of the country

» **Cebu** A nice option if you are heading to the Visayas

» **Clark** Budget flight hub north of Manila

A handful of international flights also go straight to Davao, to Mindanao, and to Kalibo near Boracay on the island of Panay.

The only feasible non-flight option is by ferry to Zamboanga (Mindanao) from Sandakan in the Malaysian state of Sabah.

Flights, tours and train tickets can all be booked online at lonelyplanet.com/bookings.

Entering the Country

Entering the country through any of the main ports is a breeze. Most nationalities are issued a free 21-day visa on the spot. Be prepared to show the airline a visa or an onward ticket before you board any flight bound for the Philippines (see p441 for more details).

If you're flying into Manila, you're bound to find NAIA and its disjointed terminals a bit confounding, especially if you have to switch terminals for a connecting flight. See the boxed text p444 for more on NAIA's terminal quagmire and tips on how to get between terminals.

Air

Airports & Airlines

Ninoy Aquino International Airport (NAIA; www.miaa.gov.ph) The country's recently upgraded flagship airport is in flux – see the boxed text, p444 for important arrival/departure information regarding terminals.

Mactan International Airport (www.mactan-cebuairport.com.ph) If you're heading to the Visayas, consider flying into Cebu City.

Diosdado Macapagal International Airport (Clark Airport; www.clarkairport.com) Clark Airport is near Angeles, a 1½- to two-hour bus ride north of downtown Manila. It has become a hot destination for Asian low-cost airlines.

Francisco Bangoy International Airport Davao has been rapidly gaining traction as a domestic hub, and is looking to translate that success into international routes.

Kalibo International Airport Boracay's skyrocketing popularity among Asian travellers has suddenly made nearby Kalibo a viable international hub. Domestic carrier Zest Air has launched flights to/from Chengdu, Pusan, Seoul, Shanghai and Taipei, and one can see that list expanding.

The Phillipines is served by many major international airlines as well as the following regional and budget airlines:

Air Asia (www.airasia.com)

Cebu Pacific (www.cebupacificair.com)

Jetstar (code 3K; ☎1-800 1611 0280; www.jetstar.com)

Philippine Airlines (www.philippineairlines.com) The country's flagship carrier.

South East Asian Airlines (SEAIR; www.flyseair.com)

Spirit of Manila Airlines (www.spiritofmanilaairlines.com) Flights from Taipei and Macau.

Tiger Airways (www.tigerairways.com)

Zest Air (www.zestair.com.ph)

Tickets

Book well in advance if you plan to arrive in the Philippines during December – expat Filipinos flood the islands to visit their families during Christmas and New Year. The lead-up to Chinese New Year in late January or early February can also get congested.

Asia

There's no shortage of direct flights to Manila, Cebu and

TERMINAL CHAOS

Plans are in place at Manila's Ninoy Aquino International Airport (NAIA) to eventually shift all international flights from the airport's dismal, antiquated Terminal 1 to the new Terminal 3. However, questions remain about the technical soundness of Terminal 3, which was built in 2002 but stood idle for six years as a dispute simmered between the builders and the Philippine government.

For now, Airphil Express and Cebu Pacific are the only airlines using Terminal 3. All Philippine Airlines (PAL) flights use yet another terminal, the relatively modern Centennial Terminal 2. All international carriers continue to use Terminal 1, while domestic carriers Zest Air and SEAIR use the old Manila Domestic Airport, located down the road from Terminal 3.

The four NAIA terminals share runways, but they are not particularly close to each other and are linked only by busy public roads. Allow plenty of time between connecting flights if you have to switch terminals.

A **shuttle bus** (P20; ⏲7am-10pm) links the four terminals.

Clark from most north and southeast Asian countries on PAL, Cebu Pacific and a host of foreign airlines, including several budget carriers. The primary Philippine low-cost carrier, Cebu Pacific, provides the best coverage, serving an ever-growing list of Asian cities, including Bangkok, Guangzhou, Hanoi, Jakarta, Kota Kinabalu, Kuala Lumpur, Saigon, Shanghai and Singapore.

Australia & New Zealand

Qantas and PAL offer the only direct flights from Australia to the Philippines (Sydney/Melbourne to Manila); otherwise, one must fly via cities such as Bangkok, Singapore, Kuala Lumpur or Hong Kong. The cheapest, if not the most convenient, flights from Australia are on Tiger Airways via Singapore.

Currently there are no direct flights between New Zealand and the Philippines; the usual route is to fly to Sydney and pick up a direct flight from there. Alternatively, it's possible to fly through an Asian city like Singapore or Hong Kong.

Continental Europe

KLM offers the only direct flights to Europe (Amsterdam); otherwise, you can fly via an Asian or Middle Eastern capital. The cheapest return fares are on the Middle Eastern carriers. Popular Asian hubs for European flights are Bangkok, Hong Kong and Singapore.

North America

PAL has the only direct flights to North America (Vancouver, San Francisco and Los Angeles). Other convenient airlines for Canada and the USA include Air Canada (via Tokyo), American Airlines (via Tokyo), Asiana (via Seoul), Cathay Pacific (via Hong Kong), China Airlines (via Taiwan), Eva Air (via Taiwan), Korean Airlines (via Seoul) and Northwest (via Tokyo).

UK & Ireland

The cheapest flights to Manila are usually with Qatar Airways or other Middle Eastern carriers. Other carriers flying between the UK and the Philippines include KLM, and Asian airlines such as Singapore Airlines or Cathay Pacific. Singapore Airlines and Cathay Pacific also offer flights into Cebu for slightly higher prices.

Sea

Although there are plenty of shipping routes within the Philippines, international services are scarce. The only route open to foreigners at the time of research was a ship from Zamboanga to Sandakan in the Malaysian state of Sabah – see the boxed text, p368. Keep in mind that travel in the Zamboanga region is considered risky (see p332).

Sporadic boats to Sabah from Palawan are off-limits to foreigners.

GETTING AROUND

Air

All of the following serve dozens of domestic destinations; consult the Getting There & Away sections of individual destination sections for specific routes.

Airphil Express (☎02-855 9000; www.airphilexpress.com)

Cebu Pacific (☎02-702 0888; www.cebupacificair.com)

ITI (☎02 851 5674; www.islandtransvoyager.com)

Mid-Sea Express (☎032-495 6976; www.midseaexpress.com)

Philippine Airlines (☎02-855 8888; www.philippineairlines.com)

SEAIR (☎02-849 0100; www.flyseair.com)

Sky Pasada (☎02-912 3333; www.skypasada.com)

Zest Air (☎02-855 3333; www.zestair.com.ph)

PAL and Cebu Pacific are the main domestic carriers and in general have the newest planes, although Cebu Pacific and PAL's budget arm, Airphil Express, continue to operate a few smaller, older planes to minor destinations. Zest Air has traditionally had the most suspect planes, but has been modernizing its fleet in an effort to play catch-up with the others. SEAIR's slick little jets – most are of the 20- to 40-seat variety – are nicer but tend to cost more.

You can always dispense with lines and crowds – and reach some areas not serviced by commercial flights – by chartering your own plane with Sky Pasada or Mid-Sea Express.

Also keep in mind the following tips when booking domestic flights:

» Healthy competition keeps domestic flights *cheap*. If you book a month or so in advance, you'll rarely pay more than P1200 (about US$28) for a one-way ticket.

» There are some exceptions to the above. Boracay and especially El Nido tend to be more expensive; and all airlines jack up rates during peak domestic travel periods like Chinese New Year, Easter and Christmas.

» You will not pay a premium for one-way tickets on most airlines.

» You will not save money by purchasing a round-trip ticket on most airlines.

» Flight routes are skewed towards Manila and (to a lesser extent) Cebu. If you want to fly between any other cities you'll likely have to purchase two tickets: one to Manila/Cebu, and then a separate onward ticket.

» Don't plan too tight a schedule for connecting flights – flight delays are a fact of life in the Philippines.

» Typhoons often ground planes from June to November. You can bank on the first few flights following a typhoon being massively overbooked.

» The duration of most flights out of both Manila and Cebu is 45 minutes to 1¼ hours, rarely longer. Accounting for delays, all flights end up being roughly the same duration.

INTERNATIONAL DEPARTURE TAX

International departure tax is P750 at NAIA and Clark, and P550 at Cebu, payable in cash only (pesos or US dollars).

DOMESTIC DEPARTURE TAX

Domestic departure tax from Manila and Cebu is P200. At smaller airports it varies from P20 to P200.

Bicycle

If you're away from the traffic and exhaust fumes of major cities, cycling can be a great way to get around quieter, less visited islands.

» You can take bicycles on domestic flights (you may have to partially disassemble the bicycle), but take heed of the baggage allowance on small planes.

» If there's room, you can stow your bike on a bus or jeepney, usually for a small charge.

» Depending on where you are, mountain bikes can be hired for P300 to P700 per day, with price very much linked to quality.

» In the big cities you will find bicycle shops where you can purchase brand-new bikes of varying quality – in Manila there are several along Chino Roces (Pasong Tamo) Ave.

Boat

The islands of the Philippines are linked by an incredible network of ferry routes, and prices are generally affordable. Ferries usually take the form of motorized outriggers (known locally as bangkas), speedy 'fastcraft' vessels, car ferries (dubbed RORO, or 'roll-on-roll-off' ferries) and, for long-haul journeys, vast multidecked passenger ferries. See the Getting There & Away sections of destination chapters for details of companies servicing individual routes.

Bangkas The jeepneys of the sea, also known as pumpboats. They are small wooden boats with two wooden or bamboo outriggers. Bangka ferries ply regular routes between islands and are also available for hire per day for diving, sightseeing or just getting around. The engines on these boats can be deafeningly loud, so bring earplugs if you plan a lot of bangka travel and you're sensitive to noise. They also aren't the most stable in rough seas, but on islands like Palawan taking a bangka can be preferable to travelling overland.

'Fastcraft' These are passenger only, and are mainly used on popular short-haul routes; they cut travel times by half but usually cost twice as much as slower RORO ferries. One modern convenience used to excess on these spiffy ships is air-conditioning, which is permanently set to 'arctic' – take a sweater or fleece. Fast-craft companies such as SuperCat and Oceanjet run every day of the year except Good Friday and New Year's Day.

ROROs (car ferries) Popular on medium-haul routes, especially along the so-called 'Nautical Highway' running from Manila to Davao in southern Mindanao.

CLIMATE CHANGE & TRAVEL

Every form of transport that relies on carbon-based fuel generates CO_2, the main cause of human-induced climate change. Modern travel is dependent on aeroplanes, which might use less fuel per kilometre per person than most cars but travel much greater distances. The altitude at which aircraft emit gases (including CO_2) and particles also contributes to their climate change impact. Many websites offer 'carbon calculators' that allow people to estimate the carbon emissions generated by their journey and, for those who wish to do so, to offset the impact of the greenhouse gases emitted with contributions to portfolios of climate-friendly initiatives throughout the world. Lonely Planet offsets the carbon footprint of all staff and author travel.

ROROs are slow but in good weather are the most enjoyable form of ocean transport, as (unlike most fastcraft) they allow you to sit outside in the open air and watch the ocean drift by.

Passenger Liners Multi-decked long-haul liners like the SuperFerry, which carry up to 4000 passengers as well as cars. They are pretty reliable but you'll need to be prepared for changes in the itinerary due to adverse weather conditions or maintenance.

Tickets

» Booking ahead is essential for long-haul liners and can be done at ticket offices or travel agencies in most cities.

» For fastcraft and bangka ferries, tickets can usually be bought at the pier before departure.

» Passenger ferries offer several levels of comfort and cost. Bunks on or below deck on 3rd or 'economy' class should be fine, as long as the ship isn't overcrowded. First class nets you a two-person stateroom.

» Before purchasing your ticket, it pays to ask about 'promo rates' (discounts), including student discounts (often 20% to 30% off).

» The website http://schedule.ph is not entirely comprehensive but it's a good place to start for ferry schedules.

Safety

For the most part, ferries are an easy, enjoyable way to hop between islands in the Philippines, but ferry accidents are not unknown. In May 2008 a Sulpicio Lines ferry went down off Romblon in Typhoon Frank; less than 60 passengers survived and more than 800 perished. It was the fourth sinking incident involving at least 150 casualties since 1987 for Sulpicio, including the largest peacetime maritime disaster in history – the 1987 sinking of the Doña Paz, in which almost 4500 people are believed to have perished.

In May 2009 an overloaded bangka ferry sank en route to Puerto Galera from Batangas. Twelve of the 60 passengers drowned. A large SuperFerry vessel went down off Mindanao in September 2009. Miraculously all but nine of the 900 passengers were rescued.

Most of the ferry accidents that have occurred in the Philippines have resulted from a combination of bad weather and the boats being overloaded. it's best to follow your instincts – if the boat looks crowded, it is, and if the sailing conditions seem wrong, they are. Bangkas during stormy weather are especially scary.

After the 2008 accident, Sulpicio Lines passenger services were suspended for three years before being reopened as we went to press. We have not included Sulpicio's routes in this book. Check the company's website, www.sulpiciolines.com, for the schedule.

Bus & Van

» Philippine buses come in all shapes and sizes. Bus depots are dotted throughout towns and the countryside, and most buses will stop if you wave them down.

» More services run in the morning – buses on unsealed roads may run only in the morning, especially in remote areas. Night services, including deluxe 27-seaters, are common between Manila and major provincial hubs in Luzon, and in Mindanao.

» Air-con minivans (along with jeepneys) shadow bus routes in many parts of the Philippines (especially Bicol, Leyte and Cebu) and in some cases have replaced buses altogether. However, you may have to play a waiting game until the vehicles are full.

» Minivans are a lot quicker than buses, but also more expensive and cramped.

» As in most countries, it pays to mind your baggage while buses load and unload.

» Reservations are useful on infrequently served routes, and are essential on the deluxe night buses heading to/from Manila (book these at least two days in advance, if possible, at the bus terminal). Otherwise, reservations can usually be skipped.

Car & Motorcycle

If time is short, driving yourself is a quicker option than relying on jeepneys and other public transport, but it's not for the faint of heart. The manic Filipino driving style is on full display in Manila, and driving the congested streets of the capital definitely takes some getting used to.

» Defensive driving is most definitely the order of the day: once you're outside of Manila, provincial roads are packed with myriad obstacles.

» It's best to avoid driving at night if you can, not least because tricycles, jeepneys and even large trucks are often without lights (many drivers believe that driving without lights saves petrol).

» Night driving in the provinces holds its own particular hazards, quite apart from the issue of potential robberies in political trouble spots (eg certain parts of Mindanao).

Motorcycle

Small and midsized Visayan islands like Camiguin, Siquijor and Bohol beg to be explored by motorcycle. You can even drive down to the Visayas via the 'Nautical Highway' – the system of car ferries that link many islands – and enjoy pleasant driving on larger islands like Cebu and Negros.

Most touristy areas have a few easy-to-find shops or guesthouses renting out motorcycles – usually in the form of 75cc to 125cc motorbikes. The typical rate is P500 per day, but you'll likely be asked for more than this in particularly popular resorts, such as Boracay and Alona Beach in Bohol. A helmet is not always included.

In more remote areas, just ask around – even if there's no rental shop, you can always find somebody willing to part with their motorcycle for as little as P300 per day.

Driving Licence

Your home country's driving licence is legally valid for 90 days in the Philippines. Technically, you are supposed to have an International Driving Permit for any period longer than this, and some car rental companies may require you to have this permit when hiring vehicles from them.

Insurance

Philippine law requires that you have third-party car insurance with a Philippines car-insurance company when you drive in the Philippines. If you rent a car, this can be arranged with the rental agency. You are required to carry a minimum of P750,000 of insurance. Car insurance is available from local insurance agencies.

Road Rules

Driving is on the right-hand side of the road. With the exception of the expressways out of Manila, most roads in the Philippines are single lane, which necessitates a lot of overtaking. Local drivers do not always overtake safely. If an overtaker coming the other way refuses to get out of your lane, they're expecting you to give way by moving into the shoulder. It's always wise to do so.

Hitching

Hitching is never entirely safe in any country in the world, and we don't recommend it. A hitchhiker is such an unusual sight in the Philippines that most regular drivers will probably ignore you if you stand on the roadside with your thumb out; the only ones who might stop are truck or jeepney drivers, who would expect a few pesos if they gave you a lift.

Needless to say, hitching in the guerrilla territory of Mindanao is not recommended.

Local Transport

Jeepney

The first jeepneys were modified army jeeps left behind by the Americans after WWII. They have been customised with Filipino touches such as chrome horses, banks of coloured headlights, radio antennae, paintings of the Virgin Mary and neon-coloured scenes from action comic books.

» Jeepneys form the main urban transport in most cities and complement the bus services between regional centres.

» Within towns, the starting fare is usually P8, rising modestly for trips outside of town. Routes are clearly written on the side of the jeepney.

» Jeepneys have a certain quirky cultural appeal, but from a tourist's perspective they have one humongous flaw: you can barely see anything through the narrow open slats that pass as windows. The best seats are up the front next to the driver.

Light Rail

Some parts of Manila are served by an elevated railway system; for details see p81.

Taxi

Metered taxis are common in Manila and most major provincial hubs. Flagfall is P40, and a 15-minute trip rarely costs more than P150. Airport taxis cost a bit more.

Most taxi drivers will turn on the meter; if they don't, politely request that they do. If the meter is 'broken' or your taxi driver says the fare is 'up to you', the best strategy is to get out and find another cab (or offer a low-ball price). Rigged taxi meters are also becoming more common, although it must be said that most taxi drivers are honest.

Though it's become less heard-of recently, there have been cases of taxi passengers being robbed at gun or knife point, sometimes with the driver in cahoots with the culprits or the driver himself holding up the passengers.

Get out of a cab straight away (in a secure populated area, of course, not in the middle of nowhere or in a slum area) if you suspect you're being taken for a ride in more ways than one.

Tricycles, Kalesa & Habal-Habal

Found in most cities and towns, the tricycle is the Philippine rickshaw – a little, roofed sidecar bolted to a motorcycle. The standard fare for local trips in most provincial towns is P8. Tricycles that wait around in front of malls, restaurants and hotels will attempt to charge five to 10 times that for a 'special trip'. Avoid these by standing roadside and flagging down a passing P8 tricycle. You can also charter tricycles for about P300 per hour or P150 per 10km if you're heading out of town.

Pedicabs Many towns also have nonmotorised push tricycles, alternately known as pedicabs, *put-put* or *padyak*, for shorter trips.

Habal-habal These are essentially motorcycle taxis with extended seats (literally translated as 'pigs copulating,' after the level of intimacy attained when sharing a seat with four people). *Habal-habal* function like tricycles, only they are a little bit cheaper. They are most common in the Visayas and northern Mindanao. In some areas they are known simply as 'motorcycle taxis'.

Kalesa Two-wheeled horse carriages found in Manila's Chinatown and Intramuros, Vigan (North Luzon) and Cebu City (where they're known as *tartanillas*).

Train

The *Bicol Express* train route south from Manila to southeast Luzon – the only functioning railway line in the country – was just being reopened at research time after a three-year hiatus (see p79).

Health

Health issues and the quality of medical facilities vary enormously depending on where and how you travel in the Philippines. Many of the major cities are now very well developed – indeed Manila and Cebu are 'medical tourism' destinations where foreigners flock for affordable yet competent health care in modern hospitals. Travel to rural areas is a different story and carries a variety of health risks.

Some travellers worry about contracting infectious diseases when in the tropics, but infections are a rare cause of serious illness or death in travellers. Pre-existing medical conditions and accidental injury (especially traffic accidents) account for most life threatening problems.

The following advice is a general guide only and does not replace the advice of a doctor trained in travel medicine.

BEFORE YOU GO

» Philippine pharmacies are usually well stocked with sterilised disposable syringes, bandages and antibiotics, but it doesn't hurt to bring your own sterilised first-aid kit, especially if you're going to be travelling off the beaten track. Contact-lens solution and spare contacts are readily available in cities.

» Pack medications in their original, clearly labelled containers. A signed and dated letter from your physician describing your medical conditions and medications, including generic names, is also a good idea. If you have a heart condition, bring a copy of your ECG taken just prior to travelling.

» If you take any regular medication bring double your needs in case of loss or theft. Philippine pharmacies generally require a doctor's prescription to issue medications. It can be difficult to find some of the newer drugs, particularly the latest antidepressant drugs, contraceptive pills and blood-pressure medications.

Insurance

» Even if you are fit and healthy, don't travel without health insurance – accidents happen.

» Declare any existing medical conditions you have (the insurance company will check if your problem is pre-existing and will not cover you if it is undeclared).

» You may require extra cover for adventure activities such as rock climbing or scuba diving.

» If you're uninsured, emergency evacuation is expensive; bills of more than US$100,000 are not uncommon.

» Ensure you keep all documentation related to any medical expenses you incur.

Vaccinations

Specialised travel-medicine clinics are your best source of information; they stock all available vaccines and will be able to give specific recommendations. The doctors will take into account factors such as past vaccination history, the length of your trip, activities you may be undertaking and underlying medical conditions.

» Visit a doctor six to eight weeks before departure, as most vaccines don't produce immunity until at least two weeks after they're given.

» Ask your doctor for an International Certificate of Vaccination (otherwise known as the 'yellow booklet'), listing all vaccinations received.

» The only vaccine required by international regulations is yellow fever. Proof of vaccination will only be required if you have visited a country in the yellow-fever zone within the six days prior to entering Southeast Asia.

Medical Checklist

Recommended items for a personal medical kit:

» antibacterial cream, eg Muciprocin

» antibiotics for diarrhoea, eg Norfloxacin or Ciprofloxacin; Azithromycin for bacterial diarrhoea; Tinidazole for giardiasis or amoebic dysentery

REQUIRED & RECOMMENDED VACCINATIONS

The World Health Organisation (WHO) recommends the following vaccinations for travellers to Southeast Asia:

» **Adult diphtheria and tetanus** Single booster recommended if none has been given in the previous 10 years. Side effects include a sore arm and fever.

» **Hepatitis A** Provides almost 100% protection for up to a year; a booster after 12 months provides at least another 20 years' protection. Mild side effects such as headache and a sore arm occur in 5% to 10% of people.

» **Hepatitis B** Now considered routine for most travellers. Given as three shots over six months. A rapid schedule is also available, as is a combined vaccination with hepatitis A. Side effects are mild and uncommon, usually headache and a sore arm. Lifetime protection occurs in 95% of people.

» **Measles, mumps and rubella** Two doses of MMR required unless you have had the diseases. Occasionally a rash and flu-like illness can develop a week after receiving the vaccine. Many young adults require a booster.

» **Polio** Only one booster is required as an adult for lifetime protection.

» **Typhoid** Recommended unless your trip is less than a week and only to developed cities. The vaccine offers around 70% protection, lasts for two to three years and comes as a single shot. Tablets are also available, however the injection is usually recommended as it has fewer side effects. A sore arm and fever may occur.

» **Varicella** If you haven't had chickenpox, discuss this vaccination with your doctor.

These are recommended only for long-term travellers (more than one month):

» **Japanese B Encephalitis** Three injections in all. Booster recommended after two years. A sore arm and headache are the most common side effects.

» **Meningitis** Single injection. There are two types of vaccination: the quadrivalent vaccine gives two to three years' protection; meningitis group C vaccine gives around 10 years' protection. Recommended for long-term travellers aged under 25.

» **Rabies** Three injections in all. A booster after one year will then provide 10 years' protection. Side effects are rare – occasionally a headache and sore arm.

» **Tuberculosis** A complex issue. Adult long-term travellers are usually recommended to have a TB skin test before and after travel, rather than vaccination. Only one vaccine is given in a lifetime.

» antibiotics for skin infections, eg Amoxicillin/Clavulanate or Cephalexin

» antifungal cream, eg Clotrimazole

» antihistamine for allergies, eg Cetrizine for daytime and Promethazine for night

» anti-inflammatories, eg Ibuprofen

» antiseptic, eg Betadine

» antispasmodic for stomach cramps, eg Buscopa

» contraceptives

» a decongestant, eg Pseudoephedrine

» DEET-based insect repellent

» diarrhoea treatment – consider an oral rehydration solution, eg Gastrolyte; diarrhoea 'stopper', eg Loperamide; and anti-nausea medication, eg Prochlorperazine

» first-aid items such as scissors, safety pins, Elastoplasts, bandages, gauze, thermometer (electronic, not mercury), tweezers, and sterile needles and syringes

» indigestion medication, eg Quick Eze or Mylanta

» iodine tablets (unless you are pregnant or have a thyroid problem) to purify water

» laxative, eg Coloxyl

» migraine medication (your personal brand), if a migraine sufferer

» paracetamol for pain

» Permethrin (to impregnate clothing and mosquito nets) for repelling insects

» steroid cream for allergic/itchy rashes, eg 1% to 2% hydrocortisone

» sunscreen

» throat lozenges

» thrush (vaginal yeast infection) treatment, eg Clotrimazole pessaries or Diflucan tablet

» Ural or equivalent if you're prone to urine infections

Internet Resources

World Health Organisation (WHO; www.who.int/ith) Publishes a superb book called *International Travel & Health*, which is revised annually and is available free online.

MD Travel Health (www.mdtravelhealth.com) Provides complete travel health recommendations for every country and is updated daily.

Centers for Disease Control and Prevention (CDC; www.cdc.gov) Good general information.

Further Reading

Healthy Travel – Asia & India (Lonely Planet) Handy pocket size, packed with useful information.

Traveller's Health by Dr Richard Dawood.

Travelling Well (www.travellingwell.com.au) by Dr Deborah Mills

IN THE PHILIPPINES

Availability Of Health Care

Good medical care is available in most major cities in the Philippines. Recommended clinics are listed under 'Information' in the city sections of regional chapters in this book. It is difficult to find reliable medical care in rural areas, although there will usually be some sort of clinic not too far away. Your embassy and insurance company are also good contacts.

If you think you may have a serious disease, especially malaria, do not waste time – travel to the nearest quality facility to receive attention. It is always better to be assessed by a doctor than to rely on self-treatment.

Infectious Diseases

Chikungunya fever

This less common viral infection poses only a small risk to travellers in the Philippines, mainly in the Visayas. Sudden pain in one or more joints, fever, headache, nausea and rash are the main symptoms.

Cutaneous Larva Migrans

This disease is caused by dog hookworm; the rash starts as a small lump, then slowly spreads in a linear fashion. It is intensely itchy, especially at night. It is easily treated with medications and should not be cut out or frozen.

Dengue Fever

This mosquito-borne disease is by far the most prevalent of the diseases you have a chance of contracting in the Philippines. It's especially common in cities, especially in metro Manila. While not usually fatal, dengue can kill; more than 300 people died from dengue in the Philippines in 2008. There is no vaccine available, so it can only be prevented by avoiding mosquito bites. The mosquito that carries dengue bites day and night. Symptoms include high fever, severe headache and body ache (dengue was previously known as 'breakbone fever'). Some people develop a rash and experience diarrhoea. There is no specific treatment, just rest and paracetamol – do not take aspirin as it increases the likelihood of haemorrhaging. See a doctor to be diagnosed and monitored.

Travellers are advised to prevent mosquito bites by taking these steps:

» Use a DEET-containing insect repellent on exposed skin. Wash this off at night, as long as you are sleeping under a mosquito net. Natural repellents such as citronella can be effective, but must be applied more frequently than products containing DEET.

» Sleep under a mosquito net impregnated with Permethrin.

» Choose accommodation with screens and fans (if not air-conditioned).

» Impregnate clothing with Permethrin in high-risk areas.

» Wear long sleeves and trousers in light colours.

» Use mosquito coils.

» Spray your room with insect repellent before going out for your evening meal.

Filariasis

This is a mosquito-borne disease that is very common in the local population, yet very rare in travellers. Mosquito-avoidance measures are the best way to prevent this disease.

Hepatitis A

A problem found throughout the region, this food- and water-borne virus infects the liver, causing jaundice (yellow skin and eyes), nausea and lethargy. There is no specific treatment for hepatitis A; you just need to allow time for the liver to heal. All travellers to Southeast Asia should be vaccinated against hepatitis A.

Hepatitis B

The only sexually transmitted disease that can be prevented by vaccination, hepatitis B is spread by body fluids, including sexual contact. In some parts of Southeast Asia up to 20% of the population are carriers of hepatitis B, and usually are unaware of this. The long-term consequences can include liver cancer and cirrhosis.

Hepatitis E

Hepatitis E is transmitted through contaminated food and water and has similar symptoms to hepatitis A, but is far less common. It is a severe problem in pregnant women and can result in the death of both mother and baby. There is currently no vaccine, and prevention is by following safe eating and drinking guidelines.

Japanese B Encephalitis

While a rare disease in travellers, at least 50,000 locals are infected each year in Southeast Asia. This viral disease is transmitted by mosquitoes. Most cases occur in rural areas and vaccination is recommended for travellers spending more than one month outside of cities. There is no treatment, and a third of infected people will die while another third will suffer permanent brain damage.

Malaria

For such a serious and potentially deadly disease, there is an enormous amount of misinformation concerning malaria. Malaria is caused by a parasite transmitted by the bite of an infected mosquito. The most important symptom of malaria is fever, but general symptoms such as headache, diarrhoea, cough or chills may also occur. Diagnosis can only be made by taking a blood sample.

According to the Centers for Disease Control and Prevention (CDC), in the Philippines there is no malaria risk in Bohol, Boracay, Catanduanes, Cebu, Manila or other urban areas. The risk of side effects from anti-malarial tablets probably outweighs the risk of getting the disease in these areas.

In general, malaria is only a concern if you plan to travel below 600m in extremely remote areas such as southern Palawan (see p383). Before you travel, seek medical advice on the right medication and dosage for you. Note that, according to the CDC, chloroquine is not an effective antimalarial drug in the Philippines.

Measles

Measles remains a problem in some parts of Southeast Asia. This highly contagious bacterial infection is spread via coughing and sneezing. Most people born before 1966 are immune as they had the disease in childhood. Measles starts with a high fever and rash and can be complicated by pneumonia and brain disease. There is no specific treatment.

Rabies

This uniformly fatal disease is spread by the bite or lick of an infected animal – most commonly a dog or monkey. You should seek medical advice immediately after any animal bite and commence post-exposure treatment. Having pre-travel vaccination means the post-bite treatment is greatly simplified. If an animal bites you, gently wash the wound with soap and water, and apply iodine-based antiseptic. If you are not pre-vaccinated you will need to receive rabies immunoglobulin as soon as possible.

Schistosomiasis

Schistosomiasis is a tiny parasite that enters your skin after you've been swimming in contaminated water. Travellers usually only get a light infection and hence have no symptoms. Schistosomiasis exists in the Philippines but it's not common and is confined to a few areas well off the tourist trail. On rare occasions, travellers may develop 'Katayama fever'. This occurs some weeks after exposure, as the parasite passes through the lungs and causes an allergic reaction – symptoms are coughing and fever. Schistosomiasis is easily treated with medications.

Tuberculosis

Tuberculosis (TB) is rare in short-term travellers. Medical and aid workers, and long-term travellers who have significant contact with the local population, should take precautions. Vaccination is usually only given to children under the age of five, but adults at risk are recommended pre- and post-travel TB testing. The main symptoms are fever, cough, weight loss, night sweats and tiredness.

Typhoid

This serious bacterial infection is spread via food and water. It gives a high and slowly progressive fever and headache, and may be accompanied by a dry cough and stomach pain. It is diagnosed by blood tests and treated with antibiotics. Vaccination is recommended if visiting smaller cities, villages or rural areas.

Typhus

Murine typhus is spread by the bite of a flea while scrub typhus is spread via a mite. These diseases are rare in travellers. Symptoms include fever, muscle pains and a rash. You can avoid these diseases by following general insect-avoidance measures. Doxycycline will also prevent them.

Traveller's Diarrhoea

Traveller's diarrhoea is by far the most common problem affecting travellers. In over 80% of cases, traveller's diarrhoea is caused by a bacteria (there are numerous potential culprits), and therefore responds promptly to treatment with antibiotics. Treatment with antibiotics will depend on your situation – how sick you are, how quickly you need to get better, where you are etc.

Traveller's diarrhoea is defined as the passage of more than three watery bowel actions within 24 hours, plus at least one other symptom such as fever, cramps, nausea, vomiting or feeling generally unwell.

Treatment consists of staying well hydrated; rehydration solutions like Gastrolyte are the best for this. Antibiotics such as Norfloxacin, Ciprofloxacin or Azithromycin will kill the bacteria quickly.

Loperamide is just a 'stopper' and doesn't get to the cause of the problem. It can be helpful, for example if you have to go on a long bus ride. Don't take Loperamide if you have a fever, or blood in your stools. See also Food, right.

Amoebic Dysentery

Amoebic dysentery is very rare in travellers but is often misdiagnosed by poor-quality labs in Southeast Asia. Symptoms are similar to bacterial diarrhoea, ie fever, bloody diarrhoea and generally feeling unwell. You should always seek reliable medical care if you have blood in your diarrhoea. Treatment involves two drugs: Tinidazole or Metroniadzole to kill the parasite in your gut and then a second drug to kill the cysts. If left untreated complications such as liver or gut abscesses can occur.

Giardiasis

Giardia lamblia is a parasite that is relatively common in travellers. Symptoms include nausea, bloating, excess gas, fatigue and intermittent diarrhoea. The parasite will eventually go away if left untreated but this can take months. The treatment of choice is Tinidazole, with Metronidazole being a second-line option.

Environmental Hazards

Air Pollution

Air pollution, particularly vehicle pollution, is a major problem in the Philippines' major cities, especially Manila. If you have severe respiratory problems speak with your doctor before travelling to any heavily polluted urban centres. This pollution can also cause minor respiratory problems such as sinusitis, dry throat and irritated eyes. If troubled by the pollution, leave the city for a few days and get some fresh air.

Diving

Divers and surfers should seek specialised advice before they travel to ensure their medical kit contains treatment for coral cuts and tropical ear infections. Divers should ensure their insurance covers them for decompression illness – get specialised dive insurance through an organisation such as **Divers Alert Network** (DAN; www.danseap.org). Have a dive medical before you leave your home country – there are certain medical conditions that are incompatible with diving, and economic considerations may override health considerations for some dive operators.

Heat

For most people it takes at least two weeks to adapt to the hot climate. Swelling of the feet and ankles is common, as are muscle cramps caused by excessive sweating. Prevent these by avoiding dehydration and excessive activity in the heat. Take

DIVING EMERGENCIES

Recompression Chambers

There are six stationary recompression chambers in the Philippines and one roving chamber operated by the **Philippine Coast Guard Search & Rescue Center** (☎02-527 8481, ext 6290/6292).

Batangas (☎043-723 2167, 0917 536 2757; www.divemed.com.ph; Batangas Hyperbaric Medicine & Wound Healing Center, St Patrick's Hospital Medical Center, Lopez Jaena St, Batangas City, Luzon) Contact Michael Perez, MD, diving medical officer. The only privately owned recompression chamber in the Philippines.

Cavite (☎046-431 6311; Sangley Recompression Chamber, Philippine Fleet, Naval Base Cavite, Sangley Point, Cavite City, Luzon) Ask for Sangley operator and request local 4490.

Cebu City (☎032-254 9262, 24hr 0919 517 5900, 235 5662; Viscom Station Hospital, Camp Lapu Lapu, Lahug, Cebu City) Contact Tonton Ortega.

Davao (☎082-227 0234, 305 3483; Wind & Waves, Sta Ana Wharf, Davao City) Contact Dr Jeffrey Ramos.

Manila (☎02-426 2701, local 6245, 0919 347 1773; Armed Forces of the Philippines Medical Center, V Luna Rd, Quezon City) Contact Jojo Bernado, MD.

Evacuation and Search & Rescue Services

The Philippine Air Force, the Coast Guard and private operators such as Subic Seaplanes can assist with evacuations. However, their range is limited and you can't expect them to miraculously appear in the middle of places like the Sulu Sea.

Philippines Air Force Search & Rescue (☎02-854 6701, 853 5013, 853 5008; Villamor Air Base, Pasay City, Manila)

Subic Seaplanes (☎047-252 2230, 0919 325 1106; Subic Bay Freeport Zone, Zambales)

it easy when you first arrive. Don't eat salt tablets (they aggravate the gut), although drinking rehydration solution or eating salty food helps. Treat cramps by stopping activity, resting, rehydrating with double-strength rehydration solution and gently stretching.

Heatstroke is a serious medical emergency. Symptoms come on suddenly and include weakness, nausea, a hot dry body with a body temperature of over 41°C, dizziness, confusion, loss of coordination, fits and eventually collapse and loss of consciousness. Seek medical help and commence cooling by getting the person out of the heat, removing their clothes, fanning them and applying cool wet cloths or ice to their body, especially to the groin and armpits.

Prickly heat is a common skin rash in the tropics, caused by sweat being trapped under the skin. The result is an itchy rash of tiny lumps. Treat by moving out of the heat and into an air-conditioned area for a few hours and by having cool showers. Creams and ointments clog the skin so they should be avoided. Locally bought prickly-heat powder can be helpful.

Insect Bites & Stings

Bedbugs don't carry disease but their bites are very itchy. They live in the cracks of furniture and walls and then migrate to the bed at night to feed on you. You can treat the itch with an antihistamine. Lice inhabit various parts of your body but most commonly your head and pubic area. Transmission is via close contact with an infected person. Lice can be difficult to treat and you may need numerous applications of a lice shampoo such as Permethrin. Pubic lice are usually contracted from sexual contact.

Ticks are contracted after walking in rural areas. If you have had a tick bite and experience symptoms such as a rash at the site of the bite or elsewhere, fever or muscle aches you should see a doctor. Doxycycline prevents tick-borne diseases.

Leeches are found in humid rainforest areas and are very common in the Philippines. They do not transmit any disease but their bites are often intensely itchy for weeks afterwards and can easily become infected. Apply an iodine-based antiseptic to any leech bite to help prevent infection.

Bee and wasp stings mainly cause problems for people who are allergic to them. Anyone with a serious bee or wasp allergy should carry an injection of adrenaline (eg Epipen) for emergency treatment. For others, pain is the main problem – apply ice and take painkillers.

Most jellyfish in Southeast Asian waters are not dangerous, just irritating. An exception is box jellyfish, which are extremely dangerous and can be fatal. They are not common in Philippine waters but they do exist, so ask around to make sure there have been no recent sightings in areas where you'll be swimming.

First aid for jellyfish stings involves pouring vinegar onto the affected area to neutralise the poison. Do not rub sand or water onto the stings. Take painkillers, and anyone who feels ill in any way after being stung should seek medical advice.

Parasites

Numerous parasites are common in local populations in Southeast Asia, however, most of these are rare in travellers. The two rules to follow if you wish to avoid parasitic infections are to wear shoes and to avoid eating raw food, especially fish, pork and vegetables. A number of parasites, including strongyloides, hookworm and cutaneous *larva migrans*, are transmitted via the skin by walking barefoot.

Skin Problems

Fungal rashes are common in humid climates. There are two common fungal rashes that affect travellers. The first occurs in moist areas that get less air, such as the groin, armpits and between the toes. It starts as a red patch that slowly spreads and is usually itchy. Treatment involves keeping the skin dry, avoiding chafing and using an antifungal cream such as Clotrimazole or Lamisil. *Tinea versicolor* is also common – this fungus causes small, light-coloured patches, most commonly on the back, chest and shoulders. Consult a doctor.

Cuts and scratches become easily infected in humid climates. Take meticulous care of any cuts and scratches to prevent complications such as abscesses. Immediately wash all wounds in clean water and apply antiseptic. If you develop signs of infection (increasing pain and redness) see a doctor. Divers and surfers should be particularly careful with coral cuts as they can become easily infected.

Snakes

Southeast Asia is home to many species of both poisonous and harmless snakes. Assume all snakes are poisonous and never try to catch one. Always wear boots and long pants if walking in an area that may have snakes. First aid in the event of a snakebite involves pressure immobilisation via an elastic bandage firmly wrapped around the affected limb, starting at the bite site and working up towards the chest. The bandage should not be so tight that the circulation is cut off, and the fingers or toes should be kept free so the circulation can be checked. Immobilise the limb with a splint and carry the victim to medical attention. Do not use tourniquets or try to suck the venom out. Antivenene is available for most species.

Language

WANT MORE?

For in-depth language information and handy phrases, check out Lonely Planet's *Filipino Phrasebook*. You'll find it at **shop.lonely planet.com**, or you can buy Lonely Planet's iPhone phrasebooks at the Apple App Store.

Tagalog, Pilipino, Filipino – the various language names might cause confusion, but they reflect the political history of the lingua franca across the 7000-island archipelago of the Philippines. Although not the mother tongue of every Philippine citizen, Filipino is spoken as a second language throughout the country (with over 165 other languages), and is an official language used for university instruction and in most legal, business and governmental transactions (the other official language being English). It belongs to the Malayo-Polynesian language family and has around 45 million speakers worldwide.

Filipino is easy to pronounce and most sounds are familiar to English speakers. In addition, the relationship between Filipino sounds and their spelling is straightforward and consistent, meaning that each letter is always pronounced the same way. If you read our coloured pronunciation guides as if they were English, you'll be understood just fine. Note that ai is pronounced as in 'aisle', ay as in 'say', ew like ee with rounded lips, oh as the 'o' in 'go', ow as in 'how' and ooy as the 'wea' in 'tweak'. The r sound is stronger than in English and rolled, and the ng combination – which is found in English words such as 'sing' or 'ringing' – can appear at the beginning of words. Filipino also has a glottal stop, which is pronounced like the pause between the two syllables in 'uh-oh'. It's indicated in our pronunciation guides by an apostrophe ('), and in written Filipino by a circumflex (ˆ), grave (ˋ) or acute (ˊ) accent over the vowel that's followed by a glottal stop.

In our pronunciation guides the stressed syllables are indicated with italics. The markers 'pol' and 'inf' indicate polite and informal forms respectively.

BASICS

Good day.	*Magandáng araw pô.* (pol)	ma·gan·*dang* *a*·row po'
	Magandáng araw. (inf)	ma·gan·*dang* *a*·row
Goodbye.	*Paalam na pô.* (pol)	pa·*a*·lam na po'
	Babay. (inf)	*ba*·bai
Yes.	*Opò.* (pol)	*o*·po'
	Oo. (inf)	*o*·o
No.	*Hindí pô.* (pol)	heen·*dee'* po'
	Hindî. (inf)	heen·*dee'*
Thank you.	*Salamat pô.* (pol)	sa·*la*·mat po'
	Salamat. (inf)	sa·*la*·mat
You're welcome.	*Walá pong anumán.* (pol)	wa·*la* pong a·noo·*man*
	Waláng anumán. (inf)	wa·*lang* a·noo·*man*

How are you?

Kumustá po kayó? (pol)	koo·moos·*ta* po ka·*yo*
Kumustá? (inf)	koo·moos·*ta*

Fine. And you?

Mabuti pô. Kayó pô? (pol)	ma·*boo*·tee po' ka·*yo* po'
Mabuti. Ikáw? (inf)	ma·*boo*·tee ee·*kow*

What's your name?

Anó pô ang pangalan ninyó? (pol)	a·*no* po' ang pa·*nga*·lan neen·*yo*
Anó ang pangalan mo? (inf)	a·*no* ang pa·*nga*·lan mo

My name is ...

Ang pangalan ko pô ay ... (pol)	ang pa·*nga*·lan ko po' ai ...
Ang pangalan ko ay ... (inf)	ang pa·*nga*·lan ko ai ...

Do you speak English?
Marunong ka ba ng Inglés? — ma·*roo*·nong ka ba nang eeng·*gles*

I don't understand.
Hindí ko náiintindihán. — heen·*dee* ko *na*·ee·een·teen·dee·*han*

ACCOMMODATION

Where's a ...?	*Násaán ang ...?*	na·sa·*an* ang ...
campsite	*kampingan*	kam·*pee*·ngan
guesthouse	*bahay-bisita*	ba·hai·bee·*see*·ta
hotel	*otél*	o·*tel*
youth hostel	*hostel para sa kabataan*	*hos*·tel *pa*·ra sa ka·ba·*ta*·an

Do you have a ... room?	*Mayroón ba kayóng kuwartong ...?*	mai·ro·*on* ba ka·*yong* koo·*war*·tong ...
single	*pang-isahan*	pang·ee·*sa*·han
double	*pandala-waha*	pan·da·la·*wa*·han
twin	*may kambál na kama*	mai kam·*bal* na *ka*·ma

How much is it per ...?	*Magkano ba para sa isáng ...?*	mag·*ka*·no ba *pa*·ra sa ee·*sang* ...
night	*gabí*	ga·*bee*
person	*katao*	ka·*ta*·o
week	*linggó*	leeng·*go*

air-con	*erkon*	*er*·kon
bathroom	*banyo*	*ba*·nyo
toilet	*kubeta*	koo·*be*·ta
window	*bintanà*	been·*ta*·na'

DIRECTIONS

Where's the (market)?
Násaán ang (palengke)? — na·sa·*an* ang (pa·*leng*·ke)

Signs

Pasukán	Entrance
Labásan	Exit
Bukás	Open
Sará	Closed
Bawal	Prohibited
CR	Toilets
Lalaki	Men
Babae	Women

How far is it?
Gaano kalayo? — ga·a·no ka·*la*·yo

What's the address?
Anó ang adrés? — a·*no* ang a·*dres*

Could you please write it down?
Pakísulat mo? — pa·*kee*·soo·lat mo

Can you show me (on the map)?
Maáari bang ipakita mo sa akin (sa mapa)? — ma·a·a·ree bang ee·pa·*kee*·ta mo sa a·keen (sa *ma*·pa)

It's ...	*Iyón ay ...*	ee·*yon* ai ...
behind ...	*nasa likurán ng ...*	*na*·sa lee·koo·*ran* nang ...
in front of ...	*sa harapán ng ...*	sa ha·ra·*pan* nang ...
near (...)	*malapit (sa ...)*	ma·*la*·peet (sa ...)
next to ...	*katabí ng ...*	ka·ta·*bee* nang ...
on the corner	*nasa kanto*	*na*·sa *kan*·to
opposite ...	*katapát ng ...*	ka·ta·*pat* nang ...
straight ahead	*diretso*	dee·*ret*·so

Turn ...	*Lumikó sa ...*	loo·mee·*ko* sa ...
at the traffic lights	*ilaw-trápiko*	ee·low·*tra*·pee·ko
left	*kaliwâ*	ka·lee·*wa'*
right	*kanan*	*ka*·nan

EATING & DRINKING

I'd like to reserve a table for ...	*Gustó kong mag-reserba ng mesa para sa ...*	goos·*to* kong mag·re·*ser*·ba nang *me*·sa *pa*·ra sa ...
(eight) o'clock	*(alás-otso)*	(a·*las*·*ot*·so)
(two) people	*(dalawáng) tao*	(da·la·*wang*) *ta*·o

I'd like the menu.
Gustó ko ng menú. — goos·*to* ko nang me·*noo*

What would you recommend?
Anó ang mairere-komendá mo? — a·*no* ang ma·ee·re·re·ko·men·*da* mo

What's in that dish?
Anó iyán? — a·*no* ee·*yan*

I don't eat (red meat).
Hindî akó kumakain ng (karné). — heen·*dee'* a·*ko* koo·ma·*ka*·een nang (kar·*ne*)

Cheers!
Tagayan tayo! — ta·ga·yan ta·yo

That was delicious!
Masaráp! ma·sa·*rap*

Please bring the bill.
Pakidalá ang tsit. pa·kee·da·*la* ang tseet

Key Words

bottle	*bote*	*bo*·te
breakfast	*almusál*	al·moo·*sal*
cafe	*kapiteryá*	ka·pee·ter·*ya*
cold	*malamíg*	ma·la·*meeg*
dinner	*hapunan*	ha·*poo*·nan
drink	*inumin*	ee·*noo*·meen
fork	*tinidór*	tee·nee·*dor*
glass	*baso*	*ba*·so
grocery	*groseryá*	gro·ser·*ya*
hot	*mainit*	ma·*ee*·neet
knife	*kutsilyo*	koot·*seel*·yo
lunch	*tanghalian*	tang·ha·*lee*·an
market	*palengke*	pa·*leng*·ke
plate	*pinggán*	peeng·*gan*
restaurant	*restoran*	res·*to*·ran
spoon	*kutsara*	koot·*sa*·ra
vegetarian	*bedyetaryan*	bed·ye·*tar*·yan
with ...	*may ...*	mai ...
without ...	*walâ ...*	wa·*la'* ...

Meat & Fish

beef	*karné*	kar·*ne*
chicken	*manók*	ma·*nok*
duck	*bibi*	*bee*·bee
fish	*isdâ*	ees·*da'*
lamb	*tupa*	*too*·pa
meat	*karné*	kar·*ne*
mussel	*paros*	*pa*·ros
oysters	*talabá*	ta·la·*ba*
pork	*karnéng baboy*	kar·*neng* *ba*·boy
prawn	*sugpô*	soog·*po'*
tuna	*tulingán*	too·lee·*ngan*
turkey	*pabo*	*pa*·bo
veal	*karnéng bulô*	kar·*neng* boo·*lo'*

Fruit & Vegetables

apple	*mansanas*	man·*sa*·nas
bean	*bin*	been
cabbage	*repolyo*	re·*pol*·yo
capsicum	*bel peper*	bel *pe*·per
cauliflower	*koliplawer*	ko·lee·*pla*·wer
cucumber	*pipino*	pee·*pee*·no
fruit	*prutas*	*proo*·tas
grapes	*ubas*	*oo*·bas
lemon	*limón*	lee·*mon*
mushroom	*kabuté*	ka·boo·*te*
nuts	*manê*	ma·*ne'*
onion	*sibuyas*	see·*boo*·yas
orange	*kahél*	ka·*hel*
pea	*gisantes*	gee·*san*·tes
peach	*pits*	peets
pineapple	*pinyá*	peen·*ya*
potatoes	*patatas*	pa·*ta*·tas
spinach	*kulitis*	koo·*lee*·tees
tomato	*kamatis*	ka·*ma*·tees
vegetable	*gulay*	*goo*·lai

Question Words

How?	*Paano?*	pa·*a*·no
What?	*Anó?*	a·*no*
When?	*Kailán?*	ka·ee·*lan*
Where?	*Saán?*	sa·*an*
Who?	*Sino?*	*see*·no
Why?	*Bakit?*	*ba*·keet

Other

bread	*tinapay*	tee·*na*·pai
butter	*mantekilya*	man·te·*keel*·ya
cheese	*keso*	*ke*·so
egg	*itlóg*	eet·*log*
garlic	*bawang*	*ba*·wang
honey	*pulót-pukyutan*	poo·*lot*·pook·*yoo*·tan
ice	*yelo*	*ye*·lo
oil	*mantikà*	man·*tee*·ka
pepper	*pamintá*	pa·meen·*ta*
rice (cooked)	*kanin*	*ka*·neen
salt	*asín*	a·*seen*
soup	*sopas*	*so*·pas
sour cream	*kremang maasim*	*kre*·mang ma·*a*·seem
sugar	*asukal*	a·*soo*·kal
vinegar	*sukà*	*soo*·ka'

Drinks

beer	*serbesa*	ser·*be*·sa
coffee	*kapé*	ka·*pe*

Numbers

1	*isá*	ee·sa
2	*dalawá*	da·la·*wa*
3	*tatló*	tat·*lo*
4	*apat*	a·pat
5	*limá*	lee·*ma*
6	*anim*	a·neem
7	*pitó*	pee·*to*
8	*waló*	wa·*lo*
9	*siyám*	see·*yam*
10	*sampû*	sam·*poo'*
20	*dalawampû*	da·la·wam·*poo'*
30	*tatlumpû*	tat·loom·*poo'*
40	*apatnapû*	a·pat·na·*poo'*
50	*limampû*	lee·mam·*poo'*
60	*animnapû*	a·neem·na·*poo'*
70	*pitumpû*	pee·toom·*poo'*
80	*walumpû*	wa·loom·*poo'*
90	*siyamnapû*	see·yam·na·*poo'*
100	*sandaán*	san·da·*an*
1000	*isáng libo*	ee·*sang* lee·bo

juice	*katás*	ka·*tas*
milk	*gatas*	*ga*·tas
tea	*tsaá*	tsa·*a*
water	*tubig*	*too*·beeg
wine	*alak*	a·lak

EMERGENCIES

Help!	*Saklolo!*	sak·*lo*·lo
Go away!	*Umalís ka!*	oo·ma·*lees* ka
Call ...!	*Tumawag ka ng ...!*	too·*ma*·wag ka nang ...
a doctor	*doktór*	dok·*tor*
the police	*pulís*	poo·*lees*

There's been an accident.
May aksidente. mai ak·see·*den*·te

I'm sick.
May sakít akó. mai sa·*keet* a·*ko*

It hurts here.
Masakít dito. ma·sa·*keet dee*·to

I'm allergic to (antibiotics).
Allergic akó sa (antibayótikó). a·*ler*·jeek a·*ko* sa (an·tee·ba·*yo*·tee·ko)

I'm lost.
Nawawalâ akó. na·wa·wa·*la'* a·*ko*

Where are the toilets?
Násaán ang kubeta? *na*·sa·*an* ang koo·*be*·ta

SHOPPING & SERVICES

I'd like to buy ...
Gustó kong bumilí ng ... goos·*to* kong boo·mee·*lee* nang ...

I'm just looking.
Tumitingín lang akó. too·mee·tee·*ngeen* lang a·*ko*

Can I look at it?
Puwede ko bang tingnán? poo·*we*·de ko bang teeng·*nan*

How much is it?
Magkano? mag·*ka*·no

That's too expensive.
Masyadong mahál. mas·*ya*·dong ma·*hal*

Can you lower the price?
Puwede mo bang ibabâ ang presyo? poo·*we*·de mo bang ee·ba·*ba'* ang *pres*·yo

There's a mistake in the bill.
May malí sa kuwenta. mai ma·*lee* sa koo·*wen*·ta

bank	*bangko*	*bang*·ko
internet cafe	*ínternet kapé*	*een*·ter·net ka·*pe*
post office	*pos opis*	pos *o*·pees
public telephone	*teléponong pampúbliko*	te·*le*·po·nong pam·*poob*·lee·ko
tourist office	*upisina ng turismo*	oo·pee·*see*·na nang too·*rees*·mo

TIME & DATES

What time is it?
Anóng oras na? a·*nong o*·ras na

It's (10) o'clock.
Alás-(diyés). a·*las*·(dee·yes)

Half past (10).
Kalahating oras makalampás ang (alás-diyés). ka·la·*ha*·teeng o·ras ma·ka·lam·*pas* ang (a·*las*·dee·*yes*)

am	*ng umaga*	nang oo·*ma*·ga
pm (12–2pm)	*ng tanghali*	nang tang·*ha*·lee'
pm (2–6pm)	*ng hapon*	nang *ha*·pon

yesterday	*kahapon ng*	ka·*ha*·pon nang
today	*sa araw na itó*	sa a·row na ee·*to*
tomorrow	*bukas ng*	*boo*·kas nang

Monday	*Lunes*	*loo*·nes
Tuesday	*Martés*	mar·*tes*
Wednesday	*Miyérkoles*	mee·*yer*·ko·les
Thursday	*Huwebes*	hoo·*we*·bes
Friday	*Biyernes*	bee·*yer*·nes
Saturday	*Sábado*	*sa*·ba·do
Sunday	*Linggó*	leeng·*go*

January	*Enero*	e·*ne*·ro
February	*Pebrero*	peb·*re*·ro
March	*Marso*	*mar*·so
April	*Abríl*	ab·*reel*
May	*Mayo*	*ma*·yo
June	*Hunyo*	*hoon*·yo
July	*Hulyo*	*hool*·yo
August	*Agosto*	a·*gos*·to
September	*Setyembre*	set·*yem*·bre
October	*Oktubre*	ok·*too*·bre
November	*Nobyembre*	nob·*yem*·bre
December	*Disyembre*	dees·*yem*·bre

TRANSPORT

Public Transport

Which ... goes to (Bataan)?	*Alíng ... ang papuntá sa (Bataan)?*	a·*leeng* ... ang pa·poon·*ta* sa (ba·ta·*an*)
boat	*bapór*	ba·*por*
catamaran	*catamaran*	*ka*·ta·ma·ran
ferry	*ferry*	*pe*·ree
Is this the ... to (Baguío)?	*Itó ba ang ... na papuntá sa (Baguío)?*	ee·*to* ba ang ... na pa·poon·*ta* sa (*ba*·gee·o)
bus	*bus*	boos
jeepney	*dyipni*	*jeep*·nee
megataxi	*mega-taksi*	me·ga·*tak*·see
train	*tren*	tren
When's the ... (bus)?	*Kailán ang ... (bus)?*	ka·ee·*lan* ang ... (boos)
first	*unang*	oo·nang
last	*hulíng*	hoo·*leeng*
next	*súsunód na*	soo·soo·*nod* na
A ... ticket (to Liliw).	*Isáng tiket ... na (papuntá sa Liliw).*	ee·*sang* tee·ket ... na (pa·poon·*ta* sa *lee*·lew)
1st-class	*1st class*	pers klas
2nd-class	*2nd class*	se·kan klas
one-way	*one way*	wan way
return	*balikan*	ba·*lee*·kan

What time does the (bus) leave?
Anóng oras áalís ang (bus)? — a·*nong* o·ras a·a·*lees* ang (boos)

What time does the (boat) get to (Samal)?
Anóng oras daratíng ang (bapór) sa (Samal)? — a·*nong* o·ras da·ra·*teeng* ang (ba·*por*) sa (sa·*mal*)

Does it stop at (Porac)?
Humihintó ba itó sa (Porac)? — hoo·mee·heen·*to* ba ee·*to* sa (*po*·rak)

Please tell me when we get to (Tagaytay).
Pakisabi lang sa akin pagdatíng natin sa (Tagaytay). — pa·kee·*sa*·bee lang sa a·keen pag·da·*teeng* *na*·teen sa (ta·*gai*·tai)

I'd like to get off at (Rizal).
Gustó kong bumabá sa (Rizal). — goos·*to* kong boo·ma·*ba* sa (ree·*sal*)

Please take me to (this address).
Pakihatíd mo akó sa (adrés na itó). — pa·kee·ha·*teed* mo a·*ko* sa (a·*dres* na ee·*to*)

bus stop	*hintuan ng bus*	heen·*too*·an nang boos
ticket office	*bilihan ng tiket*	bee·*lee*·han nang *tee*·ket
train station	*istasyón ng tren*	ees·tas·*yon* nang tren

Driving & Cycling

I'd like to hire a ...	*Gustó kong umarkilá ng ...*	goos·*to* kong oo·mar·kee·*la* nang ...
4WD	*4WD*	*por*·weel·draib
bicycle	*bisikleta*	bee·seek·*le*·ta
car	*kotse*	*kot*·se
motorbike	*motorsiklo*	mo·tor·*seek*·lo

Is this the road to (Macabebe)?
Itó ba ang daán patungo sa (Macabebe)? — ee·*to* ba ang da·*an* pa·too·ngo sa (*ma*·ka·be·be)

Can I park here?
Puwede ba akóng pumarada dito? — poo·*we*·de ba a·*kong* poo·ma·*ra*·da dee·to

The (car) has broken down at (San Miguel).
Nasiraan ang (kotse) sa (San Miguel). — na·see·*ra*·an ang (*kot*·se) sa (san mee·*gel*)

I have a flat tyre.
Plat ang gulóng ko. — plat ang goo·*long* ko

I've run out of petrol.
Naubusan akó ng gasolina. — na·oo·*boo*·san a·*ko* nang ga·so·*lee*·na

bike shop	*tindahan ng bisikleta*	teen·*da*·han nang bee·seek·*le*·ta
mechanic	*mekániko*	me·*ka*·nee·ko
petrol/gas	*gasolina*	ga·so·*lee*·na
service station	*serbis istesyon*	*ser*·bees ees·*tes*·yon

GLOSSARY

arnis de mano – pre-Hispanic style of stick-fighting (more commonly known simply as *arnis*)

bagyo – typhoon

bahala na – you could almost call this the 'national philosophy'; in the days before the advent of Christianity, god was called bathala by ancient Filipinos; the expression *bahala na* is derived from this word and expresses faith (God will provide) as well a kind of fatalism (come what may); it's somewhere between an Australian 'no worries' and Kurt Vonnegut's 'so it goes', but less individualistic than either: all things shall pass and in the meantime life is to be lived, preferably in the company of one's friends and – most importantly – family

bahay na bato – stone house

balangay – artfully crafted seagoing outrigger boat

balikbayan – an overseas Filipino returning or paying a visit to the Philippines

balisong – fan or butterfly knife

bangka – a wooden boat, usually with outriggers and powered by a cannibalised automotive engine; a pumpboat

barangay – village, neighbourhood or community, the basic sociopolitical unit of Filipino society

barkada – gang of friends

barong – a generic term to describe the Filipino local shirt (for men) that is the 'national costume'; it usually has a heavily embroidered or patterned front

Barong Tagalog – traditional Filipino formal shirt (the barong was originally for men only; it refers only to the shirt), with elaborate embroidery or patterning down the front; made of jusi or pinya

baryo – Filipiniation of the Spanish word barrio (neighbourhood). Now known as a barangay.

bayanihan – Filipino tradition wherein neighbours would help a relocating family by carrying their house to its new location. More generally, the word has come to mean a communal spirit that makes seemingly impossible feats possible through the power of unity and cooperation

BPI – Bank of the Philippine Islands

butanding – whale shark

carabao – water buffalo, sometimes called a kalabaw

CBST – Community-Based Sustainable Tourism

CR – Comfort Room (toilet)

fronton – *jai alai* court

GROs – 'Guest Relation Officers' are officially glorified waitresses; unofficially they are sex workers

haribon – the Philippine eagle, an endangered species; haribon literally means 'king of birds'

ilustrado – a 19th-century Filipino of the educated middle class

jai alai – a fast-paced ball game, and one of the more popular sports in the Philippines

jeepney – a brightly painted vehicle that looks like an extended jeep, fitted with benches, adorned with everything but a kitchen sink and crammed with passengers

jusi – fabric woven from ramie fibres; used to make a *barong*

kalesa – horse-drawn carriage

kundiman – a melancholy genre of song originating in Manila (and the Tagalog region); one of the country's most loved musical idioms

lahar – rain-induced landslide of volcanic debris or mud from volcanic ash, common around Mt Pinatubo

mestizo – Filipino of mixed (usually Chinese or Spanish) descent. A Filipino of mixed Asian ancestry other than Chinese is not called a mestizo.

MILF – Moro Islamic Liberation Front

MNLF – Moro National Liberation Front

Moro – Spanish colonial term for Muslim Filipinos, once derogatory but now worn with some pride

nara – a hardwood tree, the Philippine national tree

nipa – a type of palm tree, the leaves of which are used for making nipa huts, the typical house in rural areas

NPA – New People's Army

paraw – traditional outrigger with jib and mainsail

pasyon – Christ's Passion, sung or re-enacted every Holy Week

Philvolcs – Philippine Institute of Volcanology & Seismology

Pinoy – a term Filipinos call themselves

pinya – fabric woven from pineapple fibres; commonly used to make a *barong*

PNP – Philippine National Police

poblasyon – town centre

sabong – cockfighting

sala – living room

santo – religious statue

sari-sari – small neighbourhood store stocked with all kinds of daily necessities; *sari-sari* literally means 'assortment'

swidden farming – the cultivation of an area of land that has been cleared through the use of slash-and-burn agricultural practices

Tagalog – the dominant dialect of Manila and surrounding provinces, now the basis of the national language, Filipino

tamaraw – an endangered species of native buffalo, found only in Mindoro; one of the most endangered animals in the world

tinikling – Philippine national folk dance

tricycle – a Philippine rickshaw, formerly pedal-powered but now predominantly motorised

v-hire – local van/minibus

NOTES

NOTES

index

000 Map pages
000 Photo pages

000 Map pages
000 Photo pages

000 Map pages
000 Photo pages

behind the scenes

SEND US YOUR FEEDBACK

We love to hear from travellers – your comments keep us on our toes and help make our books better. Our well-travelled team reads every word on what you loved or loathed about this book. Although we cannot reply individually to postal submissions, we always guarantee that your feedback goes straight to the appropriate authors, in time for the next edition. Each person who sends us information is thanked in the next edition – and the most useful submissions are rewarded with a free book.

Visit **lonelyplanet.com/contact** to submit your updates and suggestions or to ask for help. Our award-winning website also features inspirational travel stories, news and discussions.

Note: We may edit, reproduce and incorporate your comments in Lonely Planet products such as guidebooks, websites and digital products, so let us know if you don't want your comments reproduced or your name acknowledged. For a copy of our privacy policy visit lonelyplanet.com/privacy.

OUR READERS

Many thanks to the travellers who used the last edition and wrote to us with helpful hints, useful advice and interesting anecdotes:
Maria Christina C Abasolo, Marie Aurousseau, Alan B, Ralph Balmer, Rob Barclay, N Barker, Luca Belis, Shyam Bera, Frederic Bergue, Lalimarie Bhagwani, Eleanor Bodling & Henrik Sundblad, Harrie Boin, Claire Brittain, Don Bronk, James Bulnes, Carisa Canepa, Carly Carratura, J Prince De Mesa Castasus, Laura Catalano, Samuel Chan, Chiara Motta, Anthony Chiu, Daniel Christen, Claudia Christl, Laurent Claudel, Christopher Clifford, Kelly Connolly, David Cook, Juliet Corpuz, Parra Didier, Peter Doelle, Liam Doherty, Patrick Doles, Murray Du Plessis, Charles Failmezger, Roger Faulkner, Phil Fawcett, Alexander Fecher, Fabien Fetter, Denis Furrer, Gabriel Gardiner, Gerhart Gerecht, Sepi Gilani, Leon Gillingham, Samantha Gould, Rachel Griffiths, Paul Guren & Eileen Synnott, Armina Gutentag, Nathalie Hagestein, Jorma Hakkarainen, Catherine Ham, Hans W Heckel, Wayne Henry, Gerard Hepsakker, Mark Hiley, Britt Hill, Wendy Hodge, Ralpha Jacobson, Wim De Jong, Martin Jordan, Sharon Keld, Piers Kelly, Teea Kemppinen, Nicole Kisslig, Paul Kraaijeveld, Virginie Lafleur Tighe, Georges Landry, Kim Leber, Louise Lee, Larry Leese, Michaela Lenger, Jill Linderwell, Ann Lond-Caulk, Fernando E Lopez Jr, Inger Lundell, Benjamin May, Jessica Maybury, Wayne McKeon, Sofie Merck, Robert Merriam, Raquel Miguel, John Miller, P Monbaron, Yorck Mothes, Claudia Mueller, Hazel Murray, Casey, Itzi, Jenni, Philippe, Ruben, Jason & Charmaine Ng, Dominik Nice, Patrick O'Dowd, Greg O'Hern, Peter Patterson, Mario Pavesi, Graham Peake, Stephanie Perillard, Violaine Pierre, Bill Pollard, Tim Pottiez, TDana Raluca, Bea Raya, Shifra Raz, Brooke Resh Sateesh, Jim Revell, Corina Risseeuw, Jean Roberrt, Fritz Roder, Noam Rumack, Robert Ruml, Bobby Russell, Jessica Sabell, Kim Serca, Wanda Serkowska, James Shannon, Ray Sinniger, Lisa Smieja, Helen Smith, Magne Stener, Stephen Johansen, Nicola Tadini, Cresil Taglo, Bart Ten Tije, Henrik Topbjerg, Homerson Uy, Hans Van Beek, Lisette Van Wylick, Paul Van Schilfgaarde, Rick Vandergraaf, Frederic Veillez, Carlos Vendrell, Intan Vermeer, Daniela Verzaro, Sabina Vogt, Ulrich Von Schroeder, Jens Walter, Jonas Wernli, Stan West, Roger Wiget, Elie Zwiebel

AUTHOR THANKS

Greg Bloom

Thanks as always to my *barkada* in Manila; you know who you are. A special nod to the Edes, Donahue, Fitzpatrick and (in Subic) Blythe clans for the hospitality; to Johnny

Weekend for tagging along and braving typhoon sea travel between Romblon and Batangas; to Glen for weathering the Boracay-to-PG route; to Peng and Will S for the research assistance; to Trisha and the many helpful PCVs I met along the way; and, most importantly, to Anna for keeping me sane on the world's worst deadline. Thanks also to her mama for holding down the fort. And to my fellow authors for their spirit of *bayanihan*.

Michael Grosberg

I'm always grateful for the warmth and kindness of Filipinos I meet along the way. Special thanks to Sonny Dison, Kublai and Min Milan in Davao; Judy Distal in El Nido; Romie Villanueva, Huber Castillo and Onyo Austria for a wonderful boat trip between El Nido and Coron; Andy and Jojo from Sangat and Jim Goll from Coron; Michele and Ulrich on Camiguin, Gerry and Susan Deegan on Siargao. And to Carly for sharing northern Palawan with me.

Trent Holden

As per usual, this book is very much a collaboration between myself, locals and travellers. The following people were a huge help: Howard and Bambi for everything Negros; Aimee Marcos, Wolfgang Dafert, Felix Constantino Cata-al for all being great interview subjects; Rene Richard A Salazar for the connections; Piers Kelly for all the great info; Nedgar Garvez, Verna Vargos, Sun Dacillo and all the great folk who work in tourist offices across the region; Mischa and Carmen. To my work colleagues, massive thanks to Ilaria Walker for giving me a shot on this title and to Greg Bloom for heaps of info and tips. Also to the production team inhouse for their tireless, great work. Finally to my family, and my amazing girlfriend Kate – particularly for letting me go away so much over the past year!

Adam Karlin

Thanks, *po*: first, the Peace Corps volunteers who made my trip so much easier, and a hell of a lot of fun too. Chelsea Sexton and Jenn Rimbach in Olongapo, Baguio and Vigan, Tracy Fooler in Baguio, Caitlin Sherman in Vigan, and big shout-outs for all the amazing research help from Dan Thalkar in Sagada, Sammy Liu in Vigan, Jessi Acuña in Marinduque and Sam West in Baguio (and, er, Tampa). Huge thanks to Filipino friends, especially Maria Teresa Madriaga and her husband in Manila, Jeff in Clark and the old men who helped me out in Zambales – I never got all your names, but bless you many times over. Big thanks to the team: Trent and Michael for fun feedback whilst co-authoring, Ilaria for ever being a supportive editor and Greg Bloom for masterfully helming the ship. Last but not least: thank you mom and dad and Rachel, for your love and support, including noteworthy, lifesaving logistical support after my passport got lifted.

ACKNOWLEDGMENTS

Climate map data adapted from Peel MC, Finlayson BL & McMahon TA (2007) 'Updated World Map of the Köppen-Geiger Climate Classification', *Hydrology and Earth System Sciences*, 11, 163344.

Bestselling guide to the Philippines - source: Nielsen BookScan, Australia, UK and USA, January 2011 to December 2011

Cover photograph: Rice paddies with Mt Mayon in background, Albay, Bicol, John Pennock/LPI

Many of the images in this guide are available for licensing from Lonely Planet Images: www.lonelyplanetimages.com.

This Book

This 11th edition of The Philippines was coordinated by Philippines aficionado Greg Bloom, who wrote all the Plan Your Trip chapters, the Understand chapters and the Survival Guide. He also researched and wrote the Manila, Around Manila and Mindoro chapters, as well as the Panay and Romblon sections of the Visayas chapter. Michael Grosberg updated the challenging Mindanao and Sulu chapter and the Palawan chapter; Trent Holden covered the Camotes, Negros, Siquijor, Bohol, Leyte, Biliran Island and Samar sections of the Visayas chapter. Adam Karlin did the Southeast Luzon and North Luzon chapters and Kate Morgan researched Cebu City. The team worked on the text from the 10th edition, which was researched and written by Greg Bloom, Michael Grosberg, Virginia Jealous and Piers Kelly; the Health chapter is based on research supplied by Dr Trish Batchelor. This guidebook was commissioned in Lonely Planet's Melbourne office, and produced by the following:

Commissioning Editors
Shawn Low, Ilaria Walker

Coordinating Editors
Jessica Crouch, Kate James

Coordinating Cartographer Csanad Csutoros

Managing Layout Designer Chris Girdler

Managing Editor
Bruce Evans

Senior Editor Susan Paterson

Managing Cartographers
Amanda Sierp, Diana Von Holdt

Layout Designer
Carlos Solarte

Assisting Editors
Janet Austin, Holly Alexander, Andrea Dobbin

Assisting Cartographers
Andras Bogdanovits, Ildiko Bogdanovits, Mick Garrett

Cover Research
Naomi Parker

Internal Image Research
Kylie McLaughlin, Rebecca Skinner

Language Content
Brana Vladisavljevic

Thanks to Ryan Evans, Yvonne Kirk, Chris Love, Katie O'Connell, Trent Paton, Martine Power, Kirsten Rawlings, Jacqui Saunders, Angela Tinson, Gerard Walker

how to use this book

These symbols will help you find the listings you want:

- Sights
- Beaches
- Activities
- Courses
- Tours
- Festivals & Events
- Sleeping
- Eating
- Drinking
- Entertainment
- Shopping
- Information/ Transport

These symbols give you the vital information for each listing:

- Telephone Numbers
- Opening Hours
- Parking
- Nonsmoking
- Air-Conditioning
- Internet Access
- Wi-Fi Access
- Swimming Pool
- Vegetarian Selection
- English-Language Menu
- Family-Friendly
- Pet-Friendly
- Bus
- Ferry
- Metro
- Subway
- London Tube
- Tram
- Train

Reviews are organised by author preference.

Look out for these icons:

- TOP CHOICE — Our author's recommendation
- FREE — No payment required
- A green or sustainable option

Our authors have nominated these places as demonstrating a strong commitment to sustainability – for example by supporting local communities and producers, operating in an environmentally friendly way, or supporting conservation projects.

Map Legend

Sights
- Beach
- Buddhist
- Castle
- Christian
- Hindu
- Islamic
- Jewish
- Monument
- Museum/Gallery
- Ruin
- Winery/Vineyard
- Zoo
- Other Sight

Activities, Courses & Tours
- Diving/Snorkelling
- Canoeing/Kayaking
- Skiing
- Surfing
- Swimming/Pool
- Walking
- Windsurfing
- Other Activity/ Course/Tour

Sleeping
- Sleeping
- Camping

Eating
- Eating

Drinking
- Drinking
- Cafe

Entertainment
- Entertainment

Shopping
- Shopping

Information
- Bank
- Embassy/ Consulate
- Hospital/Medical
- Internet
- Police
- Post Office
- Telephone
- Toilet
- Tourist Information
- Other Information

Transport
- Airport
- Border Crossing
- Bus
- Cable Car/ Funicular
- Cycling
- Ferry
- Metro
- Monorail
- Parking
- Petrol Station
- Taxi
- Train/Railway
- Tram
- Other Transport

Routes
- Tollway
- Freeway
- Primary
- Secondary
- Tertiary
- Lane
- Unsealed Road
- Plaza/Mall
- Steps
- Tunnel
- Pedestrian Overpass
- Walking Tour
- Walking Tour Detour
- Path

Geographic
- Hut/Shelter
- Lighthouse
- Lookout
- Mountain/Volcano
- Oasis
- Park
- Pass
- Picnic Area
- Waterfall

Population
- Capital (National)
- Capital (State/Province)
- City/Large Town
- Town/Village

Boundaries
- International
- State/Province
- Disputed
- Regional/Suburb
- Marine Park
- Cliff
- Wall

Hydrography
- River, Creek
- Intermittent River
- Swamp/Mangrove
- Reef
- Canal
- Water
- Dry/Salt/ Intermittent Lake
- Glacier

Areas
- Beach/Desert
- Cemetery (Christian)
- Cemetery (Other)
- Park/Forest
- Sportsground
- Sight (Building)
- Top Sight (Building)

Contributing Authors

Kate Morgan As a commissioning editor at Lonely Planet in Melbourne, Kate's job involves shipping authors off to exotic locations. Also working as a freelance writer and editor, she thought it was time to finally experience life on the road. After island-hopping on bangkas and gorging on fresh seafood in Cebu, she hopes it won't be her last authoring trip.

OUR STORY

A beat-up old car, a few dollars in the pocket and a sense of adventure. In 1972 that's all Tony and Maureen Wheeler needed for the trip of a lifetime – across Europe and Asia overland to Australia. It took several months, and at the end – broke but inspired – they sat at their kitchen table writing and stapling together their first travel guide, *Across Asia on the Cheap*. Within a week they'd sold 1500 copies. Lonely Planet was born.

Today, Lonely Planet has offices in Melbourne, London and Oakland, with more than 600 staff and writers. We share Tony's belief that 'a great guidebook should do three things: inform, educate and amuse'.

OUR WRITERS

Greg Bloom

Coordinating Author, Manila, Around Manila, Mindoro, The Visayas Greg lived in Manila for five years before moving to Phnom Penh in 2009. He has travelled all over the country in the service of Lonely Planet, experiencing many highs (diving Apo Reef, whalesharking in Donsol, spelunking in Samar) and lows (flying off out of a moving jeepney, surviving a bus crash in Bicol, being pickpocketed on the MRT) along the way. When not writing about his favourite travel destination, Greg might be found snouting around the former Soviet Union (he once called Kyiv home) or running around Asia's ultimate frisbee fields. Read about his trips at www.mytripjournal.com/bloomblogs.

Read more about Greg at:
lonelyplanet.com/members/gbloom4

Michael Grosberg

Palawan, Mindanao & Sulu This is the fourth edition of the Lonely Planet *Philippines* guidebook Michael has worked on. He's returned for various magazine assignments and loves travelling in the PI as much for the friends he's made along the way as the physical beauty of the islands. A reformed academic/journalist by trade, Michael has worked on over 17 Lonely Planet books and is based in Brooklyn, New York.

Read more about Michael at:
lonelyplanet.com/members/michaelgrosberg

Trent Holden

The Visayas Despite being a regular visitor to Southeast Asia, the Visayas is a region that's eluded Trent till now. It was well worth the wait. Exploring its eclectic islands via an endless connection of bangkas, *habal-habals* and jeepneys, he rates it right up there with some of the best beaches and friendliest people he's encountered anywhere in the world. Trent lives in Melbourne where he works as a freelance writer and editor. He's obsessed with AFL footy and everything punk rock. This is his fourth book for Lonely Planet, having co-authored titles such as *India* and *Indonesia*.

Adam Karlin

North Luzon, Southeast Luzon Adam admittedly ran into some frustrations in the Philippines. Major rains, typhoons and mudslides all came together to serve up the worst weather ever experienced on a Lonely Planet research trip. He blew a tyre out on his car at midnight in the middle of nowhere, Zambales. His wallet and passport got lifted while he was on his way to the airport. And yet – he loved the place. How can you not? The scenery is Edenic, there's giant lizards carved into dark wooden doors and the people are as friendly as all get out. Adam has authored or contributed to over 25 guidebooks for Lonely Planet.

Read more about Adam at:
lonelyplanet.com/members/adamkarlin

OVER PAGE MORE WRITERS

Published by Lonely Planet Publications Pty Ltd
ABN 36 005 607 983
11th edition – May 2012
ISBN 978 1 74179 694 0

10 9 8 7 6 5 4 3
Printed in China